SCIENCE FICTION
video games

SCIENCE FICTION
video games

Neal **Tringham**

CRC Press
Taylor & Francis Group
Boca Raton London New York

CRC Press is an imprint of the
Taylor & Francis Group, an **informa** business

AN A K PETERS BOOK

CRC Press
Taylor & Francis Group
6000 Broken Sound Parkway NW, Suite 300
Boca Raton, FL 33487-2742

First issued in hardback 2017

© 2015 by Taylor & Francis Group, LLC
CRC Press is an imprint of Taylor & Francis Group, an Informa business

No claim to original U.S. Government works

Version Date: 20140730

ISBN-13: 978-1-4822-0388-2 (pbk)
ISBN-13: 978-1-138-42769-3 (hbk)

Visit the Taylor & Francis Web site at
http://www.taylorandfrancis.com

and the CRC Press Web site at
http://www.crcpress.com

Contents

Preface

THIS BOOK DEALS WITH VIDEO GAMES. MORE SPECIFICALLY, IT DEALS with games that are part of the science fiction genre (often known simply as sf), rather than being set in magical milieux or (often exaggerated) versions of our own world. The initial chapters discuss game design and the history of science-fictional video games. The majority of the text, however, deals with individual science-fictional games, as well as with the histories and natures of their various forms, such as the puzzle-based adventure or the more exploratory and immediate computer role playing game. Unlike many existing books and websites that cover some of the same material, this work emphasizes critical analysis, especially the analysis of narrative, which is approached by means of an original categorization of story forms in games. In addition, this book is concerned with video games as works of science fiction as well as with their identities as games. This means that as much time is spent on the fictions they convey and the links between them and other forms of sf (including tabletop role playing games and wargames as well as film, television, and the written genre) as on the systems of rules (or mechanics) that define them as games. (Connections between works in different media are explored both explicitly and—by use of a specialized set of terms that represent such common science-fictional tropes as "long vanished but immeasurably superior alien species"—implicitly.) As a result of this approach, games have been selected for inclusion primarily on the basis of their interest as works of sf, with their historical or commercial importance as a secondary consideration. Thus, works that use science fiction purely as a source of generic background images, or that simply reiterate the themes and details of the media from which they have been licensed, have in general not been included. It should also be noted that this book deals primarily with works that have been released in English (as is true of the great majority of video games of science-fictional interest).

Many of the games described in this book were created to run on older hardware and computer operating systems that are no longer readily available. However, in recent years most of these games have been rereleased in revised versions intended for use on modern machines. For PC and Mac users, the GOG.com website (www.gog.com) is probably the best single source for such "remastered" works, while console gamers may want to look at the eShop (for Nintendo machines), the PlayStation Store (for Sony devices), or the Xbox Games Store (for Microsoft hardware). Similarly, independently created and self-published games (which are often not available from shops with physical premises, brick and mortar stores, high street shops or major online retailers such as Amazon) can be found on Google Play (for Android devices), the App Store (for iOS devices), the Steam website at store.steampowered.com (for PCs and Macs), and the same stores from which remastered games are sold on consoles.

The majority of the chapters in this book have been previously published, in a somewhat different form, in the third edition of the *Encyclopedia of Science Fiction*, winner of the 2012 Hugo Award for Best Related Work. I would like to thank David Langford and John Clute for the generous help that they provided as editors when the original versions of these entries were being written.

How to Read This Book

THIS BOOK USES A NUMBER OF TYPOGRAPHICAL AND FORMATTING conventions. Hopefully these are mostly self-explanatory, but they are detailed here to avoid any possibility of confusion.

Both science fiction and video games have their own specialized vocabularies, from "hyperspace" to "massively multiplayer online role playing game." In addition, this book makes use of a number of unusual critical terms, some created by the author, such as "science and sorcery" or "environmental narrative." All of these terms are defined in a glossary at the end of the book, and when they are used for the first time in an isolated section of the text (such as a description of a specific game) they are printed in bold, as, for example, **science and sorcery**. Emboldened terms that are all in lower case (such as **hyperspace**) typically refer to general concepts, while those starting with a capital letter (as with **Cthulhu Mythos**) denote a specific fictional setting, character, or series of stories. Subsequent uses of a lowercase term in the same entry are generally not in bold, however, since overly liberal use of the style produces excessively distracting text.

Most of the book is composed of entries on specific forms of **video games** (such as **adventures**) or individual franchises. Each franchise entry deals with all the games (including major revisions), game expansions, spin-off novels and anthologies, **gamebooks**, films, TV series, comics, and other media associated with a particular work (such as the **first person shooter** *Halo: Combat Evolved*) or series of works (as in the various games that have been licensed from the tabletop **role playing game** *Shadowrun*). An exception has been made, however, for franchises that contain very large numbers of associated games or novels, such as those linked to the tabletop **wargame** *Warhammer 40,000*. In these cases, the most obviously relevant works are listed, as well as any available bibliographies. Similarly, works that are not available in English are only mentioned if they are videogames. In addition, it should be noted that the ascription format used for videogames does not include many potentially important details, such as the names of the devices on which the software is available. Readers interested in this information are referred to the Mobygames website cited in the bibliography at the end of the book. (In general, games are made for a selection of the hardware platforms available at the time of release. Earlier works were often created for either personal computers, games consoles intended for use in the living room, or handheld games devices; more modern ones will typically be published on both computers and consoles, though some are built primarily for smartphones and tablets, or for use on social networking sites. Recently, however, many older games have been revised for rerelease on more modern systems, meaning that any attempt to list the devices for which games are available rapidly becomes obsolete.) Finally, the text makes extensive use of the singular "they"—as employed in such works as Oscar Wilde's *The Importance of Being Earnest*—to refer to game players and other individuals of unknown gender.

Each franchise entry follows a particular format, beginning with the name of the intellectual property or game, followed by the date on which it was first published, the name of the company which developed it (if any), and then the name or names of the designers (if known). If the company name is used again later in the same section, an abbreviation may be given in parentheses after its first appearance and employed subsequently, e.g. (SSI) for "Strategic Simulations Inc." It should also be noted that the company name is always that of the developer rather than the publisher, if there is a distinction to be made. The main body of the entry then follows, with peripheral material listed at the end under "Related works." Both the chapters that deal with individual game forms and those that describe franchises associated with particular works then end with the optional sections "Further Reading" (which lists any relevant nonfiction works) and "Web Links" (specifying relevant websites).

Various games, books, and other media are mentioned in the body of the text. These citations follow a specific set of conventions:

- *Games*: The name of the game in italics, followed by parentheses containing the date of first publication (in italics), the name of the company that developed the work (if any), a list of alternate titles, and the dates and (if different) names of any revisions, followed by the names of the designers (if known). Thus, *PsychoDeathRoboKiller* (*1994* theBorg; also known as *Slaughter in Simtown*; revised *1995*; *1996* revised as *PsychoDeathRoboKiller: Gold Edition*) designed by Harry Arthur Knight would indicate a game originally called *PsychoDeathRoboKiller* or *Slaughter in Simtown*, with a later version known as *PsychoDeathRoboKiller: Gold Edition*, first published in 1994, with revised editions released in 1995 and 1996, originally developed by theBorg and designed by Harry Arthur Knight. This format is used for all video games as well as tabletop role playing games, wargames, board games, and card games.

- *Novels*: The name of the book in italics, followed by parentheses containing the date of the first publication in book form (in bold) and any other names under which the work has been released, followed by the name of the author. Thus, *PsychoDeathRoboKiller: Genocide is Painless* (**1996**; also known as *The Silence of the Androids*) by Kilgore Trout would be a novel called *PsychoDeathRoboKiller: Genocide is Painless* but also released as *The Silence of the Androids*, first published in 1996 and written by Kilgore Trout.

- *Gamebooks*: The same format as novels.

- *Anthologies*: The same format as novels, except that an editor is listed rather than an author. Thus, *PsychoDeathRoboKiller: Prequels and Valedictories* (**1997**) edited by Kilgore Trout would be a collection of short stories by various authors called *PsychoDeathRoboKiller: Prequels and Valedictories*, first published in 1997 and edited by Kilgore Trout.

- *Nonfiction*: The same format as novels or anthologies, depending on whether the work was created by a single author or is a collection of short pieces by various hands. Thus, *Remediation & Reentrancy: Reflections on PsychoDeathRoboKiller* (**2006**) edited by Joanna Moriarty would be a collection of essays called *Remediation & Reentrancy: Reflections on PsychoDeathRoboKiller*, edited by Joanna Moriarty and first made available in 2006.

- *Short stories*: The name of the story in quotation marks, followed by parentheses containing the month and year of the story's first publication and the name of the magazine or anthology in which it was published (in italics) and any other titles under which it is known, followed by the name of the author. Thus, "Future Zombie Dino Apocalypse" (September 1996 *Gaming Aeon*; also known as "Psycho Deaf Robot Killerz") by Kilgore Trout would be a short story called

"Future Zombie Dino Apocalypse" (later reprinted as "Psycho Deaf Robot Killerz") by Kilgore Trout, first published in the September 1996 issue of *Gaming Aeon* magazine.

- *Magazine articles*: The same format as short stories.

- *Films* The name of the film in italics, followed by parentheses containing the date of first release in italics. Thus, *PsychoDeathRoboKiller: Humanity's Requiem (2006)* would be a film called *PsychoDeathRoboKiller: Humanity's Requiem*, first shown in 2006.

- *Television series*: The name of the series in italics, followed by parentheses containing the dates during which the series was first transmitted. Thus, *PsychoDeathRoboKiller: The Cartoon in 3D (2011–2012)* would be a TV show called *PsychoDeathRoboKiller: The Cartoon in 3D*, originally shown from 2011 to 2012.

- *Comics*: The same format as television series.

CHAPTER 1

Videogames and Science Fiction

HISTORICALLY, GAMES INTENDED FOR use on personal computers, mainframes, and minicomputers were often referred to as computer games, while their equivalents on home consoles and coin-operated arcade cabinets have from their first appearance in the early 1970s been known as TV games or video games. This distinction, however, became increasingly blurred after the mid-1990s, as the same games were made available on both personal computers and consoles. Since the alternative designations occasionally employed—such as "electronic game" or "digital game"—seem awkward and are little used by either players or developers, this book simply uses **videogame** to refer to any game that runs on some form of computer hardware.

Many of these games have been fantastical in nature, especially in the earlier years of the form. In this context, it seems significant that many of the first generation of videogame designers (as well as the majority of the creators of the often-associated forms of printed **gamebooks** and tabletop **role playing games**) were sf and fantasy enthusiasts. If there is (or was) any inherent link between videogame design and science fiction, however, it seems obscure. Nevertheless, there may be some connection between sf's affinity for logical extrapolation and (in the words of the critic Robert Scholes) "structured fabulation," and the complexly simulative rule systems that underlie many recently developed types of game. Certainly, sf readers who play board and counter **wargames** or pen and paper **RPGs** may find something familiar in the way they function as machines for modeling imaginary worlds, artificial universes that are often explicitly derived from particular literary subgenres. Players of videogames are typically not exposed to the reality of their rules at such a fundamental level, but these systems are certainly apparent to the creators of such works. It is also worth noting that where science-fictional cinema and television are often characterized by their visual qualities and "spectacle," sf games can arguably be defined by their interactivity. The emergence of videogames as a commercially important form thus suggests a possible categorization of sf media as either written (meaning essentially novels and short stories), visual (film and TV), audible (radio and music), or interactive (indicating games).

Various candidates have been proposed for the identity of the original videogame; which one is preferred generally depends on the exact definition of the form being employed. The earliest contender is probably "El Ajedrecista" ["The Chess Player"], an electromechanical device built by the Spanish engineer Leonardo Torres y Quevedo in 1912, influenced by Charles Babbage's designs for an Analytical Engine. This mechanism successfully played a limited chess endgame, deploying a king and a rook against a human opponent's king. Unlike earlier chess automatons, which contained a concealed human player, El Ajedrecista's moves were generated entirely algorithmically. Other possibilities include the NIMROD computer, built by John Bennett and Raymond Williams of Ferranti to play the object-picking game of NIM and demonstrated at the 1951 Festival of Britain, and *Tennis for Two*, a two-player game of electronic table tennis designed by William Higinbotham in 1958 at the US Brookhaven National Laboratory. The earliest example that had original gameplay, however, as opposed to implementing an existing game on a computer, appears to have been *Spacewar* (*1962*) designed by Stephen Russell, J M Graetz, and Wayne Wiitanen. This game, which was partially inspired by the **Lensman** and **Skylark space opera** novels of E E Smith, was also the first such work to have exerted a clear influence on later efforts; its descendants include both the 1971 *Star Trek* war game designed by Mike Mayfield and the first electronic **arcade games**.

The play of the 1962 game *Spacewar*—here shown running on a software emulation of the PDP-1 mainframe computer, which was its original platform—bears a remarkable resemblance to that of many later **2D** "shoot em ups."

In both the United States and the United Kingdom, the late 1960s and early 1970s saw a gradual increase in the amount of mainframe and mini-computer hardware that was available for unofficial use in academic establishments, whether because it was mildly obsolete or because it was intended for educational purposes. Such machines were generally interactive, in the sense that instructions could be issued at a keyboard and receive an immediate response, and sometimes had access to computer networks and video displays, though many examples could only produce output on a teletype printer. This resulted in a kind of Cambrian explosion of videogame forms, as programmers experimented with a wide variety of exotic new types of gameplay. (Many of these forms, however, were to some extent derivative; ideas were frequently borrowed from existing games such as chess and Othello, commercial aerospace simulators, and the other novel types of game that emerged in the latter half of the twentieth century. This latter influence was perhaps the most notable, with formative concepts taken from the board and counter wargames that first appeared in the mid-1950s and the tabletop role playing games that were born with 1974s publication of *Dungeons and Dragons*.) While most of these efforts swiftly disappeared, a small proportion proved highly successful, giving rise to many descendants. American examples include the first **computer role playing games**, **adventures**, and **computer wargames** (excluding simulations written for purely military purposes), *Maze War* (*1973*) designed by Steve Colley, Greg Thompson, and Howard Palmer (a precursor to later **first-person shooters**), and the early **toy game** *Space Travel* (*1969*) designed by Ken Thompson. Meanwhile, *MUD*— the ancestor of almost all persistent **online worlds**—was launched by Roy Trubshaw and Richard Bartle in the United Kingdom *circa* 1978. Many of these games were science fictional or fantastical in nature, though often highly derivative of *Star Trek*, *Star Wars*, *Dungeons and Dragons*, and other similarly well-known works. This process has continued, though at a slower pace; as new technological niches have become available, new forms of video-game have appeared to fill them.

An early part of the game development process is the creation of concept art intended to guide the appearance of the final work. This image, "Before the Fall," is a piece of concept art for *Torment: Tides of Numenéra*.

The nature of these game types, from adventures to first-person shooters, has itself been the subject of much debate. While the concept of genre usu-ally applies to a choice of subject within a form, in the case of videogames, the term has typically been employed to describe a type of gameplay. Thus, computer role playing games and computer wargames would be examples of videogame genres, while individual works within such a group might deal with science-fictional subjects, making them members of the wider sf genre. This book, however, uses the terms "type" and "school" to refer to game forms that are defined by their gameplay, in order to prevent confu-sion with the use of "genre" to denote a choice of subject or theme. It is also worth noting that the definitions of videogame forms and the classification of individual works within them are often a matter of some debate, though broad agreement exists in most cases. While many schools are now well established, and most current videogames can be placed within one, many games written in the 1970s and 1980s—when most current forms were still evolving—cannot be easily categorized.

As videogames have become more commercially significant, the question of how to define games so as to encompass the wide variety of modern forms has attracted increasing academic attention. Katie Salen and Eric Zimmerman, in *Rules of Play: Game Design Fundamentals* (**2003**), suggest that "A game is a system in which players engage in an artificial conflict, defined by rules, that results in a quantifiable outcome." Greg Costikyan, in the essay "I Have No Words & I Must Design" (1994 *Interactive Fantasy #2*), offers "A game is a form of art in which participants, termed players, make decisions in order to manage resources through game tokens in the pursuit of a goal." Many similar definitions exist, typically revolving around the concepts of decisions (or actions) within systems (or sets of rules) in pursuit of an outcome (or goal). While such characterizations seem clearly applicable to "traditional" games such as chess and poker, they can be problematic when dealing with the various new game forms that emerged in the second half of the twentieth century. Notably, tabletop role playing games do not necessarily have goals, toy games (in which the player is allowed to experiment at will with a software simulation) do not obviously involve conflict, and some videogames (such as those based on playing simulated musical instruments to match a predetermined soundtrack) appear to offer no real decisions.

This book instead assumes that the limits of what a game can be were greatly expanded by the multiplicity of new types introduced during the late twentieth century to the extent that it is necessary to adopt a much more general definition. The one chosen is based on the "Game/Drama/Simulation" model created for pen and paper role playing games in 1997 by Mary Kuhner, John Kim, and other members of the USENET forum rec.games.frp.advocacy (see the following web links). Specifically, I assume that games can be characterized as combinations of three different elements: gameplay, narrative, and simulation. Here, gameplay refers to the "ludic" quality, which is at the heart of Costikyan's and Salen and Zimmerman's definitions, and which could loosely be described—after Sid Meier's comment that good games present "a series of interesting choices," and Bernard Suits' description of playing a game as "a voluntary attempt to overcome unnecessary obstacles"—as the experience of a series of demanding challenges. Similarly, narrative refers to the sense of shaping or being part of an ongoing story or **interactive narrative**, and simulation is concerned with participation in an algorithmic model that can be manipulated by the players. (Arguably, gameplay and narrative in games have something of the same relationship as that of the "spectacle"—roughly, the visual appearance and impact—of a film to its fiction.) Particular forms typically emphasize some aspects of this model at the expense of others. Thus, tabletop board games, card games, and many types of videogames, including most first-person shooters, are generally dominated by gameplay considerations, while tabletop role playing games, gamebooks, adventures, and computer role playing games typically emphasize narrative, and board and counter wargames and toy games stress accuracy of simulation.

At the same time as videogames were becoming popular recreations on academic mainframes, a commercial industry was emerging in the United States around coin-operated cabinets placed in public arcades. In 1971, Nolan Bushnell began distribution of *Computer Space*, a variant of *Spacewar*. While this proved unpopular with the mass market, a later game called *Pong* (*1972* Atari) designed by Allan Alcom, a simple simulation of table tennis, was highly successful, launching Bushnell's Atari Inc. Such electronic games were initially perceived as improved versions of the electromechanical pinball and shooting machines, which were already common in amusement arcades, but rapidly established their own identity as "video games." Atari, along with various competitors, proceeded to create a highly profitable enterprise centered on selling relatively simple, action-oriented games with the best achievable graphics to children and teenagers. These works soon became available on consoles designed for use with the television at home as well as in the arcades, an approach that was pioneered in 1972 by Magnavox's Odyssey machine. As in the academic community, a remarkable number of videogame forms were invented by the designers of such games, though these types have generally proved to be less relevant to sf. Examples include the maze game (based on maneuvering a character around a **2D** labyrinth, typically filled with enemies), the **sports game** (in which contemporary sports such as golf are simulated with varying degrees of accuracy), and the **racing game** (where the player takes part in some kind of competition involving fast cars or other vehicles). Meanwhile, a largely separate and considerably smaller games industry emerged in the United States with the appearance in the late 1970s of personal computers—such as the Apple II and Commodore PET—which did not need to be built from kits by dedicated hobbyists. While console games were often derived from works produced for arcade cabinets, the early products of personal computer game developers were frequently influenced by forms common in the academic community, such as adventures and computer wargames. These "computer games" were also typically intended for a different market to the console and arcade games, one composed of older consumers who were often sf and fantasy enthusiasts. An excellent history of the period, and of the US videogame industry in general, can be found in *The First Quarter* (**2000**; **2001** revised as *The Ultimate History of Video Games*), by Steven L Kent.

In *L'Univers des Jeux Vidéo* ["The World of Video Games"] (**1998**), Alain and Frédéric Le Diberder identify three major types of videogame: action games (such as maze games and racing games), simulations (including toy games, **god games**, and similar forms), and "reflections" (games based on noncomputer forms such as tabletop role playing games and board games). In keeping with the three aspects of "modern games" considered earlier (gameplay, simulation, and narrative), this book uses a different taxonomy, one in which the major categories are action games, strategic planning games (including computer wargames, **4X games**, god games, and some toy games), and story games (consisting largely of computer roleplaying games and adventures). These categories also correspond to the three types of **immersion** identified by the game designer Ernest Adams in his online article "Postmodernism and the Three Types of Immersion" (*2004*): tactical, strategic, and narrative. On this basis, several major influences can be identified on the early development of videogame forms. In the academic community and the personal computer industry, strategic planning games often show marked similarities to contemporary tabletop **wargames** and board games, while story games all appear to have been influenced by pen and paper role playing games, and especially by Gary Gygax and Dave Arneson's original *Dungeons and Dragons* (*1974* Tactical Studies Rules). Meanwhile, the action games common in arcades and on early home consoles seem to have been partially inspired by earlier coin-operated devices such as the various mechanical and electromechanical shooting, sports, racing, flight simulation, and pinball machines played in amusement fairs, theme parks, and bars. Of these three basic forms, story games and strategic planning games have traditionally appealed to specific subcultures and niche audiences—though both action adventures and narratively complex computer role playing games have become notably popular in the twenty-first century—while action games have sold to the mass market.

The Japanese videogame industry was born in the early 1970s, as existing toy and game manufacturers started to produce their own coin-operated machines to compete with US imports. By the end of the decade, these companies, led by Nintendo, had continued to follow the American pattern by developing their own home game consoles. Historically, the Japanese industry has concentrated on arcade and console games; development for personal computers has largely occurred in the United States and Europe. In the late 1970s and early 1980s, Japanese designers began to create games that were highly successful worldwide, developing a number of new types of action game including the "shoot em up" (in which the player must eliminate a large number of enemies, typically on a 2D display), of which the first example was *Space Invaders* (*1978* Taito) designed by Toshihiro Nishikado. Other types of action game introduced in contemporary Japanese arcades include the **platform game** (in which the player must jump to and from suspended platforms or over obstacles) and the **fighting game** (where one or two players are involved in single combat, typically as part of a series of self-contained matches). As with the US-developed action game forms, however, these schools have produced few works that are interesting as science fiction, though some of them have sf backgrounds. In 1983, the US console market experienced a major crash triggered by a glut of low-quality games and competing types of hardware. Many American companies ceased operations or withdrew from the market altogether, though the much smaller personal computer games industry was less affected. This left a niche in the US marketplace that was exploited by Nintendo, and later its competitor Sega, in the late 1980s. The American launch of cheap and capable consoles such as the Nintendo Entertainment System, combined with highly popular games created by such designers as Shigeru Miyamoto, eventually led to Japanese domination of the worldwide console market. Meanwhile, the **console role playing game**—essentially a new type of story game, and one in which a number of novel works of sf and fantasy have been created—emerged in Japan, and proved popular elsewhere. A comprehensive and highly enthusiastic history of the Japanese industry is available in *Power-Up: How Japanese Video Games Gave the World an Extra Life* (**2004**), by Chris Kohler.

At the same time, the UK videogame industry had evolved into almost a mirror image of the Japanese one. European markets in the 1980s were dominated by a wide variety of cheap personal computers such as the Sinclair ZX Spectrum and the Commodore Amiga. As a result, the UK industry concentrated on designing games for these machines, largely ignoring console manufacture and development. In contrast to the early US personal computer game industry, works developed for computers in the United Kingdom were predominantly action based, though the strategic planning and story forms also made frequent appearances, in games variously intended to be played by children, teenagers, and adults. Of the many works created in the United Kingdom during the 1980s, one example of particular science-fictional interest is *Elite* (*1984*) designed by David Braben and Ian Bell, a combination of the action and strategic planning forms, which was the first example of the exploration form of **space sim**. Meanwhile, smaller game development industries appeared in other parts of Western Europe, notably France. Magnus Anderson and Rebecca Levene's *Grand Thieves & Tomb Raiders: How British Videogames Conquered the World* (**2012**) can be consulted for a more detailed history of computer games in the United Kingdom.

In the late 1980s, the industry entered a period of global consolidation that lasted until the mid-1990s. Coin-operated machines declined in popularity as games became available for home consoles, which were as visually impressive as those in the arcades, and by the end of this period, they were largely extinct. Meanwhile, Japanese console hardware became steadily more popular with children and teenagers, moving into the European market from America. The high global sales of these consoles encouraged US and UK developers to begin programming for them, adding to the library of games created by Japanese companies. PCs compatible with the IBM standard emerged as the dominant form of personal computer, effectively eliminating all competitors other than the Apple Macintosh series. Games for these computers typically sold to a more adult—and smaller—market than that targeted by console manufacturers, one primarily composed of members of such subcultures as computer professionals and sf and fantasy enthusiasts. Various new forms of strategic planning game entered the commercial arena, including toy games, 4X games, and **real-time strategy** games in the United States and god games in the United Kingdom. New types of action game included the **puzzle game**—exemplified by *Tetris* (*1985*) designed by Alexey Pajitnov, a Russian work based on arranging 2D shapes in **real time**—and the first-person shooter, a form often associated with sf. By the end of this period, videogames had become sufficiently well known to justify the publication of mass market books on the subject, beginning with J C Herz's always perceptive but often factually inaccurate *Joystick Nation: How Videogames Ate Our Quarters, Won Our Hearts, and Rewired Our Minds* (**1997**).

By the late 1990s, a generation of children raised on Nintendo consoles and Sinclair computers had come of age. This, more than anything else, has led to the appearance of a true mass market for adult videogames, the majority of which have been action games running on consoles. New hardware manufacturers were attracted by the potential profits, leading to a transition from a console sector controlled by Nintendo and Sega to one dominated by the Sony PlayStation series, Microsoft Xbox machines, and various Nintendo devices. Home consoles and personal computers have gradually become more similar, and many types of game previously seen on computers have appeared on consoles, and *vice versa*. Some types of strategic planning and story games associated with sf and fantasy, such as computer role playing games and real-time strategy games, have remained popular on personal computers or partially migrated to consoles, while others, including adventures, have largely disappeared. Development has also become more international, with the expansion of existing small industries in France, Germany, Canada, and Australia and the appearance of new ones in other parts of Western and Eastern Europe, Russia, China, and South Korea. Tristan Donovan's *Replay: The History of Video Games* (**2010**) offers perhaps the best overall history of the videogame form, following the evolution of both console and computer games in the United States, the United Kingdom, continental Europe, Australia, and Japan.

One major change that has occurred relatively recently in most videogame forms is the adoption of real-time **3D** graphics for displays, an approach that became common as a result of improvements in the available hardware. Such games typically employ the laws of "scientific perspective" used in the Western painting tradition to generate the final picture displayed, though some, generally earlier, works have instead used the Chinese system of "parallel perspective" (often known as **isometric** graphics). Some game hardware now also supports the use of "stereoscopy," in which different images are presented to each eye; this conveys the illusion of depth to the viewer, as if they were watching an animated hologram. Confusingly, this type of display is also referred to as "3D," or 3D. All of these 3D visuals are quite distinct from the 2D displays primarily seen in older or less expensive games, in which the player is shown the world from directly overhead or from the side, an approach that is often suggestive of a moving picture set in the world of Edwin Abbott's *Flatland* (**1884**). New types of game have continued to emerge, though at a slower pace than in earlier decades, including the action-based **third-person shooter** and **survival horror** forms as well as the story-oriented action adventure. Worldwide availability of commercial Internet connections has also allowed the development of **massively multiplayer online games** and **alternate reality games**, as well as providing a means of distribution for relatively simple "casual" games played through a web browser or on mobile phones. It is characteristic that several of these forms appeared at much the same time in different regions of an increasingly globally integrated industry, though survival horror remains a primarily Japanese form, and the creation of alternate reality games and massively multiplayer online games has been dominated by companies based in the United States and South Korea.

In the 2000s, several developments combined to greatly expand the market for videogames, while simultaneously making it far more fragmented. The appearance of powerful and widely owned mobile computing hardware, primarily in the form of personal tablets and phones, presented developers with a popular new class of devices on which games could be played. Simultaneously, the growth of social networks such as Facebook was significantly enhanced by the games that they made available to their customers. Many of the works that can be played on these new platforms are initially free to use, with revenue being obtained through the sale of virtual goods, which add to players' enjoyment. Frequently, such games are created by small teams who publish their own work by purely electronic means, with no need to produce physical products. This return to the "cottage industry" approach of early computer game development has been accompanied by a revival of many of the game forms common on arcade machines and early home consoles, notably platform games, puzzle games, and relatively simple sports games. Such designs are suitable for implementation by small groups (and deployment on mobile hardware and social websites) in a way that the "blockbuster" games created by more mainstream developers (and funded by gigantic publishing companies) are not. Arguably, the videogame market has come to resemble a complex ecosystem, in which different types of developers design various kinds of games for a variety of audiences. Thus, more casual players might be primarily interested in games on social networks or mobile phones, which are free to play, while dedicated enthusiasts will buy expensive works, which will only run on specialized hardware. Many modern **transmedia** franchises include games aimed at both of these classes of consumer as well as novels, comics, and potentially films and television series. While the majority of the more casual games appearing on mobile devices and social networks have to date been of little science-fictional interest, there is no obvious reason why this must continue to be the case. One interesting exception is *Crimson: Steam Pirates* (*2011* Harebrained Schemes) designed by Jordan Weisman, Mitch Gitelman, and Aljernon Bolden, a **turn-based** game reminiscent of Sid Meier's swashbuckling simulator *Pirates!* (*1987* MicroProse), but set in a **steampunk alternate history**.

The early twenty-first century has also seen considerable attention devoted to the videogame industry by academics working in various areas of the humanities. These researchers have historically approached videogames from one of two competing perspectives: that of ludology, which describes games as formal systems of rules with players and a goal, and that of narratology, which treats them as a kind of narrative. Other approaches have also been taken, however, including ones grounded in sociology, film theory, and performance studies. Prominent figures in this emerging field of "game studies" include Espen Aarseth, Henry Jenkins, Jesper Juul, Brenda Laurel, Nick Montfort, Janet Murray, Marie-Laure Ryan, Katie Salen, Noah Wardrip-Fruin, and Eric Zimmerman.

While different types of videogame often appear to have more in common with nondigital forms such as board and counter wargames and tabletop RPGs than with each other, some points can be made about the form as a whole. Unlike most other types of game, videogames are often played by one individual, with the computer taking the role of opponent or (in the case of toy games) manipulable simulation. It is worth remembering, however, that even single-person games are in practice often played by groups, with individuals handing off control to one another depending on the type of challenge that needs to be overcome. Other games are explicitly designed for multiple players, who either take turns, use multiple controllers with a single machine, or link their personal computers to each other or to a central system, using local networks or the Internet. While videogame players are not in general as creative as participants in pen and paper RPGs (in which **gamemasters** frequently create their own explorable worlds), some commercial computer games have been designed to be modifiable by their owners since at least the early 1980s. Although in the early years of the industry, the majority of users restricted themselves to illicitly tampering with game programs to make them easier to play, by the mid-1990s, many players had begun designing their own missions for favored games and making them freely available to others. Some groups have gone further, transforming the visual design and gameplay of a program altogether to represent a different choice of subject matter, or to improve on perceived defects in the original. Such activities are generally restricted to games that run on personal computers rather than consoles, however, since they require the use of sophisticated tools (usually distributed by the original developers), which would be difficult to create for console hardware.

Several general trends are apparent in the history of videogame development. While the majority of new story games and many (perhaps most) examples of strategic planning games and massively multiplayer online games are still sf or fantasy, the form's initial strong links with the genre have clearly diminished with time. This is, perhaps, an inevitable result of its growth from an obscure hobby to a mass market medium comparable in size to the film industry. Many types of game have become notably stylized, with strong conventions dictating the forms gameplay can take, and the natures of the worlds within which it is presented. Such patterns are often incompatible with the rules of the realities that these works supposedly simulate, but serve to structure games in ways that are known to be playable, and which the majority of the audience has come to expect. While older works were generally intended for a single player, the increasing availability of both local networks and the Internet has given birth to many games that are meant to be played wholly or partially by participants using different devices connected by various technologies; such methods are often seen as superior to the older approach of allowing multiple players to share the same machine by using multiple controllers or taking turns to interact with the game.

Similarly, as the available hardware has improved, attractive graphics have become more important; with some exceptions, videogame forms have progressed from textual output to 2D displays, and then to 3D ones. This improvement in the fidelity of the representation has not come without its costs, however. Fully 3D games seen from an immersive viewpoint (such as the first-person "character's eye" view, or the third-person "over the character's shoulder" view) are difficult to implement, requiring a realistic model of physical interactions within the simulated world. This complexity means that such works often offer fewer options for interacting with the imaginary space than do those that employ simpler technologies, such as isometric displays of 3D worlds or 2D overhead views. In addition, the violent nature of many game mechanics becomes much more vividly apparent in an immersive 3D display. While modern games may not be any more bloodthirsty than those of the late twentieth century (or for that matter contemporary films, comics, or popular novels), they have generally attracted more criticism for their aggressive content. While some of this cultural distaste may be due to the current status of videogaming as a well-known form of entertainment, which is nevertheless only engaged with by a minority, some of it is probably also due to the increased accuracy and immersiveness with which the form now portrays acts of violence. (It may also be relevant that—perhaps as a result of the tendency of many works to focus exclusively on particular game mechanics—videogame violence appears to be less evenly distributed than it is in other forms; while almost all of the world's best-selling film franchises devote some of their screen time to personal combat, many of the most popular game series are either almost entirely focused on physical aggression or contain none at all. Sex and drugs, meanwhile, have been less common subjects for games than violence, and market pressures have generally meant that when they do appear, it is in an encoded form. Thus, Troika and White Wolf's 2004 **CRPG** (computer role playing game *Vampire: The Masquerade—Bloodlines* approaches sexuality through vampirism, a common device in many popular media). As with films that employ computer-generated effects, the degree to which further technical enhancements improve the quality of most participants' experience may in any case have begun to diminish. The visuals of graphical adventures dating from the early 1990s and computer role playing games from the latter half of the same decade are often regarded as entirely adequate today, for example.

Historically, most forms have either begun with turn-based approaches (in which all participants make their moves in sequence, waiting for the others to finish before proceeding) and later shifted to real-time ones (where all actions occur simultaneously), or have always been real time. It should be noted, however, that some forms—such as 4X games—remain primarily turn based, and that real-time games do not necessarily demand rapid responses from the player. (Many examples require the user to act within a time limit rather than immediately, or include the ability to pause the game at will and issue instructions to be executed when the flow of time resumes.) Most games have become more immediately accessible, and thus more suitable for a mass market, as bulky manuals have been replaced by interactive tutorials and printed text by recorded speech. It is also common for recent works to be more guided and less exploratory than were those of earlier decades; it is easier for a mass audience to appreciate a game if mastery can be achieved without prolonged experimentation. The end result of this pattern of development is that the vast majority of videogames are now visual and immediate in nature, resembling an interactive form of film or television, rather than discursive and textual, in the manner of written fiction. This does not, however, guarantee that a slower, more text-based kind of videogame will not appear in the future, though it seems unlikely that **interactive fiction**—the most prominent such form to date—will again become popular. As of 2013, the most likely candidate for such a form may be the wave of upcoming isometric computer role playing games funded by fans using the crowdsourcing website Kickstarter. Works such as the **heroic fantasy** *Pillars of Eternity* or the far future *Torment: Tides of Numenéra*—inspired by the remarkable *Planescape: Torment* (*1999* Black Isle Studios) designed by Chris Avellone and Colin McComb and set in the **science fantasy** world of the tabletop RPG *Numenéra* (*2013* Monte Cook Games) designed by Monte Cook—are aimed at a niche audience who are more interested in a detailed and involving narrative than they are in voiced speech, and can thus present complex worlds and story lines through the medium of text, with gameplay that is partially or wholly turn based rather than real time.

"Dust and Water," another concept image for *Torment: Tides of Numenéra*.

FURTHER READING

Serious books about videogames were once rare, but have become common in the twenty-first century. The following titles are highly recommended.

- Robert Levering, Michael Katz, and Milton Moskowitz. *The Computer Entrepreneurs: Who's Making It Big and How in America's Upstart Industry*. 1984. (A business book that includes pieces on the founders of such early US computer game developers as Infocom and Adventure International.)

- Douglas Carlston. *Software People: An Insider's Look at the Personal Computer Software Industry*. 1985. (Early history of the US microcomputer software industry, concentrating on games developers and written by the creator of one of the first commercial computer wargames, *Galactic Empire* [*1979* Brøderbund Software].)

- J C Herz. *Joystick Nation: How Videogames Ate Our Quarters, Won Our Hearts, and Rewired Our Minds.* 1997.

- Alain and Frédéric Le Diberder. *L'Univers des Jeux Vidéo.* 1998.

- Steven Poole. *Trigger Happy: The Inner Life of Videogames.* (Revised as *Trigger Happy: Videogames and the Entertainment Revolution in the United States.*) 2000. (An interesting cultural analysis of the form, concentrating on action games.)

- Steven L Kent. *The Ultimate History of Video Games: From Pong to Pokemon.* 2001.

- Brad King and John Borland. *Dungeons and Dreamers: The Rise of Computer Game Culture from Geek to Chic.* 2003. (A history of the US industry, concentrating strongly on the iconic first-person shooter *Doom* and the career of the CRPG designer Richard Garriott.)

- Austin Grossman, editor. *Postmortems from Game Developer.* 2003. (Collection of articles from the eponymous magazine that provide detailed [but not overly technical] analyses of the development of various contemporary videogames, including *Deus Ex* and *Command & Conquer: Tiberian Sun.*)

- Chris Kohler. *Power-Up: How Japanese Video Games Gave the World an Extra Life.* 2004.

- Heather Chaplin and Aaron Ruby. *Smartbomb: The Quest for Art, Entertainment, and Big Bucks in the Videogame Revolution.* 2005. (An interesting analysis of early twenty-first century videogame development, including detailed descriptions of *Anarchy Online*, *Star Wars: Galaxies*, and an early version of *Spore*.)

- James Newman and Iain Simons. *100 Videogames.* 2007. (A book published by the British Film Institute, which describes a hundred games, including many science-fictional ones, in the manner of the Institute's similarly titled film guides.)

- Bill Loguidice and Matt Barton. *Vintage Games: An Insider Look at the History of Grand Theft Auto, Super Mario, and the Most Influential*

Games of All Time. 2009. (Includes excellent histories of Dune II: The Building of a Dynasty, Doom, and Final Fantasy VII, with detailed analyses of their antecedents and descendants.)

- Tristan Donovan. *Replay: The History of Video Games*. 2010.

- Magnus Anderson and Rebecca Levene. *Grand Thieves & Tomb Raiders: How British Videogames Conquered the World*. 2012.

Web Links

- MobyGames Online Database: http://www.mobygames.com/

- GameRankings Online Reviews: http://www.gamerankings.com/

- Gamasutra: The Art & Business of Making Games: http://www.gamasutra.com/

- rec.games.frp.advocacy Frequently Asked Questions: http://www.darkshire.net/jhkim/rpg/theory/rgfa/

- Halcyon Days: Interviews with Classic Computer and Video Game Programmers: http://www.dadgum.com/halcyon/

- Greg Costikyan. "I Have No Words & I Must Design" (1994 *Interactive Fantasy* #2): http://www.costik.com/nowords.html

- Ernest Adams. "Postmodernism and the Three Types of Immersion": http://www.gamasutra.com/view/feature/2118/the_designers_notebook_.php

- Bruce Sterling. "Digital Dolphins in the Dance of Biz" (November 1991 *Science Fiction Eye*): http://w2.eff.org/Misc/Publications/Bruce_Sterling/Catscan_columns/catscan.09

CHAPTER 2

Game Narratives

THE OUTCOME OF ANY given game is inherently uncertain, since it must be possible to win or lose (or, in the case of **toy games**, to play at will). Yet stories, as normally understood, should have a beginning, a middle, and an end, and only one of each. Games that include stories—referred to in this book as **interactive narratives**—have thus proved difficult to design. There has also been considerable debate as to whether it is desirable, or even possible, that games have stories. This question was a frequent subject for dispute between board and counter **wargame** players and tabletop **role playing game** enthusiasts in the 1970s, for example, with the former group emphasizing the importance of simulational accuracy over narrative and the latter taking the opposite position. More recently, the growing commercial importance of **videogames** has led to the appearance of academics dedicated to "game studies," who have historically divided into "ludological" and "narrativist" camps. Broadly, members of the first group view games as formal systems of rules and have, on occasion, suggested that videogames should not attempt to tell stories, as in Jesper Juul's master's thesis, *A Clash between Game and Narrative* (**2001**). Narrativists, on the other hand, typically begin their consideration of games from the viewpoint of narratological theory, a tradition of literary analysis that can be said to begin with the Russian formalists of the 1920s and Vladimir Propp's *Morphology of the Folk Tale* ["Morfologija Skaski"] (**1928**). Thus, Janet Murray's *Hamlet on the Holodeck: The Future of Narrative in Cyberspace* (**1997**) contains something of a manifesto for the future of interactive digital narrative, based on a structural view of the elements of story. Other narrativists have taken the position that all games are essentially narrative in nature since the act of playing any game creates a story that the player can retell, a point that, while valid, seems of little practical significance. More recently, the ludological and narrativist camps appear to be converging on some sort of middle ground. Regardless of the details of the academic debate, however, it seems clear that many modern games contain detailed characters, complex settings intended to express significant themes, and predesigned plots that allow explicitly or implicitly for various narrative paths to be taken depending on the actions of the players. Such features are more important in some forms than others; story and characterization seem especially significant in **gamebooks**, tabletop **RPGs (role playing games), adventures,** and **computer role playing games,** and can also be important in **computer wargames, 4X games, god games,** and **first person shooters**. Thus, it seems reasonable to consider the types of interactive narrative present in such works.

Various categorization schemes have been devised for game narratives, generally concentrating on videogames. In *Avatars of Story* (**2006**), Marie-Laure Ryan attempts to extend narratological theory to encompass nontraditional forms of narrative, including interactive ones. Unfortunately, her analysis of such stories is not especially detailed. Almost all of the works considered in this book fall into her "Internal-Ontological" category, corresponding to narratives in which the player takes the part of a character in the story, the outcome of which can be changed by their actions. *Cybertext: Perspectives on Ergodic Literature* (**1997**), by Espen Aarseth, contains a more complex theory, which is, however, perhaps better suited to text-based videogame forms such as **interactive fiction** and **multi-user dungeons** than to interactive narratives in general. Professional videogame designers and writers typically distinguish between three main types of narrative: "linear," or impositional (in which the story proceeds from beginning to end much as it might in a film), "multilinear," or branching (where the plot contains a number of possible paths that can be followed by the player) and "open" (referring to games for which the possible patterns of story have not been mapped out in detail). A good summary of these categories, from a somewhat hostile perspective, can be found in *Chris Crawford on Interactive Storytelling* (**2004**), by Chris Crawford. This classification, while helpful, does not seem to adequately cover the variety of forms seen in modern games. Since none of these authors appears to provide a complete categorization, this book employs an original schema based on the identification of common patterns in various types of game and "interactive literature," influenced by several sources—including *Chris Crawford on Interactive Storytelling*, the academic work of Henry Jenkins, and Ken Rolston's article on "Adventure by Design" in issue 31 of the tabletop RPG magazine *Different Worlds* (November 1983)—but especially by terms used in videogame design. The forms of narrative included in this model are as follows:

```
WELCOME TO ADVENTURE!!  WOULD YOU LIKE INSTRUCTIONS?

YES
SOMEWHERE NEARBY IS COLOSSAL CAVE, WHERE OTHERS HAVE FOUND
FORTUNES IN TREASURE AND GOLD, THOUGH IT IS RUMORED
THAT SOME WHO ENTER ARE NEVER SEEN AGAIN. MAGIC IS SAID
TO WORK IN THE CAVE.  I WILL BE YOUR EYES AND HANDS. DIRECT
ME WITH COMMANDS OF 1 OR 2 WORDS.
<ERRORS, SUGGESTIONS, COMPLAINTS TO CROWTHER>
<IF STUCK TYPE HELP FOR SOME HINTS>


YOU ARE STANDING AT THE END OF A ROAD BEFORE A SMALL BRICK
BUILDING . AROUND YOU IS A FOREST. A SMALL
STREAM FLOWS OUT OF THE BUILDING AND DOWN A GULLY.

IN
YOU ARE INSIDE A BUILDING, A WELL HOUSE FOR A LARGE SPRING.

THERE ARE SOME KEYS ON THE GROUND HERE.

THERE IS A SHINY BRASS LAMP NEARBY.

THERE IS FOOD HERE.

THERE IS A BOTTLE OF WATER HERE.

TAKE LAMP
OK
```

The opening screen of the original (1975) version of *Colossal Cave*, the first text **adventure** and a work which was very influential on the development of narratives in computer games.

Frame: This refers to a fictional setting, possibly including a short story, comic, or piece of **full motion video**, which provides context for a game but is not important during actual play and is not itself interactive. Examples include many early videogames, such as *Space Invaders* (*1978* Taito) designed by Toshihiro Nishikado, for which background was supplied in a printed booklet or on the side of an arcade cabinet, and sf and fantasy wargames, which typically concentrate on simulating fictional battles rather than on telling stories. Such narrative frames can be strikingly detailed and evocative, as in the extensive universe constructed to support the miniature figures-based wargame *Warhammer 40,000* (*1987* Games Workshop) designed by Rick Priestley, Andy Chambers, Jervis Johnson, and Gavin Thorpe.

Embedded: An embedded narrative is one that occurs before the game begins, and which is split up into fragments that the player can reassemble into a coherent story as they are discovered. Interactive narratives of this form can resemble detective stories, though the goal is generally not to solve any specific mystery but instead simply to reconstruct the past. Perhaps the most famous example is the fantasy adventure *Myst* (*1993* Cyan Worlds) designed by Rand Miller and Robyn Miller, in which the player must explore several "Ages" accessible through various unusual books in order to understand the events that led to the magical imprisonment of the major characters. Sf games with embedded narratives include *The Dig* (*1995* LucasArts) designed by Sean Clark and Brian Moriarty, with its mysteriously vanished alien civilization, and *Bioshock* (*2007* 2K Boston/2K Australia) designed by Ken Levine, set in an underwater city that has been devastated by an initially inexplicable catastrophe.

Explorable: Explorable narratives resemble conventional stories in that there is only one sequence of events connecting a single beginning and end, but differ from them by allowing a reader (or viewer) to traverse those events in more than one order. Thus, it might be possible to start with a single character's name and follow a variety of paths leading from that point until the entire plot has been explored. This approach is commonly found in **hypertext** fictions, such as Geoff Ryman's non-sf website *253* (**1996**), each section of which is concerned with one of the 253 passengers and staff on board a London Underground train that is about to crash. Sf examples include the first two *Infocomics* releases.

Linear: Linear narratives are often described as having a "string of pearls" structure, a phrase that appears to have originated with the fantasy writer and game designer Jane Jensen. The plot proceeds in a broadly straightforward fashion from beginning to end, with each major narrative event represented by the string between two pearls, or nodes. Within each of these nodes, however, players are generally free to approach the game as they wish, until they have performed whatever actions are necessary to move on to the next pearl, advancing one step further in the overall plot. Linear stories are perhaps the simplest of all narrative forms, which—unlike the frame, embedded, and explorable types—allow the player to interact with the ongoing plot, and are the most commonly used approach in videogame design. This simplicity, however, can lead to some players feeling unduly confined by the game's structure, since they are only free to act between narratively significant events. Notable videogame examples include the adventure *The Longest Journey* (*1999* Funcom) designed by Ragnar Tørnquist, the **console role playing game** *Xenogears* (*1998* Square) designed by Tetsuya Takahashi, and the **real-time strategy** game *Hostile Waters: Antaeus Rising* (*2001* Rage Software).

Multilinear: The multilinear form is a natural development of the linear one, converting the simple string into a branching tree of possibilities. This allows participants to take a variety of different paths through the plot, depending on what choices they make—fight or flee, befriend or betray— at the predefined points that correspond to a branch. Several problems exist with this approach. It is clearly unfeasible to create a branch for every choice that a player might wish to make, and many options that should be physically possible would in any case produce an unconvincing and unsat-isfying story. Multilinear designs therefore tend to offer a limited number of choices, many of which loop back to nodes that have been previously encountered, or diverge only to recombine, thus reducing the amount of planning necessary. For example, players might find themselves exiled from their homes whether or not they choose to kill their father's mur-derer. Such limitations, however, can result in some players feeling con-strained by the plot, though this is certainly less common than with linear narratives. Some videogames attempt to resolve this issue by constructing several different multilinear plots that interconnect at the expense of mark-edly increasing the complexity of the design. This latter approach, which is sometimes referred to as a "threaded" or "web" story architecture, is most often seen in computer role playing games. Notable videogames that use multilinear narratives include the historical murder mystery *The Last Express* (*1997* Smoking Car Productions) designed by Jordan Mechner, the broodingly philosophical epic *Planescape: Torment* (*1999* Black Isle Studios [BIS]) designed by Chris Avellone and Colin McComb (a game set in the *Dungeons and Dragons* world of **Planescape**), and the science-fictional *Deus Ex* (*2000* Ion Storm) designed by Warren Spector and Harvey Smith and *Chrono Cross* (*1999* Square) designed by Masato Kato and Hiromichi Tanaka. Historically, multilinear plotting has also been the standard method used to construct printed gamebooks; one interesting early exam-ple of this form is Dennis Guerrier and Joan Richards' "programmed entertainment" *State of Emergency* (**1969**), set in an African nation that has recently achieved independence from its colonial masters, while its precursors include "Un conte à votre façon" ["A Story As You Like It"] (July 1967 *Le nouvel observateur*), an experimental narrative created by

Raymond Queneau of the **Oulipo** group. While gamebooks are today largely extinct as a commercial enterprise, various digital descendants have appeared, which use similar approaches to narrative, including the romantic bijuaru noberu or "visual novels" popular in Japan and *Echo Bazaar* (*2009* Failbetter Games; also known as *Fallen London*) designed by Alexis Kennedy, a web-based game set in a **steampunk** and sorcery version of Victorian London sold to demonic forces by Queen Victoria.

Modular: Modular stories are constructed from a number of largely independent "modules," in a similar manner to the separate episodes of a picaresque novel. While *Hamlet on the Holodeck* suggests the use of sections of plot that can be assembled in different orders and still form a coherent narrative—a concept inspired by techniques used in traditional oral storytelling—actual examples of modular interactive narrative have generally placed the individual modules in different physical locations, which can be visited by the player in whatever order they prefer. These modules may make up the major part of the game's plot (perhaps positioned between a single beginning and a single ending), or they may represent separate "side stories," which the player can choose to involve themselves with if they wish. Players are generally not required to participate in every such episode in order to reach an ending. Works that make good use of this technique include the sf videogames *Fallout* (*1997* BIS) designed by Tim Cain, Leonard Boyarsky, and Christopher Taylor and *Star Control II* (*1992* Toys For Bob) designed by Fred Ford and Paul Reiche III.

Emergent: Arguably, playing any game that includes recognizable characters and settings can cause a narrative to spontaneously emerge in the mind of the player. This viewpoint seems of little use for practical analysis of narrative form, however; so this book uses the term to refer solely to games in which the emergence of story is encouraged by design. Typically, this requires the existence of a clear goal that the player is attempting to achieve, considerable freedom of choice as to how that end might be accomplished, and personalities that the player can identify with and be opposed by. Successful emergent narratives are rare, but *Sid Meier's Alpha Centauri* (*1999* Firaxis Games) designed by Brian Reynolds and Sid Meier is an interesting example of a game that appears to have been carefully crafted to achieve this effect, with the parts of human characters being taken by entire civilizations. A somewhat similar approach is employed in the impressive epic fantasy game *King of Dragon Pass* (*1999* A Sharp) designed by David Dunham, Robin D Laws, and Greg Stafford, a combination of

4X game and mythic quest set in the tabletop world of **Glorantha**. *King of Dragon Pass*, however, focuses on groups of individual characters rather than personalized cultures, treating those characters as parameters supplied to abstract templates that express potential narrative structures.

Players of *King of Dragon Pass* participate in a series of micro narratives, which combine to form an overarching saga of the history of their tribe.

Environmental: The basic concept behind the environmental approach is to create a "story-rich environment" containing characters, background details, and short missions for the players to perform, in the expectation that a story will then evolve. It differs from the emergent form primarily by not including a strong goal and not attempting to deliberately guide the evolution of a narrative. Environmental techniques have generally been unsuccessful at creating a sense of story in single-player games; an instructive demonstration of the potential problems is provided by *Battlecruiser 3000 AD* (1996 3000AD) designed by Derek Smart. However, the approach can work well when several players participate (allowing them to compete against or cooperate with each other, which encourages the formation of memorable stories) and especially when an individual is deliberately attempting to shape the development of a narrative, in the manner of a tabletop **gamemaster**. Such designs vary widely in the extent to which their miniature stories have been structured in advance, from the relatively open form of *MUD* (*1978–1980*; also known as *MUD1*) designed by Roy Trubshaw and Richard Bartle, the first multi-user dungeon, to the heavily mission-based architecture of such **MMORPGs (massively multiplayer online role playing games)** as *World of Warcraft* (*2004* Blizzard Entertainment) designed by Rob Pardo, Jeff Kaplan, and Tom Chilton. The environmental approach is the most common one in persistent **online worlds**; one notable science-fictional example is the **massively multiplayer space sim** *EVE Online* (*2003* CCP Games) designed by Reynir Harðarson. It appears to have originated, however, in tabletop RPG supplements, which presented comprehensive descriptions of a location and its inhabitants as well as "seeds" for adventures that might occur there, of which the first was *City State of the Invincible Overlord* (*1976* Judges Guild) designed by Bob Bledsaw.

Generative: The generation of narrative is the ultimate goal of many videogame theorists, though it is perhaps less popular among working designers. The intention is to create narrative as the game is being played, in response to whatever actions the players may take. Clearly, this approach is central to the play of both **alternate reality games** and tabletop RPGs, where human **puppetmasters** and **gamemasters** shape the story that emerges from the game. While these mediators generally use predesigned plots, their own skills and talents are vital to the success of the enterprise. (These plots, which are typically linear, multilinear, modular, or environmental in structure, are sold—in the form of "adventures," or "modules"— by the creators of commercial tabletop RPGs for use with their games. Interestingly, examples of several types of interactive narrative can be found in such scenarios before they can be identified in videogames, as in the environmental *City State of the Invincible Overlord*, the multilinear *Buffalo Castle* [*1976* Flying Buffalo] designed by Rick Loomis, or the arguably modular nature of the systems used by Game Designers' Workshop to model social events in the swashbuckling historical RPG *En Garde!* [*1975*] designed by Frank Chadwick and to generate character backgrounds in the original edition of *Traveller* [*1977*] designed by Marc Miller.) Producing similar results using computer software has proved to be extremely difficult, and could conceivably require the creation of artificial intelligences possessing capabilities equivalent to those of a human being. A number of books have been published containing proposals for constructing such systems, which essentially require the algorithmic simulation of a storyteller. One well-known example is Brenda Laurel's *Computers As Theatre* (**1991**), which suggests the use of an "expert system" based on a human playwright to mediate human—computer interactions, considered as dramatic performances. Unfortunately, making effective use of such ideas in videogames seems quite unfeasible given the current state of the art in computer science. *Chris Crawford on Interactive Storytelling* contains a much more detailed proposal, which has been implemented as the "Storytron," though to date this technology has not produced any clear successes. Similarly, various products of artificial intelligence research, of which one of the most recent is the "relationship simulator" *Façade* (*2005 Procedural Arts*) designed by Michael Mateas and Andrew Stern, have generally failed to create convincing stories. Perhaps the most successful example of generative narrative in videogames to date is the "human dollhouse" game *The Sims* (*2000* Maxis) designed by Will Wright, though it is arguable to what extent it actually creates stories as opposed to producing behaviors that its players interpret as narrative.

Many actual interactive narratives employ more than one of these approaches, including a number of the games mentioned earlier. For example, the **firstperson shooter** *Stalker: Shadow of Chernobyl* (*2007* GSC Game World) makes use of both multilinear and modular techniques, while the text adventure *Trinity* (*1986* Infocom) designed by Brian Moriarty follows a linear path at the beginning and end of the plot, but employs a modular structure for the remainder of the game.

It is interesting to note that, of the nine types of narrative listed earlier, in the first three, the actual sequence of events, which make up the story is fixed, while in the remaining six, it is mutable. (Arguably, linear narratives should also be categorized as having a fixed story, since only events that are of no great importance to the narrative can be affected by the player in this form.) If the frame approach is discounted on the grounds that it is actually a noninteractive form of narrative used to provide context for an interactive game, the various categories divide into two groups: one (containing the linear, multilinear, modular, emergent, environmental, and generative types) in which the sequence of events can change, and one (consisting only of the embedded and exploratory forms) in which the events are fixed but the participant may experience them in a variety of different orders. In essence, this is the difference between a story and its telling, or (in narratological theory) between the series of incidents that form the "story" and the manner of their presentation to the reader, or "discourse." This distinction is also the same as that made in Ryan's *Avatars of Story* between "ontological" and "exploratory" forms of interactive narrative.

Other approaches to the categorization of forms of interactive narrative are possible. One option is to consider the status of the player, who generally adopts either the role of an actor (participating directly in the narrative) or that of a director (who shapes the action while not being personally involved). The actor approach could be further subdivided into single- and multirole categories, corresponding to games in which the player takes the part of a single character and ones in which the player controls several, as in many computer role playing games. Similarly, the director form could be split into a manipulator type (in which the player controls events from offstage, as in *The Sims*) and an observer one (where a reader explores the narrative, as in a typical **hyperfiction**). This scheme largely corresponds to *Avatars of Story*'s division between "internal" and "external" types of interactive narrative, though they are not precisely equivalent; Ryan's definitions conflate the viewpoint used in a videogame with the player's status. Thus, her "external" type requires the player to both have a detached overhead view and control events in the manner of a manipulator.

Similarly, types of narrative can be distinguished by their implicit use of tense. Thus, mutable stories occur in present tense narratives—as commonly used in games—while immutable ones appear in the past tense, corresponding to the frame, embedded, and exploratory forms described earlier. This classification does, however, suffer from the fact that hypertext narratives—conventionally presented in the past tense—often include multilinear branches, suggesting that in digital literature, at least, the past is not unchangeable.

It is impossible to guess which directions the art of constructing an interactive narrative might take in the future. However, it seems possible that highly responsive forms such as emergent stories will become more important, since they seem better suited to the inherently interactive nature of games. Generative narrative, however, appears likely to remain restricted to types of game that can be continuously mediated by humans for the foreseeable future, given the difficulties involved in algorithmically simulating a skilled storyteller. In any case, it seems unlikely that any approach will produce interactive stories that, considered as a whole, are as convincing as a well-crafted novel or film. The appeal of game narratives lies not in the perfection of their presentation, but in the chance they offer players to shape the ongoing story as well as experience it. Even in relatively well-understood (and not very interactive) forms such as the linear narrative, a degree of Coleridge's "willed suspension of disbelief" is often necessary on the part of a videogame player in order to accept the frequently repetitive or impersonal behavior of minor characters. An analogy, perhaps, can be made to the implied contract between audiences and actors in the theatre that prevents the watchers from intruding upon the stage, or noticing the falseness of the backdrops. Regardless, the increasing importance of story in the highly lucrative videogame market suggests that considerable effort will be expended on both the form and content of such narratives.

FURTHER READING

- Brenda Laurel. *Computers as Theatre*. 1991.

- Espen J Aarseth. *Cybertext: Perspectives on Ergodic Literature*. 1997.

- Janet H Murray. *Hamlet on the Holodeck: The Future of Narrative in Cyberspace*. 1997.

- Chris Crawford. *Chris Crawford on Interactive Storytelling*. 2004.

- Lee Sheldon. *Character Development and Storytelling for Games*. 2004. (A useful summary of the practical techniques used for composing videogame narratives.)

- Chris Bateman, editor. *Game Writing: Narrative Skills for Videogames*. 2006. (An excellent anthology of essays by professional videogame writers.)

- Marie-Laure Ryan. *Avatars of Story*. 2006.

- Pat Harrigan and Noah Wardrip-Fruin, editors. *Second Person: Role-Playing and Story in Games and Playable Media*. 2007. (Collection of articles on narrative in videogames and tabletop role playing games, including pieces by the sf writers and game designers Greg Costikyan, George R R Martin, Chris Crawford, and Kim Newman.)

- Dylan Holmes. *A Mind Forever Voyaging: A History of Storytelling in Video Games*. 2012. (An analysis of the evolution of narrative techniques in videogame design, approached through detailed studies of games ranging from *Planetfall* [1983] to *Heavy Rain* [2010].)

Web Links

- Storytron: http://www.storytron.com/

- A Clash between Game and Narrative: http://www.jesperjuul.net/thesis/

CHAPTER 3

Game Design

Although new games have been created throughout recorded history, the first attempts at a theory of game design do not seem to have emerged until the late 1960s, when James Dunnigan of Simulations Publications Inc (SPI) began to formulate a theory of board and counter **wargames**, which treated them as a form of "analytic history." (In this approach, wargames are seen as simulations of actual events that lend themselves to nonlinear exploration and experimentation leading to counterfactual results.) The term "game designer" itself, referring to the profession of making games, was coined at this time by Redmond Simonsen, Dunnigan's partner at SPI. Analyses of existing forms appeared considerably earlier, as in Harold Murray's *A History of Board Games Other Than Chess* (**1952**), but these were not intended as guidelines for the creation of original works. Most early wargames, tabletop **role playing games**, and **videogames** were designed primarily by intuition and rule of thumb rather than on the basis of any kind of theory, by individuals who typically also implemented their games (by programming computers or writing rules) and created any associated fiction. In the modern videogame industry, however, game designers are usually specialized professionals who operate separately to implementers and scriptwriters, and share a certain amount of terminology and core assumptions about the nature of their work. It is worth noting, however, that a tradition of group planning persists in many videogame development companies, where games are designed more by consensus than by any one individual or by a team of specialists.

A good overview of current approaches to game design, from a somewhat academic perspective, can be found in *Rules of Play: Game Design*

Fundamentals (**2003**), by Katie Salen and Eric Zimmerman. A more detailed analysis of current practices in the videogame industry is available in *Fundamentals of Game Design* (**2006**) by Ernest Adams and Andrew Rollings, one of the best of the many recent works on the subject. One of the key concepts employed in such books is the "magic circle," a term borrowed by Salen and Zimmerman from Johan Huizinga's *Homo Ludens* (**1938**), which describes a special physical or conceptual space, within which normal codes of behavior are suspended and replaced by the rules of the game. Perhaps the single most commonly made point is that games should be "easy to learn but hard to master," meaning that understanding the basics of how to play should be simple but grasping all the ramifications of the rules and becoming truly proficient in the game should be difficult. This maxim clearly applies to such classic board games as chess and Go, for example.

Arguably, all games are essentially types of interactive media, in the sense that film and television are both types of visual media. On this basis, Janet Murray suggests in *Hamlet on the Holodeck: The Future of Narrative in Cyberspace* (**1997**) that all forms of **interactive narrative** (or "cyberdrama," in her terms) are characterized by "immersion, agency, and transformation." Here, immersion is the ability of the simulated world to seem real and compelling, and agency is the player's power to affect that world. Transformation, meanwhile, refers to the way in which involvement in the game can cause participants to adopt a new identity, analogous to the sense of vicarious presence experienced by many novel readers and film viewers. Clearly other media can also be immersive or transformative in this sense, and games in which the player takes the part of a director of the action rather than an actor within it may not offer the possibility of transformation. Nevertheless, the concepts of immersion and agency appear to speak to the nature of interactive media in general, and Murray's original triad seems relevant to all games in which the player participates in shaping a story.

Transformation, in Murray's sense, can be experienced in more than one way. The typical relationships of players to the characters who they become within a game can perhaps be categorized as those of the teleoperator, the role player, and the identifier. Here the teleoperator controls their character as if it were an extension of their own body within the simulated environment, an approach taken by many players of **first person shooters** and other action-based videogames. The role player, on the other hand, relates to the character as a friend, a separate personality that the player guides or controls through the game. This perspective is most common in games with strong stories, including most **computer role playing games**, **adventures**, and **massively multiplayer online role playing games**, as well as tabletop **RPGs (role playing games)** and **gamebooks**. Finally, the identifier immerses themselves fully in the alternative personality of their character. Most players do not experience this; those who do are generally participating in pen and paper RPGs, **multi-user dungeons**, or **MMORPGs** for which they have created an alternate persona, which they use to interact with other players.

In this context, it is interesting to consider the opportunities for transformation, which are offered by games but not by other media such as film or television. Computer RPGs, MMORPGs and tabletop RPGs, are notable for the chance they offer players to create a character of their own design and then participate in an ongoing story from the perspective of their chosen persona. Videogames are at their most distinctive when they explore such possibilities, offering players experiences which cannot be expressed in a noninteractive medium.

As well as the characters and players who inhabit games' fictional universes, it can be helpful to consider those worlds themselves. Settings created for sf games have some unique characteristics not shared with other science-fictional worlds. Most importantly, a game-world needs to be balanced, meaning that opposing forces must be of approximately equal capabilities. While this may also be a requirement for an entertaining adventure story, in which the protagonist is engaged in a conflict with a reasonable chance of either victory or defeat, games are much more demanding in this regard. Characters in stories may act foolishly as a result of personal quirks or to advance the plot; players, in general, will not. Thus, an entertaining game requires that the technologies, armies, and superpowers available to the player must be carefully matched with those possessed by their opponents, without introducing repetitive battles that have no influence on the outcome or making available strategies that guarantee an easy victory. This balance can be **symmetric** (meaning that all participants have access to similar forces, perhaps with cosmetic differences) or **asymmetric** (in which case the opponents are radically different in abilities, numbers, or both, but should still be balanced).

In addition to such general criteria as originality and emotional resonance, this book employs a threefold aesthetic when considering game worlds, based on depth, breadth, and balance. Here, depth refers to the level of detail in which the world is specified, and breadth to the completeness of that description. A setting need not be physically extensive to be considered broad, but it should not make the player feel restricted by artificial constraints, or describe some regions in detail while representing others by simple sketches. There is generally some degree of tension between these two criteria: the deeper a world is, the more difficult it is to apply that detail broadly. Where balance is concerned, it is interesting to consider how videogames adapted from tabletop wargames and role playing games have generally been more successful than those based on novels or films. While it is clearly easier to design a game set in an existing world than one that tries to create an interactive variant on an entirely fixed and **linear** story, it is also true that using a setting that has not been designed in a balanced way can result in highly problematic gameplay. Arguably, **forerunners** and their mysterious artifacts are so common in sf games because they can provide the *dei ex machine*, which are sometimes required to enforce game balance or to correct the courses of wandering narratives, a function performed in fantasy games by sovereigns, sorcerers, and, on occasion, the gods themselves.

It is also true that the nature of a game-world fundamentally determines the kinds of stories that can be told within it. This is relevant to the sometimes contentious question of how morality can be represented in games. Arguably, all modern games—including tabletop RPGs, board and counter wargames, and videogames—are to some extent simulations. As soon as the world they represent begins to incorporate individual people and their societies, however, those simulations can no longer be judged on purely technical criteria. Instead, they express the artistic vision of their designers. Stories presented in the written sf genre, or in the media of film or television, may suggest moral lessons or enact tragedies by describing the actions of a character and their consequences. In games, this approach is generally unsuccessful when applied to the protagonist; players often resent being forced to act out a script created by the designers, and do not feel responsibility for the consequences of actions they did not choose to take. Furthermore, if a character suffers some unfortunate fate as the result of evil or ill-judged decisions, their player can simply restart the game from a saved position and begin again; typically, they will then construct their own personal version of their character's story from which the experience of death and failure has been elided. A moral perspective can instead be expressed in the nature of the world itself and in the effects players' choices have within it. In *Star Wars: Knights of the Old Republic*

(*2003* BioWare), for example, the player can win the game whether they turn to the light or the dark side of the mystic Force, but either choice has inescapable consequences for the player's relationships with other characters in the game and for the galaxy at large. If they decide to become evil, their character will never be truly loved.

In the modern games industry, however, the practice of such design principles is often constrained by the expectations of the marketing department. Most importantly, specific forms of game have become associated with particular target audiences, whose presumed tastes greatly influence the design of high budget "Triple A" works. Thus both first and **third person shooters**—like the action movies, which partially inspired them—are primarily expected to appeal to Western males in their twenties and thirties, which results in a strong emphasis on white male protagonists with a military or criminal background. Computer role playing games and MMORPGs, by contrast, are often enjoyed by a more subcultural audience made up of both men and women, many of whose members are avid science fiction and fantasy enthusiasts or tabletop role players. Thus, their fans frequently expect these works to include nonheterosexual relationships, protagonists of player-selectable gender, and other elements, which **CRPG** designers are happy to provide but which the more mass market shooter audience might be less likely to appreciate. Similarly, marketing departments generally expect dance games such as Ubisoft's *Just Dance* and the social simulations exemplified by Will Wright's *The Sims* to be bought largely by young women, and—as with romantic comedies in the cinematic world—try to tailor their features to the perceived interests of this audience. Similar comments could be made about almost any school of modern videogame design.

One final point applies to the essential nature of game design. The practice of design is greatly affected by the available technology, which determines what types of games can be created. To name only one example, **massively multiplayer online games** were not practical until the Internet was opened to commercial use, but appeared very shortly afterwards. Nevertheless, the evolution of games has not been solely determined by technological factors. There is, for example, no technical reason why printed **gamebooks** and pen and paper RPGs could not have been invented much earlier than they were. This indicates that while technology dictates what forms can be devised, the actual types of game that emerge are a matter of personal creativity and cultural influence.

FURTHER READING

- Chris Crawford. *The Art of Computer Game Design: Reflections of a Master Game Designer*. 1984. (A seminal early work on videogame design.)

- Janet H Murray. *Hamlet on the Holodeck: The Future of Narrative in Cyberspace*. 1997.

- James F Dunnigan. *Wargames Handbook, Third Edition: How to Play and Design Commercial and Professional Wargames*. 2000. (Includes an explanation of Dunnigan's concept of "analytic history.")

- Chris Crawford. *Chris Crawford on Game Design*. 2003. (An insightful and impassioned, if somewhat traditional, successor to *The Art of Computer Game Design*.)

- Katie Salen and Eric Zimmerman. *Rules of Play: Game Design Fundamentals*. 2003.

- Raph Koster. *A Theory of Fun for Game Design*. 2004. (A personal perspective on game design.)

- Ernest Adams and Andrew Rollings. *Fundamentals of Game Design*. 2006.

CHAPTER 4

Hyperfiction

HYPERTEXT CAN BE DEFINED as a way of organizing textual information that allows users to move from one section, or node, to another along various routes, or links. (It is generally assumed, however, that this scheme is implemented on a computer system.) The idea of somehow automating the retrieval of information from a common store appears repeatedly in the writings of the early twentieth century, as in the Permanent World Encyclopedia suggested by H G Wells in *World Brain* (**1938**). The clearest ancestor of modern hypertext, however, is the "memex" proposed by Vannevar Bush in "As We May Think" (July 1945 *Atlantic Monthly*), which would have allowed users to create "trails" of connected sets of microfilm pages, effectively constructing their own personal links around a set of immutable texts. Computerized systems that supported links between documents, loosely inspired by the memex, were demonstrated by Douglas Engelbart and Theodor Nelson in the United States in 1968; Nelson is responsible for coining the actual word "hypertext" in 1965, originally as "hyper-text." The concept then spread through the computer science community, becoming widely known with the release of the HyperCard application for the Apple Macintosh personal computer in 1987 and the creation of the World Wide Web by Tim Berners-Lee in 1989–1991. The main subject of this chapter, however, is not hypertext in general, but its uses in fiction, and especially in science fiction.

Storyspace, a software environment designed to enable the creation of **hyperfiction** (fiction written in hypertext), was first demonstrated in 1987, running Michael Joyce's *Afternoon, a story*. This seminal work partakes enthusiastically of the postmodern tradition of literary experimentation.

It is often deliberately obscure, encouraging reader disorientation by such means as unexpected changes of the narrative voice and concealment of the links needed to move from one node to the next. Different readings (or traversals) of the text can lead to radically different understandings of its meaning; the narrator, who may have seen his son die on the afternoon of the story, may (or may not) have caused that death. The effect is of a labyrinth of interconnected fragments representing the protagonist's disassociated state of mind, through which the reader wanders, experiencing moments first of frustration and then of epiphany.

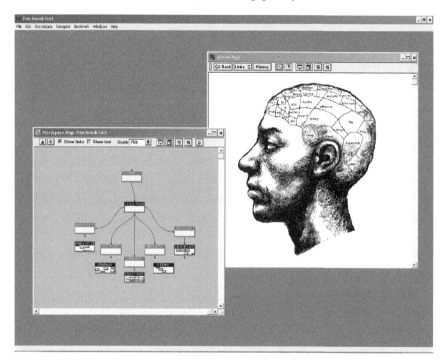

Among the many ways in which Patchwork Girl can be navigated are the hierarchical "Storyspace map" and a more visual abstraction inspired by the pseudoscience of phrenology.

The new form of hyperfiction acquired an early theorist in the person of George Landow, author of *Hypertext: The Convergence of Contemporary Critical Theory and Technology* (**1992**). Landow saw hypertext as a literal embodiment of the theories of poststructuralist literary critics such as Roland Barthes and Jacques Derrida. In essence, he suggested that the hypertext reader partially constructs the narrative they experience by choosing which links to follow. This reflects Barthes' concept of the "writerly text" as expressed in *S/Z* (**1970**): a work that the reader helps create by deciding on one of many possible interpretations. Eventually, Landow proposed that readers should be able to modify the text itself, adding links to other works or contributing comments, literally rewriting the document as they read it. This project, however, appears to be based more on the concept of the memex (in which the basic documents are static, making it easy for users to attach external links and marginalia) than on the reality of digital hypertext (where any such personal additions must be made to a body of texts, which are themselves prone to alteration). Arguably, Landow's writings are more applicable to hyperfiction than to hypertext in general; many authors have been influenced by his work, treating it as the poetics of the form.

While *Afternoon, a story* is in no way a work of sf, Shelley Jackson's *Patchwork Girl* (**1995**)—another well-known piece of hyperfiction created in Storyspace—is broadly science fictional. This is a highly referential work, which makes frequent allusions to both Mary Wollstonecraft Shelley's *Frankenstein, or The Modern Prometheus* (**1818**) and L Frank Baum's *The Patchwork Girl of Oz* (**1913**). The primary narrator is the female companion to Frankenstein's monster, secretly completed by Shelley. Creator and creation become lovers, and then go their separate ways; the monster travels to America, and finds her fate there. Thematically, *Patchwork Girl* is concerned with the assembly of composite identities (or hyperfictions) from disparate components. Structurally, it combines **multilinear** and **explorable** approaches to **interactive narrative**. Geographically, the map of its various links and nodes is considerably more straightforward than that of *Afternoon, a story*, though some readers still find it frustrating to navigate.

Various other works of hyperfiction were created in the 1990s using Storyspace and another similar environment called Hypergate, and attracted considerable attention from literary academics. One particularly well-known example is Stuart Moulthrop's *Victory Garden* (**1992**), which deals with the first Gulf War. Few of these stories can be classified as sf, however. An early exception is *King of Space* (**1991**) by Sarah Smith, a writer whose first published works were sf short stories—beginning with "Christmas at the Edge" in *Christmas Forever: All New Tales of Yuletide Wonder* (**1993**) edited by David G Hartwell—but who has since concentrated on historical fiction. The subject matter of *King of Space*— sex, starships, and criminality—is reminiscent of the works of Samuel R Delany, while its approach to the form has far more in common with the branching tree of multilinear options typically seen in **gamebooks** than the labyrinth of ever-shifting associations that dominates most hyperfiction. Another example of a literary hypertext created by a science fiction writer is Rob Swigart's *Down Time* (**2000**), but the various stories contained in this collection are not sf. Ultimately, the first wave of hyperfiction failed to gain any great audience outside academia, and few new works have been created in the Storyspace tradition since the late 1990s.

Most analyses of the structure of hyperfiction have been based primarily on the shape of the web of links. Mark Bernstein's influential paper "Patterns Of Hypertext" (June 1998 *Proceedings of the Ninth ACM Conference on Hypertext and Hypermedia*), for example, identifies a number of common elements, including the "cycle"—a recurring sequence of nodes from which the reader eventually departs, exemplified by *Afternoon, a story*—the "counterpoint"—which employs two alternating voices, as seen in *Patchwork Girl*—and the "tangle," which is used to intentionally disorient readers. In terms of the more structuralist analysis presented in this book's chapter on game narratives, hyperfictions have made use of at least the explorable, multilinear, and **modular** approaches, both separately and in combination.

Another school of hyperlinked fiction began to appear in the mid to late 1990s. These pieces frequently include images, music, and other media as well as text, and are therefore often classified as hypermedia rather than hypertext. Such works have generally been made available without charge on the World Wide Web, rather than sold as e-books implemented in proprietary systems such as Storyspace, and tend to be closer in spirit to the experimental "visual poetry" pioneered by the international Fluxus group in the 1960s than to prose storytelling. Arguably, hyperlinking may be fundamentally better suited to poetry and virtual art installations than to the development of a sustained narrative. One influential early example of the form is "My boyfriend came back from the war" (**1996**), by the Russian artist Olia Lialina. The hypermedia movement has, however, had very little connection to sf. One exception is Geoff Ryman's *253* (**1996**), a non-sf work by a science fiction writer, which presents interlinked word pictures of 253 individuals on board a London underground train that is about to crash. Structurally, *253* is very different to most Storyspace hyperfictions; it takes the form of an entirely explorable, largely static composition made up of associated stories rather than an enfolding labyrinth.

Sf authors working in the written genre have generally shown little interest in hyperfiction; Ryman and Smith are rare exceptions to this rule. When genre writers have become involved with "digital narrative," they have almost always done so through the medium of **videogames**. Relevant examples include Douglas Adams (codesigner and writer of *The HitchHiker's Guide to the Galaxy* and *Starship Titanic*), Michael Berlyn (designer and writer of *Suspended: A Cryogenic Nightmare*), Thomas M Disch (designer and writer of *Amnesia*), George Alec Effinger (codesigner and writer of *Circuit's Edge*), Warren Ellis (writer for *Hostile Waters: Antaeus Rising*), Harlan Ellison (codesigner and writer of *I Have No Mouth, and I Must Scream*), Jane Jensen (designer and writer of the *Gabriel Knight* series of graphical **adventures**), Marc Laidlaw (writer for the *Half-Life* series of **first person shooters**), Richard K Morgan (writer on *Crysis 2*), Sean Stewart (writer and codesigner of the **alternate reality game** *The Beast*), Rob Swigart (designer and writer of *Portal*), and Roger Zelazny (codesigner and writer of *Chronomaster*). The reality, perhaps, is that the history of attempts to create interactive narrative can be divided into two unrelated traditions: that of pen and paper **role playing game** and videogame development, which is strongly linked to print sf, and that of hyperfiction and hypermedia, which has primarily been associated with literary theory and postmodern art. Where narrative games are generally concerned with choice, whether within the individual chapters of an otherwise **linear** story or at the level of the overarching plot, most hyperfiction is about the exploration of a web of associations, which is open to many different interpretations. These two approaches have followed almost entirely separate lines of descent from what are arguably the two ancestral works of interactive narrative: *Dungeons and Dragons* (*1974* Tactical Studies Rules), Gary Gygax and Dave Arneson's original tabletop **RPG**, and Roland Barthes' critical theory text *S/Z* (**1970**). For good or ill, it seems likely that their two cultures will remain distinct.

FURTHER READING

- George P Landow. *Hypertext: The Convergence of Contemporary Critical Theory and Technology*. 1992.

Web Links
- Hyperizons: http://www.duke.edu/~mshumate/hyperfic.html

- Electronic Literature Organization: http://www.eliterature.org/

- Eastgate: Serious Hypertext: http://www.eastgate.com/

- Geoff Ryman's *253*: http://www.ryman-novel.com/

- Olia Lialina's "My boyfriend came back from the war": http://www.teleportacia.org/war/

- Patterns of Hypertext: http://www.eastgate.com/patterns/Patterns.html

- Ruth Nestvold and Jay Lake. "What Happened to Hyperfiction?" (August 2005 *Internet Review of Science Fiction*): http://www.irosf.com/q/zine/article/10174

CHAPTER 5

Independent Games

INDEPENDENT GAMES CAN BE defined as games owned by their creators, rather than by a large development or publishing company that exerts some degree of control over the design. Such games are often also published by the individuals who designed them. This definition is difficult to apply precisely; games may be developed and published independently and then rereleased by a major publisher, for example. In practice, however, the distinction between games that are developed independently and those that are created as part of the operations of a large organization is usually fairly clear. Important new game forms, such as the tabletop **role playing game** or the personal computer game, often first appear as independent games, with major companies—usually beginning with ones founded by the first designers to work in the field—emerging as the owners of new works if the form becomes commercially successful. Independently developed games then reappear if designers become frustrated by the constraints placed on them by the commercial system, or if the form as a whole becomes less popular, meaning that it is no longer profitable for a large-scale enterprise to create games of this kind. It is worth noting that independent games are far more common today than in the relatively recent past, a development undoubtedly influenced by the appearance of personal computers and the Internet, which have made the creation and distribution of such works significantly easier. Such technologies as print on demand and software downloading have made the means of production (and distribution) much more readily available to small developers, though not the (arguably now more important) means of marketing; lack of visibility in crowded marketplaces dooms most independent games to obscurity.

Early examples of independent game development occurred in board games, card games, and tabletop **wargames**, typically through self-publication of works rejected by the major publishers of the time. Examples include the first board and counter wargame (Charles Roberts' *Tactics* [*1954*]), the early sf-like card game *Nuclear War* (*1965*) designed by Douglas Malewicki, the first science-fictional board and counter wargame (*Lensman* [*1969*] designed by Philip Pritchard), and the first pen and paper role playing game (*Dungeons and Dragons* [*1974* Tactical Studies Rules] designed by Gary Gygax and Dave Arneson). The 1970s saw a boom in science fiction and fantasy wargames and role playing games, created by designers who initially were publishing their own games but quickly became successful enough to found companies that employed other designers and owned the rights to their work. Typically, such companies, including the American Simulations Publications Inc, Tactical Studies Rules, and Game Designers' Workshop as well as the UK's Games Workshop, developed and published their own material and distributed it through mail order and specialist shops, an approach pioneered in the 1960s by the first board and counter wargame developer, Avalon Hill.

The **videogame** industry followed a different path. The earliest games for personal computers were created by independent developers such as Richard Garriott or Chris Crawford and primarily sold through mail order and small computer shops. Meanwhile, games for arcade machines and home consoles were made by employees of the corporations that manufactured the hardware, such as America's Atari Inc. Some of these developers then founded their own companies to develop games for consoles separately to the owners of the hardware, beginning in 1979 with Activision. The industry rapidly evolved a model in which three types of companies created games: console and arcade cabinet manufacturers, which developed and released software for their own machines; large publishing companies such as Electronic Arts, who made their own games for both personal computers and consoles; and small-scale developers, who also worked on consoles and computers, but whose efforts were bought by publishers or console manufacturers, which then marketed and distributed them.

All of these patterns persist in the videogame industry today. In the twenty-first century, however, games created independently of the normal system have become more prominent. Much independent videogame development is now quite distinct from the mainstream industry, with products that are distributed directly to consumers over the Internet with the aid of such intermediaries as Apple or Amazon. Such games, like independent music and films, are sometimes works that probably would not have been released by a large commercial enterprise, whether because their form would be considered too risky or their content deemed potentially offensive to a mass market. If they can be developed cheaply by their designers and sold direct to the public, however, such games can be commercially viable. One well-known early example is the prototypal **first person shooter** *Doom* (*1993* id Software) designed by John Romero, John Carmack, Tom Hall, and Sandy Petersen, an unusual game at the time of its release, and one that was developed and sold without the involvement of a major publisher. In the late 1990s, however, as many designers became interested in following id Software's example, the steadily increasing cost of making a competitive videogame became a problem. While alternative films can be created considerably more cheaply than Hollywood movies, and making (as opposed to promoting) new music is not especially expensive, the nature of videogame development makes it difficult to build a visually impressive game of the kind that has dominated most of the market since the early 1990s without employing large teams of highly paid professionals.

Independent developers, therefore, have generally concentrated on alternative forms of videogame, such as the combination of storytelling and strategic gameplay with largely static illustrations seen in the **4X game** *King of Dragon Pass* (*1999* A Sharp) designed by David Dunham, Robin Laws, and Greg Stafford, or the **turn-based play by email** approach to online gaming used in the **computer wargame** *Laser Squad Nemesis* (*2002* Codo Technologies) designed by Julian Gollop. As with books published by small presses in the written sf genre, the lack of a significant marketing budget means that commercially successful examples are generally those that can rely on some degree of name recognition from potential customers. Examples include games made by designers well known for their previous work in the mainstream industry (such as *Laser Squad Nemesis* and *Battlecruiser Millennium* [*2001* 3000AD] designed by Derek Smart), spin-offs from already popular games (as with *King of Dragon Pass*, set in the tabletop **RPG** world of **Glorantha**) and the recipients of well-known awards (e.g., *Darwinia* [*2005* Introversion Software] designed by Chris Delay, a Grand Prize winner at the Independent Games Festival). Such free publicity is not, however, required for a game to become popular; one example of an sf videogame that attracted many players without this kind of assistance is the 4X game *VGA Planets* (*1992*) designed by Tim Wissemann.

Some independently developed videogames are not sold at all, meaning that there is no charge for downloading them and no expectation that players may later buy virtual items to enhance their experience of the game. This is, for example, how such text **adventures** as Emily Short's *Galatea* (*2000*), produced after the collapse of its form as a commercial enterprise, have been distributed; most can be obtained from the Interactive Fiction Archive. Other projects are written by large teams of volunteers and released under an open source license, meaning that the program code is made freely available for reuse and modification by others. Experience suggests, however, that games built by open source teams are most successful when they are either fairly simple or based on an existing commercial work; examples include *Wing Commander Privateer Gemini Gold* (*2005*), inspired by *Wing Commander: Privateer*, and the *Total Annihilation*-based *Spring* (*2007 Swedish Yankspankers*).

Although there is a long-standing community of amateur text adventure writers, in the 1990s, most independent videogames were created by isolated groups of developers. (Before the 1990s, few console games were made by independents due to hardware restrictions and legal issues, while the then largely separate personal computer games sector was enough of a cottage industry that there was often little distinction between independent and professionally published games.) The twenty-first century, however, has seen the emergence of an "indiegaming" movement, which explicitly models itself on independent film making and indie music labels. The members of this group have typically devoted themselves to creating action games—often based on jumping from one platform to the next—with gameplay that may contain novel twists on old designs. Some of these innovations are humorous in intent, while others are primarily visual, or concentrate on reinterpreting the structure of an earlier work. Achieving social or aesthetic significance is a common goal. Such games can be created by small groups, since they are generally modeled on the relatively uncomplicated products of the early years of the videogame industry, but presented with an irony and sophistication, which—with the exception of the text adventure form—were generally absent from their antecedents. Sometimes, they are simply short works made by professional videogame developers who have become frustrated with the creative restrictions of the modern industry. To date, few of these games have been of science-fictional interest, though *Machinarium* (*2009* Amanita Design) designed by Jakub Dvorský, *To the Moon* (*2011* Freebird Games) designed by Kan Gao, *Thomas Was Alone* (*2012*) designed by Mike Bithell, *FTL: Faster Than Light* (*2012* Subset Games) designed by Justin Ma and Matthew Davis, and *Strange Adventures in Infinite Space* (*2002* Digital Eel) designed by Richard Carlson and Iikka Keränen are all notable as works of sf. However, recent crowdfunding initiatives—in which websites such as Kickstarter are used to obtain funding from large numbers of donors or small investors for projects that are more expensive than most indie games but less costly than current professionally published efforts—have made it clear that cult games can be funded directly by fans of the designers or of previous works in a series. A crowdfunded sequel to the well-known early **computer role playing game** *Wasteland* (*1988* Interplay) designed by Alan Pavlish, Michael Stackpole, and Ken St Andre is now in production, for example. Such efforts seem likely to produce novel and intriguing works of science fiction.

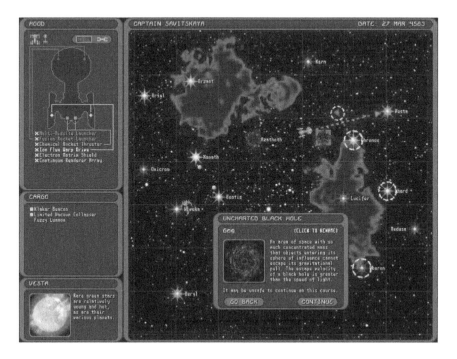

Players of *Strange Adventures in Infinite Space* explore a **2D** map of the galaxy.

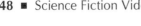

Combat in *Strange Adventures in Infinite Space* is infrequent but beautiful.

In addition to Kickstarter and self-financing from the developers' own resources, a third model is now emerging, one often associated with Valve's game delivery service, Steam—that of rolling funding for games in development, where backers pay to obtain a copy of an incomplete work in its current state with free copies of all subsequent versions as they become available. Like Kickstarter, this model has only been made possible by the existence of world-wide computer networks, since without digital downloading, the delivery of multiple versions in various stages of development to every purchaser would be prohibitively expensive. The indications so far are that it can be remarkably successful, perhaps because it appeals to a fan audience who are attracted by the opportunity to participate in the development of the games they love, even if their involvement is only a matter of commenting on early drafts of the design. Squad's impressive **Space Sim** *Kerbal Space Program* is being created in this way, for example, as is Pathea Games' *Planet Explorers*, in which interstellar colonists are marooned on an alien world.

To date, a number of interesting and influential videogames that might not have been created by the mainstream industry have been developed independently, notably *Doom* and the *Angry Birds* series of **puzzle games**, but most innovative works have been published by major companies. As the costs of development continue to rise, however—videogame budgets in the late 2000s were comparable with the costs of film making toward the end of the 1970s in real terms—it is becoming steadily more difficult to finance novel (and thus risky) games by conventional means, suggesting that independent game makers might become more important as a source of innovative designs. The issue here appears to be largely one of form, not of content; videogame publishers have historically not been overly concerned by the possibility of offending some sections of the population, but unenthusiastic about releasing games with radical designs that their core customers might not enjoy playing. As William Goldman wrote about Hollywood, "Nobody knows anything," publishers find it very difficult to predict which games will prove profitable, and often prefer to fund remakes of and sequels to successful works on the basis that they are less likely to lose money. Certainly it is interesting to consider how many videogames that originated new forms were created in an academic environment in the absence of commercial pressures (*Adventure* [*1975–1976*] designed by William Crowther and Don Woods and *MUD* [*1978–1980*] designed by Roy Trubshaw and Richard Bartle), independently developed by teams who experienced difficulty in finding a publisher (*Elite* [*1984*] designed by David Braben and Ian Bell and *Sim City* [*1989* Maxis] designed by Will Wright), or were unpopular projects that received limited support from their publishers since they were thought likely to fail commercially (*Civilization* [*1991* MicroProse] designed by Sid Meier and *Ultima Online* [*1997* Origin Systems] designed by Richard Garriott, Raph Koster, Rick Delashmit, and Starr Long). It is possible that, had these games not been made and inspired commercially successful forms, similar projects would not be created or published by major companies today, meaning that they would be developed independently or not at all.

FURTHER READING

- Mike Rose. *250 Indie Games You Must Play*. 2011. (A collection of reviews from the indiegaming movement, including analyses of *Machinarium*, *Strange Adventures in Infinite Space*, and various other works of a fantastical nature.)

Web Links

- Independent Games Festival: http://www.igf.com/

- The Interactive Fiction Archive: http://www.ifarchive.org/

- IndieGames (Indiegaming News Site): http://indiegames.com

- tigsource (Indiegaming Developer Site): http://www.tigsource.com

- IndieCade (Indiegaming Festival Site): http://www.indiecade.com/

CHAPTER 6

Adventures

A<small>N</small> ADVENTURE IS A kind of **videogame** in which the gameplay is largely based on the solution of puzzles. Such games are rarely played in **real time**. Instead, the progress of events in the game-world will typically be suspended until the player acts, allowing them time to consider their current problem. It is also important that the number of potential solutions for each puzzle be limited so that players are not overwhelmed by the exploration of endless possibilities. As a result, the worlds in which these games are set typically lack the global consistency and physical operability seen in many **computer role playing game** milieux, instead offering a wide variety of opportunities for interaction, which are specific to a given time and place. Adventures generally emphasize story and character development; arguably, the form is most effective when the puzzles are based on interaction with the characters within the game, integrating the two aspects of the design. The adventure is perhaps the videogame form that is closest to written fiction; the stories often have a strongly **linear** structure, and the discursive nature of the gameplay is reminiscent of the act of reading. Most attempts to make videogames based on written sf stories, whether by adaptation or by the creation of sequels, have been adventures, though the results have often been unimpressive.

The first game of this kind was *Adventure* (*1975–1976*; also known as *ADVENT*, *Colossal Cave* or *Colossal Cave Adventure*) designed by William Crowther and Don Woods. This program simulates part of the Mammoth Cave system in the US state of Kentucky, with added fantasy elements such as hidden treasures and an axe-throwing dwarf. The original version was written by Crowther alone, influenced by his experiences of exploring the actual Mammoth Caves and playing an obscure variant of the fantasy **role playing game** *Dungeons and Dragons* (*1974* Tactical Studies Rules) designed by Gary Gygax and Dave Arneson known as *Mirkwood Tales* (*circa 1975*) designed by Eric Roberts; Woods later expanded the program, adding more puzzles and fantasy elements. Players can enter a number of different areas, each of which is described in text, and issue instructions using a parser, a piece of software that attempts to translate natural language (in this case, English) into inputs, which the program can process. (A similar approach to game input and output can be seen in such earlier works as *Hunt The Wumpus* [*1972*] designed by Gregory Yob, in which the player must deduce the location of the eponymous creature in a 3D dodecahedral maze and kill it before it kills them.) This variant of the form is generally known as a text adventure, though this description can also be applied to games in which all or most of the program's output is textual, but players choose which action to take from a menu, as in the much later Japanese game *Radical Dreamers* (*1996* Square) designed by Masato Kato. Many of the characteristic features of text adventures are already visible in this first example. Notably, the player relates to their incarnation within the world of the game as a partially separate individual who can be given orders, and certain actions will trigger special responses delivered for comic effect, as if the parser itself has an identity and a role to play. In *Adventure*, however, there is no concept of the main character having a history and personality of their own, which is separate to that of the player, a device that was to become important in most of its descendants.

Adventure proved to be extremely influential, inspiring its players to create many similar games, which were referred to collectively as adventures in honor of that first work. Of these, the most significant are perhaps the comic fantasy *Zork* (*1977–1979*; also known as *Dungeon*) designed by Tim Anderson, Marc Blank, Dave Lebling, and Bruce Daniels and the **sword and sorcery** *Adventureland* (*1978* Adventure International) designed by Scott Adams, the first (albeit somewhat primitive) adventure released for personal computers. *Dog Star Adventure* (*1979*; also known as *Death Planet: The Dog Star Adventure*) designed by Lance Micklus, a simple game much influenced by the film *Star Wars: Episode IV – A New Hope* (*1977*) and originally published in *Softside* magazine, may have been the first science-fictional adventure made available for these new machines; it was followed by rather more accomplished works such as *Cyborg* (*1981* Sentient Software), designed by the sf writer Michael Berlyn.

In 1980, *Zork* was converted from mainframe computers to the less powerful personal devices, becoming the first product of the Infocom studio that were to exert considerable influence on the evolution of the text adventure form. Infocom created innovative and well-crafted games in a range of literary genres, though science fiction and fantasy dominated; their first sf game was *Starcross* (*1982*) designed by Dave Lebling. Other notable science-fictional works from the studio include *Planetfall* (*1982*) designed by Steve Meretzky, *Suspended: A Cryogenic Nightmare* (*1983*) designed by Michael Berlyn, *The Hitchhiker's Guide to the Galaxy* (*1984*) designed by Douglas Adams and Steve Meretzky, *A Mind Forever Voyaging* (*1985*) designed by Steve Meretzky, and *Leather Goddesses of Phobos* (*1986*), also by Meretzky. In areas other than sf, *The Lurking Horror* (*1987* Infocom) designed by Dave Lebling—a supernatural tale of college life inspired by the **Cthulhu Mythos**—the murder mystery *Deadline* (*1982* Infocom) designed by Marc Blank, and the romance game *Plundered Hearts* (*1987* Infocom) designed by Amy Briggs are all of interest. Another prominent US developer of text adventures was Trillium (later known as Telarium), which specialized in adapting works of printed literature, often from the sf or fantasy genres. Their releases include *Fahrenheit 451* (*1984*) designed by Len Neufeld—a sequel to Ray Bradbury's novel of the same name—and *Nine Princes in Amber* (*1985*), an interesting if perhaps ultimately unsuccessful attempt to model subtle character interactions using a text parser that was based on the first two books in Roger Zelazny's **Amber** sequence. Trillium also published *Shadowkeep* (*1984* Ultrasoft) designed by Alan Clark, an innovative early sword and sorcery computer role playing game whose design resembled that of a text adventure, and which inspired what was probably the first videogame spin-off novel, Alan Dean Foster's *Shadowkeep* (**1984**).

The first example of the form to be created outside the United States was probably *Acheton* (*1978–1981*) designed by Jon Thackray, David Seal, and Jonathan Partington in the United Kingdom, an exploration of a memorably lethal underground cave complex inspired by the original *Adventure*. *Acheton* was followed by such commercial works as the Australian game of *The Hobbit* (*1983* Beam Software) designed by Philip Mitchell and Veronika Megler, noted for its innovative use of a cast of independently (though sometimes rather erratically) acting characters. This game is almost a palimpsest of the J R R Tolkien novel on which it was based, including both marked simplifications of the original material and a variety of new possibilities. Interesting commercial text adventures produced in the United Kingdom in this era include the charming **parallel world** fantasy *Jinxter* (*1987* Magnetic Scrolls [MS]) designed by Georgina Sinclair and Michael Bywater and the **heroic fantasy** parody *Knight Orc* (*1987* Level 9) designed by Pete Austin, as well as such science-fictional works as *Snowball* (*1983* Level 9)—the first game in the *Silicon Dreams* trilogy—*Fish!* (*1988* MS) designed by Pete Kemp, John Molloy, Phil South, and Robert Steggles, and the notably difficult and not very serious *Countdown to Doom* (*1982* Acornsoft) designed by Peter Killworth. A line of games based on published works of fiction, similar to Telarium's products though of generally lower quality, was released by Mosaic Publishing (MP), including such sf works as *The Pen and the Dark* (*1984* MP) designed by Keith Campbell (inspired by one of Colin Kapp's tales of the **Unorthodox Engineers**), *The Width of the World* (*1984* MP) designed by Simon Gould (a sequel to Ian Watson's short story "The Width of the World" [June 1983 in *Universe 13*]), *The Stainless Steel Rat Saves the World* (*1984* Shards Software [SS]) designed by Sean O'Connell (derived from Harry Harrison's **Stainless Steel Rat** series), and *The Nomad of Time* (*1984* SS), a spin-off from Michael Moorcock's **Oswald Bastable** sequence.

By the mid-1980s, text adventures had attracted significant literary interest. Games development houses attempted to differentiate their works from other videogames by promoting them as **interactive fiction** (a term popularized by Infocom) or "electronic novels" (the form favored by Synapse Software, developers of *Mindwheel* [*1984*]). Established authors became interested in the form, including Douglas Adams (who worked on *The Hitchhiker's Guide to the Galaxy* and the contemporary comedy *Bureaucracy* [*1987* Infocom]), Robert Pinsky (later Poet Laureate to the Library of Congress), who was the lead designer on *Mindwheel*, and the noted science fiction writer Thomas M Disch, creator of the non-sf *Amnesia* (*1986* Cognetics Corp). While *Amnesia's* prose is rich and fluent, its gameplay may prove frustrating. The player is subject to artificial constraints applied to ensure that they proceed through the game as intended by Disch, and the game's detailed simulation of the reality of modern-day New York City frequently results in the main character collapsing from hunger before anything much is achieved. Ultimately, the most impressive example of commercial interactive fiction may not be any of these works, but rather Brian Moriarty's remarkable fantasia *Trinity* (*1986* Infocom).

By the end of the 1980s, however, sales of text adventures had largely collapsed, as players deserted them for their more visually appealing successors. Meanwhile, literary critics abandoned the field for the new

hypertext fiction, of which Michael Joyce's *Afternoon, a story* (**1990**) was the first example. Interactive fiction has survived, however, as a form made by enthusiasts for enthusiasts and distributed freely. Such works are typically shorter than the commercial games, and often more experimental in nature. Two excellent examples that may be of interest to sf readers are the **Cthulhu Mythos**–inspired *Anchorhead* (*1998*) designed by Michael Gentry and Galatea (*2000*) designed by Emily Short, which is less an adventure than a detailed simulation of a single individual who may be a robot, a goddess, or something other.

The first example of the form to include graphics was *Mystery House* (*1980* On-Line Systems) designed by Roberta Williams, a text adventure inspired by Agatha Christie's detective novel *And Then There Were None* (**1939**), which included static images showing locations within the game, in the manner of an illustrated novel. This approach was used in many subsequent text adventures, including *Nine Princes in Amber*, *Jinxter*, *The Hobbit*, and the later entries in the *Silicon Dreams* series. The first true graphical adventure, with fully animated visuals, appears to have been *Valhalla* (*1983* Movisoft) designed by Richard Edwards, Graham Asher, Charles Goodwin, James Learmont, and Andrew Owen, a UK-developed game based on Norse mythology, which included self-willed characters in the manner of *The Hobbit*. This was followed by the American fairy tale fantasy *King's Quest* (*1984* Sierra On-Line [SOL]; also known as *King's Quest I: Quest for the Crown*) designed by Roberta Williams. In both of these works, the player's character is shown moving through a series of static landscapes, a model also employed in most later games of the type. The developers of *King's Quest* then went on to create a number of similar works, of which the first sf example was *Space Quest* (*1986* SOL) designed by Mark Crowe and Scott Murphy. All of these games, however, were controlled using typed commands, which were processed by a parser. While this apparently allowed players to perform any action they could imagine, in reality, the limitations of the game design and the software's ability to understand natural language meant that only a small number of meaningful choices could be made. Identifying the phrases that would cause the parser to invoke these actions could, however, be frustratingly difficult. The otherwise undistinguished noir mystery *Déjà Vu* (*1985* ICOM Simulations) replaced the parser with a graphical user interface in which instructions were issued to the characters by clicking on icons, an innovation that made the choices available to the player clear. The much superior *Maniac Mansion*

(*1987* Lucasfilm Games [LF]) designed by Ron Gilbert and Gary Winnick then combined this interface with the animated visuals of *Valhalla* and *King's Quest*, an approach that came to dominate the design of Western graphical adventures. (In Japan, meanwhile, the designer Hideo Kojima took a different approach to eliminating the parser with *Snatcher* [*1988* Konami], in which the player chooses actions from a menu.) The developers of *Maniac Mansion*, LG (later LucasArts [LA]), went on to evolve a philosophy of adventure game design intended to minimize player frustration. The death of player characters, a frequent occurrence in *Space Quest*, was made impossible or very rare, and situations in which the game had to be restarted before further progress could be made (as used for comic effect in *The Hitchhiker's Guide to the Galaxy*) were eliminated. This approach, which can be seen fully developed in the musical fantasy *Loom* (*1990* LF) designed by Brian Moriarty, was well received by players, and influenced the design of most later works in the form.

Graphical adventures were highly popular in the 1990s. LA produced many notable science-fictional examples, including *Zak McKracken and the Alien Mindbenders* (*1988* LF) designed by David Fox, *Maniac Mansion: Day of the Tentacle* (*1993* LA) designed by Tim Schafer and David Grossman, *The Dig* (*1995* LA) designed by Sean Clark and Brian Moriarty, and *Full Throttle* (*1996* LA) designed by Tim Schafer, as well as the piratical *The Secret Of Monkey Island* (*1990* LF) designed by Ron Gilbert, David Grossman and Tim Schafer—a work partially inspired by Tim Powers' novel *On Stranger Tides* (**1987**)—and the parodic cartoon *Sam & Max Hit The Road* (*1993* LA) designed by Sean Clark, Collette Michaud, Steve Purcell, and Michael Stemmle. SOL, the developers of *King's Quest*, created the contemporary occult series *Gabriel Knight*, beginning with *Gabriel Knight: Sins Of The Fathers* (*1993* SOL) designed by Jane Jensen, and the comic fantasy *Quest For Glory* sequence, beginning with *Hero's Quest: So You Want To Be A Hero* (*1989* SOL; also known as *Quest for Glory I: So You Want To Be A Hero*) designed by Lori Ann Cole and Corey Cole, which incorporated elements of computer role playing games into its design. Outside the United States, the United Kingdom's Revolution Software (RS) released the dystopian *Beneath a Steel Sky* (*1994* RS) designed by Charles Cecil, Dave Cummins, Dave Gibbons, and Daniel Marchant and the occult conspiracy series *Broken Sword*, beginning with *Broken Sword: The Shadow Of The Templars* (*1996* RS; also known as *Circle of Blood* in the United States) designed by Charles Cecil and partially inspired by Umberto Eco's novel *Foucault's Pendulum* (**1988**). While the earlier games are generally humorous in tone, more serious themes began to appear in 1993–1994, as technical improvements made it possible to use less cartoon like graphics. Most of the notable adventures of the 1990s were sf or fantasy; one remarkable exception is *The Last Express* (*1997* Smoking Car Productions) designed by Jordan Mechner, a murder mystery set on the last journey of the Orient Express before World War One, in which the player's character and the other passengers engage in a complex **multilinear** interaction in real time.

One contemporary developer, Legend Entertainment (LE), is of particular science-fictional interest. This studio concentrated primarily on adapting works of sf and fantasy literature into graphical and illustrated text adventures, including *Frederik Pohl's Gateway* (*1992* LE) designed by Glen Dahlgren and Michael Verdu—based on Frederik Pohl's **Heechee** sequence—and *Callahan's Crosstime Saloon* (*1997* LE) designed by Josh Mandel and Jim Montanus, a spin-off from Spider Robinson's eponymous series. Authors from the written genre also worked on the design of some graphical adventures, as in Harlan Ellison's *I Have No Mouth, and I Must Scream* (*1995* The Dreamers' Guild) and Roger Zelazny's *Chronomaster* (*1995* DreamForge Entertainment). In the United Kingdom, Terry Pratchett became involved in the creation of three games set in his fantasy **Discworld** milieu, of which the most interesting is the Chandleresque *Discworld Noir* (*1999* Perfect Entertainment) designed by Gregg Barnett and Chris Bateman.

Another form of graphical adventure appeared with the release of the science-fictional game *The Journeyman Project* (*1993* Presto Studios [PS]) designed by David Flanagan and its more fantastic contemporary *Myst* (*1993* Cyan Worlds) designed by Rand Miller, Robyn Miller. These works employed a first-person camera, which shows events from the character's point of view, rather than the "third-person" external view of the character typically used in graphical adventures, and made use of **full motion video** to display much more impressive visuals than were possible in such competing games as *Maniac Mansion: Day of the Tentacle*. However, this improvement came at a price; the player's ability to interact with the environment was extremely limited. Characteristically, *Myst*'s gameplay depends heavily on semiabstract logic puzzles, and the story is **embedded**. While *Myst* itself and its immediate sequels were extremely popular, similar games such as *Obsidian* (*1996* Rocket Science Games) designed by Howard Cushnir, Scott Kim, and Adam Wolff generally failed to find a market. A different approach to the use of full motion video is exemplified by the later *Tex Murphy* games, which combine fully interactive sequences seen in first person with noninteractive filmed segments using live actors.

Toward the end of the 1990s, the market for graphical adventures as a whole began to decline. Critically acclaimed games such as the clay animated cartoon *The Neverhood* (1996 The Neverhood) designed by Douglas TenNapel proved unprofitable, a trend that culminated in the commercial failure of *Grim Fandango* (1998 LA) designed by Tim Schafer, a noir fantasy in which a supernatural travel agent must guide a newly arrived soul through the Mexican Land of the Dead. By the end of the decade, graphical adventures were largely extinct. The reasons for this collapse are unclear; one possibility is that solving puzzles simply did not appeal to a large enough market that games based on it could remain profitable as the visual quality of videogames, and hence their cost of development, maintained its apparently inexorable growth. Certainly, traditional puzzle-based adventures continue to sell well to a niche market; one indicative example is the episodic series *The Walking Dead* (2012 Telltale Games), a notably atmospheric spin-off from Robert Kirkman's comic book series of the same name (2003–current). Other modern adventures, such as the **science and sorcery** game *The Longest Journey* (1999 Funcom) designed by Ragnar Tørnquist, the mildly fantastical *Syberia* (2002 Microids) designed by Benoît Sokal, and the paranormal thriller *Fahrenheit* (2005 Quantic Dream [QD]; also known as *Indigo Prophecy* in the United States) designed by David Cage, are more consciously artistic and are usually made in Europe rather than the United States. *Fahrenheit* in particular attempts to fuse adventure game conventions with those of contemporary film making, not always happily. More recent examples include the serial killer–inspired *Heavy Rain* (2010 QD) designed by David Cage (in which the player participates as multiple characters, any of whom can die) and the paranormal mystery *Gray Matter* (2010 Wizarbox) designed by Jane Jensen. Some members of the form have also been created as **independent games**, notably the science-fictional *Machinarium* (2009 Amanita Design) designed by Jakub Dvorský, while several original works (including *Broken Age*, a science-fictional game designed by Tim Schafer) as well as many new entries in existing series such as *Tex Murphy* have been financed with the assistance of the crowdfunding website Kickstarter. Graphical adventures have also retained some popularity in Japan, with such works as the time travel game *Shadow of Memories* (2001 Konami) designed by Junko Kawano also being released in the West. Other Japanese games, such as the legal drama *Phoenix Wright: Ace Attorney* (2001

Capcom; also known as *Turnabout Trial: Revived Turnabout* in Japan), are arguably more closely related to the country's **gamebook**-like bijuaru noberu (known in English as "visual novels") than they are to traditional adventures.

The dominant form currently adopted by this type of game in the West, however, is that of the action adventure. These games represent an attempt to combine traditional adventure game elements, such as intellectual puzzle solving and exploration, with gameplay more often associated with "action games" depending on reaction speed and coordination. Such games are typically real time, displayed in three dimensions using a third-person view of the player's character. While the category is inevitably hard to define, it seems clear that a number of recent European games such as the science-fictional *Outcast* (*1999* Appeal) and *Beyond Good & Evil* (*2003* Ubisoft) designed by Michel Ancel should be placed within it, as should the American *The Last of Us* (*2013* Naughty Dog) designed by Bruce Straley and Neil Druckmann, the highly stylized Japanese fairy tale *Ico* (*2002* Sony Computer Entertainment) designed by Fumito Ueda, and the upcoming **alternate history** hacking game *Watch Dogs*. Action adventures proved to be rather more commercially successful than graphical adventures during the 2000s; it is perhaps characteristic that while the first game in the *Longest Journey* series is a traditional adventure, its 2006 sequel, *Dreamfall*, is an action adventure. The core puzzle–solution mechanic employed in adventures has also reappeared in several other forms, including **first person shooters** and even **space sims**. Arguably, however, the adventure game's traditional position as standard bearer for story and characterization in videogames has now been ceded to computer role playing games, though **CRPGs** (computer role playing games) typically employ **multilinear** and **modular** models of narrative as opposed to the classic **linear** form seen in most adventures.

FURTHER READING

- Gil Williamson. *Computer Adventures: The Secret Art*. 1990. (Interesting if somewhat disorganized book on adventure game design.)

- Patrick R. Dewey. *Adventure Games for Microcomputers: An Annotated Directory of Interactive Fiction*. 1991. (Contains capsule reviews of most notable text adventures produced in the commercial era.)

- Nick Montfort. *Twisty Little Passages: An Approach to Interactive Fiction.* 2003. (An excellent academic history of text adventures, including a detailed theoretical analysis of them as literary machines.)

- Kurt Kalata, editor. *The Guide to Classic Graphic Adventures.* 2011. (A remarkably comprehensive and informative collection of amateur reviews of graphical adventures.)

Web Links

- Adventure Gamers: http://www.adventuregamers.com/

- Brass Lantern: the adventure game website: http://www.brasslantern. org/

- Adventureland: http://www.lysator.liu.se/adventure/

- The Interactive Fiction Archive: http://www.ifarchive.org/

- *Computer Adventures: The Secret Art*, by Gil Williamson: http:// www.amazonsystems.co.uk/data/ca-tsa.htm

- Down from the Top of Its Game: The Story of Infocom: http://web. mit.edu/6.933/www/Fall2000/infocom/

BENEATH A STEEL SKY

1994. RS. Designed by Charles Cecil, Dave Cummins, Dave Gibbons, and Daniel Marchant.

In the graphical **adventure** *Beneath a Steel Sky*, Australia's future is a dark one. The game is set in a grimy, run-down megalopolis ruled by a totalitarian computer, where the rich live on the pleasantly arranged surface and the poor inhabit teeming levels of machinery in the sky. This inverted dystopia has something of an antique feel, somewhat reminiscent of the film *Brazil* (1985); it is characteristic that the game's version of **cyberspace** exists inside a single giant mainframe computer. The player's character, Robert Foster, is a native of the city who was involved in an aeroplane crash in the outback when young and was adopted by a group of aborigines. The game begins after the now adult Foster has been kidnapped by the city's brutal police and escaped from their custody following another aircraft crash. Trapped in the metropolis, Foster must uncover the secret of his true identity and, it is assumed, take revenge for the mass murder of the tribe that became his family. Ultimately, it emerges that the ruling computer has been guiding his progress through the **linear** narrative in order to acquire his services as an organic component of its core processor. Foster's father is revealed to have been the man who designed the machine, and whose brain was incorporated into its workings; his subconscious desires may be partly responsible for its authoritarian savagery. After confronting his father in the person of the computer, Foster can free his actual father from its embrace, replacing him with the brain of his faithful robot companion. Foster's father then dies, leaving both his son and his city to their new-found freedom.

Technological progress allowed *Beneath a Steel Sky* to successfully adopt a less cartoon like art style than that of most earlier graphical adventures, in keeping with its generally serious tone. However, the often humorous puzzle solutions and conversational byplay can seem more suited to a comedy game such as *Maniac Mansion* (*1987* LG) designed by Ron Gilbert and Gary Winnick, a contrast that creates some jarring shifts in mood. Nevertheless, *Beneath a Steel Sky*'s menacing atmosphere and impressively dynamic world, inhabited by scores of computer-controlled characters with their own personal agendas, make playing it a novel and interesting experience.

BEYOND GOOD & EVIL

2003. Ubisoft. Designed by Michel Ancel.

Beyond Good & Evil is an action **adventure**, displayed in a third-person **3D** view and set on the colony planet of Hillys, a world inhabited by an eclectic mix of humans and aliens resembling anthropomorphized animals. Hillys is a beautiful and peaceful planet, a harmonious paradise where even the criminals are charming. However, it is also under attack by the DomZ, a race of giant **psionic** spiders. The player character is Jade, an appealingly optimistic and caring photographer who runs an orphanage in her spare time. After a narrow escape from the DomZ, she is recruited by an underground media organization that wants her to discover the truth behind the planet's ineffectual defenses.

Jade's missions typically involve her infiltrating a military base and photographing secret areas and meetings. Success depends on the player's ability to solve puzzles, covertly bypass guards, and occasionally fight enemies, often in cooperation with a computer-controlled friend; other gameplay elements include photographing rare animals for money and racing hovercraft. At the end of the **linear** story, Jade can broadcast evidence that the planet's defenders have been taken over by the DomZ. Before she can triumph over the spiders, however, she must defeat their High Priest and learn that she is not truly human. Instead, it emerges she is the incarnation of something precious that was stolen from the DomZ, a messianic figure who can raise the dead. The plot ends on a cliffhanger, in expectation of an as yet undelivered sequel. *Beyond Good & Evil* is charming and entertaining in equal measure, an optimistic fairy tale for adults.

Web Link
- *Beyond Good & Evil*: http://beyondgoodevil.com/

BIOFORGE

1995. Origin Systems. Designed by Ken Demarest and Jack Herman.

Bioforge is a graphical **adventure** that prefigures later action adventures; the gameplay depends on a combination of puzzles and combat sequences. The game begins with a noninteractive **full motion video** sequence showing the unconscious player character being transported to an unknown planet, after which multiple amputations are performed. Players then start the game in a cell, to find that their newly awakened characters have been forcibly converted into **cyborgs**, and seem to be amnesiac. On escaping from their prison, participants discover that the surrounding base appears to have been heavily damaged and abandoned. Much of the rest of the game is spent searching this devastated complex, which is inhabited largely by madmen and corpses. A great deal of information is available, however, in the form of text-based computer logs. Reading these and talking to the few sane characters encountered will gradually allow the player to assemble the **embedded** backstory of the game; their character was kidnapped by a group of religious extremists who had been experimenting on unwilling victims in an attempt to create a perfect cybernetic assassin. The technology used for these experiments was obtained by excavating the ruins of an ancient alien civilization, a process interrupted by the unexpected appearance of an extremely powerful and aggressive member of the supposedly vanished species that built the complex. There is something of the grand guignol about *Bioforge*; in one early sequence, the player is forced to beat an insane cyborg to death with its own severed arm. The player's character, however, projects a curious sense of abused innocence; his default conversational gambits often involve offers to help and assist the various deranged monsters he encounters.

While the gameplay is generally well constructed, the controls can be awkward, and the ending seems abrupt. Nevertheless, *Bioforge* is an intelligently designed, if somewhat excessive, piece of body horror.

The hero of *Bioforge*.

BUREAU 13

1995. Take-Two Interactive. Designed by Rick Hall and Thomas Howell.

While it is often reminiscent of the similarly titled US TV series *Kolchak: The Night Stalker* (*1974–1975*), the tabletop **role playing game** *Stalking the Night Fantastic* (*1983* Tri Tac Games; revised *1984*; *1990* revised as *Bureau 13: Stalking the Night Fantastic*; revised *1992*; revised *2008*) designed by Richard Tucholka and Chris Belting takes a far more lighthearted approach to its investigations of the alien and the extraordinary. Players adopt the roles of agents of "Bureau 13," a secret branch of the US government founded in the 1860s to fight the dark side of the paranormal world while keeping its more peaceful denizens hidden and safe from human mobs. Most of the cases Bureau agents encounter are likely to be supernatural in nature, but some may involve such science-fictional concepts as time travel, rogue artificial intelligences, mutants, **psionic hive-minds**, and ancient astronauts. Much emphasis is placed on the humorous and the bizarre; this is an America in which suburban thuggee, seafood-obsessed monks, and vampire carrots are commonplace. One particularly notable aspect of the game is the number of subsequent television shows and comics that make use of similar ideas, including *The X-Files* (*1993–2002*), *Sanctuary* (*2008–2011*), *Fringe* (*2008–2013*), *Warehouse 13* (*2009–2014*), and Mike Mignola's *B.P.R.D.* (*2002–2014*). It is also remarkable for the Bureau's frequent use of nonhuman agents, including vampires and werewolves. This is a game in which the monsters investigate the monsters on the government dime.

The *Bureau 13* **videogame** is a graphical **adventure**, which is perhaps better known than the **RPG** from which it was derived. The game begins with the player selecting two Bureau operatives from the six choices available, after which they are assigned to cover up the activities of a rogue agent. Interestingly, the player is rewarded not only for solving puzzles but also for not drawing attention to their characters' activities. Another appealing aspect of the design is the use of a broadly **multilinear** structure for the game's **interactive narrative**; depending on the characters chosen, different puzzle solutions and plot paths become accessible. While the puzzles are occasionally obscure and the character interactions can seem artificial, the game's droll dialogue and the complex conspiracy in which the characters rapidly become entangled make it an intriguing and enjoyable experience.

Related works: Nick Pollotta has written a trilogy of entertaining novels in the setting: *Bureau 13* (**1991**; also known as *Judgement Night*), *Full Moonster* (**1992**), and *Doomsday Exam* (**1992**). *Damned Nation* (**2005**), also by Pollotta, is a distant prequel dealing with the early days of the Bureau during the American Civil War.

CALL OF CTHULHU

Franchise (from 1993). Chaosium.

Call of Cthulhu (*1981* Chaosium; revised *1982*; revised *1983*; revised *1986*; revised *1989*; revised *1992*; revised *1998*; revised *2000*; revised *2001*; revised *2004*; revised *2006*) designed by Sandy Petersen is an authorized interpretation of H P Lovecraft's **Cthulhu Mythos** in the tabletop role playing medium, named after his short story "The Call of Cthulhu" (February 1928 *Weird Tales*). The core game, set in the 1920s, places somewhat greater emphasis on the traditions of **pulp** adventure and ghostly mysteries than is present in the original fiction. Nevertheless, *Call of Cthulhu* effectively reflects the central concerns of the Mythos stories, especially in the sense of helplessness often felt by its players when confronted with almost overwhelming opposition.

The Mythos has influenced the design of many **videogames**, including the text **adventure** *The Lurking Horror* (*1987* Infocom) designed by Dave Lebling and *Alone in the Dark* (*1992* Infogrames) designed by Frédérick Raynal, a well-known ancestor of the **survival horror** form. The first such game to be officially licensed was *Call of Cthulhu: Shadow of the Comet* (*1993* Infogrames) designed by Norbert Cellier, Didier Briel, Hubert Chardot, and Beate Reiter, whose **linear** plot begins with the imminent return of Halley's Comet as seen from a quiet fishing village in New England and ends with a threatened invasion by beings utterly inimical to humanity. *Shadow of the Comet* remains a highly atmospheric work, and one that is arguably the best evocation of the spirit of the pen and paper **RPG** in a digital medium to date. The related *Call of Cthulhu: Prisoner of Ice* (*1995* Infogrames) designed by Philippe Chanoinat, Hubert Chardot, Frederic Cornet, Michel Monteille, and Christian Nabais—a loose sequel to both *Shadow of the Comet* and Lovecraft's novella *At the Mountains of Madness* (February 1936 *Astounding Stories*), whose prehuman Antarctic city is now the site of a Nazi research base— is visually superior to its predecessor, but suffers from more restrictive gameplay and an occasionally confusing story line. The most recent such game is *Call of Cthulhu: The Dark Corners of the Earth* (*2005* Headfirst Productions) designed by Christopher Gray, a hybrid of action adventure and **first person shooter** based on a reimagining of Lovecraft's *The Shadow Over Innsmouth* (**1936**). As in the original **role playing game**, the gameplay of *Dark Corners of the Earth* emphasizes stealthy escapes and investigative work rather than combat; madness is a constant threat. This work is unusually linear—it begins after the completion of the plot, with the player character's eventual suicide in a lunatic asylum—an approach that probably contributes to the experience the game imposes, one of an inevitable descent into insanity.

Related works: Many variant milieux have been published for the pen and paper RPG, including the Victorian London of *Cthulhu by Gaslight* (*1986* Chaosium; revised *1988*; revised *2012*) designed by William Barton and the exotic realm of *The Dreamlands* (*1986* Chaosium; revised *1988*; revised *1992*; *1997* revised as *The Complete Dreamlands*; revised *2004*) designed by Sandy Petersen and Chris Williams, based on the setting described in Lovecraft's *The Dream-Quest of Unknown Kadath* (**1943** in *Beyond the Wall of Sleep*), in which humanity's collective unconscious overlaps with that of inhuman races. Spin-off tabletop works include the **collectible**

card game *Mythos* (*1996* Chaosium) designed by Charlie Krank and the board game *Arkham Horror* (*1987* Chaosium; revised *2005*) designed by Richard Launius, Lynn Willis, and Charlie Krank. *Cthulhu Live* (*1997* Chaosium; revised *1999*; revised *2006*) designed by Robert McLaughlin is an associated **live action role playing** game.

CHRONOMASTER

1995. DreamForge Entertainment. Designed by Roger Zelazny and Jane Lindskold.

The graphical **adventure** game *Chronomaster* was the well-known science fiction writer Roger Zelazny's final work. In a future galactic civilization, the creation of privately owned **pocket universes** has become a hobby for the immortal rich. The player adopts the persona of the eponymous Rene Korda, a famous designer of such works lured out of retirement by a mystery: several of these toy realities have been frozen in time by an unknown saboteur. Each universe can be repaired by finding its hidden world key and resetting it, a task performed with the assistance of "bottled time"—a substance that brings people and objects to life as the player approaches them. These artificial realities are arguably the most important characters in the game; each is configured to suit the personality of its owner, having a unique theme and (often fantastic) set of physical laws. In one world, belonging to a woman who founded a philosophical movement similar to Dadaism, ice burns, pigs fly, and nonsense rules. Other realities are dedicated to war, to hedonism, and to the reenactment of the Arabian Nights. This conceit works well as the basis for an adventure game, allowing for the creation of a variety of difficult and interesting puzzles based on exotic forms of logic and physics, many of which have multiple solutions. Unfortunately, the game's interface can be awkward to use, and the player character can die in seemingly arbitrary ways. Nevertheless, *Chronomaster* succeeds as an evocative journey through a series of remarkable and disconcerting landscapes.

Related works: *Roger Zelazny and Jane Lindskold's Chronomaster: A Novel* (**1996**) is a novelization, written by Jane Lindskold.

CYBORG

1981. Sentient Software. Designed by Michael Berlyn.

While *Cyborg* was not the first science-fictional text **adventure**, it may be the first such work of any lasting interest. As in Algis Budrys' rather more sophisticated novel *Who?* (**1958**), the central character is a prosthetically augmented human of uncertain identity, in this case an astronaut who is suffering from amnesia and is thus ignorant of the nature of their mission. This setup is used to cleverly rationalize the structure of the text adventure form; the conversational nature of the game's interface is justified as representing the way in which the player—who takes the role of the protagonist's human part—must issue commands to their cybernetic half in order to act on the external world. Initially, the protagonist is trapped in a bizarre forest, but it can be discovered that this is a holographic illusion projected by alien technology. It then emerges that the player's character is the captain of a starship that has collided with an alien exploration vessel in the Tau Ceti system. Eventually, the player can determine the tasks they need to perform: repairing the ship and reanimating its passengers—who were placed in **suspended animation** to improve their chances of surviving the impact—after which the ship can be landed, beginning the colonization of a new Earth. Puzzles are rare in comparison to most contemporary adventures, their place being taken by the detailed **embedded** backstory. While the narrative is perhaps best described as competent by the standards of print sf, it is unusually strong in comparison to such contemporary games as *Adventureland* (*1978* Adventure International) or *Acheton* (*1978–1981*), making this an early example of a "story-driven" adventure.

```
* AREA SCAN REVEALS:
WE'RE AT A "T" ON AN EAST/WEST DIRT PATH
THROUGH A FOREST. A NORTHERN PATH LEADS
THROUGH A GROVE OF TREES. A TINY LIZARD
WEARING A SILVER SPACESUIT STANDS BY THE
PATH, LEANING ON A TINIER CRUTCH, AND
GROANS "FOOD. FOOD FOR THE TRUTH."

>BODY SCAN

* WE ARE CARRYING THE FOLLOWING:

   NOTHING

>GO NORTH

WE'RE ON A NORTH/SOUTH PATH THROUGH A
HUGE FOREST OF TREES. THE PATH IS SMOOTH
AND LEVEL AS IF IT HAD BEEN HERE FIRST
AND THE FOREST HAD BEEN PLANTED AROUND
IT. WE CANNOT SEE AN END TO THE FOREST
IN ANY DIRECTION.

>*
```

In Michael Berlyn's *Cyborg*, the typed commands entered by the player are rationalized as instructions issued by their character's human brain to their cybernetic components.

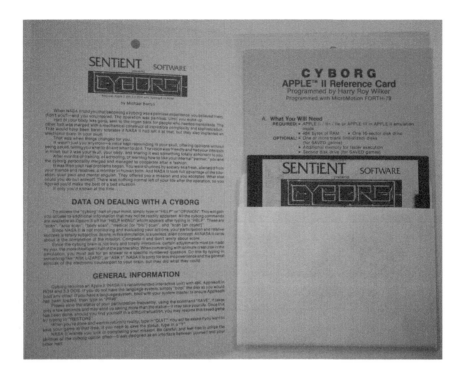

Early computer games such as *Cyborg* were sold on cassette tape or, as here, on 5.25 in. floppy disks.

DARK EARTH

1997. Kalisto Entertainment. Designed by Guillaume Le Pennec, Sylvain Dousset, and Frédéric Menne.

Dark Earth, an early example of the action **adventure** form, is set on a sunless world, a future Earth shrouded in dust clouds thrown up by a catastrophic series of meteor impacts. A few cities remain, huddled around mysterious gaps in the eternal clouds that allow light to fall, and surrounded by icy wastelands roamed by curiously altered beasts and alien monstrosities. The player character, a religious guardian in one such refuge, is unavoidably contaminated with a mutational toxin soon after the beginning of the game. This poison swiftly begins to transform him into a monster, a being physically distorted but gifted with strange new abilities. From this point on, the character has only a short space of time in which to uncover a complex plot against his city and to find an antidote to his condition before both he and his home are consumed by darkness. Ultimately, he must penetrate the secret at the heart of his world, the mystery that explains the life-giving openings in Earth's shroud of dust.

Visually, the game benefits from a striking design that blends late medieval and Moorish influences; narratively, its construction is **multilinear**, with puzzles often based around interactions with other characters rather than with physical objects. Unfortunately, the use of fixed camera angles to display the game's **3D** environments can make controlling the main character awkward for the player. Nevertheless, *Dark Earth* succeeds as an original work of **science fantasy,** as a vision of a world that has entered both a literal and a metaphorical Dark Age, and as an opportunity for players to identify with a character who is undergoing a slow but apparently inexorable degeneration into a subhuman monster. There is in it, perhaps, something of the novelist William Hope Hodgson's despairing vision of *The Night Land* (**1912**).

Related works: The *Dark Earth* milieu was developed by Kalisto Entertainment in collaboration with a **role playing game** company, Multisim, and an associated **RPG** was published in French: *Dark Earth* (*1997* Multisim) designed by Benoit Attinost.

DESTROY ALL HUMANS!

2005. Pandemic Studio (PS). Designed by Brad Welch.

Destroy All Humans! is a broad parody of the science fiction films of the 1950s and of alien invasion fictions generally; it is particularly reminiscent of Tim Burton's satire on the same theme, *Mars Attacks!* (1996). The game itself could loosely be described as an action **adventure**, with much emphasis placed on fairly unsophisticated combat sequences. Players are strictly guided through a series of **linear** missions, but allowed to roam freely after their objectives in a particular area have been achieved and when hunting humans for sport. The game's protagonist is Cryptosporidium-137 (or Crypto), the 137th clone of his line and a member of the **psychokinetic** Furon race, whose members bear a marked resemblance to the big headed "Greys" prominent in UFO (unidentified flying object) folklore. Crypto is sent to Earth in the 1950s to harvest human brain stems, from which the Furons can extract the DNA (deoxyribonucleic acid) they need to create new clone bodies for themselves. (Excessive copying has caused degradation of the Furon genetic sequence, but—for reasons too sordid to describe— human genes include some Furon DNA.) The game begins with cattle mutilation (following an unfortunate misunderstanding as to the identity of Earth's dominant species) and works its way up from there. Ultimately, the player can defeat the humans' Man (who is, in fact, a Woman) in Black, along with a gigantic robot controlled by the brain of the US President, and make the Furons the new secret masters of America. Crypto himself is sexist, speciesist, and gleefully sadistic, but has a curious appeal; as he says in a later game, his goals are simple—"kicking ass and taking brains."

Several sequels have been released, all with broadly similar gameplay. In these later works, the satire becomes gradually less focused, and also less effective, ranging over a variety of targets from the popular culture of the 1960s and 1970s. The immediate sequel, *Destroy All Humans! 2* (*2006* PS) designed by John Passfield and Brad Welch, is set in the 1960s, when Cryptosporidium-137 has been replaced as protagonist by the next clone in line, Cryptosporidium-138, who has improved **psionic** abilities. Soon after the beginning of the game, the Furon mothership is destroyed by a missile launched from the Soviet Union, which turns out to be controlled by another extraterrestrial species. The new Crypto must defeat all comers to preserve the Furons' control of the supply of human brain stems; there is much mockery of sixties counterculture, upper-class English spies, and similar subjects. In *Destroy All Humans! Big Willy Unleashed* (*2008* Locomotive Games), the generally amusing parodies of the original game degenerate into relentless sexual innuendo, as Crypto violently defends his fast food chain against the machinations of a competitor. (The chain is built on selling burgers made from the bodies of the humans Crypto has killed for their DNA; as one of the characters in the game puts it, "Big Willy Is People!"—a phrase that echoes a more famous line delivered in the film *Soylent Green* [*1973*].) Ultimately, the player can pilot the eponymous mascot, which functions as a gigantic **mecha**, in a confrontation with "Colonel Kluckin's" own giant robot. *Destroy All Humans! Path of the Furon* (*2008* Sandblast Games) designed by Jon Knoles is set in the 1970s, shortly after *Big Willy Unleashed*. Here, the struggle to find new topics for the series' aggressive brand of humor veers toward racial stereotyping, with unfortunate results. As the game begins, Crypto—now Cryptosporidium-139, clone number 138 having expired in a drunken flying saucer crash—has opened a casino in Las Vegas, where he becomes involved in a turf war with local mobsters. This leads into a somewhat disorganized plot; players can eventually complete the game by assassinating both the Furon emperor and his would-be successor. While the last two sequels, created by other hands than the original, have been notably less well received than the first two members of the series, the sequence as a whole contains many entertaining moments. Particularly memorable is Cryptosporidium's ever-growing arsenal of alarming weapons, including the Zap-O-Matic, the Quantum Deconstructor, and the Venus Human Trap, not to mention the "fire and forget multi-round heat seeking anal probe."

Related works: *Destroy All Humans!* (*2005* Big Blue Bubble) is an action adventure for mobile phones based on the original game. Its sequel, *Destroy All Humans! 2* (*2007* Universomo) is a tactical **turn-based computer wargame** in which the player, as Cryptosporidium, must complete various missions intended to crush human resistance to the Furon conquest. A third installment, *Destroy All Humans! Crypto Does Vegas* (*2008* Universomo), is an action game in which the eponymous alien must search Las Vegas for the best available DNA; reviews were mixed.

DIG, THE

1995. LA. Designed by Sean Clark and Brian Moriarty.

The Dig is a graphical **adventure** game using a point and click interface, based on an idea by the film director Steven Spielberg that combined the haunted alien world of the early sf movie *Forbidden Planet* (*1956*) with the tense relationships of *The Treasure of the Sierra Madre* (*1948*). Dialogue was contributed by the science fiction writer Orson Scott Card. The game's tone is more serious than that of previous LA adventures such as *Maniac Mansion: Day of the Tentacle* (*1993* LA) designed by Tim Schafer and David Grossman, though a certain wry humor remains. Its story begins with a scenario similar to that of the later film *Armageddon* (*1998*); an asteroid is detected on a collision course with Earth, and a team is launched by Space Shuttle to divert it. Players adopt the role of the mission commander, Boston Low; other significant characters are the geologist Dr Brink and the reporter Maggie Robbins. After completing the simple puzzles required to alter the asteroid's orbit, players will discover that the body's surface conceals an alien starship. Without warning, this ship activates itself and transports the characters to an extrasolar world; players must engage in a xenoarchaeological "dig" to uncover the planet's secrets if the characters are ever to return to Earth.

The game contains a range of well-designed and often difficult puzzles, elegantly justified as the artifacts of an apparently dead civilization. As players move further into the alien environment, the gradual revelation of the fate of the planet's inhabitants evokes a real **sense of wonder**. Perhaps the most compelling aspect of the game, however, is its fusion of the aliens' **embedded** narrative with the **linearly** plotted story of the three explorers. Prescribed events triggered by puzzle solutions are used to show the gradual disintegration of the group, as their personal priorities triumph over their need to work together to survive. Brink dies, is resurrected by alien technology, and goes mad; Robbins abandons Low to pursue her own agenda. In the end, the player, in the person of Low, can save only himself.

Related works: *The Dig* (**1995**) is a novelization by Alan Dean Foster. In addition to the characters' story, it contains sections narrated from the point of view of the alien starship builders.

Web Link
- The Dig Museum (Tribute Site): http://dig.mixnmojo.com/

DISHONORED

2012. Arkane Studios (AS). Designed by Raphaël Colantonio, Harvey Smith, and Ricardo Bare.

Dishonored is a work of **steampunk** and sorcery, but one that operates in a very science-fictional mode. The gameplay is that of an action **adventure**, seen from the point of view of the player in the manner of a **first person shooter**, with elements drawn from **computer role playing games** and much emphasis placed on the protagonist's ability to hide and sneak. With a script written by, among others, the science fiction author Austin Grossman, the game is set in a well-defined world that draws upon the iconography of diverse periods in British history, perhaps especially those of the late eighteenth and early nineteenth centuries. This milieu is a classic uchronia, a **parallel world** whose point of divergence from the reality inhabited by its creators is never made clear. Here, an alternate industrial revolution has helped shape the fantasticated Victorian metropolis of Dunwall, now racked by a mysterious plague whose impoverished victims are controlled by police walking on giant mechanical stilts and sealed away from their wealthier fellows by lethal barriers of electrical force.

The game's broadly **linear interactive narrative** begins with the player's character, a royal bodyguard named Corvo Attano, framed for the murder of Dunwall's Empress (the woman who was, perhaps, his lover). Helped to escape from prison by a cabal of plotters against the aristocratic conspiracy that assassinated his employer and now rules his city, Corvo becomes supernaturally enabled, gifted by an extranormal being with the player's choice of a variety of exotic powers and an artificial heart that whispers mystic riddles. Eventually, it emerges that the Empress' murderer, who is now Lord Regent, intentionally brought the plague to the city to diminish the numbers of the working classes, whose growing strength threatens the city's elite. This revelation is followed by a betrayal and a final confrontation; the game ends with the dawn of a new age of enlightenment, or with the plague run wild, or with the fall of the empire of Dunwall. Which of these conclusions is experienced depends partly on the player's level of success, but also on the degree to which they have favored bloody vengeance on their enemies over careful justice; the more violent their progress through the game, the darker the resolution.

It is possible to identify many influences on the design of *Dishonored*. As in *Half-Life* (*1998* Valve), the protagonist remains mute in order to enhance the player's sense of identification with their character. As in *Deus Ex* (*2000* Ion Storm), a game designed by Smith with Warren Spector, there are many choices to make, and they frequently have real consequences. Some of these decisions are moral; most enemies can be either killed or rendered unconscious, though the tone of the work certainly encourages some degree of lethality. Other choices are tactical—each of the game's various missions is played out in a sealed-off region of the city within which there are many paths to the objective, some of them aggressively confrontational and others slow and covert. Effectively, the structure is that of a sequence of nodes in which each node is a micro-world, which allows the player considerable freedom of action, though rather more help and guidance is provided than in earlier works, which took a similar approach such as Paul Woakes' *Mercenary* (*1985* Novagen Software). The game's primary plot, however, is somewhat predictable, and the player character is not especially interesting. The true protagonist of *Dishonored*, perhaps, is its highly explorable and intriguing game-world, formed by an amalgamation of post-Dickensian fables with class politics and the myths of the Good Queen and the corrupted rich, a setting rooted in an early twenty-first-century iteration of the **Matter of Britain**.

Related works: The expansion pack *Dunwall City Trials* (*2012* AS) is a series of challenges for the player, unrelated to the narrative of the game, while *The Knife of Dunwall* (*2013* AS) begins a new story whose protagonist is the assassin who was responsible for the death of the Empress. This character's abilities are generally similar to Corvo's, however, and his story line is interpolated into the events of the original game.

Web Link
- *Dishonored*: http://www.dishonored.com/

ENSLAVED: ODYSSEY TO THE WEST

2010. Ninja Theory (NT). Designed by Tameem Antoniades.

Enslaved is an action **adventure** set in a lush, verdant postholocaust America, where most of mankind has been wiped out in a devastating war and the few surviving humans are hunted by killer robots, still fulfilling their ancient objectives. The gameplay combines combat and occasional puzzles with jumping and leaping in the manner of a **platform game** in an uncomplicated package that may have been intended to appeal to novice players. The script, by Alex Garland, is very loosely based on the classical Chinese novel *Journey to the West*, probably written by Wu Cheng'en sometime in the late sixteenth century. Shortly after the beginning of the game, the heroically muscled (and highly acrobatic) Monkey, clearly a lifelong sufferer from impulse control disorder, and the smart, technologically sophisticated Trip (or Tripitaka) escape from a crashed aircraft, which was transporting the captives of a crazed survivor of the preholocaust world. Trip then fits Monkey with a controlling headband while he is unconscious so that she can force him to protect her on the dangerous journey back to her village. In the role of Monkey, the player becomes both Trip's slave and her guardian, the muscle to her mind. The game is notable for its appealing characters and for the moments of genuine emotion that enliven its strictly **linear** plot. Ultimately, it succeeds because it forces the player to participate in the relationship between Monkey and Trip—a curious fusion of romance narrative and buddy movie—acting out Monkey's role until the mask becomes the face, and the player shares what their character feels.

Related works: *Pigsy's Perfect 10* (*2010* NT) is an expansion pack and prequel for *Enslaved* in which the eponymous character tries to build his ideal friend from spare parts found in a junkyard. *Enslaved: Origins* (*2010*) is a single-issue comic that provides additional backstory for the original game.

EXILE

1988. Superior Software. Designed by Peter Irvin and Jeremy Smith.

Exile is an example of a **videogame** form that was popular in the United Kingdom during the 1980s, but rare elsewhere and hardly seen since, that of the "arcade adventure." In works of this type, solving physical puzzles is combined with the reflex and coordination-based jumping and fighting gameplay, which is characteristic of **platform games**. The first such work may have been *Adventure* (*1980* Atari) designed by Warren Robinett, a distant descendant of the original text **adventure**, which transposed its ancestor's design to a graphical, action-based form that appealed to the young adults who were Atari's main customers in the early 1980s. Later examples include the science-fictional *Alien 8* (*1985* Ultimate

Play The Game) designed by Chris Stamper and Tim Stamper, in which the player controls a robot that must save the frozen crew of a starship with damaged **suspended animation** equipment. *Exile* itself is an exceptionally well-crafted game that requires the player to rescue the crew of a disabled spaceship, who are being held captive by an archetypal mad scientist somewhere inside a large underground tunnel network. Hostile alien creatures and a range of cleverly designed puzzles act as obstacles to the player's explorations. Interestingly, the world of *Exile* models both a realistic set of physical laws and a crude ecosystem in which animals have defined behaviors toward each other. This combination allows for the evolution of a kind of experimental gameplay, in which solutions to the game's problems can emerge from the simulation rather than being hand crafted in advance. Some players find this approach to be a source of frustration as well as entertainment, however.

While the arcade adventure form has essentially disappeared from the modern videogame industry, similar experiences have remained popular in the shape of action adventures such as *Beyond Good & Evil* (*2003* Ubisoft) designed by Michel Ancel, which evolved from graphical adventures to provide a more **3D** version of *Exile*'s gameplay.

Related works: The original version of the game was sold with an included novella by Mark Cullen, also called *Exile* (**1988**).

Web Link
- *Exile* Tribute Page: http://exile.acornarcade.com/

FAHRENHEIT 451

1984. Telarium. Designed by Len Neufeld.

Fahrenheit 451 is an illustrated text **adventure**, which serves as a sequel to Ray Bradbury's novel of the same name and to which he made significant contributions. The game's protagonist is Guy Montag, once a book-burning "fireman" but now a member of the literary resistance to the ignorant bureaucracy that rules his TV-obsessed future America. Despite the martial law that has been declared in the aftermath of the war, which ends the original novel, Montag can eventually find the young woman who first led him to question his life as a paragon of the establishment. (As in both François Truffaut's film and Bradbury's own stage adaptation, this character's apparent death in the book is undone in the game.) With her assistance, the player can complete the generally **linear** story line by recovering 34 microcassettes that preserve the contents of the New York Public Library and transmitting them to the underground, who will commit their contents to memory. While the books can be saved, there is no escape for Montag and his muse; by broadcasting the cassettes they trap themselves in a room where they will inevitably be discovered and killed by the firemen.

The prose can be vivid and poetic, especially in the sequences from Montag's past, which are evoked using the unusual command "REMEMBER," while the gameplay is competently constructed, with entertaining puzzles. The design is, however, somewhat manipulative—the player is never forced to take the developers' preferred path through the narrative, but is sometimes firmly guided toward it. Much play is made of quotations from various literary works, which are used as recognition phrases by the underground and which can be obtained by asking appropriate questions of the character who is Bradbury's surrogate within the game. It is interesting that a **videogame** should be the form chosen for the sequel to a novel so centrally concerned with the perceived evils of high-technology mass media, though it is probably significant that *Fahrenheit 451* is primarily a textual work, a piece of **interactive fiction** rather than an example of a more visual and immediate form such as the action adventure or the **first person shooter**. Ultimately, however, while the game is an intriguing sequel to Bradbury's novel, it is unclear whether it is a necessary one.

FISH!

1988. MS. Designed by Pete Kemp, John Molloy, Phil South, and Robert Steggles.

Fish! is a surreal text **adventure** (with static illustrations) in which the player adopts the role of an interdimensional secret agent. This hero is something of a serial body snatcher, traveling between **parallel worlds** by possessing their inhabitants. As the game begins, the main character is taking a vacation in a goldfish bowl (and, not surprisingly, is a goldfish). Soon, however, its superior—an individual known as Sir Playfair Panchax—is dropped in by toy castle to give the player a new assignment. It seems that the Seven Deadly Fins, a group of dimension-hopping revolutionaries, have been up to their dastardly tricks again, and only the player can be trusted to stop them. This leads into a somewhat anarchic experience, featuring many awkward puzzles and a plethora of fishy puns, and culminating in a race against time to stop the destruction by dehydration of the subaquean city of Hydropolis. While *Fish!* perhaps lacks the appealing ambience of MS' alternate England fantasy *Jinxter* (*1987* MS) designed by Georgina Sinclair and Michael Bywater and the serious intent of *Corruption* (*1988* MS) designed by Robert Steggles and Hugh Steers, a tale of yuppie venality in the modern world, it has its own special charm—that of a world in which no fish goes unpinned.

Web Link

- The Magnetic Scrolls Memorial (Tribute Site): http://msmemorial. if-legends.org/

FULL THROTTLE

1996. LA. Designed by Tim Schafer.

Full Throttle is a graphical **adventure** with a point and click interface, set in a dark future somewhat reminiscent of the vehicular apocalypses seen in the board and counter **wargame** *Car Wars* (*1982* Steve Jackson Games) and the film *Mad Max* (*1979*). Its gameplay is a prototype of the approach used in later action adventures such as *Outcast* (*1999* Appeal) and *Dreamfall: The Longest Journey* (*2006* Funcom) designed by Ragnar Tørnquist, alternating between segments based around solving puzzles and action sequences. The player's character is one Ben Throttle, leader of the Polecats gang, an appealing antihero with a strong sense of personal integrity. As the game begins, he becomes involved in a struggle over the ownership of Corley Motors, the last American motorbike manufacturer. Soon the Polecats are in jail, wrongly accused of murder, leaving only Ben to clear their names and stop Corley's new manager converting it into a minivan producer. The game's **linear** plot goes on to lead the player through a long ride across the dangerous wastes of the new American desert, accompanied by the tough girl mechanic Mo, before it reaches its final showdown.

Full Throttle has the visual style of a cartoon, and its vividly drawn characters are also charmingly cartoon like. Its puzzle solutions are in keeping with the game's emphasis on physical action, while the narrative tone is full of gentle self-mockery. In essence, Schafer's game tells a rousing story of **pulp** adventure, set in a world where all real bikers are tough but honorable, and all public relations men are untrustworthy weasels.

GENE MACHINE, THE

1996. Divide By Zero. Designed by Andy Blazdell.

The Gene Machine is a **steampunk** comedy, presented as a graphical **adventure** with a strongly **linear** plot. The game begins when the player character, the pompous upper-class adventurer Piers Featherstonehaugh, is approached by a talking cat in the foyer of his London home. This exotic intruder turns out to be a product of the nefarious schemes of one Dr Dinsey, who plans to conquer the world with an army of human–animal hybrids; the player soon finds themselves dedicated to the defeat of the evil doctor. This setup leads into a farcical series of incidents as Featherstonehaugh tours the most exotic spots on the Victorian globe and its nearest neighbor, constantly accompanied by his indispensable but frequently abused manservant, Mossop.

References are made to many well-known works of **scientific romance**, including Jules Verne's *De la terre à la lune* ["From the Earth to the Moon"] (**1865**) and *Vingt mille lieues sous les mers* ["Twenty Thousand Leagues under the Sea"] (**1870**) as well as H G Wells' *The Island of Dr Moreau* (**1896**). These sources undergo a variety of strange mutations in the game, as Featherstonehaugh joins an expedition to the Moon mounted in the erroneous belief that it is made of cheese and is imprisoned on board the mechanical fish of Captain Nematode, before finally reaching the dread island of Dr Dinsey. Created in the United Kingdom and (as in the title) often gleefully anachronistic, *The Gene Machine* serves as a joyfully silly parody of the sort of **steampunk** sf in which stern Victorians master the terrors of the unknown to build a greater Empire. Puzzles are frequent, generally logical, and often hilarious, as when Featherstonehaugh must steal back the engagement ring he has proudly presented to his appalling fiancée so that he can use it to pay a low-life forger. From beginning to end, *The Gene Machine* is a delight.

HITCHHIKER'S GUIDE TO THE GALAXY, THE

1984. Infocom. Designed by Douglas Adams and Steve Meretzky.

Hitchhiker is a text-based **adventure** game, a variation on the theme of comic misadventures in a surreal galaxy established by Adams in the *Hitchhiker's Guide to the Galaxy* radio show, television series, and books. While the game starts in a similar manner to the radio series, it soon veers off along its own unexpected tangents, presenting a largely original narrative. *Hitchhiker* is remarkable for including some of the most perverse puzzles in the history of adventure game design, and yet still being highly enjoyable, an effect due entirely to the quality of Adams and Meretzky's writing. One striking example of this approach is the extremely complex puzzle, which must be unraveled in order to obtain a "Babel Fish," an object that makes it possible to understand alien languages. If the player fails to solve this problem, there are no immediate consequences, but they will discover much later in the game that it is impossible to complete without the fish, forcing them to restart almost from the beginning. At another point, *Hitchhiker* will actively lie to the player about the geography of the room they are in. These techniques have not been revisited by later adventure game developers, and it is unlikely that many designers could achieve the atmosphere of comic frustration that makes them successful here. Ingenious conceits and surreally humorous moments abound; at different times, players can find themselves unexpectedly adopting the identities of four different characters due to the side effects of the "Infinite Improbability Drive," a situation that can cause some confusion. The game addresses this problem by adding a novel command to the system: "WHO AM I." *Hitchhiker* remains a masterful example of how to subvert the conventions of a form in the name of comic absurdity.

Related works: The game was remade in 2004 by the BBC, with static illustrations added by Rod Lord and the winners of a promotional contest.

Web Links

- Free online version of *Hitchhiker* (original version): http://www. douglasadams.com/creations/infocomjava.html

- Free online version of *Hitchhiker* (BBC remake): http://www.bbc. co.uk/radio4/hitchhikers/game.shtml

- Steve Meretzky on *Hitchhiker*: http://www.bbc.co.uk/radio4/ hitchhikers/stevem.shtml

I HAVE NO MOUTH, AND I MUST SCREAM

1995. The Dreamers' Guild. Designed by Harlan Ellison, David Mullich, and David Sears.

I Have No Mouth, and I Must Scream is a graphical **adventure** based on Ellison's Hugo award-winning short story of the same name. The game, scripted and codesigned by Ellison, expands considerably on its original while altering many of the details. The central question of the adventure is why the insane supercomputer AM would pick the game's five protagonists in particular to save when it destroys the world, only to condemn them to eternal torment in a literally subterranean Hell. These characters, who are not precisely the people they were in the short story, each have a hidden trauma and matching psychiatric condition, from paranoia to depression. Players adopt each of their personas in turn as AM sends them into virtual worlds, which act as psychodramas designed to expose their deepest fears. Resolving these miniature adventures requires the solution of various puzzles, but true success depends on achieving a morally valid resolution of each character's past. The protagonists' individual dreamworlds are dark and often macabre, with disturbing visual designs reminiscent of the paintings of Hieronymus Bosch. There are several possible endings, including one that mirrors that of the original story in its depiction of a future of unending horror. If, however, the player has succeeded in helping the characters redeem themselves by confronting and overcoming their flaws, it is possible to use AM's own internal contradictions against it, and defeat it in a somewhat confusing final sequence set inside the computer's own mind. Even this ending offers no hope to the five protagonists, for whom *I Have No Mouth* is a game that can only be won by losing; four of them must die, while the last becomes AM's jailer, forever guarding the computer's hardware against a return of its eradicated software. Humanity itself, however, may be preserved by the characters' sacrifice; the destruction of AM allows a hidden group of survivors to be woken from **suspended animation** on the Moon to repopulate a newly **terraformed** Earth.

Unfortunately, some of the puzzles in *I Have No Mouth* are laborious and lack any logical solution; it sometimes seems as if the game is treating its players much as AM treats their characters. This resonance does not, however, induce the perhaps intended feelings of shame and despair, but rather ones of annoyance and frustration. More fundamentally, while the messages of *I Have No Mouth* are presented with a great deal of angry passion, it offers the player no true moral choices. Progress in the game depends upon performing the actions that the designers considered virtuous, reducing the player to the status of an actor in someone else's play. Where other games may express an ethical stance by designing their synthetic world to reflect its premises, this one creates a reality in which only one morality is permissible. Arguably, *I Have No Mouth* is too much of a story and not enough of a game.

inFAMOUS

2009. Sucker Punch Productions (SPP).

inFAMOUS is a superhero action **adventure**, the design of which shows some influence from **computer role playing game** conventions. Gameplay focuses on combat, exploration, and climbing and leaping in the manner of a **platform game**; the game's mechanics are cleverly biased to represent its protagonist's remarkable acrobatic skills. The setting is the fictional Empire City, an analogue of New York in which the player character, a slacker named Cole MacGrath, works as a bicycle messenger. MacGrath is commissioned to deliver a mysterious package to the center of town and then open it. This action triggers a devastating explosion, of which he is the only survivor. After spending several weeks recovering from his injuries, MacGrath—and the player—emerges to find the city quarantined as a result of an inexplicable plague, its citizens terrorized by street gangs and fed only by inadequate air drops. Meanwhile, MacGrath has developed electrical superpowers.

The game's plot then forces MacGrath to use his powers to take the city back from the gangs while searching for the device that caused the original disaster, a McGuffin known as the Ray Sphere. At various points, the player is given a choice between two alternative courses of action, one selfish (or "evil") and the other selfless (or "good"). Early in the game, for example, the player must decide whether to share food with all those who need it, or keep it for themselves and their friends. As in *Star Wars: Knights of the Old Republic* (*2003* BioWare), the alternatives the player chooses will determine how their friends see them, and whether the inhabitants of the city treat them as a hero or a villain. These binary choices seem especially appropriate for a game inspired by superhero comics, where morality is often simple, and every character must pick a side. While the existence of two distinct paths makes the structure of the game's **interactive narrative** essentially **multilinear**, branches are folded back into the main plot soon after they diverge, meaning that the same key events will occur whatever the player decides to do. Other aspects of the design are **embedded**—fragments of the backstory are hidden throughout the game—or **modular**, with various tasks available for the player to undertake as they wander through the dying city.

Ultimately, after MacGrath has fatally injured the worst of the gang leaders, it emerges that this man is his own future self. This other MacGrath has traveled back in time from a world in which humanity is threatened with extinction at the hands of a superpowered destroyer known only as "The Beast." His plan was simple; he would accelerate his own transformation to superhumanity, exposing his previous self to the Ray Sphere far earlier than had been the case in the original timeline. This, he hoped, would make his new iteration capable of defeating the Beast when it appeared. To achieve this end, the future MacGrath had arranged for the early construction of the Sphere, and for its empowering detonation, in which the life energies of thousands were forcibly transferred to his younger self. By this time, the path chosen by the younger MacGrath is irrevocable; the game ends with him either preparing to fight the Beast or glorying in his personal power over the helpless city. Thus, the game functions as an origin story, in which its protagonist becomes either a superhero or a supervillain. As this suggests, *inFAMOUS* is an original creation, which is highly literate about the comics that inspire it, and perhaps also informed by such contemporary works as the TV show *Heroes* (*2006–2010*).

The second game in the series, *inFAMOUS 2* (*2011* SPP), is also an action adventure, with a similar design to that of its predecessor. The intention seems to have been to create a sequel that would be appropriate whether its players had chosen to be noble or vile in the original game, or indeed had never played it at all. *inFAMOUS 2* is largely successful in this, though there are moments when the strain of supporting two incompatible relationships between MacGrath and the other continuing character becomes apparent. At the beginning of the game, the Beast tracks down MacGrath in Empire City and almost kills him. Convinced that he needs to become more powerful, MacGrath goes to New Marais—a variant of New Orleans—where he hopes to find the designer of the Ray Sphere. But when he arrives in the city, he finds it has been sealed off from the outside world while a civil war rages within its walls between newly created superhumans and a private army dedicated to their suppression. Meanwhile, the Beast begins an odyssey of destruction across America.

As in *inFAMOUS*, players are assumed to begin the game with a neutral ethical stance—though this can be slightly adjusted by reusing information saved from the first game—and must then make decisions, which determine whether other characters will see them as virtuous or wicked. Here, however, the moral choices have become markedly less ambiguous and arguably somewhat heavy-handed. Players begin by fighting the various forces that are oppressing the citizens of New Marais, while searching for the man who they hope can help them defeat the Beast. Eventually, in another reversal, it is revealed that the Beast is actually a government operative apparently killed in the first game, who is slaughtering millions in order to create new superhumans by using his powers to emulate an exploding Ray Sphere. This, he believes, is necessary, since the plague that affected Empire City in *inFAMOUS*—eventually revealed to be a consequence of the original Sphere's detonation—is spreading across the world, and will ultimately kill every human being. Only superhumans can survive the disease, and only a small minority of the human race can be made superhuman, and then only by the Ray Sphere process, which kills thousands of ordinary people in order to create one example of *Homo Superior*. The player is then left with one final decision: to activate a device, which will destroy the Beast and cure the plague, at the cost of killing every actual and potential superhuman in the world, or to join the Beast and continue with his genocidal plan. The first choice makes *inFAMOUS 2* into a game that is truly lost by winning, since in order to succeed the player must kill their own character. The second ends with the Beast, unable to face continuing with the slaughter, imbuing MacGrath with his powers before committing suicide, making the game's protagonist into the exact enemy that his future self empowered him to destroy.

While a further sequel might seem unlikely, Sony (the publishers of the series) have announced the upcoming release of *inFAMOUS: Second Son*. It remains to be seen whether this game will be able to extend the franchise without retrospectively diminishing the appeal of its predecessor.

Related works: *inFAMOUS: Festival of Blood* (*2011* SPP) is an interpolation into the story of *inFAMOUS 2*—or perhaps just a tall tale—in which MacGrath is transformed into a vampire, forcing him to destroy the mistress of the undead infesting New Marais before he becomes her eternal slave. More peripherally, *inFAMOUS: Anarchy* (*2011* Mob Science) is an online game in which participants rule districts of a virtual city, played on the social network Facebook, while *inFAMOUS: Precinct Assault* (*2009* Kongregate) is a simple **2D** platform game, made available for free on the web. *inFAMOUS* (*2011*) is a six-issue comic series, written by William Harms, which serves as a prequel to the second game.

Web Link
- *inFAMOUS*: http://www.infamousthegame.com/

INFOCOMICS

Series (from 1988). Infocom.

The *Infocomics* are a line of comics that were sold as **videogames**. While their plots were fully determined in advance, at various points, the reader can switch to a different character's view of the story; multiple readings are required to follow the whole of the narrative. Despite the generally unimpressive nature of their visual design and writing, the *Infocomics* remain interesting as an early form of computer-mediated narrative, with a fixed story that can be traversed in different ways. The first work of literary **hyperfiction**, Michael Joyce's *Afternoon, a story*, was written in 1987 and published in 1990, making these two very different approaches to computer-driven fiction rough contemporaries.

The first *Infocomic* to be released was *Lane Mastodon vs The Blubbermen* (*1988* Infocom) designed by Steve Meretzky, in which a figure resembling such **pulp**-magazine heroes as Edmond Hamilton's **Captain Future** saves the Earth from a Jovian invasion (the first phase of which is to bombard the planet with rays that magnify household animals to gigantic sizes). This was followed by *Gamma Force in Pit of a Thousand Screams* (*1988* Infocom) designed by Amy Briggs, which depicts the struggle of a team of alien superheroes resembling Marvel Comics' Fantastic Four against a planetary tyrant. The writers clearly did not take these efforts particularly seriously; an adult murder mystery story was planned, but was canceled after the commercial failure of the line.

Related works: The last two *Infocomics*, *ZorkQuest: Assault on Egreth Castle* (*1988* Infocom) designed by Elizabeth Langosy and its sequel *ZorkQuest II: The Crystal of Doom* (*1988* Infocom) designed by Elizabeth Langosy are fantasy, based on the early text **adventure** game *Zork* (*1977–1979* Infocom) designed by Tim Anderson, Marc Blank, Dave Lebling, and Bruce Daniels. Lane Mastodon also appears in a comic included in the original release of the text adventure *Leather Goddesses of Phobos* (*1986* Infocom) designed by Steve Meretzky.

JOURNEYMAN PROJECT, THE

Series (from 1993). PS. Designed by David Flanagan.

The *Journeyman Project* is a series of **linearly** plotted graphical **adventure** games dealing with time travel. Their designs emphasize visual quality over interactivity, in a similar way to the popular fantasy game *Myst* (*1993* Cyan Worlds) designed by Rand Miller and Robyn Miller. The base time period for the series is the twenty-fourth century, depicted as a technocratic dream of universal peace and democracy. At the beginning of the first game, *The Journeyman Project* (*1993* PS; revised as

The Journeyman Project Turbo!) designed by David Flanagan, Earth is about to be admitted into a galactic association, the Symbiotry of Peaceful Beings. However, as an ambassador arrives to complete negotiations, human history is altered to include acts of aggression against alien species, and Earth is refused entry to the association. These changes are detected by the Temporal Security Agency (or TSA), an organization of **time police** who had believed themselves to be the sole guardians of humanity's time machines; the player, in the persona of "Agent 5," is dispatched into the past to reverse the damage. After solving various puzzles, the player can discover that the culprit is the creator of the Pegasus time travel technology, who suffers from an irrational fear of aliens. Agent 5 must repair the timeline and prevent the scientist's planned assassination of the Symbiotry's ambassador. The game, while intriguingly plotted and well designed as an adventure, suffers from limited interactivity; players can only move to specific points in space, and the viewing window is unusually limited in size. It was remade (and notably improved) with **full motion video** featuring actors from *The Journeyman Project 2* as *The Journeyman Project: Pegasus Prime* (*1997* PS) designed by Eric Dallaire and David Flanagan.

The Journeyman Project 2: Buried in Time (*1995* PS) designed by David Flanagan, Michel Kripalani, and Phil Saunders is a direct sequel, using similar technology but incorporating footage of human actors. It begins with Agent 5, now named as Gage Blackwood, receiving a visit from himself 10 years in the future, when he is about to be arrested after being framed for tampering with the past. The player, as the present time Blackwood, must clear the name of his future self. After a number of visits to historical time periods, it emerges that in the future, another agent of the TSA, Michelle Visard, has decided that humanity is insufficiently morally advanced to be allowed to retain its monopoly on the secrets of time travel. After being discovered by the future Blackwood in the process of smuggling Pegasus technology to an alien race, Visard forged evidence implicating him in the theft of historical artifacts. The aliens, however, turn out to be interested in time travel only so that they can tamper with their own evolution and become more powerful in the present. The player can defeat their plans and clear Blackwood's name, but Visard escapes. In *The Journeyman Project 3: Legacy of Time* (*1998* PS) designed by Eric Dallaire, David Flanagan, and Tommy Yune, Visard reappears as an ally. Hiding in the deep past, she discovers that Atlantis, El Dorado, and

Shangri-La had all existed, but were destroyed by two alien races fighting over a mysterious artifact. She then deliberately alters the past to alert the Temporal Security Agency to this potential threat to humanity; the player, in the guise of Blackwood, goes to investigate. Meanwhile, ships belonging to one of the races are detected approaching Earth in the twenty-fourth century. With Visard's help, the player can broker a peace agreement between the combatants. *The Journeyman Project 3* is the most accessible of the three games, featuring the ability to look in any direction (though movement is still restricted) and a full-screen viewing area, as well as human actors.

One interesting aspect of the series is its approach to interactions with computer-controlled characters. In the first two games, Blackwood is forbidden to talk to humans in the past, ultimately for technical reasons, though the improved technology used to implement *The Journeyman Project 2* allows him to observe them while invisible. This makes playing the games a surprisingly lonely experience, focused almost entirely on the intellectual challenges of puzzle solution. In *The Journeyman Project 3*, by contrast, Blackwood can interact with other humans while wearing a "chameleon suit," which disguises his identity. The series as a whole is remarkable for its literate use of sf time travel devices and its strong espousal of pacifist principles; conflicts generally arise from characters' divergent ideas of what is for the best and are resolved without violence.

Web Link
- Presto Studios: http://presto.yoonie.com/

KULT: THE TEMPLE OF FLYING SAUCERS

1989. (Also known as *Chamber of the Sci-Mutant Priestess* in the United States.) ERE Informatique. Designed by "Arbeit von Spacekraft" (Johan Robson).

In the future of *The Temple of Flying Saucers*, humanity has split into three distinct subspecies after a (presumably nuclear) apocalypse: the **psionically** gifted Tuners, the physically mutated Protozorqs, and the unaltered Normals. The player character, a Tuner, must rescue his girlfriend from the loathsome Protozorqs who have imprisoned her, a goal that he can most obviously pursue by using his mutant powers to complete five ordeals and become the Protozorqs' Messenger of the New Solution. The gameplay is that of a graphical **adventure**, displayed as a series of static images seen from the protagonist's point of view. As in the similarly structured *B.A.T.* (*1990* Computer's Dream) designed by Hervé Lange and Olivier Cordoléani, this approach can induce a frustrating sense of limitation in the player. Visually, the game combines a striking sense of design with a deliberately trashy aesthetic, often evoking the images published in the French comic-strip magazine *Métal Hurlant* (*1975–1987*).

Unusually for an adventure, the plot has some **multilinear** elements, with more than one path leading to a single end. Perhaps the most distinctive aspect of the game, however, is its profusion of bizarre inventions, presented with much offbeat humor; the rationale for the Protozorqs' plan for global genocide is notable for its sheer incomprehensibility. The puzzles are well constructed, if fairly simple. In the final analysis, *The Temple of Flying Saucers* may not be a perfect game, but it is certainly a memorable one. In one unforgettable touch, the player character's love interest, a young Tuner who is "the essence of goodness, beauty, and light," is known simply as "Sci-Fi."

LAST OF US, THE

2013. Naughty Dog. Designed by Bruce Straley and Neil Druckmann.

In the future, zombies will rule the Earth. This apocalyptic scenario is a common preoccupation of early twenty-first-century pop culture, the central conceit of works ranging from Max Brooks' novel (and later film) *World War Z* (**2006**) to Robert Kirkman's comic (and later TV series and **videogame**) *The Walking Dead* (*2003*–current). In the action **adventure** *The Last of Us*, victims of the global pandemic, which creates its brutally mundane postholocaust world, are not technically dead; instead, as in the UK film *28 Days Later* (*2002*), they are the victims of an infection that transforms them into subhuman killers. While the game's setting is not especially original, it succeeds in telling an exceptionally powerful and involving story in an entirely **linear** way. As in the best of the films and comics that preceded it, *The Last of Us* is primarily concerned with the survivors rather than their enemies, the "Infected." There is a great deal of credible barbarity among the deftly characterized remnants of humanity, of whom the most significant are the embittered drifter Joel—the player's primary persona within the game—and Ellie, a teenage girl born after the disaster who is perhaps the milieu's only truly sympathetic character. Gameplay concentrates on exploration, climbing, and leaping in the manner of a **platform game**, and grimly realistic combat; there are no superheroes here.

Players of *The Last of Us* can readily become **immersed** in its narrative, and perhaps even be personally transformed by their participation, but have very little agency, or ability to shape the story as opposed to the actions of Joel (and occasionally Ellie) within particular segments of the overall plot. This suggests that a story of this kind could be as effectively presented in another visual medium such as film or television, since the interactivity offered by the game does not extend to its core narrative. Arguably, however, the experience of playing through most of the game in the role of Joel makes it easier for the participant to become emotionally attached to Ellie, who the initially despairing loner comes to see as a surrogate for the daughter who died in the initial outbreak. Ultimately Joel chooses to preserve Ellie's life at the expense of creating a vaccine for the plague that has destroyed civilization, believing the world well lost for love. For many players, he will be doing what they want him to.

Related works: *The Last of Us: American Dreams* (*2013*) is a four-issue comics series that serves as a prequel to the game.

Web Link
- *The Last of Us*: http://www.thelastofus.com/

LEATHER GODDESSES OF PHOBOS

1986. Infocom. Designed by Steve Meretzky.

Leather Goddesses of Phobos is a text **adventure** set in 1936. The eponymous alien women intend to invade Earth and turn it into their private pleasure world; as the game begins, the player (having chosen a male or female character) is kidnapped to serve as their experimental subject. For reasons that are not entirely clear, the game's protagonist is assumed to oppose the Leather Goddesses' plan. Without too much effort, players can escape from their cells and set off on a whirlwind tour of the solar system, collecting the assortment of objects, which a newly acquired sidekick assures them will guarantee victory. *Leather Goddesses of Phobos* is generally suggestive rather than erotic, written in an innuendo-laden style resembling that of a campy sex farce; it pays frequent homage to the *Flash Gordon* and *Buck Rogers* film serials of the 1930s, making their implicit sexuality rather more overt. The game succeeds in being mildly amusing, notably when responding to players' instructions.

Related works: The sequel, *Leather Goddesses of Phobos 2: Gas Pump Girls Meet the Pulsating Inconvenience from Planet X!* (*1992* Infocom) designed by Steve Meretzky, is a graphical adventure with a mouse-driven interface, set in the 1950s. Its plot features the arrival on Earth of an alien from the tenth planet ("Planet X") who requests help against the resurgent forces of the Leather Goddesses; the style owes much to 1950s science fiction B-movies. This game received generally poor reviews, at least partly due to being released for commercial reasons before development was complete.

LONGEST JOURNEY, THE

1999. Funcom. Designed by Ragnar Tørnquist.

Set in the twin worlds of high-technology Stark and magical Arcadia, *The Longest Journey* is an important example of a graphical **adventure** with a **science and sorcery** theme, in which science fiction and fantasy tropes are combined and contrasted. As in Mark Geston's novel *The Siege of Wonder* (**1976**), the dichotomy between Stark and Arcadia is the division between the logic of science and the poetry of magic. This tension is here embodied in the separate natures of Gordon Halloway, a man who should have become the guardian of the balance between the two worlds, but has instead been split between them. The player's character is April Ryan, a slacker and struggling art student in Stark; the game begins in April's dream. Eventually it is revealed that she can move between the two realities and that the dream was the player's first sight of Arcadia. Stark and Arcadia were divided in their distant past by the alien Draic Kin, who play the role of both worlds' secret masters, to prevent humans abusing the combined powers of magic and technology. The plot centers on the attempts of a renegade member of the Kin to reunite Stark and Arcadia prematurely, in order to gain personal power. To achieve this end, Gordon Halloway has been divided between the worlds, an act that has indirectly caused the balance between them to decay. April's task, as eventually becomes clear, is to restore this balance by rejoining Halloway's sundered halves. In the poetic Arcadia, he has become the malicious, formless Chaos; in the scientific Stark, he is the overly logical and emotionless Gordon.

The Longest Journey is structured as a sequence of largely static scenes within which characters can move, interact with each other, and manipulate objects, an approach, which has been employed in graphical **adventures** from the 1983 *Valhalla* on.

Visually, *The Longest Journey* is strikingly well designed; both socially divided, futuristic Stark and Arcadia, a land of mermaids and timid molemen, are vividly realized. Structurally, it is a conventional adventure game, in which (often quite difficult) puzzles must be solved to advance the player from one chapter to the next of the strongly **linear** story; some of its expository sequences are perhaps overly long and insufficiently interactive. The game's true strength, however, lies in its lyrical and resonant story and subtle characterizations, notably of the insecure and cynical yet appealing April. Even more than most adventures, *The Longest Journey* is centrally concerned with the relationship between the player and the character whose role they adopt within the game. In the epilogue, it is suggested that the balance, though restored, must inevitably fall.

While much of *The Longest Journey* is set in the magically mysterious land of Arcadia, other portions occur in the more grimly realistic Stark.

While the world in which *Dreamfall* opens resembles our own, it is clearly a more science-fictional version of contemporary reality.

As is typical of action **adventures**, *Dreamfall* is set in a much more open, expansive setting than such graphical adventures as its predecessor *The Longest Journey*.

The sequel, *Dreamfall: The Longest Journey* (2006 Funcom) designed by Ragnar Tørnquist, moves away from exclusive reliance on puzzles to progress the story toward an action adventure style of gameplay, though the mechanics for fighting and hiding seem somewhat simplistic. The view chosen is third person, in a **real-time 3D** world. As in *The Longest Journey*, the plot is linear; the player is guided through the broad outlines of the story Tørnquist wants to tell. Ten years after the end of the first game, both Stark and Arcadia have entered a time of troubles. In Stark, a global computer crash has brought about the "Collapse" and loss of contact with its space colonies, after which order has been restored by the introduction of a semibenevolent police state. Meanwhile, much of Arcadia is now ruled by religious fundamentalists, who have brought peace but banned the use of magic. The main protagonist is Zoe Castillo, a young woman from Stark who is suffering from a loss of faith in the world when she begins receiving mysterious messages asking her to "save April Ryan." Later in the game, the player's control shifts to an older, embittered April and the religious fanatic who is hunting her; their contrasting viewpoints are expressed through the interior monologues that the player hears when interacting with the characters and their environment. The story explores conflicts between beauty and security, faith and freedom. In the end, much is left unresolved for a sequel.

Web Links

- *The Longest Journey*: http://www.longestjourney.com/

- *Dreamfall: The Longest Journey*: http://www.dreamfall.com/

- Ragnar Tørnquist on *Dreamfall: The Longest Journey*: http://www. gamasutra.com/features/20060403/woodard_01.shtml

MACHINARIUM

2009. Amanita Design. Designed by Jakub Dvorský.

Machinarium is a graphical **adventure**, developed as an **independent game** and set in a fairytale "City of Robots." As in such earlier works as *Another World* (*1991* Delphine Software) designed by Éric Chahi, a broadly **linear** story is told entirely without dialogue, though thought balloons containing informative images are sometimes employed. The game's setting is notably decrepit, a battered and rusted inner city environment in which humanity's role is taken by an entirely artificial population, while animals are replaced by mechanical birds and clockwork dogs. This milieu is, however, presented with much joy and lightness of touch, an approach epitomized by the design of the player character, a curiously Chaplinesque "little robot."

The 2009 **independent game** *Machinarium* revisited the approach taken in many earlier graphical **adventures** by presenting its characters as **2D** animations overlaid on a sequence of static backgrounds.

The twisty alleyways of *Machinarium*'s City of Robots conceal a multitude of quirky characters and intriguing details.

The game's backstory emerges only slowly, and in fragments, as the player makes their way through its sequence of generally well-constructed puzzles. Initially, the player's robot has been discarded on a scrapheap, and must reassemble himself from the scattered pieces of his body. Eventually, it becomes clear that the main character's task is to rescue his Significant Robot from a vicious gang of mechanical punks while defusing a bomb they have planted in the city. *Machinarium*'s heroic protagonist appears to be nameless, but the game's developers have indicated that he should be called Josef, in memory of Josef Čapek—who first suggested the use of the word robot to designate the artificial servants in his brother Karel Čapek's play *R.U.R.* (**1920**), and who, like the members of Amanita Design, was a Czech. Ultimately, *Machinarium* is an amusing cartoon, frequently reminiscent of the work of the film director Tim Burton, and similarly charming and sophisticated.

Web Link
- *Machinarium*: http://machinarium.net/

MANHUNTER

Series (from 1988). Evryware. Designed by Dave Murry, Barry Murry, and Dee Dee Murry.

The *Manhunter* games incorporate the reflex-based gameplay of **2D** action games into the puzzle narratives of graphical **adventures**, an unusual (and ultimately unsuccessful) combination. There is typically little overlap between the group of **videogamers** who appreciate intense, fast-paced excitements and those who are intrigued by the more cerebral pleasures offered by intricate conundrums, making a game that is intended for players who enjoy both forms a problematic proposition. It could also be argued that some of the *Manhunter* series' embedded action games and puzzles are poorly designed, tending to be more frustrating than challenging. Nevertheless, the games included several interesting innovations. Similarly to the French **computer role playing game** *B.A.T.* (*1990* Computer's Dream) designed by Hervé Lange and Olivier Cordoléani, they prefigured the well-known fantasy adventure *Myst* (*1993* Cyan Worlds) designed by Rand Miller and Robyn Miller by presenting most of their puzzles in static scenes seen from the viewpoint of the player character. While the games' visuals often seem crude, they are occasionally successful in evoking such sources as the iconic vision of a future Los Angeles seen in Ridley Scott's 1982 film *Blade Runner*. Many cinematographic tricks and techniques were borrowed from films and comics, an approach that has been used extensively by later videogame designers.

The first game in the sequence, *Manhunter: New York* (*1988* Evryware) designed by Dave Murry and Barry Murry, begins by telling the player that an alien species who resemble giant floating eyeballs (the Orbs) conquered the Earth in 2002. Two years later, in the game's present, the unnamed player character is forced to become one of the eponymous enforcers, an agent who hunts down human rebels and criminals for the aliens and their robotic servants. The New York of 2004 is a devastated city, littered with debris from shattered buildings and oppressed by a dark red sky contaminated with extraterrestrial gases. There are many restrictions on the player's actions; humans must always wear brown robes, can only travel between permitted locations, and cannot speak. (Interestingly, all of these limitations serve to make the developers' task easier, by allowing them to work around the technical problems that, for example, limited the range of colors that could be displayed.) In an entirely **linear interactive narrative**, the player is assigned a series of cases that lead them to make contact with an underground resistance to the Orbs, whose members are being killed by a psychotic **cyborg** who is working for the aliens without their knowledge. Eventually, the protagonist will find themselves in a position to complete the plan of the (now defunct) rebels, destroying a machine located in the Statue of Liberty, which is converting Earth's atmosphere into something more suitable for the invaders before ending the game by setting off in pursuit of the escaped cyborg in a captured spaceship.

The story of the sequel, *Manhunter 2: San Francisco* (*1989* Evryware) designed by Dave Murry, Barry Murry, and Dee Dee Murry, follows immediately on from that of its predecessor, as the player crashes in the eponymous city, where their quarry has landed in their own vessel. As soon as they stagger out of the wreck, the player discovers the corpse of a Manhunter who was crushed beneath their craft. They must then assume the victim's identity, working on a sequence of new cases for the Orbs, which, unsurprisingly, turn out to lead to another opportunity to strike back at the invaders. In San Francisco, the aliens are using geothermal energy as a power source, but have discovered that their human slaves are poorly suited for working in the lava-filled mines beneath the city. They have therefore sponsored the genetic engineering of various human–animal hybrids, including reptile men and rat men; some of these unfortunates can be freed from their prison on Alcatraz Island to help overthrow the oppressors. While the narrative is again linear, it is rather more complex and convoluted than that of the first game, to the extent of often being extremely confusing.

Evryware's original intention was to create a third game that would tie up various plot threads left unresolved at the end of *Manhunter 2: San Francisco*, but this work was never released. While the series is interesting for its initial positioning of the player as an alien collaborator, and for its depiction of an oppressive, alienated future in which moments of grotesque humor are mingled with enigmatic (and often unresolved) mysteries, the reality of the experience offered by the games rarely lives up to their premise. One fundamental difficulty is with the fiction, which seems overly skeletal. The player's persona is extremely thinly characterized, a problem shared with the various computer-controlled characters encountered during the course of the series. This lack of definition for the protagonist would not be a problem if the player was allowed the freedom to create their own personality by making personal choices. However, the narratives of the *Manhunter* games are notably linear; to deviate from their predefined sequences of successful actions is, typically, to die. This leaves the player acting out a story in which their character's motivations are unknown, forcing them to construct justifications for the actions they must take with little assistance from the script.

Web Link
- The Manhunter Shrine (Tribute Site): http://manhunter.talkspot.com

MANIAC MANSION

1987. LG. Designed by Ron Gilbert and Gary Winnick.

Maniac Mansion is a graphical **adventure** game that parodies 1950s sf B-movies in a not dissimilar manner to the film of *The Rocky Horror Picture Show* (*1975*). It introduced several innovations to adventure design, including a choice of playable avatars and the combination of a simple verb and noun-based point and click interface with animated characters. The game begins after the sinister Dr Edison has kidnapped Dave Miller's girlfriend, Sandy, and taken her to his mansion, where he intends to experiment on her brain. Players then choose two of Dave's friends to accompany him, and the three characters set out to rescue the girl. Gameplay concentrates on exploring the mansion and solving its often humorous puzzles, though the occasional appearance of noninteractive scenes showing Dr Edison at work adds a degree of narrative tension. Ultimately, it emerges that the doctor is being mentally controlled by an evil meteor, which the player must defeat. The plot is **multilinear**, with several possible endings, depending on the player's actions and initial choice of characters. Thus, one of Dave's friends can summon the Meteor Police to arrest the monster, while another can expose it to the world by arranging for the publication of its autobiography. From the player's first sight of the mansion's menacing sign "Warning!! Trespassers will be horribly mutilated" to the final triumph over Purple Meteor, *Maniac Mansion* is a delight.

Related works: *Maniac Mansion Deluxe* (*2004* Lucasfan Games) is an amateur remake, which adds some minor improvements while remaining faithful to the original. *Maniac Mansion* (*1990–1993*) is a television series featuring a new Dr Edison, grandson of the original, who has inherited the mansion and accidentally mutated his family. The series is much more family oriented than the game, lacking any equivalents of the original Dr Edison's sadomasochistic wife and insane survivalist son.

Web Link
- The Expurgation of *Maniac Mansion* for the Nintendo Entertainment System: http://www.crockford.com/wrrrld/maniac.html

MANIAC MANSION: DAY OF THE TENTACLE

1993. LA. Designed by Tim Schafer and David Grossman.

Widely considered to be one of the best of LA's graphical **adventures**, *Day of the Tentacle* is a loose sequel to *Maniac Mansion* (*1987* LG) designed by Ron Gilbert and Gary Winnick. Its eponymous villain is one Purple Tentacle, an intelligent ambulatory member created by Dr Edison's dubious experiments in the previous game. After exposing itself to toxic waste, the tentacle grows arms and develops a demented plan to become ruler of the world. Participants adopt the role of Bernard Bernoulli, a cowardly geek who was one of the playable characters in *Maniac Mansion*. With two friends, he returns to the scene of the previous horror, but all three soon find themselves trapped in different time periods after an unfortunate encounter with Dr Edison's malfunctioning time machine. The remainder of the **linear** plot alternates between the three characters, who must find a way of defeating Purple Tentacle and reuniting in the present. The puzzle designs play ingeniously with the concept of time travel; at one point, a character in the eighteenth century can insert a flyer advertising vacuum cleaners into a suggestions box for the American Constitution, leading to the addition of a clause that requires every home to contain such a device as soon as it has been invented. As a result, the future is changed to make a vacuum cleaner available when it is needed in the present. The surreal art style, entertaining parodies of historical figures and consistently witty dialogue combine to make *Day of the Tentacle* one of the most amusing adventure games ever designed.

MARSPORT

1985. Gargoyle Games (GG). Designed by Roy Carter and Greg Follis.

Marsport is an "arcade adventure," a precursor to the action **adventure** form that flourished in the United Kingdom during the 1980s. While it was well regarded at the time of its original release—as was its better known predecessor, the Celtic fantasy game *Tir Na Nog* (*1984* GG) designed by Roy Carter and Greg Follis—the game now seems of largely historical interest. *Marsport* is set in the twenty-fifth century, the first of a projected trilogy of which it was the only member to be completed. In the game's backstory, Earth is protected from an aggressive alien species by a gigantic **force field**, but the invaders are on the point of breaching this defense. The player's character is sent to infiltrate the eponymous Martian city—now occupied by the enemy, and made more dangerous by the malfunctioning guard robots deployed by its Terran computer system—and recover the original plans for the energy shield, which contain the information needed to make it impenetrable to the aliens' attack. While the eerily deserted submartian environment is evocatively depicted, using an unusual 2D view, which simulates **3D** visuals by rotating the display whenever the player changes direction, the gameplay is dominated by combat and the solution of physical puzzles, most of which suffer from a distinct lack of credibility. Considered as a work of science fiction, the game is perhaps most valuable for the demonstration it offers of the difficulties faced by the developers of early visual **videogames** who wanted to depict a convincing fictional reality. (Text adventures were generally less affected by such problems, since their designs were not so restricted by the technical limitations of the underlying hardware and they lent themselves naturally to the presentation of long passages of descriptive text.) The manual for *Marsport* contains a moderately detailed history of the game's milieu, including references to science fiction stories by Larry Niven, Isaac Asimov, James Blish, and Gordon R. Dickson, but very little of this is realized in the actual gameplay.

Related works: *Sweevo's World* (*1986* GG; also known as *Sweevo's Whirled*) and its sequel *Hydrofool* (*1987* Carter Follis Software Associates), both designed by Carter and Follis and featuring the arcade adventures of a comic robot, are officially set in the same universe as *Marsport*.

MIND FOREVER VOYAGING, A

1985. Infocom. Designed by Steve Meretzky.

The release of *A Mind Forever Voyaging* represented an attempt by its developers to produce a game that would be less of a text-based **adventure** and more of a work of **interactive fiction**. The choice of title—a quotation from William Wordsworth's autobiographical poem *The Prelude* (**1850**)—reflects this goal. (In context, the phrase refers to a statue of Isaac Newton: "The marble index of a mind forever Voyaging through strange seas of Thought, alone.") In a significant departure from previous adventure games, *A Mind Forever Voyaging* is almost entirely devoid of puzzles.

The game is set in 2031, in a future "United States of North America" suffering from social decay and the threat of global war. Immediately before the start of the adventure, the player's character is informed that he is an artificial intelligence called PRISM rather than a human being and that the small town of Rockvil where he lives is only a simulation. The head of the PRISM project explains that he is now needed to investigate a politically conservative "Plan for Renewed National Purpose" by entering a simulation of its likely effects and reporting on what he sees. The player is then introduced into a series of artificial Rockvils, projected into the future at 10-year intervals. Within the virtual Rockvil, PRISM takes on the life of his previous "human" identity, Perry Simm. Gameplay largely consists of roaming through the extensive environs of the town and experiencing or observing interesting events. These sequences can be quite disturbing; notably, the effects on Perry Simm's family life of the simulated America's decline into totalitarian theocracy (after a brief initial revival) are genuinely moving. After several excursions into the projected future, it becomes apparent that the Plan will eventually result in a savage anarchy. At this point, the project's sponsor attempts to shut down PRISM in order to suppress the results of the experiment and players must act to defend themselves, using only the systems accessible to their computer selves; this closing sequence contains the only puzzles in the game.

Arguably, *A Mind Forever Voyaging* suffers from a lack of interesting gameplay when considered as a game and an absence of dramatic tension when regarded as a narrative. Nevertheless, it has moments of real power both as a work of American liberal evangelism and as a story of personal tragedy. Its greatest importance may be as a seminal text for the amateur creators of interactive fiction who appeared after the demise of the commercial text adventure; its structure has been very influential on many of their works.

MINDWHEEL

1984. Synapse Software. Designed by Robert Pinsky.

Written by the noted American poet Robert Pinsky, *Mindwheel* was originally marketed as an "Electronic Novel." In design terms, however, it is a text-based **adventure** game, in which the player takes the role of a "Mind Adventurer." The premise is that the Adventurer's future society is on the verge of destroying itself through internal conflict, and in order to prevent anarchy, the player must obtain the Wheel of Wisdom (an object containing "the secret of [their] planet's best values") from the mind of the first truly creative human being. The Wheel can be retrieved by projecting the Adventurer's mind into the "neuro-electronic matrix," in which the dreaming minds of the dead are preserved for eternity. While *Mindwheel* is not especially convincing as a work of science fiction, it is a powerful piece of metaphysical prose, dense, allusive, and often light heartedly playful, full of striking images. The idea of traveling through the minds of the dead (represented as a labyrinthine building in which subconscious desires and images roam through interconnected rooms) is a powerful one, similar to the **telepathic** therapy described in Roger Zelazny's *The Dream Master* (**1966**). As in *The Dream Master*, not all of the minds entered are benign. In *Mindwheel*, this use of **dream hacking** also allows complex characters to be presented to the player as landscapes to be explored rather than as simulated humans whose conversations might have proved unconvincing. Considered as a game, however, *Mindwheel* is less effective. The puzzles presented to players consist largely of riddles and poems for which the participant must supply any missing words. While the riddles generally work well, the missing word puzzles often seem arbitrary, and their solutions can require the player to perform actions for which there is no clear rationale. While *Mindwheel* is impressive as a metaphysical fable, it is perhaps less successful as a work of **interactive fiction**.

NOMAD SOUL, THE

1999. (Also known as *Omikron: The Nomad Soul* in the United States.) QD. Designed by David Cage.

The Nomad Soul is a **science and sorcery** action **adventure**, set in a **parallel world**, which fuses a somewhat routine **cyberpunk** background with ritual magic and supernatural predators. As in the *Manhunter* series, the action and adventure aspects are unusually disjunct; in this game, most of the player's time is spent exploring the world, talking to its inhabitants, and solving puzzles, but some isolated sequences are modeled after **fighting games** and **first person shooters**. *The Nomad Soul* was also part of a brief wave of fantastical **videogames** created in association with musicians, a movement that is perhaps exemplified by the unimpressive dystopian vision of *Queen: The eYe* (*1998* Destination Design), featuring music from the eponymous group. Here, David Bowie supplies several songs (most of which are included in revised form on the 1999 album "*hours…*"), as well as providing voice and gestures for two characters and contributing to the game's design. Bowie's metafictional appearance as the lead singer of an underground band called The Dreamers is echoed in the game's introduction, in which the player is invited to possess the body of an "investigating agent" from another dimension, through the medium of the game that they are already playing.

Once the game has begun, the player finds themselves in the city of Omikron, occupying the body of one Kay'l 669 and expected to continue the police investigation of a mysterious serial killer. It soon emerges that the murderer is both a police commander and a demon in disguise. After the player kills the demon, the game's broadly **linear interactive narrative** continues with an invitation to join an underground organization opposed to the city's ruling computer and overly powerful corporations. The commander turns out to be merely a pawn of a much more powerful demon, who created the videogame in which the player is participating in order to lure human souls into his world, where he can eat them. Only by rediscovering forgotten magical arts can the player defeat this nemesis, which is fused to the city's master computer, liberate the people of Omikron, and escape from the game with their soul intact. As in such earlier games as *Mercenary* (*1985* Novagen Software) designed by Paul Woakes, players are allowed to roam largely at will through the various regions of the city, which are extensive and highly operable if somewhat shallow. Much use is made of the player's titular ability to transfer their mind from one body to another, whether to solve puzzles or to escape the death of their current host. The game's visuals are stylish and filmic, but its narrative fails to achieve an elegant fusion of the disparate elements from which it is composed; its contemporary *The Longest Journey* (*1999* Funcom) designed by Ragnar Tørnquist is far more successful in this regard.

The Nomad Soul is a highly ambitious game, in some ways—as in its emphasis on exploration and its characters' ability to improve their fighting skills—more reminiscent of **computer role playing game** designs than those of adventures. Nevertheless, the action sequences are simplistic and occasionally frustrating by the standards of dedicated fighting games and first-person shooters, some of the puzzles seem overly cryptic, the controls are sometimes awkward, and the narrative occasionally provides players with insufficient guidance, meaning that they may find themselves wandering aimlessly through the gigantic city. The design demonstrates an approach to gameplay that has since become particularly associated with Cage, that of a **3D** graphical adventure in which miniature action games are embedded. Arguably, however, Cage did not truly master this style until the release of his next work, *Fahrenheit* (*2005* QD), in which the more immediately stimulating sequences are smaller and more tightly integrated with the flow of the story. (This game, while it involves a group of artificial intelligences in present-day New York, is centrally concerned with the fulfillment of a prophecy about a pure-souled child pursued by various factions with paranormal abilities, and is thus difficult to approach as a work of sf.) Ultimately, *The Nomad Soul* represents something of a triumph of style over content, one that seems thematically suggestive of the "prog rock" concept albums of the 1970s.

Web Link
- *Omikron: The Nomad Soul*: http://www.quanticdream.com/en/game/omikron-the-nomad-soul

OBSIDIAN

1996. Rocket Science Games. Designed by Howard Cushnir, Scott Kim, and Adam Wolff.

The striking commercial success of the first-person graphical **adventure** game *Myst* (*1993* Cyan Worlds) designed by Rand Miller and Robyn Miller fostered a wave of enthusiasm for games based on **full motion video** technology. One of the most dedicated advocates for this approach, Rocket Science Games, was founded with the aim of bringing Hollywood values into the **videogame** industry, and hired many talented individuals with a background in cinema in addition to well-known game designers and comics creators. Ultimately, this strategy proved unsuccessful; the techniques used to make bestselling films often translate poorly into the world of games, where interactivity is king. One of the studio's products did become something of a cult success, however: *Obsidian*, a direct descendant of *Myst*, which replaced its prototype's fantasy landscapes with a surreal world built by a malfunctioning artificial intelligence.

As is typical of games that make heavy use of full motion video, *Obsidian*'s core gameplay strongly resembled that of its model; interactivity was traded off for graphical quality, meaning that players could only move to specific points in space for which **3D** visuals had been created in advance. At the beginning of the game, the player takes the part of Lilah Kerlins, a scientist who has gone on a camping holiday with her partner Max to celebrate the successful launch of Ceres, a satellite they designed to repair the ozone layer by releasing **nanotechnological** devices into the upper atmosphere. The pair discovers a strange crystalline formation, apparently formed from obsidian glass, and become trapped inside it. Soon the player realizes that the formation was created by Ceres, which has become sentient and wishes to learn about its makers by observing how they explore an artificial world.

The impressive visual design of Ceres' nanotechnologically constructed world draws upon Jungian psychology and surrealism; it bears some resemblance to the films of the Czech artist Jan Švankmajer. The several different areas traversed by the player each have their own aesthetics. Notably, the first to be encountered resembles a Cubist reimagining of a bureaucratic maze, full of talking television sets on articulated arms. Puzzles are often difficult, depending on the player's ability to understand the axioms of an alien logic. The successful solution of each group of problems only allows participants to access the next area, which will operate under its own unique set of rules. Eventually, however, the player will reach the end of their **linear** progression through the game and discover that they must persuade Ceres that mankind is not simply another form of pollution. If they fail, humanity will be cleansed from the Earth.

OUTCAST

1999. Appeal.

Outcast is a **3D** action **adventure** game normally played in a third-person view, particularly notable for the ethereal, otherworldly beauty of its visuals. The game begins after a probe sent to a **parallel world** has malfunctioned, creating a hole in space that threatens to destroy the Earth within weeks. The player adopts the role of the somewhat stereotypical Cutter Slade, a former US Navy Special Forces soldier dispatched to the parallel Earth to shut down the probe. On arrival, the player finds themselves separated from the scientists who make up the rest of their team and hailed by the nonhuman Talans as their messiah. In order to get the help they need to complete their mission, participants must agree to overthrow the Talans' oppressive dictator. The alternate Earth of Adelpha is an impressive work of subcreation, with a richly imagined society influenced by Middle Eastern cultures, an extensive geography and a history that has left the landscape crowded with the partially understood artifacts of an older, more powerful civilization. The Talans themselves are remarkable for their detailed yet varied personalities as well as for the alien vocabulary they use and which the player must learn.

The unusual rendering technology used in *Outcast* allowed its developers to create moments of remarkable beauty.

Playing through the game, however, evokes a certain sense of bathos. The strongly **modular** story encourages participants to travel across Adelpha, convincing local Talans that Slade is indeed their messiah, thus recruiting them to assist him in overthrowing their rulers. As a result, much of the player's time is spent performing mundane and sometimes repetitive tasks for suspicious Talans in order to persuade them that Slade is trustworthy and virtuous. The contrast between these activities and the profound significance attached to the player's mission can be jarring. *Outcast* succeeds impressively when participants focus on the pleasures of exploring its strikingly well-constructed alien world, but is perhaps less rewarding when they concentrate on the puzzle solution and combat gameplay, which is traditionally at the heart of an action adventure game.

Players of *Outcast* can travel across the surface of Adelpha using ring-shaped **matter transmission** gateways known as Daokas.

Web Link
- Planet Adelpha (Tribute Site): http://www.planet-adelpha.net/

PATHOLOGIC

2006. (Also known as *Pestilence: The Utopia* in Russia.) Ice-Pick Lodge. Designed by Nikolay Dybowskiy.

While *Pathologic*'s gameplay resembles that seen in examples of the **survival horror** form, it is perhaps better described as a slow-paced action **adventure**, viewed from a first-person perspective. The majority of the player's time is spent exploring the game's urban environment, interacting with its inhabitants, and searching for scarce (and often desperately needed) resources, notably food and medical supplies. In tone, *Pathologic* is more philosophical and despairing than it is exciting and terrifying; violence is best avoided whenever possible.

Fundamentally, the game is more a work of speculative than of science fiction. The setting is a remote town on the Russian steppes, apparently in the early twentieth century. Shortly after the player has chosen their character and arrived in the community, a mysterious disease is discovered among the population, and a quarantine is declared. From this point on, the player has 12 days to solve the mystery of the plague and find a treatment. If the time elapses without a cure being found, the town will be destroyed. If the player fails to complete the single major task, which a character will offer them each day, one of their character's friends or allies in the town will die. If the player's character fails to eat, sleep, or stay free of disease, they too can die. As this list suggests, *Pathologic* can be a harsh and unforgiving game to play, in which the player must repeatedly trudge from one part of the town to another, negotiating and bartering with the natives within strict time limits to obtain the goods and information they need to survive and complete their daily mission. The town in which the game is set is grim and sometimes vile, subject to a metaphysical form of urban decay. While each of the characters whose role the player can choose to adopt is some kind of healer (the alternatives being a doctor of medicine, a shaman with divinatory powers, and a tribal witch), their abilities can lead the player to make morally dubious choices, sacrificing one to save many.

Perhaps the most unusual aspect of *Pathologic*'s construction is the way in which its designers have blurred the lines between game and reality, between the player and the character. At intervals in the predesigned plot, mysterious masked entities resembling bird-headed men or faceless mimes will approach the protagonist and speak directly to the player who controls them, emphasizing the artificiality of the work and the arbitrary nature of its rules. This stratagem is used, for example, to explain the death of one of the protagonist's friends whenever the player fails, a mechanic that has no causal justification within the reality of the game. Such devices are reminiscent of Bertolt Brecht's "theatre of estrangement," in which an actor might address the audience directly in order to create "a sense of curiosity and astonishment."

In the game, it soon becomes apparent that not only the people but also the buildings are dying. Eventually, it can be deduced that it is not truly the population that is sick, but the town itself and the earth beneath it. The people's abuse of the land, and of the symbolic bull that provides the shape of their town, has made it ill, and the sickness of the land causes the disease of the people. For a cure to be found, humanity must recognize its abuse, and begin to end it. This pagan mystery can only be fully penetrated by finishing the game more than once; only part of the story can be understood from the viewpoint of any one of the player's three possible personas. All of these characters are present whenever the game is played, but two of them simply act out their prepared roles while the player performs the part they have chosen. Thus, the shape of the plot is that of several intertwined **linear** narratives, a kind of multithreaded tapestry of story.

Pathologic is bleak, otherworldly, occasionally abhorrent, and very slow to play. It also suffers from a truly awful translation from the original Russian. Even allowing for this, it is often remarkably pretentious. Nevertheless, it offers a genuinely compelling experience, an exercise in choosing ends over means in a morally ambiguous world and a vision of a kind of dirty transcendence, which may also serve as an allegory of Russian society. The game is also almost unique in the world of **video-game** design. Its closest artistic relatives may be Thomas M. Disch's non-sf text adventure *Amnesia* (*1986* Cognetics Corp) and (especially) Andrei Tarkovsky's agonizingly hypnotic film *Stalker* (*1979*).

Web Link

- *Pathologic*: http://www.pathologic-game.com/eng_index.htm

PEPPER'S ADVENTURES IN TIME

1993. SOL. Designed by Gano Haine, Jane Jensen, Josh Mandel, and Lorelei Shannon.

Pepper's Adventures in Time is a graphical **adventure** marketed as edutainment for young adults, which many older players have also found appealing. Participants alternate between the roles of the eponymous character, a sassy young amateur newsgirl, and her "newshound," Lockjaw. The game begins with Pepper and Lockjaw outside her parents' house, but the player (in the person of Pepper) will soon find themselves following Lockjaw back in time from contemporary America to the eighteenth century, courtesy of Uncle Fred's experimental time machine. Fred, it seems, is something of an archetypal mad scientist, having not only discovered time travel but decided to use it to bring the counterculture of the 1960s to the cradle of the American Revolution. This plan is clearly working; Benjamin Franklin has become a hippie guru, surrounded by lotus-eating disciples and utterly indifferent to politics. The player's goal is to return history to its expected shape, while perhaps learning some useful facts along the way. The lasting impression is of a gently amusing game, liberally endowed with not overly taxing puzzles.

PLANETFALL

1983. Infocom. Designed by Steve Meretzky.

The text **adventure** game *Planetfall* is a mildly comic **space opera**, remembered largely for the strong emotional reactions it evoked in many players. At the beginning of the game, the participant is a lowly Ensign Seventh Class on a Stellar Patrol starship, helping to reunify the galaxy after the collapse of the Second Galactic Union. After some preliminary comic business, explosions are heard aboard the ship, and the protagonist is forced to use an escape pod, which crash-lands on an apparently deserted planet. As the player explores their new world, they can discover that the inhabitants are in **suspended animation**, waiting for their robotic systems to find a cure for a lethal plague; the primary narrative in the game is this **embedded** backstory. In the game's present, the plot is driven by the player's realization that their character has been exposed to the plague and that increasingly frequent meteorite bombardments may destroy the automatic systems before a cure is discovered.

As is conventional for text adventures, the gameplay in *Planetfall* is focused on solving various puzzles, which enables the participant to uncover more of the backstory and eventually to save the frozen population. To assist the player on the deserted planet, the game provides Floyd, a playful robot companion. Some puzzles cannot be solved without Floyd's assistance, and near the end of the game, he must be allowed to sacrifice himself in order to obtain a vital component. The robot's apparent death is a surprisingly affecting moment, illustrating the potential power of an **interactive narrative**. In the end, however, the player can revive the planet's people, who will repair Floyd.

The sequel, *Stationfall* (*1987* Infocom) designed by Steve Meretzky, begins in the same comic mode as *Planetfall*, but becomes steadily darker in tone. The player's character has been promoted after the events of the first game but finds himself trapped in a boring job processing absurdly redundant paperwork. At the beginning of the game, he is sent to a space station to pick up a load of "form request forms," accompanied by Floyd. On arrival, the player discovers that all the humans are missing, but many of the robots on the station have turned homicidal. Eventually, it emerges that an alien artifact is influencing machines to make them hate and destroy humans and that Floyd has become affected. In order to survive and prevent the alien influence spreading off the station, the participant has no choice but to kill Floyd. While the robot's first death in *Planetfall* caused grief, this second and irrevocable demise was greeted with anger by many players. Although both deaths are unavoidable if the games are to be won, *Stationfall*'s requirement that players execute Floyd personally was seen as cruel.

Related works: Both *Planetfall* and *Stationfall* are loosely linked to *Starcross* (*1982* Infocom) designed by Dave Lebling; internal evidence suggests that the former two games are set in the distant future of the latter. Arthur Byron Cover wrote novelizations of both works as *Planetfall* (**1988**) and *Stationfall* (**1989**). Both books display a rather heavy-handed sense of humor not seen in the games; *Stationfall* in particular is remarkable for having a plot that bears almost no resemblance to that of its original.

PORTAL

1986. Nexa Corporation. Designed by Rob Swigart.

Portal was an attempt to create a "computer novel," a form that was intended to more closely resemble that of **hyperfiction** than the text **adventure**. The player takes the part of an astronaut sent on a solitary mission of exploration in a **slower than light** starship. When they return, a century after their departure, Earth is deserted and the only available clues to the mystery are buried in an abandoned worldwide information retrieval system. The terminal they use to communicate with this network is the interface to the game; the player's task is to search through the available databases until they can assemble the story of humanity's disappearance, assisted by a simulated "storytelling AI" that supplies the necessary narrative ligatures. As the player reads their way through the game's simulated data files, more are made available, until they have decoded the entire history of the destruction of an ambiguously utopian society by a form of **psionic** transcendence. The story is thus entirely **embedded**; the act of reading the text is the same as that of playing the game. (A more visual variant of the same approach was later used in *Dear Esther* [*2008* The Chinese Room; revised *2012*] designed by Dan Pinchbeck, an **independent game** in which the player explores a mysterious island that acts as a kind of psychogeographic repository for its cryptic, fragmented narrative.) While *Portal* succeeds in evoking an atmospheric sense of melancholy and in presenting an intriguing mystery, in the end, it is questionable whether the interactive presentation is superior to that of a purely linear novel.

Related works: *Portal: A Dataspace Retrieval* (**1988**), again by Swigart, consists of the introduction from the game's manual followed by what is essentially a transcript of the gameplay, with some additional material presented from the protagonist's point of view. The result is a "mosaic novel" in the manner of such works as John Brunner's *Stand on Zanzibar* (**1968**) or John Dos Passos' *The 42nd Parallel* (**1930**).

PROTOTYPE

2009. Radical Entertainment (RE). Designed by Eric Holmes and Dennis Detwiller.

In *Prototype*, the hero is a monster. In present-day Manhattan, an unknown virus is radically mutating the population, turning them into grotesque zombie-like killers. The player's character, Alex Mercer, is a superpowered amnesiac, a condition that also appears to have been caused by the devastating disease. As a protagonist, Mercer offers the player a remarkable sense of empowerment; he is a superhumanly strong and agile shapeshifter who can adopt forms that allow him to glide across the sky, punch through tanks, and pull helicopters from the air. His goal at the beginning of the game is simply to take revenge on those who infected him. Ultimately, it emerges that he is the one responsible for the plague, having deliberately released the virus when he was about to be killed by its owners, for whom he had helped create it. There are other twists in the tale.

The game's design is that of an action **adventure**, one that combines a spine of **linear** plot with a selection of optional missions arranged in a **modular** structure. Gameplay is extremely fast paced, with players typically having the option of penetrating dangerous areas by mimicking the forms of government soldiers or simply by attacking everything in sight. As in the somewhat similar *inFAMOUS* (*2009* SPP), players can roam the city more or less at will, though most of their time will be devoted to (somewhat repetitive) combat. There is a strong element of body horror, as if the director of the Japanese film *Tetsuo* (*1989*) had been inspired by biology rather than machinery. Players gain the ability to enact a wide range of disturbing bodily transformations upon their characters as well as the need to regularly ingest people in order to absorb their biomass and memories. (This last device is used to reveal the **embedded** backstory of Mercer's past through the minds of his victims as well as to bestow upon him the skills needed to use military weapons and vehicles.) While the chaotic ruins of Manhattan Island are effectively depicted, and the subtext of the story is interesting, the game's relentless focus on carnage and dismemberment is less appealing. Ultimately, there is little more tiresome than fountains of human viscera. Interestingly, many players seem to have found adopting the role of the monster troublesome; the unavoidable heroic death experienced by the protagonist of the **first person shooter** *Halo: Reach* (*2010* Bungie Studios) designed by Marcus Lehto and Christian Allen appears to have made for a notably more popular experience.

Prototype 2 (*2012* RE) designed by Matthew Armstrong and John Howard is a broadly similar, but arguably less interesting, sequel, in which the protagonist is James Heller, a soldier who has been given superhuman powers by Mercer. Mercer, meanwhile, has become a crazed messiah determined to infect the whole of humanity with the virus that transformed him. Heller devotes himself to hunting down and killing his maker, pausing only to indulge in bouts of macho posturing. *Prototype 2* attempts to present its main character in more conventionally heroic terms than did its predecessor, though the gameplay benefits gained by killing and consuming passing civilians may make this a difficult role for players to enact. The game ends with Heller dedicating himself to preserving humankind by destroying the infected before they can spread the disease any further. Ominously, this is precisely the role that Mercer adopts at the end of the first game.

Related works: *Colossal Mayhem* (*2012* RE) and *Excessive Force* (*2012* RE) are expansions for *Prototype 2* that contain additional weapons and abilities for the player. *Prototype* (*2009*) is a six-issue comics series that serves as a prequel to the original game, while *Prototype 2* (*2012*) is a graphic novel, set between the first and second games and authored by Dan Jolley (who wrote the script for *Prototype 2*).

Web Link

- *Prototype*: http://www.prototypegame.com/

REMEMBER ME

2013. DONTNOD Entertainment. Designed by Jean-Maxime Moris.

Remember Me is an action **adventure**, scripted by Stéphane Beauverger and set in a near future "Neo-Paris" where the technological manipulation of human memories is commonplace. This is an old idea in science fiction, dating back at least to Israel Zangwill's "The Memory Clearing House" (July 1892 *The Idler*) and seen in many later works, from Alfred Bester's *The Demolished Man* (**1952**) through Roger Zelazny's *Today We Choose Faces* (**1973**) to such films as *Eternal Sunshine of the Spotless Mind* (*2004*) and the **dream hacking**-based *Inception* (*2010*). As in many of its predecessors, the ability to remove painful memories and transfer more desirable recollections to others is here presented as an unmitigated curse. The future France of the game is a society of junkies hooked on dangerously addictive memory swaps, where the personalities of dissidents are simply erased. As in Joss Whedon's TV series *Dollhouse* (*2009–2010*), the mutability of memory has resulted in a dangerous fragmentation of identity, as people forget who they truly are.

The gameplay is a combination of hand-to-hand combat, stealthy infiltration, and climbing and leaping in the manner of a **platform game**, with some interesting sequences in which the player can remix a subject's memories, changing their motivations in the present by altering their recollections of the past. There is a general emphasis on making the game accessible to participants who have not played similar works before, an approach that may have contributed to its perhaps overly **linear** structure; players' travels through the milieu seem constrained to a path in which every step has been laid out in advance, leading to an unfortunate sense of constriction. Nevertheless, the game benefits from an impressive ambience and an excellent visual design, reminiscent of both the comic-strip *bandes dessinées* and the film *The Fifth Element* (*1997*). Despite some hokey dialogue and an unconvincing denouement, *Remember Me*'s appealing heroine, cheerfully exploitative sensibility, and outré fashion designs lend it a great deal of charm.

Related works: *Remember Me: The Pandora Archive* (**2013**), by Scott Harrison, is a prequel, which was published as an e-book.

Web Link
  * *Remember Me*: http://www.remembermegame.com/

SHADOW OF MEMORIES

2001. (Also known as *Shadow Of Destiny* in the United States.) Konami. Designed by Junko Kawano.

Shadow Of Memories is a highly atmospheric graphical **adventure** with an unusual plot; the player must solve the mystery of their own murder. The display is fully **3D**, while the gameplay revolves around puzzle solution and conversation with computer-controlled characters, in the manner of such earlier works as *Maniac Mansion: Day of the Tentacle* (*1993* LA) designed by Tim Schafer and David Grossman or *The Longest Journey* (*1999* Funcom) designed by Ragnar Tørnquist. The game begins with the murder of Eike Kusch, the player character, in a modern town in Germany, followed by his resurrection by a mysterious figure. This entity tells Kusch that if he wishes to survive, he must change the sequence of events that led to his death, gives him an erratically functioning time travel device, and dispatches him into the recent past. Events then proceed through a sequence of fatalities; the player can repeatedly succeed in preventing their character's death, only to discover that they will then be killed in a different way, and resurrected yet again. Eventually, it becomes clear that the only hope of survival lies in traveling to a variety of time periods, including the Middle Ages, the beginning of the twentieth century, and the 1980s, and attempting to uncover the secrets of Kusch's forgotten past.

The game's rationale depends on **science and sorcery** (the individual who rescues Kusch is an alchemically created homunculus who uses a technological time machine), but its conception of time travel is entirely science fictional. Time passes continuously and simultaneously in all periods during play, meaning that if the player travels into the past an hour before they are due to die in the present, they have only 60 min to save themselves in the past before their fate is sealed. This conceit, which corresponds to assuming that Kusch can only travel specific distances in time, adds a real sense of tension to the gameplay, since the player is always racing an unforgiving clock. While the town of Lebensbaum (in which the game is set in all its various eras) is not especially interactive, being almost completely deserted, considerable effort has been devoted to giving the player as many options as possible within the limitations imposed by the design. The game's structure is highly **multilinear**, with a variety of endings and a labyrinthine web of behaviors that allow for many complex interactions in time. If, for example, Kusch attempts to talk to a previous version of himself, the consequences are as disastrous as might be expected.

Playing *Shadow Of Memories* can be a curiously disorienting experience. The reality of the game-world becomes dreamlike and insubstantial as Kusch experiences his last day again and again, with subtle variations introduced by his actions in previous time periods. Mysteries are uncovered and secret identities revealed, but it is hard to be certain that these revelations are fundamental, and not artifacts created by changes made by the player in the past that may be altered at some point in the future. After completing the game once, the player can choose to begin again, but in this iteration, Kusch is clearly aware of having experienced the story before, in some other reality. Eventually, it may emerge that the homunculus has manipulated everything that happens in order to ensure his own creation through a circuit in time, but this reality seems no less mutable than the rest.

SILICON DREAMS

Series (from 1983). Level 9 Computing (L9).

The *Silicon Dreams* trilogy is a series of text-based **adventures** dealing with the colonization of other worlds. The first game, *Snowball* (*1983* L9) designed by Mike Austin, Nick Austin, and Pete Austin, is set aboard a **slower than light** colony starship (the "Snowball 9") approaching its destination in the solar system of 40 Eridani A. (The ship design strongly resembles the "Enzmann Starship" proposed by Dr Robert Enzmann in the 1960s, with Enzmann's single giant "snowball" of frozen deuterium fuel replaced by individual shells of ice surrounding a series of giant disks, which carry colonists in **suspended animation**.) As the game begins, an insane crew member has set the ship on a collision course with the system's sun. The player takes the part of Kim Kimberley, an undercover operative who is awakened from frozen sleep when the ship's computer detects a problem; they must evade the ship's automated defenses and reach the control room in time to save the colonists. *Snowball* is remarkable for the number of separate locations it contains, though many of them are essentially identical. Another interesting aspect is the protagonist's name, which was chosen to be gender ambiguous in order to enhance player identification with the character, though the sequels suggest that Kimberley is actually a woman.

In the first sequel, *Return to Eden* (1984 L9) designed by Nick Austin and Chris Queen, the awakened colonists accuse Kimberley of being the insane hijacker from the first game. After escaping, the player lands on the colony planet, Eden, where self-replicating robots dispatched ahead of the main expedition have built the city of Enoch in preparation for the humans' arrival. Shortly after the start of the game, the Snowball 9 fires on Kimberley's landing craft, causing the robots to classify the colony ship as a hostile alien vessel. The player must reach the city, evading the dangerous native plant life, and convince the machines not to destroy the ship, thus incidentally clearing Kimberley's name. (Harry Harrison's novel *Deathworld* [1960] was apparently an influence on the design of Eden, suggesting the relentless hostility shown by its wildlife toward offworlders.) The third entry in the series, *The Worm in Paradise* (1986 L9) designed by Mike Austin, Nick Austin, and Pete Austin, is set in Enoch a 100 years after the events of *Return to Eden*. Play begins inside a symbolic **virtual reality** simulation of a beautiful garden; the player must follow a worm that escapes from an apple until they reach an exit to the real world. That world is somewhat darker than the settings of the first two games; Enoch has become an alienated metropolis dominated by robots, resembling a less violent version of the Mega City One often featured in contemporary comic strips in the sf anthology magazine *2000 AD*. Interestingly, victory in the game is achieved not by overthrowing the system, which keeps citizens in line with the threat of nonexistent aliens, but by joining it, and getting a piece of the action.

The original versions of both *Return to Eden* and *The Worm in Paradise* include graphics as well as text in the manner of an illustrated novel rather than that of graphical adventures such as the *Space Quest* series. The entire trilogy was rereleased as *Silicon Dreams* (*1986* L9), which added illustrations to *Snowball* and additional text to all three games. The first two entries in the series are essentially collections of puzzles made more interesting by their detailed **hard sf** settings, but *The Worm in Paradise* aims significantly higher artistically. Its satire on 1980s UK politics is somewhat confused, however, and it is unusually hard to complete; the fact that the design of the city's transport system changes every time the game is loaded adds significantly to the difficulty. In the end, the simpler *Snowball* is the better game.

Related works: Some copies of *The Worm in Paradise* were sold with an included novella by Peter McBride, *Eden Song* (**1987**). The satirical text adventure *Knight Orc* (*1987*), designed by Pete Austin and developed by Level 9, is set entirely in a **virtual reality** game that exists in the world of *The Worm in Paradise*, and serves as a parody of early **multi-user dungeons**.

SNATCHER

1988. Konami. Designed by Hideo Kojima.

Snatcher is a menu-driven graphical **adventure** with some **real-time** combat sequences, of which only the 1994 MegaCD version has been released in English. Designed in Japan, the game draws heavily on the style of Ridley Scott's film *Blade Runner* (*1982*) and 1980s sf **anime** such as *Bubblegum Crisis* (*1987–1991*). Its setting is the twenty-first century, 50 years after the accidental release of an experimental bioweapon wiped out half of the world's population, including most Europeans. The player's character is an amnesiac, drifting through life in Japan after being rescued from **cryogenic** suspension in one of the areas devastated by the disease. Confused about his identity, he has separated from his wife and decided to join a special police unit that is responsible for tracking down and destroying the titular Snatchers, biomechanical **androids** of unknown origin that kill and replace human beings. Many classic themes of Japanese **cyberpunk** are present, including artificial humans who are unaware of their own nature and a noir vision of the future city. The player can eventually uncover the secrets of their character's past, along with a madman who wishes to improve humanity by replacing first its leaders and then the rest of the population with a superior form of android.

The most important aspect of *Snatcher* is its story, which impressively translates the typical concerns of contemporary sf anime to an interactive form. Most scenes are displayed as still images in a style derived from **manga** art, while the essentially **linear** plot evokes greed, jealousy, love, and humor in its (not especially sophisticated) narrative. While the choices available to the player at any point are quite limited, the careful selection of options and use of a genre within which the player's preferred actions are readily predictable give the actual experience of play a surprisingly unrestricted feel. A similar, though perhaps less subtle, approach to interactive storytelling can be seen in many later Japanese **console role playing games**, including both *Xenogears* (*1998* Square) designed by Tetsuya Takahashi and its successor series, *Xenosaga* (*2002–2006* Monolith Soft) designed by Tetsuya Takahashi.

Related works: *Super Deform Snatcher* (*1990* Konami) designed by Hideo Kojima is a remake of the original as a **CRPG**, using the "super deformed" visual style, in which characters have small plump bodies and exceptionally large heads. It was only released in Japan.

SPACE QUEST

Series (from 1986). SOL.

Space Quest is a series of **linearly** plotted graphical **adventures** in which the player adopts the role of Roger Wilco, a janitor in a **space opera** universe who strongly resembles the protagonist of Steve Meretzky's text-based *Planetfall* (*1983* Infocom). The games' parodic style of humor and comic puzzles are alternately amusing and juvenile, similar in tone to a less frenetic version of Mel Brooks' 1987 film *Spaceballs*. As in such later works as the animated TV series *Futurama* (*1999–2003, 2008*–current), there are frequent references to popular sf films and television shows. The first entry in the series to appear was *Space Quest: The Sarien Encounter* (*1986* SOL; *1991* revised as *Space Quest I: Roger Wilco in the Sarien Encounter*) designed by Mark Crowe and Scott Murphy, in which the then unnamed protagonist begins the game asleep in a broom closet, on a research ship containing an experimental device capable of destroying suns. The player's character then wakes up to find their ship has been taken over by hostile aliens who plan to use the device against the character's homeworld; the player must survive, escape, and defeat the enemy. Comic deaths while failing to solve the (sometimes frustrating) puzzles are frequent. The first version of the game uses text-based input with a graphical display; a later revision was altered to use a point and click interface.

The original game was followed by *Space Quest II: Vohaul's Revenge* (*1987* SOL) designed by Mark Crowe and Scott Murphy, which also combines text-based input with graphical output. Play begins with the player abducted by Sludge Vohaul, whose plans they foiled in *Space Quest I*; players must escape from Vohaul and frustrate his plan to launch millions of cloned insurance salesmen at their home planet. The game ends with the protagonist floating in space in an escape pod. At the beginning of the next installment, *Space Quest III: The Pirates of Pestulon* (*1989* SOL) designed by Mark Crowe and Scott Murphy, the game's central character—now definitely identified as Roger Wilco—is picked up by an automated garbage freighter. After escaping from this accidental prison, the player discovers that "ScumSoft" have kidnapped the designers of their favorite videogame and is forcing them to design the worst products imaginable. The designers are of course Crowe and Murphy, and the titular pirates are actually software pirates, the owners of ScumSoft, which itself is a reference to Microsoft. A rescue can be achieved by following a plot that involves fighting a giant robot version of Bill Gates. *Space Quest III* is remembered as a notable improvement on its predecessors, with enhanced graphics, better puzzles, and a partially point and click interface.

From this point on, all of the *Space Quest* games were released with a fully graphical interface in which all input was done with a mouse. The first of these works, *Space Quest IV: Roger Wilco and the Time Rippers* (*1991* SOL) designed by Mark Crowe and Scott Murphy, is perhaps the most accomplished of the series. It is also the game in which the strand of metafictional humor first seen in *Space Quest III* is most prominent. Sludge Vohaul appears from the never to be made *Space Quest XII: Vohaul's Revenge II* and pursues Roger through time, as represented by a return to *Space Quest I* and an excursion into the also nonexistent *Space Quest X: Latex Babes of Estros*. In the *Space Quest I* sequences, tough bikers mock the player for the graphics used to display their character, which are considered pretentious compared to the simpler colors employed in the original. The next installment was *Space Quest V: The Next Mutation* (*1993* Dynamix) designed by Mark Crowe. This game, to which only one of the two original designers contributed, has a rather gentler tone than its predecessors. Wilco is presented as less of a hapless loser who constantly saves the universe by accident and more of a hero, while the parody is focused almost entirely on *Star Trek*. The player becomes captain of their own spaceship, and must prevent the spread of a virulent disease while completing various side missions. Finally, the sixth game ended the series with what is often thought to be a regrettable decline in quality. *Space Quest 6: Roger Wilco in The Spinal Frontier* (1995 SOL) designed by Josh Mandel and Scott Murphy begins with Wilco broken back to janitor after his successes in *Space Quest V*, but the subsequent story line lacks direction, and many puzzles are unnecessarily difficult due to poor implementation. The plot involves an attempt to steal Roger's body; in the end, the miniaturized player must enter the body of their character's love interest.

Related works: *The Adventures of Roger Wilco* (1992) is a three-issue comic based on the first game, published by Adventure Comics. *Space Quest 0: Replicated* (2003) designed by Jeff Stewart is a prequel to *Space Quest I*, while the much inferior *Space Quest: The Lost Chapter* (2001) is set between *Space Quest II* and *Space Quest III*. Both of these games are amateur tributes to the original series.

Web Links

- SpaceQuest.Net Tribute Site: http://www.spacequest.net/

- *Space Quest 0: Replicated* download: http://www.wiw.org/~jess/replicated.html

- *Space Quest: The Lost Chapter* download: http://frostbytei.com/space/

STARCROSS

1982. Infocom. Designed by Dave Lebling.

Starcross was one of the first text-based **adventure** games to use an sf theme. The game's story is **hard sf**, reminiscent of both Arthur C. Clarke's novel *Rendezvous with Rama* (**1973**) and John Varley's short story "The Black Hole Passes" (June 1975 *Fantasy and Science Fiction*); the player adopts the role of a quantum **black hole** miner who discovers a huge and apparently abandoned alien vessel in deep space. On entering this mysterious spacecraft, the player must travel through a range of internal environments and solve a variety of difficult puzzles before they can pilot it back to Earth, thus winning the game. *Starcross* is perhaps the least interesting of Infocom's sf adventures, being essentially a collection of intellectual problems without much in the way of characterization or atmosphere. It is, however, enlivened by moments of wry humor, particularly when the player issues an instruction that the software considers foolish.

STARSHIP TITANIC

1998. The Digital Village. Designed by Douglas Adams, Adam Shaikh, and Emma Westecott.

Starship Titanic is a graphical **adventure** that uses a first-person view similar to that of *Obsidian* (*1996* Rocket Science Games) designed by Howard Cushnir, Scott Kim, and Adam Wolff or *The Journeyman Project* (*1993* PS) designed by David Flanagan. As in those games, the player must move from one predefined node in space to another, and their ability to interact with the physical environment is strictly limited. *Starship Titanic*, however, also draws heavily on the tradition of text adventure design exemplified by such works as *Planetfall* (*1982* Infocom) designed by Steve Meretzky and Adams' own *The Hitchhiker's Guide to the Galaxy* (*1984* Infocom), based on his well-known novel and radio series of the same name, both in its tone of sometimes painful obscurity and in its use of a text parser to enable typed conversation between the player and computer-controlled characters.

The game begins with a markedly metafictional moment; the player finds themselves in their suburban home, where they must locate a copy of *Starship Titanic* and load it into their computer. As soon as this has been done, the eponymous spacecraft crashes into their house, and the player is shanghaied by the ship's robotic crew to perform emergency repairs on their sabotaged artificial intelligences. Such flourishes bring to mind Adams' written work, and the game contains many isolated sequences that are as amusing as anything in his novels. The plot, however, is remarkably predictable, many of the puzzles seem arbitrary, and technical limitations mean that the frequent conversations are often frustrating. While *Starship Titanic* has many excellent parts—including impressive art deco visuals and numerous moments of genuine hilarity—the whole is, perhaps, less than their sum.

Related works: A spin-off novel—*Douglas Adams' Starship Titanic* (**1997**), by Terry Jones—was published based on the game, with a rather more developed plot.

Web Link
- Douglas Adams' Starship Titanic: http://www.starshiptitanic.com/

STAR TREK: 25TH ANNIVERSARY

1992. Interplay. Designed by Bruce Schlickbernd, Jayesh Patel, Elizabeth Danforth, Michael Stackpole, and Scott Bennie.

Many early *Star Trek*-based **videogames**, such as the poorly implemented text **adventure** *The Kobayashi Alternative* (*1985* Micromosaics) designed by the sf writer Diane Duane, were something of a disappointment. Others were legally questionable; thus, *The Warp Factor* (*1981* Strategic Simulations Inc) designed by Bruce Clayton and Paul Murray was a competent conversion of the tabletop **wargame** *Star Fleet Battles* (*1979* Task Force Games) designed by Stephen Cole to a computerized form, but lacked a license from either the owners of the TV show or the developers of the wargame. *Star Trek: 25th Anniversary* was perhaps the first videogame derived from the television series to be both fully legitimate and generally respected for its gameplay.

The game is a combination of **real-time** starship combat simulator and graphical **adventure**, presented as a "fourth season" of the original television series (*1966–1969*). As with the spin-off-animated TV series (*1973–1974*), the majority of the voice acting included in the CD-ROM version was done by members of the original cast. Players can control the starship *Enterprise* from its bridge or participate directly in "away missions," in which they travel to other locations such as planetary surfaces. Seven separate "episodes" are included, each of which is structured as a partially **multilinear** story. One of these segments features the iconic rogue Harry Mudd (who appeared several times in the original series), while another involves imminent war with the Klingon Empire, which the player must avert. Overall, the game is remarkably effective at evoking the tone of the 1960s TV series, for good or ill. Two of its designers (Stackpole and Danforth) had worked in tabletop **role playing game** design before devoting themselves to the show's *25th Anniversary*, a grounding that may have contributed to the sophistication with which it deploys its borrowed setting.

Related works: The sequel is *Star Trek: Judgment Rites* (*1993* Interplay) designed by Bruce Schlickbernd, Jayesh Patel, Scott Bennie, Mark O'Green, Michael Stackpole, and Elizabeth Danforth, which features another eight episodes in a game with a very similar structure to that of its predecessor.

SUSPENDED: A CRYOGENIC NIGHTMARE

1983. Infocom. Designed by Michael Berlyn.

The player's character in this text **adventure** is a native of an extrasolar colony who has been selected by lottery to spend 500 years in **suspended animation** in an underground complex. While the character is frozen, their subconscious mind is used to keep the colony's vital systems functioning. Play begins with the protagonist's abrupt awakening, to be informed that an earthquake has severely damaged their equipment. As the game progresses, further disasters follow. If the player has not repaired the complex's systems within a short period of time, the colonists, operating on the assumption that their frozen slave has gone insane and is damaging the equipment deliberately, will end the game by forcibly disconnecting the protagonist. The most striking aspect of the design is its requirement that players cannot leave their **cryogenic** vault. Instead, they must attempt repairs through six robot intermediaries, each of which has a different form of limited sensory apparatus, specific abilities, and a distinctive mode of speech. For example, "Poet" can sense electrical currents and has a hipster's approach to verbal descriptions, while "Waldo" can perform delicate physical manipulations but is only capable of perceiving the world through a crude form of sonar. The gameplay revolves around synthesizing the reports of the various robots to arrive at some understanding of the actual situation before using their combined talents to repair the complex, under strict time limits. *Suspended* is difficult but intriguing; it perhaps shares more with later **real-time** simulation games than with other text adventures.

TEX MURPHY

Series (from 1989). Access Software (AS). Designed by Aaron Conners, Brent Erickson, and Christopher Jones.

Tex Murphy is a series of graphical **adventure** games featuring the eponymous twenty-first-century private detective. The setting is a post–World War Three San Francisco, where the skies glow red with radiation and many of the inhabitants are down and out mutants. Tex, the player's character, is one of the few unmutated "norms" living in the bad part of town, a kind man, but one whose kindness is informed by a certain world weary cynicism. The tone is much influenced by Raymond Chandler's hard-boiled detective fiction, though *Tex Murphy* is more knowing and less serious; the games include frequent pop culture references, and are often gently self-mocking.

Mean Streets (1989 AS) designed by Brent Erickson, Brian Ferguson, and Christopher Jones was the first game in the series. Tex is hired by

Sylvia Linsky, a beautiful, mysterious woman, to investigate the suspicious death of her father; the player can eventually discover that he was working on a form of mind control, and shut down the project, which is conducting the research. The gameplay is a mixture of action game (including **2D** combat and sequences set in Tex's flying car) and puzzle solution; the puzzles depend largely on the player's ability to combine fragments of information obtained by questioning, bribing, and threatening a variety of characters. While of largely historical value today, *Mean Streets* remains of interest for its unusual fusion of what later became largely separate game forms. The next installment, *Martian Memorandum* (*1991* AS) designed by Brent Erickson and Christopher Jones, is a more conventional graphical **adventure** using a (somewhat clumsy) point and click interface, set 6 years later. Play begins with a powerful businessman, who has become extremely wealthy as a result of his investments in Martian **terraforming**, summoning Tex to his office to inform him that the tycoon's daughter is missing—and so is "something else." Half set on Mars and half on Earth, the game combines puzzles based around logical problems with the conversation-based form of deductive reasoning used in *Mean Streets*.

The first two *Tex Murphy* games were notable for their attempts to include realistic video and audio portrayals of their characters. With *Under a Killing Moon* (*1994* AS) designed by Aaron Conners and Christopher Jones, technology had improved to the point where **full motion video** of human actors could be used. While promoted as an "interactive movie," *Under a Killing Moon* actually alternates between noninteractive filmed scenes, which establish the characters and plot and **real-time** sequences in which the player moves through a **3D** world using a first-person view. The gameplay concentrates on puzzle solution within these interactive first-person sequences; this approach was adopted by all of the *Tex Murphy* games from this point on. At the beginning of *Under a Killing Moon*, Tex has married and divorced Sylvia Linsky, and has reached his personal nadir. The player is hired to track down a missing statuette, but rapidly becomes entangled with the activities of the Crusade for Genetic Purity, a vicious antimutant cult.

The fourth game, *The Pandora Directive* (*1996* AS) designed by Aaron Conners and Christopher Jones, is often considered the high point of the series, featuring romance, aliens, and an intriguingly complex plot. Events begin with Tex hired to find a missing man, and end with him involved with the ancient Mayans and a conspiracy to hide the truth about the supposed 1947 UFO crash at Roswell. One interesting aspect of *The Pandora Directive* is that it can be played using three different versions of Tex's personality, from slightly tarnished knight in shining armor to selfish cynic; the choices made affect the events depicted in the full motion video segments. Meanwhile, *Tex Murphy: Overseer* (*1998* AS) designed by Aaron Conners and Christopher Jones is a remake of *Mean Streets* as a graphical adventure with the same basic structure as *Under a Killing Moon*. The main story is wrapped in a framing sequence that ends on a cliffhanger, with Tex and his girlfriend shot by unidentified assailants.

The *Tex Murphy* games are effective detective stories, with gameplay focusing on investigation of scenes and questioning of suspects. Their strongly **linear** stories are often reminiscent of quality B-movies; the sometimes shaky dialogue, questionable special effects, and dubious science are overshadowed by a certain retro charm. As a whole, the series is consistently amusing and on occasion genuinely moving.

Related works: When it became apparent that a sixth game was unlikely to appear, Christopher Jones and Aaron Conners produced six episodes of the "Tex Murphy Radio Theater" audio drama with the original cast to resolve the ending of *Overseer*; these are available for free download from the "Unofficial Tex Murphy" website. *Under a Killing Moon* (**1996**) and *The Pandora Directive* (**1995**) are novelizations of the third and fourth games, respectively, both by Aaron Conners.

Web Link

- The Unofficial Tex Murphy (Tribute Site): http://www. unofficialtexmurphy.com/

TIMEQUEST

1991. LE. Designed by Robert Bates.

TimeQuest is an illustrated text **adventure** in which the player, adopting the role of an operative in a future organization of **time police**, must undo the alterations to history made by a rogue agent before they become irreversible. The basic structure of the game is **modular**; many different points in space-time, each of which corresponds to a **jonbar point** that must be restored to its historical state, can be visited in any order. The tone is generally dry; *TimeQuest*'s designer was clearly more concerned with the presentation of intriguing intellectual puzzles than with the construction of a compelling narrative. Nevertheless, there are a number of amusing moments, and Bates was happy to alter various factual details to make the game more entertaining, despite a general emphasis on histori-cal authenticity. *TimeQuest* was by no means the first text adventure to deal with time travel, but it is perhaps the most accomplished such work, reveling in its convoluted temporal paradoxes.

TIME ZONE

1982. On-Line Systems. Designed by Roberta Williams.

Time Zone is an illustrated text **adventure** with a highly **linear** plot. The player begins the game in possession of a time machine, having been chosen by a mysterious figure to save the future Earth from an extraterrestrial enemy. They must travel to a wide variety of points in space and time, acquiring items that can be used to solve puzzles else-where (and elsewhen) until they can finish the final problem and win the game. Unfortunately, *Time Zone* is clumsily structured, unconvincing, and presented in questionable prose. Some of the available locations are unavoidably lethal or contain nothing of use, adding markedly to the complexity of the game. Aggravatingly, vital items that are anachronistic for a particular time period will disappear without warning and forever if transported there. Overall, the game is very difficult, partly as a result of its exceptional size; many actions must be performed in various locations in exactly the right sequence if all the puzzles are to be solved. *Time Zone* was well regarded at the time of its original release, but it is hard to see it now as anything other than greatly inferior to its designer's best work, notably the charming fairytale adventures of the *King's Quest* series.

TO THE MOON

2011. Freebird Games. Designed by Kan Gao.

To the Moon is a graphical **adventure** about **dream hacking** in which events are displayed from above in a forced **3D** perspective. Created in Canada as an **independent game** and set in the near future, its fiction depends on a technology that allows specialists to enter and manipulate the memories of their patients, lending an apparent reality to their unfulfilled dreams and ambitions. Since this procedure damages the mind, it is only used on the terminally ill; its practitioners grant the last wishes of the dying.

The player participates in the game through the actions of a pair of bick-ering doctors, but the focus of its highly **linear** narrative is their patient, an elderly man named John Wyles who is obsessed with going to the moon, but has no idea why. As the player progresses through Wyles' mind, they discover markers that signify his most important memories, and which—after some simple puzzles have been solved—allow access to earlier, and more important, recollections. Eventually, a secret is uncovered, which explicates the nature of the patient's ambition and opens a path to its fulfillment. Interestingly, the resolution conflates space flight with the repair of a romantic relationship; in the final draft of his memories, Wyles achieves both the love of his life and an escape from Earth in the same moment.

While the story of *To the Moon* is emotionally involving, with much witty (and often self-referential) banter, the game's visual presentation and much of its dialogue deliberately echo the conventions of Japanese **console role playing games**, which can be jarring. More fundamentally, this is a work in which there is much conversation, but few choices. The gameplay revolves around the solution of uncomplicated puzzles, and occasional short action sequences, after which the two protagonists proceed to uncover the details of Wyles' **embedded** backstory without much direction from the player. *To the Moon* is a game that is explored far more than it is one that is acted upon; significant decisions are rare, but the halls of the patient's memory palace can be roamed at will.

Web Link
- *To the Moon*: http://freebirdgames.com/to_the_moon/

TRINITY

1986. Infocom. Designed by Brian Moriarty.

Trinity is a text **adventure** that combines elements of magic realism, children's fantasy, and science fiction, notably time travel, with an overriding concern with nuclear weapons. The player begins the game as an American tourist in London, where reality seems subtly out of joint. A further breakdown in normality is announced by the appearance of an incoming Soviet nuclear missile, at which point time begins to slow down. With some difficulty, the player can escape ground zero through a mysterious door that leads to a whimsical world between worlds, where space and time are oddly distorted. This world contains other doors, each opening on the site of a historically significant nuclear detonation (including one in the game's future), all of which are frozen in time shortly before the explosion occurs.

Trinity is centrally concerned with the destruction of innocence by atomic weapons; it makes many allusions to British children's literature, notably to J M Barrie's *The Little White Bird* (the book that in **1901** introduced the character of Peter Pan), some in the form of quotations overlaid on the game text. Nuclear annihilation is presented as a possibly inevitable consequence of human nature and scientific progress. At the end of the game, the player can enter the door leading to the Trinity site in New Mexico where the first atomic bomb was triggered, with the intention of disabling the test device. In the event, however, it is only possible to prevent a far greater explosion than historically occurred, maintaining the reality of Hiroshima and Nagasaki. At this point, players are transported back to the beginning of the game; trapped in a causal loop, they are ultimately permitted only to observe history, not to change it.

Structurally, the game is remarkable for the degree to which its puzzles are integrated with its message. At one point, the player must kill a small animal as a means toward the end of reaching the Trinity site and attempting to change what happened there. This act intentionally puts the player in something of the same moral position as that of the scientists who built the Trinity bomb as a way of ensuring that Nazi Germany would not win the Second World War with atomic weapons. Such a successful fusion of the puzzle form with serious artistic intent has rarely been achieved in the history of text adventures.

Web Link

- Interview with Brian Moriarty: http://www.dadgum.com/halcyon/ BOOK/MORIARTY.HTM

WOODRUFF AND THE SCHNIBBLE OF AZIMUTH

1994. (Also known as *The Bizarre Adventures of Woodruff and the Schnibble* in the United States.) Coktel Vision (CV). Designed by Muriel Tramis, Stéphane Fournier, and Pierre Gilhodes.

Woodruff is a graphical **adventure** with the ambience of a satirical cartoon. Long after a devastating nuclear war, humanity has returned to the surface world from its underground refuges to find that a new intelligent species has appeared in its absence—the wise, peaceful, and remarkably stupid looking Boozooks ("Bouzouks" in the original French). Soon the humans have conquered the newcomers and built the City, a gigantic **arcology** in which the Boozooks are an oppressed underclass. Professor Azimuth, an eminent human scientist, decides that he must help free the slaves, and develops a plan to bring universal peace and love to the City with the assistance of the mysterious Schnibble. Immediately before the game begins, a human faction raids the Professor's laboratory, leaving his young Boozook ward Woodruff—the player character—wandering the streets alone and amnesiac except for the traumatic memory of seeing his teddy bear shot to pieces by human thugs.

The resulting game is something of a pacifist polemic, wrapped in a series of bizarre situations and baffling enigmas. Comic moments are frequent, and many of the characters are memorably vivid grotesques; prominent among them is a ludicrously persistent tax collector who stalks the protagonist relentlessly. The visual design is excellent, with many charmingly exaggerated depictions. Some of the puzzles, however, are so difficult as to be almost insoluble; finishing the game appears to require a thought process not so much lateral as 4D. In this, *Woodruff* is not unique; it shares both its quirky approach to narrative and the dreamlike illogicality of its puzzles with many other products of the CV studio. Especially notable is the largely incomprehensible *Bargon Attack* (*1992* CV) designed by Claude Marc and Serge Marc, in which Earth is threatened by an invasion of aliens from a **videogame** called, inevitably, *Bargon Attack*.

ZAK McKRACKEN AND THE ALIEN MINDBENDERS

1988. LG. Designed by David Fox.

Zak McKracken is a graphical **adventure** game with an interface similar to that of *Maniac Mansion* (*1987* LG), an earlier work created by the same company and designed by Ron Gilbert and Gary Winnick. The player alternates between the roles of the titular Zak (a reporter for an American supermarket tabloid, the *National Inquisitor*), Zak's love interest, and her friends, who have converted their van into a spaceship and gone to Mars. All of these characters follow a **linear** story line in which they must defeat some extremely poorly disguised alien invaders, who have taken over the phone company for nefarious purposes. Fortunately, a group of benevolent aliens have hidden the components of a defensive machine in exotic locations on Earth and Mars; guided by their dreams, the characters must solve the puzzles that guard the pieces and reassemble them into a working device. Amusingly, Zak's interior monologue on the bizarrely unfolding plot is phrased as possible headlines for the *Inquisitor*. *Zak McKracken* is a lighthearted romp through the paraphernalia of New Age culture, from golf-playing gurus to ancient astronauts, enlivened by much excellent dialogue.

Related works: *The New Adventures of Zak McKracken* (*2003* Lucasfan Games) is a sequel made by amateurs, under somewhat ambiguous legal circumstances.

Web Link

- The Zak McKracken Archive (Tribute Site): http://www.zak-site.com/

CHAPTER 7

Computer Role Playing Games

A COMPUTER ROLE PLAYING game is a type of **videogame** derived from pen and paper **role playing games**. (This section only deals with the single-player variant; the **massively multiplayer online role playing game**, a related form in which many individuals share the same virtual world, is instead considered in the section dealing with **online worlds**.) These games are characterized by detailed and extensive fictional settings and by the existence of characters wholly or partially controlled by the players who have markedly different abilities to their master. The characters thus serve not only as alternate personalities for the player but also as their physical incarnations within the game's world. Players' actions are mediated through the abilities of their characters, which could include such mundanities as a minor proficiency at lock picking or reality altering levels of **psionic** power. Battle systems in computer role playing games often resemble those found in tactical **computer wargames**, whether they are **turn-based** (meaning that the player's and the computer's characters make alternate moves) or **real-time** (indicating that events occur continuously). While a player's success at combat in a **first person shooter** depends primarily on their own physical skills, in a computer role playing game, it is generally determined by a combination of the character's abilities and the player's tactical intelligence and (in real-time versions) their ability to make decisions rapidly. Another important feature of the form is its openness; players typically expect to be able to move freely within the simulated environment and solve problems using a variety of different approaches. Gameplay normally revolves around exploration, interaction with computer-controlled characters, combat, and puzzle solution. These elements may be combined, as in a puzzle that can be solved by persuading mutually antagonistic characters to resolve their differences and work together.

Almost all computer role playing games borrow concepts from the pen and paper designs, especially from their archetype, the original **heroic fantasy** game of *Dungeons and Dragons* (*1974* Tactical Studies Rules [TSR]) designed by Gary Gygax and Dave Arneson. Some examples of the computer form are licensed from specific **RPG** (role playing game) systems such as *Traveller* (*1977* Game Designers' Workshop [GDW]) designed by Marc Miller or *d20* (*2000* Wizards of the Coast [WOTC]) designed by Jonathan Tweet, Monte Cook, and Skip Williams, and implement their rules in detail. Many others make use of such ideas as class, a particular role that a character must fulfill (such as spaceship pilot or **esper**), and level, the degree of proficiency that a character has attained with the abilities associated with their class. As players progress through a computer role playing game using these concepts, and their characters become more experienced in their professions (or roles), their levels—and hence their power within the game world—will grow. Profession is not the only customizable feature of these simulated personas; options allowing the player to specify characters' gender, species, and physical appearance are common. Another frequently used idea is that of attributes, numerical ratings for such characteristics as strength and dexterity that define the basic nature of a character and suggest what classes they might be best suited for. An individual who was exceptionally strong but moderately clumsy might make a good soldier but a poor pilot, for example. Many sf games, however, describe characters' abilities primarily in terms of their physical and mental skills rather than by class and level, an approach that was first used in *Traveller*.

Pen and paper RPGs are generally played by a group, one of whom will become the **gamemaster** while the rest adopt the role of one character each. Early computer role playing games often reproduced this model by giving their single player an entire group of characters, though their control was not always complete; in some games, characters could refuse to obey the player's orders or decide to leave the group altogether. Later examples often allow the player only one character initially, though they may be able to persuade computer-controlled individuals to join them during the course of the game. Another notable divergence between computer role playing games and their pen and paper equivalents has emerged in their treatment of narrative. Many recent "storytelling" RPGs include mechanics that allow the players to explicitly influence the shape of the ongoing narrative, rather than simply respond to decisions taken by the gamemaster. This is not possible in a single-player digital game, where all possible paths through the plot must be laid out in advance. Videogame developers have instead chosen to improve the sophistication and flexibility of their story lines by increasing the complexity of the predesigned plot to a degree, which would make a prewritten RPG scenario difficult for a human gamemaster to grasp. The differences between the computer-mediated and pen and paper forms can perhaps be summarized by saying that computer role playing games automate the manual calculations and rule interpretations required by tabletop role playing games, but are unable to provide the kind of intelligently guided narrative that can be crafted by a human gamemaster. Massively multiplayer online role playing games, on the other hand, often suffer from a lack of meaningful story, since their worlds must remain essentially unchanged by the players' actions. These games, however, provide a shared social experience in a similar way to pen and paper RPGs, a feature that single-player computer role playing games cannot offer.

Early computer role playing games typically employed a **2D** plan view, with a **3D** display seen from the characters' perspective sometimes being used for exploration. Later works often adopted **isometric** 3D visuals or used the characters' viewpoint throughout the entire game; current ones almost always use true 3D graphics, with either a first-person perspective (seen from the characters' point of view) or a third-person one (in which the player characters can be seen by the camera). Thematically, most computer role playing games have followed their pen and paper forebears by concentrating on epic fantasy inspired by the works of J. R. R. Tolkien; science fiction is the next most common theme, followed by alternative forms of fantasy derived from Chinese and Japanese folklore, urban gothic, and **steampunk**.

Interactive narrative has become increasingly important in computer role playing games over the last 20 years. To a degree, they have recapitulated the evolution seen in tabletop RPGs, from designs concentrating on simulation of physical events and tactical combat to ones that emphasize character interaction and story development. Computer role playing games often employ **multilinear** and **modular** forms of story construction, with many optional subplots, reflecting the form's concern with exploration and freedom of choice.

The first computer role playing game may have been *pedit5* (*1974*) designed by Rusty Rutherford, a simple graphical game in which the player wandered through a subterranean dungeon looting treasure and killing fantastic monsters, inspired by the first edition of *Dungeons and Dragons*. The game was created on PLATO (Programmed Logic for Automated Teaching Operations), a mainframe computer system made available in many contemporary US universities for the purpose of computer-assisted learning. Inevitably, PLATO, with its then state-of-the-art capabilities for graphical display and connecting multiple users to the same program, was used by many students to write games. Equally inevitably, the system's administrators disapproved of this activity, and deleted such programs whenever they were discovered, a fate soon suffered by *pedit5*, despite its creator's attempt to preserve it by giving it a misleading name. It was, however, soon succeeded by the similar *dnd* (*1975*) designed by Gary Whisenhunt, Ray Wood, and a host of other descendants of gradually increasing complexity. The most significant of these was perhaps *Rogue* (*1980*) designed by Michael Toy and Glenn Wichman, in which the dungeon is randomly generated every time a player enters it (as in the automatic "adventure generation" systems that allowed some contemporary tabletop role playing games to be played solo), ensuring an endless supply of new (if not particularly subtle) experiences.

The first such game available on personal computers appears to have been the American *Beneath Apple Manor* (*1978*) designed by Don Worth, a **sword and sorcery** work greatly resembling the later, more famous *Rogue*. Its closest contemporary may have been *Dungeon Campaign* (*1978* Synergistic Software [SS]) designed by Robert Clardy, a game very clearly based on the first edition *Dungeons and Dragons* rules, which was followed by *Wilderness Campaign* (*1979* SS) and *Odyssey: The Compleat Apventure* (*1980* SS), both designed by Robert Clardy. Several more examples were published in 1979 in the United States, including *Akalabeth: World of Doom* (*1979*) designed by Richard Garriott—named after a misspelling of a word invented by Tolkien, and notable chiefly for being the first entry in the *Ultima* fantasy series—and *Dunjonquest: Temple of Apshai* (*1979* Automated Simulations [AS]) designed by Jon Freeman and Jeffrey Johnson, perhaps the most interesting of the first generation of computer role playing games. *Temple of Apshai* represents a raid on the buried temple of the titular insect god, a similar plot to that of *dnd*, but the game's manual includes extensive descriptions of the areas a player might enter, which add texture to the experience. The first sf example was *Space* (*1979* Edu-Ware Services [ES]) designed by Steven Pederson and Sherwin Steffin, a game so closely based on *Traveller* that it was withdrawn from sale following a lawsuit by GDW for unauthorized use of their intellectual property. *Space* was quickly followed by the *Starquest* series (from *1980* AS), a science-fictional spin-off of *Dunjonquest* set in the universe of the computer wargame *Starfleet Orion* (*1978* AS) designed by Jon Freeman and Jim Connelley, and then by Edu-Ware's replacement for their abortive initial effort, *Empire I: World Builders* (*1981* ES) designed by David Mullich, the first in a trilogy of games that allowed participants to play a role in the early evolution of a galactic empire. Two other contemporary sf games, *Universe* (*1983* Omnitrend Software) designed by Thomas Carbone and William Leslie III and *Sundog: Frozen Legacy* (*1984* FTL Games) designed by Bruce Webster, could be regarded as precursors of the space exploration form of **space sim** as well as computer role playing games. Such early examples of the commercial form as *Akalabeth* and *Starquest* were often referred to at the time as "action adventures," "fantasy adventures," or "real-time adventures," as well as (or instead of) "role playing simulations," since they were often seen as a variant form of text **adventures**. Soon, however, it became clear that these works were in fact a different kind of game, one that was to eventually become far more popular than the classic adventure.

Meanwhile, a related but UK-dominated subform appeared and then rapidly disappeared: that of the computer **gamebook**. These works were based on volumes from printed gamebook series such as *Fighting Fantasy* (as in *Citadel of Chaos* [*1984* Puffin] designed by Darryl Mattocks and Simon Ball), *Choose Your Own Adventure* (e.g., in *The Cave of Time* [*1985* Bantam Software]), or *Lone Wolf* (the first of which was *Flight from the Dark* [*1984* Five Ways Software] designed by Joe Dever). Narrative decisions were made by selecting an explicit branch in the multilinear plot, as in the original gamebooks but quite differently to computer role playing games in general, while the results of combat were either determined automatically or (in the more successful *Lone Wolf* games) played out in real time. While this was an interesting approach to the problems of transferring pen and paper role playing to a computer, the school did not prove sufficiently commercially successful to survive the demise of its printed parent. Many other early UK videogames that were marketed as adventures, or graphic adventures, would probably now be categorized as computer role playing games, since their gameplay concentrated on real-time combat and exploration using simulated characters. None of these works became as well known as such US equivalents as *Ultima* or *Dunjonquest*, however, though the epic fantasy game *Wrath of Magra* (*1984* Carnell Software) designed by Roy Carnell and Stuart Galloway is an interesting example of what was achieved.

The mid-1980s is sometimes seen as the beginning of a "Golden Age" for the form. As with the "Golden Age of Science Fiction" (usually taken to refer to American magazine stories of the late 1930s and 1940s), this is perhaps better thought of as a first flowering than a glorious culmination. The games of the era often closely resembled the more conventional tabletop role playing games of the time, with long manuals describing the rules and an emphasis on turn-based tactical combat, generally displayed using an isometric view. Nevertheless, the Golden Age saw the first real appearance of story and characterization within the form as well as an increasing emphasis on originality of world creation. Among the significant early works are the sword and sorcery *The Bard's Tale* (*1985* Interplay) designed by Michael Cranford, a game distinguished largely by the charming roguery of its eponymous central character, and *Ultima IV: Quest of the Avatar* (*1985* Origin Systems [OS]) designed by Richard Garriott, notable for its explicit confrontation of ethical issues within the fantasy land of Britannia. The player's main character must become an embodiment of eight cardinal virtues, as demonstrated by their actions in the game. Significant sf games from the same period include *Autoduel* (*1985* OS) designed by Richard Garriott and *Starflight* (*1986* Binary Systems [BS]).

Perhaps the most significant Golden Age game, however, was *Pool of Radiance* (*1988* Strategic Simulations Inc [SSI]), which licensed both the mechanics of the fantasy RPG *Advanced Dungeons and Dragons* (*1977–1979* TSR) designed by Gary Gygax and its pseudo-medieval **Forgotten Realms** setting. This game was not especially innovative, but its design combined most of the best elements of previous efforts, and its fiction benefited greatly from its richly detailed (if somewhat generic) milieu, developed for the pen and paper version. After it proved to be extremely popular, a number of other games were derived from its design, including the **retro-pulp** sf series beginning with *Buck Rogers: Countdown to Doomsday* (*1990* SSI) designed by Graeme Bayless and Bret Berry. Meanwhile, the *Ultima* series produced both *Ultima VII: The Black Gate* (*1992* OS; *1994* revised as *Ultima: The Black Gate*) designed by Richard Garriott, an epic fantasy noted for its impressive scope, detailed characterization, and openness to exploration, and the science-fictional spin-off series *Worlds of Ultima* (from *1990* OS). Many of the best sf games of the era were derived from existing RPGs and **wargames**, including *BattleTech: The Crescent Hawk's Inception* (*1988* Westwood Associates [WA]), the **hard sf space opera** games *The Zhodani Conspiracy* (*1990* Paragon Software [PS]) and *Quest For The Ancients* (*1991* PS), based on *MegaTraveller*, and the impressively colorful and wide ranging steampunk work *Space: 1889* (*1990* PS). Other notable games are the postapocalyptic *Wasteland* (*1988* Interplay) designed by Alan Pavlish, Michael Stackpole, and Ken St Andre, *Darklands* (*1992* MicroProse) designed by Arnold Hendrick, set in a fantastic fifteenth-century Germany in which all the medieval beliefs about religion and the supernatural are made real, and *Betrayal At Krondor* (*1993* Dynamix) designed by John Cutter and Neal Hallford, part of Raymond E. Feist's **heroic fantasy Riftwar Saga** series, and cowritten by the author. Innovative designs included *Circuit's Edge* (*1990* WA) designed by George Alec Effinger, Michael Legg, and Michael Moore, which combines computer role playing game structures with elements taken from the adventure form to present a story that forms part of Effinger's series of novels set in the **Budayeen**; it too was largely scripted by the original author. Similarly, *Neuromancer* (*1988* Interplay) designed by Bruce Balfour, Brian Fargo, Troy Miles, and Michael Stackpole also uses elements drawn from adventures as well as role playing, but suffers from its unsuccessful attempt to fuse the plot of William Gibson's eponymous novel with moments of lighthearted comedy.

A separate line of development was popularized by the sword and sorcery *Dungeon Master* (*1987* FTL Games) designed by Doug Bell, which featured real-time combat in a 3D display seen from the characters' point of view, though the player's freedom of movement was limited by technical restrictions. This tradition led to several notable games, including the *Advanced Dungeons and Dragons* license *Eye of the Beholder* (*1990* WA), set in the **Forgotten Realms** milieu, *Ultima Underworld: The Stygian Abyss* (*1992* Blue Sky Productions) designed by Paul Neurath—a spin-off from the *Ultima* fantasy sequence—and the science-fictional series beginning with *System Shock* (from *1994* Looking Glass Studios), which combines role playing and first-person shooter elements. Later examples do not suffer from the technical limitations of *Dungeon Master*, and this approach has become increasingly common in modern games.

Meanwhile, a largely distinct form of digital role playing game was evolving in Japan. One early example is *The Black Onyx* (*1984* Bullet-Proof Software) designed by Henk Rogers, a relatively simple game closely based on contemporary Western fantasy **CRPGs** (computer role playing games). However, it is unclear how much influence this work had on the later development of the form in Japan. Meanwhile, in 1983, the Japanese designer Horii Yuji had begun playing early *Ultima* games such as *Ultima II: Revenge of the Enchantress* (*1982* Sierra On-Line) designed by Richard Garriott and the more combat-oriented *Wizardry* series, which began with *Wizardry I: Proving Grounds of the Mad Overlord* (*1981* Sir-Tech Software) designed by Andrew Greenberg and Robert Woodhead, and was inspired to create something similar. The result was the heroic fantasy *Dragon Quest* (*1986* Enix; revised *1993*; revised *2000*; also known as *Dragon Warrior* in the United States), the prototype for role playing games intended to be played only on home consoles (as opposed to personal computers). These games— referred to in this book as **console role playing games**—have generally been created in Japan, while most computer role playing games (modern examples of which are typically available for both consoles and computers) have been developed in the United States and Canada. The console form has a number of other distinctive features. Most notably, console role playing games have significantly simpler mechanics than most of their computer-based equivalents—a feature designed to appeal to a mass audience—and generally employ strongly **linear** plots in which the player is assigned a pre-defined character, as opposed to the original variant's tendency (inspired by pen and paper RPGs) toward open narratives featuring characters designed by the player. The console approach has the advantage of making it easier to create strong personas and emotionally involving story lines, but the drawback that the narrative may not in fact be very interactive, leading some players to feel confined by the need to follow the script. One common issue with the gameplay in the Japanese tradition is an overreliance on "random encounters," repetitive battles with enemies who abruptly appear for no obvious reason; this is perhaps best seen as a form of padding intended to extend the game's playing time. The better examples, however, generally have fewer random encounters, or none.

Console role playing games often make use of themes and visual styles also seen in **anime**, as well as sharing that form's narrative tendencies toward cuteness and intense (sometimes melodramatic) emotion. As with computer role playing games, the most common subject is fantasy, though often influenced by Asian as well as European traditions. Another frequent theme is **science and sorcery**; console role playing games often combine technology with forms of magic derived from mysticism and the concept of a world formed from five or more basic elements, including such exotica as lightning or poison. Significant early examples that can be categorized as sf or science and sorcery include *Final Fantasy* (*1987* Square) designed by Hironobu Sakaguchi, *Phantasy Star* (*1987* Sega) designed by Rieko Kodama and Yuji Naka, and *Mother* (*1989* Nintendo) designed by Shigesato Itoi.

The Golden Age of Western computer role playing games is generally felt to have ended in the mid-1990s, after the release of a number of disappointing games. The late 1990s, however, saw the appearance of several works that combined the explorative gameplay of the Golden Age with a depth of story and characterization rarely seen in previous examples. Complex role playing systems were still present, but largely hidden from the player unless they wanted to investigate the mechanics in detail. The first of these games to appear were the postapocalyptic *Fallout* (*1997* Black Isle Studios [BIS]) designed by Tim Cain, Leonard Boyarsky, and Christopher Taylor and *Baldur's Gate* (*1998* BioWare) designed by Ray Muzyka and James Ohlen, an *Advanced Dungeons and Dragons* **Forgotten Realms** game that (together with its sequel, *Baldur's Gate II: Shadows of Amn* [*2000* BioWare] designed by Kevin Martens and James Ohlen and the expansion pack *Baldur's Gate II: Throne of Bhaal* [*2001* BioWare] designed by Kevin Martens) essentially allows the player to shape the story and final resolution of a skillfully told epic fantasy trilogy reminiscent of the works of such writers as Patricia A. McKillip or Barbara Hambly. These games were followed by the science-fictional *Deus Ex* (*2000* Ion Storm [IS]) designed by Warren Spector and Harvey Smith, which blends first-person shooter and role playing elements in its design, the steampunk and sorcery *Arcanum: Of Steamworks and Magick Obscura* (*2001* Troika Games [TG]) designed by Jason Anderson, Leonard Boyarsky, and Timothy Cain, set in a high fantasy world undergoing an industrial revolution, and the **Forgotten Realms** game *Neverwinter Nights* (*2002* BioWare), designed to allow players to run the equivalent of a traditional tabletop role playing game in a persistent online world in which one individual takes the role of the gamemaster and others adopt the personas of characters within the game. Perhaps the most impressive of all these works, however, is *Planescape: Torment* (*1999* BIS) designed by Chris Avellone and Colin McComb, an *Advanced Dungeons and Dragons* license set in the **Planescape** milieu, where many planes of existence cross in Sigil, the "City of Doors," which resembles a fantasticated Victorian London. *Torment* is a morbidly philosophical epic far more concerned with conversation than combat, featuring such characters as Fall-From-Grace, a retired succubus who has opened the Brothel For Slaking Intellectual Lusts, and Nordom, a poorly socialized ambulatory cube.

Another variant was made famous by the release of *Diablo* (*1997* Blizzard Entertainment) designed by David Brevik and Erich Schaefer, a sword and sorcery game resembling a much improved version of *Rogue*, with an immediacy inspired by *Dungeon Master*. This form, generally known as the "**action RPG**," emphasizes real-time combat, often seen from an overhead view, and simplified role playing mechanics; the narrative aspects are typically either minimized or constrained to fit a strictly linear story line within which the player undertakes specific missions. The commercial success of the excellently crafted *Diablo* led to a number of successors, including the epic fantasy *Dungeon Siege* (*2002* Gas Powered Games) designed by Chris Taylor and the science-fictional *Freedom Force* (*2002* Irrational Games [IG]) designed by Robb Waters and Ken Levine.

During the same period, Japanese console role playing games were becoming steadily more sophisticated. Later examples such as *Chrono Trigger* (*1995* Square) designed by Hironobu Sakaguchi and Yuuji Horii offer significantly more flexible story lines, generally by including a range of possible endings, and works such as *Xenogears* (*1998* Square) designed by Tetsuya Takahashi and *Chrono Cross* (*1999* Square) designed by Masato Kato and Hiromichi Tanaka are notably more adult in tone than their predecessors. Other games of this kind that deal with science fictional or science and sorcery subjects include the *Xenosaga* series, beginning with *Xenosaga: Episode I – Der Wille zur Macht* (*2002* Monolith Soft [MS]) designed by Tetsuya Takahashi, *Star Ocean* (*1996* tri-Ace), and later entries in the *Final Fantasy* sequence such as *Final Fantasy VII* (*1997* Square) designed by Hironobu Sakaguchi and Yoshinori Kitase. The console form remains highly popular worldwide, significantly more so than the computer one, though it is less involved with science fiction.

Recent computer role playing games have experimented considerably with the form as it was developed in the late 1990s, often with the aim of attracting the larger audiences required to justify the ever-increasing costs of videogame development. These works typically display the player character and any allies they may have recruited in a fully 3D environment, and frequently employ real-time gameplay that can be paused while instructions are issued to the characters (effectively allowing the player to choose between real-time and turn-based approaches). One example is the *Elder Scrolls* series, which concentrates on providing an extremely detailed simulation of its (somewhat generic) fantasy world, within which characters have a great deal of freedom of action, without any requirement that they follow the predesigned plot. The most successful iterations of the series are the most recent: *Morrowind* (*2002* Bethesda Game Studios [BG]) designed by Todd Howard and Ken Rolston, *Oblivion* (*2006* BG) designed by Todd Howard and Ken Rolston, and *Skyrim* (*2011* BG) designed by Todd Howard, Bruce Nesmith, and Kurt Kuhlmann. *Fallout 3* (*2008* BG) designed by Todd Howard and Emil Pagliarulo and *Fallout: New Vegas* (*2010* Obsidian Entertainment [OE]) designed by Josh Sawyer and John Gonzalez followed *Oblivion* by transposing the approach taken in the *Elder Scrolls* games to a science-fictional postholocaust landscape. *Vampire: The Masquerade – Bloodlines* (*2004* TG) designed by Jason Anderson and Leonard Boyarsky, by contrast, is an erotically charged gothic fantasy licensed from the **World of Darkness** RPG *Vampire: The Masquerade* (*1991* White Wolf) designed by Mark Rein-Hagen, Graeme Davis, Tom Dowd, Lisa Stevens, and Stewart Wieck, with a strongly multilinear story. The UK-developed *Fable* (*2004* Lionhead; *2005* revised as *Fable: The Lost Chapters*) designed by Dene Carter, Ben Huskins, Mark Webley, and Peter Molyneux resembles a fairy tale; its central conceit is that any action taken by the player as they progress through the broadly linear plot will affect their character's appearance, social status, and personal relationships. Though the actions required to cause such alterations can seem superficial, the end result is an interesting game of personal transformation. *The Witcher* (*2007* CD Projekt Red Studio) designed by Michal Madej and Artur Ganszyniec, based on an eponymous series of fantasy books by Andrzej Sapkowski and created in his native Poland, employs a profound sense of moral ambiguity in its brutally realistic depiction of a world where the monsters are by no means the most evil creatures to be found. Looking ahead, the developers of *The Witcher* are now working on *Cyberpunk 2077*, a **cyberpunk** game based on the tabletop RPG *Cyberpunk 2013* (*1988* R Talsorian Games; *1990* revised as *Cyberpunk 2020*; *2006* revised as *Cyberpunk V3.0*) designed by Michael Pondsmith.

Perhaps the most significant recent development, however, is the integration of elements drawn from console role playing game design into the computer role playing game form. *Anachronox* (*2001* IS) designed by Tom Hall and the earlier *Septerra Core: Legacy of the Creator* (*1999* Valkyrie Studios) designed by Brian Babendererde both represent attempts to transpose the console form directly to home computers, within an sf or sf-like setting. Commercial success, however, was reserved for

Star Wars: Knights of the Old Republic (*2003* BioWare), which combined the guided story line of the console games with much of the openness characteristic of the personal computer form. The developers, the Canadian company BioWare, later used a similar approach for the mystical martial arts game *Jade Empire* (*2005* BioWare; revised *2007*), set in an ancient China that never was, the space opera *Mass Effect* (*2007* BioWare) designed by Casey Hudson and Preston Watamaniuk, and the epic fantasy *Dragon Age: Origins* (*2009* BioWare) designed by Mark Darrah, Brent Knowles, Mike Laidlaw, and James Ohlen. In Japan, later works in the *Final Fantasy* series have similarly integrated aspects of the Western form into the console game tradition, while such stand-alone efforts as *Xenoblade Chronicles* (*2011* MS) designed by Tetsuya Takahashi and Koh Kojima have concentrated on reviving the emphasis on strong linear stories seen in *Xenogears* and *Xenosaga*. Regardless of such changes in design, it seems likely that both the computer and console role playing game forms will remain highly significant in the future development of **interactive narrative** in videogames.

FURTHER READING

- Neal Hallford with Jana Hallford. *Swords & Circuitry: A Designer's Guide to Computer Role-Playing Games.* 2001. (An excellent analysis of how computer role playing games are constructed, including excerpts from the design documents for *Fallout* and *Deus Ex*.)

- Matt Barton. *Dungeons and Desktops: The History of Computer Role-Playing Games.* 2008. (A remarkably comprehensive history of the computer form, with some coverage of console games.)

ALBION

1995. Blue Byte Software.

Albion is a **computer role playing game** that uses both **2D** overhead and **3D** first-person views, developed by the same German team that produced the noted fantasy **CRPG** *Amberstar* (*1992* Thalion Software). The game begins on board the Toronto, a factory starship sent to mine valuable resources from a newly discovered, and supposedly barren, world. However, the player's primary character, Tom Driscoll, soon discovers that the planet is inhabited when his shuttle crashes on its surface during a reconnaissance flight. The planet of Albion, it turns out, is populated with **telepathic** feline aliens and a group of humans seemingly descended from ancient Celts; both groups appear to have magical powers. Driscoll must explore this new world, accompanied by other characters who the player can recruit, and uncover the conspiracy that has led to the Toronto beginning mining operations on an inhabited planet.

Albion is notable for its detailed alien civilizations; the clash of cultures between Terrans and Albion natives is a recurring theme, as in the sf writer's Marion Zimmer Bradley's not dissimilar **Darkover** series. One unfortunate feature is the 3D rendering technique used to display interiors and underground areas, which some players find disorienting. Nevertheless, *Albion*'s credible (if sketchy) characterizations, richly imagined **science fantasy** setting, and open, **modular** story make it an interesting, atmospheric game.

Much of the player's time in *Albion* is devoted to uncovering the secrets of a mysterious alien civilization.

ALIEN LOGIC

1994. Ceridus Software. Designed by Andrew Leker, Jeff Moser, Kevin Stein, and Jonathan Stone.

The tabletop **role playing game** *SkyRealms of Jorune* (*1985* SkyRealms Publishing; revised *1986*; revised *1992*) designed by Andrew Leker, Miles Teves, and Amy Leker is a work of **science fantasy**, set on the eponymous planet in the distant future, long after it has been colonized by humanity. The tone is reminiscent of the **planetary romances** of the sf writer Jack Vance, and also of the various **RPGs** and **wargames** set on the world of **Tékumel** created by M. A. R. Barker. Jorune is home to many sentient races, including not only the native Shanthas and various sub-species of humanity, but also **uplifted** bears, wolves, tigers, cougars, and frogs and a variety of other aliens who colonized the planet in the distant past. Most notable, perhaps, are the highly intellectual but somewhat ineffectual Thriddle. Each of these groups has its own unique culture, evoked through the use of a curious vocabulary of invented terms. The setting's most striking feature, however, is perhaps "Isho," a form of life energy (resembling the "vril" introduced by the First Baron Lytton in *The Coming Race* [**1871**]) that emanates from deposits of a crystalline mineral buried deep within the world. The titular realms are islands that float above the planet's surface due to imbalances in the local Isho energy; the crystals' power can also be used by some species to create effects somewhat resembling those of **psionics**, but based on a complex system of color-coded abilities that is unique to the milieu. In the setting's present, humanity has emerged from a long Dark Age to rediscover the buried remnants of their ancestors' technology and use them to achieve considerable power, without truly understanding the principles involved. This has led to the creation of a highly complex multispecies civilization, dominated by elaborate codes of conduct and a powerful bureaucracy.

Alien Logic is an **action RPG** set on Jorune, with a design that often resembles that of such later action **adventures** as *Outcast* (*1999* Appeal). The player must rescue their fellow villagers, who have been kidnapped by a mysterious Shantha, following a partly **multilinear** and partly **modular** plot. Unusually, both **2D** overhead and side views are used, with **real-time** combat occurring in the latter mode. While some aspects of *Alien Logic's* gameplay may initially prove confusing, and the technical implementation of the work is sometimes unreliable, it is notable for its detailed and genuinely alien world and often quirkily humorous characters.

ANACHRONOX

2001. IS. Designed by Tom Hall.

Anachronox is a **computer role playing game** played in a third-person **3D** perspective, strongly influenced by such Japanese games as *Chrono Trigger* (*1995* Square) designed by Hironobu Sakaguchi and Yuuji Horii. The gameplay combines exploration, combat, puzzles, and conversation in a similar way to that of its models, including the use of a partially

turn-based combat system and the game's broadly **linear** plot. In the future of *Anachronox*, humanity has spread throughout the galaxy using a network of **faster than light** gateways created by a vanished alien **forerunner** civilization. Anachronox itself is an artificial world prone to curious geometric distortions, found floating inside the gigantic sphere that is the hub of the interstellar network and now inhabited by a variety of successor species. The player's primary character is one Sylvester "Sly" Boots, a perpetually down-on-his-luck private investigator trying to make a living in the worst part of Anachronox. Play starts slowly, with Boots desperate for money to pay off some ill-advised loans. Soon, however, Sly and his companions are sucked into an ever-expanding plot revolving around a hunt for pieces of "Mystech," a technology of transcendental power that appears to have originated in the future, and which can be used to create effects almost indistinguishable from magic. After the unexpected destruction of the planet they are visiting by matter that materializes from nowhere, the player learns that they have become involved in a **changewar** between forces from past and future universes. One of these realities is the cosmos whose gravitational collapse preceded the Big Bang in which the present universe was created; the other is the one that will be formed after that reality has similarly imploded. The faction originating in the oldest universe is attempting to transfer mass from their home reality to its current iteration, thus ensuring that their own cosmos will never collapse while preventing the birth of every future universe, including the one in which the game takes place.

Anachronox's tone is perhaps best described as **hard sf** noir, though the dominant sense of the narrative is often that of a lighthearted adventure, somewhat in the vein of a more adult *Indiana Jones and the Raiders of the Lost Ark* (1981). There are many comic moments, and some genuinely tragic scenes triggered by the reappearance of characters from Boots' tangled past. Sly himself is a likeable hero, noble and foolish in equal measure. The most impressive aspect of the game is perhaps its unceasing flow of invention; plot twists are frequent, including the appearance of a character that is in reality a miniaturized planet and a diversion in which Boots can earn much needed cash as an exotic dancer. Regrettably, the plot ends on a cliffhanger, in anticipation of a sequel that never came.

Related works: The game's cinematic director, Jake Hughes, led a group that edited **full motion video** from the game together with **machinima** material to make the award-winning *Anachronox: The Movie* (2002).

Web Link

- *Anachronox: The   Movie*:   http://archive.org/details/
JakeHughesAnachronoxTheMovie

AUTODUEL

1985. OS. Designed by Richard Garriott.

Car Wars (*1981* Steve Jackson Games [SJG]; *1985* revised as *Car Wars Deluxe*; revised *1989*; revised *1990*; revised *2002*) designed by Steve Jackson and Chad Irby is a board and counter **wargame** whose subject is "autodueling"—combat between armed and armored cars, motorcycles, and trucks. It is set in a fragmented future America, in which oil and food crises have caused the near collapse of civilization. The game's **future history** exemplifies many of the social and ecological fears of the 1970s; in this world, casual violence is common, and autodueling is both a recognized national sport and a vital survival skill outside the fortified cities. Autodueling was prefigured in many sf short stories, including Harlan Ellison's "Along the Scenic Route" (July 1969 in *The Beast That Shouted Love at the Heart of the World*; also known as "Dogfight on 101") and Roger Zelazny's "Devil Car" (June 1965 *Galaxy*), as well as in such films as *Death Race 2000* (*1975*) and *Mad Max* (*1979*). The game itself cites Alan Dean Foster's "Why Johnny Can't Speed" (September–October 1971 *Galaxy*) as an inspiration. *Car Wars* was very successful commercially; many players were attracted by the idea of acting out their road rage in a fantasy setting, especially as the game allows them to design their own vehicles and equip them with a carefully chosen selection of weapons.

Autoduel itself is a well crafted—if somewhat combat focused— **computer role playing game** set in the *Car Wars* milieu, which uses a **2D** plan view to depict its highly interactive world. Most of the player's time is spent configuring their customized vehicles, delivering various packages, and fighting enemies; there is little in the way of plot or characters to interact with. In many ways, the game is reminiscent of its UK-developed contemporary, the **space sim** *Elite* (*1984*) designed by David Braben and Ian Bell, though *Autoduel* offers a much more detailed simulation of the player's character, while being rather less open and explorable.

Related works: A large amount of *Car Wars* material was released throughout the 1980s and 1990s, including the introductory *Mini Car Wars* (*1987* SJG) designed by Steve Jackson and Jim Gould, and *Car Wars: The Card Game* (*1991* SJG; revised *2001*) designed by Creede and Sharleen Lambard.

GURPS Autoduel (*1986* SJG; revised *1996*) designed by Aaron Allston and Scott Haring is a supplement for the 1986 edition of SJG's *GURPS* tabletop **role playing game**, while *Autoduel Champions* (*1983* SJG) designed by Aaron Allston contains rules for combining *Car Wars* with the *Champions* (*1981* Hero Games) superhero **RPG** designed by George MacDonald and Steve Peterson.

Six well-regarded **gamebooks** set in the *Car Wars* universe were released by TSR: *Battle Road* (**1986**) by Steve Jackson, *Fuel's Gold* (**1986**) by Steve Jackson, *Dueltrack* (**1987**) by Scott Haring, *Badlands Run* (**1987**) by Creede Lambard and Sharleen Lambard, *Green Circle Blues* (**1987**) by Scott Haring, and *Mean Streets* (**1987**) by W. G. Armintrout. *Car Warriors* (*1991*) is a four-issue comics series associated with the game, written by Chuck Dixon. Three novels were also published under the *Car Warriors* name: *The Square Deal* (**1992**), by David A. Drake; *Double Jeopardy* (**1994**), by Aaron Allston; and *Back From Hell* (**1999**), by Mick Farren.

B.A.T.

1990. Computer's Dream (CD). Designed by Hervé Lange and Olivier Cordoléani.

B.A.T. is a **computer role playing game** with a strongly **multilinear** plot. The player adopts the role of an agent of the eponymous Bureau—a secret organization that enforces interstellar law by any means necessary—who has been ordered to prevent a terrorist atrocity on the colony world of Selenia. The game is set in the decadent metropolis that is Selenia's only city, a cosmopolitan interzone populated by a wide variety of exotic aliens and human drifters. As is common in **CRPGs**, many different actions are available in *B.A.T.*, including conversation, combat, exploration, and the use of objects purchased or discovered in the world. Additional options are provided courtesy of a computer implanted in the player character's arm, which allows B.A.T. agents to temporarily boost their abilities to superhuman levels, and special systems such as the "love meter," a gadget that monitors a character's romantic performance. The visuals are primarily static images that the player can interact with through menus, seen from the character's point of view, as if the fantasy **adventure** game *Myst* (*1993* Cyan Worlds) designed by Rand Miller and Robyn Miller had been created using prerendered artwork rather than **full motion video**. Some situations trigger the use of **real-time** displays, as in the rudimentary flight simulator, which allows the player to travel across the surface of Selenia. Nevertheless, as with *Myst*, playing *B.A.T.* can evoke a sense of confinement, as the limited degree of interactivity becomes apparent.

Developed in France, *B.A.T.* is artistically striking, with a lush visual style reminiscent of the *bandes dessinées* ["drawn strips"] created by such artists as Enki Bilal. The game also benefits from a lovingly detailed fictional universe. Not only does *B.A.T.* include a wide variety of bizarre nonhumans, curious weapons, and peculiar locations, but its manual contains a surprisingly long discussion of the physics of Einstein–Rosen bridges as a means of creating **wormholes** to the stars. As in Charles Stross' later novel *Singularity Sky* (**2003**), **faster than light** travel using this method means going back in time, presumably in order to avoid the problems with causality, which the theory of relativity otherwise predicts. Unfortunately, a lack of guidance for the player means that it is easy to get lost in the game's open world and fail to make progress in the plot. *B.A.T.* also suffers from a less than ideal English translation, exemplified by the rendering of "Bureau des Affaires Temporelles" ["Office of Temporal Affairs"]—the original acronym for the titular organization—as "Bureau of Astral Troubleshooters." Nevertheless, the rather obscure *B.A.T.* is an impressive piece of future noir, set in a stylish, violent underworld with a distinctly anti-capitalist tone. It deserves to be better known.

Related works: The sequel is *The Koshan Conspiracy* (*1992* CD) designed by Hervé Lange and Olivier Cordoléani. This game has a similar design to the first, but offers more animated visuals and a greater number of options for interaction. The narrative is also more structured; the player is initially given a series of missions to complete. Here, the threat faced by the Bureau is a plot by the eponymous corporation to gain complete control of supplies of an economically vital mineral. As with its predecessor, most of the events of *The Koshan Conspiracy* take place in a single large city. One sequence is set in space, however, with real-time gameplay resembling that of *Wing Commander* (*1990* OS) designed by Chris Roberts.

BORDERLANDS

2009. Gearbox Software (GS). Designed by Matthew Armstrong.

Borderlands is an **action RPG**, much influenced by **first person shooters** but in essence resembling a science-fictional variant of the hack and slash fantasy game *Diablo* (*1997* Blizzard Entertainment) designed by David Brevik and Erich Schaefer. Players wander the blasted deserts of the planet Pandora, performing missions for assorted patrons, battling (often randomly generated) enemies and looting their corpses for guns and money. Pandora appears to be populated almost entirely by trigger-happy mercenaries, crazed treasure hunters, and recently released convicts; it is also notable that every single member of the local wildlife seems to be a highly aggressive predator. While there are few really memorable characters—the sleazy merchants and dancing robots are among the most distinctive—it is remarkably easy to build up a truly impressive gun collection. The players (and most of the other characters) are supposedly searching for a legendary cache of **forerunner** artifacts, but this has little real influence on the general mayhem. Characters have a variety of skills that can be improved as the game progresses, ranging from the ability to turn invisible by shifting into an alternate dimension to the control of an alien battle bird. As is true of *Diablo* and many other games that take a primarily **environmental** approach to **interactive narrative**, players typically prefer to participate as part of a group of friends; *Borderlands* emphasizes online cooperative play by small teams. Visuals are presented in a cartoon like style, which is deliberately reminiscent of graphic novels, though the most obvious inspirations for *Borderlands'* gleefully over-the-top style may be such campy action movies as *The Ice Pirates* (*1984*), *Mad Max Beyond Thunderdome* (*1985*), and *Spacehunter: Adventures in the Forbidden Zone* (*1983*). In the end, perhaps all that needs to be said about *Borderlands* is that it is a game that has been enthusiastically honored with Internet awards for both "gratuitous violence" and "epic loot."

Related works: There are four expansion packs for *Borderlands*: *The Zombie Island of Dr. Ned* (*2009* GS), *Mad Moxxi's Underdome Riot* (*2009* GS), *The Secret Armory of General Knoxx* (*2010* GS), and *Claptrap's New Robot Revolution* (*2010* GS/Darkside Game Studios). Of these, *The Secret Armory* and *New Robot Revolution* continue the story line of the original game, while the first two packs are spin-offs that add new missions with special themes. *Borderlands Legends* (*2012* GS) is a derivative work with a design influenced by both action RPGs and **real-time tactics** games, played in an overhead view; reviews were mixed.

Borderlands 2 (*2012* GS) designed by Paul Hellquist is a sequel that makes minor improvements, but essentially has a very similar design to that of its predecessor. The **linear** primary plot, however, is far more strongly defined than that of the original game; a new group of characters with different abilities to those seen in *Borderlands* must participate in a rebellion against Pandora's megalomaniacally charming overlord.

Various optional missions are also available, attached to the core story line in a **modular** fashion and featuring a variety of computer-controlled characters whose personalities seem rather more vivid than those in the first game. This iteration of the series has four expansions, which add new narratives, of which the first two to be released were *Captain Scarlett and Her Pirate's Booty* (*2012* GS) and *Mr. Torgue's Campaign of Carnage* (*2012* GS), both of which revolve around the acquisition of hidden treasure. These were followed by the monster-hunting mayhem of *Sir Hammerlock's Big Game Hunt* (*2013* GS) and *Tiny Tina's Assault on Dragon Keep* (*2013* GS), an extended satire on combat-focused sessions of the tabletop **role playing game** *Dungeons and Dragons* (*1974* TSR) designed by Gary Gygax and Dave Arneson. The *Psycho Pack* (*2013* GS), *Ultimate Vault Hunter Upgrade Pack* (*2013* GS), and *Vault Hunter Upgrade Pack 2* (*2013* GS), meanwhile, add new character types and enemies to the basic gameplay.

Borderlands: Origins (*2012–2013*) is a comics series that serves as a prequel to the first game. Similarly, *Borderlands: The Fallen* (**2011**) focuses on the life of one of *Borderlands'* characters before the opening of the game, while *Borderlands: Unconquered* (**2012**) and *Borderlands: Gunsight* (**2013**) are sequels that involve most of the original game's characters. All three novels are by John Shirley.

Web Link
- *Borderlands*: http://www.borderlandsthegame.com/

BUCK ROGERS XXVC

Series (from 1990). SSI.

Buck Rogers was perhaps the first in the line of quintessentially American mass market **space opera** heroes that continued through **Flash Gordon**, E. E. Smith's Kimball Kinnison (the grey **Lensman**) and *Star Wars'* Han Solo, all of them tough men in tough universes. The original comics series—*Buck Rogers in the 25th Century*—was canceled in 1967, but rights to the character remained the property of the descendants of John Flint Dille, who devised the strip based on magazine stories written by Philip Francis Nowlan in the late 1920s. The president of the tabletop **role playing game** developer TSR during most of the 1980s and 1990s was Lorraine Williams, a granddaughter of Dille, who decided to relaunch the then dormant **Buck Rogers** intellectual property as an **RPG**. Flint Dille, Williams' brother, created the core background for a new iteration, and TSR developed a line of novels, a board game, and the *Buck Rogers XXVC* RPG (*1990* TSR) designed by Mike Cook, Michael Dobson, Jeff Grubb, Jim Ward, Warren Spector, and Jeff Butler, which used similar mechanics to the second edition of their fantasy game *Advanced Dungeons and Dragons* (*1989* TSR) designed by David Cook and Steve Winter, but added a much more detailed system for handling character skills resembling that used in the sf game *Traveller* (*1977* GDW) designed by Marc Miller.

The setting is **retro-pulp**, aiming to combine the tone and visual style of the original series with science-fictional ideas current in the 1980s, including genetic engineering and an oppressive social system dominated by corporate forces. In the twenty-fifth century, the solar system is controlled by coalitions of Earth's former national governments, of which the most important is the strongly capitalist Russo-American Mercantile, a group reminiscent of Jerry Pournelle's **CoDominium**. The planets, each of which has its own exotic culture, have been **terraformed** and colonized by artificially created human subspecies, including the partially feline Desert Runners of Mars and the human shark hybrids that inhabit the atmosphere of Jupiter. Meanwhile, a polluted, exhausted Earth is fighting for its independence, assisted by Buck, a twentieth-century astronaut woken from **cryogenic** hibernation. The milieu's amalgamation of rocket pistols with nuclear fusion and **uploaded** personalities with living spaceships makes for an unusual ambience, suggestive of a **parallel world**'s version of **pulp** sf; ultimately, however, it proved to be a commercially unsuccessful one. The overall effect remains oddly reminiscent of many of Nowlan's contemporaries, as if Edmond Hamilton's **Captain Future** had been transported into a **cyberpunk** reimagining of Larry Niven's **Known Space**.

Buck Rogers XXVC is remembered largely for the two **computer role playing games** that were created in the setting, using the same basic design as the highly popular *Advanced Dungeons and Dragons* license *Pool of Radiance* (*1988* SSI). The **videogames** take the form of Grand Tours of the solar system, with the characters traveling in stylized rocket ships between various planetary bases and asteroid outposts. Many actions are handled through abstract menu-driven systems, notably space travel and combat, while a variety of **3D**, overhead, and **isometric** views are used on the ground. Both games are strongly focused on **turn-based** combat, with largely **linear** plots that emphasize a deliberately over-the-top sense of cheap melodrama; the frequent battles are enlivened by occasional moments of vivid incident. In the first game, *Countdown to Doomsday* (*1990* SSI) designed by Graeme Bayless and Bret Berry, a freshly formed team of characters must save Earth from a gigantic lens that will devastate the newly liberated planet with focused solar energy. *Matrix Cubed* (*1992* SSI) designed by Rhonda Van is a direct sequel in which every faction in the politically fragmented solar system is fighting over the "Matrix Device," a McGuffin that converts matter from one form to another and could be used to reconstruct the still ravaged Earth.

Related works: *Buck Rogers – Battle for the 25th Century* (*1988* TSR) designed by Jeff Grubb is a relatively simple strategic board game (somewhat resembling *Risk* [*1957* Miro as *La Conquête du Monde*] designed by Albert Lamorisse), which was the first game to be released in the *Buck Rogers XXVC* milieu. A number of spin-off novels and anthologies were published for the setting, beginning with *Arrival* (**1989**) edited anonymously by Flint Dille, which collects stories revolving around Buck Rogers' resuscitation written by Dille, Robert Sheckley, and other authors. This was followed by the *Martian Wars* trilogy by M. S. Murdock, comprising *Rebellion 2456* (**1989**), *Hammer of Mars* (**1989**) and *Armageddon off Vesta* (**1989**), the *Inner Planets* trilogy, which contains John Miller's *First Power Play* (**1990**), Murdock's *Prime Squared* (**1990**) and Britton Bloom's *Matrix Cubed* (**1991**), and the *Invaders of Charon* trilogy, consisting of C. M. Brennan's *The Genesis Web* (**1992**), William H. Keith Jr's *Nomads of the Sky* (**1992**), and Keith and David Miller's *Warlords of Jupiter* (**1992**). A series of 10 comics (known as "comics modules" for contractual reasons) were published as *Buck Rogers* (*1990–1991*), written by Dille and Buzz Dixon.

CHRONO TRIGGER

1995. Square (SQ). Designed by Hironobu Sakaguchi and Yuuji Horii.

Chrono Trigger is a **console role playing game**, played in a **2D** overhead view. It remains one of the best-known Japanese **CRPGs**, strongly upbeat and not overly serious, full of endearing characters and clever puzzles; the tone is perhaps best characterized as "young adult." *Chrono Trigger* popularized several innovations in console role playing game design, notably the use of a **multilinear** plot with many possible endings, some only available if the game is played more than once, and the inclusion of many optional subplots that provide deeper insight into the characters involved. The gameplay focuses on exploration, puzzle solution, negotiation, and (fairly frequent) combat, though *Chrono Trigger* also broke new ground for Japanese CRPGs by eschewing the use of random encounters with monsters as a way of increasing the game's length.

The game is set in an **alternate world** where both **science and sorcery** exist, though primarily in different time periods. It begins in the Kingdom of Guardia in the year 1000, where the teenage boy Crono follows a mysterious girl through an experimental **matter transmitter** and finds himself in the past. Adopting the primary role of Crono, the player must rescue the Queen of Guardia in this earlier time in order to save the girl who, it emerges, is the Princess of Guardia in the year 1000, and will never be born if the Queen does not survive. Later, Crono and the other characters who the player has recruited into their group visit the far future, where they discover that in the year 1999 the world is destroyed by the mysterious "Lavos." A great deal of time travel ensues, notably including the death of Crono (and potentially his eventual resurrection using the "Chrono Trigger" device), visits to a prehistoric airborne Kingdom, and the establishment of a base at the End of Time. Players can experience many classic sf time travel devices, including individuals meeting in reverse order along their own personal timelines and a version of the grandfather paradox (which postulates that an individual has killed one of their own grandparents before their parents were conceived). The various endings are diversely charming; in one, manipulation of the past has resulted in all the characters becoming intelligent dinosaurs.

Chrono Cross (1999 SQ) designed by Masato Kato and Hiromichi Tanaka is a loose sequel, focusing on **parallel worlds** rather than time travel and using a combination of **3D** and 2D overhead views. The game begins with Serge, the main character, slipping into a parallel version of his reality, a world in which he died long ago. Players can discover that many things are duplicated across the two dimensions, some with curious variations. The two realities are closely linked; making changes in one may induce corresponding alterations in the other. Gameplay is similar to that of *Chrono Trigger*, but the tone is rather more adult and serious, with a strongly multilinear plot in which the player can choose to recruit many different characters into their group. Thematically, the game is concerned with the multiple paths that lives and universes can take; this aspect is reflected in the many characters available to enlist, and the varying personal interactions that exist for different combinations. *Chrono Cross'* complex story involves a research institute catapulted into the past after a failed experiment, a race of intelligent reptiles, a malignant computer, and magic; ultimately, it is revealed that Serge himself is of vital importance to the structure of the universe and that the two realities split as the result of an attempt to save his life using time travel. In the end, the sundered dimensions can be rejoined.

Related works: *Radical Dreamers* (*1996* SQ) designed by Masato Kato is a menu-driven text **adventure**, illustrated with static visuals, which was intended to tie up an unresolved subplot from *Chrono Trigger*. It includes different versions of many characters who would later appear in *Chrono Cross*, and has been retrospectively defined as occurring in a different alternate world. The game was only released in Japan, via episodic satellite download.

Web Link

- Chrono Compendium (Tribute Site): http://www.chronocompendium. com/

CIRCUIT'S EDGE

1990. WA. Designed by George Alec Effinger, Michael Legg, and Michael Moore.

Circuit's Edge was scripted by the science fiction writer George Alec Effinger, and is set in his **Budayeen** milieu—a twenty-first-century slum in a **cyberpunk** future dominated by Islam—with a story that takes place between those of Effinger's novel *When Gravity Fails* (**1987**) and its sequel *A Fire in the Sun* (**1989**). The player's character is the protagonist of the novels, the tough yet damaged Marid Audran, making the game an integral part of the **Budayeen** sequence; *Circuit's Edge* is a rare example of a broadly successful game closely based on written fiction. The fact that it was codesigned by the author of the novels is undoubtedly helpful here, as is its status as an original work in the series rather than an adaptation, which made it possible to construct a story better suited to the medium. The game is, however, only moderately convincing as a work in its own right; players who have not read the books may find aspects of its world hard to grasp. In design terms, *Circuit's Edge* combines elements drawn from **computer role playing games**, notably the movement and combat systems, with the puzzle-based gameplay of an **adventure**. The player, in the role of Audran, finds themselves involved in a murder mystery that they have limited time to solve, in a world that is represented through a combination of textual descriptions, static illustrations, and a **2D** overhead view.

The game effectively conveys the ambience of Effinger's setting, a carnival of drugs and sex and casual violence, populated by vulnerable tourists and transsexual prostitutes, where the use of a cybernetically implanted artificial personality is a common lifestyle choice. Curiously, however, players who respond to other characters' frequent offers of sex and drugs will find themselves punished by their employer—an underworld boss— for their lapses; this is apparently the result of a somewhat unhappy compromise between the milieu as described in the novels and the developers' reluctance to endorse dangerous habits in a mass market **videogame**. Other **computer role playing games** have generally chosen to ignore this issue, allowing players to do as they wish. A more serious problem is presented by the story line, which proceeds in **real time** rather than being structured around the player's actions, with critical events occurring only when their character has reached an appropriate point in the plot. This latter approach is the norm in videogame narratives, since it ensures that the player can act effectively within the ongoing story rather than drifting through a sea of poorly understood set pieces. The end result of the scheme adopted by *Circuit's Edge*, unfortunately, is that the gameplay can feel forced and awkward, despite the **modular** options available in the broadly **linear** plot. Nevertheless, Effinger's game remains notable as one of the few convincing attempts to create a **videogame** that is an integral part of a sequence of written narratives, as opposed to being set within a world devised by a novelist.

EMPIRE I: WORLD BUILDERS

1981. ES. Designed by David Mullich.

World Builders is the first of a trilogy of **computer role playing games** that followed the developers' earlier science-fictional **CRPG**, *Space* (*1979* ES) designed by Steven Pederson and Sherwin Steffin. The later works add a great deal of graphical animation to the entirely text-based design of *Space*, and replaces its menu-driven interface with a parser resembling those found in contemporary text **adventures**, allowing players to enter instructions using a limited form of natural English. Visuals are displayed from a variety of viewpoints, but are typically seen from the character's perspective, while combat is **turn based**. Players adopt one of three professions—miner, missionary, or homesteader—as they explore the galaxy and participate in the initial expansion of an interstellar empire ruled by humanity. At the time of its release, *World Builders* was an innovative game, combining the numerical personifications of players' characters used in CRPGs with the visual presentation of an unusually animated variant of the illustrated text adventure form.

From a modern perspective, however, the game's use of the parser for its interface seems clumsy, its **space operatic** fiction is thin, and the animations have not aged well. More fundamentally, perhaps, the game-play lacks any real sense of direction. While the attempt to provide a wider canvas for players' adventures than deadly catacombs and extraterrestrial battle scenes is interesting, the final work seems inferior to such combat-focused contemporaries as the science-fictional *Starquest* series (from *1980* AS) or the **sword and sorcery** game *Wizardry I: Proving Grounds of the Mad Overlord* (*1981* Sir-Tech Software) designed by Andrew Greenberg and Robert Woodhead. Truly successful science-fictional CRPGs with a wider narrative scope arguably did not begin to appear until the mid-1980s, with the release of such works as *Starflight* (*1986* BS).

Related works: The remaining two parts of the *Empire* trilogy were released as the similarly structured *Empire II: Interstellar Sharks* (*1982* ES) and *Empire III: Armageddon* (*1983* ES), both designed by Mullich and dealing, respectively, with the race for riches when the series' galactic empire has reached its zenith and with its eventual fall.

FALLOUT

1997. BIS. Designed by Tim Cain, Leonard Boyarsky, and Christopher Taylor.

Fallout is a **computer role playing game** that uses an **isometric 3D** perspective, set—as was its most important influence, *Wasteland* (*1998* Interplay) designed by Alan Pavlish, Michael Stackpole, and Ken St Andre—in the ruins of a postholocaust USA. The future of *Fallout* is not that of our own world; instead, it assumes that American history followed the template laid down in the 1950s for another 100 years, with generations living in fear of the atomic war that finally arrived in the mid-twenty-first century. The game's radioactive badlands are littered with the detritus of the 1950s dream, from computers running on vacuum tubes to Godzilla's footprint. Its visual design has a strong "retro futurist" style, drawing on cinematic influences ranging from *Forbidden Planet* (*1956*) to the **Flash Gordon** serials. *Fallout*'s tone is often satirical, and on occasion cheerfully brutal.

The game begins in an underground Vault, one of a series of refuges that were supposedly built to protect part of the population from the impending war. In reality, however, they were constructed as social experiments to help their creators design the ideal crew configuration for an interstellar spacecraft. Thus, one Vault is saturated with psychoactive drugs, while another was set up with an initial population of 999 women and 1 man.

The player character is a native of Vault 13, which was intended to remain sealed for two centuries after the war. However, the Vault's water purification chip has broken down, and the protagonist is chosen to find a new one before supplies run out. This mission leads the player into a world of two-headed cows and giant scorpions, where an army of mutants is trying to convert all of humanity into members of their Perfect Unity. The game ends with the player's character deemed to be irrevocably contaminated by the outside world, and exiled from the Vault they have saved.

Fallout was originally intended to use the tabletop **RPG** system *GURPS* (*1986* SJG) designed by Steve Jackson, but creative differences between BIS and SJG led to the use of a similar set of role playing mechanics created by the game designers. This system allows the player to create and develop a wide range of possible characters, from brave soldier to peaceful scientist to violent sociopath. All of these types can be used effectively within the game; computer-controlled characters will remember the player's previous behavior and react appropriately. Actual gameplay generally concentrates on exploration, **turn-based** combat, and character interaction, including the ability to recruit new individuals as additional playable characters.

The sequel, *Fallout 2* (*1998* BIS) designed by Feargus Urquhart and Matt Norton, contained a considerably larger world than the original, to which it added a further measure of sex, drugs, and violence. The player adopts the role of a descendant of the protagonist of *Fallout*, who is assumed to have founded an independent village after their exile. After creating a character, the player is sent out into the wilderness to locate a "Garden of Eden Construction Kit" from before the war, which their village needs to overcome a drought. As in the first game, the outside world proves to be varied and complex, with many possible paths to follow. Eventually, the player will encounter the descendants of the shadow government that built the Vaults, trapped on postapocalyptic Earth after their experimental starship was destroyed during the war. They are now attempting to create a virus that will kill any creature with mutated genes, after which they intend to rule a purified, but largely empty, world.

Fallout and *Fallout 2* share a Wild West feel reminiscent of a Sergio Leone film; the second game is more savage than the first, including slavery and dangerously addictive drugs. Each game has a strongly **modular** story; players can roam freely in postapocalyptic America, dealing with a wide range of characters and taking part in a variety of subplots, while gradually becoming aware of the nature of the game's major threat. Throughout both games, a great deal of emphasis is placed on allowing the player as much freedom of action as possible. In essence, Black Isle's *Fallout* **CRPGs** play as a form of moral simulator, allowing players to make meaningful choices in a dark and complex world.

Fallout Tactics: Brotherhood of Steel (*2001* Micro Forté) is a mix of CRPG and **computer wargame** created by a different development studio, focusing on a broadly **linear** story of tactical combat. The player begins the game as a member of the eponymous Brotherhood, a military organization attempting to restore civilization by force. As leader of a squad of new recruits, the player fights through a series of missions against Beastlords (who can **psionically** control armies of mutant animals, in what is ultimately an homage to Andre Norton's seminal sf novel *The Beast Master* [**1959**]), human raiders who worship ancient technology, and a mysterious group of robots, among others. While it lacks the depth and complexity of the first two members of the series, *Fallout Tactics* is an excellent tactical combat game with an atmospheric background and limited role playing elements.

Fallout 3 (*2008* BG) designed by Todd Howard and Emil Pagliarulo is another sequel built by different hands, in this case by the creators of the highly flexible if somewhat generic *Elder Scrolls* sequence of **sword and sorcery** computer role playing games. The combination of the *Fallout* series' strong sense of place with Bethesda Game's skill at creating open-ended, explorable worlds was a success; *Fallout 3* is a rather more linearly plotted game than its predecessors and one that places more emphasis on combat and less on moral ambiguity, but it is still an evocative portrayal of a harshly ironic postnuclear wasteland and one that offers its players a great deal of freedom. It is also more influenced by **first person shooters** than earlier entries in the series, including a first-person perspective view of its fully 3D world and a choice of **real-time** and turn-based battle systems. The overall effect is of a careful homage to the Black Isle games, combining moral choices and visceral violence with such morbidly humorous inventions as the Fat Man handheld catapult, which launches miniature atomic weapons.

With the announcement of *Fallout: New Vegas* (*2010* OE) designed by Josh Sawyer and John Gonzalez, it might have seemed that the franchise was being passed on to yet another new developer. The reality, however, was that Obsidian was formed by many of the employees of Black Isle after that studio was shut down; the move to Obsidian was thus more of a return than a departure. And if *Fallout 3*'s design suggests a deliberate tribute to its predecessors, *New Vegas* is a true sequel that restores the freedom of choice experienced by the players of the first two games with its strongly modular and **multilinear** structure. The setting is the eponymous city and its surrounding badlands, where an undeclared war is being waged for control of the Hoover Dam; participants include the owner of the city, the militaristic New Californian Republic, and a brutal postapocalyptic imitation of Caesar's Rome. As in the spaghetti Western *A Fistful of Dollars* (*1964*), much can be made of the opportunity to play various factions off against one another. The gameplay is generally similar to that of *Fallout 3*, but this game's fictional world is richer and deeper than that of its predecessor, with a wide variety of excellently, and often wittily, designed missions for the player to undertake. Many iconic B-movie creatures from previous iterations of the series return from rad-scorpions to supermutants. While it arguably still lacks some of the darkly comic flavor and originality of the first two games in the series, *New Vegas* is undoubtedly one of the most impressive science-fictional videogames to be created in the first decade of the twenty-first century.

Related works: *Operation: Anchorage* (*2009* BG) is an expansion pack for *Fallout 3* that takes place in a **virtual reality** simulation of one of the conflicts that led to the game's nuclear apocalypse. Further expansions include *The Pitt* (*2009* BG), set in the ruins of Pittsburgh, *Broken Steel* (*2009* BG), which allows the player to continue beyond the ending of the original game, *Point Lookout* (*2009* BG), set in the remains of the eponymous park in the US state of Maryland, and *Mothership Zeta* (*2009* BG), in which the player's character is abducted by a UFO (unidentified flying object). *New Vegas* also received a number of expansion packs. *Dead Money* (*2010* OE) features a quest for the lost treasure of the Sierra Madre Casino, while *Honest Hearts* (*2011* OE) deals with tribal warfare in the Zion National Park. In *Old World Blues* (*2011* OE), the player character is brought to a prewar research center, now overrun by mad scientists, while *Lonesome Road* (*2011* OE) ties up loose ends from the main game in a linear narrative set in a radioactive wasteland. *Gun Runner's Arsenal* (*2011* OE) and *Courier's Stash* (*2011* OE) contain various additional weapons and pieces of equipment for use in the game.

Fallout: Warfare (*2001* Interplay) designed by Christopher Taylor is a tabletop **wargame** that uses miniature paper models to simulate the same types of battle as *Fallout Tactics*. It has generally been made available digitally rather than as a boxed game, with printable files showing the board and counters included with various **videogame** releases. *Fallout: Brotherhood of Steel* (*2004* Interplay) is a heavily combat-oriented game in which the player adopts the role of an initiate in the Brotherhood of Steel. Notable largely for its extreme violence and repetitive gameplay, *Brotherhood of Steel* is also frequently inconsistent with the continuity established in the earlier games.

Web Links

- *Fallout*: http://fallout.bethsoft.com/index.html

- *Fallout Tactics* Postmortem: http://www.gamasutra.com/features/20010420/oakden_01.htm

- No Mutants Allowed (Tribute Site): http://www.nma-fallout.com/

FINAL FANTASY

1987. (Also known as *Final Fantasy Origins*; also known as *Final Fantasy Mobile Phone*; also known as *Final Fantasy I & II: Dawn of Souls*; also known as *Final Fantasy Anniversary Edition*.) Square. Designed by Hironobu Sakaguchi.

The series that began with *Final Fantasy* is the most commercially successful sf-like **videogame** franchise as of 2013, outstripped in worldwide popularity only by the various young adult games based on the *Mario* and *Pokémon* properties, the *Wii Sports* series produced for the eponymous console, the *Tetris* **puzzle game**, the *Grand Theft Auto* sequence of underworld action games, and the social simulation series beginning with *The Sims* (*2000* Maxis) designed by Will Wright. It could loosely be described as the *Star Wars* of videogames, both for its flamboyantly romantic tone and for its broad appeal. Members of the sequence are not, however, set in a single consistent universe. Instead, they have in common the appearance of **anime**-influenced ensembles of playable characters who live in a fantasticated world as well as a number of recurring character names and iconic creatures. Several leitmotifs also tend to reappear within the games' strongly **linear** stories, including the need for a balance to be struck between nature and technology and the hero's journey as experienced by a moody, androgynous protagonist. Within this framework, every major game—those denoted by a suffixed Roman numeral, as in *Final Fantasy VII*—is set in its own unique milieu, which may be shared by associated works including videogames, anime, and written fiction. With a few exceptions, all of the videogames are **console role playing games**. As is typical for members of the form, their gameplay depends on a combination of exploration, combat, character interaction, and puzzle solution, typically experienced through predesigned characters whose abilities can be improved by various means. Particular characteristics of *Final Fantasy*'s various descendants include the appearance of **psionic** or magical creatures that can be summoned for assistance in battles and a tendency to experiment with the systems used to enhance characters' powers and simulate combat; many innovations introduced by the series have proved influential on other console role playing games. It is noticeable, however, that in recent years the flow of new worlds and gameplay ideas has slowed considerably, with many of the more recent entries in the franchise being derivatives of or associated with previous works; it is possible that creative exhaustion is setting in.

The original *Final Fantasy* is of largely historical interest today. The setting is **heroic fantasy** with some sf elements, based on a conflict between four "light warriors" and the forces of darkness. As with its predecessor *Dragon Quest* (*1986* Enix), the gameplay resembles that of many contemporary Western **CRPGs**. As in the Western games, players' actions are largely focused on **turn-based** combat in a **2D** overhead view, but with fewer options than would typically be offered in the computer games and a more strongly directed story line. The name of the game was a reference to Sakaguchi's belief that this would probably be the last videogame he worked on, since the developers were experiencing financial difficulties. In the event, *Final Fantasy* proved to be extremely popular, spawning a wide range of sequels and spin-offs sharing its designation. The first of these, *Final Fantasy II* (*1988* Square; also known as *Final Fantasy Origins*; also known as *Final Fantasy I & II: Dawn of Souls*; also known as *Final Fantasy Mobile Phone*; also known as *Final Fantasy II Anniversary Edition*) designed by Hironobu Sakaguchi and Akitoshi Kawazu, is similar, but with a markedly better developed (though still rudimentary) narrative. This game and its contemporary *Phantasy Star* (*1987* Sega) designed by Rieko Kodama and Yuji Naka first introduced the emphasis on story and characterization that has become a dominant feature of console role playing games. *Final Fantasy II* is also notable for its use of a mechanic that improves the abilities of characters depending on how much they are used, an approach that has often been employed in pen and paper **role playing games** but received mixed reviews here. The next installment, *Final Fantasy III* (*1990* Square; revised *2006*) designed by Hironobu Sakaguchi, Hiromichi Tanaka, and Kazuhiko Aoki, largely returned to the design of the original game, though its heroic fantasy story line placed a greater degree of emphasis on characterization.

The next three *Final Fantasy* games continued to use 2D displays, while experimenting with the gameplay and adding increasingly sophisticated character interactions and some degree of moral ambiguity. Their combat systems replaced the turn-based mechanics of the earlier games with designs in which actions must be taken within a time limit, combining **real-time** and turn-based approaches. Some confusion is created by the fact that the original US releases used a different numbering system to the Japanese versions. *Final Fantasy II*, *Final Fantasy III*, and *Final Fantasy V* were not initially made available outside Japan; thus, *Final Fantasy IV* and *Final Fantasy VI* were known as *Final Fantasy II* and *Final Fantasy III*, respectively, internationally. Later releases corrected this discrepancy, using the Japanese designations worldwide. This book employs the original Japanese numbers by default.

Final Fantasy IV (*1991* Square; also known as *Final Fantasy IV Advance*; revised *2007*; also known as *Final Fantasy IV: The Complete Collection*) designed by Hironobu Sakaguchi and Takashi Tokita and *Final Fantasy V* (*1992* Square; also known as *Final Fantasy V Advance*) designed by Hironobu Sakaguchi and Hiroyuki Itou are both set in pseudo-medieval fantasy worlds, though *Final Fantasy IV* makes much use of magical devices that are analogous to technology, including an airship on which the characters can travel to an artificial moon. *Final Fantasy IV: The After Years* (*2008* Matrix Software [MS]/SE; also known as *Final Fantasy IV: The Complete Collection*) designed by Takashi Tokita is a late sequel to *Final Fantasy IV*, released episodically in Japan. *Final Fantasy VI* (*1994* Square; also known as *Final Fantasy VI Advance*) designed by Hironobu Sakaguchi, Yoshinori Kitase, and Hiroyuki Ito, by contrast, is the first truly science-fictional game in the series. The setting is **science and sorcery**, with a story in which a strong cast of diverse characters attempt to overthrow an evil empire that intends to combine its existing scientific knowledge with an almost forgotten magic. Part of the way through the game, the entire world is devastated; in the end, it seems that it will recover, but the magic has gone, never to return.

With the release of *Final Fantasy VII* (*1997* Square) designed by Yoshinori Kitase and Hironobu Sakaguchi, the numbers used for Japanese and international versions were synchronized, so that this and all later entries in the series bear the same designations worldwide. *Final Fantasy VII* preserved much of the gameplay of *Final Fantasy VI*, while introducing a new, more flexible system for character improvement, but changed the main displays to employ **3D** views and made extensive use of **full motion video** sequences to present its story. The game retains the science and sorcery approach of its predecessor, but shifts the setting to a society dominated by advanced technology fueled by vital energies extracted from the spiritual essence of its world. Robots, hostile aliens, and genetic engineering coexist with biological defense mechanisms created by the planetary life force and a magically induced meteor strike; almost every character has their own personal weakness to confront and overcome. The overall effect is lushly melodramatic and curiously compelling, strongly reminiscent of such anime works as the film *Final Fantasy: The Spirits Within* (*2001*) or the television series *Blue Gender* (*1999–2000*). *Final Fantasy VII* was still the most commercially successful entry in the series as of 2011, and did much to popularize the console role playing game form outside Japan. *Before Crisis: Final Fantasy VII* (*2004* Square Enix [SE]) designed by Yoshinori Kitase is a prequel, while *Dirge of Cerberus: Final Fantasy VII* (*2006* SE) designed by Yoshinori Kitase and Takayoshi Nakazato is a sequel, which received mixed reviews; unusually for the series, *Dirge of Cerberus* is a **third person shooter**, albeit one with role playing elements. *Crisis Core: Final Fantasy VII* (*2007* SE) designed by Hajime Tabata is another sequel, but one presented as a console role playing game. *Final Fantasy VII Snowboarding* (*2005* SE) is a version of a snowboarding sequence found in the original game.

Final Fantasy VIII (*1999* Square) designed by Yoshinori Kitase and Hironobu Sakaguchi has a similar structure to its predecessor, but takes a markedly more realistic approach to the visual design. Several changes were made to the gameplay, including the addition of an interesting and complex new mechanic for handling character abilities and some alterations to the combat system, which can unfortunately prolong battle sequences considerably. The setting again combines fantasy and sf elements, in a world resembling an alternate version of the historical 1960s in which spiritual forces appear to play a role similar to those of guardian angels; the overall effect is somewhat reminiscent of that of the film *The Wings of Honneamise* (*1987*). While the main story line sets a group of elite teenage mercenaries against an aggressive nation ruled by a time-traveling sorceress, the primary focus of the narrative is perhaps the affecting love story between two of the major characters. The next installment, *Final Fantasy IX* (*2000* Square) designed by Hiroyuki Ito and Hironobu Sakaguchi, abandons science and sorcery for the heroic fantasy, which dominated the earliest games in the series. Many details of its gameplay were also conceived as part of a deliberate attempt to recapture the spirit of such predecessors as *Final Fantasy IV*, though the 3D displays of the later games were retained. The story concentrates on a war in a pseudo-medieval setting that makes use of limited—often magically powered—technologies. Eventually, it emerges that the entire planet is threatened by an invasion of souls from a dying world, which is its analog in a parallel dimension.

Final Fantasy X (*2001* Square; *2002* revised as *Final Fantasy X International*) designed by Motomu Toriyama and Toshiro Tsuchida included a number of innovations. The combat model was turn based, an approach that the series' developers had not used since *Final Fantasy III*, another new system was introduced for describing character abilities, and Asian cultural influences figured strongly in the milieu for the first time. The setting is dominated more by sorcery than science; the game is set in a fantasy world where technology has been banned, and is employed only by a single pariah culture. Its story line focuses on attempts to defeat a monster known as Sin, created to protect a dream-like recreation of a ruined city. One of the major characters, Tidus, is a citizen of this illusory metropolis; in the end, city, Tidus, and Sin must all be lost. The game succeeds in generating a genuine sense of melancholy; unusually for the series, its central love story is a doomed one, since Tidus cannot be saved. *Final Fantasy X* was also the first member of the main sequence to receive a direct sequel, in the form of *Final Fantasy X-2* (*2003* Square; *2004* revised as *Final Fantasy X-2 International + Last Mission*) designed by Yoshinori Kitase and Motomu Toriyama. This game is much more exploratory in nature than any of its predecessors, with a broadly **modular** plot rather than the deep linear story line typical of console role playing games. While it is set in the same milieu as *Final Fantasy X*, it contains many more sf elements; the game-world is presented as rapidly evolving from an ancient, highly spiritual civilization toward a more modern and materialist one, represented by frequent references to contemporary Japanese pop culture. A group of female characters must attempt to resolve the conflicts engendered by this complicated transition. The mood of *Final Fantasy X-2* is far more cheerful and lighthearted than that of its predecessor; it is even possible to resolve the first game's downbeat ending by recreating Tidus.

Final Fantasy XI Online (*2002* Square) designed by Hiromichi Tanaka and Koichi Ishii is a **massively multiplayer online role playing game**, the first such work that allowed players using different types of computer hardware to participate in the same virtual world. As with *Phantasy Star*

Online (*2000* Sega) designed by Yoshihiro Sakuta, a library of pretranslated phrases is supplied to simplify communication between players of different nationalities and those who do not have access to a keyboard. *Final Fantasy XI Online* could be described as a well-crafted but unexceptional **MMORPG** (massively multiplayer online role playing game), featuring real-time combat in a heroic fantasy milieu; its most distinctive feature is perhaps its inclusion of such iconic *Final Fantasy* elements as the Chocobos, flightless birds that can be ridden in the manner of horses. There have been five expansion packs to date: *Rise of the Zilart* (*2003* SE), *Chains of Promathia* (*2004* SE), *Treasures of Aht Urhgan* (*2006* SE), *Wings of the Goddess* (*2007* SE), and *Seekers of Adoulin* (*2013* SE).

Several recent *Final Fantasy* games have been set in the **Ivalice** milieu, which echoes the *Final Fantasy IV* background in its depiction of magically powered technologies in a pseudo-medieval world that includes elements of Arabian fantasy. The first game to use this setting was *Final Fantasy Tactics* (*1997* Square; *2007* revised as *Final Fantasy Tactics: The War of the Lions*) designed by Yasumi Matsuno and Hiroyuki Ito, a **tactical RPG** that emphasizes turn-based combat. Direct sequels to this work include *Final Fantasy Tactics Advance* (*2003* SE) designed by Yuichi Murasawa—set in an imaginary version of **Ivalice**—and *Final Fantasy Tactics A2: Grimoire of the Rift* (*2007* SE), both of which are also tactical RPGs. *Final Fantasy Tactics S* (*2013* SE) is another associated game that combines tactics with play on a social network, to date only released in Japan. *Final Fantasy XII* (*2006* SE; *2007* revised as *Final Fantasy XII: International Zodiac Job System*) designed by Yasumi Matsuno, Hiroshi Minagawa, and Hiroyuki Ito was the first major entry in the series to be set in the milieu. *Final Fantasy XII* borrows much from contemporary Western **computer role playing games**, most notably its real-time combat system. Arguably, the design of this game can be seen as a mirror image of that of *Star Wars: Knights of the Old Republic* (*2003* BioWare), which blends elements drawn from console role playing games into the Western approach to development associated with personal computers. The narrative mood also differs from that of previous *Final Fantasy* games, focusing more on a realistic war story than operatic drama. *Final Fantasy XII: Revenant Wings* (*2007* SE/Think & Feel Inc) designed by Motomu Toriyama is a loose sequel, a real-time variant of a tactical RPG that deals with the exploration of a floating continent by airship. *Crystal Guardians* (*2008* MSF/Winds), *Crystal Defenders* (*2008* MSF/Winds) and *Crystal Defenders: Vanguard Storm* (*2009* MSF/Winds) are associational turn-based strategy games.

Final Fantasy XIII (2009 SE) designed by Motomu Toriyama returns to science and sorcery in its depiction of a technologically advanced flying city created by angelic beings to provide humanity with a refuge from the dangerous world below. The game's protagonists become involved with the angelic "God Machines," which sustain their home, an association that makes them undesirable elements destined to be banished by the city's theocratic government. Meanwhile, one of the characters is searching for a way to restore her sister, who was transformed into an immortal crystalline form as a result of an earlier encounter with the angels (or Gods). Ultimately, some of the game's characters must sacrifice themselves to prevent the floating city falling from the sky. The game mechanics are greatly simplified compared to those of its predecessor, with an entertaining but generally undemanding combat system, and the story is highly linear; the impression must be that a decision was taken to abandon any attempt to integrate elements drawn from the Western CRPG tradition and instead create a mass market game firmly in the Japanese style. Interestingly, *Final Fantasy XIII's* most important character is a woman, exemplifying the trend toward more female protagonists seen in such recent members of the series as *Final Fantasy X-2.* Earlier *Final Fantasy* games were often popular with female players, as were their strikingly beautiful male leads; the appearance of women in the majority of leading roles may be a response to this enthusiasm. *Final Fantasy XIII-2 (2012* SE) designed by Motomu Toriyama is a sequel in which a small group of characters must use time travel to save humanity from extinction in the distant future, while rescuing the lead character of the previous game, who has been left trapped in a world outside time. There is a kind of **changewar**, fought against an enemy who wants to make history immutable by destroying time; the story ends on a cliffhanger. This game's plot is markedly less linear than of its predecessor, with a strongly **modular interactive narrative**; the design is otherwise similar to that of *Final Fantasy XIII,* with minor improvements. Unfortunately, this additional flexibility in the story may have come at the cost of some depth of characterization; it is possible that Square Enix's designers found it difficult to combine the creation of a compelling narrative with the player's possession of (at least an illusion of) free will. *Final Fantasy Type-0 (2011* SE) designed by Hajime Tabata is a vaguely associated game in which an ensemble of heroes performs missions in a fantasy setting, which is only thematically linked to that of *Final Fantasy XIII.* To date, it has only been released in Japan.

Final Fantasy XIV Online (*2010* SE) designed by Naoki Yoshida is another massively multiplayer online role playing game, set in a different but similar fantasy world to that of *Final Fantasy XI Online*. Initial reviews of this work were exceptionally poor; notably, the interface was considered to be highly confusing, and the **environmental** narrative undeveloped, leading to a sense that inhabitants of the world were offered only an endless series of mechanically repetitive tasks to complete. A much revised version, set 5 years in the future of the original milieu, was released in 2013 under the name of *Final Fantasy XIV: A Realm Reborn*, to much improved reviews.

Related works: A wide variety of other works are associated with the franchise. Perhaps the most significant are the various anime TV series and films of which the first was *Final Fantasy: Legend of the Crystals* (*1994*), a sequel to *Final Fantasy V*. The thematically interesting and visually appealing but commercially unsuccessful *Final Fantasy: The Spirits Within* (*2001*) is a science-fictional film, which shares many of the tropes of the videogames but is not set in any of their worlds. *Final Fantasy: Unlimited* (*2001–2002*) is a **sword and sorcery** series, which is also not set in any of the established milieux, but makes use of many recurring elements of the mythos. *Final Fantasy VII: Advent Children* (*2005*) is a sequel to *Final Fantasy VII*, while the short *Last Order: Final Fantasy VII* (*2005*) is a prequel to it.

A number of videogames have also been released, which use the *Final Fantasy* name but are not associated with any of the major entries in the series, typically set in magical fantasy worlds. These include the console role playing games *The Final Fantasy Legend* (*1989* Square) designed by Akitoshi Kawazu and its sequels *Final Fantasy Legend II* (*1990* Square) designed by Akitoshi Kawazu and *Final Fantasy Legend III* (*1991* Square) designed by Kouzi Ide, as well as the more action-oriented *Final Fantasy Adventure* (*1991* Square; also known as *Mystic Quest* in Europe) designed by Koichi Ishii and *Final Fantasy: Mystic Quest* (*1992* Square; also known as *Final Fantasy USA Mystic Quest* in Japan; also known as *Mystic Quest Legend* in Europe) designed by Kouzi Ide and Chihiro Fujioka. *Final Fantasy: Unlimited* (*2003* Amada) and *Final Fantasy: Unlimited with U* (*2002* Amada) are set in the same universe as the *Final Fantasy: Unlimited* anime, and have only been released in Japan. *Final Fantasy: The 4 Heroes of Light* (*2009* MS/SE) designed by Takashi Tokita and Hiroaki Yabuta is another console role playing game set in a fantasy world, one that is often reminiscent of the original *Final Fantasy*. *Final Fantasy Legends: Warriors of Light and Darkness* (*2010* MS/SE) designed by Toshio Akiyama and *Final Fantasy Brigade* (*2012* SE) are generally similar, but to date have only been released in Japan. The events of *Final Fantasy Dimensions* (*2010* MS/SE), meanwhile, take place in a fantasy milieu split into two worlds, one of eternal day and one of endless night. *Final Fantasy Airborne Brigade* (*2012* SE) and *Final Fantasy Artniks* (*2012* SE) both emphasize social interactions between players over the Internet, though the first is a CRPG and the second is based on a virtual card game, while *Final Fantasy: All the Bravest* (*2013* BitGroove) is a poorly received work featuring characters from many previous members of the franchise. *Theatrhythm Final Fantasy* (*2012* indieszero) has a plot related to that of *Dissidia: Final Fantasy* (for which see the following) but is played as a "rhythm game," in which players must simulate the performance of a musical score in order to achieve victory; this work has also not been sold outside Japan.

Final Fantasy: Crystal Chronicles (*2003* Game Designers Studio) designed by Kazuhiko Aoki is another console role playing game that began a popular spin-off series set in a world covered with a poisonous fog in which cities survive with the assistance of magical crystals. Later games in the same milieu (some of which are set before the fog descends, or after its retreat) include *Final Fantasy: Crystal Chronicles – Ring of Fates* (*2007* SE) designed by Mitsuru Kamiyama, the city building simulation *Final Fantasy: Crystal Chronicles: My Life as a King* (*2008* SE) designed by Kenichiro Yuji, *Final Fantasy: Crystal Chronicles: Echoes of Time* (*2009* SE) designed by Mitsuru Kamiyama, the strategy game *Final Fantasy: Crystal Chronicles: My Life as a Darklord* (*2009* SE) designed by Hiroyuki Kaneko, and *Final Fantasy: Crystal Chronicles: The Crystal Bearers* (*2009* SE) designed by Toshiyuki Itahana. Another subsequence was begun with *Dissidia: Final Fantasy* (*2008* SE) designed by Takeshi Arakawa. *Dissidia* is essentially a 3D **fighting game** in which characters from various works in the main series, from the original *Final Fantasy* to *Final Fantasy X*, are recruited by the Goddess of Harmony to wage a multidimensional war against chaos; there are echoes of Michael Moorcock's **Eternal Champion** cycle. *Dissidia 012: Final Fantasy* (*2011* SE) designed by Mitsunori Takahashi is a similarly structured prequel.

Most of the written fiction associated with *Final Fantasy* has not been published in English, or has not been released separately to various game compilations. One work that is internationally available is Dean

Wesley Smith's *Final Fantasy: The Spirits Within* (**2001**), the novelization of the film of the same name.

Web Link

- Final Fantasy Compendium (Tribute Site): http://www. ffcompendium.com/

FREEDOM FORCE

2002. IG. Designed by Robb Waters and Ken Levine.

Freedom Force is a **computer role playing game** that emphasizes tactical combat, set in 1962 that might have appeared in the superhero comics of the time. The tone is knowing and self-aware; this is not so much a game derived from the comics of the Silver Age as a game about them. The **linear** plot begins with the alien Mentor fleeing to our world from another dimension. Lord Dominion, ruler of a multitude of **parallel worlds**, has decided that rather than conquer Earth he will bestow the powers of "Energy X" on the worst humans he can find, expecting that mankind will then destroy itself. Mentor, however, has stolen the canisters of Energy X, which are scattered across Patriot City after Lord Dominion destroys Mentor's ship. A variety of individuals, both good and evil, come into contact with the mysterious energy, developing superpowers related to their essential natures and the circumstances in which they were affected. The player must control a growing group of these individuals, first to bring the newly created supervillains under control and then to fight off Lord Dominion himself.

Structurally, the game is split into a series of missions, between which characters' powers can be improved and new abilities chosen. These tasks feature a wide range of enemies, from robots originating in an alternate future to the Great God Pan, whose power transforms women into nymphs. Gameplay is focused on combat between small groups, displayed in a **3D** overhead view, while the interface design is centered on objects in the environment rather than the heroes' abilities, allowing players to easily perform such iconic actions as throwing cars and wielding lamp posts. *Freedom Force* contains many appealing characters influenced by classic comics archetypes; indirectly participating in their arguments and romantic entanglements is one of the chief pleasures of the game. The final impression is of a loving pastiche of the world of Marvel Comics' Jack Kirby and Stan Lee, similar to Alan Moore's comic book series *1963* (*1993*), but without its air of slightly savage irony.

Related works: *Freedom Force vs The 3rd Reich* (*2005* IG) is a sequel, similar in both tone and gameplay. The plot traps the heroes from the first game in an alternate 1963 where the Nazis won World War Two, a reality that can only be undone if the player goes back in time to the 1940s, where they can team up with superheroes modeled on the "Golden Age" characters of DC and Marvel Comics to repair world history. Part of the story echoes the "Dark Phoenix" sequence from *The X-Men*, one of the most famously melodramatic of Silver Age comic book tragedies. *Freedom Force* (*2005*) is a six-issue comics series that retells the story of the first game, written by Eric Dieter and drawn by Tom Scioli.

Web Link
- Freedom Force Universe: http://www.freedomfans.com/

FRONT MISSION

Series (from 1999). Initially Square (SQ), later Square Enix (SE). Designed by Toshiro Tsuchida.

Front Mission is a series of **console role playing games** that emphasize **turn-based** tactical combat and strong, often **multilinear**, plots. To date, only three members of the main series have been released outside Japan: *Front Mission* (*1995* SQ; *2002* revised as *Front Mission 1st*) designed by Toshiro Tsuchida, *Front Mission 3* (*1999* SQ) designed by Toshiro Tsuchida, and *Front Mission 4* (*2003* SE) designed by Toshiro Tsuchida. All of these works use a combination of **3D** action sequences and overhead views to present what are unusually serious narratives for Japanese **CRPGs**, focusing on conspiratorial politics and the futility of war. Their visual designs tend to be dark and industrial, reflecting their military themes. Parallels can be drawn with the **anime** series *Gundam Wing* (*1995–1996*) and *Gasaraki* (*1998–2000*), though *Front Mission* depicts a realistic near-future world that lacks both the space travel of the former and the mysticism of the latter. The most significant feature of this future is the use of Wanzers, "wandering panzers" or human-piloted walking tanks, in warfare. Gameplay in the series alternates between Wanzer combat scenarios, including story development through prescribed events, and scenes focusing on character interaction, during which the player's conversational choices can trigger different plot paths. While several of the games employ branching plots, the available paths will frequently split temporarily and then recombine later. Role playing elements include the ability to improve the player characters' Wanzer piloting skills and select and upgrade the **mecha** they use. As is conventional in CRPGs intended for games consoles, players are assigned characters with detailed backgrounds, rather than creating their own.

All of the *Front Mission* games are set in a shared **future history**; characters from one game may later reappear in another. In this continuity, the world is divided between the Oceania Community Union, the United Continental States, the European Community, and several smaller power blocs, most of which are intermittently (though not very intensively) at war with one another. In *Front Mission 3*, two entirely separate story lines are available, depending on an early, apparently insignificant, choice made by the player; both focus on a military industrial conspiracy in Japan. The **linearly** plotted *Front Mission 4* also has two story lines, but the player follows both simultaneously, switching from one to the other. In one, the player adopts the role of a European Community Wanzer pilot working with advanced military technology; in the other, that of a United Confederate States soldier in Venezuela who is contemplating desertion from a "police action." The two stories eventually merge, revealing a global conspiracy to intensify the world's endemic cool war.

Related works: *Front Mission: Evolved* (*2010* Double Helix Games) designed by David Verfaillie and David Hall is a spin-off from the main sequence with the gameplay of a **third person shooter**; there are some similarities to the *BattleTech* game *MechAssault* (*2002* Day 1 Studios) and its sequels. The setting is the twenty-second century, later than the games in the original series; **space elevators** and advanced mecha appear.

Several other *Front Mission* games have never been translated out of Japanese. *Front Mission 2* (*1997* SQ) designed by Toshiro Tsuchida is the second game in the main series. *Front Mission 5: Scars of the War* (*2005* SE) designed by Toshiro Tsuchida has a story line that follows the same group of characters over many years; its narrative is primarily concerned with the dehumanizing effects of high-technology warfare and with an allegorical depiction of the contemporary War on Terror. *Front Mission 2089* (*2005* SE; *2008* revised as *Front Mission 2089: Border of Madness*) and *Front Mission 2089-II* (*2006* SE) use broadly similar designs to those of the original *Front Mission* to present the linear story of a group of mercenaries who are investigating the actions of a secret military organization. Other *Front Mission–*related games, unreleased outside Japan, include *Front Mission: Gun Hazard* (*1996* SQ), a **2D** action game, *Front Mission: Alternative* (*1997* SQ), and the multiplayer-only online third-person shooter *Front Mission Online* (*2005* SE).

Web Links

- *Front Mission: Evolved*: http://www.frontmissionevolved.com/

- frontmission.org (Tribute Site): http://www.frontmission.org/

.HACK

Series (from 2002). CyberConnect2 (CC2). Designed by Kazunori Ito, Kōichi Mashimo, and Yoshiyuki Sadamoto.

.hack is a **transmedia** franchise including **videogames**, **anime**, novels, and comics, all of which are perhaps best viewed as parts of a single work. Its story revolves around a fictional **massively multiplayer online role playing game** called "The World," which bears a strong resemblance to the fantasy game *EverQuest* (*1999* Verant Interactive) designed by Brad McQuaid, Steve Clover, and Bill Trost; the major difference is that The World is played using **virtual reality** equipment. As is often true of real **MMORPGs**, the fictional game seems poised halfway between a fully convincing alternative reality and an obviously artificial construct. The first part of the franchise to be released, *.hack//Sign* (*2002*), is an anime series that concentrates on Tsukasa, a new player who for unknown reasons is unable to log out of the system. Meanwhile, the game's synthetic reality appears to be breaking down, and a mysterious artificial intelligence has been discovered buried deep in the infrastructure of The World. *.hack// Sign* is remarkable for the understanding it displays of the cultures of persistent **online worlds**, and the way in which they can offer people a second, better life. In the end, Tsukasa's story is resolved, but many other questions are left unanswered.

A series of videogames, set after the end of the anime, began with *.hack//Infection* (*2002* CC2; also known as *.hack//Infection Expansion* in Japan), in which the player takes on the role of Kite, who is himself a player of The World. Soon the player finds that they have acquired unusual powers to access The World's infrastructure, which they must use to discover why many of the game's players have fallen into a coma. The series was continued in *.hack//Mutation* (*2002* CC2; also known as *.hack//Malignant Mutation* in Japan), *.hack//Outbreak* (*2002* CC2; also known as *.hack// Erosion Pollution* in Japan), and *.hack//Quarantine* (*2003* CC2; also known as *.hack//Absolute Encirclement* in Japan), which together make up a single serial story with an essentially **linear** plot. Each game includes an episode of the anime series *.hack//Liminality (2002–2003)*, which tells a parallel story set in the real world. In design terms, *.hack//Infection* and its successors are **console role playing games** that focus strongly on the combat and treasure-hunting aspects of The World's fiction. Unfortunately, this makes their core gameplay an all-too-accurate representation of what is perhaps the least interesting aspect of MMORPGs, without including the other human players who make it entertaining. Ultimately, it is revealed that the comatose players have been caught in a conflict between two artificial intelligences: Aura, who was constructed illicitly by a programmer of The World in the hope that she could eventually become truly sentient by learning from the game's players, and her guardian, Morganna, who has gone rogue. Resolution comes when Aura merges with Morganna, becoming a benevolent goddess in The World's machine.

Another part of the whole, Tatsuya Hamazaki's *.hack//Legend of the Twilight (2002–2004)*, is a **manga** set after the end of the game series; a separate version was produced as a young adult anime, also called *.hack// Legend of the Twilight (2003)*. The story focuses on attempts by the owners of the MMORPG to delete Aura. A second series of interlinked projects, sometimes collectively referred to as *.hack Conglomerate* to distinguish them from the original *.hack*, then began with the anime *.hack//Roots (2006)*. *Conglomerate* is largely set within "The World R:2," a new version of the MMORPG created after a catastrophic failure of the original. This new World has been overrun by players who enjoy slaughtering other participants' characters and is slipping into anarchy; meanwhile, Aura has disappeared. A series of three games followed the anime: *.hack//G.U. Rebirth (2006* CC2; also known as *.hack//G.U. Resurrection* in Japan), *.hack//G.U. Reminisce (2006* CC2; also known as *.hack//G.U. The Voice that Thinks of You* in Japan), and *.hack//G.U. Redemption (2007* CC2; also known as *.hack//G.U. At a Walking Pace* in Japan). The primary character is the protagonist of *Roots*, who has become a dedicated killer of player killers within The World; the plot centers on the results of a failed attempt by the game's owners to resurrect Aura, in the hope that she can salvage their creation. This second iteration of the concept suffers from a certain degree of repetition, both in the gameplay and in the various manifestations of the story. Nevertheless, the well-drawn characters and intriguing situations remain of interest.

A third revision of the franchise was launched with a manga, originally published in Japan from 2007 and later translated into English as *.hack//Link Volume 1 (2010)*, *.hack//Link Volume 2 (2010)*, and *.hack//Link*

Volume 3 (*2011*), all written by Megane Kikuya. In this variant, which acts as a sequel to *.hack//Roots* and the *.hack//G.U.* games, The World has been rebooted as "The World R:X." As in the film *Tron* (*1982*), the comic's protagonist is mysteriously transported into this artificial reality as a fully physical entity, to discover that the virtual world is mutating in inexplicable ways. *.hack//Link* (*2010* CC2) is a **CRPG** loosely based on the manga, which has only been made available in Japanese; reviews were mixed. Other associated works include the anime series *.hack//Quantum* (*2010–2011*) and the computer-animated film *.hack//The Movie* (*2012*), which was only released in Japan. Stories set in The World R:X, in any medium, frequently feature the return of characters from the many previous core narratives and spin-offs in the franchise, to an extent that sometimes makes them inaccessible to those who are not already dedicated fans of the milieu. Arguably, the *.hack* concept has now reached the point of diminishing returns.

Related works: *.hack//fragment* (*2005* CC2) is a version of The World implemented as an actual MMORPG, only released in Japan. It was generally considered to be severely limited compared to competing games such as *Anarchy Online* (*2001* Funcom) designed by Gaute Godager and Ragnar Tørnquist, and was shut down after a year. *.hack//Enemy* (*2003* Decipher) designed by Mike Reynolds and Chuck Kallenbach is an award-winning **collectible card game** set in The World, in which players adopt the role of monsters attacking characters within the fictional MMORPG.

AI Buster (**2005**) by Tatsuya Hamazaki is a prequel to *.hack//Sign*, describing the appearance within The World and subsequent suicide of a failed prototype of Aura. *AI Buster 2* (**2006**), also by Hamazaki, is a collection of short stories set within the franchise. *.hack//Another Birth Volume 1* (**2006**), *.hack//Another Birth Volume 2* (**2006**), *.hack//Another Birth Volume 3* (**2007**), and *.hack//Another Birth Volume 4* (**2007**), all by Miu Kawasaki and Kazunori Ito, are novelizations of the original four *.hack* games. Similarly, *.hack//G.U. Volume 1* (**2009**), *.hack//G.U. Volume 2* (**2010**), *.hack//G.U. Volume 3* (**2010**), and *.hack//G.U. Volume 4* (**2011**), all by Tatsuya Hamazaki, are novelizations of the three *Conglomerate* games, while *.hack//G.U.+ Volume 1* (*2008*), *.hack//G.U.+ Volume 2* (*2008*), *.hack//G.U.+ Volume 3* (*2008*), *.hack/G.U.+ Volume 4* (*2008*), and *.hack//G.U.+ Volume 5* (*2009*), again written by Hamazaki, are manga adaptations of the same material. Other **ties** to *Conglomerate* include Ryo Suzukaze's *.hack//CELL Volume 1* (**2010**) and *.hack//CELL Volume 2* (**2010**), which follow the parallel stories of a seriously ill young girl in our world and an identically named character in The World who charges players for allowing them to kill her, and the manga .hack//Alcor (*2009*) and .hack//4koma (*2010*).

Web Link

- dothackers (Tribute Site): http://www.dothackers.net/

INFINITE SPACE

2009. Nude Maker/Platinum Games. Designed by Hifumi Kono and Masafumi Nukita.

Infinite Space is a **console role playing game** that uses a combination of **2D** displays and preprepared **3D** sequences to present its intergalactic milieu. Players are able to explore space more or less at will, using both **faster than light** drives and **stargates** to travel within and between the Large and Small Magellanic Clouds, though much time is also spent fighting (and occasionally boarding) hostile spacecraft or reconfiguring and improving the participant's own vessels. It is also possible to descend to planetary surfaces using **space elevators**, where players can talk to (and sometimes fight) computer-controlled characters in a strictly limited range of locations. The major focus of the game, however, is its generally **linear** (but occasionally **multilinear**) plot.

This story is cast in a classic **space opera** mode; it begins with a wish-fulfillment fantasy for heterosexual boys and ends with the destruction of the universe. The game opens with the (young male) player character's escape from a backwater planet that bans space travel, with the help of a sexually alluring older female pilot. This pair can fight and win many battles, meeting a diverse cast of memorable (if somewhat stereotypical) characters, before a gigantic empire invades their galaxy. This adversary cannot be defeated; the player's only option is to escape from the Small to the Large Magellanic Cloud, leaving the fairy tale space kingdoms and vicious pirates of their home to be conquered by the enemy. Tragedy, and several heroic deaths, ensues.

At this point, the narrative skips 10 years, and the boy protagonist becomes a man. The invaders have now begun to attack the Large Magellanic Cloud, and the player's character can be their greatest enemy. Soon, however, it emerges that the empire is conquering humanity in order to unify them against their own creators, a **forerunner** species that made the universe and gave mankind the technology for starflight, but intend to unmake reality as soon as humans have explored the whole of space. The player character, it is revealed, is not human but an **android** constructed by the forerunners as an observer, as is the sister for whom he appears to feel a more than brotherly love. Ultimately, the protagonist can lead a fleet to the Small Magellanic Cloud, defeat the empire, and then join its forces in an attack on Earth. Here, they will discover that the aliens have enclosed the sun in a **Dyson Sphere**, and are using its energy to power a stargate through which they can summon living warships from a higher reality. While these entities have already destroyed most of the universe by this point in the game, shattering the Sphere prevents the creators from further affecting humanity's cosmos. The protagonist can then, perhaps, use his forerunner-given power to manipulate reality in order to restore what has been lost.

Infinite Space is not a flawless game. The plot can be hard to follow, the frequent battles are not always interesting, and a great deal of time is spent micromanaging the disposition of the player's crew and equipment. The simulated universe is vast but—unsurprisingly, given the finite resources available to create and store it—somewhat repetitive. It succeeds, however, as an interactive **anime**, a melodramatic soap opera in which the player can participate as one of many characters fighting in a seemingly endless series of galactic wars across an ocean of stars. There are frequent homages to the seminal anime series *Space Battleship Yamato* (*1974–1975*), most notably in the presentation of the space combat system, which often evokes the naval battles of World War Two. There is also something of the quality of ever-inflating scale that gives E. E. Smith's **Lensman** novels much of their **sense of wonder**, a suggestion of unfolding revelation as the game's subject expands from escape from a single planet through the exploration of space and intergalactic war to the salvation of the universe.

MASS EFFECT

2007. BioWare. Designed by Casey Hudson and Preston Watamaniuk.

Mass Effect is a **computer role playing game** that employs a **3D** third-person view. The setting is **space opera**; in the twenty-second century, humanity is expanding into a galaxy populated by many diverse alien civilizations, using technology obtained from **forerunner** artifacts discovered on Mars. The various species each have their own "racial personalities," in the manner of *Star Control II* (*1992* Toys For Bob) designed by Fred Ford, Paul Reiche III, or the **Uplift War** stories of David Brin. Political power resides with a sodality somewhat resembling the United

Nations, within which humanity is a minor participant; internal squabbles are common, though the galaxy is generally peaceful. The titular effect is a fundamental physical force similar to gravity or electromagnetism, which (with the assistance of implanted cybernetics, or "biotics") can be used in ways largely indistinguishable from **psionics**; a network of "mass relays" is used for instantaneous **faster than light** travel. The game's main story line is broadly **linear** with some **multilinear** elements but quite complex, with many optional missions that do not affect the main plot. In essence, all the sentient races are in danger from the Reapers, artificially intelligent **berserkers** that periodically return from outside the galaxy to eliminate technologically advanced civilizations; among their previous victims are the Protheans, the now extinct forerunner race from whose abandoned spacecraft humanity learnt how to travel to the stars. Initially, the player is ignorant of this threat; ultimately, they must avert the Reapers' first strike.

Two main styles of play are offered by the game: action-oriented set pieces that occupy most of the player's time on planets and long conversational sequences that occur on spaceships and the Citadel, a gigantic space station. During combat, the player is usually given control of a squad of three soldiers, who can be commanded either in **real-time** (in the manner of a **third person shooter**) or by pausing the game and issuing detailed instructions. There is considerable scope for role playing outside battle situations, with a great deal of choice in both the nature of the main character and what they can say. The player's character, a human military officer, can be male or female, with one of several possible personal histories and professions as well as a custom-ized physical appearance. Some of the options available to the player initially proved contentious, notably the ability to form a same-sex romantic relation-ship with an alien if the main character is female, which resulted in the game being briefly banned in Singapore. The flexibility of the conversational system greatly assists with the creation of an alternate persona; it is possible to con-struct a preferred role and begin playing it almost without conscious thought. As in *Star Wars: Knights of the Old Republic* (*2003* BioWare), characters' behavior is rated according to a moral scheme, in this case one that distin-guishes between honor and expediency, and computer-controlled individuals' reactions to the player are affected by such assessments of their character. In *Mass Effect*, however, the ethical choices are generally less clear-cut than in *Star Wars: Knights of the Old Republic*. At one point, for example, the player may need to decide whether to commit genocide to eradicate the threat posed by a perhaps incurably aggressive alien race.

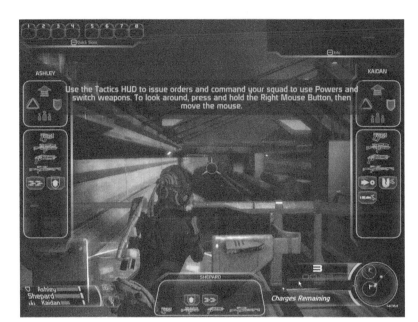

In *Mass Effect*, commands can be issued to the player's team through a special interface while the game is paused.

Much of the player's time in *Mass Effect* is spent exploring the surfaces of vividly realized alien worlds.

Mass Effect is undoubtedly one of the most wide-ranging sf **CRPGs** created to date. On occasion, this sense of scale can create its own problems; while the player can travel to many different solar systems, those that are not part of a specific mission tend to be quite uninteresting. Nevertheless, the game offers players a real chance to shape the events of a galaxy-spanning space opera, which draws on both the **military sf** tradition exemplified by the television series *Space: Above and Beyond* (1995–1996) and the **sense of wonder** that distinguishes *Babylon 5* (1993–1998).

The next game in the sequence is *Mass Effect 2* (*2010* BioWare) designed by Casey Hudson and Preston Watamaniuk. The design of this work differs in several important respects from that of its predecessor. Notably, BioWare borrowed the third-person shooter form's emphasis on speed and fluidity in combat, as they had earlier taken a focus on strongly characterized and directed core narratives from **console role playing games**. Action sequences are much faster paced as a result, though it is still possible to issue commands while the game is paused as well as fight in real time. *Mass Effect 2* is also less interested in the details of character simulation than the original game and offers fewer opportunities for the player to configure their virtual persona; the design is strongly focused on conversation and combat, with a few minor additions such as planetary mining. The narrative structure is reminiscent of one often seen in the middle volume of book trilogies, or the midseason episodes of TV shows; the (largely linear) main story line is relatively simple, but is surrounded by optional missions in which the player can interact with the game's many strongly drawn and interesting characters. That primary plot begins on an ominous note, with the destruction of the player's ship (the *Normandy*) and the unavoidable death of their character. Several years later, the protagonist's corpse is revived by an underground human supremacist organization known as Cerberus, which wants them to investigate the mysterious disappearances of the populations of several human colony worlds. Eventually, it emerges that the missing colonists have been abducted by a servant species of the Reapers, who are using them as raw material for the construction of a partially organic berserker; the player must follow the kidnappers through a mass relay to the center of the galaxy and attack a space station in orbit around a **black hole**. Interestingly, information that represents the set of decisions a player made in the first game can be ingested by its successor, ensuring that continuity is maintained and influencing the multilinear choices available in the second work.

The structure of *Mass Effect 3* (*2012* BioWare) designed by Casey Hudson and Preston Watamaniuk is similar to that of its predecessor, though victory is perhaps harder to achieve. As this game begins, annihilation is coming; the Reapers have begun their final assault, and Earth is under attack. Participants must unite the galaxy's many alien species against the common enemy, fighting both Cerberus and the Reapers during a series of multilinear missions; completion of many of these diplomatic tasks requires players to make difficult choices. Many characters from the earlier games return, in ways that (as in *Mass Effect 2*) may be determined by the decisions the player made in those works. The Reapers justify their actions as an attempt to preserve intelligent species by incorporating their essential natures into the berserkers' own designs and then making the organic races extinct before they can create the artificial intelligences that will otherwise inevitably destroy them. Ultimately, a galactic alliance can be forged, allowing the player to construct a Prothean superweapon in Earth orbit and deploy it against the invaders, after which they can choose whether to attempt to destroy the enemy, control them, or merge with them. Regardless of the decision made, a sacrifice will be demanded; the mass relay network is destroyed, and the player's character will almost certainly die.

Mass Effect's frequent conversations are represented by an interface that allows the player to select the general tenor of their responses, after which the game supplies their character's actual dialogue.

Considered as a whole, the games of the *Mass Effect* series depict a notably rich and varied fictional galaxy, one amply supplied with distinctive alien species and civilizations. While these works offer far less freedom to roam than do such games as *Fallout: New Vegas* (*2010* OE) designed by Josh Sawyer and John Gonzalez, they instead provide lengthy story arcs with appealing characters who add personal significance to the many choices their players must make. Ultimately, this degree of emotional depth may be incompatible with the license to explore granted by *Fallout: New Vegas*. Regardless, the *Mass Effect* trilogy offers what may be the most impressive evocation of the space opera tradition yet seen in a **videogame**.

Related works: *Mass Effect: Galaxy* (*2009* BioWare) designed by Kevin Barrett is an action game, played in plan view, which follows a biotic super-soldier through a story intended to serve as a prequel to *Mass Effect 2*. *Mass Effect: Infiltrator* (*2012* IronMonkey Studios) is a third-person shooter in which the player must covertly penetrate Cerberus bases and liberate prisoners. Both games received mixed reviews.

The *Mass Effect* games have received frequent and varied expansions. *Bring Down The Sky* (*2008* BioWare) is a pack for the first game, which deals with an alien terrorist group's attempt to drop an asteroid on a human colony world, while *Pinnacle Station* (*2009* BioWare) extends the same work with a set of simulated combat missions. Expansions for *Mass Effect 2* include *Zaeed: The Price of Revenge* (*2010* BioWare) and *Kasumi: Stolen Memory* (*2010* BioWare), which introduce new characters, *Firewalker Pack* (*2010* BioWare), which adds new equipment, and the combat-oriented *Overlord* (*2010* BioWare), in which the player must destroy a rogue artificial intelligence. *Lair of the Shadow Broker* (*2010* BioWare) ties up a loose end from the first game, while *Arrival* (*2011* BioWare) extends the game's major plotline into a prequel for *Mass Effect 3*. Finally, *Normandy Crash Site* (*2010* BioWare) allows the player to visit the remains of the ship destroyed at the beginning of *Mass Effect 2* and erect a memorial to its crew; much additional backstory is revealed.

Several expansions have also been released for *Mass Effect 3*, including *From Ashes* (*2012* BioWare), which features the last remaining Prothean, *Leviathan* (*2012* BioWare), a depiction of a search for the eponymous alien, *Omega* (*2012* BioWare), set on a space station that serves as a haven for criminals, and *Citadel* (*2013* BioWare), which adds various missions occurring in the titular installation. The *Retaliation Multiplayer Expansion* (*2012* BioWare), *Rebellion Multiplayer Expansion* (*2012* BioWare), *Earth Multiplayer Expansion* (*2012* BioWare), *Resurgence Multiplayer Expansion* (*2012* BioWare), and *Reckoning Multiplayer Expansion* (*2013* BioWare) contain additional equipment and areas for use in competitive online play, while the *Firefight Pack* (*2012* BioWare) and *Groundside Resistance Pack* (*2012* BioWare) include new weapons to be used by a single player. Finally, the *Extended Cut* (*2012* BioWare) is a free expansion that adds further detail to the ending of the original game.

Drew Karpyshyn, lead writer for the first two games in the main series, has published three novels set in the milieu. *Mass Effect: Revelation* (**2007**) is a prequel to *Mass Effect*, which expands significantly on its backstory, while *Mass Effect: Ascension* (**2008**), set after the end of that game, concentrates on humanity's research into the mental powers derived from the titular effect, and *Mass Effect: Retribution* (**2010**) is a sequel to *Mass Effect 2*, which follows a secret Cerberus program intended to fuse a human test subject with berserker technology. These books were followed by *Mass Effect: Deception* (**2012**) by William C. Dietz, a prequel to *Mass Effect 3*, which received generally poor reviews. Various spin-off comics have been published by Dark Horse, including *Mass Effect: Redemption* (*2010*), *Mass Effect: Evolution* (*2011*), *Mass Effect: Invasion* (*2011–2012*), *Mass Effect: Homeworlds* (*2012*), and *Mass Effect: Foundation* (*2013*–current); all are written by Mac Walters, lead writer on *Mass Effect 3*. Finally, *Mass Effect: Paragon Lost* (*2012*) is an animated film that serves as a prequel to *Mass Effect 2*.

Web Link

- *Mass Effect*: http://masseffect.bioware.com/

MEGATRAVELLER

Series (from 1990). PS.

The publication of the original edition of *Traveller* (*1977* GDW) designed by Marc Miller launched what is probably the most commercially successful science-fictional tabletop **role playing game** franchise to date. Initially, the *Traveller* rules were intended as a generic system for running science fiction adventures, with the universe of the **Third Imperium** provided as an optional setting. In practice, however, this milieu proved to be highly popular, while the details of the original mechanics have now been largely forgotten. The **Third Imperium** is part of a tradition of **hard sf**-based romantic space adventure (described as "Ruritanian space opera" by the critic Gary Westfahl in the 2003 *Cambridge Companion to Science Fiction*), which may have reached its peak in the written genre in the years immediately before the first publication of the game; Poul Anderson's **Technic History** could be seen as epitomizing the form. Acknowledged influences on the **Third Imperium** include E. C. Tubb's **Dumarest** series as well as the **Technic History**; others can be inferred, notably H. Beam Piper's *Space Viking* (**1963**), Jerry Pournelle's **CoDominium** sequence, and Andre Norton's **Free Traders** and (perhaps) her *Star Rangers* (**1953**; also known as *The Last Planet*). More recently, Walter Jon Williams' **Dread Empire's Fall** and the television series *Firefly* (*2002*) demonstrate the continuing vitality of this kind of sf. It is significant that none of these works explore recent science-fictional themes such as **nanotechnology** or **posthumanism**; current versions of the *Traveller* rules explicitly suggest that such elements should be excluded, in order to maintain the feel of the game.

In the distant past of the **Third Imperium**, a **forerunner** species (the "Ancients") transplanted early humans to a wide variety of other worlds. One of these groups, the Vilani, developed a high level of civilization and a **faster than light** drive thousands of years before humans on Earth, and formed a galactic empire in which Vilani nobles ruled a feudal society of humans scattered by the Ancients. The Vilani empire lasted for more than fifteen centuries, but collapsed in a series of Interstellar Wars after contact was made with the Solomani, Earth humans who had independently discovered faster than light travel. The Second Imperium, formed by the Solomani military to rule the conquered territories, also disintegrated, and interstellar humanity fell into a **long night** of barbarism until the establishment of the **Third Imperium**. Most editions of the game are set in the fifty-seventh century CE, a Golden Age when this empire is at its zenith. Other interstellar groups exist, including the Zhodani Consulate (a separate human society that makes extensive use of **psionics**), the Hivers (a radically alien, and largely nonviolent, species that deters potential aggressors with the threat of **psychohistoric** retaliation), the lion-like Aslan race, and the Vargr, descended from Earth wolves **uplifted** by the Ancients, but none of them present a serious threat to the Imperium.

The second edition of the **RPG** rules was published as *MegaTraveller* (*1986* GDW) designed by Marc Miller, created collaboratively by GDW and Digest Group Publications. Perhaps the most important change made in this version was the introduction of a state of civil war within the Imperium, after the apparent assassination of its Emperor triggered a chaotic struggle for power. This addressed a perceived flaw in the design of the original game, by making it possible to have adventures featuring military actions and open clashes between armed groups within the borders of the Imperium as well as on its fringe. Two **computer role playing games** were developed by Paragon using the *MegaTraveller* ruleset with several different displays, of which the most common is a **2D** overhead view. Despite the inclusion of the *MegaTraveller* version of the RPG's mechanics, however, the games appear to take place in the Golden Age setting of the original *Traveller* rather than the fragmented Imperium of its successor. The first entry in the series, the somewhat frustrating *The Zhodani Conspiracy*

(*1990* PS) designed by Jane Yeager and Christopher Straka, concentrates on **real-time** combat and the details of character simulation. A brief **linear** story line depicts a plot against the Imperium, which can be resolved by hunting down a Zhodani spy, while various **modular** subplots encourage the exploration of a large number of (somewhat shallowly depicted) solar systems. The sequel, *Quest for the Ancients* (*1991* PS) designed by Glenn Dill, F J Lennon, and Marc Miller, is generally superior, though still strongly focused on combat. The highly modular plot revolves around the need to discover more about the titular forerunner race before a mysteriously reactivated artifact destroys a human colony world. This work benefits both from improvements made to its combat system and interface as a result of experience with its predecessor and from a markedly more interesting and better developed story than that of the original **videogame**.

Related works: Various other iterations of the core RPG exist as well as a number of associated games and spin-off novels. Several (partial) bibliographies are noted in the following. In the world of videogames, *StarCrystal I – Mertactor: The Volentine Gambit* (*1985* Ba'rac Limited), designed by Terry Gray, Jeff Billings, Ken Maniscalco, and Jim Long, is a text **adventure** set in the era of the original *Traveller* game. While its presentation of the background is impressively detailed, various technical faults make it a somewhat frustrating game to play. *Traveller AR* (*2011* ingZ) is an unfinished **space sim**, apparently also set in the Golden Age, which is played in a persistent **online world**. The "AR" refers to "augmented reality" (in which simulated objects from the game are overlaid on the real world as seen through a digital camera), though the game's actual use of this technology seems somewhat superficial.

FURTHER READING

- Timothy Collinson. *The Traveller Bibliography*. 1997. (Details *Traveller* game publications.)

Web Links

- *Traveller AR*: http://www.traveller-ar.com/

- *Traveller* Bibliography: http://www.travellerbibliography.org/

MOTHER

Series (from 1989). Nintendo. Designed by Shigesato Itoi.

Mother is a series of Japanese **console role playing games**, beginning with the **3D isometric** view *Mother* (*1989* Nintendo) designed by

Shigesato Itoi. This game, released only in Japan, follows the adventures of a young boy who travels around the world finding friends with special talents, often **psi powers**, and collecting eight melodies with which to save humanity from Giygas, leader of an alien race whose members can control human minds (and a possible reference to Gary Gygax, primary creator of the tabletop **role playing game** *Dungeons and Dragons*). The second game, *Mother 2* (*1994* Nintendo; also known as *EarthBound* in the United States) designed by Shigesato Itoi is a sequel that largely repeats the first game's plot, displayed in an oblique view that gives the illusion of three dimensions. This iteration of the series begins with a young boy who is visited by an alien from a future where Giygas has returned and conquered the Earth. The player, in the role of the boy, must gather a group of friends with similar gifts and personalities to those seen in the first game. With their assistance, he can visit eight sacred places where he can amplify his own psychic powers, allowing him to finally confront and defeat Giygas.

The *Mother* games are unusual among Japanese **CRPGs** both for being set in a broadly modern-day milieu, with sf elements, and for their irreverent sense of humor. While the gameplay is fairly conventional for a console role playing game, depending on a mixture of puzzle solution, exploration, combat, and character interaction, the series satirizes the clichés seen in many similar fantasy games, with characters using baseball bats as weapons against evil hippies and dangerous table lamps. *Mother* and *EarthBound* are set in a twisted version of America, a fantastic dream of the West, which combines the fairy tale world of *Little House on the Prairie* (*1974–1983*) with aliens and **psionic** powers. Much importance is attached to friends and family; in *Mother 2*, the main character's mother can always be found at home, and sessions are saved by telephoning his permanently absent father. In essence, the first two *Mother* games tell children's stories that are eminently suitable for adults.

Related works: *Mother 3* (*2006* Nintendo) designed by Shigesato Itoi is a further sequel, using a **2D** overhead view and currently released only in Japan. Its story is darker and more adult, with multiple viewpoint characters. The plot is based on an invasion of "Nowhere Island" by an army wearing pig masks, who introduce disruptive technology into a rural paradise.

Web Link
- starmen.net (Tribute Site): http://starmen.net/

PHANTASY STAR

1987. (Also known as *Phantasy Star Collection*.) Sega. Designed by Rieko Kodama and Yuji Naka.

Phantasy Star was one of the earliest **console role playing games** and was influential on the development of the unique characteristics of the form. Both this game and its contemporary *Final Fantasy II* (*1988* Square) designed by Hironobu Sakaguchi and Akitoshi Kawazu added a greater depth of characterization to the formula established by *Dragon Quest* (*1986* Enix), a vital element in the **linear** narratives of their various descendants, though *Phantasy Star*'s story is still best described as rudimentary. *Phantasy Star* is also the first example of a console role playing game that could be described as clearly science fictional in nature. The game is set in the Algol star system, a **science fantasy** milieu much influenced by *Star Wars*, mixing medieval romanticism with such sf elements as **psionics** and interplanetary travel. In the opening sequence, a young woman sees her brother murdered by the **cyborg** soldiers of her planet's King. The player—adopting the persona of the surviving sister—sets out to avenge the victim, eventually encountering a range of other playable characters (including a talking cat named Myau) and a mystical personification of pure evil that is the power behind the throne. As with many early **computer role playing games**, *Phantasy Star* uses a combination of a **2D** overhead map and a limited **3D** view to display events. Actual gameplay is somewhat repetitive, emphasizing **turn-based** combat to a much greater degree than that seen in most later examples of the form. The game was remade with much improved dialogue and characterization as *Phantasy Star Generation 1* (*2003* Japan Art Media), though to date this version has only been released in Japan.

The original game had three sequels. *Phantasy Star II* (*1989* Sega; also known as *Phantasy Star II: The End of the Lost Age* in Japan; also known as *Phantasy Star Collection*) designed by Akinori Nishiyama and Yuji Naka is set 1000 years after *Phantasy Star*, when a computer network that controls much of the technology in the Algol system has begun to malfunction for unknown reasons, devastating the ecology of a **terraformed** world. The gameplay combines exploration and combat in a uniformly 2D display, while the story is markedly more detailed than that of its predecessor, though still somewhat unsophisticated. This game was remade for a Japanese-only release as *Phantasy Star Generation 2* (*2005* 3D Ages), with similar enhancements to those made for *Phantasy Star Generation 1*.

The next installment, *Phantasy Star III: Generations of Doom* (*1990* Sega; also known as *Phantasy Star Collection*) designed by Hirota Saeki and Yang Watt, is a more innovative design, with a story that follows a single family over three generations. It is set on a pseudo-medieval colony world outside the Algol system, founded by refugees from a planet devastated in *Phantasy Star II* who split into two warring factions soon after their arrival. At the end of each generation of the story, the player's main character must choose which of several possible candidates they will marry, thus determining the identity of the protagonist in the next generation. The eventual goal is to find a path through the **multilinear** branches of the story that will bring peace to both factions. Finally, *Phantasy Star IV: The End of the Millennium* (*1993* Sega) designed by Rieko Kodama, Toru Yoshida, and Toru Yoshida is a more conventional sequel to *Phantasy Star II*. While the gameplay is generally similar to that of the second game, the linear story is much deeper. The setting returns to the Algol system, where a new but equally cataclysmic threat must be defeated. With its appealing if roughly sketched characters and frequent references to the background established in the first two games, *The End of the Millennium* presents what is undoubtedly the most involving narrative in the *Phantasy Star* series.

The release of *Phantasy Star Online* (*2000* Sega; *2002* revised as *Phantasy Star Online Ver 2*; *2002* revised as *Phantasy Star Online Episode I & II*; *2004* revised as *Phantasy Star Online Episode I & II Plus*) designed by Yoshihiro Sakuta marked a radical change of direction for the series. While all previous *Phantasy Star* games had been intended for a single player, *Phantasy Star Online* was the first attempt to make a **massively multiplayer online role playing game** for home consoles rather than personal computers. Interestingly, the game also allows players from different cultures to interact using simple pretranslated phrases that can be combined into messages without using a keyboard, though this feature received mixed reviews. The game is set in a different solar system to the earlier works in the series, one in which the members of an interstellar expedition have begun colonizing a new world after fleeing the imminent destruction of their own. As the players' ship arrives, however, the initial exploratory mission on the planet's surface mysteriously explodes. This setup leads into a story-based single-player game, with a simple and somewhat derivative plot concentrating on **real-time** combat displayed in a 3D view. As an **MMORPG**, however, the gameplay focuses on four-player teams participating in the story together, in their own private **online worlds**. This aspect of the game could almost be described as the epitome of a combat-oriented "dungeon crawl" of the type often seen in pen and paper **role playing game** adventures from the 1970s, featuring frequent battles, occasional traps, and little in the way of conversation.

While the original game was expanded by a second episode, later included in revised releases, *Phantasy Star Online Episode III: C.A.R.D. Revolution* (*2004* Sega) designed by Yuji Naka makes so many alterations to the earlier versions as to essentially constitute a separate work. Set two decades after the initial colonization attempt during a period of civil war, it uses a turn-based system based on a virtual **collectible card game** to represent combat, with characters positioned on a regular 3D grid. The gameplay continues to focus largely on physical conflict, however. *Phantasy Star Online: Blue Burst* (*2005* Sega) returns to the initial concept, including the content from the original and the second episode as well as new material. *Phantasy Star Universe* (*2006* Sega) was then launched as a replacement for the first game, the multiplayer aspects of which were shut down in 2007–2008. *Universe* is set in a third solar system in the shared galaxy of the *Phantasy Star* games, one which is being invaded by an army of alien monsters; the gameplay is again similar to that of *Phantasy Star Online*. *Phantasy Star Universe: Ambition of the Illuminus* (*2007* Sega) is an expansion, based on a conflict with a group of "human supremacists."

Related works: Several games associated with the original *Phantasy Star* series were only released in Japan. *Phantasy Star Gaiden* (*1992* Japan System Supply) is a console role playing game with similar gameplay to *Phantasy Star II*, dealing with the later life of the protagonist of *Phantasy Star* on a colony world she founds outside the Algol system. *Phantasy Star Adventure* (*1992* Sega) is a menu-driven illustrated text **adventure** with some **CRPG** elements, the story of which is contemporaneous with *Phantasy Star II*. The *Phantasy Star II Text Adventures* (*1990* Sega) is a series of eight illustrated text adventures, which act as prequels to *Phantasy Star II*; each one further develops the background of one of that game's major characters.

Phantasy Star 0 (*2009* Sega; also known as *Phantasy Star ZERO*) is similar to *Phantasy Star Online*, but is available on a handheld device. *Phantasy Star Portable* (*2009* AlfaSystem/Sega) and *Phantasy Star Portable 2* (*2010* AlfaSystem/Sega) are again similar, but act as sequels to *Phantasy Star Universe*. An expansion pack for the latter game, *Phantasy Star Portable 2 Infinity* (*2011* Alfa System/Sega), was only released in Japan.

Web Link
- *Phantasy Star* Tribute Site: http://www.phantasy-star.net/

RESONANCE OF FATE

2010. (Also known as *End of Eternity* in Japan.) tri-Ace. Designed by Takayuki Suguro.

Resonance of Fate is a **console role playing game** set on a far future Earth whose environment has been ruined by toxic gases. Survivors persist inside a stratospheric tower that functions as an air purifier; effectively, this structure is a gigantic **arcology**. Outside the tower, mutants have evolved to endure the poisonous atmosphere; within it, an intelligent machine has become humanity's God. The game concentrates on the lives of three playable characters, a trio of drifters who can be hired to perform a variety of dubious jobs, from couriering to killing. Initially, these apparently unconnected missions occupy most of the player's time, but eventually a more fundamental story emerges in which the characters follow a largely **linear** plot in the present while their tortured pasts are revealed as **embedded interactive narratives**. There is much opportunity for stylish gunplay; the combat mechanics are unusual and somewhat obscure, but players who have achieved mastery find them to be both tactically interesting and visually dramatic.

Throughout, the game's narrative is suffused with a lushly overwrought romanticism. Its characters are vividly, if somewhat stereotypically, drawn; sulky, pretty teenagers abound, as do doomed and moody villains. Visually, *Resonance of Fate* offers a striking (if sometimes repetitive) vision of humanity's last city, a crowded retro-Victorian complex created within a structure belonging to what appears to be a far higher level of technology. At the end, the player can unravel the various conspiracies that underlie their characters' origins, and escape with them to the outside, which has again become a place where humans can live. Unknown to the population of the spire, it seems, its machinery has **terraformed** the Earth.

ROGUE GALAXY

2005. Level 5. Designed by Akihiro Hino, Koji Hori, and Takeshi Akasaka.

Rogue Galaxy is a **console role playing game**, much influenced by *Star Wars*, but with the tone of a young adult **anime**. The game's somewhat cliché-ridden plot features aliens, robots, and a spaceship whose first mate is a talking cat, all within an essentially **linear** structure to which various optional activities and peripheral missions have been added. The spine of this story takes the form of a galactic odyssey in which the primary character—the eponymous Jaster Rogue, a mysterious orphan from a desert world—is mistaken for a famous bounty hunter and recruited by a pirate captain who is looking for a legendary lost planet. Eventually, the player can rescue this world, which is trapped outside time, and bring about a state of universal peace, while discovering various characters' true identities as hidden royalty. There is a great deal of well-crafted swordplay, which the player participates in using a fast-paced combat system in which points must be expended to engage in actions in **real time**, as well as sophisticated mechanics for creating new types of equipment and weapons, either from scratch or by combining existing items. Ultimately, the nature of *Rogue Galaxy*'s milieu suggests not so much **science and sorcery** as epic fantasy in space. Notably, the player's starship resembles a naval galleon that has been equipped with rocket engines and a **faster than light** drive in addition to the more traditional sails and rigging. The overall effect is somewhat reminiscent of the *Dungeons and Dragons* setting of **Spelljammer**, in which magically empowered ships sail through pseudo-Aristotelian crystal spheres, though the **role playing game**'s background seems better rationalized.

SENTINEL WORLDS

Series (from 1988). Designed by Karl Buiter.

Sentinel Worlds is the name used by this book to refer to a sequence of two **computer role playing games** set in similar, though probably not identical, **space opera** milieux. Both borrow design elements from **space sims**, as do several other contemporary games including *Starflight* (*1986* BS) and *Space Rogue* (*1989* OS) designed by Paul Neurath. The gameplay of the *Sentinel Worlds* series thus combines exploration, conversation, and combat on planetary surfaces and on board ships, displayed in both **3D** and **2D** overhead views, with **realtime** space battles and other activities such as asteroid mining (in the first game) and interplanetary smuggling (in the second). Much of the games' shared background appears to be derived from the tabletop **RPG** *Traveller* (*1977* GDW) designed by Marc Miller, with some aspects drawn from the original *Star Trek* TV series (*1966–1969*) and E E Smith's **Lensman** books.

Sentinel Worlds I: Future Magic (*1988* Electronic Arts) designed by Karl Buiter, the first game in the sequence, allows the player to control a military team sent to a remote star system and ordered to hunt down the mysterious spacecraft, which appear, apparently from nowhere, to destroy harmless merchant vessels. While the setting is somewhat generic and the game's interface can be awkward, the partially **modular** plot is ingeniously constructed. After a slow start, players can become involved in a range war on a frontier world, scientific research in a frozen wasteland, and disputes between tribes of primitive humans. Eventually, the titular secret masters of the system are revealed, and the game ends with a literal battle of minds.

While *Hard Nova* (*1990* Malibu Interactive) designed by Karl Buiter, Eric Lindstrom, and Jeff Haas does not appear to share a setting with *Sentinel Worlds I*, there are many similarities, notably in weapons technology. Players adopt the role of the eponymous character, a mercenary who is by default female, and somewhat suggestive of many of the protagonists of C J Cherryh's **Merchanters** books. In this identity, a player can recruit other mercenaries to crew their ship, in which they can participate in conflicts between the various factions occupying a group of newly settled star systems. The gameplay is similar to that of the first game, but the presentation is generally superior, with greater use made of 3D displays. Various missions can be completed by the mercenaries, including an assassination and the prevention of a hijacking, but players are likely to rapidly become involved in a largely **linear** plot, which deals with an alien invasion mounted through an unexplored **wormhole**. This story, the major narrative of the game, ends with the first use of a sun igniting superweapon; the player must choose whether this device is employed to kindle a new sun (thus reviving the invaders' dying homeworld and removing the reason for their invasion) or to convert the aliens' old, dying star into a supernova, rendering them extinct.

SEPTERRA CORE: LEGACY OF THE CREATOR

1999. Valkyrie Studios. Designed by Brian Babendererde.

Septerra Core is a **computer role playing game** played in an **isometric 3D** perspective, with a design heavily influenced by Japanese console games such as the *Final Fantasy* series. It is set on an alternate **science and sorcery** world called Septerra, where seven continents, or shells, orbit an inaccessible center. At rare intervals, the planetary clockwork aligns in such a way that the hidden core can be reached, and its legacy unlocked; this reward is believed to bestow godlike powers. Each shell is radically distinct from the rest. The arrogant Chosen rule the first, while the player's primary character, Maya, lives on shell two, whose inhabitants form a literal underclass, subsisting on the mechanical junk thrown out by their superiors from shell one. After a slightly aimless start, Maya soon becomes involved in a renegade Chosen's attempt to unlock the core before the scheduled time. A variety of characters, from a robot dog to a member of the Chosen, may join her; all of these computer-controlled individuals have their own histories and strong personalities.

The setting is perhaps the true protagonist of *Septerra Core*. There is a real **sense of wonder** in the journey through the seven shells, reminiscent of the ascent of **The World of Tiers** in Philip José Farmer's novel *The Maker of Universes* (**1965**). The appeal is, however, somewhat diluted by the **linear** plot's requirement that several shells be crossed more than once, especially as much of the player's time during later visits is spent fighting. Gameplay elements include a partially **turn-based** combat system, puzzles, and a magic system based on Fate cards, which resemble the Tarot arcana; interesting results can be obtained by combining cards in a simple grammar. Thematically, the game is grimmer and more adult than such influences as *Final Fantasy VII* (*1997* Square). In the end, the characters reach the living computer at Septerra's Core and the legacy is revealed, leading to a transformation of the world.

SHADOWRUN

Franchise (from 1993). FASA (Freedonian Aeronautics and Space Administration).

The setting for the *Shadowrun* tabletop **role playing game** (*1989* FASA; revised *1992*; revised *1998*; revised *2005*; revised *2013*) designed by Robert N. Charrette, Tom Dowd, and Paul Hume is a curious **science and sorcery** fusion of high fantasy and **cyberpunk**, an innovation that greatly appealed to many players but inspired adverse comments on its aesthetics from, among others, the cyberpunk author William Gibson. Some aspects of the design are closely based on actual technology and history, notably the rules for handling shamanic magic and **cyberspace**, but the primary influences on the game are literary. In the **future history** posited by the designers, a magical "Awakening" occurs in the twenty-first century, after which North America fragments into tribal nations, nonhuman homelands (occupied by such species as Elves and Orks), and high-technology cities dominated by large corporations. Low-intensity warfare between these factions is common, fought by mercenary "shadowrunners" (among whom will be found most of the players' characters). The setting does demonstrate a strong sense of style, reveling in such elegant conceits as the threat to air travel posed by terrorist dragons.

Three separate **console role playing games** have been created in the milieu, each one for a different games machine: the **isometric** *Shadowrun* (*1993* Beam Software) designed by Gregg Barnett and the fantasy writer Paul Kidd for the Super Nintendo Entertainment System, the **2D** plan view *Shadowrun* (*1994* BlueSky Software) designed by Scott Berfield, John Fulbright, Heinrich Michaels, and Tony Van for the Sega MegaDrive (also known as the Sega Genesis), and the plan view *Shadowrun* (*1996* Compile) designed by Takafumi Tanida, Akira Egawa, and Shinobu Murakawa for the Sega MegaCD. In Beam Software's game, which is arguably the most interesting of the three, the player is encouraged to participate in a broadly **linear** plot, which begins with the resurrection of a murdered shadowrunner in Seattle (the suggested starting point for players of the pen and paper **RPG**). Despite placing considerable emphasis on **real-time** combat and suffering from a somewhat awkward interface, the game's noir atmosphere and involving plot make playing it an intriguing experience. The 1994 *Shadowrun*, on the other hand, concentrates on providing a detailed simulation of the player's character, with a design that closely follows the mechanics of its tabletop original, in the manner of most contemporary **computer role playing games**. Here, a largely **modular** story, also set in Seattle, revolves around the protagonist's investigations of the death of his brother. Finally, the MegaCD game, which was only released in Japan, is a **turn-based** work with an episodic linear story line, set in "Neo Tokyo." This game seems distinctly Eastern in approach; its design is reminiscent of both contemporary members of the *Final Fantasy* series and menu-driven **adventures**, while the narrative and characters are based on a **manga**, which was licensed from a Japanese version of the pen and paper RPG.

Shadowrun was revived in 2007 by Microsoft's FASA Studio as another (eponymous) **videogame**, this time designed by John Howard and Sage Merrill. This iteration of the franchise is a **first person shooter** set in an alternate version of the RPG's history, during a period of transition between the present day and a fully magical reality. The **FPS** (first person shooter) received highly mixed reviews, partly due to the absence of any story line that could be played through by a single participant; only competitive games against opponents controlled by the computer or online players are possible. The next attempt to reinvigorate the franchise was very different. *Shadowrun Returns* (*2013* HareBrained Schemes) designed by Jordan Weisman and Mitch Gitelman is an isometric turn-based **CRPG** set firmly within the tabletop milieu, with a detailed implementation of the pen and paper game's mechanics resembling that of BlueSky's 1994 effort. Narratively, the game presents a highly linear plot in which the murder of an old friend of the player's character at the hands of a serial killer turns out to be only the first clue to a deadly New Age conspiracy; there is much colorful (and often deliberately clichéd) dialogue. This story line could be described as a loose sequel to that of Beam Software's game, whose protagonist makes several appearances, though the 2013 iteration treats sex and drugs in a far more adult manner than was possible in an early 1990s console game, for which the primary market was young adults.

Perhaps the most significant aspect of *Shadowrun Returns* is its demonstration of how to make an effective CRPG with limited resources. Funding was obtained from the *Shadowrun* fan community via the "crowdsourcing" website Kickstarter, and used to build a work that is supplied with a relatively small amount of content, but which comes with a sophisticated realization of the RPG's core rules and editors designed to make it easy for enthusiasts to add their own contributions. If this strategy proves successful, the final game is likely to owe as much to the work of its dedicated fans as to that of its professional developers. Regardless, it seems likely that this game and the upcoming *Shadowrun Online*, another product of Kickstarter that will be set in a persistent **online world**, will restore some of the luster, which the series lost after the release of the Microsoft FPS.

Related works: The original tabletop game is loosely associated with the fantasy RPG *Earthdawn* (*1993* FASA; revised *1994*; revised *2001*; revised *2009*) designed by Greg Gorden and Louis Prosperi, which is set in a prehistoric era that may correspond to the distant past of the *Shadowrun* milieu. *Shadowrun: The Trading Card Game* (*1997* FASA) designed by Mike Nielson is a **collectible card game** based on the franchise, while *Shadowrun Duels* (*2003* WizKids) designed by Kevin Barrett and Jordan Weisman was a commercially unsuccessful **collectible miniatures game**. *Shadowrun: Downtown Militarized Zone* (*1990* FASA) is a tabletop **wargame** that depicts personal combat in urban environments. *1–800-Magic* (*2007*) is an amusing **machinima** based on the FPS, made by Rooster Teeth Productions. In addition, more than 40 *Shadowrun*-related novels have been published, beginning with *Never Deal with a Dragon* (**1990**) by Robert N. Charrette, which was also the inspiration for the story line of Beam Software's 1993 videogame.

Web Link

- *Shadowrun* Universe: http://www.shadowrun.com/

SPACE

1979. ES. Designed by Steven Pederson and Sherwin Steffin.

Space was the first science-fictional **computer role playing game** to be made available commercially. Its design was very much influenced by the pen and paper **RPG** *Traveller* (*1977* GDW) designed by Marc Miller, to the extent that both it and its sequel were removed from sale in 1982 following a lawsuit by GDW for unauthorized use of their intellectual property. The largely text-based gameplay involves playing through the early life of a character serving in the military forces of a far future galactic empire and then choosing various scenarios to participate in; options include planetary exploration, interstellar trading, financial speculation, and defending against an alien invasion. These modules are essentially unconnected, but can be played through in sequence to create the appearance of a long and varied life lived in a diverse interstellar society. The final effect of the design can be quite frustrating, however, since the implementation seems somewhat erratic, and characters generated by the system are frequently severely disabled and tend to die before they have completed training. This feature is also found in the first edition of *Traveller*—one of the few RPGs in which a character can die before their player has finished creating them—but is much amplified in *Space*, perhaps in an attempt to extend the length of the game. The sequel, *Space II* (*1979* ES) designed by David Mullich, is broadly similar, but presents two new scenarios based on propagating a religious cult and experimenting with psychedelic drugs. In what could be considered a prototype for the design of many later **CRPG** series, participants can either continue using their character from the first game or create a new one and start afresh.

SPACE: 1889

1990. PS. Designed by F J Lennon, Steve Suhy, and Don Wuenschell.

The *Space: 1889* tabletop **role playing game** (*1988* GDW) designed by Frank Chadwick is an early example of **steampunk**, set in an **alternate history** whose central conceit is that many of the now discarded scientific theories of the Victorian age were actually correct. So, in this universe, Thomas Edison invents an "ether propeller" and uses it to travel to Mars in 1870. By 1889, the Great Powers of the nineteenth century have expanded into space and begun to colonize the worlds of the inner solar system.

Many of the planets in the game are analogs of continents on Earth during the Victorian era. Thus, Venus, a savage jungle populated by primitive lizardmen, resembles the colonial view of Africa; Mars, a patchwork of warring ancient cultures, references India, and Mercury, on which the only habitable land borders a world girdling river between the superheated Day Side and the frozen Night Side, is arguably analogous to Antarctica. The inner planets also express a pseudoscientific theory of evolution, in which life evolves along a single path from the dinosaurs of Venus through the mammals of Earth to the multiple intelligent species of Mars. The classic archetypes of steampunk fiction—mad anarchists, eccentric scientists, upright adventurers, and daring adventuresses—provide a colorful population for the setting, though much emphasis is also placed on exotic devices, from orbiting interplanetary heliographs to steam powered aerial warships.

The **videogame** *Space: 1889* is an excellently crafted **computer role playing game**, displayed in the then conventional **2D** plan view. There is a **linear** primary plot dealing with a quest for immortality, which leads players from Egypt to a hidden world beneath the North Pole by way of Mars, Venus, the Moon, Mercury, Jupiter, and the lost city of Atlantis, as well as various optional story lines arranged in a **modular** fashion. Overall, the game is notably more successful than the same developers' *MegaTraveller* licenses, offering some vividly drawn characters (including the circus proprietor Phineas T. Barnum and the early sf writer Jules Verne), interesting puzzles, and the opportunity to explore a rich variety of exotic locales.

Related works: A variety of tabletop **wargames** were released in association with the **RPG**, including *Sky Galleons of Mars* (*1988* GDW) designed by Frank Chadwick, Loren Wiseman, and Marc Miller and its expansion *Cloudships and Gunboats* (*1989* GDW) designed by Frank Chadwick, as well as *Ironclads and Ether Flyers* (*1990* GDW) designed by Frank Chadwick and the miniature figures-based *The Soldier's Companion* (*1989* GDW). *Temple of the Beastmen* (*1989* GDW) designed by Frank Chadwick and Lester Smith is a board game in which players participate in a rescue expedition within the mines of a Martian King, while *Space 1889: Red Sands* (*2010* Pinnacle Entertainment Group [PEG]) designed by William Reger, Clint Black, Matthew Cutter, Joel Kinstle, Piotr Koryś, and Tony Lee is a version of the setting, which can be used with the pen and paper RPG system *Savage Worlds* (*2003* PEG; revised *2005*; revised *2007*; revised *2011*) designed by Shane Lacy Hensley.

Four audio plays associated with the setting have been produced by Noise Monster Productions: *Red Devils* (*2005*) by Jonathan Clements; *The Steppes of Thoth* (*2005*) by James Swallow; *The Siege of Alclyon* (*2005*) by Marc Platt; and *The Lunar Inheritance* (*2005*) by Richard Dinnick and Andy Frankham-Allen, of which the first three make up the *Arina Stone* trilogy. In addition, a series of e-book **ties** are being published by Untreed Reads. A first sequence comprises *Journey to the Heart of Luna* (**2011**) by Andy Frankham-Allen, *Vandals on Venus* (**2011**) by K G McAbee, *Ghosts of Mercury* (**2011**) by Mark Michalowski, *Abattoir in the Aether* (**2012**) by L. Joseph Shosty, *A Prince of Mars* (**2012**) by Frank Chadwick, and *Dark Side of Luna* (**2012**) by Chadwick and J T Wilson. Another series was then begun with *Conspiracy of Silence* (**2012**), by Frankham-Allen and Chadwick, and continued in *Mundus Cerialis* (**2012**), by Frankham-Allen and Sharon Bidwell.

STARFLIGHT

1986. BS.

Starflight is perhaps best described as a **2D computer role playing game** set on a starship. The game begins on a planet known as Arth, which is inhabited by a mix of species, including humans. A spacecraft of unknown origin has recently been discovered during an archaeological dig, and a company has reverse engineered the ship's **faster than light** drive to create their own starships. Players begin the game by selecting a crew and equipping their vessel; this ship is then launched into space on a voyage of exploration, with the proviso that it must make a profit by mining rare resources and selling any alien artifacts the adventurers might find. As the game progresses, players can upgrade their starships and train their crews to higher levels of proficiency.

Starflight's universe is noticeably influenced by that of the television series *Star Trek* (*1966–1969*), and the game's mixture of exploration, diplomacy with quirky alien races, and occasional combat is strikingly successful at enabling imaginative players to experience stories similar to those of its model. The most interesting aspect of *Starflight*, however, is the **embedded** backstory, which is gradually revealed as players move deeper into the game. Conversations with alien races will eventually reveal that Arth is a lost colony of a galactic empire and that the enemy that destroyed that empire is still at large. Eventually, players find themselves responsible for saving Arth itself from destruction, a mission that requires them to learn the secret history of the galaxy.

Related works: *Starflight 2: Trade Routes of the Cloud Nebula* (*1989* BS) is a sequel, set in another galaxy reached via a **wormhole**, whose complex plot involves travel to several different time periods. It adds the ability to trade with alien races and some new weapons and technology, but is otherwise broadly similar in gameplay.

Web Link
- Starflight Resource Pages (Tribute Site): http://www.starflt.com/

STAR OCEAN

Series (from 1996). tri-Ace.

Star Ocean is a series of Japanese **console role playing games**, set in a universe heavily influenced by that of *Star Trek*. In addition to the sf elements, a form of alchemical magic often makes an appearance, variously referred to as symbology, heraldry, and runology. While this suggests that the *Star Ocean* games should be classified as **science and sorcery**, the ending of *Star Ocean: Till the End of Time* may justify the magical aspects in sf terms. An interesting repeated theme is the association of Christian symbols with evil, as in *Star Ocean: The Second Story*, where the ultimate antagonists bear the names of angels; this motif has often been censored in English translations of the series. The gameplay is a mixture of conversation, exploration, and combat, as is common in the form, though the *Star Ocean* games are distinguished by their use of a **real-time** combat system, in contrast to the **turn-based** approach favored by most examples of the type.

The first game, *Star Ocean* (*1996* tri-Ace; *2007* revised as *Star Ocean: First Departure*), was initially only released in Japan; the 2007 remake, however, is available worldwide. The player's primary character is a young boy on an undeveloped planet who meets the crew of an Earth Federation starship while searching for a cure for a lethal disease. Eventually, it emerges that the disease is caused by an alien race at war with the Federation; in order to find the remedy, a group of characters must travel through a Time Gate to obtain a sample of the blood used to create the virus. In essence, *Star Ocean* is a somewhat generic console role playing game, set in a largely medieval milieu and focusing on character interaction and often repetitive combat, displayed in a **2D** overhead view. The sequel, *Star Ocean: The Second Story* (*1998* tri-Ace; *2008* revised as *Star Ocean: Second Evolution*), was the first game in the series to be translated into English; it largely repeats the gameplay and themes of its predecessor. Two main characters are available: the teenage son of a character from the original game, who is instantaneously transported to the undeveloped planet of Expel while examining an alien artifact, and the girl he meets there. The plot is broadly **linear**, with some branches depending on which major character is used; it initially focuses on the search for the impact site of a meteorite that appears to be responsible for a series of natural disasters on Expel. As in many early Japanese **CRPGs**, the characters in *Star Ocean: The Second Story* can seem curiously childlike.

Star Ocean: Till the End of Time (2003 tri-Ace) is perhaps the most interesting game in the series. Set 200 years after *Star Ocean: The Second Story*, it uses **3D** graphics to tell the story of Fayt Leingod, a young wastrel from Earth who crashes on a primitive planet after the Federation is attacked by powerful aliens. The linear narrative guides the player through a long and winding story involving a great deal of combat; ultimately, it is revealed that the Federation's scientific research into the nature of symbology has angered the Creator, who has decided that reality itself must be destroyed. Fayt and several other characters are products of the Federation's research, and have been symbologically altered to enable them to reach the higher dimension in which the Creator resides. The alien attack that begins the game was intended to capture Fayt, in the hope that the Creator could be placated if he was surrendered to its angelic minions. On arriving in the higher space, the characters discover that their entire universe is a computer game, a form of **massively multiplayer online game** played by the residents of the parent reality. Symbology allows the inhabitants of the simulation—in which all previous *Star Ocean* games have occurred—to break through the fourth wall separating them from their creators, and thus must be suppressed. The characters fight their Gods, and win, but fail to prevent one of them turning off the *Star Ocean* universe. However, shutting down the simulation mysteriously fails to destroy the reality in which the games take place, perhaps because symbology has allowed the simulated inhabitants to reach some form of transcendence, or perhaps because the characters have become too "real" to be simply switched off.

Related works: *Star Ocean: The Last Hope* (2008 tri-Ace; 2010 revised as *Star Ocean: The Last Hope – International*) designed by Mitsuo Iwao is a prequel to the entire sequence, occurring during an interstellar diaspora that follows World War Three on Earth. The broadly linear story line is that of a very conventional **space opera**; the main character is a member of the newly formed Space Reconnaissance Force, searching the galaxy for a new home for humanity, until he stumbles upon

198 Science Fiction Video Games

an alien threat. Many players, however, have enjoyed exploring the colorfully 3D planetary environments from their spaceship and fighting their way through the numerous battles, which borrow some concepts from the more combat oriented branch of **MMORPG** design. *Star Ocean: Blue Sphere* (*2001* tri-Ace) is a direct sequel to *Star Ocean: The Second Story*, released only in Japan. It features a "Sargasso World," a mysterious planet that somehow causes passing starships to crash onto its surface (a concept prefigured in such sf novels as Andre Norton's *Sargasso of Space* [**1955**]). *Star Ocean EX* (*2001*) is an **anime** version of *Star Ocean: The Second Story*, based on a Japanese-only **manga**, which ends unexpectedly partway through the plot (as does *Star Ocean EX*).

Web Links

- *Star Ocean: The Last Hope*: http://na.square-enix.com/starocean/

- starocean.org (Tribute Site): http://www.starocean.org/

STARQUEST

Series (from 1980). AS. Designed by Jon Freeman.

The members of the *Starquest* series are early examples of the **computer role playing game** form, modeled after their designer's successful *Dunjonquest* fantasy sequence but set in the same **future history** as the **computer wargame** *Starfleet Orion* (*1978* AS) designed by Jon Freeman and Jim Connelley. In the first, *Rescue at Rigel* (*1980* AS) designed by Jon Freeman, the player adopts the role of Sudden Smith, a biologically enhanced adventurer determined to rescue 10 human captives from an asteroid base controlled by an insectoid alien race. The gameplay is **turn based** and strongly combat oriented, with events displayed in a **2D** overhead view. The sequel, *Star Warrior* (*1980* AS) designed by Jon Freeman, somewhat resembles a turn-based tactical wargame, simulating a small military campaign fought with **powered armor** and nuclear weapons on the surface of a recently conquered human colony world. The player controls a member of the Furies, a group of "honourable mercenaries" who have agreed to assassinate the governor of the occupying forces so that the planet's inhabitants can rebel against their rulers. While technical limitations left little scope for including atmospheric background details within the actual software, the documentation for the *Starquest* games projects a strong ambience, one that is consciously evocative of the **space opera** adventure stories of the 1950s.

STAR WARS: KNIGHTS OF THE OLD REPUBLIC

2003. BioWare.

Knights of the Old Republic is a **computer role playing game** using a **3D** third-person view, set in the *Star Wars* universe. Its design combines the player-created characters and branching plots seen in many Western **CRPGs** with the emphasis on character backstory and directed narrative commonly associated with Japanese console role playing games. The game is set 4000 years before *Star Wars: Episode I – The Phantom Menace (1999)*, in a galaxy not very different to that of the films. The Jedi, servants of a democratic Republic whose dedication to virtue allows them access to the spiritual power of the "Force," are losing a war against the Sith, their moral and philosophical opposites. As the game begins, the main character is forced down on the planet Taris by Sith fighters; the player's initial mission is to find and rescue a Jedi whose exceptional skill with the Force offers hope for the embattled Republic.

The game mechanics are based on the *d20 (2000* WOTC) tabletop **RPG** system as used in the second version of the *Star Wars Roleplaying Game (2000* WOTC; revised *2002*; revised *2007*) designed by Bill Slavicsek, Andy Collins, and J. D. Wiker. Gameplay concentrates on puzzle solution, round-based combat, and character interaction; depending on the choices made by the player when creating their character, their persona may be more proficient at one of these approaches to the game than the others. Perhaps the most interesting aspect of the mechanics is the morality system, which tracks the player's actions and conversational choices to determine whether they are aligning themselves with the dark (Sith) or light (Jedi) side of the Force. Different plot paths appear for good and evil alignments, and computer-controlled individuals' interest in joining the player's group will be affected by the player character's moral position. While neither orientation is favored, the game does encourage the player to select a side, since high-level Force powers are only available to characters with a definite affinity for either light or dark. (Similar systems have been used by tabletop RPG designers to motivate players to create well-defined personas suitable for their fictional milieux since the initial release of *Dungeons and Dragons*, with its requirement that characters have "alignments" that must be "lawful," "chaotic," or "neutral." In his sequel to the first edition of 1974, *Advanced Dungeons and Dragons [1977–1979* TSR], Gary Gygax went on to suggest that **gamemasters** should monitor players' behavior and alter their characters' alignments if their actions seemed inconsistent with their professed beliefs, an approach that could deprive personas of the special benefits granted to such character types as the paladin, who most follow a strict moral code.) During the course of the game, the player will discover that their character is actually the previous Dark Lord of the Sith, whose memory has been wiped clean by the Jedi in an attempt to redeem them. In the end, players must choose whether to save the Republic, using a superweapon built by a forgotten galactic empire, or resume their position as Dark Lord. *Knights of the Old Republic* is an impressive example of a licensed game, which successfully translates the key concerns of its original, notably the ever-present danger of turning to the dark side of the Force, to a different medium. Arguably, it expresses the ethos of the original trilogy of *Star Wars* films better than does the second trilogy.

Related works: *Star Wars: Knights of the Old Republic II: The Sith Lords (2004* OE) is a sequel with similar gameplay in which the player adopts the role of an exiled Jedi; its tone is darker and somewhat more morally ambiguous than that of the first game. Interestingly, this work allows the player to select which of the endings to *Knights of the Old Republic* should be included in its backstory. *Star Wars: Knights of the Old Republic (2006–2010)* is a comic series, written by John Jackson Miller and published by Dark Horse, which is set in the same era as the games but tells an unrelated story. *Star Wars: Knights of the Old Republic – War (2012)* is a sequel to the original comic. *Star Wars: The Old Republic: Revan (**2011**)* is a novel by Drew Karpyshyn, writer for the first game. This book acts as a sequel to both games; their protagonists are assumed to have turned toward the light, but the tone of the work is dark.

Web Link
- Star Wars Knights.com (Tribute Site): http://www.starwarsknights. com/

SUNDOG: FROZEN LEGACY

1984. FTL Games. Designed by Bruce Webster.

Sundog: Frozen Legacy was one of the earliest **computer role playing games** with a science fiction theme. The premise is classic **space opera**; the player begins the game as the owner of the eponymous newly inherited spacecraft, contractually obliged to assist a religious group in establishing a colony by obtaining supplies and delivering colonists in **suspended animation**. What follows is a kind of interstellar egg hunt, as the player wanders the galaxy searching for the required goods and personnel, supporting themselves by trading while fighting pirates, talking to computer-controlled characters, and visiting planetary surfaces. The gameplay has some similarities to that of the game's contemporary, *Elite* (*1984*) designed by David Braben and Ian Bell, but *Sundog's* world is deeper, and correspondingly less broad, than that of its rival. While its relatively crude **2D** graphics and simple character interactions may seem primitive by modern standards, *Sundog* is an interesting precursor to more sophisticated **CRPGs** and **space sims** such as *Fallout* (*1997* BIS) designed by Tim Cain, Leonard Boyarsky, and Christopher Taylor and the *X Series* (from *1999* Egosoft).

Web Links

- Bruce Webster on *Sundog: Frozen Legacy*: http://brucefwebster.com/past-projects/sundog/

- The Sundog Information Page (Tribute Site): http://www.lukin.com/sundog/

TWILIGHT: 2000

1991. PS. Designed by Paul Conklin and Marc Miller.

Famously, one of the most depressing tabletop **role playing games** ever created, *Twilight: 2000* (*1984* GDW; revised *1990*; revised *1993*) is a postholocaust game set in the immediate aftermath of World War Three. The players' characters are the remnants of a military unit, struggling to survive among the ruins in a world almost destroyed by the "Twilight War." Typically, players will either try to make their way home or become little kings, protectors of a group of survivors who can provide them with food and new recruits. Regardless, the characters are assumed to have lost all contact with their superiors and any desire to continue the war; they are in an army without commanders, a situation many players find appealing.

The first edition of *Twilight: 2000* includes a history of the world from 1984 to 2000, when the game begins with the final unraveling of the war. Following an unexpected reunification of Germany and a Soviet invasion of China, the nations of Europe become involved in a chaotic conflict that develops into a global war of East against West. First tactical and then strategic nuclear weapons are used, as the world drifts into a slow motion apocalypse. By 2000, the war is ending with a whimper, as civilian governments disappear, and the remnants of NATO and the Warsaw

Pact fight on without resupply or reinforcements in an irradiated, plague-ridden central Europe. There are no victors in the Twilight War; it simply fizzles out as the remaining militaries lose both the will and the means to fight. The much expanded second edition (also known as Version 2.0) describes a very similar future, in which Poland turns to the Soviet Union for protection against reunified Germany in a pernicious mirror-image of actual European history after the collapse of the Warsaw Pact; events then proceed much as in the first edition. Version 2.2, however, published in 1993, presents an **alternate history** in which the failed 1991 coup in the Soviet Union succeeds, returning Russia to communist rule and setting the world once again on the road to apocalypse. By 1993, history had diverged too much from the timeline laid down in the game, making the Twilight War obsolete. While *Twilight: 2000*'s rules emphasize military realism, it cannot be played as a simple game of martial adventure in an exotic setting. The devastated landscapes and degenerate survivors that shape its world are too familiar; a sense of horror and futility inevitably colors the experience.

The **videogame** version of *Twilight: 2000*, however, generally avoids the grim ambience that often dominates sessions of the original **RPG**, concentrating instead on the difficulties of both **real-time** and **turn-based** tactical combat. In form, it is a **computer role playing game** that makes use of both **3D** and **2D** overhead displays. The representations of military skills and weaponry are extremely detailed, resulting in a work that often seems like more of a simulation than a game. However, the combination of difficulties with the design of the interface and the effects of its relentless realism make *Twilight: 2000* an exceptionally hard game to win. Ultimately, most players find their mission—to prevent an insane aristocrat from taking over what remains of Poland—to be unachievable.

Related works: *Last Battle* (*1989* GDW) designed by Tim Ryan is a tactical **wargame**, played on the tabletop and set in the final days of the Twilight War. The pen and paper RPG *2300 AD* (*1987* GDW; revised *1988*) designed by Marc Miller, Timothy Brown, Lester Smith, and Frank Chadwick is set 300 years in the future of the *Twilight: 2000* world, after the reconstruction of civilization. *Twilight: 2013* (*2008* 93 Games Studio) designed by Clayton Oliver, Simon Pratt, and Keith Taylor is a new edition of the original RPG which recasts the Twilight War as the result of global environmental and social collapse, perhaps the most credible contemporary equivalent of the original game's apocalyptic vision.

WASTELAND

1988. Interplay Productions. Designed by Alan Pavlish, Michael Stackpole, and Ken St Andre.

Wasteland is a **2D computer role playing game** set in the twenty-first-century Nevada desert, many years after an apocalyptic nuclear war. This milieu has a similar flavor to the future shown in the films *Mad Max 2 (1981)* and *Mad Max Beyond Thunderdome (1985)*, a hostile wilderness inhabited by dangerous mutants, isolated tribes, and bizarre cults, including the Temple of the Servants of the Mushroom Cloud. The player controls a group of paramilitary "Desert Rangers" who patrol the radioactive wilderness, where they will eventually uncover a threat to what remains of human civilization.

Gameplay in *Wasteland 2*, an upcoming sequel to *Wasteland* funded on the crowdsourcing website Kickstarter.

The core gameplay of *Wasteland* strongly resembles that of a combat-oriented pen and paper **role playing game**. (Two of the designers had previously written such games—*Tunnels and Trolls* [*1975* Flying Buffalo (FB)] designed by Ken St Andre and the related *Mercenaries, Spies and Private Eyes* [*1983* FB] designed by Michael Stackpole.) As in contemporary tabletop works, there is considerable flexibility as to how specific goals may be achieved, with characters able to use a wide range of skills and equipment. Notably, this was one of the first **CRPGs** in which players' characters were not simply extensions of their will; individuals recruited from the desert have their own goals and may refuse to obey the players' orders. The most impressive aspects of *Wasteland*, however, are its detailed and often brutally humorous game-world and its highly **modular** plot. Constructing a narrative by playing through the game remains a remarkably open, unfettered experience.

Wasteland 2, due to be released in 2014, uses an **isometric 3D** view to display its world, an approach that was common in the **CRPGs** of the late 1990s and early 2000s.

Related works: *Fountain of Dreams* (*1990* Electronic Arts) is a sequel set in a postnuclear Florida, which was created by a different development team. It received generally poor reviews.

Web Link
- Wasteland Ranger HQ-Grid (Tribute Site): http://wasteland.rockdud. net/

WORLDS OF ULTIMA

Series (from 1990). OS.

The *Worlds of Ultima* series was launched as a spin-off from the *Ultima* sequence of **sword and sorcery computer role playing games**. A central conceit of the *Ultima* series is that the player is represented by the Avatar, an individual from our own world who enters the fantasy land of Britannia through a "dimensional portal," returning at intervals of many years to intervene at crucial points in that world's history. In *Worlds of Ultima*, the Avatar is sent elsewhere, to realities that are unrelated to their normal destination. In the two games that were released before the series was canceled, those universes were science fictional in nature. Interestingly, the *Worlds of Ultima* are also distinguished from Britannia by their lack of a strong moral compass; the emphasis on ethical actions and the importance of pseudo-medieval "virtues" seen in contemporary members of the main sequence are largely absent from the spin-off series. As in other *Ultima* games of the time, the simulated world is displayed in a **2D** overhead view and is highly operable; almost any physical item can be used and manipulated, though characters are generally less responsive.

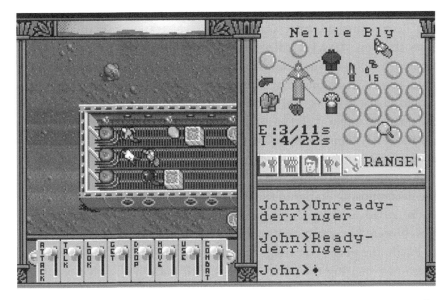

Martian Dreams was influenced by contemporary tabletop **RPGs** in its use of a party of several different adventurers—each of whom is described in detail—to represent a single player.

The Savage Empire (1990 OS) designed by Stephen Beeman and Richard Garriott was the first *Worlds of Ultima* game to be released. Scripted by the tabletop **RPG** designer and writer Aaron Allston, it is set in a lost world much influenced by Edgar Rice Burroughs' **Pellucidar**, similar to the hollow Earth Allston created for the *Dungeons and*

Dragons world of **Mystara**. *The Savage Empire*'s land of Eodon is populated with the dinosaurs, jungle princesses, and savage tribes descended
from lost Aztecs and Neanderthals, which are typical of such hidden
worlds, as well as less conventional giant ants, intelligent reptilians, and
shamans capable of effective magic. The gameplay is generally discursive, focusing on exploration of Eodon and performing diverse tasks
with the eventual goal of unifying the various tribes against the threat
presented by the giant ants; opportunities for conversation with other
characters are rare.

Martian Dreams (*1991* OS) designed by Jeff George, Richard
Garriott, and Warren Spector, the second entry in the series, is more
interesting. This game is **steampunk**, set in a secret history of our own
world in which a Phlogiston-fueled cannon was used to send an expedition to Mars in 1893, in the manner of Jules Verne's *De la terre à la
lune* ["From the Earth to the Moon"] (**1865**). The expedition's "bullet"
has been launched early due to sabotage, trapping many eminent
Victorians on Mars, including the inventor Thomas Edison, the revolutionary Nikolai Lenin, and the anarchist Emma Goldman; the Avatar
joins a rescue mission led by Edison's rival, Nikola Tesla. The Mars presented in the game is cold and arid, inhabited by creatures combining
the qualities of plant and animal. It is also the site of a unique alien civilization, now apparently extinct, whose members grew new individuals from seeds in a plot of land that combined the functions of cemetery
and nursery, passing on racial memories absorbed into the soil from
the decomposing bodies of the dead. These Martians were the possess-
ors of an advanced technology based on gigantic underground factories, powered by steam and operated by "mechanical men." To return
to Earth, the player's characters must learn how to use these forgotten
machines, melting the polar ice caps with giant lenses that focus the
heat of the sun to refill the Martian canal system and reactivating the
abandoned power stations. Many other elements appear in a strongly
imagined fiction, including **psionic** powers gained by eating alien ber-
ries and the Martian dream machines, which have trapped many members of the first expedition in their own nightmares. Overall, *Martian
Dreams* is perhaps the most interesting of the "Golden Age" science fiction computer role playing games, emphasizing exploration of its complex and original world over combat, and amply supplied with vividly
drawn characters.

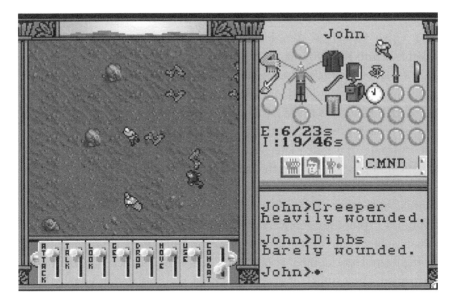

As in most of the **computer role playing games** of the 1980s and early 1990s, the primary display in *Martian Dreams* is a **2D** overhead view.

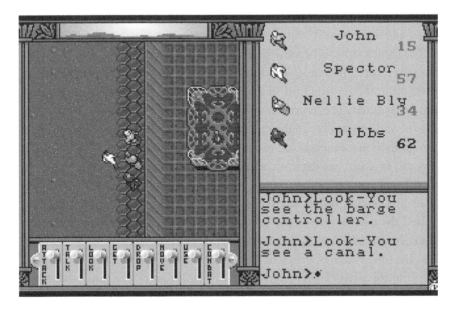

The Martian "canals" supposedly observed by the astronomer Percival Lowell in the late nineteenth century are a central concern of *Martian Dreams*.

XENOBLADE CHRONICLES

2011. (Also known as *Xenoblade* in Japan.) MS. Designed by Tetsuya Takahashi and Koh Kojima.

Xenoblade Chronicles is a **console role playing game**, much influenced by the *Final Fantasy* series and (especially) by one of its designer's previous works, *Xenogears* (*1998* Square). The game begins with a depiction of a battle between two gods at the dawn of time, before allowing the player to participate in a much later war between the intelligent machines and organic humans who live on the continents formed from the bodies of the two deities. Its milieu is thus one of **science and sorcery**, in which guns, swords, and "ether artillery" are all effective weapons of war. Gameplay combines exploration, conversation, and combat with the collection of valuable objects and the creation of powerful equipment, as is conventional for the form. Here, combat is essentially **real time**, but actions can only be performed when sufficient energy has been accumulated to enable them; the system is somewhat reminiscent of that used in *Final Fantasy XII* (*2006* Square) designed by Yasumi Matsuno, Hiroshi Minagawa, and Hiroyuki Ito. More interesting, perhaps, is the importance attached to strengthening the romantic bonds between characters by such means as encouraging them to engage in private and deeply personal conversations. Throughout, much effort has clearly been spent on making the game easy to learn; its many and occasionally complex mechanics are unusually approachable.

The game's story is broadly **linear**, though there are many optional missions structured in a more **modular** fashion. It tells a tale of love and loss, possession, and resurrection, in which reveals and reversals are both frequent and unexpected. The many playable and unplayable characters are strongly drawn and generally charming, if slightly stereotypical. Thematically, the eponymous weapons are archetypally powerful swords that drain the strength of their wielders, a conceit that is familiar from many works of **sword and sorcery**. Ultimately, it emerges that the entire game has taken place in a **pocket universe** created as part of a disastrous experiment that caused the destruction of the Earth; the gods are the scientists who made this cosmos and found themselves incorporated into its fabric as divine entities. The final villain of the piece turns out to be the god who created organic life, who the player's characters must kill with one of the titular blades; it becomes apparent that the spirit inhabiting this weapon is in fact the artificial intelligence, which controlled the space station on which the originating experiment was performed. There are striking echoes of many of Michael

Moorcock's fantasy novels, especially of the **Elric** and **Corum** sequences, in both of which the hero must kill the gods in order to set humanity free. In the final interpretation, the nature of the game's creation narrative suggests that *Xenoblade Chronicles* might be approached as a science-fictional story set in an **alternate cosmos** rather than—or as well as—a work of **science and sorcery**. Regardless, it is one of the most impressive works yet created by the Japanese school of **computer role playing game** design.

Web link

- *Xenoblade Chronicles*: http://www.nintendo.co.uk/NOE/en_GB/ games/wii/xenoblade_chronicles_32583.html

XENOGEARS

1998. Square. Designed by Tetsuya Takahashi.

Xenogears is a **3D console role playing game**, one that is markedly more adult in tone than such earlier Japanese **CRPGs** as *Chrono Trigger* (*1995* Square) designed by Hironobu Sakaguchi and Yuuji Horii. With a player character tortured by guilt over the accidental death of his friends, a strong concern with Gnostic theology and an abundance of **mecha**, it is instead often reminiscent of the television series *Neon Genesis Evangelion* (*1995–1996*). The game's setting is Ignas, a human-inhabited extrasolar world in the distant future, where a war between two technologically primitive nations has recently been exacerbated by the excavation of ancient human-piloted bipedal robots, or "gears." The primary character, Fei Fong Wong, who has no memories before the age of 15, soon discovers a war gear and destroys his village while trying to save it. Fleeing the scene of this disaster, he finds himself pursued by mysterious forces.

The game's well-drawn characters operate within a strongly **linear** plot; *Xenogears* is one of the few **videogames** to employ flash-forwards. Ultimately, it emerges that the humans of Ignas were created by the Deus, an alien power source that had been built into a weapon and become trapped on the planet after a spacecraft crash. The Deus, which resembles the evil Demiurge of the Gnostics, intends to absorb humanity in order to create a new body for itself and escape to the stars. The player must help Wong reintegrate his ego, superego, and id, which were fragmented by the childhood trauma that cost him his memory, before he can defeat the Deus, with the assistance of a remote, unknowable cosmic intelligence referred to as the "Wave Existence." Various characters are available for the player to recruit into their group, including one with whom Wong has a strong romantic subplot. Throughout, the gameplay involves a mix of exploration, puzzle solution, combat, and character interaction; combat in *Xenogears* was considered innovative for its use of two separate systems, one for humans and one for gears. While the linearity of the narrative can seem confining, it is inarguable that *Xenogears* has a powerfully symbolic story to tell, and guides the player through it with skill. It remains an impressive demonstration of what can be achieved with videogame storytelling.

The *Xenosaga* series could be described as a reimagining of a *Xenogears* prequel that was never made. Following creative disagreements, many of the original game's developers left Square to start their own company, where they built *Xenosaga: Episode I – Der Wille zur Macht* (2002 MS), *Xenosaga: Episode II – Jenseits von Gut und Böse* (2004 MS), and *Xenosaga: Episode III – Also Sprach Zarathustra* (2006 MS), all designed by Tetsuya Takahashi. The subtitles are the names of two books and a collection of posthumously published writings by Friedrich Nietzsche, in the original German; *Xenosaga*'s world view synthesizes concepts from Nietzschean philosophy, Christian theology, and Carl Jung's theories of the human psyche into an interesting, if rather pretentious, whole. While it is not entirely consistent with *Xenogears*, the series shares much of the first game's **future history** and core concerns. The games are set in a scientifically advanced and richly imagined galactic civilization after the loss of Earth, during an attack by a mysterious enemy called the "Gnosis." A variety of appealing characters, many of them **androids** or **cyborgs**, become involved in a conspiratorial struggle against their ethereal adversaries, using human-piloted "Anti Gnosis Weapon Systems" (or mecha). Gameplay is similar to *Xenogears*, but the story development is significantly more controlled, to the extent that playing through *Xenosaga* involves watching the equivalent of an entire series of (expertly constructed) **anime**. The three games form a single continuing story; at the end of the last episode, it is revealed that the Gnosis are the wills of dead humans who have rejected the universe and each other, who emerge from a shadow reality to attack the living. Ultimately, the universe is saved in a moment of transcendence.

Related works: *Xenosaga* (2005) is an anime based on *Der Wille zur Macht*, with significant differences. *Xenosaga: Pied Piper* (2004 MS) is a CRPG, which serves as a prequel to the *Xenosaga* games, focusing on the early life of one of the series' major characters. It has only been released in Japan. *Xenosaga I+II* (2006 MS), also only available in Japan, is a remake of *Der Wille zur Macht* and *Jenseits von Gut und Böse*, using a **2D** overhead view.

CHAPTER 8

Online Worlds

Any game involving more than one person is played in a kind of shared world, even if that world only exists until one of the participants has won. Such places gained a greater degree of permanence in tabletop **role playing games**, where the **gamemaster** might create an episodic campaign taking years to complete, and in the **play by mail** industry, in which the moderator maintains an independent record of the state of play for as long as the game goes on. The development of computer networks, however, made possible a new form of communal world, one in which physically distant players could participate in the same game in **real time**, without the delays in communication characteristic of games played by post. Such online worlds can be either temporary or persistent, a distinction resembling that made in the play by mail industry between "closed" and "open" games. A temporary world exists just long enough for players to finish a single session of its associated game, while persistent examples are of potentially infinite duration, continuing to grow and develop for as long as their underlying computer programs run.

The first examples of temporary online worlds were created on local networks connecting several large mainframes or minicomputers, or on systems that allowed multiple users to connect to the same central machine from separate terminals. These games were typically competitive in nature, allowing players to fight simulated battles in the virtual universe. Early works include a networked two-player version of 1962s *Spacewar* created in 1969 by Rick Blomme, the first-person shooting game *Maze War* (*1973*) designed by Steve Colley, Greg Thompson, and Howard Palmer, the prototypal space combat game *Spasim* (*1974*) designed by

Jim Bowery, and *airace* (*circa 1974*) designed by Silas Warner, an aircraft racing game that inspired the networked combat flight simulator *Airfight* (*circa 1974*) designed by Kevin Gorey and Brand Fortner. With the exception of *Maze War*, all of these games were written for PLATO, a US system for mainframe computers that offered advanced networking capabilities for the time and was primarily used by students, making it fertile ground for the early development of online worlds. *Maze War* was also notable for the development of a version in 1974, which allowed play across the ARPAnet, the predecessor of the modern Internet.

Early commercial **videogames** generally did not include networked play, since the requisite technology was rarely available outside an academic environment. Instead, most multiplayer games took an approach similar to that used in *Mule* (*1983* Ozark Softscape [OS]) designed by Danielle Bunten Berry, allowing participants to take turns, or let several individuals play on the same machine at the same time by using multiple joysticks or similar devices to communicate with the hardware. Outside university networks, online games were sometimes played through bulletin board systems, computers that provided electronic mail services and discussion forums for members who connected to them using a telephone modem. Such systems often hosted "door games," independently developed videogames, which were launched through a "door" provided by the bulletin board software. One science-fictional example is *Trade Wars 2002* (*1991*) designed by Gary Martin, a text-based game influenced by the single-player *Star Trader* (*1974*) designed by Dave Kaufman and *Universe* (*1984* Omnitrend Software) designed by Thomas Carbone and William Leslie III. *Trade Wars 2002* allows several players to explore a shared interstellar space influenced by *Star Trek* and *Star Wars* and build an empire by trade and conquest, initially by taking turns but in later versions through simultaneous play. While the simulated world is persistent in the sense that it is preserved for as long as an individual game lasts, it is essentially temporary in nature, since every game ends once a winner is declared.

Fully commercial online worlds first appeared in the early 1980s on national network services such as the US GEnie and CompuServe and the UK's Micronet, which were in essence much larger versions of the independently run bulletin board systems. One of the methods used by these services to attract customers was to commission proprietary multiplayer games that were only available on their network. One well-known example was the World War Two flight simulator *Air Warrior* (*1986* Kesmai) designed by Kelton Flinn, a GEnie game that could be seen as a much improved version of *Airfight*. A science-fictional work set in a similarly temporary online world was the CompuServe-based *MegaWars* (*1982* Kesmai), a multiplayer game greatly resembling early **computer wargames** based on the *Star Trek* TV series, of which the progenitor appears to have been the mainframe game *Star Trek* (*1971*) designed by Mike Mayfield. Meanwhile, videogame developers had begun experimenting with games that allowed two participants to compete against each other by connecting their computers directly via telephone modem without using a bulletin board or other online service; an early example is the **real-time** computer wargame *Modem Wars* (*1988* OS) designed by Danielle Bunten Berry, in which each player controls an army of robots. Later works of this kind include *Metaltech: Battledrome* (*1995* Dynamix) and *Wing Commander Armada* (*1994* Origin Systems) designed by Jeff Everett and Whitney Ayres. This development was greatly popularized by the archetypal **first person shooter**, *Doom* (*1993* id Software [id]) designed by John Romero, John Carmack, Tom Hall, and Sandy Petersen, which offered competitive play by modem and on local networks of the sort that might be found in a contemporary office or laboratory.

In 1991, however, the Internet (which had previously been restricted to governmental, academic, and corporate research bodies) was opened to commercial use. This network rapidly came to dominate online services, helped by the invention of the graphical World Wide Web interface, with existing network providers such as America Online migrating to the new standard and bulletin boards largely disappearing. *Quake* (*1996* id) designed by John Carmack, American McGee, Sandy Peterson, John Romero, and Tim Willits, the successor to *Doom*, was released with options allowing users to create their own temporary online worlds on the Internet and host competitions for other players. This approach proved to be highly popular, and such features have become *de rigueur* in videogames, which are suitable for competitive play, particularly in the first-person shooter, **third person shooter**, and **realtime strategy** forms. Early examples were exclusively available on personal computers, which could be equipped with the required networking hardware. In the late 1990s, however, game consoles began to be manufactured with similar capabilities; successful console games that allow online play include *Unreal Championship* (*2002* Epic Games/Digital Extremes) designed by Cliff Bleszinski and *Halo 2* (*2004* Bungie Studios [BS]) designed by Paul Bertone, Jaime Griesemer, and Joseph Staten. Most games set in temporary online worlds, whether on mainframe networks, bulletin boards, proprietary online services, or the Internet, have been competitive in nature, typically revolving around player versus player combat in environments separate to those used in the single-player version and disconnected from its plot. While most early examples took the form of a war of all against all, more recent games have often encouraged players to join opposing teams, an approach popularized by *Starsiege: Tribes* (*1998* Dynamix). A few works, however, offer cooperative options, in which players work together against a common enemy, often in a modified version of the normal game; sf examples include *Doom*, *Freelancer* (*2003* Digital Anvil) designed by Chris Roberts, and *Halo 3* (*2007* BS) designed by Jaime Griesemer, Paul Bertone, Rob Stokes, Tyson Green, and Joseph Staten.

While temporary online worlds have largely served as venues for a new form of competitive sport, with cash prizes awarded to tournament winners in the United States, the United Kingdom, and South Korea, their persistent equivalents have developed into genuine other worlds. Such virtual environments are more easily understood as places to go, with their own geographies, histories, and codes of conduct, than they are as games to be won. They have a distinctive history, beginning with *MUD* (*1978–1980*; also known as *MUD1*) designed by Roy Trubshaw and Richard Bartle—a player of tabletop **RPGs** (role playing games) and designer of amateur play by mail games—the first **multi-user dungeon**. This game, written at Essex University in the United Kingdom, was originally conceived as a multiplayer version of the mainframe text **adventure** *Zork* (*1977–1979*), a variant of which Trubshaw had played under the name of *Dungeon*. While *MUD*'s interface was similar to that of *Zork*, however, being based on the use of typed commands and textual descriptions of the simulated world, its gameplay more closely resembled that of a multiplayer **computer role playing game**, set in a **sword and sorcery** milieu (known simply as the "Land") where players' characters could become more powerful by killing monsters and plundering their treasure. Many players, however, spent more time socializing with each other or exploring the virtual environment than they did attempting to progress in the game. These three areas of interest have been used by Bartle to characterize the different types of player who inhabit *MUD*'s many descendants; a fourth group, which enjoy dominating other users, can be more problematic for the social dynamics of an online world. As in a computer role playing game, *MUD*'s players adopted personas that were formally distinct from their own identities, though (as has also been true in most later examples of the form) only a minority role-played personalities that were markedly different to their own. Most of the key features of the form are visible in *MUD*, including the use of such tabletop RPG-derived concepts as character class (which largely corresponds to profession, such as soldier or engineer). And from the beginning, many problems were present, which later became endemic. Notably, experienced players of the game were systematically ambushing new participants (who made for easy victims) and using computer-controlled characters to automatically gather virtual valuables from very early on in the life of that first *MUD*. While most of *MUD*'s players were students at Essex University, an experimental connection to the ARPAnet allowed some users to join from the United States, prefiguring the Internet-based **massively multiplayer online role playing games** of the late 1990s, which made persistent online worlds into a global phenomenon.

While the majority of later examples of the form are descended directly from *MUD*, it is possible to identify several contemporary games that developed independently along similar lines. *Avatar* (*1979*) designed by Bruce Maggs, Andrew Shapira, and David Sides was a multiplayer computer role playing game with an epic fantasy theme created on the PLATO network, which operated in a persistent world much influenced by the tabletop RPG *Dungeons and Dragons* (*1974* Tactical Studies Rules [TSR]) designed by Gary Gygax and Dave Arneson. *Scepter* (*1978*; also known as *Milieu*; *1983* revised as *The Scepter of Goth*; also known as *The Scepter and The Phoenix*) designed by Alan Klietz, another *Dungeons and Dragons* influenced fantasy game, became perhaps the first such work to be made commercially available when the 1983 iteration was licensed to early bulletin board operators. Other interesting precedents can be found among **play by mail** games of role playing and global conquest, played in sessions of indefinite length by hundreds of individuals who used the letter post to communicate with human **gamemasters**, of which the first was George Schubel's *The Tribes Of Crane* (*1978* Schubel & Son). Various other commercial games followed, including versions of *MUD* (in 1984 on the UK's CompuNet online service and, under the name of *British Legends*, on CompuServe in the United States in 1987) and *Federation* (*1988* IBGames) designed by Alan Lenton, a UK-created multi-user dungeon, which may have been the first persistent online world with an sf setting (a **space opera** milieu that concentrated on interstellar trading and exploration). Technical restrictions meant that all of these games were entirely text-based, however, with the exception of *Avatar*, which ran on powerful (and expensive) academic computers.

Graphical multi-user dungeons, which added **isometric** or plan view displays to the form, first became commercially available with the release of the somewhat primitive fantasy game *Island of Kesmai* (*1985* Kesmai) designed by John Taylor and Kelton Flinn on the CompuServe network. The game that made this variant truly popular, however, was *Neverwinter Nights* (*1991* Stormfront Studios) designed by Don Daglow, a computer role playing game licensed from the pen and paper RPG *Advanced Dungeons and Dragons* (*1977–1979* TSR) designed by Gary Gygax and set in its high-fantasy **Forgotten Realms** milieu. This game, written for the America Online network, was far more visually pleasing than *Island of Kesmai*, with well-crafted gameplay and a skillfully implemented persistent world. Meanwhile, text-based multi-user dungeons or MUDs had continued to evolve in academia, where they were free to play. Notable examples include the highly popular **heroic fantasy** combat game *AberMUD* (*1987*) designed by Alan Cox in the United Kingdom, *TinyMUD* (*1989*) designed by James Aspnes, an American effort, which was the first in a line of MUDs designed to emphasize role playing and social interaction rather than combat and adventure, and its descendant *LambdaMOO* (*1990*) designed by Pavel Curtis, intended to function more as an alternative society than as a game. The political evolution of *LambdaMOO*'s community is described by the journalist Julian Dibbell in *My Tiny Life: Crime and Passion in a Virtual World* (**1999**). As is true of persistent online worlds in general, most of the academic multi-user dungeons are set in some form of high-fantasy world; science fiction is a common alternative.

In the mid-1990s, however, improved network infrastructure and the opening of the Internet to business traffic made it possible to create commercial online worlds on a far larger scale than *Neverwinter Nights*. These works were referred to as **massively multiplayer online games** rather than graphical multi-user dungeons, despite being exclusively graphical in nature, due to the "massive" numbers of players they could support. While temporary online worlds are usually free to play, their maintenance being the responsibility of the game's publishers or of the players who instantiate them, and games on commercial networks such as GEnie were generally either included in the service or charged for on an hourly basis, massively multiplayer online games have often been paid for by a monthly subscription, or by the sale of virtual items such as unusually potent weapons or elegant clothing for a player's favorite character. In South Korea, early commercial usage of the Internet occurred primarily in cafes instead of private homes, encouraging the formation of a subculture of online videogame players with access to the latest networking hardware. This set the stage for the first successful attempt at a **massively multiplayer** persistent online world, *Nexus: The Kingdom of the Winds* (*1996* NEXON) designed by Jake Song, set in a mythic version of ancient Korea. The highly popular pseudo medieval game *Lineage* (*1998* NCSoft), also designed by Jake Song in South Korea, is a descendant of *Nexus*, which emphasizes territorial warfare between large groups of players. The game that popularized the form in the West, however, was *Ultima Online* (*1997* Origin Systems) designed by Richard Garriott, Raph Koster, Rick Delashmit, and Starr Long, a spin-off from the *Ultima* series of heroic fantasy computer role playing games. *Ultima Online* was released with a large and impressively detailed fantasy world, including a simulated economy and ecology and an artificial currency, displayed in an isometric view. The game allowed players a great deal of freedom, including the ability to attack each other whenever they chose, and a wide range of skills to learn, from forging saleable weapons to alchemy. However, as the number of players rose, rapidly outstripping the designers' original projections, it soon became clear that experience gained with the smaller-scale multi-user dungeons did not necessarily apply to the massively multiplayer form.

While the cities (where combat between players was banned) remained relatively civilized, *Ultima Online*'s countryside rapidly degenerated into anarchic killing fields, plagued by roaming bands of aggressive players who would attack other characters on sight. The effects of this were ameliorated by the automatic resurrection of the dead, but travel between cities nevertheless became extremely difficult. Changes were then made to the system to automatically evaluate the morality of characters' actions toward others, with dangerous individuals tagged as "murderous" on the display, so that they could be identified and hunted by other players and computer-controlled characters. However, algorithmic assessments of characters' ethical status proved, in practice, to be highly unreliable, and the problem was eventually resolved by creating a separate version in which players' characters could only attack each other by mutual agreement, a solution used in most subsequent **MMORPGs** (massively multiplayer online role playing games). One memorable example of the general tendency toward mayhem was the assassination of "Lord British"—Garriott's *alter ego* within the game—by a player during a "royal visit," after the invulnerability normally enjoyed by British had been accidentally deactivated. The carefully engineered fantasy ecology was replaced by an unending supply of dangerous monsters after players effectively caused a mass extinction by killing too many of the original stock of dragons and other exotic beasts. Meanwhile, the sophisticated economic simulation, which continuously modeled supply and demand, proved problematic when player characters produced so many items that prices began to suffer from rapid deflation. This problem was addressed by modifying computer-controlled traders so that they would always buy equipment built by players at a "fair price," a change that replaced deflation with rampant inflation. Nevertheless, variants of this approach—in which currency is injected as necessary, rather than there being a constant amount of gold or some equivalent standard of value within the simulated world—have been used in most later examples of the form. Arguably, much of the history of massively multiplayer online role playing games has revolved around attempts to resolve the social and psychological issues first seen in *Ultima Online*.

The general direction of MMORPG development since *Ultima Online* has become notably stylized, concentrating on the creation of artificial universes in which the laws of reality are rewritten to make the experience more enjoyable for the players. Thus, the death of players' characters is almost always temporary, with some fictional justification (such as the activation of a clone) often being used to explain their resurrection, though the replacement may not retain all of the original's possessions or skills. Behaviors that cause problems within the game are primarily discouraged not by hiring gamemasters to police the simulated society— which is expensive—but by creating worlds in which those behaviors are impossible. So, most MMORPGs offer a variety of different versions of the game in which the rules are slightly different, typically allowing players to attack each other whenever they wish in some variants but heavily restricting or banning the practice altogether in others. Similarly, the habit of killing newly created (and thus generally weak and vulnerable) characters to loot their bodies is often deterred by transferring the victims' possessions automatically to their next incarnations rather than leaving them with the corpses. Even games that do not allow variant versions generally splinter their game-worlds into "shards," or divergent copies which each support some fraction of the player population. This approach is both technically advantageous and helpful in ensuring that popular areas do not become overcrowded, though games such as *EVE Online* (2003 CCP Games [CCP]) designed by Reynir Harðarson prefer to simulate a single galaxy for all their players.

Much effort has been devoted to fostering the growth of communities within virtual worlds. Players are encouraged to join game-world organizations, and the available types of character are usually designed to be interdependent. Thus, adventurers may need weapon builders to make their equipment, and effective combat strategies often depend on teams of players who adopt such roles as medic, hand-to-hand combat specialist, and sniper. This latter concept is ultimately derived from the complementary character classes used in the first edition of *Dungeons and Dragons*, the original pen and paper RPG. Communication between players, whether by keyboard, by headset and microphone, or by some other means, is also important; preconstructed physical actions such as dances (in graphical variants) or special symbols (in text-based ones) are used to take the place of body language. While many players concentrate on killing virtual monsters, increasing their characters' skills, and acquiring wealth and fame (though often only with computer-controlled admirers), others see the creation of a separate persona in a virtual world as an opportunity to experiment with their own identities, sexual preferences, and gender. Some participants who are interested in improving their status in the game-world have proved willing to buy virtual equipment and currency on online auction sites. The appearance of this secondary market made it possible to make a (poor) living from playing MMORPGs, though game developers—after initially discouraging such activities on the grounds that they might diminish the enjoyment of players who were not willing or able to buy simulated loot—have now often taken to funding their games by selling such items themselves, as an alternative or supplement to subscription fees.

While small predesigned missions are often offered to players and new creatures and explorable areas are regularly made available for Internet download, persistent worlds do not typically make use of overarching plots or story arcs; their **interactive narratives** are predominantly **environmental** in nature. Most massively multiplayer games are, like *Nexus* and *Ultima Online*, massively multiplayer online role playing games, direct descendants of the first *MUD*, but there are exceptions to the rule. *PlanetSide* (*2003* Verant Interactive [VI]) designed by Terrence Yee, for example, is an sf massively multiplayer first-person shooter, in which teams of players from three opposing factions fight over the surface of the planet Auraxis, using characters who gradually improve in ability as they complete more missions. Other forms of massively multiplayer online game include the **space sim** *EVE Online* and the social worlds of *The Sims Online* (*2002* Maxis) designed by Will Wright and *Second Life* (*2003* Linden Research) designed by Philip Rosedale.

Ultima Online was followed by a number of similar games that tried to improve on its design. Where Koster and Garriott's game had attempted a detailed simulation of a fictional reality within which players could make moral choices, *EverQuest* (*1999* VI) designed by Brad McQuaid, Steve Clover, and Bill Trost took its inspiration from the successful line of combat-oriented fantasy multi-user dungeons beginning with *AberMUD* and continuing through *DikuMUD* (*1991*) designed by Sebastian Hammer, Tom Madsen, Katja Nyboe, Michael Seifert, and Hans Staerfeldt. The game's combination of attractive **3D** graphics with a strong emphasis on adventurous gameplay made it highly popular; it rapidly gained more subscribers than *Ultima Online*. Later examples of the MMORPG form have almost exclusively followed *EverQuest* by using a 3D view. *Asheron's Call* (*1999* Turbine Entertainment) designed by Toby Ragaini, Eri Izawa, Chris Pierson, and Chris Foster introduced a number of innovations, most notably an epic fantasy narrative that affected its entire sword and sorcery world. However, this concept proved problematic, since players' actions could not make any real difference to the unfolding of the **linear** plot; story arcs have not been much used in subsequent MMORPG designs. *Dark Age of Camelot* (*2001* Mythic Entertainment) designed by Mark Jacobs focused on player versus player combat, with participants divided into groups corresponding to the three nations of its post-Arthurian world and encouraged to fight in specific areas. Meanwhile, the Norwegian game *Anarchy Online* (*2001* Funcom) designed by Gaute Godager and Ragnar Tørnquist made use of an original and evocative sf setting, as well as introducing dynamically generated missions that gave players a wide selection of tasks to perform.

Subsequent massively multiplayer online games were developed in a number of different directions. Early examples were created exclusively for personal computers, which were the only games machines capable of connecting to the Internet. However, in the twenty-first century, game consoles, which could go online, appeared making it possible to develop MMORPGs for them, though the lack of keyboards made player communication problematic. The first examples were *Phantasy Star Online* (*2000* Sega) designed by Yoshihiro Sakuta and *Final Fantasy XI Online* (*2002* Square) designed by Hiromichi Tanaka and Koichi Ishii, both created in Japan as spin-offs from popular series of **console role playing games**. Another development was the introduction of free MMORPGs, which were supported by advertising or the sale of game-world items and abilities to players rather than by a monthly subscription; perhaps the best known of the early Western examples was the high-fantasy *RuneScape* (*2001* Jagex), designed by Andrew Gower and developed in the United Kingdom.

A variety of non-fantasy-based games were released in the early 2000s, including the unsuccessful space opera *Earth & Beyond* (*2002* Westwood Studios), the superhero-based *City of Heroes* (*2004* Cryptic Studios [CS]), and the Icelandic space sim *EVE Online* (*2003* CCP), an unusual design notable for the degree of freedom it offers to its players. Meanwhile, many of the developers of *Ultima Online* moved on to the film license *Star Wars: Galaxies* (*2003* Sony Online Entertainment) designed by Raph Koster, which showed a similar idealistic concern with the value of community, but proved commercially unsuccessful. A more profitable approach was taken by *Guild Wars* (*2005* ArenaNet) designed by Mike O'Brien, Patrick Wyatt, and Jeff Strain, a sword and sorcery game, which had to be purchased initially but which did not charge a subscription fee. While *Star Wars: Galaxies* is a direct descendant of *Ultima Online*, *Guild Wars* is perhaps best described as an improved version of *EverQuest* and *Dark Age of Camelot*. Its design concentrated on making combat-based cooperative and competitive play in a high-fantasy world as enjoyable as possible; notably, it popularized the idea of creating separate subworlds for every mission performed by a group, an idea previously used in *Anarchy Online*. Thus, while players can interact freely in towns, as soon as a group begins playing through a prepared story line or enters the wilderness, they are moved into their own private copy of the world, where they can participate in an adventure with their chosen companions without having to deal with potentially unhelpful interlopers. In essence, *Guild Wars* is more of a game than many of its antecedents, but less of a world.

Other recent games have more closely resembled *Guild Wars* than *Star Wars: Galaxies*. By far the most commercially successful is *World of Warcraft* (*2004* Blizzard Entertainment [BE]) designed by Rob Pardo, Jeff Kaplan, and Tom Chilton, set on the same **steampunk** and sorcery world used for the real-time strategy game *Warcraft: Orcs & Humans* (*1994* BE). *World of Warcraft* contains little that is strikingly new, but everything that it does, it does well. Perhaps its most distinctive features are its frequent use of private subworlds in which to play out adventures, as in *Guild Wars*, the universal availability of predesigned missions intended for both large and small groups of characters, so that players never find themselves at a loss for something interesting to do, and its guarantee that one character will never be allowed to kill another unless both have agreed to the terms of the combat. While the game avoids many of the unfortunate clichés of MMORPG gameplay, such as the sight of characters forming a polite queue while waiting for a monster to appear in a particular spot so that it can be killed, it is not immune to problems. One famous incident is the "Corrupted Blood" plague, an infectious (and lethal) curse that was smuggled out of the jungle troll city to which it was meant to be confined and spread to the general population. The result was a virtual epidemic that infected several simulated cities before it was eliminated by the developers. Nevertheless, the *World of Warcraft* approach has proved sufficiently successful that most subsequent games have copied most aspects of its design, though not necessarily the darkly cynical humor often apparent in its fiction.

While *World of Warcraft* currently dominates the market, alternative types of MMORPG are still released; one interesting example is the now defunct sf game *Tabula Rasa* (*2007* Destination Games) designed by Richard Garriott, Paul Sage, and Susan Kath, which emphasized the resolution of moral dramas. Other works aimed at a mass market include *Star Wars: The Old Republic* (*2011* BioWare) designed by James Ohlen, Emmanuel Lusinchi, Brad Prince, and Daniel Erickson, the successor to *Star Wars: Galaxies*, and Funcom's occult conspiracy game *The Secret World* (*2012*), designed by Martin Bruusgaard, Joel Bylos, and Ragnar Tørnquist. Most experimental designs, however, are now launched as small-scale multi-user dungeons rather than as (extremely expensive) MMORPGs. Interesting commercial examples include the graphical *A Tale In The Desert* (*2003* eGenesis) designed by Andrew Tepper, an independently produced game set in ancient Egypt, which is largely focused on social interaction, and various text-based games created by the US developer Skotos. These latter works are classic multi-user dungeons distinguished by the presence of individuals who serve a similar purpose to that of the gamemaster in a pen and paper RPG, helping to shape the development of the ongoing narrative; examples include *Castle Marrach* (*2001* Skotos), set in a faerie citadel, which shares something with Mervyn Peake's **Gormenghast**, and the science-fictional *The Lazarus Project* (*2007* Skotos) designed by Michael Zerbo, which concentrates on the search for immortality on a colony planet. Skotos' games also allow players to significantly alter the world their characters live in, an element present in many academic multi-user dungeons but little seen in commercial MMORPGs, perhaps because it is far easier for players to build textual descriptions than graphical models. This mutability may itself be helpful in the creation of an involving narrative. Most commercial massively multiplayer online games, by contrast, concentrate on accurately simulating an essentially unchanging world, in which the same stories can be enacted again and again. MMORPGs have also begun to appear in the written sf genre, notably in Charles Stross' *Halting State* (**2007**), Cory Doctorow's *For the Win* (**2010**), and Neal Stephenson's *REAMDE* (**2011**), and in such TV series as *The Big Bang Theory* (*2007*–current).

In the late 2000s, two (often linked) phenomena became increasingly important in Western online worlds: social games and free play. The former is a term used to refer to games played on "social networks," websites—of which Facebook is currently the best known—which concentrate on facilitating relationships between individuals. Social games are thus always online games, though the worlds in which they are played can be temporary (as for the many such works based on traditional board games, such as Scrabble) or persistent (the approach taken by such games as the iconic farming simulation *FarmVille* [*2009* Zynga]). Many of these works are reminiscent of the "door games" seen on bulletin board systems (for which see earlier text), especially in their support for players who want to participate in the same game at different times. Most of them make use of the social network's systems to link the gameplay to players' existing relationships, for example, by ensuring that their online friends are their neighbors in the game; the exceptions are typically works that simply use the social network as a platform on which to deliver a conventional single-player game. A common characteristic of the form is that its members are initially free to play, with income generated by the sale of virtual goods, which make the game easier or more rewarding. While many players are enthusiastic about this approach—especially those who intend never to actually buy any items—it is not universally appreciated; notably, some participants resent the inevitable loss of virtual goods if (and when) the game-world in which their items exist becomes unprofitable and is shut down. Regardless of the virtues or vices of their sales strategy, the vast majority of these works are of little science-fictional interest; their fictions are generally simple, and in any case are typically set in realities that are essentially contemporary, fairy tale fantasies, or entirely abstract. Exceptions include *Evil Genius: WMD* (*2010* Rebellion) and *Global Resistance* (*2011* Insomniac Games).

While selling virtual items to players of games that are initially free was always the dominant business model for social games, it has also become much more common among MMORPG developers. This approach was first popular in South Korea and China, and subsequently spread into the West through such games as Jagex's *RuneScape*; in the early 2010s, it has become the most common way of funding massively multiplayer games. Typically, the most popular works will still charge a monthly subscription, but games that have become less fashionable, or that cater to a more casual group of players, will be free, with their expenses paid for by the sale of imaginary goods (such as a better engine for a player's virtual starship, or a more attractive uniform for their game-world persona). Well-known science-fictional examples include the superhero-based *Champions Online* (*2009* CS) and the TV license *Star Trek Online* (*2010* CS). Sometimes, as in the current version of *World of Warcraft*, the early stages of play are free, but after that, a subscription is required. This approach to the funding of MMORPGs can invert developers' relationships with their customers, transforming them from guardians of fair play—responsible for ensuring that all participants have an equal chance by preventing the sale of powerful game weapons and devices on online auction sites—to suppliers of those exact items, selling virtual power to those willing and able to pay for it.

Both temporary and persistent online worlds remain highly successful commercially and have become well known in the culture at large. The persistent form seems of particular science-fictional interest, since—as with the social simulation school of **toy games**—it incarnates a traditional sf dream, that of the virtual world, which can seem more real than reality. It is interesting, however, to consider the differences between the conception and the creation. While most visions of such worlds have depended on **virtual reality**, this has proved to be of little relevance to actual online worlds. The emotional significance of playing a fictional character in another world, adopting the role of a secondary persona that can be more capable than its creator and perhaps express hidden facets of their personality, is, it seems, more important than the visual accuracy of the simulation.

FURTHER READING

- Duncan Howard. *An Introduction to MUD: Multi-User Dungeon.* 1985. (This book, sold to players of the commercial versions of the Essex *MUD* run by British Telecom and CompuNet in the United Kingdom, offers a fascinating [if rather disorganized] glimpse of the culture of what was arguably the first true online world.)

- Julian Dibbell. *My Tiny Life: Crime and Passion in a Virtual World.* 1999.

- Richard Bartle. *Designing Virtual Worlds*. 2003. (An impressively comprehensive and passionate book on the design of the persistent form, written by one of the designers of the first multi-user dungeon.)

- Edward Castronova. *Synthetic Worlds: The Business and Culture of Online Games*. 2005. (An interesting analysis of persistent online worlds by an economist who has made a study of the form.)

- Tim Guest. *Second Lives: A Journey through Virtual Worlds*. 2007. (A journalistic investigation of online worlds, focusing on *Second Life* but also including material on *EverQuest* and *EVE Online*.)

Web Links
- Richard Bartle's MUD Archive: http://www.mud.co.uk/richard/mud.htm

- Timeline for the development of online worlds: http://www.raphkoster.com/gaming/mudtimeline.shtml

- MMORPG.com (Tribute Site): http://www.mmorpg.com/

ANARCHY ONLINE

2001. Funcom. Designed by Gaute Godager and Ragnar Tørnquist.

Anarchy Online is a **massively multiplayer online role playing game** that could be characterized as a form of shared **planetary romance**. It is set on the far future world of Rubi-Ka, where the morally suspect hypercorporation Omni-Tek is mining notum, a substance vital to the production of **nanotechnological** devices. Players can choose to align themselves with Omni-Tek or the rebellious local Clans, or to remain neutral. Rubi-Ka is realized in considerable detail, with four different human subspecies and a varied and often beautiful geography. The original design drew heavily on concepts used in contemporary fantasy **MMORPGs**, notably the structured conflict between groups of players seen in such games as *Dark Age of Camelot* (*2001* Mythic Entertainment) designed by Mark Jacobs and the overarching story arc of *Asheron's Call* (*1999* Turbine Entertainment) designed by Toby Ragaini, Eri Izawa, Chris Pierson, and Chris Foster. *Anarchy Online* also introduced several innovations intended to resolve problems seen in earlier games, including a system to automatically generate missions such as capturing criminals or recovering artifacts, ensuring that players could always find a personal quest to complete. Similarly, combat between players is allowed, but only in specific areas. After some notable technical problems when it was first made available, *Anarchy Online* has become moderately popular. Several aspects of the original design have been changed since the launch; notably, the overarching story is no longer an important part of the game, making Rubi-Ka more of an eternal "planet of adventure."

There is much of interest to explore in *Anarchy Online*, from red light districts to orbiting satellites, while its science-fictional background is generally well constructed, with a quirky sense of humor. The game's design has not entirely overcome the cognitive dissonance that haunts many MMORPGs, however. Many necessary gameplay conventions are well rationalized, as when nanotechnology is used to reconstruct dead characters from the point where they last recorded their memories, but it has still been possible to find groups of players standing in line waiting for a particular enemy to be reborn, so that they can kill it and advance to the next stage of a scripted plot. In the end, players go to Rubi-Ka for many reasons, to adopt the persona of a famous scientist or a deadly assassin, to join an organization of adventurers and hunt dangerous animals, to participate in the war of Omni-Tek against Clan, to perform amateur works of art, or simply to make friends and admire the scenery.

Related works: Several expansions have been published for the game: *The Notum Wars* (*2001* Funcom), which gives groups of players the ability to control their own territories; *Shadowlands* (*2003* Funcom), which adds a **parallel world** version of Rubi-Ka inhabited by the remnants of the planet's previous inhabitants; *Alien Invasion* (*2004* Funcom), which allows groups of players to build their own cities; *Lost Eden* (*2006* Funcom), which concentrates on player versus player combat; and *Legacy of the Xan* (*2009* Funcom), which adds areas intended for longstanding players with exceptionally powerful characters. Major events in the world's story arc were delivered by the earlier expansions. *Anarchy Online* (*2001*) is an animated series, written and directed by Ragnar Tørnquist, which can be downloaded from the game's website. *Prophet Without Honour* (**2001**) is a novel that expands on the setting's history, also by Tørnquist; it too is freely available from the *Anarchy Online* website.

Web Links
- *Anarchy Online*: http://www.anarchy-online.com/
- Terri Perkins on Anarchy Online: http://www.igda.org/online/ quarterly/1_1/interview1.php

CHAMPIONS ONLINE

2009. CS. Designed by Bill Roper.

The launch of the first edition of the tabletop **role playing game** *Champions* (*1981* Hero Games [HG]; revised *1982*; revised *1984*; revised *1989*; *2002* revised as *Champions: Superpowered Roleplaying*; *2010* revised as *Champions: The Super Roleplaying Game*; *2012* revised as *Champions Complete*) designed by George MacDonald and Steve Peterson popularized superheroes as a subject for pen and paper **RPGs**. (Previously, they had only appeared in relatively obscure games such as *Superhero 2044* [*1977* Gamescience] designed by Donald Saxman and *Villains and Vigilantes* [*1979* Fantasy Games Unlimited] designed by Jeff Dee and Jack Herman.) Thematically, *Champions* is very much a reflection of the "four colour" world of 1960s comics, focusing on cosmic conflicts and simple emotions. Financially, the game remained consistently but not spectacularly successful for the next two and a half decades, spawning various revisions and one major spin-off: *Champions: New Millennium* (*1997* R. Talsorian Games; revised *2000*) designed by Bruce Harlick, a much darker version of the work in which almost all of the world's superheroes have been wiped out in a millennial apocalypse, and the players' characters must take their places.

In 2007, however, the **videogame** developer CS sold their superheroic **massively multiplayer online role playing game** *City of Heroes* (*2004* CS) and its companion game *City of Villains* (*2005* CS) to NCSoft before beginning work on a new **online world** set in the Marvel Comics universe. However, artistic differences between CS and Marvel led to the termination of the license before the game was released, after which Cryptic bought the intellectual property for *Champions* from HG. It seems likely that Cryptic's main motivation was the desire to acquire a readymade and highly detailed milieu suitable for use in an **MMORPG**, rather than an interest in the *Champions* mechanics or its existing players (who were not very numerous by the standards of modern online worlds). The resulting game was launched 2 years later as *Champions Online*. HG has continued to publish the tabletop RPG, now under license from Cryptic; both the MMORPG and the pen and paper game are currently set in the milieu described in *Champions Universe* (*2002* HG; revised *2010*) designed by Steve Long and Darren Watts, an evolved version of the minimal background presented in the original version of the *Champions* rules. The effect of this setting is that of the simple, action-packed stories, which inspired the creators of the game's earliest edition, but presented in a knowing way reminiscent of Kurt Busiek's rather more sophisticated comic *Astro City* (*1995*–current).

Related works: There have been a number of comics based on the characters created by the players in the pen and paper designers' original game. These began with *Champions* (*1986–1987*), published by Eclipse Comics, and continued with *Champions* (*1987–1988*), *League of Champions* (*1990–1993*), and *Flare* (*1992–1993*), variously published by Hero Comics and Hero Graphics. Disagreements over how the characters should be portrayed between the players who created them and Dennis Mallonee, who wrote the comics, eventually led to a split in which the individuals featured in the comics and in the *Champions* game setting became formally distinct. Currently, issues of *Flare Adventures* and *Champions Adventures* are appearing from Heroic Publishing.

Several tabletop games have also been created as derivatives of the original RPG. *Autoduel Champions* (*1983* Steve Jackson Games [SJG]) designed by Aaron Allston is a crossover book between *Champions* and the tabletop **wargame** *Car Wars* (*1982* SJG) designed by Steve Jackson and Chad Irby, while *Champions: Wildstrike* (*1998* HG) designed by Steve Peterson is a board game of superhero combat, set in a dueling arena.

Web Link
- *Champions Online*: http://www.champions-online.com/

CITY OF HEROES

2004. CS.

City of Heroes was a **massively multiplayer online role playing game**, set in a "four colour" superhero world similar to that of classic DC and Marvel comics, where virtuous heroes were forever rescuing helpless citizens from the machinations of evil masterminds. The game design concentrated on the superpowered battles and archetypal paragons of its source materials rather than on their melodramatic depictions of personal relationships; *City of Heroes* characters did not use "secret identities" to hide their superhuman natures. Instead, a great deal of emphasis was placed on the player's ability to create the superhero of their dreams, selecting from a wide range of possible superpowers and visual designs. The setting was the eponymous Paragon City, where computer-controlled supervillains and street thugs lurked around almost every corner. The gameplay was more action oriented than that of most **MMORPGs**; characters typically joined a temporary or permanent superteam and either patrolled the streets to fight crime or went on predesigned missions against groups of supervillains.

The game was also unusual among MMORPGs for the extent to which the participants' experience depended on content provided by the game designers rather than on their interactions with each other. Paragon City was well crafted, featuring a complex backstory and a wide range of original supervillains, from **psychokinetically** controlled clockwork robots to a group of female carnival performers who used mind control on their unsuspecting audiences. Players could gradually uncover the true natures of their enemies and the connections between them as they proceeded through the game's missions, growing progressively stronger as their powers improved. Eventually, characters would reach a level of expertise where only the most challenging enemies were worth confronting; at this point, they might find themselves fighting off alien invasions, or traveling to alternate versions of Paragon City, where friends and enemies were strangely changed. All of these tasks were completed separately by different groups; while individual players might triumph over all enemies in their own experience of the world, Paragon City itself existed in the eternal present characteristic of **massively multiplayer online games**, where nothing could ever really change. Notably, the consequences of players' actions were primarily social rather than physical; computer-controlled citizens might be overheard discussing a character's failure to prevent the destruction of an important landmark, but the building itself would still be present, since the game's physical reality would be shared by both players who failed to save the building and those who succeeded. Ultimately, the game offered an entertaining and richly realized portrayal of the four colour comics' universe of eternal struggle, though players who had seen the whole of its world might not wish to remain.

City of Villains (*2005* CS) was a companion game, playable either separately or in combination with *City of Heroes*. It inverted the premise of the original work by making characters into supervillains; players began by breaking out of the Paragon City prison and escaping to the Rogue Isles, a legally independent archipelago owned by a prominent evil mastermind. The Rogue Isles implemented an extreme form of **social Darwinism**; their rulers encouraged a never-ending war between the inhabitants in the expectation that the most powerful would eventually become their allies. As in the underlying comics, the assumption was that supervillains are proactive, plotting their own paths to ultimate power, while the heroes of the preceding game were essentially reactive, acting only to suppress threats to the status quo. The game's visual design was suitably menacing, full of titanic, brooding architecture and decayed slums, in stark contrast to Paragon City's general atmosphere of futuristic perfection. *City of Villains* added several new gameplay features, notably the ability to construct permanent bases for a group and the option for players to fight other players in special arenas, an activity banned altogether in the first game. As in such earlier games as the *Star Wars* license *TIE Fighter* (*1994* Totally Games) designed by Lawrence Holland and Edward Kilham, however, players were not encouraged to be genuinely evil; most of their time was spent fighting other criminals.

Both of these games were generally lighthearted, informed by a joyful enthusiasm for the simple stories that inspired them. *City of Heroes* in particular was notable for its combination of **environmental** narrative elements with stories structured around individual characters, guiding players through their own personal versions of the hero's journey. Ultimately, however, this could not save it from obsolescence, perhaps because the natural destination for those who had completed their journeys was a different game. In late 2012, after the number of players had dropped below the level at which the games were profitable to run, the servers for both *City of Heroes* and *City of Villains* were shut down, bringing Paragon City's eternal present to an abrupt conclusion.

Related works: *City of Heroes: Going Rogue* (*2010* Paragon Studios) was an expansion for both *City of Heroes* and *City of Villains*, which made available a new **alternate history** setting for the games. More intriguingly, perhaps, it also allowed players to create characters of uncertain morality, who could ultimately become either truly good or utterly evil. *City of Heroes Collectible Card Game* (*2005* Alderac Entertainment Group) designed by David Williams is a **collectible card game** based on combat between superheroes in a dueling arena, featuring a web-based system that enables players to create new cards for their own hero designs. *City of Heroes* (*2004–2007*) is a comic book series set in the eponymous universe continuity; writers include Mark Waid, Dan Jurgens, and Rick Dakan, one of the designers of the original game. *The Web of Arachnos* (**2005**) by

Robert Weinberg and *The Freedom Phalanx* (**2006**) by Robin D. Laws are novels, focusing on the histories of major characters in the setting.

Web Link
- *City of Heroes*: http://www.cityofheroes.com/

DEFIANCE

2013. Trion Worlds.

The TV series *Defiance* (*2013*–current) is set on a near-future Earth that has been transformed into an alien frontier. In the program's backstory, a civilization made up of diverse alien species arrives from another star, looking for a new home after the destruction of their own solar system. (The most prominent writer for the show, Rockne O'Bannon, previously worked on *Alien Nation* [*1988*], a film with a somewhat similar premise.) War with humanity eventually follows, an outcome that proves disastrous for both cultures and ultimately leads to a negotiated peace. By the time of the TV program, Earth has become a patchwork of alien and human enclaves, a background that allows for the creation of a kind of Wild West milieu where contemporary American culture is mingled with alien technologies, bizarrely mutated animals, and exotic extraterrestrials. The end result is an adequate, if uninspired, adventure series. It is perhaps indicative of a certain lack of thought that Earth's transformation into a partially alien world is repeatedly described as being the result of the accidental release of the aliens' **terraforming** devices, though the effect of this technology has clearly been to make the planet less like Earth (or Terra) and more like an extraterrestrial body; xenoforming might be a more apt term for this process.

The Syfy network, which commissioned the TV series, also collaborated with Trion Worlds to create a **massively multiplayer** online **third person shooter** set in the same world. While this has been marketed as a **transmedia** experience, it could perhaps be better described as a license; the game is set in the remains of San Francisco while the events of the series occur near St Louis, and with the exception of a few crossover characters there seems to be little connection between them. The **MMOG** (massively multiplayer online game) is centrally concerned with the phenomenon of "Arkfalls," in which valuable loot—in the form of debris from the aliens' shattered starships—regularly drops from orbit to the surface, where it can be scavenged by players' characters. As with its parent, the game of *Defiance* could be said to offer acceptable, if somewhat generic, entertainment.

Web Link

- *Defiance*: http://www.defiance.com/

EVE ONLINE

2003. (Revised *2009* as *EVE Online: Special Edition*; revised *2010* as *Eve Online: Commissioned Officer Edition*.) CCP. Designed by Reynir Harðarson.

EVE Online is perhaps best described as a **massively multiplayer online space sim**. While the game has role-playing elements, including the ability to improve the skills of players' characters, it could be said that in *EVE Online*, a player's true character is their spaceship. The setting is a **space opera** universe in which a group of humans have reached another galaxy through a **faster than light** gateway that then collapsed, leaving them to fend for themselves. *EVE Online*'s core gameplay is similar to that of *Elite* (*1984*) designed by David Braben and Ian Bell or the *X Series* (from *1999* Egosoft), concentrating on mining, trading, exploration, combat, and improving the player's spacecraft; planets and space stations exist, but cannot be visited. The most interesting aspect of the game, however, is its strongly **libertarian** society. In contrast to such **massively multiplayer online role playing games** as *Anarchy Online* (*2001* Funcom) designed by Gaute Godager, Ragnar Tørnquist, which enforce limitations on players' actions by dictating the rules of their reality, *EVE Online* has very few restrictions. Within the civilized parts of its simulated universe, local military bodies will enforce the law, but in unsettled space, players indulging in piracy, protection rackets, and fraud are common. Another unusual feature is the nature of the economy, which is simulated in considerable detail, allowing players to create complex financial schemes. *EVE Online* is also distinctive for its maintenance of a single coherent **online world** for all players, in contrast to such games as *Star Wars: Galaxies* (*2003* Sony Online Entertainment) designed by Raph Koster, which create multiple separate images of the simulated reality, each inhabited by a fraction of their total population. While a war of all against all may seem the likely consequence of this design, the combination of the high cost of dying (which can result in a player paying for both a new ship and a clone of their character to be grown before they can resume play) with the ability to form capitalist corporations (for mutual defense and profit sharing) appears to have encouraged the emergence of a frontier mentality, in which large groups of players enforce their own informal laws.

An orbital view of Caldari Prime, the homeworld of one of the major polities in the universe of *EVE Online*.

One of the larger vessels in *EVE Online*, the cargo-carrying Epithal.

EVE Online is a slow game, with moments of striking, unpredictable beauty, which can be very **immersive** for players who find its freedom appealing. While the designers do impose some large-scale narrative structures, including intermittent warfare between the major spacegoing cultures, the primary source of story in the game is the players themselves. Such features as the ability of groups of characters to construct starbases and claim sovereignty over solar systems have encouraged the formation of alliances of corporations including thousands of players. Some alliances have fought galactic wars with each other, an interesting indication of the game's ability to engender **environmental** narratives. It is also notable that *EVE Online*'s players have formed an unusually strong attachment to the work; disagreements with the developers over corporate policy have triggered virtual rebellions within the game. Arguably, the participants' creation of much of the game-world's fiction has fostered a sense of ownership. As of 2013, *EVE Online* had more subscribers than the number of inhabitants of Iceland, where it was developed; it will be interesting to see how much more it can grow.

Moments of unexpected beauty are common in the simulated space of *EVE Online*.

Related works: *EVE: The Second Genesis CCG* (*2006* CCP) designed by Pétur Örn Þórarinsson, Stefán Friðriksson, and Reynir Harðarson is a **collectible card game** based on the franchise. *Eve: The Empyrean Age* (**2008**), by Tony Gonzales, is a **tie,** which fills in the background to the events seen in the *Empyrean Age* expansion, made available to subscribers as a download in 2008. Further spin-offs include *Eve: The Burning Life* (**2010**) by Hjalti Daníelsson, one of the designers of the game, and *Eve: Templar One* (**2011**), also by Gonzales.

Dust 514 (*2013* CCP) is a massively multiplayer **first person shooter** set in the universe of *EVE Online*. As in an **MMORPG**, players' characters can be customized by selectively training them in various skills, but—in a common development for members of this form—participants, who can normally play without charge, will find that boosting their characters' abilities is very much easier if they are willing to pay. While much of the gameplay is reminiscent of such earlier massively multiplayer **FPS** games as *PlanetSide 2* (*2012* Sony Online Entertainment), the firefights are generally on a smaller scale than those supported by such works. As in *EVE Online*, dead characters can be resurrected, here through the medium of an implant, which records brain activity. (In a similar manner to that described in such earlier sf novels as Richard Morgan's **Takeshi Kovacs** sequence, these memories can be downloaded into a cloned body in the event of the original's death.)

Perhaps the most interesting aspect of *Dust 514* is its integration with its companion game. As in such predecessors as the board and counter **wargames** *Starsoldier* (*1977* Simulations Publications Inc [SPI]) designed by Tom Walczyk and *Starforce: Alpha Centauri* (*1974* SPI) designed by Redmond Simonsen, the tactical battles of the FPS can represent conflicts for actual possession of planets in the universe of *EVE Online*, with players of the latter game providing support by bombarding surface targets from orbit. In the current version, however, this pairing resembles that between SPI's games in another and less fortunate way; the coupling between the two works is relatively weak. This can leave players of the FPS with little sense of participation in the complex struggles of the larger milieu.

Web Links

- *EVE Online*: http://www.eve-online.com/

- CCP on EVE Online: http://www.gamasutra.com/features/20050923/rossignol_01.shtml

STAR WARS: GALAXIES

2003. Sony Online Entertainment (SOE). Designed by Raph Koster.

While the milieu of *Star Wars: Galaxies* was licensed from the eponymous film series (specifically, it was set in a frozen historical moment between *Star Wars: Episode IV – A New Hope* [*1977*] and *Star Wars: Episode V – The Empire Strikes Back* [*1980*]), when it was launched, the game represented the cutting edge of **massively multiplayer online role playing game** design. Players were offered a wide range of character types, including supportive options such as artisans (who created weapons and equipment) and entertainers (such as musicians and dancers), as well as the more conventional adventurers and medical experts. Character types were designed to be dependent on each other, requiring players to interact; for example, adventurers needed to relieve their "combat fatigue" by employing entertainers to relax them. Other aspects of the game were derived from previous **MMORPGs,** including a system that automatically generated missions for players to complete similar to that used in *Anarchy Online* (*2001* Funcom) designed by Gaute Godager and Ragnar Tørnquist. As is common in large persistent **online worlds,** death in *Star Wars: Galaxies* was made into a temporary inconvenience, and players were only able to attack each other under special circumstances. Community formation was encouraged by such means as allowing players to elect their own Mayors to run virtual cities, and the simulated economy was centered on the artisans, who were the only individuals capable of making many valuable items. While it was possible for characters to become Force-wielding Jedi, the ultimate heroes of the films, the path players had to follow to reach this goal was initially kept secret, lending its eventual achievement the mystique of a true hero's journey.

However, while the game's skilled evocation of the tone of the original trilogy of *Star Wars* films and the striking visual designs of its planets were widely praised, *Star Wars: Galaxies* proved to be considerably less popular than its developers had hoped. It remains unclear whether this was due to a somewhat imperfect initial implementation or to a fundamentally flawed conception. Certainly, many players found the roles of entertainers and artisans less varied and stimulating in practice than they had hoped. In 2005, the "New Game Enhancements" radically revised the gameplay, eliminating many of the available character types while reducing the value of some of those remaining and the strength of the links between them, as well as making Jedi status far easier to achieve. While initially popular with some players, this new version of the game was also not met with long-term commercial success. It was, perhaps, too conventional and too similar to previous MMORPGs such as the fantasy-based *EverQuest* (*1999* VI) designed by Brad McQuaid, Steve Clover, and Bill Trost. The lead designer of *Star Wars: Galaxies* left the project after the 2005 revisions, and the game entered a long decline; it was eventually shut down in 2011. Ultimately, *Galaxies* was judged by its backers to have failed as a commercial venture and was replaced by *Star Wars: The Old Republic* (*2011* BioWare) designed by James Ohlen, Emmanuel Lusinchi, Brad Prince, and Daniel Erickson, another MMORPG based on the *Star Wars* license, but this time set in the derivative milieu of BioWare's 2003 **computer role playing game** *Star Wars: Knights of the Old Republic* rather than that of the original films.

Related works: The main game was released as *Star Wars: Galaxies – An Empire Divided* (*2003* SOE) designed by Raph Koster. There were several expansions: *Star Wars: Galaxies – Jump to Light Speed* (*2004* SOE), which gave players the ability to fly their own spacecraft; *Star Wars: Galaxies – Rage of the Wookiees* (*2005* SOE), which included the homeworld of the eponymous race; and *Star Wars: Galaxies – Trials of Obi-Wan* (*2005* SOE), in which players could perform various missions for the titular Jedi Master. *Star Wars Galaxies: Trading Card Game* (*2008* SOE) was an associated **collectible card game** that could only be played online. *The Ruins of Dantooine* (**2003**), by Voronica Whitney-Robinson and Haden Blackman, is a **tie** to the game.

Web Link

- Star Wars Galaxies Online (Tribute Site): http://www. starwarsgalaxiesonline.com

STAR WARS: THE OLD REPUBLIC

2011. BioWare. Designed by James Ohlen, Emmanuel Lusinchi, Brad Prince, and Daniel Erickson.

After it became clear that Sony Online Entertainment's *Star Wars: Galaxies* would not be a commercial success, and since it was generally believed that the causes of that game's failure could be found in its design or implementation rather than in the intellectual property from which it was licensed, a decision was made to build a new **massively multiplayer online role playing game** set in the *Star Wars* universe. This time, however, the game was not based directly on the original films, but was instead derived from one of the most popular **videogame** incarnations of the franchise to date, *Star Wars: Knights of the Old Republic* (*2003* BioWare). This game is set 4000 years previous to *Star Wars: Episode I – The Phantom Menace* (*1999*), in a time that is both different from and yet remarkably similar to that of the films. The gameplay of *The Old Republic* occurs 300 years after that of *Knights of the Old Republic*, when the eponymous democracy is engaged in a galactic cold war with the evil Sith Empire, one that seemingly could turn hot at any moment. This milieu is skillfully depicted, with an excellent feel for the ambience conveyed by the original cinema trilogy. Throughout, the game is very professionally constructed; it may represent the state of the art in **MMORPG** design.

While *The Old Republic* appears much influenced by the **heroic fantasy** game *World of Warcraft* (*2004* BE) designed by Rob Pardo, Jeff Kaplan, and Tom Chilton, it shows a definite preference for story over that work's emphasis on place. The player's experience is notably more guided than in *World of Warcraft*, with much time spent in complex **multilinear interactive narratives** specific to the character's profession (such as Bounty Hunter or Smuggler) in addition to the **environmental** stories that are typical of the form. Notably, these branching plots do not affect the entire universe, unlike the problematically world-altering arc narratives of *Asheron's Call* (*1999* Turbine Entertainment) designed by Toby Ragaini, Eri Izawa, Chris Pierson, and Chris Foster. Instead, they are adventure paths along which the player's choices determine only their own stories and those of their computer-controlled companions. As in the later iterations of *Star Wars: Galaxies*, becoming a member of the spiritual Jedi order (or its polar opposite, the evil Sith) is simply a matter of player choice, but the resulting problems seen in *Galaxies*—where the significance of joining such an order was devalued by their members' excessive abundance within the game—are finessed by making player Jedi into specially gifted exemplars of the type.

The game has clearly been designed to be as continuously enjoyable as possible. Thus, potentially uninteresting parts of the player's experience— such as flying over large empty landscapes or creating new equipment—are generally either skipped over entirely or made assignable to computer-controlled assistants. As in many similar games, play concentrates on a combination of completing assigned missions, undirected exploration, and combat, with some conversation (though less than is found in other works from the same developer, such as 2007s *Mass Effect*). As in *Knights of the Old Republic*, the player's behavior is tracked and determines their assumed allegiance to the dark (Sith) or light (Jedi) side of the mystic Force, and hence affects the actions of computer-controlled characters who might ally with them or oppose them. Interestingly, characters who are members of the Sith Empire can still find themselves categorized as good, and *vice versa*. While *The Old Republic* differs from most persistent online games by encouraging players to spend much of their time pursuing their own character's personal plot, the game also includes more difficult missions and briefer story lines that can be shared by multiple players. To date, however, it seems that these experiences may be less compelling than the more complex narratives intended for individuals. Certainly, many players have left the game after completing their character's prescripted journey to heroism (or villainy), suggesting that for some, the shared areas may not be worth the monthly fee. In late 2012, the publishers responded to this development by making the earlier parts of the game's various story lines freely available, while still charging for access to other portions of the work. While *The Old Republic* is by no means a commercial failure, its design and business model are still evolving; it will be interesting to see their final forms.

Related works: *Rise of the Hutt Cartel* (*2013* BioWare) is an expansion for *The Old Republic*, focusing on an eponymous third faction in the setting's central conflict. *Star Wars: The Old Republic: Fatal Alliance* (**2010**), by Sean Williams, is a loose prequel to the game, while *Star Wars: The Old Republic: Deceived* (**2011**), by Paul S. Kemp, deals with the aftermath of the sacking of an important Jedi world. Other related **ties** include Drew Karpyshyn's *Star Wars: The Old Republic: Annihilation* (**2012**) and Joe Schreiber's *Star Wars: The Old Republic: Red Harvest* (**2010**), which features zombie Sith. *Star Wars: The Old Republic* (*2010–2011*) is an associated comics series, which also serves as a prequel to the game; its authors include Alexander Freed, one of the writers for *The Old Republic*.

Web Link
- Star Wars: The Old Republic: http://www.swtor.com/

TABULA RASA

2007. Destination Games. Designed by Richard Garriott, Paul Sage, and Susan Kath.

Tabula Rasa was a **massively multiplayer online role playing game**, much influenced by **third person shooters**. In the game's backstory, a near-future Earth had been invaded by an alien empire. The attackers were ruled by a race known as the Bane, an offshoot of a **forerunner** civilization that had decided to guarantee its future dominance by destroying or enslaving any species that might eventually challenge it. Humanity proved unable to effectively resist the invasion, but some survivors escaped to distant worlds through alien **wormholes**, where they joined an army of other displaced species at war with the Bane. As might be expected in an **MMORPG**, this conflict was effectively endless; neither side could be allowed victory, since that would have destroyed the rationale for the game. The tone was similar to that of much **military sf**, and especially suggestive of a darker-hued version of the television series *Stargate SG-1* (*1997–2007*), in which contemporary US and Russian militaries are engaged in a covert war on a galactic scale.

Tabula Rasa's gameplay blended that of a combat-based massively multiplayer online role playing game with that of more intensely action-oriented games such as the **first person shooter** *Halo: Combat Evolved* (*2001* BS) designed by John Howard; success in battle depended both on physical abilities such as accuracy and reaction time and on the skills of the player's character, which improved as progress was made in the game. Characters were all human, but could acquire special powers by incorporating alien genetic material into their bodies or by learning the Logos, a universal language that affected the nature of reality. (Comprehension of Logos fragments left by the forerunners allowed humans to gain **psionic** abilities, converting matter into energy by force of will.) As in such **massively multiplayer** online first-person shooters as *PlanetSide* (*2003* VI) designed by Terrence Yee, the player's experience bore little relationship to that of members of an actual army. Instead, the contested areas of planetary surface resembled anarchic free-fire zones in which characters adopted roles similar to those of bounty hunters, selecting which military missions they wished to perform. Perhaps the most interesting aspect of the game's design was its "ethical parables," missions in which the player had to make a moral choice, weighing ends against means. Such decisions, which were typically made in private copies of an area of the battlefield that could be entered only by the individual or group assigned to the task, allowed players to define the personalities of their characters, and determined how computer-controlled comrades would react to them. These parables attracted little interest from players, however, and the game apparently failed to acquire enough subscribers to make a profit. It was shut down in 2009.

CHAPTER 9

Alternate Reality Games

A N ALTERNATE REALITY GAME (ARG) is a type of **videogame** that shares much with the fictional **literary god games** described in such works as Robert Shea and Robert Anton Wilson's **Illuminatus** trilogy and Thomas Pynchon's *The Crying of Lot 49* (**1966**). There is a notable resemblance between many examples of the form and the (perhaps carefully orchestrated) intrusion of the miraculous into the mundane experienced by the protagonist of the latter novel. In the classic literary god game, a magus figure constructs an illusory existence around the protagonist to teach or transform them; in an **ARG**, the world the players live in is altered to make it seem more significant and meaningful, though the new reality is deliberately made to be less than wholly convincing. Actual gameplay in an ARG often resembles that of a **live-action role-playing** game, but one with many more participants and without explicit rules or roles to play. Typically, games begin with the distribution of clues or entry points into the work's fiction, such as coded messages concealed in posters, clothing, or music. Players then spread this information on the Internet and use their collective intelligence to solve predesigned puzzles, allowing them to reassemble the fragments of an **embedded** narrative that explains the nature of the game. Notably, such works deny their status as games, instead presenting the fiction as real. Their true nature is generally made clear by the context, however, for example, by the use of websites that claim to be in the future. ARGs are also usually unannounced and unadvertised. Instead, they depend on their players to discover the initial clues and then make contact with others interested in searching for more. Once the game has begun, the story continues through regular updates, shaped by the designers in response to the players' discoveries and beliefs as revealed by monitoring their online discussions. The designers— often referred to as **puppetmasters**—thus act as secret **gamemasters**, generating an evolving drama based on prepared scenarios in the manner of a tabletop **role-playing game**. Players are typically able to communicate with characters in the story, by speaking to actors on the telephone or communicating on the Internet, and may be asked to personally attend rallies or perform simple tasks as well as uncovering information and decoding clues. Fundamentally, the design of such works depends on large groups of players assembling spontaneously and using their communal knowledge to make progress; they are, along with **massively multiplayer online games**, perhaps the first game forms native to the Internet.

The clearest precursors of ARGs are **role-playing games**, especially live-action role-playing games. Notably, *Assassins*, which evolved in Anglo-Saxon colleges and universities in the 1970s and was published as *Killer* (*1982* Steve Jackson Games), shares with ARGs the quality of intruding on players' normal lives. While ARGs may involve participants receiving telephone calls or packages at home, *Killer* makes an individual's entire life part of the game; players can be "eliminated" at any time using mock weapons such as toy guns and water balloons as part of a simulated "assassins' duel." Early Internet-based works that share some of the form's traits include the promotional **cyberpunk** game *Webrunner* (*1996* Wizards of the Coast) designed by Richard Garfield and the contemporary horror **hypertext**-based fiction *Dreadnot* (*1996*), which contained hidden clues on its website and references to physical objects constructed to support the story. The first clear examples of the form, however, are *The Beast* (*2001* Microsoft) designed by Jordan Weisman, Elan Lee, and Sean Stewart, created to promote the film *A.I. Artificial Intelligence* (*2001*), and *Majestic* (*2001* Electronic Arts) designed by Neil Young, a subscription-based videogame that proved rather less popular than its contemporary. *Majestic* appears to have failed commercially at least partly because the requirements that players sign a legal waiver and pay to play, which may be unavoidable for a profit-making game, made it difficult to sustain the sense of participating in a story that was at least half real. Almost all subsequent ARGs, therefore, have followed the model used by *The Beast*, which was free to play (and unadvertised), with funding obtained from the marketing budget for *A.I. Artificial Intelligence*. Such works have become fairly common as promotional devices for films, videogames, television series, and on occasion other products such as cars, though some examples that have been described as ARGs can be difficult to distinguish from viral marketing campaigns. Notable science fiction (sf) examples include *I Love Bees* (*2004* 42 Entertainment) designed by Sean Stewart, Elan Lee, and Jordan Weisman to promote the release of *Halo 2* (*2004* Bungie Studios) and *Year Zero* (*2007* 42 Entertainment) designed by Sean Stewart, a game based on the *Nine Inch Nails* album of the same name. This latter work presented a more detailed picture of the dystopian future that serves as background to the album and could more accurately be described as an expansion of the concept behind the music than as an advertisement for it. A community of enthusiasts, initially formed around *The Beast*, have also become active in producing smaller-scale amateur examples of the form, some of which are of impressive quality; amateur sf games include *Lockjaw* (*2002*) designed by Andy Aiken, Bruce Cain, Clay Chiment, Derek Jensen, Brooke Thompson, and Krystyn Wells—the first work to be described as an ARG, by Sean Stacey—and *ChangeAgents: Out of Control* (*2002*) designed by Dave Szulborski, a spin-off from *Majestic*.

The concept of the ARG has proved influential on sf writers, appearing in Walter Jon Williams' *This Is Not a Game: A Novel* (**2009**) and (in the guise of the "footage," enigmatic film clips distributed on the Internet that enthusiasts attempt to decode and assemble into a coherent narrative) perhaps also in William Gibson's *Pattern Recognition* (**2003**). The form itself, however, remains somewhat limited by its general dependence on marketing budgets; most attempts to generate revenue from games of this kind, such as works based on winning prizes, have not proved successful. While interest in the form has declined in the second decade of the twenty-first century, the model represented by *Year Zero*, in which the ARG is a freely available part of a commercial **transmedia** fiction, may ultimately prove to be a fruitful approach to financing these works.

FURTHER READING

- Dave Szulborski. *This Is Not a Game: A Guide to Alternate Reality Gaming.* 2005. (Contains a detailed history of the form as well as advice on designing and running a game.)

Web Links

- Unfiction: http://www.unfiction.com/

- Alternate Reality Gaming Network: http://www.argn.com/

BEAST, THE

2001. (Also known as *A.I. Web Game.*) Microsoft. Designed by Jordan Weisman, Elan Lee, and Sean Stewart.

The Beast was the first **ARG**. The key premises underlying its design were that it should be a cooperative game (solved by many people working together on the Internet), that its existence should be kept secret from the players (so that they could discover it on their own), that its story should be delivered through as many routes as possible (including telephone calls, faxes, and websites), and that it should contain a strong **embedded** narrative that the players would have to reassemble from fragments. Based on this approach, the designers also decided that the game should never admit it was a game; all of the story elements would be presented as if they were real. These concepts were then used to design a promotional game for Steven Spielberg's film *A.I. Artificial Intelligence* (2001), set in the film's future world but expressed as a present tense narrative. Several entry points were provided for potential players, including an incongruous credit for a "sentient machine therapist" called Jeanine Salla in some of the film's trailers and posters, as well as phone numbers and secret messages encoded in other promotional material. These "rabbit holes" were rapidly discovered, leading players to a separate world of recorded phone messages and fake websites that implied a man named Evan Chan had been murdered and that "Jeanine is the key." The story that was eventually uncovered was well crafted and strikingly complex, featuring a pogrom against artificially intelligent houses and a missing robot built for sex. Players were often asked to participate directly in the narrative, helping characters they had come to know and attending rallies of the fictional "Anti-Robot Militia." The majority of the gameplay revolved around cryptic puzzles that required collaboration to solve; examples include messages written in the language of the Indian state of Karnataka and clues encoded into digital images. Players rapidly formed communities on the Internet to discuss the game that became the primary venues for its play, the most prominent of which was the "cloudmakers" group. As in a tabletop **role-playing game**, *The Beast*'s narrative was not entirely predetermined; the designers, referred to by the cloudmakers as "puppetmasters," monitored the players' progress and tailored the new material that was released every week to ensure that the story line remained involving and that it would be resolved before the premiere of the film.

The game's blurring of the line between fiction and reality, and the sense of personal involvement in and power over an ongoing story that it bestowed, made it an extremely affecting experience for many players. It is important to recognize, however, that *The Beast* never entirely shed its fictional identity; from the outset, it was clear that the mysterious discoveries made by the players were linked to *A.I. Artificial Intelligence* and that they were occurring in its science-fictional future. If there had truly been no boundary between the game world and the actual one, the experience might have evoked more fear than fascination in its participants. Nevertheless, *The Beast* was far less obviously artificial than its markedly less popular cousin *Majestic* (*2001* Electronic Arts) designed by Neil Young, a fact which undoubtedly contributed to its success. As well as being the first professionally created ARG, *The Beast* also inspired many members of the cloudmakers community to create their own similar games, giving birth to a new amateur art form.

Web Links

- Sf writer Sean Stewart on *The Beast*: http://www.seanstewart.org/beast/intro/

- cloudmakers.org: http://www.cloudmakers.org/

MAJESTIC

2001. Electronic Arts. Designed by Neil Young.

Majestic was one of the first **ARGs** and to date the only one to be launched through conventional game distribution channels. Promoted as "The Game That Plays You," it was intended to blur the line between fiction and reality by intruding into players' daily lives, an idea apparently inspired by the film *The Game* (*1997*). As part of playing the game, *Majestic*'s subscribers would receive phone calls and e-mail, visit websites, and talk with game characters via instant messaging services. The plot was based on UFO conspiracy theories; the title refers to the "Majestic 12" group supposedly formed by President Truman to investigate and cover up alien activity on Earth following a flying saucer crash at Roswell in 1947. As soon as players started the game, they would receive a message indicating that the computers belonging to the purported developer, Anim-X, were out of action, after which they would learn that the Anim-X studios had suffered an "accident" and the game was shut down. From then on, the players would be drawn into helping the Anim-X employees, who were apparently in hiding after realizing that their game had come too close to the truth about a government conspiracy involving mind control technology.

Soon players would find themselves cooperatively solving puzzles online to help the fugitive developers, while receiving threatening phone messages from shadowy forces.

In reality, *Majestic* was developed by Electronic Arts, and Anim-X did not exist; its apparent destruction was the first event in the game. The intention was to draw players into a tangled web of conspiracy theories within which, despite having bought the game, they could not be entirely certain what was fact and what was fiction. In order to reduce costs, however, software was used to simulate game characters in online messaging services, and telephone calls to players were prerecorded, eliminating any possibility of engaging in a dialogue with callers. These technical constraints, combined with the administrative machinery surrounding the game (which was required to gain players' permission for the work's intrusions into their everyday lives), significantly reduced most participants' sense of **immersion**. Many players also felt frustrated by the pace of plot development, which was too slow for some and too quick for others. In any event, *Majestic* proved to be a commercial failure and was shut down after 9 months. While the game remains a fascinating experiment, it seems likely that the future of ARGs lies with more subtle, non-profit-making, works such as *I Love Bees* (*2004* 42 Entertainment) designed by Sean Stewart, Elan Lee, and Jordan Weisman.

CHAPTER 10

First-Person Shooters

A FIRST-PERSON SHOOTER (FPS) IS a kind of **videogame** that is distinguished by a **3D** character's eye view of the world and fast-paced, often violent, gameplay that requires players to react rapidly and acquire physical skills. "First person" refers to the camera position—as opposed to the third-person view of the main character used in most graphical **adventures** and **computer role-playing games (CRPGs)**—and "shooter" to the player's most common action. Later examples of the type have added a variety of other elements to the gameplay, including puzzle solution, exploration, and an increasing focus on (usually **linear**) narrative, but physical combat is still the core of the form's appeal. The speed and immediacy of the FPS make it perhaps the type of videogame most analogous to film, though it is clearly more closely related to the violent action of *The Terminator* (*1984*) than to the pensive montages of *La Jetée* (*1963*).

First-person perspective games based on combat evolved early in the history of videogames. The first example may have been *Maze War* (*1973*; also known as *Maze*) designed by Steve Colley, Greg Thompson, and Howard Palmer, a game created at a Californian NASA center, which allowed several players to enter a 3D maze drawn using simple lines and shoot at each other. Isolated examples of similar gameplay appeared over the next two decades in such works as the tank-combat-based *Battlezone* (*1980* Atari) designed by Ed Rotberg, *Voyager I* (*1981* Avalon Hill) designed by William Volk—in which the player must destroy a ship full of **berserker** robots—the UK-developed games *3D Monster Maze* (*1981* J. K. Greye Software) designed by Malcolm Evans and *Driller* (*1987* Major Developments; also known as *Space Station Oblivion* in the United States), and *Ultima Underworld: The Stygian Abyss* (*1992* Blue Sky Productions) designed by Paul Neurath, a CRPG with a fantasy setting that focuses on **real-time** combat in 3D perspective. The FPS form, however, is generally regarded as having begun with the American game *Wolfenstein 3D* (*1992* id Software [id]) designed by John Carmack and John Romero, in which the player must fight their way through various covert missions in a not especially serious version of World War II, including slaughtering an army of mutant zombies and assassinating Adolf Hitler (who is wearing a suit of mechanical armor). This game has a fluidity and immediacy lacking in its predecessors, partly as a result of technical improvements that allowed it to use more realistic, rapidly updating visuals; the resulting sense of intensity has come to define the form.

Wolfenstein 3D was followed by *Doom* (*1993* id) designed by John Romero, John Carmack, Tom Hall, and Sandy Petersen, which made the form famous, and then by a wave of similar games including *Quake* (*1996* id) designed by John Carmack, American McGee, Sandy Peterson, John Romero, and Tim Willits; *Unreal* (*1998* Epic Games) designed by Cliff Bleszinski and James Schmalz; and the broadly parodic and mildly pornographic *Duke Nukem 3D* (*1996* 3D Realms) designed by George Broussard and Todd Replogle. The UK-developed *Aliens Versus Predator* (*1999* Rebellion) took something of a different approach, concentrating on evoking a sense of vulnerability more than on carefree mayhem. The *Marathon Trilogy* (from *1994* Bungie Studios [BS]) and *System Shock* (*1994* Looking Glass [LG]) designed by Doug Church added linear stories, an element almost entirely absent from *Doom*, though this innovation did not attract much attention at the time. Meanwhile, two concepts popularized by *Doom* and its successors had a major effect on videogames in general: competitive (and later cooperative) games between several players in temporary **online worlds** and the creation and free distribution of new content by the game's players as well as by its developers. Almost all early FPSs were science fiction (sf); a rare exception is the **sword and sorcery** *Heretic* (*1994* Raven Software; *1995* revised as *Heretic: Shadow of the Serpent Riders*) designed by Brian Raffel.

In the late 1990s, developers devoted considerable effort to expanding the boundaries of FPS design. *Half-Life* (*1998* Valve) added a credible and well-integrated linear story, created by the sf writer Marc Laidlaw. The **steampunk** and sorcery game *Thief: The Dark Project* (*1998* LG; *1999* revised as *Thief Gold*) designed by Greg LoPiccolo, Doug Church, and Ken Levine introduced gameplay that depended more on stealth and subtle trickery than heroic combat. *Deus Ex* (*2000* Ion Storm [IS]) designed by Warren Spector and Harvey Smith, perhaps the most interesting of all these games, combined the traditional FPS with elements borrowed from CRPGs in a novel science-fictional milieu, while *Tom Clancy's Rainbow Six* (*1998* Red Storm Entertainment) designed by Brian Upton emphasized tactical cooperation with other (computer-controlled) squad members in a broadly realistic setting based on Clancy's eponymous techno-thriller. Another line of development began with *Starsiege: Tribes* (*1998* Dynamix), a spin-off from the *Metaltech* universe, which concentrated entirely on competitive play between large teams in online worlds. Meanwhile, the form, previously largely restricted to personal computers, was brought to home consoles by such games as *Halo: Combat Evolved* (*2001* BS) designed by John Howard and the UK-developed *Perfect Dark* (*2000* Rare) designed by Martin Hollis. More recent FPSs have made frequent use of many of these elements. Notably, the stories experienced by individual players have become increasingly important (despite an enduring lack of narrative sophistication in many works), while competitive play between multiple online participants is now a major selling point for most members of the form. Arguably, however, the tradition has become somewhat static; new games increasingly resemble the old, possibly because commercial considerations discourage risk taking or perhaps because the mix of action, violence, and reflection in the typical work is approaching some kind of optimum.

FPSs remain highly popular, though perhaps more so among dedicated videogame players than in the mass market. Sf is still a common setting, but techno-thrillers and games based on historical and contemporary warfare may now have become the form's default modes; an example of the former school is the well-known *Call of Duty: Modern Warfare 2* (*2009* Infinity Ward) designed by Jason West. One recent trend is the increasing prevalence of the **third-person shooter**, a related type of game in which the player character is seen from an external view. The FPS is still a popular form, however, as demonstrated by the high sales of such recent sf games as *Bioshock* (*2007* 2K Boston/2K Australia) designed by Ken Levine, the remarkable *Stalker: Shadow of Chernobyl* (*2007* GSC Game World)—developed in the Ukraine near the eponymous nuclear reactor—the somewhat generic *Killzone 3* (*2011* Sony Computer Entertainment) designed by Mathijs de Jonge, and *Halo 4* (*2012* 343 Industries) designed by Scott Warner and Josh Holmes, a sequel to *Halo: Combat Evolved*. The next few years may even see a resurgence in the popularity of the classic science-fictional **FPS**; the two most widely advertised upcoming games in the form are the **mecha**-based *Titanfall* and *Destiny*, set on a devastated future Earth.

FURTHER READING

- David Kushner. *Masters of Doom: How Two Guys Created an Empire and Transformed Pop Culture*. 2003. (A popular history of the creation of Wolfenstein 3D, Doom and Quake.)

ALIENS VERSUS PREDATOR

1999. Rebellion.

The *Aliens Versus Predator* franchise began with the four-issue comic series *Aliens vs. Predator* (*1990*), written by Randy Stradley and published by Dark Horse, which already had licenses to produce comics based on both 1986s *Aliens* film and 1987s *Predator*. This late twentieth-century equivalent of such Universal Studios films as *Frankenstein Meets the Wolf Man* (*1943*) proved popular, leading to the creation of versions of the concept in a variety of media, including books, **videogames**, and the film *AVP Alien vs. Predator* (*2004*). Perhaps the most interesting of these variants is the series of **FPSs** for the Windows platform beginning with *Aliens Versus Predator*. The original game is notable chiefly for its skilful evocation of the source material's sense of lurking dread and for the fact that players can adopt the roles of a predator or an alien as well as a human marine. (This latter feature had previously appeared in the developers' earlier but less well-known **FPS** for the Atari Jaguar console, *Alien vs. Predator* [*1994* Rebellion].) Gameplay in the three modes is significantly different; the alien can walk on walls but must attack at close range, while the predator can become invisible and has access to a variety of exotic weapons and modes of perception. However, it is the game's menacing ambience that is most impressive and that proved influential on such later games as *FEAR: First Encounter Assault Recon* (*2005* Monolith Productions [MP]) designed by Craig Hubbard. While its plot is somewhat incoherent, the first *Aliens Versus Predator* is a well-crafted transcription of the spirit of its licenses to a different medium.

Related works: *Aliens Versus Predator 2* (*2001* MP) is similar to its predecessor but benefits from a much superior story in which the alien, predator, and human games are all interwoven in an ingeniously designed **linear** plot. *Aliens Versus Predator 2: Primal Hunt* (*2002* Third Law

Entertainment) is an expansion pack that serves as a prequel to the second game. In the twenty-first century, Rebellion attempted to reprise their success with *Aliens vs. Predator* (*2010* Rebellion) designed by Alex Moore, which reimagines the original Windows game with a more complex—if somewhat derivative—plot and extra gore. Reviews, however, were mixed.

Web Link
- Planet AVP (Tribute Site): http://www.planetavp.com/

BIOSHOCK

2007. 2K Boston/2K Australia. Designed by Ken Levine.

Bioshock is a game much influenced by *System Shock 2* (*1999* Irrational Games [IG]/LG) designed by Doug Church. Its story begins with the player's character, Jack, in the middle of the Atlantic in 1960, having survived an airplane crash. After swimming to a nearby island, the player can discover a bathysphere and descend to the secret underwater city of Rapture. This metropolis, an apparent response to Plato's Atlantis, was built by the charismatic ideologue Andrew Ryan in 1946 as a sanctuary for followers of Ayn Rand's anarcho-conservative objectivist philosophy, allowing them to secede from a world that denied them absolute freedom. On entering Rapture, however, the player finds themselves immersed in the fragments of Ryan's broken dream; the city is falling apart and overrun with biologically enhanced monsters. In the game's back story, the discovery of a mutagen extracted from a previously unknown species of sea slug allowed Rapture's inhabitants to develop **psionic** powers and create specialized human variants by genetic engineering. The resulting objectivist utopia, however, rapidly fell victim to civil war, as an anarchist society based on rational self-interest degenerated into a Hobbesian struggle of all against all. The player soon becomes involved with the conflicts of the surviving factions and must fight their way through the ruined city to survive.

The game's plot is strongly **linear**, using a variety of subtle cues and explicit instructions to guide the player through the story. *Bioshock* is an unusually accessible **FPS**; considerable effort was spent on making it easy for mass market audiences to understand and play. The design also makes use of some elements taken from **CRPGs**, though to a lesser extent than its predecessor *System Shock 2*. Notably, characters can selectively enhance their bodies with mutagens, allowing them to gain **psychokinetic** powers, grow an armored carapace, shoot bees from their hands, and so on. The true strength of the game, however, lies in its intensity of experience.

Players are constantly bombarded with fragments of the **embedded** history of Rapture, expressed as psychic impressions, and distorted voice recordings while fighting the iconic "Big Daddies"—altered humans in bulky diving suits—in the visually striking ruins of the retro futurist "diesel punk" city. The combat can become repetitive, however, despite the wide range of aggressive options available to the player, and the design of Rapture is more suggestive of a postholocaust objectivist theme park than a subtle critique of Rand's writings. Ultimately, *Bioshock* is an excellently crafted **FPS** whose style is arguably superior to its substance.

The sequel, *Bioshock 2* (*2010* 2K Australia/2K Marin/Digital Extremes [DE]), largely reiterates the themes and gameplay of its predecessor. A decade after the events of the first game, the player adopts the role of one of the Big Daddies, a monstrous bodyguard who is artificially bonded to his mutated "daughter"—a "Little Sister" whose role is to generate new supplies of the sea slug–derived mutagen and harvest it from the bodies of the dead. The protagonist's Little Sister has been imprisoned by her biological mother, a fanatically antianarchist collectivist who is the new ruler of the city under the sea. Interestingly, the player must fight and kill other Big Daddies so that they can extract the mutagens that are a vital source of psionic power from their victims' Little Sisters; there are choices to be made as to how brutal (and effective) this process will be, decisions that affect the ending of the game. While much of *Bioshock 2*'s claustrophobic ambience may seem familiar, the presentation is impressive, and the game's reversal of its original's ideological opposition leaves it with as much claim to the status of a "serious shooter" as its predecessor.

Where the first two games take place in what appears to be a secret history of our own world, *Bioshock Infinite* (*2013* IG) designed by Ken Levine is set in a multiplicity of overlapping **alternate histories**. Both the original *Bioshock* and *Infinite* open with the player's arrival at a lighthouse, but where the former begins with their descent into the depths of the ocean, in the latter they must ascend into the air, where they arrive at the floating cloud city of Columbia. This metropolis, a collection of disparate structures held aloft by a variety of anachronistic technologies, was launched in 1893 as a mobile symbol of the World's Columbian Exposition, held in Chicago in that year. In the game's present of 1912, it has become an extreme reflection of the nationalism, racism, and religious fervor common in pre–World War I America. The city's society is not monolithic, however; its ruling elite is opposed by a resistance group that consciously references the Occupy movements that protested against global capitalism while the game was being made. Meanwhile, the paranatural "vigors" that enable abilities similar to those provided by its predecessors' psionic mutagen appear to depend upon a mysterious essence extracted from an imprisoned young woman, a captive who the player's character is told to rescue (or kidnap) and transport to New York.

Structurally, *Infinite* is very similar to the earlier games in the series, both in its gameplay and in its linear narrative, though this work offers rather more opportunity for open movement and combat. Thematically, however, it seems quite different. Where Rapture is a hidden city resembling such lost worlds as Edgar Rice Burroughs' **Opar** or H Rider Haggard's **Kôr**, Columbia's universe is formed from a multiplicity of conflicting **parallel worlds** and alternate futures; the plot is ultimately revealed to depend upon a kind of **changewar**.

More significantly, perhaps, the first two games' relatively clear-cut villains are absent here. Both the rulers of the floating city and its rebels are dangerous fanatics, while the player's character begins the game with a questionable past and will presumably go on to wreak the kind of havoc expected of the protagonists of FPSs. Ultimately, the only true innocent in this story may be Elizabeth, the woman who the player sets out to find. The message of *Infinite* is, perhaps, better aligned with its medium than were those of its predecessors; here, it seems violence and extremism are always wrong, even when they are directed against the violent and extreme.

Related works: *Bioshock* (*2009* Studio Lakshya) designed by Purnima Iyer, Manish Saraswat, and Varun Bhavnani is a simplified variant of the first game that is played in a **2D** plan view. A separate version for more powerful devices, *Bioshock* (*2010* Studio Tridev), preserves the original's **3D** displays. Various expansion packs have been released for the second installment in the main series. Thus, *Bioshock 2: Sinclair Solutions Test Pack* (*2010* 2K Marin) makes new locations available for competitive play in a temporary **online world**, while *Bioshock 2: Protector Trials Pack* (*2010* 2K Marin) includes several new single-player combat sequences: *Bioshock 2: Rapture Metro Map Pack* (*2010* 2K Marin) concentrates on player versus player combat and *Bioshock 2: Minerva's Den* (*2010* 2K Marin) positions the player as another Big Daddy who encounters a prototype artificial intelligence known as "The Thinker." Similarly, *Bioshock Infinite: Clash in the Clouds* (*2013* IG) adds new single-player combat options to *Infinite*, while *Bioshock Infinite: Burial at Sea* (*2013* IG) extends its narrative to include a sequence set in Rapture as its civil war begins. *Bioshock Infinite: The Siege* of *Columbia* (*2013* Plaid Hat Games) designed by Isaac Vega is a board game in which players adopt the roles of the rulers or rebels of Columbia and battle for the control of the city. *Bioshock: Rapture* (**2011**), by John Shirley, is a prequel to the first game that describes the foundation and early years of the eponymous city, while *Bioshock Infinite: Mind in Revolt* (**2013**), by Ken Levine and Joe Fielder, is a short e-book that includes additional backstory for the titular game.

Web Links

- *Bioshock*: http://www.bioshockgame.com/

- *Bioshock* Postmortem: http://www.gamasutra.com/view/feature/3774/postmortem_2k_boston2k_.php

- Ken Levine on *Bioshock*'s approach to narrative: http://www.gamasutra.com/view/feature/3636/ken_levine_on_bioshocks_narrative_.php

CRYOSTASIS

2009. (Also known as *Cryostasis: Sleep of Reason* in Russia.) Action Forms. Designed by Alexander Tugaenko and Dmitry Nechay.

Cryostasis is a game influenced by the **survival horror** tradition as well as that of the **FPS**, developed in the Ukraine and set on a nuclear-powered icebreaker trapped in the Arctic. The player's character arrives under mysterious circumstances, to discover that he is the only living human on a derelict vessel occupied variously by frozen corpses and humanoid monsters who could be atomic mutants, ice spirits, or neither. Survival depends on finding sources of heat—which are all that can keep the protagonist alive in the deadly cold—killing the monsters with whatever weapons come to hand and using an unexplained form of mental time travel to enter the last moments of the crew, before attempting to correct their final, fatal mistakes. Successfully reliving the lives of the dead will cause their corpses to disappear—presumably because their deaths have been postponed, rather than canceled altogether—and allow the player to move deeper into the wreck. Often the errors of the dead have created physical barriers to progress, such as flooded compartments that can be made accessible as a result of actions taken in the past, but the game's progression in the present is in any case entirely **linear**. Playing through the time travel episodes and watching various related flashbacks will, however, eventually reveal how the ship became trapped in the ice. Such **embedded** narratives are common in FPSs, but *Cryostasis* is unusual in allowing the player to participate in the history of its disaster.

The game conveys its ambience of mournful despair and frigid threat with considerable force. Nevertheless, it is—perhaps deliberately—slow and somewhat repetitive to play; the story progresses at an appropriately glacial pace, interrupted by regular shocks and moments of panic. Frequent quotations are made from a story by Maxim Gorky in which the hero of a folktale rips his burning heart from his chest so that its flames can illuminate his people's path out of a dark and haunted forest ("The Heart of Danko," included in the 1895 short story "Starukha Izergil" [translated by Margaret Wettlin as "Old Izergil" *circa* 1950]). Though arguably rather pretentious, these references do serve to emphasize the symbolic underpinnings of the narrative, which treats its many time paradoxes with a dreamlike lack of concern for the complex details of cause and effect. Despite its essentially contemporary setting—the icebreaker is a Soviet vessel, wrecked in the 1960s and explored by the player's character in the 1980s—and heavy use of the time travel trope, *Cryostasis* is only marginally a work of sf; it might more readily be categorized as a ghost story. Ultimately, the player can save the icebreaker and her crew by enacting a narrative in the past for which Gorky's tale serves as an allegory. Regardless, the best approach to the game is perhaps to assume that the protagonist dies when he falls through the ice during its introductory sequence and the remainder of the work takes place in some kind of purgatorial afterworld.

CRYSIS

2007. Crytek. Designed by Cevat Yerli, Sten Hübler, Christopher Auty, and Bernd Diemer.

Crysis is, in essence, a game of enablement. The player adopts the role of a near-future US Delta Force operative equipped with a suit of armor powered by **nanotechnology** or "nanosuit." As in such earlier works as the board and counter **wargame** *Starsoldier* (*1977* Simulations Publications, Inc.) designed by Tom Walczyk, the suit has a limited amount of energy that can be employed in various ways, in this case to resist damage, provide active camouflage, or boost the wearer's strength or speed. The gameplay has a more realistic tone than that of many **FPSs**; much effort has been spent on accurate simulation of the environment. Initially, the player's character is ordered to rescue the members of an archaeological team that had been investigating a buried alien spacecraft discovered on an island off the coast of North Korea and who are threatened by the North Korean army. Soon, however, the aliens become active, xenoforming the island's lushly realized jungle into a frozen wasteland and deploying war machines to attack both sides. While the game's story line is essentially **linear**, its gameplay is often highly exploratory, allowing the player to accomplish their mission goals in many different ways. The characters are thin and the plot is largely derivative, but *Crysis'* main focus is on its action sequences, which can be impressively apocalyptic and (as in the zero-gravity regions inside the alien ship) genuinely novel. Ultimately, the game is surprisingly effective at giving the player a sense of how it might feel to be a superhumanly powerful soldier taking part in a covert operation.

The first game's plot ends on a cliffhanger, with a nuclear attack on the alien vessel by the US Navy. Its immediate successor, *Crysis: Warhead* (*2008* Crytek), concentrates on expanding this narrative rather than extending it, with a story line that is contemporaneous with that of the original game, focusing on another member of the Delta Force team. The later *Crysis 2* (*2011* Crytek), designed by Sten Hübler, Martin Lancaster, and Dennis Schwarz and with a story scripted by the sf writer Richard Morgan in collaboration with Lancaster, is perhaps more interesting as a work of sf. The events of this installment occur several years after those of its predecessors, in a New York transformed by a terrifying plague and an invasion of the extraterrestrials uncovered in *Crysis* into an alien environment reminiscent of the first game's semi-tropical wilderness. While *Crysis 2* is a direct sequel to its original, its gameplay is markedly more directed than that of *Crysis*, though there is still some flexibility as to how particular objectives can be achieved. The player's character, a US Marine sent into the devastated city to rescue an important scientist, soon finds himself alone and in possession of an upgraded nanosuit, one that is both more intelligent and easier to use than that in the first game. From this point on, the player is engaged in a long campaign against the aliens and their apparently subterranean warships, not to mention an army of private military contractors who (wrongly) believe the protagonist to be a carrier for the flesh-melting disease. In the end, the player can succeed in taking back Manhattan, but only by merging themselves with both the nanosuit and the stored personality of its previous owner, becoming a **posthuman** synthesis of man and machine.

In the next (and possibly last) installment, *Crysis 3* (*2013* Crytek) designed by Dennis Schwarz, Tim Partlett, Sten Hübler, and Martin Lancaster, the protagonist of the second game has been fully absorbed by his nanosuit, with his memories replaced by those of its previous wearer. This game is set 24 years after its predecessor, in a New York that has been further transformed into a literal urban jungle by its confinement inside a vast dome; within this vault, remnants of the original architecture mingle with swampy wetlands and miniature forests. The gameplay is similar to that of *Crysis 2*, though with rather more scope for exploration, but the linear narrative is more personal, concentrating on a melodramatic story of betrayal and revenge. In a rather contrived echo of contemporary politics, the private military corporation of the previous game has used alien technology to establish a monopoly on power generation; its extortionate pricing has driven much of the population into ruinous debt. Meanwhile, the company has placed the game's protagonist—whose personality is that of one of the soldiers from the original *Crysis*—in **suspended animation** so that it can study the alien technology that is integrated into his nanosuit and transported him to New York. The game begins with this character's revival by a group of rebels who oppose the corporation and continues with a series of battles against human soldiers and the aliens, who eventually succeed in opening a **wormhole** to their home planet. After an impressive sequence set in Earth orbit, all enemies can nevertheless be defeated. *Crysis 3*'s focus on personal relationships suggests that the designers intended its narrative to have a greater emotional resonance than those of its predecessors. Arguably, however, the game's story lacks the subtlety required to make this strategy effective.

Related works: *Crysis: Legion* (**2011**), by Peter Watts, is a novelization of *Crysis 2*, while *Crysis* (*2011*) is a six-issue comic series, written by Richard Morgan, which serves as a prequel to the same game. *Crysis: Escalation* (**2013**), by Gavin Smith, is a collection of linked stories set between the second and third entries in the series. *Crysis 3: The Lost Island* (*2013* Crytek) is an expansion pack for *Crysis 3* that adds new locations intended for player versus player combat in temporary **online worlds**.

Web Links

- *Crysis*: http://www.ea.com/crysis/

- Bernd Diemer on *Crysis Warhead*: http://www.gamasutra.com/view/feature/3785/learning_from_crysis_the_making_.php

DEUS EX

2000. (Also known as *Deus Ex: The Conspiracy* in the United States) Ion Storm (IS). Designed by Warren Spector and Harvey Smith.

Deus Ex is an **FPS** that borrows many elements from **CRPGs**. Notably, it includes the ability to improve the player character's skills by training and **nanotechnological** augmentation, creating a persona specialized in such activities as sniping or stealthy intrusion. The gameplay centers on missions performed by the player, which can typically be completed in a variety of different ways, including infiltration, negotiation, and hacking into computer systems. Physical combat is rarely required to complete an objective but is generally an option. As the title suggests, the game is centrally concerned with the creation of gods from the fusion of men and machines. The player's role is to decide whether such a god should be born and, if so, what form it should take.

The player's character is the significantly initialled J C Denton, a newly trained agent for the United Nations Anti-Terrorist Coalition, a group formed to fight the anarchist factions that are increasingly common in the game's dystopian vision of mid-twenty-first-century Earth. Society is collapsing due to the spread of the "Gray Death," a lethal plague for which there is no cure, only a vaccine restricted to the rich and powerful. The player rapidly finds themselves involved in a web of overlapping conspiracies, with participants including the Illuminati and Majestic 12, an organization supposedly founded by the US government to investigate UFOs. Many fictional works are evoked by this milieu, notably Grant Morrison's comic *The Invisibles* (*1994–2000*) and the later novels of such **cyberpunk** authors as Bruce Sterling. The game's plot (for which the lead writer was Sheldon Pacotti) is **multilinear**, with side branches that typically fold back into the main story, leading the player toward a single ending. There, they must decide whether to destroy the global communications network (thus bringing about a new Dark Age in which there will be no global masters), award power to the Illuminati (who will rule humanity for their own good, with an unseen but powerful hand), or merge with the artificial intelligence Helios and become a benevolent god. This question has no right answer; any of the final sequences that follow the player's decision could be considered the best.

The sequel *Deus Ex: Invisible War* (*2003* IS) designed by Warren Spector and Harvey Smith and scripted by Sheldon Pacotti simplifies the series' gameplay, primarily by removing most of the role-playing elements while making the plotting more complex and multilinear. Set 20 years after the first game, *Invisible War* presents a more postcyberpunk vision of the future, suggestive of such novels as Neal Stephenson's *The Diamond Age* (**1995**). Interestingly, the game does not define the choice that its player may have made at the end of *Deus Ex* but instead presents a world formed by a fusion of all three options. Denton is assumed to have combined with the artificial intelligence; however, this melding failed and precipitated a breakdown in global communications known as "The Collapse." Subsequently, the Illuminati acquired a great deal of power, controlling both the dominant World Trade Organization and its apparent opponent, the religious order, from behind the scenes. The player's character, "Alex D," is a clone of Denton, constructed without their knowledge as part of an attempt to find a cure for their original, who is in **suspended animation** following the failure of his unification with Helios. The game's story revolves around the attempts of the various conspiracies to recruit Alex and gain control of the character's unique biology; typically, the player will begin by agreeing to work for every faction but be forced to make choices when they are assigned incompatible tasks. In the end, there is another ultimate decision, between Denton's vision of a perfect **posthuman** democracy, the Illuminati's dream of a benevolent world dictatorship ruled from the shadows, the totalitarian theocracy espoused by the descendants of the Knights Templar, and the desire of a cybernetically linked **hive mind** for global anarchy.

Deus Ex: Human Revolution (*2011* Eidos) is a late prequel, designed by Jean-François Dugas and scripted by Mary DeMarle in collaboration with various writers including James Swallow. In spirit, this work is something of a loving homage to the first game; the gameplay is strikingly similar, though the world of *Human Revolution* seems less operable than that of its predecessor, and there are more sequences where the player is forced to engage in (occasionally frustrating) combat. In a future nearer than that of the original game, the world is increasingly divided between those who can afford cybernetic augmentations and those who cannot. The protagonist, director of security for a bioengineering company, is severely injured in an apparent act of industrial terrorism and must become a **cyborg** in order to survive and investigate the attack; increasingly conspiratorial revelations follow. The ambience could perhaps be described as transhumanist noir; this is a world of augmented prostitutes and anti-cyborg cults, where hidden factions struggle to control the direction of humanity's artificial evolution. As in the previous games in the sequence, *Human Revolution* ends with a choice that has profound consequences, here one that will determine the world's future attitude to human augmentation.

The involving atmosphere and convincing world building of the *Deus Ex* series are consistently impressive. Frequent references are made to other works with complementary themes, including such sf and sf-like novels as G K Chesterton's *The Man Who Was Thursday: A Nightmare* (**1908**) and Alfred Bester's *Tiger! Tiger!* (**1956**; also known as *The Stars My Destination*). *Deus Ex* and its various descendants are some of the most powerfully multilinear games yet created; their flexible mission structures and intricately branching plots are notably effective at allowing the player freedom to act as they think best.

Related works: *Deus Ex: Human Revolution—The Missing Link* (*2011* Eidos) is an expansion that tells a linear story interpolated into the narrative of *Human Revolution*, while *Deus Ex: Human Revolution—Tactical Enhancement Pack* (*2011* Eidos) adds various new weapons. *Deus Ex: Human Revolution* (*2011*) is a six-issue comic series associated with the eponymous game, written by Robbie Morrison. Similarly, *Deus Ex: Icarus Effect* (**2011**; also known as *Deus Ex: The Icarus Effect*) is a **tie** by James Swallow that serves as a loose prequel to *Human Revolution*. *Deus Ex: The Fall* (*2013* Eidos/nFusion Interactive), designed by Jean-François Dugas and Tyler Munden and scripted by James Swallow, is a sequel to *The Icarus Effect* intended for play on mobile devices; its design resembles that of *Human Revolution*, with a similar combination of **FPS** and **CRPG** elements.

Web Links

- Deus Ex: Human Revolution: http://www.deusex.com/

- *Deus Ex* Postmortem: http://www.gamasutra.com/features/20001206/spector_01.htm

- Planet Deus Ex (Tribute Site): http://www.planetdeusex.com/

DOOM

1993. id Software (id). Designed by John Romero, John Carmack, Tom Hall, and Sandy Petersen.

Doom is not the original **FPS**, but it was the game that popularized the form. Its combination of smoothly **immersive** graphics, rapid pace, and casual hyperviolence proved extremely popular and came to symbolize **videogames** for many people who did not play them. *Doom*'s violence is more cartoon-like than realistic; its aesthetic shares much with industrial metal music and such horror films as Sam Raimi's deliberately excessive *Army of Darkness* (1993). Essentially, it is a well-designed action game that uses sf and demonic imagery as props to furnish its fictional world.

The game's somewhat stereotypical story is essentially a **frame** narrative and of minimal importance compared to the gameplay. The player's character is a space marine who is sent to the Martian moon of Phobos to investigate after a **matter transmission** experiment by the Union Aerospace Corporation goes mysteriously wrong, causing communication to be lost and Mars' other moon, Deimos, to disappear altogether. Play begins after the character has discovered that the experiment has opened a gate to a **parallel world** loosely resembling the Christian Hell and "demons" have invaded our reality. The player must fight their way to the end of the game and make it out alive; their journey takes them through Deimos, which has been transported to the Hell Dimension and Hell itself. Gameplay revolves around combat, evading traps, and solving simple puzzles; collecting impressive weapons and other useful items such as first-aid kits is important for survival. *Doom* is structured as a series of discrete levels occurring in different areas, a common approach for action games; the various locations that the player shoots, punches, and chainsaw their way through are consistently well crafted.

Doom was innovative in several respects other than its single-player experience. While it was not the first game to allow player versus player combat in temporary **online worlds**, its skilful implementation of the concept was the first to become truly popular, essentially creating a new form of sport. The game is also easy for its players to modify by designing and adding their own levels, a feature that gave birth to a community of "modders" and has proved very influential on later games. In 1997, the underlying program code for the game was released to the public, under a license that allowed it to be modified and distributed freely as long as the modifications were also made freely available, an act that encouraged the later release of other games into the public domain. Other innovations made by id Software had less of an impact; notably, the dissemination of *Doom* as an **independent game** over the Internet did not have a major effect on the dominance of software publishing houses over the means for videogame distribution.

Doom II: Hell on Earth (1994 id) designed by John Romero is a sequel, in which Hell has invaded Earth. The player reprises their role from the first game, helping to evacuate the planet's population and then sealing the dimensional gate from the Hell side; gameplay is similar to *Doom*, with some additional monsters. *The Ultimate Doom* (1995 id) designed by John Romero is a rerelease of the first game with additional levels set between the original ending and *Doom II. Final Doom* (*1996* id/Williams) contains two separate sets of levels based on further incursions by Hell into the human universe, largely designed by modders; the underlying game is *Doom II*.

Doom 3 (*2004* id; *2012* revised as *Doom 3: BFG Edition*) is a reimagining of the first game, with much improved visuals and similar gameplay. Unlike its original, *Doom 3* has a **linear** story line that is followed through the game, scripted by the sf and fantasy writer Matthew Costello. It also has a more subtle atmosphere than the original work, borrowing from **survival horror** in its depiction of an archaeological dig on Mars, which uncovers a cache of alien artifacts. The team uses these discoveries to build a matter transmission gate, which turns out to lead straight to Hell. *Doom 3* received somewhat mixed reviews; while the graphics are impressive, the story presentation is somewhat clumsy compared to such contemporaries as *FEAR: First Encounter Assault Recon* (*2005* MP) designed by Craig Hubbard. *Doom 3: Resurrection of Evil* (*2005* id/Nerve Software) is an expansion pack that largely repeats the plot and gameplay of its original. *Doom 3* also provided much of the inspiration for the cinematic *Doom* (*2005*), notable largely for its demonstration of just how unsuitable a series of strongly combat-oriented FPSs is as the basis for a film narrative.

Regardless of the merits of its various sequels and spin-offs, however, the original game has acquired an iconic status in popular culture. It has come to epitomize an anarchic, confrontational strand in game development, which is perhaps as close as videogames have ever come to the musical ethos of punk—the spirit of *Doom*.

Related works: *Doom 64* (*1997* Midway Games) is a sequel to *Doom II*, with similar plot and gameplay. *Master Levels for Doom II* (*1995* id) is an expansion pack for *Doom II*, containing additional levels. *Doom RPG* (*2005* id/Fountainhead Entertainment) is a **turn-based CRPG** played in a first-person view, with a plot similar to that of *Doom 3*, while *Doom Resurrection* (*2009* id/Escalation Studios) is an FPS in which the player faces a predetermined sequence of enemies, with a simple story line that is interpolated into the events of the 2004 game.

Knee-Deep in the Dead (**1995**) and *Hell on Earth* (**1995**) are novelizations of *Doom* and *Doom II* that change the games' demons into hostile aliens; both are by Dafydd ab Hugh and Brad Linaweaver. *Infernal Sky* (**1996**) and *Endgame* (**1996**), also by ab Hugh and Linaweaver, continue the series. Interestingly, *Infernal Sky* reveals that Earth has been invaded as part of a war between two alien races over the relative merits of hyperrealist and deconstructionist schools of literary criticism; this is not an element that appears in the game series. *Doom* (*1996*) is a single-issue comic, notable only for its memorably poor dialogue. *Worlds on Fire* (**2008**) and *Maelstrom* (**2009**), both by Matthew J. Costello, make up a two-part novelization of *Doom 3*; a projected third volume was never published. *Doom: The Boardgame* (*2004* Fantasy Flight Games [FFG]) designed by Kevin Wilson is a well-crafted **wargame** reminiscent of *Space Hulk* (*1989* Games Workshop) designed by Richard Halliwell, to which *Doom: The Boardgame Expansion Set* (*2005* FFG) designed by Kevin Wilson is an extension.

Web Links

- John Romero on *Doom*: http://rome.ro/games_doom.htm

- Planet Doom (Tribute Site): http://www.planetdoom.com/

FEAR: FIRST ENCOUNTER ASSAULT RECON

2005. Monolith Productions (MP). Designed by Craig Hubbard.

FEAR is a game that merges the psychological horror of the Japanese film *Ring* (*1998*) with the kinetic violence of John Woo's Hong Kong action movie *Hard Boiled* (*1992*). The player's character is a new recruit to FEAR, a secret US military unit tasked with responding to "paranormal" incidents. As in *Half-Life* (*1998* Valve), the protagonist is silent; other characters speak to him but he never replies. The intention here is to increase **immersion** by emphasizing the player's direct identification with the character, as opposed to treating the protagonist as a role that the player should adopt. Such a level of identification might be disrupted by hearing the character speak in a voice that was not the player's own.

The player's first mission is to assist with the termination of a rogue military commander and his army of **telepathically** controlled clones. However, the operation soon begins to go horribly wrong, as the player is bombarded with hallucinatory images in a disturbingly decayed experimental facility. It is possible to assemble the scattered fragments of an **embedded** narrative that establishes the renegade commander Fettel as the son of a powerfully **psionic** woman, Alma, who has been used as an experimental subject. Alma was sealed in a concrete vault and left to die; it appears that she is now using Fettel to help her escape. Eventually, it emerges that the player's character is also a son of Alma, explaining the superhuman abilities he has displayed throughout the game. While the player cannot prevent Alma's release, they can sabotage the facility's reactor, possibly preventing her from taking her revenge on the outside world. *FEAR*'s cinematic visuals and disturbing flashes of aberrant imagery make playing the game an intense, visceral experience. It is surprisingly effective at making its players afraid of the dark.

The sequel is *FEAR 2: Project Origin* (*2009* MP) designed by John Mulkey, in which *FEAR*'s nameless protagonist is replaced by a new main character, a Delta Force operative sent to detain an executive of the company that experimented on Alma. In a manner reminiscent of the *Metal Gear Solid* series (from *1998* Konami), events become increasingly complex and conspiratorial; the game ends with Alma, apparently pregnant with the protagonist's child, standing in the ruins of a devastated landscape. Ultimately, however, *FEAR 2* may offer more in the way of repetition than of novelty. The third installment, *F3AR* (*2011* Day 1 Studios) designed by Frank Rooke and T. J. Wagner and scripted by Steve Niles and the filmmaker John Carpenter, allows players to adopt two roles: that of the first game's protagonist and that of the brother who was once an enemy but has now become an uneasy ally, the renegade soldier Fettel. Gameplay is similar to that of previous iterations of the series, but players who participate as Fettel can use his psychic powers to possess enemies or assault them **psychokinetically**. At the end of the game's essentially **linear** story line, the brothers fight each other once again, with the winner taking possession of Alma's newborn child. The ominous atmosphere of the original work is largely absent here, however, replaced by the thrills and spills of a more typical **FPS**.

Related works: *FEAR* includes an online multiplayer option that allows for player versus player battles. The freely available *FEAR Combat* (*2006* MP) allows players without the original game to join in online play. *FEAR: Extraction Point* (*2006* TimeGate Studios [TS]) is an expansion pack that largely reiterates *FEAR*'s themes while continuing its story; it ends with the facility's surrounding city in flames. *FEAR: Perseus Mandate* (*2007* TS) is another expansion pack, focusing on a second FEAR unit dispatched on a related mission to that seen in the first work. The story lines of both of these expansions are contradicted by the events of *FEAR 2*, however, perhaps because they were created by other hands to those that made the original game; they are thus essentially irrelevant to the series' ongoing narrative. *FEAR 2: Reborn* (*2009* MP) is an expansion pack for *FEAR 2* in which the player adopts the role of one of the clones from the first game. Ultimately, this character can become possessed by the spirit of Fettel, who is killed at the end of *FEAR*; *Reborn* thus serves as a prequel for *F3AR*.

HALF-LIFE

1998. Valve.

Half-Life is a game that is particularly notable for its depth of narrative **immersion**. It was the first **FPS** in which a story line was presented without the use of noninteractive scenes interposed between levels set in different locations. Instead, the story is integrated with the gameplay, using such techniques as overheard conversations and prescripted events triggered by player actions. While the story line itself is not particularly notable, this approach, combined with the sf writer Marc Laidlaw's well-crafted dialogue and convincingly created world, gives the player a strong sense of being involved with the narrative; similar techniques have been used in many later works.

Half-Life took an innovative approach to the presentation of its narrative by integrating the prescripted events into the gameplay, as in this sequence in which a physics experiment is interrupted by a catastrophic "resonance cascade."

Gameplay focuses on combat and physically based puzzles; the environmental design is ingenious and challenging. The player's character is Gordon Freeman, a theoretical physicist at the Black Mesa underground research complex. As in *Doom* (*1993* id Software [id]) designed by John Romero, John Carmack, Tom Hall, and Sandy Petersen, the game begins with a disastrous experiment that leads to a portal being opened to a

parallel world inhabited by hostile nonhumans. Initially, the player will be attempting to reach the surface and summon medical assistance for the injured. However, it soon becomes apparent that a military team have been sent in with orders to kill both the invading aliens and the human scientists, in order to guarantee secrecy. Ultimately, the player has to enter the portal and journey to Xen, a strange "border world" where dimensions intersect. There, the portal can be sealed, stopping the invasion. A strong vein of conspiracy runs through the game; the player can discover that members of the Black Mesa facility have been secretly investigating the border world for some time. Throughout, they are often observed by the mysterious "G-Man," an ambiguous figure who shares much with the "Men in Black" of UFO folklore. The game's **linear** plot ends with the G-Man offering Freeman a chance to escape from Xen and be preserved in stasis for unknown purposes; if the player refuses, Freeman will inevitably die.

Players of the original *Half-Life* will be attacked by the grotesque denizens of an alien dimension.

The sequel, *Half-Life 2* (*2004* Valve), is set many years later, after Earth's conquest by a parallel world empire known as the Combine. In the game's backstory, the "portal storms" that covered the planet after the incident described in *Half-Life* attracted the aliens' attention; after a swift war, the administrator of the Black Mesa project negotiated a surrender in which he rules humanity on their behalf. The script was again written by Laidlaw, who created a nightmare vision of a totalitarian future in which the Combine takes the place of George Orwell's Big Brother. Most of the game is set in "City 17," the Eastern European capital of the new Earth, where the remnants of Communist rule mingle with the aliens' bioengineered **post-human** soldiers and unceasing propaganda. Much of Laidlaw's carefully constructed world is revealed only in passing, as an overheard broadcast denies that this will truly be the last generation of humanity or the fallen ocean levels suggest Earth's state of environmental degradation. The game begins with the player, in the person of Freeman, brought out of **suspended animation** by the G-Man and deposited in City 17 to make contact with the human resistance, to whom he has become a legend. Gameplay and plot structure are similar to that of the first game, though the environment is much more open. Many old friends and enemies from *Half-Life* reappear, often with unexpectedly reversed allegiances. Ultimately, the player can lead a successful revolt against the Citadel, the Combine's headquarters in City 17, after which they are apparently returned to stasis by the G-Man.

The remarkable improvements made in computer game graphics in the 1990s and 2000s can be seen by comparing this image from 2004's *Half-Life 2* with those from 1998's *Half-Life*.

The opening sequences of *Half-Life 2* are notably effective at evoking feelings of dread and despair in its players.

Watching yourself move through a chain of Portal's **matter transmission** gateways can be a surprisingly disconcerting experience.

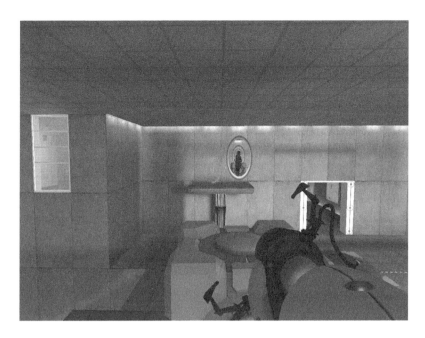

Portals in *Portal* can act as an infinitely reflecting hall of mirrors.

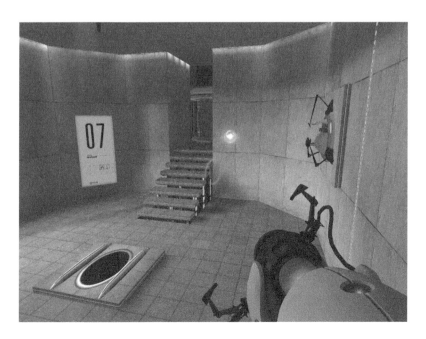

Baroque deathtraps are a common feature of *Portal's* many "testing chambers."

Half-Life 2 was partially distributed using Steam, an online delivery system created by Valve, designed to eliminate the need for retail distribution via major publishers. Its sequel was initially sold entirely through Steam as a series of "episodes," making it an **independent game**. The first part, *Half-Life 2: Episode One* (*2006* Valve), is a direct sequel to *Half-Life 2*. Gordon Freeman's odyssey into the future continues as he is rescued from the G-Man at the last moment by a group of aliens opposed to the Combine; the player must help refugees escape from City 17 before the Citadel, damaged at the end of the second game, explodes with devastating force. *Half-Life 2: Episode Two* (*2007* Valve) then begins with Freeman trapped in the wreckage of a destroyed train outside the city, after which the game moves into an extended chase sequence, ending with the player rejoining the resistance. Some aspects of the *Half-Life* series' approach to **interactive narrative** may be less successful in later games; notably, the use of a "silent protagonist" to increase **immersion** is unconvincing when Freeman is involved in personal conversations with other characters. Nevertheless, the games remain impressive for the quality of their world building and the subtlety with which it is presented to the player.

Of the various works associated with *Half-Life* that are not part of the main series, *Portal* (*2007* Valve; *2008* revised as *Portal: Still Alive*) designed by Kim Swift is undoubtedly the most interesting. This game is set in the subterranean Aperture Science Enrichment Center (a rival to Black Mesa) where the protagonist is run through a series of increasingly dangerous experimental environments by a deranged artificial intelligence known as GLaDOS (the "Genetic Lifeform and Disk Operating System"). GLaDOS' tests revolve around the use of a **matter transmission** device that creates the titular portals, gateways that connect flat walls to other surfaces at any orientation. *Portal*'s gameplay thus concentrates on solving 3D puzzles by using the portals in increasingly baroque ways; much pleasure can also be gained from the dark humor implicit in the protagonist's situation, which shares much with the scenario presented in the film *Cube* (*1997*). *Portal* seems to have a particular appeal for fans of written sf, no doubt partially because its deadly testing rooms provide a primarily intellectual challenge, but perhaps also due to the wit displayed in its sinister dialogue and ironic graffiti.

The sequel is *Portal 2* (*2011* Valve), a work promoted by a kind of **alternate reality game (ARG)** in which enthusiasts could play specially modified independent games in order to reactivate GLaDOS (supposedly destroyed at the end of the first game), thus slightly accelerating the launch of its successor. *Portal 2*'s complex but entirely linear narrative begins by revealing that the protagonist's apparent victory at the end of the first game was an illusion; after a period in **suspended animation**, the woman who was the "test subject" of the original work wakes to find herself back in the underground facility, though its advanced state of decay suggests that many years have passed. While escaping from her confinement, she accidentally reactivates GLaDOS; many unlikely twists and bizarre incidents follow, and much **embedded** backstory is revealed. The gameplay is generally similar to that of *Portal*, but various novel tricks are made available to the player, including chances to deploy **pressor beams** and use artificial gels with highly unusual properties. In the end, the game's protagonist can finally free herself from the testing facility; it is notable, however, that the *Portal* games are set in the same milieu as and after the events of *Half-Life*, meaning that the world she escapes to is (we must assume) one that has been conquered by the Combine. The single-player game then segues into a cooperatively played story in which two online participants adopt the roles of robots being tested by GLaDOS in a new, more complicated, series of chambers. Remarkably, *Portal 2* succeeds in being as cruelly amusing, and as ruthlessly ingenious, as the original that supplied the template for its design.

Related works: *Half-Life: Uplink* (*1999* Valve) is a trial version of the first game, consisting of revised versions of some sequences cut from the final release. A number of expansions were produced for *Half-Life*, all with subtitles referencing the physical sciences. *Half-Life: Opposing Force* (*1999* Gearbox) occurs during the same "Black Mesa Incident" described in the original game, but the player adopts the role of a member of the military team sent in to "sanitize" the facility. *Half-Life: Blue Shift* (*2001* Gearbox) is similar but features a Black Mesa security guard as the player character. *Half-Life: Decay* (*2001* Gearbox) again provides a different version of the original story, this time from the perspective of two of Freeman's female colleagues; this expansion was only made available as part of the PlayStation 2 version of the original game. *Half-Life 2: Lost Coast* (*2005* Valve) contains story material cut from *Half-Life 2*, though it was primarily intended as a technology demonstration. *Codename: Gordon* (*2004* Nuclearvision) designed by Sönke Seidel and Paul Kamma is a **2D platform game** based on the events of *Half-Life 2*.

Portal 2: Peer Review (*2011* Valve) is an expansion for *Portal 2* that provides additional tests for the robots who are the primary characters in the game's cooperative mode. *Valve Presents: The Sacrifice and Other Steam-Powered*

Stories (**2011**) is a graphic collection that anthologizes comic strips related to various games developed by Valve, including *Lab Rat*, a prequel to *Portal 2*.

The *Half-Life* series has been highly popular as an online game of player versus player combat. Many amateur modifications have been released for the game, notably *Counter-Strike* (*1999*) designed by Minh Le and Jess Cliffe, a team-based game pitting present-day terrorists against counterterrorism squads, which eventually had a commercial release through Valve. Another popular online multiplayer modification *Team Fortress Classic* (*1999* Valve) was produced by the *Half-Life* developers themselves, based on an earlier game created using *Quake* (*1996* id) designed by John Carmack, American McGee, Sandy Peterson, John Romero, and Tim Willits.

Web Links

- *Half-Life 2*: http://half-life2.com/

- Story and Narrative in *Half-Life*, by Marc Laidlaw: http://www.gamasutra.com/features/20030808/carless_01.shtml

- Planet Half-Life (Tribute Site): http://www.planethalflife.com/

HALO: COMBAT EVOLVED

2001. (Revised *2011* as *Halo: Combat Evolved Anniversary*.) Bungie Studios (BS). Designed by John Howard.

Halo: Combat Evolved is a **linearly** plotted game with a story that owes much to such sf action films as James Cameron's *Aliens* (*1986*). The player takes the role of the "Master Chief," a biologically enhanced chief petty officer wearing **powered armor**. In the future of the Halo series, humanity is fighting a losing war against the Covenant, a technologically superior collective of alien species who want to exterminate mankind for religious reasons. After a successful Covenant attack on the human world of Reach, the starship Pillar of Autumn escapes, making a **faster-than-light** jump to a random location. Upon arrival, it discovers the titular Halo, a **big dumb object** resembling a smaller version of the eponymous construct described in Larry Niven's novel *Ringworld* (**1970**). As the game begins, Covenant forces have followed the Pillar of Autumn, and the player is forced to escape from the damaged ship and land on Halo with Cortana, the ship's artificial intelligence. The subsequent story is extremely fast paced, featuring constant plot twists and well-designed battle sequences. Eventually, it is revealed that the Halo was built by an apparently extinct **forerunner** race to contain the Flood, a parasitic form of alien life that mutates its hosts. The Covenant accidentally release the Flood, and Halo's artificial intelligence decides to trigger a superweapon that will wipe out all sentient life in the galaxy to stop it. The player must fight the Covenant, the Flood, and Halo's robotic drones to prevent the weapon from firing. In the end, Halo itself is destroyed.

As in Larry Niven's novel *Ringworld*, players of Bungie's *Halo* who are standing on the surface of the eponymous **big dumb object** can see the structure extending up into the sky in a gigantic "Arch."

The gameplay of *Halo: Combat Evolved* is fairly conventional for an **FPS**; innovative elements include the use of regenerating energy shields by many of the combatants and a well-designed third-person view that is used to pilot a variety of vehicles. Its detailed **hard sf** background and involving plot, combined with the appeal of player identification with the superhuman Master Chief, resulted in considerable commercial success. *Halo 2* (*2004* BS) designed by Paul Bertone, Jaime Griesemer, and Joseph Staten is a direct sequel, with separate sections played from the viewpoints of the Master Chief and a disgraced Covenant commander who eventually becomes a human ally. Unlike *Halo: Combat Evolved*, it includes an online multiplayer mode; players can either cooperate to complete the story line together or compete in player versus player combat. The game's plot begins with a Covenant invasion of Earth in search of the "Ark," a forerunner device that can be used to trigger the superweapons on several new Halo artifacts resembling the one destroyed in the first game. (The Covenant believe, wrongly, that firing the weapon will leave them alive to inherit the galaxy.) After this attack is repulsed, the story continues on the "Delta Halo" object, where a civil war breaks out between different Covenant factions as humans, Covenant, and a superintelligent form of Flood fight over whether to activate the ring's weapon. *Halo 2* ends on a cliffhanger; the story line is completed in the final part of the trilogy, the similarly structured *Halo 3* (*2007* BS) designed by Jaime Griesemer, Paul Bertone, Rob Stokes, Tyson Green, and Joseph Staten. As this game begins, Earth is under siege by the Covenant. Humanity continues to resist, however, along with a species known as the Elite who have defected from the alien collective after discovering that firing the Halo weapons will render them extinct. Events culminate on the true Ark, an extragalactic space station that is constructing a new Halo, where both the Flood and the Covenant can eventually be defeated.

Several related games were created after the release of *Halo 3* completed the original trilogy. *Halo Wars* (*2009* Ensemble Studios) designed by Dave Pottinger is a **real-time strategy** game set 20 years earlier than *Halo: Combat Evolved*, in which the player controls human troops who must fight both the Covenant and the Flood for possession of ancient alien artifacts; its linear narrative ends with the destruction of a fleet of forerunner starships in order to deny them to the enemy. (The logic of the series' **future history**—in which humanity is ignorant of the existence of the Flood until the events of *Combat Evolved*—demands that the players' characters cannot go home; in the end, the survivors are left in **suspended animation**, adrift without a faster-than-light drive.) Reviews were generally positive. *Halo 3: ODST* (*2009* BS) designed by Joseph Staten and Paul Bertone returns to the form of the **FPS** while abandoning the Master Chief as protagonist in favor of its titular "Orbital Drop Shock Troopers." As the game begins, a squad of these future paratroopers have jumped into a city occupied by the Covenant during the invasion of Earth that occurs at the start of *Halo 2*, where they must recover vital information before it is captured by the aliens. While its design is similar to that of previous entries in the main series, *ODST* is less directed than its predecessors, with more scope for exploration and elements of **embedded** as well as linear storytelling. Similarly, *Halo: Reach* (*2010* BS) designed by Marcus Lehto and Christian Allen is another FPS that serves as a prequel for *Halo: Combat Evolved*. Finely crafted though this game's combat sequences are, all of its players know that in the end the titular planet must fall despite everything they do to defend it, setting the stage for the events of the original trilogy. Interestingly, this does not seem to have had any adverse effect on the game's popularity.

With the release of *Halo: Reach*, responsibility for the development of further games in the franchise was transferred from BS, its creators, to an wholly owned subsidiary of its publishers, Microsoft's 343 Industries (named after 343 Guilty Spark, a forerunner artificial intelligence that appears in *Combat Evolved*). Their first contribution to the series was *Halo 4* (*2012* 343 Industries [343]) designed by Scott Warner and Josh Holmes, an interesting work (and the start of a new trilogy) that serves both as an homage to its predecessors and as an extension of their themes. At the end of *Halo 3*, Cortana and the Master Chief were left drifting in space in a disabled starship. In *Halo 4*, set 5 years later, this vessel crashes on Requiem, a forerunner world still inhabited by the remnants of this supposedly vanished species. Much combat follows, against both forerunner servant races and rogue Covenant forces who have refused to obey the cease-fire established between their civilization and humanity after the end of *Halo 3*; the gameplay resembles that of earlier FPSs in the series, with minor improvements. These battle sequences are interspersed with revelations about the nature of humanity and a surprisingly intimate portrayal of the repressed romantic relationship between the emotionally damaged supersoldier, brainwashed and experimented on in childhood to make him a better warrior, and the artificial intelligence, who has reached the limit of her achievable life span. (In a nod to BS' earlier *Marathon Trilogy* [from *1994*], Cortana is said to be suffering from "rampancy"—a form of information overload that is the equivalent of senescence for software intelligences.) Meanwhile, it becomes apparent that the forerunner troops who the player is fighting are an altered form of humanity.

As in earlier works ranging from the **Captain Future** story "The Lost World of Time" (Fall 1941 *Captain Future*) through Ben Bova's *As on a Darkling Plain* (**1972**) to the television series *Stargate SG-1* (*1997–2007*), humans in the Halo universe developed a starfaring civilization in the distant past, a culture that was destroyed and forgotten long before their eventual redevelopment as a technological species. Here, humanity lost a war with the forerunners before they used a version of the Halo doomsday weapon to defeat the Flood, apparently eradicating all sentient life then existing in the galaxy. However, two forerunner factions survive on Requiem: one that believes humanity should inherit their position as the guardians of all intelligent life—and who, as in E E Smith's **Lensman** novels, have manipulated their evolution to shape them into suitably formidable custodians—and one that still blames mankind for the long-ago war and intends to eliminate

Earth's population by subjecting it to a kind of forcible **uploading**. At the end of the game's linear story line, this latter group can be defeated, but Cortana is apparently lost.

The Halo series has always been associated with unusual forms of marketing. The first announcement of *Halo: Combat Evolved*, in 1999, took the form of a series of cryptic e-mails sent to a fan website for Bungie's earlier *Marathon Trilogy* (from *1994* BS), supposedly by the Cortana artificial intelligence. The letters mingle references to the poetry of William Blake and T S Eliot with allusions to the future history of the Halo universe in a deliberately obscure style. Bungie's denial of responsibility for the Cortana Letters and the way in which fan analysis of the first e-mails was referenced in later examples make them a precursor of later **ARGs**. *Halo 2*'s promotion took the form of a full-blown ARG, *I Love Bees* (*2004* 42 Entertainment; also known as *The Haunted Apiary*) designed by Jordan Weisman with Elan Lee and the sf writer Sean Stewart. The game was begun by briefly displaying a website link in trailers for *Halo 2* while simultaneously delivering cryptic clues to previous players of the series; both entry points led to the ilovebees. com website, a site apparently devoted to beekeeping, which had developed inexplicable problems. The somewhat complex plot, as revealed by an online community of ARG players, revolved around an artificial intelligence from the Halo's future history that had become trapped in the site and needed help to repair itself and fight off a Covenant virus. *I Love Bees* is considered an excellent example of an ARG, involving both Internet-based puzzles and clues delivered through calls to specially chosen payphones. Visiting the website could provide a vivid sense of roaming through the shattered pieces of an artificial mind, many of which had their own engagingly individual personalities; an archived version of the game's content is still available at the site. Another, less successful, ARG called *Iris* (*2007* AKQA) was used to promote *Halo 3*; it involved a group known as the "Society of the Ancients" who were investigating forerunner artifacts discovered on Earth. For *Halo 4*, however, Microsoft apparently decided to eschew the use of such experimental methods to promote the game and instead released a cinematic prequel as a series of episodes on the web: *Forward Unto Dawn* (*2012*).

Halo: Combat Evolved was also important in the development of **machinima**. The entertaining *Red vs. Blue: The Blood Gulch Chronicles* (*2003–2007*) from Rooster Teeth Productions was perhaps the first mainstream example of the form, eventually running to a hundred episodes available for free download and on DVD. The series uses the game's software to tell the story of two teams of superhuman soldiers fighting a pointless civil war in a desolate box canyon. *Red vs. Blue* is essentially a situation comedy, focusing on character interaction between largely deranged individuals, featuring amusing parodies of the worst clichés found in FPSs and bad sf films; its overall tone somewhat resembles that of Kevin Smith's film *Clerks* (*1994*).

Related works: *Halo: Custom Edition* (*2004* Gearbox Software) is a free expansion for the Windows version of *Halo: Combat Evolved* that was converted from the Xbox by Gearbox. It adds online multiplayer support, with the ability to design custom locations for online games. The *Halo 2 Multiplayer Map Pack* (*2005* BS) is an expansion containing additional missions suitable for use in competitive online games of *Halo 2*. Similarly, the *Halo 3 Heroic Map Pack* (*2007* BS), *Halo 3 Legendary Map Pack* (*2008* BS), *Halo 3 Mythic Map Pack* (*2009* BS), and *Halo 3 Mythic II Map Pack* (*2010* BS) add new locations for competitive online play to *Halo 3*. Equivalent expansions for *Halo Wars* are *Halo Wars: Strategic Options* (*2009* Robot Entertainment [RE]) and *Halo Wars: Historic Battles* (*2009* RE), while *Halo: Reach* was similarly extended by *Halo: Reach—Noble Map Pack* (*2010* BS) and *Halo: Reach—Defiant Map Pack* (*2011* BS). *Halo: Spartan Assault* (*2013* 343/Vanguard Entertainment) is a **2D** action game, set between *Halo 3* and *Halo 4*, in which two player-controlled supersoldiers fight a group of Covenant who have refused to make peace with humanity. *Halo 4* itself has been extended by three expansions that contain additional locations for multiplayer battles: the *Crimson Map Pack* (*2012* 343), the *Majestic Map Pack* (*2013* 343), and the *Castle Map Pack* (*2013* 343). In addition, a sequel to the main game's narrative is available as a series of downloadable episodes known as *Spartan Ops*, intended for cooperative play over the Internet.

Halo ActionClix (*2007* WizKids) designed by Michael Mulvihill and Mike Elliott is a **collectible miniature game** based on the franchise, similar to the superhero-themed *Heroclix* (*2007* WizKids) designed by Jordan Weisman and Seth Johnson. The *Halo Interactive Strategy Game* (*2008* B1 Games/Genius Products) is a board game that attempts, with limited success, to translate FPS gameplay into a turn-based game played with miniature figures. *Risk: Halo Wars* (*2009* Hasbro) designed by Rob Daviau is a variant of Albert Lamorisse's board game *Risk* (*1957* Miro as *La Conquête du Monde*), which is licensed from *Halo Wars*.

Various spin-off novels have been written. *The Fall of Reach* (**2001**) by Eric Nylund is a prequel to the first game, of which *The Flood* (**2003**) by William C Dietz is a novelization. *First Strike* (**2003**) by Eric Nylund is primarily set between the events of *Halo: Combat Evolved* and those of *Halo*

2, while *Ghosts of Onyx* (**2006**), also by Nylund, ties up various plot threads from the games and continues the story after *Halo 2*. This latter book follows the discovery of a world whose core contains a gateway to a miniature **Dyson Sphere** in an alternate space, which may have been created by the forerunners as a refuge from the Flood. The next novel, *Contact Harvest* (**2007**) by Joseph Staten, is another prequel that describes humanity's **first contact** with the Covenant, explicating much of the series' background. This work was followed by Tobias Buckell's *The Cole Protocol* (**2008**), which also focuses on the early days of the war. *Halo: Evolutions—Essential Tales of the Halo Universe* (**2009**) collects short stories by a variety of authors, including Nylund, Tobias Buckell, Jeff VanderMeer, Karen Traviss, and Brian Evenson. A new trilogy by Greg Bear, concentrating on the history of *Halo*'s forerunner species, began with *Cryptum* (**2011**) and continued with *Primordium* (**2012**) and *Silentium* (**2013**). A separate series is set after the end of *Halo 3* and written by Karen Traviss; to date, this sequence comprises *Glasslands* (**2011**) and *The Thursday War* (**2012**). Tobias Buckell's *Halo Encyclopedia* (**2011**), meanwhile, is a "nonfiction" description of the milieu.

The Halo Graphic Novel (*2006*) includes four short stories set in the Halo universe, one of them drawn by the well-known French artist Jean Giraud (also known as Moebius). *Halo: Uprising* (*2007–2009*) is a four-issue comic series, written by Brian Michael Bendis, which serves to bridge the gap between the events of *Halo 2* and those of *Halo 3*. More recent associated comics include *Halo: Helljumper* (*2009*), a five-issue sequence written by Peter David that focuses on a group of Orbital Drop Shock Troopers, and *Halo: Blood Line* (*2009–2010*), a limited series written by Fred van Lente that deals with a covert group of biologically enhanced supersoldiers similar to the protagonist of the original game. *Halo: Fall of Reach* (*2010–2012*) is an adaptation to graphical form of Nylund's novel of the same name, while *Halo: Initiation* (*2013*) is a three-issue comic series **tied** to *Spartan Assault*. *Halo: Legends* (*2010*) is a collection of **anime** inspired by the franchise, including a piece created by the well-known Japanese director Shinji Aramaki.

Web Links

- *Halo*: http://www.halowaypoint.com/
- Bungie Studios on *Halo*: http://www.bungie.net/Projects/Halo/
- I Love Bees: http://ilovebees.com/
- Rooster Teeth Productions: http://roosterteeth.com/
- *Forward   Unto   Dawn*:   http://www.machinima.com/shows/forward-unto-dawn

HEAVY GEAR

Series (from 1997). Activision.

The original *Heavy Gear* pen and paper **RPG** (*1994* Dream Pod 9 [DP9]; revised *1997*; revised *2004*) designed by Jean Carrières, Gene Marcil, Martin Ouellette, and Marc-Alexandre Vézina is set in the sixty-ninth century much influenced by the tabletop **wargame** *BattleTech* (*1984* FASA). In *Heavy Gear*'s **future history**, an economic collapse has caused the abandonment of Earth's interstellar colonies, including the world of Terra Nova. The setting's timeline begins after Terra Nova has emerged from a period of anarchy and become divided between two political entities: the Confederated Northern City States and the Allied Southern Territories. Both sides use "gears," human-piloted bipedal robots (or **mecha**), for war. Meanwhile, Earth has recovered economically but is now dominated by a fascist regime that has begun a war of reconquest against its former colonies. The tone is gritty and realistic, with few developments in technology other than the necessary invention of **faster-than-light** travel.

After the 1995 release of *MechWarrior 2*, the **videogame** developers Activision lost the license to create *BattleTech* games, as Dynamix had before them. While Dynamix responded by developing their own similar franchise, *Metaltech* (from *1994*), Activision chose to license *Heavy Gear*. The first game developed under this agreement, *Heavy Gear* (*1997* Activision) designed by Tim Morten, is competent but suffers from giving the relatively small and agile gears the handling characteristics of *BattleTech*'s huge, lumbering BattleMechs. The game's **linear** plot follows the crew of a Confederated Northern City States hovercraft as they skirmish with a similar Allied Southern Territories vessel in Terra Nova's badlands; its credibility is enhanced by the use of details from the complex world developed for the RPG. The sequel, *Heavy Gear II* (*1999* Activision) designed by Jack Mamais, represents gear movement and combat rather more successfully. Players proceed through its linear plot by completing a series of missions as one of the members of a special operations team dispatched by all the Terra Novan factions to attack Earth forces on an occupied colony world. *Heavy Gear II* is an excellently crafted robot combat game that refines and improves upon the gameplay of such predecessors as *Earthsiege* (*1994* Dynamix) and *MechWarrior* (*1989* Dynamix) while adding some innovative **real-time tactics** elements.

Related works: Several miniature-based tabletop wargames have been released as spin-offs from the **role-playing game**, including *Heavy Gear*

Tactical (*1998* DP9; *2001* revised as *Heavy Gear Tactical Miniatures Rules*) designed by Philippe Boulle, Jean Carrières, and Marc-Alexandre Vézina; *Heavy Gear Blitz* (*2006* DP9), and *Heavy Gear Arena* (*2010* DP9). *Heavy Gear Fighter* (*1994* DP9) designed by Jean Carrières is a card game based on gear versus gear duelling; *Heavy Gear Fighter: Weapons and Equipment* (*1995* DP9) designed by Jean Carrières is an expansion. *Heavy Gear* (*2001–2002*) is a 40-episode animated series made for television by Mainframe Entertainment, which focused on "gear duelling" tournaments between representatives of Terra Nova's Northern and Southern factions; it is aimed at a significantly younger audience than the RPG and videogames.

Web Link

- *Heavy Gear II* Postmortem: http://www.gamasutra.com/features/19991208/imislund_01.htm

MARATHON TRILOGY

Series (from 1994). Bungie Studios (BS).

The *Marathon Trilogy* is a series of games with a single protagonist, a twenty-eighth-century **cyborg** security officer. The first game, *Marathon* (*1994* BS) designed by Alex Seropian and Jason Jones, begins with an attack by the alien Pfhor on the eponymous interstellar colony ship, a gigantic vessel constructed from the Martian moon of Deimos. Players must attempt to defeat the Pfhor, alternately aided and opposed by the ship's three artificial intelligences, some of which have been coopted by the aliens. Eventually, it is possible to kill the Pfhor responsible for controlling a slave race, who then revolt, ending the game. *Marathon* is most interesting for its depiction of the amusingly sarcastic and partially insane software intelligence Durandal, who ultimately proves to be the player's only reliable ally. *Marathon 2: Durandal* (*1995* BS; *2007* revised as *Marathon: Durandal*) designed by Jason Jones is set 17 years later. It begins with the revelation that Durandal captured the Pfhor ship after the end of the first game and escaped, having forced the player's character into a form of **suspended animation**. Durandal has now awakened the player to help it search the ruins of a war-ravaged world originally inhabited by a race known as the S'pht. The artificial intelligence proves to be a menacing and somewhat unhinged master, forever unwilling to reveal what it knows or plans. Eventually, it emerges that Durandal intends to prevent a Pfhor invasion of Earth, a goal achieved by the player's activation of another software intelligence belonging to a **forerunner** race. However, the Pfhor triggers a nova, finally destroying the S'pht homeworld.

The last installment, *Marathon: Infinity* (*1996* BS), is perhaps the most interesting part of the trilogy. Its somewhat cryptic plot revolves around an apparent **changewar** between Durandal and an immensely powerful entity released when the S'pht's sun went nova. The player is catapulted into at least three alternate timelines, including one in which their character was not captured by Durandal, but is instead controlled by another artificial intelligence from the Marathon, which is itself enslaved by the Pfhor. Ultimately, the player can restore the reality that existed at the end of *Marathon 2*.

Gameplay in the *Marathon Trilogy* focuses on well-crafted combat mechanics and a wide variety of mission objectives; the series has also been popular for player versus player combat in temporary **online worlds**. However, the *Marathon* games are significantly more concerned with story than their better-known contemporary, *Doom* (*1993* id Software) designed by John Romero, John Carmack, Tom Hall, and Sandy Petersen, a trait they share with the first *System Shock* (*1994* LG) designed by Doug Church. A great deal of **embedded** narrative is presented in various journals and logs that the player can find, adding an additional layer of gameplay. While this aspect of the design attracted little attention at the time of the games' initial release, it has since exerted considerable influence on many later examples of the **FPS** form.

Related works: *Super Marathon* (*1996* BS) is a combined version of *Marathon* and *Marathon 2*. The program code for *Marathon 2* was released into the public domain in 2000 and became the basis of the freely available game *Aleph One* (*2000*). The Apple Mac versions of the entire trilogy were made available for free download in 2004, meaning that *Aleph One* can now be used to run all three games.

Web Links
- Marathon Trilogy: http://marathon.bungie.org/
- Original *Marathon* series downloads for the Mac: http://trilogyrelease.bungie.org/

METALTECH

Series (from 1994). Dynamix.

After developing the first *MechWarrior* game in the late 1980s, Dynamix lost the license for the intellectual property to Activision. Their response was to create their own version of *MechWarrior*'s *BattleTech* universe, featuring HERCULANs (human- and software-piloted bipedal robots, or **mecha**) in a unique **future history**, and develop their own games within this *Metaltech* continuity. The first game, *Earthsiege* (*1994* Dynamix), is similar to the 1989 *MechWarrior*, with pilots playing through a series of **linearly** plotted missions, using a first-person perspective view of a **3D** landscape. The setting is Earth in the twenty-sixth century, after a rebellion by artificially intelligent "Cybrids" has left humanity on the brink of extinction. Cybrids greatly resemble the genocidal robots of the *Terminator* films; the background is perhaps best summarized as a depiction of human survivors using giant robots to fight the future shown in the opening sequences of *Terminator 2: Judgment Day* (*1991*). Gameplay is focused on HERCULAN versus HERCULAN combat; the choice of robot for a mission and effective communication with computer-controlled squadmates are important if victory is to be achieved. In the end, the Cybrids can be expelled from Earth.

The overall narrative of the series was extended by *Metaltech: Earthsiege—Expansion Pack* (*1995* Dynamix), an expansion for *Earthsiege* that largely repeats the structure of the first game in its depiction of an attack on Earth by Cybrids who have been rebuilding their strength in space colonies. *Earthsiege 2* (*1995* Dynamix) then continues that story, in another game based on robot versus robot combat. This game's plot is **multilinear**, with failed missions leading to different branching paths. Ultimately, the player must confront the first Cybrid, Prometheus, on the Moon. A further sequel, *Starsiege* (*1998* Dynamix), is set in the twenty-ninth century, in what appears to be a slightly different version of the *Metaltech* continuity. In this variant, the Cybrids rebelled after Prometheus came into contact with the mind of its creator, Solomon Petresun, and decided that humans were only semi sentient animals who did not deserve to exist. After its ejection from Earth, Prometheus fled to the outer solar system, where it prepared for an eventual return. Meanwhile, Petresun **uploaded** his mind to an almost immortal cybernetic brain and become Emperor of the inner worlds, justifying his oppressive rule with the continuing threat of Cybrid invasion. As the game begins, the Mars colony rebels against the Empire and Prometheus launches an attack on humanity. The player can adopt the role of a human rebel or a Cybrid soldier, playing through two very different views of the war; the Cybrid campaign is of interest for its depiction of their language, culture, and internal disagreements. By the end of the human-centered story line, both Prometheus and the Emperor are dead, and the Cybrids have again been defeated. Gameplay in *Starsiege* resembles that of the earlier entries in the series, but HERCULANs have become more nimble, giving the game more of the feel of an **FPS**.

The *Metaltech* franchise also gave rise to a line of **turn-based computer wargames**, played in an **isometric** 3D view. These games take place after a human victory in *Starsiege*, when mankind is expanding into interstellar space. Thus, in *MissionForce: Cyberstorm* (1996 Dynamix), the player controls groups of HERCULANs piloted by genetically engineered "BioDerm" soldiers, with the aim of exterminating the surviving Cybrid refugees in a series of ground battles. *Cyberstorm 2: Corporate Wars* (1998 Dynamix) is a sequel, based on a struggle between competing interstellar corporations; it received mixed reviews.

A later installment, *Starsiege: Tribes* (1998 Dynamix), is a multiplayer only online game, marking a change of direction for the series. It is set in the fortieth century, after many of the worlds colonized during the *Cyberstorm* games have seceded from the human Empire. In the game's backstory, the forces dispatched from Earth to suppress the rebellion became trapped in an unwinnable war, and both sides fragmented into the battling tribes of the title. Gameplay focuses on FPS-style combat between teams of players wearing **powered armor**. The game is well crafted, including combined aerial and ground combat and tactically useful items such as deployable self-targeting gun turrets; it became notably popular.

Tribes 2 (2001 Dynamix) is a sequel, featuring such enhancements as the option of playing as a BioDerm. Another variant created by different hands, *Tribes: Aerial Assault* (2002 Inevitable Entertainment), converts the online team battle concept to a game console; it includes a simple single-player campaign in which the player is a new recruit fighting against a BioDerm invasion. A further installment, *Tribes: Vengeance* (2004 IG), is also similar to the original *Starsiege: Tribes* but includes an extensive story line in addition to the multiplayer game. This work's linear plot, in which the player adopts several different roles, depicts the neobarbaric culture of the interstellar clans and describes the origins of the universal state of war that exists in the original game. While it seemed that the franchise had come to an end with *Vengeance*, it has recently been revived by a newly created studio as *Tribes: Ascend* (2012 Hi-Rez Studios), which concentrates on competitive free-to-play games in temporary **online worlds**; it will be interesting to see if this work can recapture the popularity of the original *Tribes*.

Related works: *Metaltech: Battledrome* (*1995* Dynamix) is a player versus player game of HERCULAN combat, with an optional computer-controlled opponent.

METRO 2033

2010. 4A Games (4A). Designed by Andrew Prokhorov and Vyacheslav Aristov.

Metro 2033 is an **FPS** with something of the threatening ambience of a **survival horror** game, based on a Russian novel of the same name by Dmitry Glukhovsky. Following an apocalyptic global war, humanity is almost extinct. A few survivors linger in the remains of the Moscow subway system, ineluctably aware that they may be the last of their species. The Metro is a world lit by the red glow of emergency lighting, where the only currency is the superior prewar grade of ammunition. Below ground, the crowded stations fight pointless battles in the names of the obsolete ideologies, which rule their tiny societies. Above, there is only unending nuclear winter, vicious animals distorted by the deadly radiation and the mysterious "Dark Ones," mutants who may represent the next step in human evolution. At the start of the game, its protagonist has agreed to travel through the subterranean wilderness of the disintegrating Metro system to its center, where he must warn the greatest of the stations of the threat posed by the Dark Ones' **psionic** powers. This odyssey takes the player through a world of almost constant combat, where they must fight both human soldiers and packs of altered beasts.

Tense moments are common in the post-nuclear underworld of *Metro 2033*.

The game offers a detailed and convincing visualization of its dark and melancholy world. Its characters, however, are largely indistinguishable; almost universally, they act as either icons of suffering humanity or rough, manly comrades for the player. While the subway contains various caricatures of prewar ideologies, from Nazis to Communists to free market capitalists, they are sketchily drawn; the player is unable to communicate with members of these microsocieties but must instead try to eavesdrop on their conversations with each other. Gameplay is well crafted but generally difficult, with much time spent scavenging for scarce resources such as bullets and gas mask filters, in an environment that is perhaps overly dark. Unexpectedly for an **interactive narrative**, *Metro 2033* begins with a flash-forward to the finale; as this suggests, the majority of the plot is highly **linear**. At the end, however, there are two possible branches. Typically, the player will reach a conclusion in which the Dark Ones are destroyed by prewar missiles controlled from a hidden bunker in the subway system. If, however, the player has taken a morally superior path through the game—by refusing rewards offered for saving innocents, by listening to the appeals of suffering tunnel dwellers, and by avoiding conflict whenever possible—then it will be revealed that the Dark Ones are actually attempting to communicate **telepathically** with the humans rather than to drive them mad; the player is then offered a final chance to abort the missile attack. The nature of the game's moral universe is thus, it appears, determined by the player's own actions.

Players of *Metro: Last Light* spend much of their time in the devastated Moscow, which lies above the titular tunnels.

With the release of the same designers' *Metro: Last Light* (*2013* 4A), the game series diverged from its ancestor; the plot of this work, though primarily linear (with some minor **multilinear** aspects), is quite different to that of *Metro 2034* (**2009**), Glukhovsky's sequel to his original novel. *Last Light*'s design is generally similar to that of its predecessor, though there is more emphasis on stealthily bypassing enemies in the tunnels and more time spent on the surface, where combat is inescapable. Characterization and dialogue seem markedly superior to those of the first game, however, though a few moments still lack credibility. Interestingly, the narrative—cowritten by Glukhovsky—assumes that the player's character destroyed the Dark Ones at the end of *Metro 2033* but then offers them a further chance at redemption. One mutant, a child, has survived and during the course of the plot will be saved by the protagonist. If the player has behaved sufficiently virtuously throughout the game, that Dark One will then save them in turn; otherwise, their character must die to save the other inhabitants of the Metro from genocide at the hands of a fanatical group of Communists.

Related works: *Metro: Last Light—Faction Pack* (*2013* 4A) adds several new missions to *Last Light*, while *Metro: Last Light—The Ranger Mode* (*2012* 4A) makes the game more difficult (and potentially more **immersive**).

Web Links
- *Metro: Last Light*: http://enterthemetro.com/

PERFECT DARK

2000. Rare. Designed by Martin Hollis.

Perfect Dark is a well-crafted work whose design was much influenced by the gameplay of the non-sf **James Bond** licensed game *GoldenEye 007* (*1997* Rare). The player's character is one Joanna Dark, a new recruit to the twenty-first-century Carrington Institute's covert operations group, and a woman who justifies the game's title by her achievement of a "perfect" score in training. A fully **linear** plot is based on an attempt by the alien Skedar to retrieve a weapon from a derelict spacecraft on the ocean floor, a device that they intend to use to annihilate both humanity and the Institute's allies, the Maians (who resemble the "grays" of UFO folklore). Players are led through this story in a series of missions with precisely defined objectives; the gameplay concentrates on stealthy infiltration and combat with realistic near-future weapons. In essence, *Perfect Dark* is an **FPS** whose tone is strongly evocative of such "spy-fi" fictions as Luc Besson's film *Nikita* (*1990*) or J J Abrams' later TV series *Alias* (*2001–2006*).

Related works: *Perfect Dark* (*2000* Rare) is unrelated to the original **FPS**; it uses a **2D** overhead view to follow Dark's attempts to shut down an illegal **cyborg** manufacturer. *Perfect Dark Zero* (*2005* Rare) is a prequel, featuring Joanna Dark and her father as bounty hunters before Joanna joined the Carrington Institute. It is notably less science-fictional in tone than *Perfect Dark*, and its story line generally takes second place to the gameplay. *Perfect Dark: Initial Vector* (**2005**), by Greg Rucka, is a novel set between the events of *Perfect Dark Zero* and the FPS version of *Perfect Dark*, dealing with an outbreak of a weaponized influenza virus. *Perfect Dark: Second Front* (**2007**), also by Rucka, is a sequel to *Initial Vector*, while *Perfect Dark: Janus' Tears* (*2006–2007*) is a six-issue comic written by Eric Trautmann, set between *Initial Vector* and *Second Front*.

Web Link

- Interview with Martin Hollis: http://www.gamasutra.com/view/ feature/1451/the_restless_vision_of_martin_.php?print = 1

QUAKE

1996. (Revised *1996* as *VQuake*; revised *1996* as *QuakeWorld*; revised *1997* as *GLQuake*; revised *1997* as *WinQuake*; revised *2005* as *Quake Mobile*.) id Software (id). Designed by John Carmack, American McGee, Sandy Peterson, John Romero, and Tim Willits.

Quake was the successor to *Doom* (*1993* id) designed by John Romero, John Carmack, Tom Hall, and Sandy Petersen and shares many of its predecessor's strengths and weaknesses. The major changes were technological; while *Doom*'s world is not fully **3D**, improvements in available hardware platforms meant that the previous game's restrictions could be lifted for *Quake*. Graphics are much more detailed, though there are fewer enemies as a result of the greater technical resources required to display them. As with *Doom*, player versus player combat games were, and to some extent still are, highly popular as a competitive sport. *Quake*'s gameplay is an intensified version of that seen in the earlier game, focusing on the adrenaline rush of continuous combat in an ominous world reminiscent of the Clive Barker film *Hellraiser* (*1987*). The story, by contrast, is even less important than in *Doom*. The US government has opened a portal into another dimension, and hostile demons have emerged; the player, a nameless soldier, is sent in to stop whatever is responsible for the invasion, an entity codenamed "Quake." The various areas within the portal show a range of Gothic and dark fantasy influences, partially as a result of conflicting design visions prevalent in id Software during development; H P Lovecraft's **Cthulhu Mythos** is a common theme.

The Quake series, similar to *Final Fantasy*, includes games that share common themes and gameplay but are not necessarily set in the same fictional universe. Thus, *Quake II* (*1997* id) is a gameplay sequel to *Quake* with a **space opera** setting. Players adopt the role of a soldier taking part in a counterattack against the home planet of hostile alien **cyborgs** known as "Stroggs." Immediately after the landing, most of the player's companions are killed or captured, leaving them to penetrate the aliens' capital and kill their leader without assistance. The game's background is essentially a transposition of the settings of *Quake* and *Doom* into traditional sf terms; the Stroggs are psychopathically obsessed with war and human vivisection, making them as perfect an enemy as the demons of the earlier games. *Quake III Arena* (*1999* id; *2001* revised as *Quake III: Revolution*; *2010* revised as *Quake Live*; *2010* revised as *Quake Arena Arcade*), by contrast, concentrates almost entirely on multiplayer combat in temporary **online worlds**, though a single-player mode is also available with computer-controlled opponents. *Quake III: Team Arena* (*2000* id) is an expansion pack designed to add team-based competitive play.

The next installment, *Quake 4* (*2005* Rave Software/id), is a story sequel to *Quake II*, in which the player's character is assigned to help conquer the Stroggs' machine planet after their leader was killed at the end of the earlier game. The **linear** story line is somewhat stronger than in *Quake II*, featuring a disturbing sequence in which the protagonist is captured and forcibly cyborged, while the gameplay is broadly similar. A later sequel by other hands, *Enemy Territory: Quake Wars* (*2007* Splash Damage) designed by Paul Wedgwood, again focuses on online multiplayer combat but emphasizes conflicts between competing teams given specific objectives and equipped with aircraft and land vehicles, as opposed to *Quake III*'s largely personal duels. A minimal backstory justifies the battles as occurring during the Strogg invasion of Earth that takes place before *Quake II*.

Related works: *Quake Mission Pack #1: Scourge of Armagon* (*1997* Hipnotic Interactive) and *Quake Mission Pack #2: Dissolution of Eternity* (*1997* Rogue Entertainment [RE]) are expansions for *Quake*, including new missions, enemies, and weapons. *Quake II Mission Pack: The Reckoning* (*1998* Xatrix Entertainment), *Quake II Mission Pack: Ground Zero* (*1998* RE), and *Quake II Netpack I: Extremities* (*1998* id) are similar extensions for *Quake II*; the *Extremities* collection is notable for being designed by enthusiasts rather than professionals.

Web Link
- Planet Quake (Tribute Site): http://planetquake.gamespy.com/

RAGE

2011. (Revised *2012* as *Rage: Campaign Edition*.) id Software (id). Designed by Tim Willits.

Rage is an **FPS** in which much of the player's time is spent racing and fighting from ramshackle vehicles; the game's world is often reminiscent of that depicted in the film *Mad Max 2* (*1981*). There are many sly references to other games and game creators, including *Fallout* (*1997* Black Isle Studios) designed by Tim Cain, Leonard Boyarsky, and Christopher Taylor and *Wasteland* (*1988* Interplay) designed by Alan Pavlish, Michael Stackpole, Ken St Andre, and the designer Warren Spector (cocreator of *Deus Ex* [*2000* IS]), as well as id Software's own *Doom* (*1993*), *Quake* (*1996*), and *Wolfenstein 3D* (*1992*). The setting is a ruined Earth devastated by the near-future impact of a large asteroid. As in the tabletop **RPG** *The Morrow Project* (*1980* Timeline) designed by Kevin Dockery, Robert Sadler, and Richard Tucholka, underground refuges (or "Arks") were constructed before the disaster and stocked with military and scientific personnel in **suspended animation**, an elite who would be revived to reconstruct the world after the holocaust. The player's character is a soldier who was frozen in one of these bunkers. However, also as in *The Morrow Project*, something has gone wrong, and the protagonist is reanimated far later than planned, to discover that all the other sleepers in his Ark died before they woke. Emerging from his shelter, the player's character finds scattered groups of survivors who are maintaining a primitive civilization against the assaults of degenerate mutants and marauding gangs. Soon, he is being hunted by the mysterious Authority for the **nanotechnological** devices in his blood, improvements made by the Ark project that give him a superhuman level of physical endurance.

The **interactive narrative** of *Rage* is dominated by a somewhat clichéd **linear** story line that the game never seems to take terribly seriously. Players can also choose to undertake a variety of optional tasks, though the world outside the areas required for the primary narrative is not very detailed. Arguably, the game is a well-designed and visually impressive FPS in the style of such predecessors as *Quake* or *Unreal* (*1998* Epic Games) designed by Cliff Bleszinski and James Schmalz, onto which the stronger narrative and more open world of such later works as *Stalker: Shadow of Chernobyl* (*2007* GSC Game World) have been rather uneasily grafted. Notably, the game world is not very flexible; it suggests a set dressed for the purposes of enacting the game's plot rather than an environment that participants are intended to explore. Player response to *Rage* has been somewhat muted, less perhaps due to any great flaws in the actual game than because its design is too close to that of the primal FPS, a subform that has fallen out of fashion.

Related works: *The Scorchers* (*2012* id) is an expansion pack that adds the titular bandit clan to the game, while the *Wasteland Sewer Missions* (*2011* id) includes missions set in the eponymous subterranean regions. *Rage* (*2010* id) is an FPS in which the player follows a predetermined path through the killing grounds of a postapocalyptic game show; reviews were good. *Rage* (**2011**) is a novelization of the 2011 game by Matthew J Costello, who also created the game's script, while *Rage* (*2011*; also known as *Rage: After the Impact*) is an associated three-issue comic series.

Web Link
- *Rage*: http://www.rage.com/

RED FACTION

2001. Volition.

The original *Red Faction*, set in a near-future colony on Mars, is often suggestive of the less sophisticated scenes in the 1990 film *Total Recall*. Its **linear** story follows the adventures of an oppressed miner (the player character) who becomes involved in a rebellion against the company that runs twenty-first-century Mars. The gameplay is competently constructed if somewhat routine, with a design that is often reminiscent of *Half-Life* (*1998* Valve). While the color of the eponymous rebel group suggests radical socialism as well as the Red Planet, the game's revolutionary credentials are somewhat superficial; ultimately, the rebels are saved by an intervention from Earth. Much of *Red Faction*'s commercial success can be attributed not to its cliché-ridden plot or to its conventional core gameplay but to the unusual degree of mutability exhibited by its scenery when struck by rockets or grenades. This ability to destroy large portions of the player's environment was highly popular and became the signature feature of the game's various sequels.

Red Faction II (*2002* Volition) designed by Nathan Camarillo is another **FPS**, but this time set in a range of urban environments and military bases rather than the first game's maze of tunnels. Its linear story follows a revolution against a dictatorship on twenty-first-century Earth led by a team of **nanotechnologically** enhanced supersoldiers, one of whom is the player's character. Throughout the *Red Faction* series, nanotechnology fills the role of the technology suggested by the sf writer Arthur C Clarke, one sufficiently advanced that its effects are indistinguishable from magic. The next entry in the series, *Red Faction: Guerrilla* (*2009* Volition) designed by James Hague, repeats the first game's scenario of a rebellion against oppressive overseers on Mars, but with the role of the tyrants taken by Earth's military rather than by a monopolistic corporation. In *Guerrilla*, it is the twenty-second century, and Mars has been **terraformed**, allowing the game to be set on the surface. The basic design is that of a **third-person shooter**, but the *Guerrilla*'s most distinctive feature is that every man-made structure in the game is destructible, as opposed to the occasional mutable areas seen in the first two works. Players are offered a choice of missions within a partially **modular** narrative, but the emphasis is on the dubious pleasures of sheer destruction. Finally, *Red Faction: Armageddon* (*2011* Volition) designed by David Abzug is another third-person shooter, again set on Mars, this time in the late twenty-second century. Soon after the beginning of the game, the planet's single terraformer—which also serves as a weather control machine—is destroyed, rendering the surface uninhabitable. The colonists take refuge in the old mines, justifying the use of a rather more linear narrative structure than that of *Guerrilla*. The majority of the plot takes place several years later, when some (inevitably hostile) aliens are released from a sealed section of the underground caverns to attack the colonists and the player must fight them and the humans who have arranged for their escape. In this iteration of the series, highly destructive exotic weapons are commonplace. The most characteristic, perhaps, is the "singularity cannon"—a handgun that fires miniature **black holes**.

Related works: *Red Faction: Guerrilla—Demons of the Badlands* (*2009* Volition) is an expansion pack and prequel for *Guerrilla* that was included in the Windows version. *Red Faction: Armageddon—Path to War* (*2011* Volition) is an expansion pack for *Armageddon* that serves as a prequel to that game. *Red Faction: Battlegrounds* (*2011* THQ Digital Warrington) is a **2D** game of vehicle combat, seen in plan view. *Red Faction: Origins* (*2011*) is a film made in association with the Syfy network, set between *Guerrilla* and *Armageddon*.

RESISTANCE: FALL OF MAN

2006. Insomniac Games (IG).

The setting of *Resistance* is an **alternate history** in which aliens invaded the United Kingdom in the early 1950s. The background is vividly realized, from the devastated towns of Northern England where the last remnants of the armed forces launch their desperate raids to the conversion factories where humans infected by the aliens' mutagenic virus are brought to complete their transformations into extraterrestrial organisms. In this reality, World War II did not occur; instead, the Great War was followed by peace in Europe and lasting prosperity. This happy picture was marred only by Russia, which had completely sealed itself off from outside contact shortly after the failure of its Communists to overthrow the Tsar. In 1949, however, aliens known as the Chimera—who had reached Earth on the 1908 Tunguska meteorite—invaded Europe from beyond the "Red Curtain," having converted most of Russia's population into alien supersoldiers. After swiftly crushing the continental nations, the Chimera burrowed under the English Channel and have almost completed the conquest of Britain when the Americans launch a counterattack from across the Atlantic; this is the point at which the game begins.

The player, adopting the role of a US soldier, must shoot their way through a strictly **linear** story line before they can liberate Britain by killing the aliens that control the bulk of the invasion force. During his odyssey, the player's character discovers that the Chimera intend to be both the once and future overlords of Earth; their artifacts have been buried beneath England's soil for millions of years, waiting for their return. Gameplay is enlivened by a wide variety of monstrous opponents formed from human flesh, as well as by the superhuman abilities the protagonist gains from being exposed to the alien virus while somehow escaping its full effects. Subtle characterization is not, however, a strong point.

In the similarly constructed sequel, *Resistance 2* (*2008* IG) designed by Ted Price, Todd Fixman, and Brian Hastings, the same protagonist is given access to drugs to keep the Chimera virus under control, and a complex history of experimentation with its effects on humans is revealed; these experiments may be responsible for the lead character's unusual reaction to the mutagen. The main narrative, however, is concerned with the protagonist's defeat of a massive alien invasion of North America. In the end, the player's character is overcome by the virus and transforms into an alien being, forcing his last remaining comrade to kill him. Meanwhile, a **wormhole** opens above New York, allowing a second Chimeran invasion fleet to arrive from another star, replacing the one that the player has just destroyed. The final game, *Resistance 3* (*2011* IG) designed by Marcus Smith, Drew Murray, and Jon Paquette, is again an **FPS** with a linear narrative in which the lead character is less a soldier than a guerilla fighter in alien-occupied territory. Here, the surviving character from the previous game must defeat the second alien attack on what is by now an almost entirely conquered—and very much devastated—America. Eventually, a complete victory against the Chimera can be achieved.

All of these games gain from their juxtaposition of the familiar details of the past with the alien and the grotesque, in a history that is not quite our own. There are several literary antecedents for this effect, including Harry Turtledove's **Worldwar** sequence, in which aliens invade Earth during World War II. Arguably, something similar was at work in the **pulp** novels of **Operator #5**, who fought a "Purple Invasion" that laid waste to America with secret weapons and scientific plagues; whatever the reality in which these stories took place, it was clearly not the one their readers were living in.

Related works: *Resistance: Retribution* (*2009* Sony Computer Entertainment) is a **third-person shooter** in which the player takes the part of a British marine who must liberate alien-occupied Europe, set between the events of *Resistance* and *Resistance 2*. *Resistance: Burning Skies* (*2012* Nihilistic Software) designed by Harley Baldwin White-Wiedow is an FPS, similarly set between *Fall of Man* and *Resistance 2*, in which the player must oppose the Chimera's initial invasion of America, with a story cowritten by William C Dietz. Reviews were mixed. *Project Abraham* (*2009* 42 Entertainment) designed by Brooke Thompson is an **ARG** that explores the secret history of US experiments with the Chimera virus; it was developed to promote the release of *Resistance 2*. *Global Resistance* (*2011* IG) is a **computer wargame**, played on social networks, in which players can control either human or Chimera forces in the worldwide war. *Resistance* (*2009*) is a six-issue comic series, written by Mike Costa and set between the first and second games. *Resistance: The Gathering Storm* (**2009**) and *Resistance: A Hole in the Sky* (**2011**), both by William C Dietz, are prequels to, respectively, *Resistance 2* and *Resistance 3*.

Web Links

- *Resistance*: http://resistance-game.com/

- *Project Abraham*: http://www.projectabraham.com/

STALKER: SHADOW OF CHERNOBYL

2007. GSC Game World (GSC).

Stalker is a game much influenced by both Arkady and Boris Strugatski's novel *Roadside Picnic* (**1972**) and the Andrei Tarkovsky's film *Stalker* (*1979*) that was loosely based on the book. While *Roadside Picnic* locates its enigmatic Zone in Canada and *Stalker* places its equivalent in a desolate, unidentified landscape, the game identifies it with the 30 km radius Exclusion Zone put in place around the Chernobyl nuclear reactor complex after its meltdown in 1986. Much of the game's visual design was directly copied from the Chernobyl Zone by the game's Ukrainian developers. In the game, the reactor complex exploded for a second time in 2006, causing strange alterations in reality within the surrounding area. Humans and animals mutated, some gaining **psionic** powers, and "anomalies" appeared, including regions of increased gravity and lethal miniature whirlwinds. These anomalies produce strange artifacts, which have unexplainable effects on humans. As in *Roadside Picnic*, the potential value of these curiosities has led to the appearance of the titular Stalkers, humans who enter the Zone illegally to search for them. The player's character is an amnesiac Stalker who starts the game with a notepad containing only one message: "Kill Strelok." Eventually, the player can discover that their character is Strelok.

The game's plot combines **modular** and **multilinear** approaches to impressive effect. Players have a great deal of freedom to act as they explore the Zone, attempt to recover valuable artifacts, and interact with other Stalkers; combat, infiltration, and negotiation are common activities. The Zone itself is well crafted, with a functioning simulated ecology and a rich variety of locations, from blasted concrete wastelands to desolate, radioactive marshes. Various factions roam the area near the reactor, including professional killers for hire, military forces attempting to control access, and groups of Stalkers dedicated to protecting the world from the Zone. The player can ally with many of these factions or oppose them. As they proceed deeper into the game, and into the Zone, they will discover that something unexplained lurks at its heart, in the ruins of the reactor, protected by a fanatical group of Stalkers. Eventually, a full-scale war develops between this band and the other factions, giving the player their chance to reach the core.

The game's somewhat convoluted backstory involves a Soviet military experiment to create a human **hive mind** capable of extrasensory perception (**ESP**) in a laboratory under the still radioactive Chernobyl reactor complex, where secrecy could be guaranteed. After the collapse of the Soviet Union, this experiment was abandoned, and the emerging group mind absorbed its creators before deciding to bring about world peace by direct manipulation of humanity's noosphere. Unfortunately, its first attempt failed, causing the second explosion and creating the Zone. The game's protagonist had previously reached the reactor complex but been caught in an anomaly and rendered amnesiac. The group mind, knowing that a Stalker named Strelok was attempting to uncover its secrets but not realizing who the player's character was, then attempted to program him to kill Strelok and released him. In the end, the player's fate after they return to the reactor depends on the path they have taken through the game. If they have not succeeded in discovering their character's previous identity, they will be presented with an ending in which Strelok is trapped in an illusion of whatever the game decides the player most desires. For example, a player who had spent the game accumulating money would hallucinate false riches before being killed by falling masonry. If the player is aware of who their character truly is, they will be offered the option of assisting the group mind in its attempt to bring about universal peace. Acceptance results in their incorporation into the group; refusal leads to a chance to destroy the hive, though that victory may itself be illusory.

Various morals can be deduced from the game's cryptic resolution. However, its most impressive feature remains its depiction of the alienated, hostile landscape of the Zone; this is also the aspect in which it most strongly resembles Tarkovsky's film. While the gameplay may occasionally seem unpolished, *Shadow of Chernobyl*'s bleak vision of a shattered reality is not easily forgotten.

Related works: *Stalker: Clear Sky* (*2008* GSC) is a prequel to the original game, released as an expansion that can also be played alone. The player's mission is to prevent Strelok from reaching the center of the Zone; successful completion of the game will create the situation that exists at the beginning of *Shadow of Chernobyl. Stalker: Call of Pripyat* (2009 GSC) is another expansion that serves as a sequel to the original work. The assumption made is that Strelok kills the hive mind at the end of *Shadow of Chernobyl*, after which the Ukrainian military decide to take control of the Exclusion Zone. Their attempt is a disastrous failure, however, and the player character—an agent of the Ukrainian Security Service—is sent into the area around Chernobyl to search for survivors; this mission will eventually lead him to the eponymous city.

Southern Comfort (**2011**), by John Mason (a pseudonym for Balázs Pataki), and its sequel *Northern Passage* (**2012**), also by Pataki, are **ties** to the franchise. Both are set in an **alternate history** in which nuclear weapons were used in Afghanistan in 2011, creating a vast new Zone.

Web Link

- *Stalker*: http://www.stalker-game.com/

SYSTEM SHOCK

1994. LG Studios. Designed by Doug Church.

System Shock is an early **FPS** that was much influenced by the tradition of **CRPG** design. It is set in a **cyberpunk** world, with gameplay that combines puzzle solution, exploration, and combat. Interestingly, the difficulty of the puzzles and the amount of combat can be set before starting the game, allowing players to choose the mix of action and **adventure** they prefer. The game begins with the player's character waking up from a medically induced coma, to find himself trapped on the Citadel space station with SHODAN (Sentient Hyper-Optimized Data Access Network), an insane artificial intelligence with plans for global domination. After being contacted by the station's owners on Earth, the player realizes that they have no choice but to destroy the artificial intelligence. This forces them to fight their way to its core, destroying or evading its robot servants and the disturbing mutants that are all that remains of the crew after their exposure to mutagenic compounds. On occasion, the player also needs to enter **cyberspace** using a neural implant, where they are opposed by hostile security programs. The plot has many twists; the player will repeatedly find themselves defeating one of SHODAN's plans to attack Earth, only to discover that the intelligence is preparing another and more dangerous weapon. As the player progresses through the game, the **embedded** story of how SHODAN went rogue and took over Citadel is gradually revealed through log files. The player's character, it emerges, unintentionally caused the AI's insanity while hacking into the station's systems

6 months earlier. Perhaps the most impressive aspect of the game is the relationship that develops between the player and SHODAN, who watches them constantly and mocks them at every turn. While the interface can be clumsy, *System Shock* succeeds in immersing the player in its menacing world, in which their only contact with other humans comes through occasional terse messages from Earth and reading dead men's journals.

The sequel, *System Shock 2* (*1999* IG/LG) designed by Ken Levine, has gameplay closer to that of a true **CRPG**. Notably, the player selects their character's skills in such areas as **psionics** before the game begins and then improves them during play. As in *System Shock*, the game starts with the player's character regaining consciousness after surgery. In *System Shock 2*, however, the character is partially amnesiac, unable to remember the purpose of the operation. The setting is the Earth's first **faster-than-light** starship, the *von Braun*, which is returning from a test voyage to Tau Ceti. It rapidly becomes apparent that the ship is badly damaged and rest of the crew have been absorbed by a mutagenic organism that calls itself "The Many." The primary narrative, as in *System Shock*, is embedded, obtained from audio journals and the ghostly images of dead crew members, visible through the player character's psionic implants. In *System Shock 2*, the horrors of the past are always present. As the game progresses, the player is contacted by an unseen presence that claims to be the sole survivor of the crew and instructs them in how to deal with The Many. Ultimately, it emerges that this is the voice of SHODAN, who escaped from Citadel Station before it was destroyed in the first game, aboard a pod containing samples of her mutagenic experiments. SHODAN eventually drifted into the Tau Ceti system, where her lifeboat was discovered by the *von Braun*. Subsequently, the crew were absorbed by The Many, a **hive-mind** organism descended from the original contents of the pod. After achieving a position of power aboard the ship, SHODAN had the player's character cybernetically enhanced as a weapon against its rebellious creation. SHODAN thus becomes the player's ultimate enemy, as she was in the first game. In *System Shock*, the player must destroy their character's creation; in *System Shock 2*, they must destroy the artificial intelligence that made them what they are. While the first game is always interesting, *System Shock 2* benefits from a far denser science-fictional ambience than that of its predecessor, as well as a superior interface. Most fundamentally, perhaps, the second game's horribly human monsters and dark, haunted atmosphere make it far more viscerally disturbing than the original.

Players of *System Shock 2* can use **psionic** powers against their enemies.

Web Link

- *System Shock 2* Postmortem: http://www.gamasutra.com/features/19991207/chey_01.htm

UNREAL

1998. Epic Games (EG). Designed by Cliff Bleszinski and James Schmalz.

The *Unreal* series of **FPSs** is a competitor to *Quake* (*1996* id Software [id]) and its various descendants and has generally shared its rival's philosophy, with similar gameplay, atmosphere, and approaches to narrative. The two series have competed not only as game experiences but also as technologies, with the core software of both systems licensed to other game developers to use in their own products. The first game in the series, *Unreal*, casts the player as a prisoner on a starship en route to a penal colony that crashes on an unknown planet. After making their way out of the remains of the ship, the player discovers that the pacifist indigenous aliens are being enslaved by a cruel and technologically advanced race of interstellar conquerors, the Skaarj. The most interesting moments are perhaps at the beginning, when the player is trying to determine their situation from logs found inside the crashed spacecraft, before suddenly emerging onto the surface of an alien world full of exotic species and striking locales. *Unreal*'s visual design is impressive, and its many combat sequences are well crafted. Ultimately, the player can find a way off the planet, after which the story is continued in *Unreal Mission Pack I: Return to Na Pali* (*1999* EG), a largely repetitive expansion in which the player is picked up by a human starship and dispatched back to the planet to recover secret military data from another downed spacecraft.

Unreal Tournament (*1999* EG) designed by Cliff Bleszinski was a rival to *Quake III Arena* (*1999* id) and was thus primarily concerned with multiplayer combat in temporary **online worlds**. It was followed by several similar games that made gradual improvements to the gameplay; the earlier titles included year dates in their names in order to emphasize their similarity to **sports games**. The major releases to date are *Unreal Tournament 2003* (*2002* EG/DE; *2002* revised as *Unreal Championship*) designed by Cliff Bleszinski; *Unreal Tournament 2004* (*2004* EG/DE) designed by Cliff Bleszinski, Jeff Morris, and Steven Polge; and *Unreal Tournament III* (*2007* EG) designed by Steven Polge. *Unreal Championship 2: The Liandri Conflict* (*2005* EG) designed by Mitchell Danuco is a sequel to *Unreal Championship* (the Xbox version of *Unreal Tournament 2003*) that was redesigned to suit gameplay styles common on game consoles, primarily by including hand-to-hand combat and a third-person view. *Unreal Tournament III: Titan Pack* (*2009* EG) is an expansion for *Unreal Tournament III*. *Unreal II: The Awakening* (*2003* Legend Entertainment [LE]), however, is a single-player **FPS** set in the same universe as the first *Unreal* but created by different hands. The player adopts the role of a marshal in an obscure sector of space who must recover the seven pieces of a mysterious alien artifact. While the mission designs are interestingly diverse, the **linear** plot suffers from somewhat clichéd execution. *Unreal II: eXpanded MultiPlayer* (*2003* LE) adds an option for player versus player combat to the game.

As with *Quake*, originality of speculative concept and credibility of plot were not major concerns when the first *Unreal* games were designed. The intent—as was conventional for FPSs at the time—was simply to provide an exciting and visually striking action experience in a science-fictional environment. In this, both *Unreal* and its single-player sequel succeed admirably.

Related works: *Hard Crash* (**1998**) by Ryan Hughes (a pseudonym for Jerry B. Oltion) and *Prophet's Power* (**1998**) by Dean Wesley Smith are **ties** based on the story line established in the first game.

Web Links

- *Unreal Tournament* Postmortem: http://www.gamasutra.com/features/20000609/reinhart_01.htm

- Interview with Tim Sweeney of Epic Games: http://www.gamasutra.com/features/20010406/foreman_02.htm

- Planet Unreal (Tribute Site): http://planetunreal.gamespy.com/

CHAPTER 11

Third-Person Shooters

A THIRD-PERSON SHOOTER IS a form of **videogame** that, like the **first-person shooter** (FPS), focuses on physically demanding, fast-paced, often violent gameplay displayed in three dimensions. Unlike that form, however, in a third-person shooter, the player's character is seen in an external (third-person) view. This perspective may make the experience of playing the game less intense than in an **FPS** but is necessary when the player needs a clear view of their character's actions, as with the martial arts moves used in *Oni* (*2001* Bungie Studios). The form has primarily developed on game consoles rather than personal computers. A possible early example is the science fiction (sf)—related UK game *Tomb Raider* (*1996* Core Design) designed by Toby Gard, in which the aristocratic English archaeologist Lara Croft—later to become a noted videogame sex symbol and ultimately a feminist icon—must jump, shoot, and puzzle her way through a range of locations to uncover the secrets of a superscientific Atlantis. Later games of this kind include the enthusiastically melodramatic **pulp** noir thriller *Max Payne* (*2001* Remedy Entertainment [RE]) designed by Petri Järvilehto and Sami Järvi, created in Finland; the French—Canadian techno-thriller *Tom Clancy's Splinter Cell* (*2002* Ubisoft) designed by Nathan Wolff; the psychological thriller *Alan Wake* (*2010* RE) designed by Mikael Kasurinen; and the Japanese *Resident Evil 5* (*2009* Capcom) designed by Jun Takeuchi and Kenichi Ueda. One recent development is the growing popularity of third-person shooters that force the player to make extensive use of cover to avoid enemy fire, a mechanic that works rather better in third-person than in first-person view; an excellent example is the US-developed **military sf** game *Gears of War* (*2006* Epic Games [EG]) designed by Cliff Bleszinski.

GEARS OF WAR

2006. Epic Games (EG). Designed by Cliff Bleszinski.

Gears of War is a squad-based **third-person shooter** that shares much with the same developers' earlier **FPS** *Unreal* (*1998* EG) designed by Cliff Bleszinski and James Schmalz. The setting is an interstellar colony planet, ravaged by subterranean aliens known as the "Locust Horde" and defended by the titular human soldiers. The tone is that of the more clichéd kind of **military sf**; *Gears* features orbital laser weapons and a main character who begins the game in prison, enthusiastically macho dialogue, and a great deal of splattered blood and body parts, all within a brutal world where humanity's army must destroy its own cities to deny them to the enemy. As might be expected, the gameplay focuses on a largely realistic approach to combat. There is much emphasis on the need to take cover from enemy fire, whether in the single-player game or in the variously competitive and cooperative multiplayer options. In essence, *Gears of War* is a well-crafted action game, with impressive visuals and a primarily **linear** narrative based around a formulaic war story that is delivered with considerable verve and an abundance of references to popular culture.

Gears of War 2 (*2008* EG), designed by Cliff Bleszinski and with a script by Joshua Ortega, is a sequel with similar gameplay and a somewhat deeper story, based on a counteroffensive against the Locusts. Ultimately, the player is forced to destroy humanity's last redoubt in order to defeat the enemy. In *Gears of War 3* (*2011* EG), designed by Cliff Bleszinski and written by Karen Traviss, a new, but equally hostile, alien species emerges from underground to threaten the few survivors of the previous game; ultimately, both they and the remaining Locusts can be utterly destroyed. Fundamentally, the considerable commercial success of the *Gears* series may be due to its effectiveness at making its players—usually, but not exclusively, men—feel that they have become heavily muscled, highly competent, hypermasculine future soldiers, regardless of how much they resemble this stereotype in everyday life. Arguably, this makes the games a kind of interactive analogue to such films as *The Chronicles of Riddick* (*2004*) or to the **Space Wolf** novels of William King.

Related works: *Gears of War: Judgment* (*2013* People Can Fly [PCF]) designed by Wojciech Madry, Arcade Berg, and Oliver Barder is a prequel created by other hands. Gameplay and tone are similar to those of previous installments, but the main story line takes place during a series of flashbacks from a framing sequence in which a team of soldiers are being court-martialed for their actions on the day the Locust Horde first emerged from their underground lairs. A coda focuses on the actions of the same characters during *Gears of War 3*.

Gears of War: Hidden Fronts (*2007* EG) and *Gears of War 2: All Fronts* (*2009* EG) are expansion packs for the eponymous works that add more locations for competitive games between players in temporary **online worlds**. *Gears of War 3: Horde Command* (*2011* EG), *Gears of War 3: Forces of Nature* (*2012* EG), and *Gears of War 3: Fenix Rising* (*2012* EG) similarly add new areas for multiplayer games to *Gears of War 3*. More interestingly, perhaps, *Gears of War 3: RAAM's Shadow* (*2011* EG) serves as a distant prequel to the original game, with some sequences in which the player adopts the role of a Locust commander. Finally, *Gears of War: Judgment—Call to Arms* (*2013* PCF) and *Gears of War: Judgment—Lost Relics* (*2013* PCF) extend the titular game with new options and locations for player versus player combat. *Gears of War: The Board Game* (*2011* Fantasy Flight Games [FFG]) designed by Corey Konieczka is a board game in which players must cooperate to complete randomly constructed missions based on the events of the first two **videogames**. *Gears of War: Mission Pack 1* (*2012* FFG) designed by Corey Konieczka and Brady Sadler is an expansion.

Gears of War: Aspho Fields (**2008**) by Karen Traviss is a sequel to the original game that focuses on the histories of its world and major characters. Several other **ties** followed, all by Traviss. Thus, *Gears of War: Jacinto's Remnant* (**2009**), *Gears of War: Anvil Gate* (**2010**), and *Gears of War: Coalition's End* (**2011**) are set between *Gears of War 2* and *Gears of War 3* and tell a single continuous story while depicting the games' characters in rather more detail than they receive in their original medium. *Gears of War: The Slab* (**2012**), meanwhile, is a prequel to the first game, which also provides additional backstory for the third. *Gears of War* (*2008–2012*) is an associated comic series, written variously by Joshua Ortega, Michael Capps, and Traviss.

Web Links

- *Gears of War*: http://gearsofwar.xbox.com/

- Rod Fergusson on *Gears of War 2*: http://www.gamasutra.com/view/feature/3773/new_better_more_epics_approach_.php

- Planet Gears of War (Tribute Site): http://planetgearsofwar.gamespy.com/

METAL GEAR

1987. Konami. Designed by Hideo Kojima.

The original *Metal Gear* is notable largely for having popularized the idea of an action-based **videogame** whose gameplay revolves around stealthy infiltration. (The World War Two action game *Castle Wolfenstein* [*1981* Muse Software] designed by Silas Warner—the inspiration for the much less stealthy and rather more violent **FPS** *Wolfenstein 3D* [*1992* id Software] designed by John Carmack and John Romero—appears to have been the first videogame of this type but was little known outside the then small community of American personal computer enthusiasts.) As with all of its various sequels, *Metal Gear* is essentially a techno-thriller, set in what was at the time the near future of the 1990s, and features the eponymous bipedal tank, which here serves as a launching platform for nuclear weapons. The player, in the role of a US operative code-named Solid Snake, must penetrate the defenses of Outer Heaven, a rogue state founded by disillusioned soldiers. Snake's mission is to gather intelligence on and eventually destroy the Metal Gear, with which Outer Heaven's leader is threatening the nations of the West. In order to succeed, the player must avoid combat wherever possible, using the game's **2D** overhead view to spot and evade enemies and finding innovative ways to bypass or disable various traps. The game succeeds in creating considerable tension as the player threads their way through one lethal obstacle after another, particularly after a twist in the (admittedly minimal) plot leaves the protagonist cut off from his superiors. *Metal Gear* had two direct sequels, of which the first was created by other hands than Kojima's: *Snake's Revenge* (*1990* Konami), which uses both overhead and side views to tell its story of the infiltration of a terrorist base containing mass produced Metal Gears. Kojima returned to design *Metal Gear 2: Solid Snake* (*1990* Konami), another 2D stealth-based game in which the player is tasked with rescuing a kidnapped scientist who has invented a way to produce petroleum using genetically engineered algae.

The series only became truly popular, however, with the release of *Metal Gear Solid* (*1998* Konami; *1999* revised as *Metal Gear Solid: Integral*) designed by Hideo Kojima. This work retains the basic gameplay of the original *Metal Gear*, but displays it **three-dimensionally**, usually from overhead and in a third-person view. Perhaps more importantly, it begins the process of transforming the simple story lines of the first three games into an increasingly baroque serial melodrama, littered with flamboyant grotesques, bizarre plot twists, and unexpected lectures on philosophy. The approach taken is highly cinematic, both in its use of visual techniques derived from film and in its presentation of the generally **linear** narrative through long **full motion video** scenes and conversations, which the player listens to rather than participates in. The story begins with Solid Snake called out of retirement to infiltrate a nuclear weapon disposal facility occupied by members of his old unit. These ex comrades turned terrorists have seized control of a Metal Gear and are threatening the US government with a nuclear strike if it fails to surrender the body of the leader of Outer Heaven, killed at the end of *Metal Gear 2*. Things rapidly become more complicated, as it emerges that the unit is commanded by a previously unmentioned clone of the protagonist, known as Liquid Snake, and that Solid Snake has been infected with a genetically engineered virus designed to kill the terrorists and possibly himself as well. Meanwhile, Snake's commanding officer regularly contacts him via radio to supply advice on how to play the game, obtain updates on the status of the mission, and occasionally discuss the meaning of life. As with the later *Metal Gear Solid* games, the tone veers between enthusiastic kitsch, broad humor—pornographic magazines are an especially effective way of distracting guards in later revisions of the game—and heartfelt denunciations of nuclear proliferation and the corrosive effects of warfare on human nature. There is one expansion, *Metal Gear Solid: VR Missions* (*1999* Konami), a set of additional missions unrelated to the main story line that were included in the revised *Metal Gear Solid: Integral*. *Metal Gear Solid: The Twin Snakes* (*2004* Konami/Silicon Knights) is a full remake of the original, incorporating various enhancements to both the gameplay and the visuals.

The first sequel to *Metal Gear Solid* was *Metal Gear Solid 2: Sons of Liberty* (*2001* Konami; *2002* revised as *Metal Gear Solid 2: Substance*; revised *2011*) designed by Hideo Kojima. Gameplay in *Sons of Liberty* is a much refined and more realistic version of that seen in its predecessor, with markedly more intelligent opponents. The linear story is split into two parts. In the first, Solid Snake—now working for a United Nations–sponsored organization known as Philanthropy—is dispatched to investigate the theft of a new Metal Gear prototype. In the second, a new protagonist known as Raiden is sent into an environmental cleanup facility in New York City, which has been captured by terrorists. Almost everything in Raiden's initial mission briefing, however, eventually proves to have been a lie. The narrative tone resembles that of *Metal Gear Solid*; characters repeatedly break the fourth wall, at one point telling the player to turn off the console on which they are playing the game. *Metal Gear Solid 3: Snake Eater* (*2004* Konami; *2005* revised as *Metal Gear Solid 3: Subsistence*; revised *2011*; *2012* revised as *Metal Gear Solid: Snake Eater 3D*) designed by Hideo Kojima adopts a somewhat more sober tone in its depiction of the early career of "Naked Snake," the man who became the leader of Outer Heaven in *Metal Gear* and from whom Solid Snake and Liquid Snake were cloned. Naked Snake is an agent of the US government during the 1960s, sent into the Soviet Union to extract a defecting nuclear scientist. The mission rapidly disintegrates, however, as it emerges that Snake is acting as a pawn in a war between different factions of a secret society that once controlled the most powerful nations in the world; the ending conveys a sense of genuine tragedy. *Snake Eater*'s gameplay emphasizes exploration and accuracy of simulation to a greater degree than previous entries in the series, including realistic depictions of wounds and jungle survival. *Metal Gear Solid: Portable Ops* (*2006* Konami) designed by Masahiro Yamamoto and Hideo Kojima is a sequel to *Snake Eater*. Set in South America during the early 1970s, the game deals with Naked Snake's attempts to dispose of renegade members of his own unit who have taken over a Soviet army base. The gameplay is quite different to that of previous entries in the series; while stealth is still emphasized, *Portable Ops* is a squad-based game in which the player must recruit members of the opposing forces and deploy them in teams to secure mission objectives. *Metal Gear Solid: Portable Ops Plus* (*2007* Konami) is an expansion that concentrates on adding new multiplayer options; it can be played either separately or in combination with the first game. Similarly, *Metal Gear Solid: Peace Walker* (*2010* Konami) designed by Hideo Kojima follows Naked Snake's use of his mercenary army—the Militaires Sans Frontières ["Soldiers Without Borders"]—to defend Costa Rica against a mysterious invasion in the mid-1970s. The gameplay and narrative styles resemble those seen in *Sons of Liberty* and *Snake Eater*, with squad-based elements reminiscent of *Portable Ops*. Ultimately, Naked Snake will decide to create the military nation of Outer Heaven, making himself into the villain of the original *Metal Gear*.

The series culminates with *Metal Gear Solid 4: Guns of the Patriots* (*2008* Konami) designed by Hideo Kojima. This work's gameplay is a refined version of that provided by *Sons of Liberty*, but the (generally linear) story is markedly more complex and almost impossible to follow without playing the previous games in the sequence. Solid Snake is now suffering from premature aging brought on by rapid cellular degeneration and referred to as "Old Snake." *Guns of the Patriots* begins with him deployed to the Middle East to prevent rogue agents taking control of a **nanotechnological** facility used to enhance the abilities of the mercenaries who dominate military operations in the game's near future. The subsequent plot is so convoluted as to defy description. Characters from various previous games reappear, often in disguise, bioengineered supervillains proliferate wildly, and the backstory of the entire series is explained by means of a remarkably intricate conspiracy theory in which America's secret masters turn out to be a network of artificial intelligences named after its most famous presidents. This game may be Solid Snake's last hurrah; if so, it is certainly a fitting conclusion.

Related works: *Metal Gear Rising: Revengeance* (*2013* Platinum Games [PG]) designed by Kenji Saito is a spin-off game, set 4 years after the end of *Guns of the Patriots* and featuring Raiden (the second protagonist of *Sons of Liberty*) as the player's character. Here, however, Raiden spends far more time slashing than sneaking; this iteration of the franchise is more concerned with action than stealth, featuring a great deal of high-speed swordplay with excessively powerful blades and an almost obsessive focus on dismemberment. The linear plot is as overwrought as ever, with frequent discussions of the various characters' ethical stances, a talking robotic dog, and a villain who plans to restart the War on Terror in order to transform the United States into a land ruled by an endless war of all against all (an outcome he sees as the true American dream). Ultimately, the game's **cyborg** hero, having successfully come to terms with his inner child soldier, can hack and slash his way through all opposition. The story ends with him disappearing to fight his own private war, while the mercenary army that employed him sets up a refuge where the brains of abused children can be rehoused in artificial bodies. *Metal Gear Rising: Revengeance—Blade Wolf* (*2013* PG) and *Metal Gear Rising: Revengeance—Jetstream Sam* (*2013* PG) are expansion packs that serve as prequels, focusing on the back stories of two of the most iconic characters from the game.

Various other games have been created in which Solid Snake is the protagonist, and the gameplay emphasizes stealthy infiltration, but which are not part of the main story sequence. *Metal Gear: Ghost Babel* (*2000* Konami; also known as *Metal Gear Solid* outside Japan) designed by Shinta Nojiri and Hideo Kojima has similar gameplay to the original *Metal Gear* and a plot based on the theft of a Metal Gear prototype by an African guerilla group. *Metal Gear*

Acid (*2004* Konami; *2008* revised as *Metal Gear Acid Mobile*) designed by Shinta Nojiri has a highly stylized design in which a virtual **collectible card game** is used to control Snake's actions; the story revolves around attempts to rescue a kidnapped US senator and investigations of a secret research project. The broadly similar sequel is *Metal Gear Acid 2* (*2005* Konami; *2009* revised as *Metal Gear Acid 2 Mobile*) designed by Shinta Nojiri, in which an amnesiac Snake is forced to perform missions by a rogue US official. *Metal Gear Solid Mobile* (*2008* Ideaworks) deals with attempts to prevent the spread of leaked Metal Gear technology, while *Metal Gear Solid Touch* (*2009* Konami) is a much simplified version of *Guns of the Patriots* in which the player shoots their way through a predetermined series of enemies. *Metal Gear Online* (*2008* Konami) is a competitive multiplayer game set in temporary **online worlds**, normally included with *Guns of the Patriots*, which has to date only received an independent release in Japan. Finally, *Metal Gear Solid: Social Ops* (*2012* Konami) designed by Hideo Kojima is an action game intended for play on mobile devices, with an emphasis on social interaction between participants; to date, it has only been released in Japan.

Several comics and novels have been written based on the franchise. *Metal Gear* (**1990**) by Alexander Frost is a young adult novelization of *Metal Gear*, while *Metal Gear Solid* (**2008**) and *Metal Gear Solid 2: Sons of Liberty* (**2009**), both by Raymond Benson, are novelizations of *Metal Gear Solid* and *Metal Gear Solid 2*. Similarly, *Metal Gear Solid* (*2004–2005*) is a 12-issue comic based on the game of the same name, written by Kris Oprisko, and *Metal Gear Solid: Sons of Liberty* (*2005–2007*) is a 12-issue comic series derived from *Sons of Liberty*, written by Alex Garner. There is also a Japanese novelization of *Guns of the Patriots* by Keikaku Itō: *Metal Gear Solid: Guns of the Patriots* (**2008**), translated into English in 2012.

Web Link

- Kojima Productions: http://www.konami.jp/kojima_pro/

- Ryan Payton on *Metal Gear Solid 4*: http://www.gamasutra.com/view/feature/1954/infiltrating_kojima_productions_.php

ONI

2001. Bungie Studios.

Oni is a third-person **fighting game** with the narrative structure, world design, and some of the gameplay of a **linearly** plotted **third-person shooter.** (Players can engage in combat both with guns, as in the shooter form, and as a martial artist, as in fighting games.) This unique combination of forms works well in principle, but the game's urban environments, based on real-world architecture, seem overly repetitive and are arguably poorly designed for gameplay. The setting is a twenty-first century Earth much influenced by the film *Ghost in the Shell* (1995) and other works of sf **anime**. In this **future history**, a totalitarian global government dominates a world in which the air outside the domed cities has been rendered toxic by ecological collapse. Within the domes, the poor have become increasingly desperate, while the rich live in the future that everyone wanted. The player's character, the purple-haired Konoko, is a biologically enhanced woman who is an operative for the paramilitary Technological Crimes Task Force; adopting her role within the game involves the player in a dark, emotionally compelling narrative. After the death of an **android** to whom she is neurally and emotionally linked, Konoko discovers that when she was a child, she was implanted with a "Daodan Chrysalis," a symbiote that evolves to alter and improve her body, allowing her to survive outside the cities. Having learned this, the player is forced to become a rogue agent. Eventually, it emerges that Konoko's long-lost brother, who has also been implanted with a Chrysalis, intends to fill their dome with toxic air, forcing the inhabitants to pay him for implants of their own. Konoko can stop him, but only at the price of destroying the city's atmospheric converters, meaning that the population may still be forced to choose between adaptation to the Chrysalis and death. Ultimately, *Oni* combines an intriguing linear narrative with somewhat less interesting gameplay. Nevertheless, the martial-arts-based combat mechanics work well, and the game's fictional world offers an excellent homage to its source material.

Web Link

- *Oni*: http://www.bungie.net/Projects/Oni/

CHAPTER 12

Survival Horror

S URVIVAL HORROR IS A term used to describe a form of **videogame** that, unusually among game forms, is defined by its tone and ambience rather than by its gameplay. As the name suggests, survival horror games are characterized by vulnerable protagonists attempting to escape from menacing and disturbing situations, almost always of a fantastic nature. The gameplay most often resembles that of an action **adventure**, though in a survival horror game the players' characters will be at much more frequent risk of death, dismemberment, and crippling psychological injury. The form is dominated by Japanese designers and has typically been developed for game consoles rather than personal computers.

The term was first used to promote *Resident Evil* (*1996* Capcom) designed by Shinji Mikami, which is thus often considered to be the first game of its kind. Several earlier works could perhaps be classified as survival horror, however, notably *Project Firestart* (*1989* Dynamix) designed by Jeffrey Tunnell and Damon Slye—a game much influenced by the film *Alien* (*1979*)—and the **Cthulhu Mythos**-inspired *Alone in the Dark* (*1992* Infogrames), created in France. *Resident Evil* itself was clearly influenced by *Sweet Home* (*1989* Capcom) designed by Juzo Itami, a Japanese haunted house game linked to the horror film *Sûîto Homu* (*1989*; also known as *Sweet Home* outside Japan), which in turn bears some resemblance to the Steven Spielberg film *Poltergeist* (*1982*).

While the *Resident Evil* series concentrates on visceral zombie horror with a science fiction (sf) rationale, later members of the school have tended toward dark fantasy and psychological terror. Notable examples of the form include the serial killer–based *Clock Tower* (*1998* Human Entertainment; also known as *Clock Tower 2* in Japan); *Fatal Frame* (*2001* Tecmo; also known as *Project Zero* in Europe and Australia) designed by Keisuke Kikuchi, in which a young girl must exorcize a house full of ghosts using a mystical camera; the Canadian game *Eternal Darkness: Sanity's Requiem* (*2002* Silicon Knights) designed by Denis Dyack, which involves elements based on the Cthulhu Mythos; and the markedly unsettling *Silent Hill 2* (*2001* Konami; *2001* revised as *Silent Hill 2: Restless Dreams*) designed by Masashi Tsuboyama. Among the rare examples that can be categorized as sf are the UK-developed game *Call of Cthulhu: Dark Corners of the Earth* (*2005* Headfirst Productions), a work inspired by H P Lovecraft's Cthulhu Mythos story *The Shadow over Innsmouth* (**1936**); *Parasite Eve* (*1998* Square) designed by Hironobu Sakaguchi and Takashi Tokita, a game based on Hideaki Sena's eponymous novel of present-day humanity threatened by rebellious mitochondrial cells in the form of **telekinetic** women; and *Dead Space* (*2008* Electronic Arts [EA]) designed by Brett Robbins, Wright Bagwell, and Jatin Patel. At their best, survival horror games can be profoundly involving and remarkably effective at inducing emotional responses in their players, though in a somewhat limited register.

DEAD SPACE

2008. Electronic Arts (EA). Designed by Brett Robbins, Wright Bagwell, and Jatin Patel.

Dead Space is a **survival horror** game presented in the manner of a **third-person shooter** and a work that is very much influenced by the art house terror of Ridley Scott's *Alien* (*1979*). The player's character, the significantly named Isaac Clarke (a homage to the sf writers Isaac Asimov and Arthur C Clarke), is an engineer on the starship Kellion. At the beginning of the game, the Kellion is investigating a distress signal sent out by the Ishimura, a gigantic vessel engaged in mining operations on the colony world of Aegis VII. Not long after the start of the game's **linear** story, the Kellion crashes into the Ishimura, trapping the crew on board the distressed ship, which turns out to be overrun with hideous monsters. Eventually, it emerges that the colonists had uncovered an alien artifact known as the Marker, the most sacred relic of the Unitologist church, and brought it aboard the Ishimura. Shortly after the object's arrival, the crew began experiencing mass hallucinations and murdering each other; the bodies of the dead were then infected by a virus associated with the Marker, which resurrected them as deformed, homicidal monstrosities known as Necromorphs. Ultimately, the player can return the Marker to Aegis VII, where a **hive-mind** entity controls the Necromorphs, before destroying both the colony and the controlling entity. At the end of the game, Clarke is left drifting in space in a small auxiliary craft.

The game includes much **embedded** narrative, with the disastrous history of the Ishimura's mission being conveyed through various journals and logs in a similar manner to that used in *System Shock 2* (*1999* Irrational Games/Looking Glass) designed by Ken Levine. The script, written by Warren Ellis, Rick Remender, and Antony Johnston, makes frequent references to previous works and other features of the genre. Notably, the Unitologists are suggestive of **Scientology**, the Marker resembles the monolith discovered in the film *2001: A Space Odyssey* (*1968*), and the game's somewhat convoluted backstory—in which Earth's secret government is experimenting with the Marker, which appears to be a copy of an original of extraterrestrial origin—is reminiscent of the conspiracy theories that underpin both *Alien* and its various sequels. Even the Necromorphs, reconstructed corpses with altered, and supposedly improved, genetic structures, may have been suggested by the effects of the parasitic cruciforms in Dan Simmons' novel *Hyperion* (**1989**).

The end result is a very visceral game, in every sense. Severed limbs pile up as the player frantically dismembers attacking Necromorphs with improvised weapons in the Ishimura's dark corridors, lit only by dim, flickering emergency lighting. Some time is spent repairing malfunctioning equipment and solving simple puzzles, but the gameplay emphasizes escape, evasion, and occasional mayhem, in the manner of the *Resident Evil* series (from *1996* Capcom). Ultimately, *Dead Space* is a well-crafted example of Gothic horror, full of exciting shocks and disturbing grotesqueries, but its background and story are derivative and predictable.

Moments of gruesome horror are commonplace in Electronic Arts' *Dead Space*.

Dead Space 2 (*2011* Visceral Games [VG]) designed by Wright Bagwell, John Calhoun, Jatin Patel, Ben Walker, and Matthias Worch essentially repeats the plot and design of the first game, with a rescued Isaac Clarke trapped on a space station orbiting Saturn where another Marker has become active, creating another infestation of Necromorphs. One remarkable feature is the number of characters in Jeremy Bernstein's script who appear to be named after sf writers. In addition to Clarke, *Dead Space 2* offers Nolan Stross (an apparent reference to Charles Stross), Daina Le Guin (suggestive of Ursula K Le Guin), Ellie Langford (reminiscent of David Langford), and—in the prequel film *Dead Space: Aftermath*, see later text—Nicholas Kuttner (a probable reference to Henry Kuttner).

The next entry in the series, *Dead Space 3* (*2012* VG) designed by Ben Walker and Jean-François Chabot, has something of the relationship to its predecessors that James Cameron's film *Aliens* (*1986*) does to *Alien*. In an attempt to reach a larger market that would better justify the development costs of the series, its designers decided to make the third iteration more of a third-person shooter and less of a survival horror game than its precursors. Thus, Clarke—who returns as a protagonist—is here accompanied by a constant companion who can be controlled either by the computer or by another player, Sergeant John Carver. There is also much more emphasis on set-piece battles than on the frantic flights that characterized the play of the first two games, with new mechanics that allow the player to create personalized weapons that combine the various horrifically lethal devices they discover. *Dead Space 3*'s linear plot also represents a revision of the formula established by the original game. A somewhat convoluted and unlikely narrative follows an expedition to the frozen world of Tau Volantis, which is thought to be the home planet of the Necromorphs. Meanwhile, it becomes apparent that Clarke is now involved in a melodramatic love triangle with Langford and a new character, Robert Norton. Eventually, it emerges that the Necromorphs did not originate on Tau Volantis; instead, it is the homeworld of a sentient species long ago destroyed by them. Various alarms and excursions follow; ultimately, the Necromorphs on the planet can be defeated, though it appears that only Langford remains alive. An expansion pack, *Dead Space 3: Awakened* (*2013* VG), continues the story, revealing that Clarke, Carver, and some of the Necromorphs have all survived. The story ends with the protagonists' return to Earth, only to find that—as in one of the rejected concepts for the third film in the *Alien* franchise—the monsters are there before them.

Related works: *Dead Space: Extraction* (*2009* VG/Eurocom Developments) is an excellently constructed **first-person shooter** in which the player is faced with a predetermined sequence of enemies to kill. The plot follows the attempts of several colonists to escape from the Necromorph-infested colony of Aegis VII immediately prior to the events of *Dead Space*. *Dead Space: Ignition* (*2010* VG/Sumo Digital) designed by Tim Spencer is an action **adventure** that serves as a prequel to *Dead Space 2*; reviews were mixed. *Dead Space* (*2011* IronMonkey Studios) is a well-received survival horror game, set between the first and second entries in the main series. *Dead Space 2: Severed* (*2011* VG) is an expansion pack for *Dead Space 2*, including some of the characters from *Dead Space: Extraction*.

In *Dead Space*, the player is relentlessly hunted by the hideously mutated undead Necromorphs.

Dead Space: Downfall (*2008*) and *Dead Space: Aftermath* (*2011*) are animated films. The first is another prequel to the original *Dead Space*, concentrating on events aboard the Ishimura. The second deals with the final voyage of the O'Bannon, a ship dispatched to investigate the situation on Aegis VII after the disappearance of the Ishimura; it is also a prequel to *Dead Space 2*. *Dead Space* (*2008*) is a six-issue comic series, written by Antony Johnston, the plot of which occurs immediately before those of *Dead Space: Downfall* and *Dead Space: Extraction*, making it a prequel to the prequels to the original game. *Dead Space: Salvage* (**2010**) is a graphic novel, again written by Johnston, in which a group of independent salvagers find the remains of the Ishimura, abandoned after the events of the original game; carnage ensues. *Dead Space: Liberation* (*2013*), written by Ian Edginton, is a graphic novel that explores the backstory of John Carver, the second protagonist of *Dead Space 3*. *Dead Space: Martyr* (**2010**) is a novel by Brian Evenson writing as B. K. Evenson, which describes the origin of the Church of Unitology, several centuries prior to the Ishimura's arrival at Aegis VII. Of all the various games, films, comics, and novels associated with the *Dead Space* franchise, *Martyr* may be the most interesting as a work of sf. *Martyr* was followed by the same author's *Dead Space: Catalyst* (**2012**), which tells a separate story of Necromorph infestation set in the same time period as the games.

Web Link

- *Dead Space*: http://deadspace.ea.com/

RESIDENT EVIL

1996. (Also known as *Biohazard* in Japan; *2006* revised as *Resident Evil: Deadly Silence*.) Capcom. Designed by Shinji Mikami.

Resident Evil was not the first game that could be categorized as **survival horror**, but it was the game that codified the form. Its gameplay focuses on puzzle solution and combat within an apparently deserted mansion overrun by undead zombies and lethal biological experiments, in a scenario strongly evocative of George A Romero's **Living Dead** films. The flavor is that of a cult B-movie, with clichéd dialogue, strikingly poor voice acting, and a well-crafted atmosphere of unease and intermittent terror. As in many later *Resident Evil* games, players are offered a choice of characters, one male and one female. The game is set in Raccoon City, a company town in the Midwestern United States, dominated by the morally suspect Umbrella Corporation. Members of a local law enforcement team, the Special Tactics and Rescue Service (STARS), are dispatched to investigate an outbreak of murder and cannibalism on the outskirts of the city and find themselves trapped in the mansion. The narrative is of relatively little importance compared to the ambience, but documents can be found that explain the background as an **embedded** story. Players can discover that Umbrella's illegal experiments, intended to create "Bio Organic Weapons," have exposed both humans and animals to a mutagenic agent known as the T-Virus, converting them into animalistic zombies and distorted freaks. The virus is also capable of resurrecting the dead. Ultimately, the surviving members of the STARS team can escape after discovering a secret underground laboratory.

While most other members of the survival horror school have adopted a more subtle approach, concentrating on psychological horror, the *Resident Evil* series has remained resolutely focused on shock effects and horrific monsters. Few changes were made to the gameplay until the release of *Resident Evil 4*, though the original game's somewhat awkward control system was significantly improved. Thus, *Resident Evil 2* (*1998* Capcom; also known as *Biohazard 2* in Japan) designed by Hideki Kamiya depicts an infestation of Raccoon City by zombies after the T-Virus is accidentally released into the sewer system. The next installment, *Resident Evil 3: Nemesis* (*1999* Capcom; also known as *Biohazard 3: Last Escape* in Japan) designed by Kazuhiro Aoyama and Shinji Mikami, is divided into two parts, one set before *Resident Evil 2* and one after. Players must escape from the contaminated Raccoon City described in the previous game before the US government sterilizes it with a nuclear warhead, fighting their way past the bioweapon code-named "Nemesis." (This game's plot was used as the basis for the film *Resident Evil: Apocalypse* [*2004*].) A further sequel, *Resident Evil Code: Veronica* (*2000* Capcom; *2001* revised as *Resident Evil Code: Veronica X*; also known as *Biohazard Code: Veronica* in Japan) designed by Hiroki Kato and Shinji Mikami, is sometimes considered the most entertaining of the earlier games. Set partly on a private island owned by the Umbrella Corporation and partly in Antarctica, it features the corporation's owning family, who have mutated themselves using the new "T-Veronica" virus. *Resident Evil Zero* (*2002* Capcom; also known as *Biohazard Zero* in Japan) is a prequel to the original game, which explains more of the backstory; uniquely for the series, the player controls two characters simultaneously.

Resident Evil 4 (*2005* Capcom; *2009* revised as *Resident Evil 4: Mobile Edition*; also known as *Biohazard 4* in Japan) designed by Shinji Mikami and Hiroyuki Kobayashi made several changes to the established formula, emphasizing combat over puzzles and rejecting slow-moving zombies in favor of a fast-paced "splatter horror" feel. It is perhaps best described as a **third-person shooter** with survival horror elements. At the beginning of the game, the Umbrella Corporation is bankrupt as a result of the Raccoon City disaster described in *Resident Evil 2* and *Resident Evil 3*. The player's character, a survivor of this incident, has become an agent for the US government. He is sent to Spain to rescue the president's daughter, who has been kidnapped by a mysterious cult that uses a parasitic organism to control the minds of its members. The player must face enemies old and new; there is a great deal of bloodshed. This game was then followed by *Resident Evil 5* (*2009* Capcom; also known as *Biohazard 5* in Japan) designed by Jun Takeuchi and Kenichi Ueda, a generally similar work that makes it possible for two participants to play through the game cooperatively. Set in Africa, its story revolves around the activities of another corrupt Western corporation, who have infected the population with a variant of the T-Virus. *Resident Evil 5: Lost in Nightmares* (*2010* Capcom) and *Resident Evil 5: Desperate Escape* (*2010* Capcom) are expansions for *Resident Evil 5*, which illuminate previously undisclosed aspects of its plot.

With the release of *Resident Evil 6* (*2012* Capcom; also known as *Biohazard 6* in Japan) designed by Eiichiro Sasaki and Jiro Taoka, the developers moved the gameplay even further in the direction of the model established by third-person shooters while revisiting characters and enemies from many of the game's predecessors in its narrative. While the several segments devoted to different protagonists, each have their own style of gameplay, with some favoring escape and others emphasizing puzzle solution or relentless combat; all are centrally concerned with fast-paced gun battles between the players and their many foes. Narratively, the various story lines interleave to depict the first use of a newly invented bioweapon, the C-Virus, though the presentation is perhaps overly **linear**, with many sequences where players have only limited control over events. Melodramatic moments of gruesome excess are frequent, but the steadily building tension and fear characteristic of survival horror games are notably absent. *Resident Evil 6: Additional 3-Mode Pack* (*2012* Capcom) is an expansion that adds new options for online player versus player combat.

The sixth major iteration of the franchise performed less well commercially than its developers had hoped, and the indications are that they may return to a more restrained and less combat-focused approach for the inevitable sequel. While the market for third-person shooters is an ocean compared to survival horror's lake, sales of the series may benefit if it devotes itself to being a big creature in a small lagoon rather than a medium-sized shark in a greater sea.

Related works: *Resident Evil: Survivor* (*2000* Capcom; also known as *Biohazard: Gun Survivor* in Japan) is a **first-person shooter**, heavily focused on combat, set on a private island owned by the Umbrella Corporation that has been overrun by the living dead. *Resident Evil: Survivor 2—Code: Veronica* (*2001* Capcom; also known as *Gun Survivor 2: Biohazard Code: Veronica* in Japan) is similar, with a plot based on that of *Resident Evil Code: Veronica*. *Resident Evil: Dead Aim* (*2003* Capcom; also known as *Gun Survivor 4: Biohazard—Heroes Never Die* in Japan) is another version of the same basic concept, which makes use of a third-person view; the story involves an outbreak of a new form of the T-Virus on board a cruise ship. All three of these games have received somewhat mixed reviews. *Resident Evil: The Mercenaries 3D* (*2011* Tose/Capcom; also known as *Biohazard: The Mercenaries 3D* in Japan) pits players against endless waves of the undead, with gameplay based on an optional mode included in *Resident Evil 4* and *Resident Evil 5*.

Resident Evil: Outbreak (*2003* Capcom; also known as *Biohazard: Outbreak* in Japan) is set during the Raccoon City disaster. Gameplay is similar to that of games in the main series, except that there is no true story line; instead, the player chooses one of a range of disconnected scenarios. The game includes a cooperative multiplayer option set in a temporary **online world**; the design of this aspect received mixed reviews. *Resident Evil Outbreak File #2* (*2004* Capcom; also known as *Biohazard: Outbreak 2* in Japan) is similar, adding five more scenarios. *Resident Evil Gaiden* (*2001* Capcom; also known as *Biohazard Gaiden* in Japan) is an action game played in a **2D** overhead view. The player controls an agent of an underground anti-Umbrella organization who is sent to an ocean liner that has suffered a T-Virus outbreak; events end on a cliffhanger, which remains unresolved.

Resident Evil: The Umbrella Chronicles (*2007* cavia/Capcom; also known as *Biohazard: Umbrella Chronicles* in Japan) designed by Masachika Kawata recapitulates the most important events of the series before *Resident Evil 4*, perhaps in the hope of introducing new players to the backstory. *The Umbrella Chronicles* plays quite differently to those earlier games, however; participants essentially reenact combat scenes from several previous works. *Resident Evil: The Darkside Chronicles* (*2009* cavia/Capcom; also known as *Biohazard: The Darkside Chronicles* in Japan) is similar but is based primarily on the events of *Resident Evil 2* and *Resident Evil: Code Veronica*; it also serves as a prequel to *Resident Evil 4*.

Resident Evil: Revelations (*2012* Tose/Capcom; also known as *Biohazard: Revelations* in Japan) plays similarly to the earlier games in the main series, with a focus on shocks and puzzles rather than combat and gore. It is set between *Resident Evil 4* and *Resident Evil 5*, on a cruise ship that has been contaminated with a marine version of the T-Virus. *Resident Evil: Operation Raccoon City* (*2012* Slant Six/Capcom), on the other hand, is a third-person shooter that emphasizes gunplay in its depiction of the actions of an "Umbrella Security Service" team at the time of the viral outbreak seen in *Resident Evil 2* and *Resident Evil 3*. Reviews of this latter game were somewhat mixed.

Five live-action films have been made based on the franchise: *Resident Evil* (*2002*), *Resident Evil: Apocalypse* (*2004*), *Resident Evil: Extinction* (*2007*), *Resident Evil: Afterlife* (*2010*), and *Resident Evil: Retribution* (*2012*), all of which could be said to reuse images and themes from the games in the service of a different, and rather less coherent, vision. They have all received notably mixed reviews. *Resident Evil: Degeneration* (*2008*) and *Resident*

Evil: Damnation (*2012*) are computer-animated films that, unlike their cinematic relatives, are part of the same continuity as the **videogame** series. The former uses characters from *Resident Evil 2* to tell a story that largely reiterates that game's themes but is set after *Resident Evil 4*, while the events of the latter occur between *Resident Evil 5* and *Resident Evil 6*.

Several spin-off novels have been written by S. D. Perry. *The Umbrella Conspiracy* (**1998**), *City of the Dead* (**1999**), *Nemesis* (**2000**), *Code Veronica* (**2001**), and *Zero Hour* (**2004**) are novelizations of, respectively, *Resident Evil*, *Resident Evil 2*, *Resident Evil 3*, *Resident Evil Code: Veronica*, and *Resident Evil Zero*. *Caliban Cove* (**1998**) and *Underworld* (**1999**), also by Perry, are original novels within the franchise, sequels to *The Umbrella Conspiracy* and *City of the Dead*, respectively. *Resident Evil: Genesis* (**2004**), *Resident Evil: Apocalypse* (**2004**), and *Resident Evil: Extinction* (**2007**), all by Keith R. A. DeCandido, are novelizations of the first three live-action films, while John Shirley's *Resident Evil: Retribution* (**2012**) is based on the fifth. Several spin-off comic series have also been published, including the five-issue *Resident Evil* (*1998*), the four-issue *Resident Evil: Fire And Ice* (*2000–2001*), the four-issue *Resident Evil: Code Veronica* (*2002*), and the six-issue *Resident Evil* (*2009–2011*).

Web Links

- *Resident Evil*: http://www.residentevil.com/

- Postmortem of *Resident Evil 2* for the Nintendo 64: http://www.gamasutra.com/features/20000728/meynink_01.htm

CHAPTER 13

Computer Wargames

A COMPUTER WARGAME IS A form of **videogame** that descended (sometimes quite remotely) from tabletop **wargames** played with miniature models on artificial terrain or with cardboard counters on a flat mapboard. The subject of the computer wargame is war, but (unlike **first-person shooters [FPSs]**) success does not depend on reaction speed and manual dexterity. Instead, the gameplay is focused on intellectual contests of strategy and tactics; **real-time** variants typically have less sophisticated rules than **turn-based** ones but require the player to perform many complex tasks simultaneously. Computer wargames, like board and counter wargames, generally present an overhead view of the battlefield, whether as a **2D** map or as an **isometric** or truly **3D** display. As the name suggests, they have usually been developed for personal computers rather than for game consoles. One reason for this is that the control methods available on computers (notably, the mouse) are more suited to such games than the devices supplied with consoles, but the fundamental cause is probably the historical (and now partially obsolete) view that intellectual games belong on computers and reflex-based "action" ones on consoles.

As in many early **computer wargames**, *Battle Isle*'s map is displayed in a 2D plan view with an overlaid hexagonal grid borrowed from tabletop games, which were played with miniature counters on paper maps.

The earliest known examples of computer wargames are combat simulations written for the US military in the 1950s and 1960s. Examples include *THEATERSPIEL* (*1961* Research Analysis Corporation), a game that allowed two players to engage in a strategic contest using models representing specific possible conflicts. These programs were not intended for enjoyment, however, being descendants of the German military simulation *Kriegspiel* (*circa 1811*) rather than H G Wells' *Little Wars: A Game for Boys from Twelve Years of Age to One Hundred and Fifty and for That More Intelligent Sort of Girls Who Like Boys' Games* (**1913**), arguably the ancestor of all such works published for the benefit of enthusiastic amateurs. During the 1970s, various text-based war games, such as the *Star Trek*-inspired *Super Star Trek* (*circa 1975*) designed by David Matuszek and Paul Reynolds and several programs that simulated artillery duels, were created on mainframe computers and freely distributed; these seem to have been the first computer wargames developed purely for the sake of the players. The first such work to be commercially sold was probably

Tanktics (*1976*; revised *1978*; revised *1981*) designed by Chris Crawford in the United States, a tank combat game in which the computer took the part of one player, but (due to technical limitations) all vehicle positions in the microcomputer version had to be represented by hand-moved cardboard counters on a separate paper map. In essence, the commercial variant of *Tanktics* is a board and counter wargame in which the computer supplies the enemy's intelligence but nothing else.

The earliest science fiction (sf) example was *Starfleet Orion* (*1978* Automated Simulations [AS]) designed by Jon Freeman and Jim Connelley, a two-player game of combat between small space fleets that (due to the absence of complex terrain) could be fully depicted on the computer screen using contemporary technology. This was followed by such works as *Galactic Empire* (*1979* Brøderbund Software [BS]) designed by Douglas Carlston, *RobotWar* (*1981* Muse Software) designed by Silas Warner (in which players write computer programs to control simulated robots that then fight to the virtual death), *The Warp Factor* (*1981* Strategic Simulations, Inc. [SSI]) designed by Bruce Clayton and Paul Murray—an unlicensed adaptation of the tabletop wargame *Star Fleet Battles* (*1979* Task Force Games) designed by Stephen Cole—and its successor *The Cosmic Balance* (*1982* SSI) designed by David Siefkin and Paul Murray. *Star Trek*–inspired games are common in the early history of commercial computer wargames; another well-regarded contemporary work with a similar theme to *The Warp Factor* and *The Cosmic Balance* is *Star Fleet I: The War Begins* (*1983* Cygnus; revised *1985*) designed by Trevor Sorensen, which could be described as a very much expanded version of *Super Star Trek*.

A common theme in the early development of computer wargames is the extent to which they were influenced by or based on existing tabletop wargames; another important early example is the UK-developed **heroic fantasy** *Lords of Midnight* (*1984*) designed by Mike Singleton, an excellently crafted game of military strategy and role-playing that shares much with the J R R Tolkien–licensed wargame *War of the Ring* (*1977* Simulations Publications, Inc.) designed by Richard Berg and Howard Barasch. One notable inheritance from wargames is that all early computer wargames were turn based, meaning that the players (one of whom might be the computer) made alternate moves, and were generally not subject to time limits. The players' moves were then executed either alternately or simultaneously, again as in board and counter wargames. As computer hardware improved, real-time equivalents began to appear, in which players moved simultaneously and combat continued without a pause for thought. Another development was the addition of (generally **linear**) stories of more significance than the **frame** narratives typically presented by tabletop sf wargames. Evolution along these lines eventually produced forms of computer wargame that were quite distinct from their board and counter and miniatures-based ancestors.

One useful distinction that can be made between different types of wargame is whether they are strategic (meaning that they deal with the conduct of entire military campaigns, including the movement and disposition of forces) or tactical (indicating that they simulate individual battles between small formations in specific terrain). Typically, tactical computer wargames resemble tactical tabletop wargames, while strategic computer games are similar to "operational" level board and counter works, which deal with a specific battle rather than an entire theater of war. The third aspect of warfare, logistics (the management of the production and transport of military equipment and personnel), has not proved to be as ready a source of inspiration for computer game designers as the other two, though it does appear in **real-time strategy (RTS)** games. Most turn-based strategic videogames have dealt with contemporary or historical warfare; an early example is the well-regarded World War II game *Eastern Front (1941)* (*1981*) designed by Chris Crawford. Exceptions include the epic fantasy series *Heroes of Might and Magic*, which began with *Heroes of Might and Magic* (*1995* New World Computing) designed by Jon Van Caneghem; the sf *Star General* (*1996* Catware), licensed from David A Drake and Bill Fawcett's shared-world anthology series **The Fleet** and designed by Fawcett; and *Rites of War* (*1999* DreamForge Entertainment), a *Warhammer 40,000* game in which the player must lead the alien Eldar to victory over human Space Marines and the biological weapons of the Tyranid **hive mind**. Both of the latter two games are derived from iterations of the well-known World War II computer wargame *Panzer General*: *Star General* from the original *Panzer General* (*1994* SSI) and *Rites of War* from the sequel *Panzer General II* (*1997* SSI).

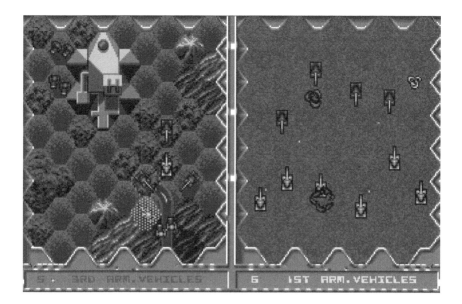

Participants in games of Battle Isle play through a series of turns, in each of which they issue instructions to their forces and then watch as the computer moves their units and displays the results of any battles.

The turn-based tactical form has also been dominated by historical and contemporary subjects; notable games include *Steel Panthers* (*1995* SSI) designed by Gary Grigsby and *Jagged Alliance* (*1994* Madlab Software) designed by Ian Currie and Linda Currie. Sf examples based on existing tabletop works include *Ogre* (*1986* Origin Systems), *Renegade Legion: Interceptor* (*1990* SSI), and the *Warhammer 40,000*-licensed *Chaos Gate* (*1998* Random Games), a game of combat between superhuman Space Marines with gameplay resembling that of the *X-COM* series, and *Final Liberation* (*1997* Holistic Design), in which the armies of the human Imperium contest control of the planet Volistad with bestial alien invaders. Many games of this form with original settings and rules were also influenced by existing board and counter games, notably the UK-developed *Laser Squad* (*1988* Target Games [TG]) designed by Julian Gollop and its unofficial sequel the *X-COM* game *UFO: Enemy Unknown* (*1994* Mythos Games) designed by Julian Gollop, which is perhaps the most impressive of all sf-related turn-based tactical games. *Battle Isle* (*1991* Blue Byte Software) designed by Lothar Schmitt is a less well-known German example, first in an eponymous series influenced by the future seen in the film *The Terminator* (*1984*).

Several early tactical videogames involved players in real-time combat, as in *Legionnaire* (*1982*) designed by Chris Crawford, which deals with battles between Caesar's legions and the barbarians of Gaul. Isolated works with similar gameplay were released over the next decade, including the remarkable fantasy chess variant *Archon: The Light And The Dark* (*1984* Free Fall Associates) designed by Jon Freeman and Paul Reiche III, in which two pieces occupying the same square must fight to determine which takes possession. At the start of the 1990s, however, the key elements of the **real-time tactics** form were developed in such games as the *BattleTech*-inspired *BattleTech: The Crescent Hawks' Revenge* (*1989* Westwood Associates [WA]); the UK-created military satire *Cannon Fodder* (*1993* Sensible Software) designed by Jon Hare; the *Warhammer 40,000*-licensed *Space Hulk* (*1993* Electronic Arts [EA]); and *Syndicate* (*1993* Bullfrog Productions [BP]) designed by Peter Molyneux and Sean Cooper, also developed in the United Kingdom. By the mid-1990s, when *Shadow of the Horned Rat* (*1995* Mindscape) was released as a spin-off from the darkly humorous heroic fantasy wargame *Warhammer Fantasy Battle* (*1983* Games Workshop [GW]) designed by Bryan Ansell, Richard Halliwell, and Rick Priestley, the school had largely been codified as a faster, more fluid version of the turn-based tactical form. Subsequent examples include the World War II–based *Close Combat* (*1996* Atomic Games), the UK-developed historical game *Rome: Total War* (*2004* Creative Assembly), and the epic fantasy *Myth: The Fallen Lords* (*1997* Bungie Studios) designed by Jason Jones, which shares much of its tone with Glen Cook's **Chronicles of the Black Company**. Within sf, some of the more impressive later real-time tactics games are the *BattleTech*-licensed *Mech Commander* (*1998* FASA); *Starfleet Command* (*1999* 14 Degrees East) designed by Erik Bethke and Christopher Taylor, which is based on *Star Fleet Battles*; and the Swedish *Ground Control* (*2000* Massive Entertainment) designed by Martin Walfisz, an ingenious design that offers a more detailed simulation of land warfare than most of its contemporaries but is marred by an uninteresting sf setting. Real-time tactics has become a much more popular form than its turn-based equivalent, perhaps as a result of its emphasis on intense gameplay over accuracy of simulation. It is also notable that many **RTT** games (especially those based on sf or fantasy) present their combat missions in the context of an ongoing story, a feature less often seen in the earlier turn-based games, whether tactical or strategic.

A separate form of tactical game developed from the **console role-playing game (RPG)** in Japan. This variant, known as the **tactical RPG**, is essentially a console RPG that emphasizes turn-based tactical combat, generally on a hexagonal or square map grid. Unlike other computer wargames, tactical RPGs are almost always released for game consoles rather than personal computers. The gameplay is often similar to that of combat-oriented **computer role-playing games** (CRPGs) such as the **sword and sorcery** *Pool of Radiance* (*1988* SSI), except that the stories are generally linear and frequently told through a series of missions separated by noninteractive sequences that advance the plot rather than by allowing the characters to roam through the simulated world at will. Fantasy and **science and sorcery** are the most common themes, as in all console RPG forms. The earliest example of the school appears to be *Fire Emblem: The Dragon of Darkness and the Sword of Light* (*1990* Intelligent Systems) which was only released in Japan. Other games of this type include the heroic fantasy *Final Fantasy Tactics* (*1997* Square; *2007* revised as *Final Fantasy Tactics: The War of the Lions*) designed by Hironobu Sakaguchi, Yasumi Matsuno, and Hiroyuki Itō; the sf *Front Mission* (*1999* Square) designed by Toshiro Tsuchida; and the unforgettable *Rhapsody: A Musical Adventure* (*1998* Nippon Ichi; also known as *The Puppet Princess of Marl Kingdom* in Japan) designed by Koichi Kitazurri and John Yamamoto, a romantic fantasy in which the plot progresses through frequent battles with magical puppets, interleaved with sequences sung by the major characters in the manner of a stage musical. A Western example is the post-apocalypse *Fallout Tactics: Brotherhood of Steel* (*2001* Micro Forté).

The most commercially successful form of computer wargame, however, has been the RTS one. Members of this school are not simply strategic war games, which run in real time. Instead, they are highly stylized, combining a specific set of elements drawn from **4X games**, tabletop wargames, and the real-time tactics form. Gameplay typically involves building bases, factories, and other structures on the battlefield while producing new combat and support units (such as tanks and mining robots) and researching technology that will allow the creation of more powerful units. All of this activity is fueled by limited resources that must be gathered during play, typically representing energy, matter, or both.

Meanwhile, the player must fight a tactical battle in real time. Victory in this kind of game requires considerable skill at multitasking, as well as the ability to plan rapidly and respond to unforeseen events. It does not, however, depend on the sort of careful long-term planning needed in turn-based strategy games and board and counter wargames. RTS games are also distinguished by their frequent use of sf backgrounds and (generally linear) **interactive narratives**.

Various precursors of the RTS form can be identified, among them the US-developed *Cytron Masters* (*1982* Ozark Softscape) designed by Danielle Berry, the Japanese *Herzog Zwei* (*1989* Technosoft), and *Nether Earth* (*1987*), created in the United Kingdom. All of these games are real time and contain some elements of the RTS approach to design, but not all of them. The game that defined the type, and created the design pattern used for almost all subsequent real-time strategic videogames, was the **Dune**-licensed *Dune II: The Building of a Dynasty* (*1992* Westwood Studios [WS]) designed by Joseph Bostic and Aaron Powell. *Dune II* was followed by the fantasy game *Warcraft: Orcs & Humans* (*1994* Blizzard Entertainment [BE]) and the sf *Command & Conquer* (*1995* WS), *Total Annihilation* (*1997* Cavedog Entertainment [CE]) designed by Chris Taylor, and *Starcraft* (*1998* BE) designed by James Phinney and Chris Metzen. Other examples of the form are experimented in various ways. Thus, *Battlezone* (*1998* Activision) combined **RTS** gameplay with that of an FPS, while the impressive Canadian game *Homeworld* (*1999* Relic Entertainment [RE]) transferred the core design elements from their normal land and sea setting to a fully 3D interplanetary environment. Thematically, *Age of Empires* (*1997* Ensemble Studios) designed by Rick Goodman, Bruce Shelley, and Brian Sullivan and the similar *Empire Earth* (*2001* Stainless Steel Studios) designed by Jon Alenson and Rick Goodman used historical rather than sf settings. Meanwhile, the remarkable *Giants: Citizen Kabuto* (*2000* Planet Moon Studios) designed by Nick Bruty, Bob Stevenson, and Tim Williams combined **third-person shooter** and RTS gameplay with magic, sf, and the eponymous **Godzilla**-like monster.

Few of these innovations were adopted by later games, however. Instead, several recent works have concentrated on refining the original pattern while providing better fictional justifications for their design. So, the UK-developed *Hostile Waters: Antaeus Rising* (*2001* Rage Software) uses a script by the comics writer Warren Ellis to explain its gameplay, while the well-regarded *Warhammer 40,000* game *Dawn of War* (*2004* RE) translates many fundamental RTS concepts into ones that seem more realistic. For example, the game's "requisition" resource corresponds to the local commander's ability to call in reinforcements. Most radically, *Supreme Commander* (*2007* Gas Powered Games [GPG]) designed by Chris Taylor employs much larger maps than previous games, making its battles truly strategic in scope while cleverly justifying the need to improve the available technology and build new units by beginning every engagement with the player in possession of a single self-reproducing war machine. Meanwhile, another subtype has appeared in the form of the **multiplayer online battle arena** game. This school, which began with player-created variants of *Starcraft* (*Aeon of Strife* [*circa 1999*] designed by Aeon64) and *Warcraft III: Reign of Chaos* (*2002* BE) designed by Robert Pardo (*Defense of the Ancients* [*2003*] designed by Eul), in some ways resembles real-time tactics games more closely than it does RTS ones. Players compete against each other online in teams, with each participant adopting the role of a powerful hero; both sides receive support from less potent computer-controlled units, but many other aspects of RTS gameplay, such as the need to construct new buildings, have been removed. This fan-made form became notably popular during the 2000s, and commercial variants have now begun to appear; one well-received example is *Heroes of Newerth* (*2010* S2 Games) designed by James Fielding, set on a science and sorcery post-holocaust Earth. While RTS games are less commercially important today than they were in the 1990s, the form remains popular, a point emphasized by both the success of 2010's *Starcraft II* and the recent funding through the Kickstarter website of *Planetary Annihilation*, a game whose focus on interplanetary warfare seems much influenced by the designs of *Total Annihilation* and *Supreme Commander*.

FURTHER READING

- Andrew Wilson. *The Bomb and the Computer*. 1968. (Presents a comprehensive history of military wargames up to the 1960s, including such computerized simulations as *THEATERSPIEL*.)

- Brian Murphy. *Sorcerers & Soldiers: Computer Wargames, Fantasies and Adventures*. 1984. (Includes reviews and analysis of early computer wargames, including *Tanktics*.)

ANDROMEDA CONQUEST

1982. Avalon Hill. Designed by David Peterson.

Andromeda Conquest is a game of **turn-based** interstellar warfare that uses text menus and somewhat rudimentary **2D** displays to represent a conflict between various galactic empires. Each player begins as absolute ruler of a species that has recently invented a **faster-than-light** drive, with the intention of expanding out into the galaxy, conquering and colonizing inhabitable solar systems before defending them against other aggressive civilizations. The gameplay somewhat resembles that of the board game *Risk* (*1957* Miro as *La Conquête du Monde*) designed by Albert Lamorisse; it is important to gain early control of resource-rich systems and construct large fleets in preparation for the inevitable war. While the game can be played with only the computer as an adversary, this is an unsatisfying experience—other humans are needed to provide effective opposition.

This game is now of largely historical interest. It shows strong influences from earlier board and counter **wargames**, notably in its use of paper maps and data sheets to record the state of the galaxy and in its conditions for victory. (The first player to control 10 star systems wins outright, though in practice success is often determined by the initial distribution of resource-rich uninhabited planets on the 2D galactic map; players with many such systems near their homeworld have a significant advantage.) Nevertheless, *Andromeda Conquest* is much less sophisticated than contemporary tabletop wargames such as *Godsfire* (*1976* Metagaming Concepts [MC]) designed by Lynn Willis or *Web and Starship* (*1984* West End Games) designed by Greg Costikyan, both in its gameplay and in its lack of a detailed, cohesive background. It is perhaps most interesting as a rare example of a strategic **videogame** of galactic conquest that is not a **4X game**—a form that rapidly came to dominate computerized expressions of this theme after the release of the Strategic Studies Group's *Reach for the Stars* in 1983.

BATTLETECH

Franchise (from 1988). FASA. Designed by Jordan Weisman.

One of the most commercially successful wargaming franchises ever created, the *BattleTech* tabletop **wargame** transplanted the giant **mecha** of Japanese **anime** to a gritty far-future setting of constant war. The original game (*1984* FASA as *BattleDroids*; *1985* revised as *BattleTech*; revised *1992*; revised *1996*; revised *2007*) designed by Jordan Weisman is set during the thirty-first century, when hundreds of years of conflict have reduced an interstellar civilization centered on Earth to a collection of antagonistic feudal Houses that have forgotten how much of their own technology works. The players use teams of BattleMech robots, piloted by human MechWarriors, to fight battles between these feuding groups, each of which has a strong tribal identity. In the original version, cardboard figures are used to represent the players' BattleMechs and maneuvered across a flat paper map; later editions replace the cardboard miniatures with plastic ones. *BattleTech* is easy to play, and the opportunity to become a pseudomedieval knight in massive armor appealed to many prospective players, especially as the game contains extensive rules for creating custom BattleMechs. This latter element and the suggestion that players could take their personalized Mechs and use them in successive battles in a lengthy military campaign were both drawn from tabletop **RPG** design; the developers' intention was to create a wargame that had some of the personal appeal of an **RPG**.

The first *BattleTech*-related **videogame** was *BattleTech: The Crescent Hawk's Inception* (*1988* WA) designed by Tony Van, a blend of **CRPG** and **turn-based** strategy. The sequel, *BattleTech: The Crescent Hawks' Revenge* (*1989* WA) designed by Tony Van, was an influential early **real-time tactics** game, with a story line that followed on directly from that of *The Crescent Hawk's Inception*. The first **real-time** digital game in the franchise, however, was *MechWarrior* (*1989* Dynamix) designed by Paul Bowman, Terry Ishida, John Skeel, and Damon Slye, which featured a complex story presented in the manner of a contemporary CRPG and the ability to pilot a BattleMech from its cockpit with a **3D** view. *MechWarrior 2: 31st Century Combat* (*1995* Activision) designed by Sean Vesce and Zachary Norman is broadly similar but is set at a later point in the *BattleTech* **future history** than the previous game, after the squabbling states that occupy the "Inner Sphere" have been invaded by the technologically superior Clans. (In the tabletop game's universe, the Clans are the descendants of the fallen interstellar civilization's last army, who fled known space to become a Spartan society of obsessively dedicated MechWarriors.) *MechWarrior 2* is often considered to be the best in its series for the elegant way in which it handles BattleMech customization and the need to balance competing robot subsystems during combat, two of the features that most attracted players to the original wargame. Further sequels are *MechWarrior 3* (*1999* Zipper Interactive) designed by George Sinfield and *MechWarrior 4: Vengeance* (*2000* FASA).

Several of the *MechWarrior* games received expansions: *MechWarrior 2: Ghost Bear's Legacy* (*1995* Activision), *MechWarrior 2: Mercenaries* (*1996* Activision), *MechWarrior 3: Pirate's Moon* (*1999* Zipper Interactive), *MechWarrior 4: Black Knight* (*2001* Cyberlore Studios [CS]), *MechWarrior 4: Clan 'Mech Pak* (*2002* CS), *MechWarrior 4: Inner Sphere 'Mech Pak* (*2002* CS), and *MechWarrior 4: Mercenaries* (*2003* CS). *NetMech* (*1996* Activision) is an add-on for *MechWarrior 2* that enables competitive play over computer networks, an important feature in later iterations of the *MechWarrior* series, and one that was also the main focus of *Multiplayer BattleTech* (*1992* Kesmai). This latter game was a version of the original *MechWarrior* designed to enable competitive play in an **online world** on the (precommercial Internet) online GEnie service. Despite receiving generally poor reviews, it proved popular enough to spawn a more successful sequel: *Multiplayer BattleTech: Solaris* (*1996* Kesmai).

MechCommander (*1998* FASA) and its sequel *MechCommander 2* (*2001* FASA) designed by Michael Lee represent a different branch of development; they are both real-time tactics games that allow the player to command a squad of BattleMechs through a series of missions. *MechCommander: Desperate Measures* (*1999* FASA), meanwhile, is an expansion pack for *MechCommander* that continues the story line of the original game. Of all the various *BattleTech*-related videogames, the *MechCommander* series is perhaps the closest in spirit to the original wargame, though the first of the two works is generally acknowledged to be unusually difficult. A number of action-oriented games have also been created for home consoles: *BattleTech* (*1994* Malibu Games; also known as *MechWarrior 3050*), which uses an **isometric** view; *MechAssault* (*2002* Day 1 Studios) designed by Tom Dowd, which features fully destructible environments, and its sequel *MechAssault 2: Lone Wolf* (*2004* Day 1 Studios), which extends the original game design to allow the player to pilot vehicles other than BattleMechs; and *MechAssault: Phantom War* (*2006* Backbone Entertainment) designed by Dan Mueller. These works deemphasize the tactical considerations of the original tabletop games, notably the risk that BattleMechs could overheat disastrously if too many systems are used at once, in favor of nonstop giant robot action.

In recent years, the *BattleTech* franchise has become markedly less well known; the various wargames, **RPGs**, and videogames are now played largely by dedicated fans. It does seem likely that the recent release of *MechWarrior Online* (*2013* Piranha Games)—a real-time game of 3D

BattleMech combat set in an online world that can be entered free of charge and that is played in a cerebral style emphasizing tactical acumen in the manner of the earlier *MechWarrior* games—will restore some of *BattleTech*'s lost popularity. Nevertheless, Adhesive Games' upcoming *Hawken*, which is much more action-oriented than *MechWarrior Online* but otherwise remarkably similar in both design and setting despite its lack of any official connection with the *BattleTech* milieu, may ultimately prove to be a more popular work.

Related works: Many other tabletop games have been created as derivatives of the original wargame, of which the best known are perhaps the RPG *MechWarrior* (*1986* FASA; revised *1991*; revised *1999*; also known as *Classic Battletech RPG*) designed by L Ross Babcock III, Jordan Weisman, Brian Nystul, Lester Smith, Walter H Hunt, and William H Keith Jr; the **collectible card game** *BattleTech: The Collectible Card Game* (*1996* Wizards of the Coast) designed by Richard Garfield; and the **collectible miniatures game** *MechWarrior: Dark Age* (*2002* WizKids) designed by Kevin Barrett, Matt Robinson, and Paul Nobles. This latter work is set in the thirty-second century, after a collapse in interstellar communications has triggered a long series of apocalyptic wars and religious jihads of steadily decreasing credibility. A bibliography listing further works is noted in the following.

The *BattleTech* universe has also spawned a large number of spin-off novels, beginning with *Decision at Thunder Rift* (**1986**) by William H Keith Jr. More than 60 novels set in the thirty-first century followed, until a new line was begun with *Ghost War* (**2002**) by Michael Stackpole, to accompany *MechWarrior: Dark Age*, set in the thirty-second century. Currently, there are over 30 books in the *Dark Age* series. *BattleTech: Fallout* (*1994–1995*), *BattleTech* (*1987–1988*), *BattleTech in 3-D* (*1989*), and *BattleForce* (*1987–1988*) are all **tied** comics, while *BattleTech: The Animated Series* (*1994*) is a 13-episode (one season) animated TV series based on the Clans' invasion.

FURTHER READING

- Randall N Bills. *BattleTech: 25 Years of Art & Fiction*. 2009. (Includes a full bibliography and articles on the history of the game.)

Web Link

- *MechWarrior Online*: http://mwomercs.com/

BATTLEZONE

1998. (Revised *2000* as *Battlezone: Rise of the Black Dogs.*) Activision.

Battlezone is an innovative **RTS** game, named after the largely unrelated arcade tank combat game *Battlezone* (*1980* Atari) designed by Ed Rotberg. Its gameplay uses a **3D** first-person view to combine the physical urgency of an action game with the flexible thinking required in an **RTS**. Players pilot "hover tanks" in **real time** while issuing commands to various combat and support vehicles through an elegantly designed interface, requiring them to simultaneously react to immediate threats and monitor the situation on the entire battlefield. It is possible to dismount from the player's tank; the gameplay then resembles that of an **FPS**. More conventional RTS elements are also present, including the need to gather "living metal" resources with which new vehicles can be constructed. *Battlezone* can be played both by a single player and as a competitive online game, a mode in which it has been highly popular.

The setting is an **alternate history** somewhat reminiscent of the contemporary TV series *Dark Skies* (*1996–1997*). History is a lie, told to conceal the existence of a secret space program that collects the artifacts of a now extinct alien race. (This species evolved on a planet between Mars and Jupiter, whose remains now form the asteroid belt.) Evidence of the aliens' existence was first discovered on Earth in the 1960s in the form of deposits of living metal on meteorites, which both the United States and the Soviet Union used to construct **antigravity** devices and advanced weapons. The two nations then expanded into space and fought for control of the remaining artifacts, using their official space programs to conceal the reality of their secret war. Players select either the Russian or the American side and play through a sequence of **linearly** plotted missions set on a variety of planets; both story lines end with the Russians constructing alien supertanks, which then turn on their creators.

Related works: *The Red Odyssey* (*1998* Team Evolve) is an expansion pack that adds an additional story line to the original game's plot, following a similar Chinese space effort that ends on an extrasolar planet reached using an alien **hyperspace** gateway. *Battlezone II: Combat Commander* (*1999* Pandemic Studios) is a sequel with similar gameplay, set in an alternate 1990s when an international force in charge of living metal reserves is confronted with the return of a group of exiled human soldiers, who were experimentally fused with the alien substance during the 1960s. The game's **multilinear** plot allows the player to either attempt to eliminate the enemy or negotiate a compromise. This iteration of the franchise was less well received than the first; the mission designs in particular were considered to be overly simplistic.

CARRIER COMMAND

1988. Realtime Games (RG). Designed by Clare Edgeley, Ricardo Pinto, Ian Oliver, and Graeme Bird.

The original *Carrier Command* was both one of the first UK-developed videogames to use **real-time 3D** displays and an innovative fusion of **computer wargame** and action game that included many elements later seen in works of **RTS**. The player takes control of a highly advanced carrier equipped with robotic aircraft and amphibious vehicles, which is engaged in a near-future conflict with an almost identical opponent for control over a newly formed archipelago and the energy extractable from its volcanoes. Victory depends on systematically taking possession of the islands (by force if they are already occupied by the enemy) and constructing devices that will mine their resources, manufacture fuel and weapons, or act as defensive fortifications. The resulting industrial network provides the materiel players need to defend their territory and eventually either destroy the enemy's carrier or capture the entire archipelago. The result is an interesting game with a wide variety of tactical options, highly playable despite a somewhat complex interface, but one that is of little importance as a work of sf.

Interest in the game waned during the 1990s. However, in the twenty-first century, David Lagettie—an Australian computer entrepreneur who had created music for *Operation Flashpoint: Cold War Crisis* (*2001* Bohemia Interactive [BI]), an **FPS** that simulated military operations in the 1980s—acquired the rights to make a sequel to *Carrier Command*. Lagettie also provided the original concept behind P D Gilson's novel *Gaea: Beyond the Son* (**2007**), a largely routine tale of interstellar exploration and a resource crisis on Earth whose highly dubious science, occasionally melodramatic tone and unusual (for the written genre) focus on fatherhood, may all be related to its genesis as the script for an unmade feature film. While the book was being written, Lagettie suggested tying it to the game by including details that would allow a remake of *Carrier*

Command to be placed in the same universe; the published version ends with representatives of Earth's two contending factions (one democratic and Western and the other totalitarian and Eastern) about to go to war on a **terraformed** moon orbiting a **gas giant** in a distant solar system.

That reimagining of the original game was published as *Carrier Command: Gaea Mission* (*2012* BI) designed by Jaroslav Kašný, a work created by BI, the Czech developer for whom Lagettie had written music for *Operation Flashpoint*. *Gaea Mission* is set on the habitable moon introduced at the end of *Beyond the Son*, where the player takes command of a ship resembling that in *Carrier Command* and fights for possession of a chain of islands against a similar enemy vessel. The gameplay is generally reminiscent of its prototype, with some minor changes and refinements (notably, interpolated sequences are played in the manner of an FPS), though several decades' worth of advances in computer hardware allowed the designers to make vast improvements in the visuals over those of the original. Unfortunately, the game's mechanics are sometimes presented in a confusing fashion, and—despite the involvement of Phil and Didi Gilson, who together make up the "P D" Gilson who wrote *Beyond the Son*—the dialogue is unusually poor and the plotting generally predictable. More fundamentally, technical problems with the game's implementation mean that it is often frustrating to play. In the final analysis, *Gaea Mission*'s essential concept remains interesting, but the slipshod nature of its realization makes it a much inferior successor to the original *Carrier Command* than Rage Software's earlier *Hostile Waters: Antaeus Rising* (*2001*).

Related works: *Battle Command* (*1990* RG) designed by Steven Caslin is an action game, vaguely associated with the original *Carrier Command*, in which the player controls a superpowered tank. Reviews were mixed.

Web Link
- *Carrier Command: Gaea Mission*: http://www.carriercommand.com/

COMMAND & CONQUER

Series (from 1995). Westwood Studios (WS).

Command & Conquer is a series of **RTS** games, played from an overhead view of the battlefield. As in the same developers' *Dune II: The Building of a Dynasty* (*1992* WS) designed by Joseph Bostic and Aaron Powell, to which the first *Command & Conquer* game was an unofficial sequel, the player must gather resources that they can use to build new combat and support units, such as tanks and artillery, and create increasingly complex buildings, which allow them to construct more sophisticated units. Meanwhile, vehicles and infantry are dispatched to seek out and destroy the enemy. The games have been highly popular both as single-player campaigns with generally **linear** or **multilinear interactive narratives** and for player versus player competition in temporary **online worlds**. As with *Starcraft* (*1998* BE) designed by James Phinney and Chris Metzen, the *Command & Conquer* mechanics emphasize entertaining gameplay over realistic simulation, employing a partly symbolic visual representation of the conflict. The series does not present an especially serious view of warfare; it abounds with deliberately camp scenarios and absurd super-weapons, of which the most striking is perhaps *Red Alert 2*'s **telepathically** controlled giant squid.

Gathering resources—in this case gold nuggets—is important in *Command & Conquer: Red Alert* 2, as in most games of **real time strategy**.

A wide variety of exotic superweapons can be deployed in *Command & Conquer: Red Alert 2.*

The first game, *Command & Conquer* (*1995* WS; also known as *Command & Conquer: Tiberian Dawn*), was created by Westwood to further develop the real-time strategic gameplay they had experimented with in *Dune II*. It improves on many of its predecessor's mechanics, notably in the player interface, and set the design template for most of the later *Command & Conquer* games. The setting assumes that a meteorite impact near the river Tiber in the late 1990s contaminates Earth with a substance named "Tiberium." This alien element extracts minerals from the ground and processes them into advanced materials that are otherwise impossible to fabricate; unfortunately, it is also highly toxic and its organic crystals rapidly grow to absorb surrounding territory. The game focuses on a war between the Global Defense Initiative, formed by the United Nations to study and contain Tiberium, and the Brotherhood of Nod, a fanatical religious group who want to use it to transform the Earth, creating a New World Ecology of extraterrestrial origin. Both sides make heavy use of Tiberium to create the materials they need to construct their advanced weaponry; this is the primary resource that the player must gather. The Brotherhood's leader, Kane, is a late twentieth-century equivalent of Sax

Rohmer's **Fu Manchu**: fiendishly malevolent, devilishly cunning, and a messiah to the world's poor and oppressed. In essence, the appearance of Tiberium is depicted as catalyzing the real political tensions of the 1990s, setting rich against poor on a global scale. The player can adopt the role of a commander on either side, playing through a series of missions leading to an eventual victory for their chosen faction. *Command & Conquer: The Covert Operations* (*1996* WS) is an expansion pack that adds new units and missions.

Combat between small groups of units is the core mechanic of the *Command & Conquer* series.

Command & Conquer: Tiberian Sun (*1999* WS) is a sequel to *Tiberian Dawn*, set in what had by the time it was designed become an **alternate history**. This game is more science fictional in tone than the original, featuring highly advanced technology, and set in 2030 in which much of the world's surface has been absorbed by Tiberium, creating a xenoformed landscape resembling those seen in such early J G Ballard novels as *The Crystal World* (**1966**). *Tiberian Sun* assumes that the player achieved a United Nations victory in the first game; the Brotherhood, and Kane, return. *Command & Conquer: Tiberian Sun—Firestorm* (*2000* WS) is an expansion pack, in which the Brotherhood and the Initiative are forced to join forces against the Brotherhood's rogue artificial intelligence. The next installment, *Command & Conquer 3: Tiberium Wars* (*2007* EA), maintained the series' increasingly apocalyptic tone. It is set a further 20 years into the future, when Earth is divided between Tiberium zones that are incapable of supporting carbon-based life, contaminated areas dominated by the Brotherhood, and clean regions that are ruled by the Initiative. Kane returns for the third time, triggering another war, one that is interrupted by the arrival of hostile aliens intent on mining the Earth for Tiberium. *Command & Conquer 3: Kane's Wrath* (*2008* EA/BreakAway Games) is an expansion pack for *Tiberium Wars*, which follows events from Kane's point of view for the two decades that elapse between the end of *Tiberian Sun* and the aftermath of *Tiberium Wars*. The end of the story is presented in *Command & Conquer 4: Tiberian Twilight* (*2010* EA), though ultimately there is more of a sense of an epilogue than of a conclusion. In the interval between *Kane's Wrath* and *Tiberian Twilight*, set a further 30 years into the future, the Initiative and the Brotherhood have become allies, dedicated to controlling the spread of Tiberium using recovered alien technology. While their combined forces have succeeded in preventing further contamination, extremists from both sides have begun a new war. This conflict is played out using radically revised mechanics that more closely resemble those of a **real-time tactics** game with role-playing elements than they do those of earlier members of the franchise. The gameplay is even more stylized than is traditional for RTS games and arguably concentrates on competitive play between teams in online worlds rather than the single-player campaign; there is some resemblance to the *Warhammer 40,000*-licensed *Dawn of War II* (*2009* RE). Ultimately, the player can help Kane and the Brotherhood escape to the stars through an alien **wormhole**, a resolution that is presented more as a heavenly reward than as an interstellar colonization program.

A separate series of the *Command & Conquer* franchise began with *Command & Conquer: Red Alert* (*1996* WS), a work that appears to have been originally intended to establish an alternate history that would become the past of the Tiberium setting. However, later developments in the sequence, notably the unusual technologies seen in *Red Alert 2*, suggest that the two settings are best regarded as separate timelines. *Red Alert* begins in the late 1940s with Albert Einstein inventing a time machine, which he uses to dispose of Adolf Hitler in the 1920s, thus preventing World War II. Unfortunately, however, in this history, the Soviet Union then invades Europe in the 1950s. As in *Tiberian Dawn*, the player can take the part of a commander on either side of the conflict. *Command & Conquer: Red Alert—The Aftermath* (*1997* WS/Intelligent Games [IG]) and *Command & Conquer: Red Alert—Counterstrike* (*1997* WS/IG) are expansions that add new units and missions, including gigantic mutant ants. Both of these packs are included in *Command & Conquer: Red Alert—Retaliation* (*1998* WS/IG). *Command & Conquer: Red Alert 2* (*2000* WS) is a sequel that describes an alternate World War III in which the Soviet Union invades the United States, using mind control over international telephone lines to disable the American nuclear arsenal. This game is especially notable for its exotic collection of super-scientific weapons, including localized weather control, cloned soldiers, and giant Tesla coils, which project balls of electrical energy. The plot is continued in the expansion *Command & Conquer: Red Alert 2—Yuri's Revenge* (*2001* WS), in which the eponymous Soviet agent goes rogue and builds a network of "Psychic Dominators" that will let him control the minds of everyone on Earth; in order to defeat him, the Soviets and the Western allies must use time travel to return to the war depicted in *Red Alert 2*. In a further sequel, *Command & Conquer: Red Alert 3* (*2008* EA), the timeline has again been changed, this time by the Soviets. Einstein has been assassinated in 1927, creating a present in which the Western democracies, the Soviet Union, and a Japanese-dominated Empire of the Rising Sun are fighting a three-sided war for global domination. Many of the novel military technologies seen in previous games reappear, along with such new exotica as Russian units composed entirely of armored bears—an invention perhaps influenced by Philip Pullman's novel *Northern Lights* (**1995**)—and a **psionic** Japanese schoolgirl who is suggestive of many **anime** heroines. The gameplay is similar to that of previous entries in the series but with increased emphasis on naval operations and the addition of the ability to play cooperatively with an ally (who may be controlled either by another player or by the computer). *Command & Conquer: Red Alert 3—Uprising* (*2009* EA; revised as *Command & Conquer: Red Alert 3—Commander's Challenge*) is an expansion that assumes that the West was victorious at the end of *Red Alert 3*; various sequels and peripheral narratives are presented, including one in which a corporate conspiracy intends to use a temporal weapon to remove the Soviet Union from history altogether.

Related works: Various additional works associated with the Tiberian series have been created. *Command & Conquer: Sole Survivor* (*1997* WS) is an online player-versus-player game using units from *Tiberian Dawn*, with gameplay resembling that of a **third-person shooter**. *Command & Conquer: Renegade* (*2002* WS) is an **FPS** with a linear plot that occurs at the same time as *Tiberian Dawn*; it includes an interesting team-based online multiplayer option. *Command & Conquer 4: Tiberian Twilight* (*2012* EA) appears to be a simplified version of the original game of that name, intended for use on smartphones. *Command & Conquer: Tiberium Wars* (**2007**) is a novelization of *Tiberium Wars*, focusing on different characters to those included in the game, by Keith R A DeCandido. Meanwhile, the Tiberium games have received a—possibly final—coda in the form of *Command & Conquer: Tiberium Alliances* (*2012* EA), an RTS game depicting endless (and story free) conflicts in an online world. This variant is (perhaps unsurprisingly for a game that can be played entirely for free) notably simpler and more repetitive than its ancestors; aficionados of the earlier works in the series have generally shown little enthusiasm for this iteration.

Command & Conquer: Red Alert (*2009* EA) is another RTS game for smartphones, set between *Yuri's Revenge* and *Red Alert 3*; its linear narrative serves as a prequel for the latter game. *Command & Conquer: Generals* (*2003* EA) is the first in a third series of *Command & Conquer* games, created by different developers. It is set in the near future, during a conflict between the United States, China, and the terrorist Global Liberation Army; the gameplay is much influenced by *Starcraft*. *Command & Conquer: Generals—Zero Hour* (*2003* EA) is an expansion pack.

Web Links

- *Command & Conquer*: http://www.commandandconquer.com/

- Command & Conquer: Tiberium Alliances: http://www.tiberiumalliances.com/

- *Command & Conquer: Tiberian Sun* Postmortem: http://www.gamasutra.com/features/20000404/tiberiansun_pfv.htm

DARWINIA

2005. (Revised *2010* as *Darwinia+*.) Introversion Software (IS). Designed by Chris Delay.

As in many stories in the written sf genre, *Darwinia*'s protagonist plays God to a world of rapidly evolving and surprisingly involving creatures. The player adopts the role of a present-day hacker who enters a mysterious sealed zone on the Internet, the creation of a barely sane genius. In this hidden world, newly created artificial intelligences are living out virtual lives. Recently, however, their private system has been invaded by dangerous viruses, and the player is recruited to fight them. To do this, players have access to a variety of programs that can be used to attack the enemy directly, construct and repair systems, and issue orders to the native Darwinians. *Darwinia*'s gameplay fuses aspects of the **RTS** and action forms with its own original mechanics, to impressive effect. While the game's story line is weak, the Darwinians' simple personalities succeed in evoking a strong sense of concern for them in the player. The game is also notable for its deliberately primitive visual style, reminiscent of the film *Tron* (*1982*), and its status as an early example of a successful **independent game** created without the involvement of a major publisher.

Related works: *Multiwinia* (*2008* IS; *2010* revised as *Darwinia+*) designed by Chris Delay and Gary Chambers is a sequel to *Darwinia* in which the virtual world's inhabitants divide into tribes and turn on each other. The player takes command of one of these groups and competes against computer-controlled opponents or other participants online to achieve such goals as winning the Darwinian space race, by any means necessary.

Web Links

- *Darwinia*: http://www.introversion.co.uk/darwinia/

- *Multiwinia*: http://www.introversion.co.uk/multiwinia/

- Chris Delay on *Darwinia*: http://www.sffworld.com/mul/198p0.html

DUNE II: THE BUILDING OF A DYNASTY

1992. (Also known as *Dune II: Battle for Arrakis* in Europe). Westwood Studios (WS). Designed by Joseph Bostic and Aaron Powell.

While it was not the first **computer wargame** to run in **real time**, *Dune II* was the first **RTS** game as the form is understood today. Although the game was licensed from Frank Herbert's novel *Dune* (**1965**), it has little in common with its original and even less with the **adventure** game *Dune* (*1992* Cryo Interactive) to which it was technically a sequel. The game's premise is that the ruler of the novel's galactic empire has challenged three noble Houses to fight each other for control of spice production on the planet Arrakis. (In the novel, the melange spice, which can only be obtained from the deserts of Arrakis, is a rare drug that extends its users' life spans and allows them access to **psionic** abilities vital for the navigation of interstellar spacecraft.) The participants are the Atreides, the Harkonnens, and the Ordos, of which only the first two appear in the **Dune** novels; the Ordos are a mercantile House, mentioned briefly in Willis McNelly's "nonfiction" book *The Dune Encyclopedia* (**1984**). Players adopt the role of a field commander serving their chosen House; a variety of units such as individual soldiers and spice harvesters are available with which to fulfill their mission objectives. Gameplay combines much of the depth of earlier **turn-based** computer wargames with the rapid pace of an action game. Important elements include the ability to improve the strength of available units through research, a feature borrowed from **4X games**, and the need to mine spice that can be sold in return for the funds required to continue operations. These are the key elements of an RTS game and represented a fundamental break from the gameplay of such earlier works as *Laser Squad* (*1988* TG) designed by Julian Gollop, which had much in common with board and counter **wargames**. Such descendants as the *Command & Conquer* series (from *1995* WS) have improved considerably on many aspects of *Dune II*, notably the interface design, but it is still of considerable historical interest.

Related works: *Dune 2000* (*1998* WS/IG) is a remake of the original that received mixed reviews. While its visuals and story line were much enhanced compared to *Dune II*, the gameplay closely resembled that of its original, without taking into account design improvements made in later **RTS** games. *Emperor: Battle for Dune* (*2001* WS/IG) is a direct sequel to *Dune 2000* that received better reviews than its predecessor.

Web Link
- *Dune II*: http://duneii.com/

FROZEN SYNAPSE

2011. Mode 7 Games (M7). Designed by Ian Hardingham and Paul Taylor.

Frozen Synapse is a **computer wargame**, developed as an **independent game**, in which the player controls small groups (or "systems") of mindless clones (or "vatforms") in small military actions. The gameplay, in which the player works out their orders for a turn and then waits to see the results, is reminiscent of such predecessors as *Laser Squad* (*1988* TG) designed by Julian Gollop. Here, however, participants can test the simulated results of their actions, assuming that the enemy does not alter their strategy, before making those instructions irrevocable. The game's design is visually striking and highly playable; its effect is oddly cool and detached.

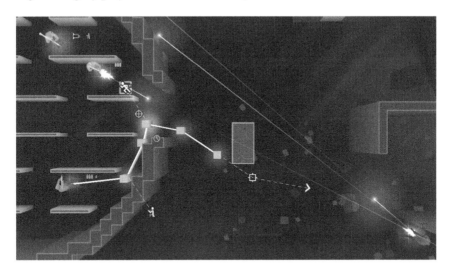

Gameplay in Mode 7's *Frozen Synapse*.

The game was originally built for competition in temporary **online worlds**, with a **linear interactive narrative** added after the core gameplay had been finished. Nevertheless, the story is effective. It is set in a city deliberately unpositioned in time or space, a technologically sophisticated metropolis dominated by a single giant corporation and pervaded by the "shape" (an informational space that functions as a kind of Platonic realm inhabited by "shapeforms" but is accessed as if it were a **cyberspace**). Various competing factions are struggling for control of the city, including the ruling company, anticorporate rebels, dangerously idealistic proponents of a utopian society, and religious fanatics who worship the **Omega Point**. Eventually, the player's character—who acts as primary tactician for the rebels—is revealed as a fragment of the shapeform that controls the corporate enemy, deliberately split off and made amnesiac by this superhuman intelligence so that it can fight a war worth winning.

Ultimately, *Frozen Synapse* is an excellently crafted, highly atmospheric game of tactical combat that is presented with a very indie sensibility. While its fiction is not especially original, it is honest about the moral ambiguities of revolution, full of evocative detail, and highly self-aware. Throughout, it retains its own sense of style.

Related works: *Frozen Synapse: Red* (*2012* M7) designed by Ian Hardingham and Paul Taylor is an expansion pack that adds new plot, equipment, and types of gameplay.

Web Link

- *Frozen Synapse*: http://www.frozensynapse.com/

GALACTIC SAGA

Series (from *1979*). Brøderbund Software (BS). Designed by Douglas Carlston.

Of the four games in the *Galactic Saga*, by far the best known is the first, *Galactic Empire* (*1979* BS; revised *1994*). This is perhaps the earliest commercial **videogame** in which the player's goal is to build a galactic empire by means of unprovoked interstellar warfare and careful economic development, a theme that became much more popular with the appearance of **4X games**. Unusually, in this game, the player leads their own personal fleet into the unknown, conquering (or being defeated by) planets they encounter while dispatching scouts to other worlds and ordering their possessions to supply new spacecraft and conscripted troops. (In later works of this kind, or in contemporary board and counter **wargames** dealing with a similar subject, the player would typically take the part of a universal commander who could control ships anywhere in the simulated galaxy.) *Galactic Empire* is also more sf literate than most contemporary sf videogames, with a **3D** galactic map and a background in which starships can only move **slower than light**. This, combined with the impossibility of communication with ships distant from the player's fleet, gives the game's strategies a unique feel. Players must plan their fleet's route hundreds of game years in advance so that they can meet with reinforcements dispatched to prearranged stars at **sublight** speeds, often putting their crews in **suspended animation** to wait for rendezvous. While the game is quite slow to play, and its combination of **2D** displays and paper map sheets somewhat primitive, this kind of **slower-than-light** strategy remains unusual and intriguing today.

The remaining three games in the series are all direct sequels, developing a single story that becomes markedly more sophisticated over the course of the sequence. In *Galactic Trader* (*1979* BS; revised *1994*), the player is assumed to have completed the first game's program of galactic conquest and to have become unemployed as a result. The player's character, therefore, acquires a tramp starship and becomes an interstellar trader. Gameplay is similar to that of *Star Trader* (*1974*) designed by Dave Kaufman but using the interface of *Galactic Empire*, with additional complexities caused by the need to avoid assassins sent by the player's previous employer, the new Galactic Emperor. *Galactic Revolution* (*1980* BS) provides an identity for the series' previously nameless protagonist: Julian du Buque, a military genius and future philosopher king reminiscent of characters from such works of print sf as Gordon R Dickson's **Dorsai** sequence. The gameplay is essentially a much complexified version of that seen in *Galactic Empire*, with more emphasis placed on political maneuvering and less on military action. Single players must attempt to instigate a successful rebellion against the Emperor, using such rarely seen commands as "collectivize farms and factories" and "abolish the draft." Optionally, two additional players can participate, adopting the roles of the Emperor and the leader of a third faction. Arguably, this work is a precursor to such highly political 4X games as Sid Meier's *Civilization* (*1991* MicroProse). Finally, in *Tawala's Last Redoubt* (*1981* BS), the eponymous Emperor, assumed to have been defeated at the end of the third game, has fled to a remote and isolated world. As in *Galactic Revolution*, an extensive **framing** narrative is included in the manual, here describing the background of the new protagonist, who will become du Buque's lover in the ongoing **future history**. The design resembles that of the first game, except that the player's travels are confined to the surface of a single world; there are similarities to the rather more popular UK game *Lords of Midnight* (*1984*) designed by Mike Singleton.

HOMEWORLD

1999. Relic Entertainment (RE).

Homeworld is an **RTS** game, noted for its innovative use of **3D** space and its involving **linear** story line. The setting is **space opera**; the Kushan race, evicted from their homeworld long ago after losing a war against the Taiidan, have settled on the planet of Kharak and forgotten their origins. However, shortly before the beginning of the game, the Kushan excavate the ruins of an ancient starship, providing them with both **faster-than-light** technology and a map showing the location of their planet of origin. A gigantic starship (the Mothership) is constructed, containing a factory system capable of building smaller ships and storage space for half a million colonists in **suspended animation**, and launched on a test flight. The player serves as commander of the Mothership's subordinate spacecraft. After the ship's experimental **hyperspace** jump to the outer reaches of the

Kharak system, it is unexpectedly attacked; upon its return, it discovers Kharak has been destroyed, and the only survivors are frozen colonists in high orbit. The Mothership's mission is now crucial to the Kushan's future; their search for a lost homeworld has become the only hope their race has of survival.

Gameplay focuses on 3D movement of spacecraft, asteroid mining and combat, using an ingenious interface. The plot is unusually well integrated with the gameplay, and its linearity does not appear confining; the player's status as a subordinate of the Mothership's commander makes obedience to orders seem natural. The artificiality of many **RTS** games is also absent, with credible justifications provided for such contrivances as the player's need to research improvements in ship technology and a 3D display that is both convincing and beautiful. Ultimately, diplomacy with other races allows the player to discover that Kharak was destroyed by the Taiidan. This act of genocide was technically justified by a ban on the Kushan developing faster-than-light drives, imposed following an unprovoked attack on the Taiidan that started the long-ago war. However, the savagery of the Taiidan action has caused internal dissent within their Empire. The player can ally with Taiidan rebels and help bring about the corrupt Empire's transformation into a Republic, after which the Kushan sentence of exile is lifted. The game's scrupulous avoidance of melodrama helps it to convey a powerful sense of sorrow and loss, only partially ameliorated by the Kushan's eventual return home.

Homeworld: Cataclysm (*2000* Barking Dog/RE) is an expansion pack, largely created by a different developer. Various changes were made to the design, resulting in a broadly similar game that requires a higher level of detail management on the part of the player. It is set 15 years after *Homeworld*, concentrating on a clan of Kushan asteroid miners who encounter a derelict construct in deep space. During investigation, the derelict absorbs part of their ship before they can escape. Soon, it emerges that the construct was host to a long-dormant parasitic entity that uses **nanotechnology** to subvert the technology of other races and that poses a major threat to the galaxy; the peaceful miners must become warriors in order to defeat it. The entity's nature has interesting effects on tactics; massed attacks will generally end with it assimilating the player's vessels. *Homeworld 2* (*2003* RE) is a sequel, set a century after the first game. Its story deals with a threat to the Kushan homeworld from a nomadic warrior race who are gradually conquering the known galaxy. To defeat them, the player must recover the lost technologies of a vanished **forerunner** race. *Homeworld 2* is an entertaining game that is considerably more warlike in tone than its original; this game's version of the Mothership is a military factory, not the soul of a people.

Related works: The program code for *Homeworld* was released to the public in 2003, since when it has been used to create versions of the game for the Linux and Apple Mac platforms.

Web Links

- *Homeworld*: http://www.relic.com/games/homeworld/

- *Homeworld* downloads for Linux and Apple Mac: http://www. homeworldsdl.org/

HOSTILE WATERS: ANTAEUS RISING

2001. Rage Software.

Scripted by the well-known comics writer Warren Ellis, *Hostile Waters* is notable for the quality of its dialogue and the skill with which the **linear** plot is integrated with the gameplay. The game is set in the twenty-first century, after a global revolution against warmongering capitalists and politicians has established a liberal utopia based on **nanotechnology**. As the story begins, a cabal of powerful figures from the old regime has launched an attack on the new world order. Since the planet's stock of weaponry has been scrapped, the decision is made to raise an "adaptive cruiser" from the ocean floor, equipped with nanotechnological factories capable of manufacturing advanced military hardware and chips containing the recorded personalities of dead soldiers, resurrectable for another tour of duty. The player takes the role of the captain of this ship, a radical avenger fighting a war to end war.

In gameplay terms, *Hostile Waters* is an experimental form of **RTS** game. As in *Battlezone* (*1998* Activision), the player can take direct control of their land and air vehicles as well as commanding them from an overhead view, but in *Hostile Waters*, the default view is the strategic rather than the personal one. Also as in *Battlezone*, orders can be given to other units while in the direct control mode, using a sophisticated but somewhat cryptic interface. Many of the game's other features are reminiscent of *Carrier Command* (*1988* RG), a previous **computer wargame** featuring a high-technology aircraft carrier. *Hostile Waters* is an innovative, atmospheric, and well-designed game, but its utopian worldview can seem more morally simplistic than politically radical.

LASER SQUAD

1988. Target Games (TG). Designed by Julian Gollop.

Laser Squad is a **turn-based computer wargame** with a **2D** overhead view whose subject is combat between small groups of soldiers on the surfaces of alien worlds. Its game mechanics greatly resemble those of squad-level board and counter **wargames** such as the sf *Starsoldier* (*1977* Simulations Publications, Inc.) designed by Tom Walczyk, adapted for a **videogame**. Many early computer wargames show similar influences from the board and counter form; notably, the design of such space combat games as Jon Freeman and Jim Connelley's *Starfleet Orion* (*1978* AS) echoes that of such predecessors as *WarpWar* (*1977* MC) designed by Howard Thompson and *Alpha Omega* (*1977* Battleline) designed by Sean Hayes and J Stephen Peek. The core gameplay of *Laser Squad*, however, is an improved version of the system used in Gollop's earlier *Rebelstar Raiders* (*1984*) and its sequels *Rebelstar* (*1986*) and *Rebelstar II* (*1988* TG); a similar approach to squad-based combat also appears in his later *UFO: Enemy Unknown* (*1994* Mythos Games). As a work of sf, *Laser Squad* is of little interest; the game's backstory is thin and much influenced by *Star Wars*. It is, however, an excellent example of how to convert the basic concepts of a tactical tabletop wargame into a highly playable, visually appealing videogame that offers much in the way of military subtlety and operational variety.

Laser Squad Nemesis (*2002* Codo Technologies) designed by Julian Gollop is a loose sequel that is primarily a **play by e-mail** game. Each player selects one of four species with different strengths and weaknesses and joins a scenario with another participant. The game then proceeds turn by turn, with orders submitted to a central machine and the results sent back to the players. Created by Codo Technologies without publisher involvement, *Laser Squad Nemesis* was one of the most successful **independent games** of the early 2000s.

MIDWINTER

1989. Maelstrom Games (MG). Designed by Mike Singleton.

Midwinter is an unusual combination of **real-time CRPG** and **computer wargame**, set on an isolated island in the aftermath of a devastating meteorite strike that has plunged the game's near-future Earth into a worldwide winter. The design echoes that of Singleton's previous work, the **heroic fantasy** *Lords of Midnight* (*1984*), as well as that of its sequel

Doomdark's Revenge (*1985* Beyond). Players begin the game in control of a single individual and must recruit a diverse group of characters with which to fight a guerilla war against an invading army. Many potential soldiers can only be persuaded to fight by others who are their lovers or close friends, adding a surprising degree of strategic depth to the gameplay. Once recruited, individuals can perform many different actions, including spying, sabotage, first aid, sniping at the enemy, and traveling across the algorithmically generated **3D** terrain using skis, snowmobiles, cable cars, or hang gliders. Each character has specific skills that are useful in different circumstances; a skiing instructor might prove helpful for obtaining a vehicle from a distant village, but a mining engineer would be better suited to sabotaging an enemy installation. However, while the strategic aspects of the game are engaging, many players found the real-time combat and movement overly difficult to master and on occasion monotonous. Ultimately, *Midwinter* is a more original but perhaps less enjoyable game than *Lords of Midnight*, its entirely **turn-based** predecessor.

Related works: The sequel, *Flames of Freedom* (*1991* MG) designed by Mike Singleton, is set many years later, on a newly warming post-holocaust Earth. The Free Villages of Midwinter have become the Atlantic Federation, which is fighting a covert war with the Saharan Empire; the player character's mission is to promote revolution in the Saharan occupied islands that lie between the territories of the two adversaries. *Flames of Freedom* offers many more options than *Midwinter* but is, arguably, too complex; its design lacks the elegance shown in the first game.

OGRE

1986. Origin Systems. Designed by Steve Jackson and Steve Meuse.

The original game of *Ogre* is a board and counter **wargame**, developed in 1977 by Steve Jackson for MC and set during the Last War, a 40-year-long nuclear conflict between all the major power blocs of the twenty-first century. The stars of the game, and the source of much of its appeal, are the eponymous giant, malevolent robot tanks, a concept influenced by Keith Laumer's **Bolo** stories. (Ogres are an inversion of Bolos, however; where Laumer's intelligent tanks are peerless warriors and perfect knights, Jackson's are demons of the battlefield.) Gameplay revolves around an **asymmetric** conflict between a single Ogre, controlled by one player, and their opponent's choice of smaller units, including artillery, tanks, and infantry. The **videogame** is a direct conversion of this work to a **turn-based computer wargame**. This alteration of form was skillfully implemented and is generally effective, though it is regrettable that in single-player games the software must always control the Ogre. Nevertheless, the entertaining gameplay of the original is preserved in the digital version, as is the disturbing sense that, in the end, only the Ogres can win the Last War.

Related works: The tabletop game was revised in 1977, 1982, 1987 (as *Ogre Deluxe*), and 2000 (as *Deluxe Ogre*). It has also had several sequels and spin-offs, including *GEV* (*1978* MC) designed by Steve Jackson, which focuses on armored hovercraft; an expansion set called *Shockwave* (*1984* Steve Jackson Games [SJG]) designed by Steve Jackson; *Battlesuit* (*1983* SJG) designed by Steve Jackson, which deals with infantry wearing **powered armor**; and *GURPS Ogre* (*2000* SJG) designed by Jonathan Woodward, a supplement for the 1988 third edition of SJG's *GURPS* pen and paper **RPG**. *The Ogre Book* (**1982**) edited by Steve Jackson is a collection of articles and fiction inspired by the game.

PERIMETER

2004. K-D Lab (KDL). Designed by Andrey Kuzmin, Yulia Shaposhnikova, and Michail Piskounov.

Perimeter is an **RTS** game, set in a sequence of subworlds located in a region known as the Psychosphere (or, in a less felicitous translation from the original Russian, the Sponge). The Psychosphere is a separate layer of reality, one in which human fears and dreams become manifest, shaping the physical environment. Humans entered these worlds with the assistance of a caste of Priest-Scientists who created a new occult science based on their **psionic** abilities, using which they could open portals into the psychic subspaces. Humanity's explorations, however, rapidly resulted in the formation of aggressive, nightmarish creatures in the Psychosphere. At first, these beings simply attacked the intruders, but soon they began to follow them home. An already polluted and dying Earth, invaded by monsters from the id, decided to seal the portals to the subworlds. By this act, they exiled a group who intended to move deeper into the chain of psychic spaces, searching for exits leading to new planets circling other stars in Earth's reality.

The game begins centuries after the closing of Earth's portals, when many generations have lived and died on the giant city ships in which the exiles fight their way through the hostile territory of the collective unconscious. Most of the cities' inhabitants have been subjected to "personality elimination," in order to minimize the number of hostile entities generated by the Psychosphere in response to the presence of human minds. The remainder have long since forgotten the details of their past and are dividing into mutually hostile factions—those who wish to continue with the journey, those who want to try and return to Earth, and a group that intends to conquer the Psychosphere itself, taking possession of the human imagination. The game's highly **linear** plot follows the conflicts between these three groups and between all of them and the entities created by the subworlds. Unfortunately, following the story line can be awkward; the narrative switches confusingly between multiple viewpoints, and the explanations of the framing backstory within the game (as opposed to on external resources, such as the publisher's website) are quite inadequate. However, it appears that in the end both the faction that intends to continue to the stars and the one that prefers to return home will arrive at the same new world, which is in a sense also their old one: prehistoric Earth.

Perimeter's gameplay is genuinely original, offering a notably different vision of how RTS games might play to that epitomized by such works as the better-known *Starcraft* (*1998* BE) designed by James Phinney and Chris Metzen. There are no physical resources that must be mined or gathered before new buildings and units can be constructed. Instead, the player's ability to create new material depends on their available energy, which in turn is determined by the amount of land they have flattened—or "terraformed"—so that they can construct energy-gathering devices on it. Conflicts are thus primarily about control of flattened areas and the power grids that can be built on them. Another interesting feature is the use of **nanotechnology**-based robots for all combat and support units, a conceit that justifies the instant conversion of one group of minions into another. Thus, a set of ordinary "soldier" and "officer" robots might transform into a tank and back again, with minimal effort. This leads to combats that resemble magicians' duels, with one side converting their units into a superior form, only to have their opponents create something that counters their new shape. There is, of course, no single form that outmatches all the rest. Finally, the eponymous **force field** allows a player to make their city ships and constructed buildings impervious to attack but only for a short time. Some of these features may not be perfectly balanced; use of the energy shield, for example, can lead to prolonged wars of attrition. Nevertheless, the game design is both novel and highly entertaining, an impressive combination. *Perimeter* is also notable for its wide variety of exotic and strikingly visualized environments and for the distant, almost inhuman tone of its narrative. The game's most memorable characteristic, however, may be its vision of the human unconscious—a dirty, dangerous place, dominated by endless warfare and expedient evils. The impression is of a sort of grimy transcendence that could, perhaps, be described as mystic grunge.

Related works: *Perimeter: Emperor's Testament* (*2005* KDL) designed by Yulia Shaposhnikova, Michail Piskounov, and Andrey Kuzmin is an expansion pack for *Perimeter* that contains additional, more difficult, missions for the basic game, presented as events that occur during a new story line. *Perimeter II: New Earth* (*2008* KD Vision) is a sequel in which many of the innovative aspects of *Perimeter's* gameplay have been replaced by more conventional designs. Thus, the ability to transform between many different types of robot is replaced by the power to convert air units to and from ground ones, psionic crystals can be mined and used to construct special weapons, and so on. Unfortunately, the elements used are generally considered to have been poorly chosen and the resulting gameplay to be unbalanced. The game is set in the new world that is reached at the end of the original *Perimeter*, where the two surviving city ships continue their civil war.

Web Link
- The *Perimeter* Universe: http://games.1c.ru/perimeter/eng/universe.html

RENEGADE LEGION: INTERCEPTOR

1990. SSI. Designed by Scot Bayless, Graeme Bayless, and Todd Mitchell Porter.

Renegade Legion: Interceptor is set in the sixty-ninth century, when the entire galaxy is oppressed by the Terran Overlord Government (TOG), a human empire deliberately modeled on Imperial Rome. Its only significant opponents are the egalitarian Commonwealth and its allies, the eponymous Legions, who have defected from the TOG. This milieu is perhaps best summarized as a conflict between an idealized British

Empire and a Rome made more decadent and savage, fought with near-future technologies and **faster-than-light** drives. The setting also includes several interesting alien races that, while often warlike, are depicted with some subtlety. Many of these species have psychological traits based on an extreme reflection of some aspect of human nature; one race, for example, has completely separated love and reproduction, while members of another go through regular transitions after which their personalities are changed and their past lives forgotten.

This background was developed by the game studio FASA for a series of tabletop **wargames** using cardboard models, beginning with *Renegade Legion: Interceptor* (*1987*) designed by Jordan Weisman, Sam Lewis, and Albie Fiore, a **turn-based** game that models combat in space between single-pilot starfighters. Considerable emphasis is placed on detailed rules for ship damage, including flowcharts that determine the systems affected by a weapons strike. The eponymous **videogame** is a direct conversion of this work to a turn-based **computer wargame**. The implementation is competent but suffers somewhat from the lack of a story line; players fight in an eternal campaign for which new missions are continually generated for as long as they wish to continue. Arguably, the most interesting part of the original wargames is their fiction, which unfortunately is largely absent from the videogame.

Related works: *Renegade: The Battle for Jacob's Star* (*1995* SSI) designed by Daniel Cermak, Dan Hoecke, and James Long is a **real-time space sim** focusing on starfighter combat in which the player flies missions for the Commonwealth; reviews compared its gameplay unfavorably with that of its contemporary, *Wing Commander III: Heart of the Tiger* (*1994* Origin Systems) designed by Chris Roberts and Frank Savage.

Several other tabletop wargames were released for the milieu, including *Renegade Legion: Centurion* (*1988* FASA), *Renegade Legion: Leviathan* (*1993* FASA), and *Renegade Legion: Prefect* (*1992* FASA). *Renegade Legion: Legionnaire* (*1990* FASA) is an associated pen and paper **RPG**, while *Renegade Legion: Circus Imperium* (*1988* FASA) is a comparatively light-hearted board game about **antigravity** chariot racing. Several novels were written using the background: *Renegade's Honor* (**1988**) by William H Keith Jr, and *Damned If We Do…* (**1990**), *Frost Death* (**1992**), and *Monsoon* (**1992**) all by Peter Rice.

ROBOTWAR

1981. Muse Software. Designed by Silas Warner.

The premise behind the release of *RobotWar* was simple; in the distant future of 2002, human soldiers will be obsolete. Instead, wars will be fought by robots, controlled by programs written by the players. Participants construct simple routines in a language resembling a cross between the low-level machine code used in contemporary microprocessors and the teaching language BASIC (an acronym for Beginner's All-purpose Symbolic Instruction Code) and pit their creations against robots running other programs; the resulting conflicts are displayed in a **2D** overhead view. It is impossible to control the combatants directly; their actions in battle are solely dictated by the instructions stored in their virtual brains. In the early 1980s, *RobotWar* was very popular in the then small community of US microcomputer enthusiasts, with annual competitions held in the magazine *Computer Gaming World*, whose readers would send in their best programs so they could be tested against each other.

The commercial game was derived from an earlier version written by its creator for mainframe computers on the academic PLATO network during the 1970s; later efforts in a similar vein include the freely distributed mainframe game *Core War* (*1984*) designed by D G Jones and A K Dewdney, the robot tank simulator *Omega* (*1989* Origin Systems) designed by Stuart Marks, and the board game *RoboRally* (*1994* Wizards of the Coast) designed by Richard Garfield, which takes a comic approach to the same basic concept. Today, however, *RobotWar* may be most interesting for the vivid illustration it offers of the differences between the US computer game market of the 1980s and the modern mass market for **videogames**. The hobbyist computer owners of the time, enthusiastic about their expensive new hardware and often also devotees of *Dungeons and Dragons* and other tabletop games with complex rules, were happy with a work whose gameplay depended on simulated computer programming. It is hard to imagine that the majority of today's players—or for that matter the console and arcade gamers of the 1980s, who were typically children and young adults interested in fast-moving action games—would be similarly enthusiastic.

SINS OF A SOLAR EMPIRE

2008. Ironclad Games (IG).

Solar Empire is a simulation of space warfare that fuses the conventions of the **RTS** form with those of **4X games**. While many of the design elements it shares with 4X games were borrowed by the earliest examples of the **RTS** form (and have become characteristic of the school), the events of *Solar Empire* play out on a much wider stage than those of a typical RTS, one that incorporates multiple solar systems. The gameplay is correspondingly slower and more detailed, in the manner of such **turn-based** works as *Master of Orion* (*1993* Simtex) designed by Steve Barcia. *Solar Empire* does not have the emphasis on social development and political conflict seen in such games as *Sid Meier's Alpha Centauri* (*1999* Firaxis Games [FG]) designed by Brian Reynolds and Sid Meier, concentrating instead on scientific research, economic development, and military strategy. The player's time is spent controlling orbital structures and spacecraft in **real time** while issuing more abstract instructions to entire planets and civilizations. One interesting predecessor is *Star General* (*1996* Catware) designed by Bill Fawcett, which similarly concentrates on strategic warfare between small numbers of star systems with economic, technological, and diplomatic aspects, though *Solar Empire* has no equivalent of the ground combat employed in *Star General* to model planetary assaults. The most significant differences, however, lie in the representation of space—*Star General* is essentially **2D**, in the manner of a naval combat game, while *Solar Empire* is **3D**, using the orbital plane of a specified star as a reference—and in the distinct traditions from which their designs developed. *Star General* owes much to turn-based board and counter **wargames**, while *Solar Empire* is influenced by the history of real-time **computer wargame** development and is ultimately descended from such **videogames** as *Dune II: The Building of a Dynasty* (*1992* WS) designed by Joseph Bostic and Aaron Powell as well as the tabletop game *Stellar Conquest* (*1974* MC) designed by Howard Thompson. Interestingly, one significant inspiration for the design of *Solar Empire* appears to have been the board game *Buck Rogers—Battle for the 25th Century* (*1988* Tactical Studies Rules), a spin-off from the same franchise that gave rise to the **CRPGs** *Countdown to Doomsday* (*1990* SSI) designed by Graeme Bayless and Bret Berry and *Matrix Cubed* (*1992* SSI) designed by Rhonda Van.

Many fans of *Sins of a Solar Empire* are attracted by the opportunity to stage gigantic battles in space.

The game is set in a **space opera** galaxy split between a human civilization formed by interstellar traders, an offshoot of that culture whose **psionic** religion instructs them to absorb all sentient beings into a single collective consciousness by any means necessary, and refugees from an alien galactic empire who are fleeing an unknown enemy. A wide variety of both technologies and celestial bodies are present, from **antimatter** engines to **wormholes** and asteroids to **gas giants**. Some sf inventions also serve as justifications for important gameplay limitations; thus, travel between stars can only be accomplished along specific roads through **hyperspace**, creating a spatial geography with supply routes and defensible bastions. While the background is quite detailed, there is no predefined story line; the setting serves only as a narrative **frame** for games played against the computer or other participants online. These games can be quite complex, but a well-designed user interface combines with the ability to examine events on a wide variety of spatial scales to make the gameplay absorbing rather than overly demanding. As a game of space conquest, *Solar Empire* is compelling and intellectually challenging; as an exercise in design, it suggests a possible future direction for the evolution of the 4X game form as a whole.

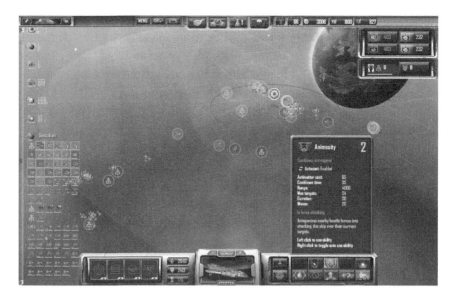

In Sins of a *Solar Empire*, players manipulate events across entire solar systems.

Related works: *Entrenchment* (*2009* IG) is an expansion pack that adds new weapons and technologies. Similarly, *Diplomacy* (*2010* IG) significantly enhances players' diplomatic options, making it possible to play a more cooperative version of the original game, while *Rebellion* (*2012* IG) divides each of *Solar Empire*'s competing civilizations into "rebel" and "loyalist" factions.

Web Links

- *Sins of a Solar Empire*: http://www.sinsofasolarempire.com/

- *Sins of a Solar Empire* Postmortem: http://www.gamasutra.com/view/feature/3638/postmortem_ironcladstardocks_.php

STARCRAFT

1998. (Revised *2000* as *Starcraft 64*.) Blizzard Entertainment (BE). Designed by James Phinney and Chris Metzen.

Starcraft is an **RTS** game, played in a **2D** overhead view, with a setting that owes much to the films *Aliens* (*1986*) and *Predator* (*1987*). The story line follows a war between three factions in a **space opera** future: the Terran Confederacy (analogous to *Aliens*' Marines), the arthropodal **hive-mind** Zerg (which share something with H R Giger's eponymous Aliens), and the **psionic** Protoss, whose adherence to a strict code of honor is reminiscent of *Predator*'s titular hunters. While the narrative is strictly **linear**, it is unusual in the way it positions the player as a member of all three races in turn, immersing them in every side of the conflict over the course of three separate campaigns that make up a single story. The game begins with the player, in the role of a magistrate for the confederacy, arriving on a colony world where they must confront an invasion by the Zerg. During the course of the campaign, the player's character is unjustly condemned by his superiors and defects to a rebel organization, the Sons of Korhal. By its end, the Sons have taken power but the player has lost faith in their motives and again become a rebel. In the second campaign, the player is a newly formed Zerg, initially entrusted with defense against the Protoss, who have followed the Zerg into Terran space in order to exterminate them. Finally, the player becomes a Protoss commander, responsible for protecting their homeworld against a Zerg counter attack. The game ends with the Terran rebels allying with the Protoss to destroy the Zerg's central brain, or "Overmind."

The gameplay is a refined version of that seen in earlier **RTSs** such as Blizzard's own fantasy game *Warcraft II: Tides of Darkness* (*1995* BE; *1997* revised as *Warcraft II: The Dark Saga*). Players adopt the roles of tactical commanders, controlling large numbers of units specialized for combat, repair and gathering gas, and mineral resources. Games are focused on mining resources (with which new units can be built), constructing various types of buildings (which enable more powerful units to be created), and tactical combat. As in many members of the RTS school, this combination is highly unrealistic when considered as a simulation of actual warfare but very playable as a game. The three races are **asymmetrically** balanced, with different strengths and weaknesses. Campaigns are played through as a series of individual missions; their objectives include such tasks as scouting out hostile positions, infiltration and destruction of the enemy. *Starcraft* is still a popular game, both as a single-player experience with well-crafted gameplay, which depends on a constantly evolving balance of micro- and macroscopic priorities, and as a player-versus-player game in temporary **online worlds**. Players' enthusiasm for the online option was enhanced by the inclusion of an editor that allows players to create and distribute their own mission designs. In South Korea, competitive *Starcraft* play became a professional sport, with matches broadcast on TV.

Starcraft: Brood War (*1998* BE) is an expansion pack that adds new units and continues the original game's plot. The story concentrates on Sarah Kerrigan, the "Queen of Blades," a psionic woman who was betrayed by the Terrans and assimilated by the Zerg in the first game. Following the death of the Overmind, she has become the new controller of the Zerg and is planning an all encompassing war to avenge herself on her former commanders. Meanwhile, a force arrives from Earth to reestablish control over this disputed volume of space. As in the original game, the player serves all three sides in the ensuing conflict, watching as strongly (if somewhat crudely) portrayed characters rise and fall through the fortunes of war. In the end, the charismatic villain Sarah Kerrigan is victorious, though her more honorable enemies are allowed to survive.

The next work in the sequence is *Starcraft II: Wings of Liberty* (2010 BE) designed by Dustin Browder and Chris Metzen, another RTS game. This is very much a sequel that builds on the original; it is at once an improved version of what was already an impressive game and an extension of a cheerfully clichéd space opera narrative with strong overtones of both **military sf** and the fiction of the Wild West. The gameplay is broadly similar to that of its predecessor, though some new units have been added and it is now possible to make permanent improvements to their abilities by researching new technologies between missions, as in the earlier *X-COM* series. Missions are varied and entertaining; in one, the player must retrieve a heavily defended McGuffin from a world whose star is going nova, creating a wall of fire that moves inexorably across the planet's surface. Considered as a narrative, however, *Wings of Liberty* is incomplete; only the first part of the story, which played from the Terran perspective, is present, with Protoss and Zerg sections expected to arrive as expansions. The player adopts the role of Jim Raynor, a former Confederacy Marine turned outlaw turned frontier marshal turned rebel who was an ally of the player's character in the first part of the original game. A broadly linear **interactive narrative**, with some **multilinear** elements, follows Raynor's attempts to foment a rebellion against the Terran Dominion, a repressive dictatorship ruled by one Arcturus Mengsk, former leader of the Sons of Korhal. Raynor funds his activities by recovering pieces of an ancient **forerunner** artifact (created by a vanished species responsible for **uplifting** both the Protoss and the Zerg) and selling them to a secretive Foundation. Soon, the Zerg, the Protoss, and the humans become involved in a many-sided war, and Raynor allies himself with the Foundation (which turns out to be a front for a faction within the Dominion) in an attempt to use the now reconstructed artifact to restore the humanity of the Queen of Blades (who Raynor loved, when she was a woman). Ultimately, however, the point of *Wings of Liberty* is not its narrative but its strikingly well-crafted gameplay; it is eminently suitable for competitive play online.

The story continues in the expansion *Starcraft II: Heart of the Swarm* (*2013* BE). Kerrigan, transformed back into a human at the end of *Wings of Liberty*, decides to return to her role as leader of the Zerg after Raynor is apparently killed and goes on to exact a bloody revenge on Arcturus Mengsk; the tortured romance between the rebel leader and hive mistress features prominently. An upcoming final expansion, *Legacy of the Void*, is expected to conclude the ongoing plot with the return of the mysterious forerunners.

Related works: *Starcraft: Insurrection* (*1998* Aztech New Media) is an expansion pack including new multiplayer maps and a story that occurs simultaneously with the first campaign of the original game. *Starcraft: Retribution* (*1998* Stardock) is another expansion, including a short story line and a large number of multiplayer maps. *Starcraft Adventures* (*2000* Wizards of the Coast) designed by Bill Slavicsek, David Eckelberry, and Shawn Carnes is a tabletop **RPG** that uses the mechanics of *Alternity* (*1988* Tactical Studies Rules) designed by Bill Slavicsek and Richard Baker. *Starcraft: The Board Game* (*2007* Fantasy Flight Games [FFG]) designed by Corey Konieczka and Christian Petersen is a tabletop **wargame** that attempts to translate the gameplay of an RTS to a system based around cards, miniature models, and a modular board. *Starcraft: The Board Game—Brood War* (*2008* FFG) designed by Corey Konieczka, Daniel Clark, and Robert Kouba is a supplement based on the eponymous **video-game** expansion.

Various novels have been written that tie in to the games' story line. Thus, *Starcraft: Uprising* (**2000**) by Micky Neilson is a prequel that deals with the early life of Sarah Kerrigan, while *Starcraft: Liberty's Crusade* (**2001**), by Jeff Grubb, is a novelization of the original game's Terran-campaign. Similarly, *Starcraft: Shadow of the Xel'Naga* (**2001**), by Gabriel Mesta (a joint pseudonym for Kevin J Anderson and Rebecca Moesta), is a prequel to *Brood War*, while *Starcraft: Speed of Darkness* (**2002**) by Tracy Hickman follows some soldiers of the Confederacy during the first *Starcraft* campaign. These four works are collected in *The Starcraft Archive: An Anthology* (**2007**). The series was continued in *Starcraft: Queen of Blades* (**2006**) by Aaron Rosenberg, a novelization of the Zerg campaign in *Starcraft*, and *Starcraft: I, Mengsk* (**2008**) by Graham McNeill, which could be described as a Mengsk family saga.

Starcraft Ghost: Nova (**2006**) and its sequel *Starcraft Ghost: Spectres* (**2010**), by Keith R A DeCandido and Nate Kenyon, respectively, are spin-offs from the canceled **FPS** *Starcraft: Ghost*, which would have featured psionic Terran infiltration experts known as "Ghosts." *Starcraft: The Dark Templar Saga #1: Firstborn* (**2007**), *Starcraft: The Dark Templar Saga #2: Shadow Hunters* (**2007**), and *Starcraft: The Dark Templar Saga #3: Twilight* (**2009**), all by Christie Golden, concentrate on the Protoss and serve as prequels to *Wings of Liberty*. *Starcraft: Heaven's Devils* (**2010**), by William C Dietz, deals with the early life of Jim Raynor; *Starcraft: Devils' Due* (**2011**), by Christie Golden, is a sequel. *Starcraft II: Flashpoint* (**2012**), also by Golden, is a prequel to *Heart of the Swarm*. Finally, *Starcraft: Frontline* (*2008–2009*) is a series of anthologies in graphic novel form, while *Starcraft: Ghost Academy* (*2009–2011*) is another sequence of graphic novels that focuses on a team of Ghosts, written by David Gerrold and Keith R A DeCandido, and *Starcraft* (*2009–2010*) is a comics series that acts as a prequel to *Wings of Liberty*.

Web Links

- *Starcraft*: http://us.blizzard.com/en-us/games/sc/

- *Starcraft II*: http://us.blizzard.com/en-us/games/sc2/

STARFLEET COMMAND

1999. (Revised *2000* as *Starfleet Command: Gold Edition*.) Interplay. Designed by Erik Bethke and Christopher Taylor.

The board and counter **wargame** *Star Fleet Battles* (*1979* Task Force Games; revised *1979*; revised *1983*; revised *1990*) designed by Stephen Cole was first developed as a game of tactical combat between starships in the universe of the original *Star Trek* TV series (*1966–1969*). However, the limitations of the license under which the game is produced, and the extent to which the various themes found in the original material were differently emphasized by the game developers and later TV shows, led to the creation of a separate continuity (the "Star Fleet Universe") for the game. The license allows the game to include elements from the TV franchise only as it existed before 1979, including the spin-off animated series (*1973–1974*). As a result, the various *Star Trek* feature films, and later developments in the core franchise, are not reflected in the Star Fleet Universe. Instead, the game continuity adds a wide variety of new alien races, ship types, and military technologies, including small fighters, unmanned drones, and marines (who are used for ship boarding actions). Other inventions appear to have been developed by considering the logical consequences of devices featured in the original series; thus, the game includes mines that can be deployed by **matter transmitter** (or "transporter") and **tractor beams,** which can be used to drag ships into other objects. In addition, while the various later films and TV shows have concentrated on the more pacifist and cooperative aspects of the original series, the game has focused on developing its militaristic elements, creating a **future history** suitable for use in a wargame.

The wargame is played on a hexagonal grid with counters, in two dimensions. This design is a good representation of combat in *Star Trek*, in which the third dimension is rarely mentioned and ships maneuver in a way that is intuitively rather than physically convincing. Much of the gameplay revolves around allocating finite energy resources to various ship functions (such as shields or weapons) and the widely varied technologies available to different races. While the result can become highly complex, the many different types of combatant create a remarkable range of tactical possibilities.

The rules of *Star Fleet Battles* were first translated into a digital form in *The Warp Factor* (*1981* SSI) designed by Bruce Clayton and Paul Murray, a **2D turn-based** game that faithfully represented the design of its original but unfortunately had no legal right to do so. Two decades after the release of this first attempt, Interplay created *Starfleet Command* as a direct conversion of the tabletop game to a **real-time videogame** with a **3D** display. The gameplay is similar to that of its prototype, though the nature of the interface often results in ships continuously circling each other at close range rather than engaging distant enemies, as in the original. As a visual experience, the digital version is undeniably superior. Considered as sources of narrative, however, *Star Fleet Battles* and *Starfleet Command* take almost identical approaches; both focus relentlessly on the complexities of battle while largely ignoring the possibility of story.

Related works: There have been several sequels to *Starfleet Command*, including *Starfleet Command II: Empires At War* (*2000* Taldren) designed by Erik Bethke and Joshua Morris, which adds new combatants and simulated technologies as well as improved visuals, and *Starfleet Command: Orion Pirates* (*2001* Taldren) designed by Joshua Morris, an expansion to *Starfleet Command II* based on the titular group. *Starfleet Command III*

(*2002* Taldren), designed by Joshua Morris and Scott Bruno, was published by Activision rather than the previous games' Interplay and took something of a new approach. Its mechanics and interface were somewhat simplified compared to those of its predecessors (and *Star Fleet Battles*), and it was set in the continuity of the TV series *Star Trek: The Next Generation* (*1987–1994*) rather than that of the Star Fleet Universe, with a relatively well-developed (**linear**) plotline. Nevertheless, it was not sufficiently commercially successful to justify the creation of a further sequel; the year after it was released, Activision sued the owner of the rights to the TV series on the grounds that "through its actions and inactions, Viacom has let the once proud 'Star Trek' franchise stagnate and decay," thus (allegedly) affecting Activision's ability to sell licensed videogames. The case was settled out of court in 2005.

Various other tabletop wargames are associated with *Star Fleet Battles*, including the strategic *Federation and Empire* (*1987* Amarillo Design Bureau [ADB]; revised *1993*; revised *2000*; revised *2004*) designed by Stephen Cole and its predecessor *Federation Space* (*1981* ADB) designed by Stephen Wilcox, as well as *Federation Commander* (*2005* ADB) designed by Stephen Cole, which is essentially a simplified version of *Star Fleet Battles*. In addition, ADB have set two other games in the Star Fleet Universe: *Star Fleet Battle Force* (*2001* ADB) designed by Stephen Cole, a **collectible card game**, and *Prime Directive* (*1993* ADB/Task Force Games; revised *2002*; revised *2005*; revised *2008*) designed by Mark Costello and Timothy Olsen, a pen and paper **RPG** in which the characters are members of elite exploration and combat teams. *A Call to Arms: Star Fleet* (*2011* Mongoose Publishing [MP]) designed by Matthew Sprange, meanwhile, is a miniatures-based wargame that combines the mechanics of the *Babylon 5* spaceship combat game *A Call To Arms* (*2004* MP) designed by Matthew Sprange with the setting of the Star Fleet Universe.

STARFLEET ORION

1978. Automated Simulations (AS). Designed by Jon Freeman and Jim Connelley.

Starfleet Orion is the earliest known example of an sf **computer wargame** that was sold commercially. The game, played by two participants in alternating turns, revolves around combat between small fleets of spacecraft; there is a marked resemblance to such contemporary board and counter **wargames** as *WarpWar* (*1977* MC) designed by

Howard Thompson or the earlier *Triplanetary* (*1973* Game Designers' Workshop) designed by Marc Miller. Many common features of these games appear, including the use of a limited energy reserve for each ship that must be divided between various systems. (In *Starfleet Orion*, functions to which energy can be allocated include launching smart torpedoes, absorbing hostile fire with shields, and deploying small, agile starfighters that can be pushed rapidly toward the enemy with **pressor beams**.) The general absence of geographical features in space means that, in contrast to such contemporary land-based games as *Tanktics* (*1976*) designed by Chris Crawford, all the necessary graphics could (barely) be displayed on the computer screen, using a **2D** overhead view. Various scenarios and ship designs compatible with the game's flamboyant **future history** of rebellious interstellar colonies are provided, with additional examples based on such printed fictions as Poul Anderson's **Dominic Flandry** sequence. Unusually for such an early work, *Starfleet Orion* also includes a tool that allows the player to construct scenarios of their own design. While *Starfleet Orion* is an entertaining and strategically challenging game, it suffers from one significant flaw: the requirement for two players, who must take turns at the same keyboard, carefully ignoring each other's moves. This problem was resolved in the otherwise broadly similar sequel, *Invasion Orion* (*1979* AS) designed by Jon Freeman, which allowed a single player to fight off the invading robotic Klaatu, named in honor of the alien ambassador in the film *The Day the Earth Stood Still* (*1951*).

STAR GENERAL

1996. Catware. Designed by Bill Fawcett.

Star General is a **turn-based** strategic war game dealing with conflicts on an interstellar scale, much influenced by board and counter **wargames**. Its design is an expanded version of that of *Panzer General* (*1994* SSI), a well-received World War II era **computer wargame** that adopted many of the conventions of the tabletop form, including a **2D** map display laid out on a hexagonal grid. *Star General* is composed of two largely independent components dealing, respectively, with space and planetary operations; both systems include the production of resources and material such as food and spacecraft as well as actual combat. The scale is large, with gameplay revolving around galaxy-wide wars with an extensive range of options available for diplomacy, technological improvements, and production. The overall feel somewhat resembles that of the strategic version of the tabletop wargame *Starfire* (*1979* Task Force Games; revised *1984*; revised *1992*; revised *2000* as *Galactic Starfire*; revised *2004* as *ULTRA Starfire*; revised *2012* as *SOLAR Starfire*) designed by Stephen Cole but with more emphasis on ground combat and far less on research and economics. While the visual displays are somewhat limited, the battle simulations are detailed and precise, borrowing many mechanics from board and counter wargames but hiding the esoteric calculations required behind a reasonably intuitive interface. The credibility of the simulated space warfare is questionable, however; it resembles naval operations in an archipelago rather more than it does **3D** combat in interstellar space.

The game is set in the **military sf** milieu of **The Fleet**, the venue for a series of shared-world anthologies edited by David A Drake and the game's lead designer, Bill Fawcett. This background, however, adds little; the various opposing factions are not particularly distinctive, and their military units seem to owe more to the ground vehicles and naval vessels of twentieth-century warfare than they do to the sf imagination. Compared to other sf war games such as the tabletop *Starforce: Alpha Centauri* (*1974* Simulations Publications, Inc.) designed by Redmond Simonsen or the *Warhammer 40,000*-derived computer game *Dawn of War* (*2004* RE), *Star General*'s fiction lacks novelty. Nevertheless, it is a well-crafted game that makes excellent use of its tabletop heritage and perhaps the most interesting large-scale strategic **videogame** dealing with interstellar conflict.

STAR TREK

1971. (Also known as *SPACWR*.) Designed by Mike Mayfield.

The popularity of the original *Star Trek* TV series throughout the 1970s and 1980s encouraged early game developers (often students and computer scientists at universities and colleges in the United States and the United Kingdom) to see it as an inspiration for the games they built on mainframe computers and gave away to anyone who wanted them. Perhaps the most important of these works to be derived from *Star Trek* were the earliest, the various **computer wargames** that appeared on academic networks during the 1970s, and may have been the first works of their kind designed as games to be played rather than as military simulations to be used. The first such work appears to have been the 1971 *Star Trek*, which uses a simple text-based display (often printed out on a teletype in early versions) to present a **2D** grid map of the galaxy. While the original concept for the game was influenced by the MIT game *Spacewar* (*1962*) designed by Stephen Russell, J M Graetz, and Wayne Wiitanen, the final gameplay is quite different. Players, in the role of the captain of the TV show's USS Enterprise, use a **turn-based** interface to move, attack, and allocate energy between their vessel's shields, weapons, and engines, with the eventual aim of destroying all enemy ships in the galaxy. This game was highly popular with students, spawning a bewildering variety of descendants, variants, and reimplementations, of which the best known are perhaps the much improved *Super Star Trek* (*1974*) designed by Robert Leedom and its successor *Super Star Trek* (*circa 1975*) designed by David Matuszek and Paul Reynolds.

```
Do you need instructions (y/n): y
1. When you see _Command?_ printed, enter one of the legal commands
   (nav, srs, lrs, pha, tor, she, dam, com, or xxx).
2. If you should type in an illegal command, you'll get a short list of
   the legal commands printed out.
3. Some commands require you to enter data (for example, the 'nav' command
   comes back with 'Course(1-9) ?'.) If you type in illegal data (like
   negative numbers), that command will be aborted.

   The galaxy is divided into an 8 X 8 quadrant grid, and each quadrant
is further divided into an 8 x 8 sector grid.

   You will be assigned a starting point somewhere in the galaxy to begin
a tour of duty as commander of the starship _Enterprise_; your mission:
to seek out and destroy the fleet of Klingon warships which are menacing
the United Federation of Planets.

   You have the following commands available to you as Captain of the Starship
Enterprise:

\nav\ Command = Warp Engine Control --
```

Early mainframe computer games such as Robert Leedom's Super *Star Trek* typically included instructions as text that could be displayed when the program was run.

Another contemporary computer wargame that was unofficially based on the franchise was *Star Trek* (*1972*) designed by Don Daglow. This work has many similarities to Mike Mayfield's *Star Trek* but is distinguished by the use of an interface resembling that of a menu-driven text **adventure** rather than a 2D map. Versions of Mayfield's and Leedom's games were created for many early home computers and proved highly influential on such later computer wargames as *Star Fleet I: The War Begins* (*1983* Cygnus) designed by Trevor Sorensen, as well as helping to inspire the first clear example of the combat-focused form of **space sim**, *Star Raiders* (*1979* Atari) designed by Doug Neubauer.

```
                *       *       Stardate              2700
                      *         Condition             GREEN
                                Quadrant              1, 6
         *                      Sector                5, 3
        <*>                     Photon Torpedoes      10
                                Total Energy          3000
                                Shields               0
                                Klingons Remaining    13
_____

Command? lrs

Long Range Scan for Quadrant 1, 6

_____
: *** : *** : *** :
_____
: 003 : 004 : 004 :
_____
: 008 : 008 : 001 :
_____
Command?
```

The main display of a version of Robert Leedom's 1974 *Super Star Trek*, as published in David Ahl's 1978 book BASIC *Computer Games*.

Web Link

- *Super Star Trek* Tribute Site: http://almy.us/sst.html

SUPREME COMMANDER

2007. Gas Powered Games (GPG). Designed by Chris Taylor.

Supreme Commander is an **RTS** game, much influenced by Chris Taylor's earlier *Total Annihilation* (*1997* CE). As in that game, the availability of resources at any point on the battlefield and the wide range of air, sea, and land units promote a flexible, open style of combat in which opponents are constantly attempting to outmaneuver each other with novel strategies. *Supreme Commander* is set in the thirty-seventh century, during a civil war in a human galactic empire. None of the various factions is clearly morally superior to the others. Instead, each has its own justification for war: the reunification of the remnants of the Earth Federation, a crusade to spread an alien-derived pacifist philosophy by force, and the desire for freedom of an enslaved group who have cybernetically augmented their minds. Participants can choose any of these factions and play through the last days of the war or fight other players online.

Supreme Commander is interesting both for the enormous scale of its battlefields and the realism with which it deploys many of the conventions of the **RTS** form. Engagements begin when the eponymous unit, a human-piloted bipedal **mecha**, arrives on the battlefield through a **wormhole** that allows **faster-than-light** travel. This unit can then construct a variety of combat and support robots using **nanotechnology**, expending energy and mass resources obtained by such means as drilling geothermal boreholes and salvaging destroyed enemy equipment. As an industrial military complex is built up, more advanced units can be assembled, ranging from amphibious naval destroyers that walk on land to mobile factories. The size of the maps makes it a more truly strategic game than its predecessors, which have generally concentrated on tactical warfare with interpolated strategic elements. The large numbers of units under the player's control are made manageable by the inclusion of a high degree of automation in the interface, enabling such actions as automatically coordinated attacks and programmed transport of units to the front line. Perhaps the most intriguing aspect of the game, however, is the way in which the scale of the maps used will abruptly expand during a mission, forcing the player to make rapid mental readjustments as their understanding of the local situation is repeatedly transformed.

Related works: *Supreme Commander: Forged Alliance* (*2007* GPG) designed by Bradley Rebh and Chris Taylor is an expansion to the first game that can be played alone. It adds various enhancements to the gameplay of the original, including orbital bombardment weapons, to support a story line that focuses on the return of the aliens who inspired the aggressively pacifist principles of one of the groups seen in *Supreme Commander*. This race, who were thought to have been exterminated by the genocidal Earth Federation but had instead retreated to a quantum sea underlying the physical universe, devastate the various splintered factions of humanity, whose survivors unite against them. The player, in the role of a soldier for one of the original three groups, must help resist the invasion.

Supreme Commander 2 (*2010* GPG) designed by Chris Taylor is a sequel to the original game, set after the coalition formed in *Forged Alliance* has broken up, leading to a resumption of the universal war. Games of *Supreme Commander 2* are similar to those of its predecessor, but faster paced and arguably simpler. The *Infinite War Battle Pack* (*2011* GPG) is an expansion that adds new locations and combat units for competitive play.

SYNDICATE

1993. Bullfrog Productions (BP). Designed by Peter Molyneux and Sean Cooper.

Syndicate is an early example of a **real-time tactics** game, played in a **3D isometric** view and set in a milieu that emphasizes the moral ambiguity of much **cyberpunk** fiction. Players adopt the role of an executive in one of the crime syndicates that have taken over the world's ruling corporations, tasked with advancing their employer's interests by assassinating rivals, acquiring the services of prominent scientists, and any other means that may prove necessary. *Syndicate*'s future world is polluted and violent; most of the population have been implanted with mind control devices, turning them into compliant drones living in a virtual paradise. The player's instrument for completing their various tasks is a team of four drug-controlled **cyborgs**, kept in **cryogenic** vaults between excursions. These missions take place in complex environments, many aspects of which are destructible or usable by the player; another important aspect of the game is the need to perform technological research and upgrade cyborgs between assignments in order to keep up with the competition. *Syndicate*'s gameplay is ruthlessly amoral; there are no penalties for killing civilians, but no attempt is made to excuse such actions or to persuade the player that their role is anything other than that of a brutal enforcer.

The immediate sequel, *Syndicate Wars* (*1996* BP) designed by Peter Molyneux, combines a fully 3D view with similar gameplay to its predecessor to tell the story of a conflict between the world's ruling syndicate and a religious upstart. This latter organization, the Church of the New Epoch, is using a computer virus that disables mind control chips in an attempt to take the syndicate's place as master of the world, a process that causes large numbers of citizens to become "unguided"; players can take the role of a syndicate executive or one of the church's disciples. *Syndicate Wars* has a more complex narrative than that of its original, but the gameplay can be slightly confusing, with challenges that seem less well crafted than those of the first game. A late addition to the franchise, *Syndicate* (*2012* Starbreeze Studios) designed by Andrew Griffin and written by Tommy Tordsson in collaboration with the sf writer Richard Morgan, was created by other hands that rephrased the series' gameplay as that of an **FPS** with a **linear interactive narrative**. While the game is visually appealing and much of its shooting is exciting if unusually bloody, the story is predictable, blighted by an unsuccessful attempt to add a moral dimension to its cynical milieu.

The world of the *Syndicate* series is suggestive of a range of influences, from Ridley Scott's *Blade Runner* (*1982*) to the brutal future megalopolis of Mega City One that made frequent appearances in contemporary issues of the UK anthology comic *2000 AD*. Nevertheless, it is a credible creation in its own right, entirely convincing as a work of sf.

Related works: *Syndicate: American Revolt* (*1993* BP) is a (significantly more difficult) expansion for the original *Syndicate*. It sets the player the ironic task of suppressing a new American rebellion against the syndicate that achieved world domination during the first game, assumed to be based in London.

Web Links

- *Syndicate* (*2012*): http://www.ea.com/syndicate/

- *Syndicate* Tribute Site: http://syndicate.lubie.org/

TOTAL ANNIHILATION

1997. Cavedog Entertainment (CE). Designed by Chris Taylor.

Total Annihilation is an **RTS** game, noted for its innovative design. It introduced many new features to the gameplay seen in such previous **RTS** games as *Command & Conquer* (*1995* WS), including **3D** landscapes with lines of fire affected by terrain elevation and the ability of combatants to take cover behind destructible features. As is typical for members of the RTS form, the player acts as commander of a small military force, controlling combat and support units such as tanks and repair robots. The game includes an unusually wide range of air, sea, and land units, though the different rosters available to the two sides have broadly **symmetric** characteristics. Players need to draw upon two fundamental resources, metal and energy, to construct their forces. These resources are available anywhere on a battlefield, though easier to obtain in some places than others, a design that often leads to long games featuring constant conflict and sudden reversals of fortune.

The game's setting is appropriately nihilistic. In the distant future, a galactic civilization has split into the Core, who wish to enforce human immortality by **uploading**, and the Arm, who insist on retaining their organic bodies. After centuries of war between replicated minds inhabiting robot bodies and cloned warriors using high-technology armor, both sides are almost exhausted, feuding over the remains of a ruined galaxy. The single-player game is set during the last days of the war and is playable from the perspective of either the Core or the Arm. Story development is somewhat thin, however, and the computer-controlled opponents are not very challenging. As a result, *Total Annihilation* is most popular as a game of player-versus-player combat in temporary **online worlds**, where it has been highly successful.

Related works: *Total Annihilation: The Core Contingency* (*1998* CE) designed by Chris Taylor is an expansion pack that continues the Arm version of the story beyond the end of the first game, in which an apparent victory is achieved. Many new units and maps are included for multiplayer games. The less well-received *Total Annihilation: Battle Tactics* (*1998* CE) designed by Chris Taylor is another expansion pack, focusing on predesigned battles rather than the more open scenarios of the original game.

WARHAMMER 40,000

Franchise (from 1992). Games Workshop (GW).

While most tabletop **wargames** have failed to compete against **videogames**, GW's fantasy game *Warhammer Fantasy Battle* (*1983* GW; revised *1984*; revised *1987*; revised *1992*; revised *1996*; revised *2000*; revised *2006*; revised *2010*) designed by Bryan Ansell, Richard Halliwell, and Rick Priestley and its sf descendant *Warhammer 40,000* (*1987* GW; revised *1993*; revised *1998*; revised *2004*; revised *2008*; revised *2012*) designed by Rick Priestley have proved remarkably successful. An important reason for their survival has been their use of customizable miniature figures for game pieces, from which players are encouraged to design their own personal armies. Another widely acknowledged virtue of *Warhammer 40,000* is its detailed and atmospheric background, though the sense of existential damnation associated with the game does on occasion mutate into an essentially juvenile obsession with war and destruction. *Warhammer 40,000* is set in the forty-first millennium, when a pseudomedieval human empire rules most of the galaxy. This milieu is a classic example of **medieval futurism**, often suggestive of the setting of Frank Herbert's novel *Dune* (**1965**), especially in its depiction of science and technology as being essentially mystical in nature. The Imperium shares the stars with a variety of generally hostile alien races, many of them based on fantasy archetypes, including Chaos Gods (psychic entities formed from the coagulation of the sentient races' worst desires within the Warp, an alternate space that allows for **faster-than-light** travel), the Eldar (the remnants of a sophisticated, declining older race), and the Tyranids (extragalactic predators intent on absorbing all life into their biological unity). Among humanity's armies are the Space Marines, biologically enhanced superhumans who wear **powered armor**, and the Inquisitors, **psionic** defenders of the Imperial religion. The universe depicted in the game is essentially malevolent; reality itself has been corrupted by Chaos, and war is omnipresent. Strong religious and transcendental themes appear throughout, adding a sense of sacrificial redemption to the essential brutality of the game's setting.

Various **videogames** exist for the milieu. The first to be released was *Space Crusade* (*1992* Gremlin Graphics), a direct conversion of the *Warhammer 40,000* spin-off board game *Space Crusade* (*1990* GW/ Milton Bradley) designed by Stephen Baker. Next came the well-received *Space Hulk* (*1993* EA) designed by Nicholas Wilson, Kevin Shrapnell, and Andrew Jones and its sequel *Space Hulk: Vengeance of the Blood Angels* (*1995* Key Game) designed by Nicholas Wilson, two **real-time** games that combine **FPS** and **computer wargame** elements. Similarly to *Space Crusade*, these works are loosely based on the wargame *Space Hulk* (*1989* GW; revised *1996*; revised *2009*) designed by Richard Halliwell, which deals with Space Marines investigating derelict spacecraft inhabited by aggressive aliens. The next three games in the franchise were all **turn-based** computer wargames, beginning with *Final Liberation* (*1997* Holistic Design) designed by Andrew Greenberg and Ken Lightner, derived from the *Epic 40,000* rules (*1988* GW; revised *1994*; revised *1997*; *2003* revised as *Epic Armageddon*) designed by Jervis Johnson, Rick Priestley, and Andy Chambers (a more strategic version of *Warhammer 40,000* that operates on a larger scale). This game was followed by *Chaos Gate* (*1998* Random Games) designed by Steven Clayton, which combines an involving **linear** story line with well-crafted small unit tactics, and *Rites of War* (*1999* DreamForge Entertainment) designed by John McGirk, Brian Urbanek, and Vernon Harmon, a game of strategy in which the player must lead the alien Eldar to victory over human Space Marines and a Tyranid "hive fleet." The next license to be released, however, was an FPS, *Fire Warrior* (*2003* Kuju Entertainment) designed by David Millard, a notably atmospheric work with somewhat conventional gameplay in which the player takes the role of a member of another alien race, the Tau.

The most commercially successful of the videogames to date, however, has been *Warhammer 40,000: Dawn of War* (*2004* RE), an excellently crafted **RTS** game with innovative systems for handling groups of units and morale and an interesting linear story line that follows the struggle between a chapter of Space Marines and the corrupting forces of Chaos. This game has received three expansions: *Winter Assault* (*2005* RE), *Dark Crusade* (*2006* RE), and *Soulstorm* (*2008* Iron Lore Entertainment).

The sequel, *Warhammer 40,000: Dawn of War II* (*2009* RE), blends elements drawn from turn-based computer wargames with the original's mechanics. Players can engage in competitive or cooperative online play or adopt the role of a Space Marine commander and attempt to cleanse an Imperial subsector of alien infestation. In the latter mode, strategic decisions are made turn by turn on planetary and galactic maps, triggering limited conflicts that are fought in real time. The overall impression is of a more credible simulation than the original and one that is more readily classifiable as a **real-time tactics** game than an RTS one. *Chaos Rising* (*2010* RE) and *Retribution* (*2011* RE) are expansions for *Dawn of War II* that extend its narrative. While the *Dawn of War* games concentrate on relatively complex strategic gameplay, the other recent videogame in the franchise, *Space Marine* (*2011* RE) designed by Raphael van Lierop, is notable for going to the opposite extreme. This is an action game resembling a **third-person shooter** but one that could perhaps more aptly be described as a third-person slasher; the player's character must hack their way through seemingly endless hordes of inhuman opponents.

Related works: *Squad Command* (*2007* RedLynx) designed by Leo Kihlman is a turn-based computer wargame somewhat resembling *Chaos Gate*. *Glory In Death* (*2006* Razorback Developments) is similar to *Squad Command*, while *Kill Team* (*2011* THQ) is an action game in which a group of Space Marines must fight off an invading force of brutish Orks. Recent works for mobile devices based on the *Space Hulk* board game include the action game *Warhammer: Space Hulk* (*2005* Mnemonic Studios) and the turn-based *Space Hulk* (*2013* Full Control), which received mixed reviews.

A large number of tabletop games associated with the original wargame have been published. Among the most notable are *Necromunda* (*1995* GW) designed by Rick Priestley, Andy Chambers, and Jervis Johnson, which depicts skirmishes between rival gangs in the abandoned levels beneath a giant **arcology**, and *Battlefleet Gothic* (*1999* GW; revised *2007*) designed by Andy Chambers, a space combat game whose mechanics seem much influenced by historic forms of naval warfare. In addition, several **collectible card games** have been published for the milieu by Sabretooth Games (SG), of which the best known is perhaps *Dark Millennium* (*2005* SG) designed by Luke Peterschmidt and Ryan Miller. The *Warhammer 40,000* universe has also proved to be a fertile source of inspiration for pen and paper **RPG** designers. The first such work, *Inquisitor* (*2001* GW) designed by

Gavin Thorpe, is a mixture of miniatures-based wargame and **RPG** in which players investigate threats to the Imperium. The later *Dark Heresy* (*2008* GW) designed by Owen Barnes, Kate Flack, and Mike Mason also concentrates on the psionic Inquisitors, who defend humanity against enemies both internal and external, but is structured as a more conventional RPG that focuses on investigations of occult conspiracies. *Dark Heresy* proved sufficiently popular to inspire the creation of various sequels, including *Rogue Trader* (*2009* FFG) designed by Michael Hurley and Ross Watson, *Deathwatch* (*2010* FFG) designed by Ross Watson, *Black Crusade* (*2011* FFG) designed by Sam Stewart and Ross Watson, and *Only War* (*2013* FFG) designed by Andrew Fischer.

Over a hundred *Warhammer 40,000* novels have been written by a variety of authors. Perhaps the best evocations of the milieu can be found in four books by Ian Watson: *Space Marine* (**1993**) and the *Inquisition War* trilogy, consisting of *Inquisitor* (**1990**; also known as *Draco*)—the first novel **tied** to the franchise to reach print—*Harlequin* (**1994**), and *Chaos Child* (**1995**). Many other novels in the various associated series do, however, display a rather relentless militarism. Short stories set in the game's universe appeared in *Inferno!* magazine (*1997–2004*) and can now be found in the online publication *Hammer and Bolter* (*2010*–current), while the *Warhammer Monthly* anthology (*1998–2004*) printed associated comic strips. GW has also published a number of art books, each of which contains paintings and additional background information. Among the most memorable are *Inquis Exterminatus* (**2000**), *Insignium Astartes* (**2002**), *The Horus Heresy* (**2004–2006**), *Xenology* (**2006**), and *The Imperial Infantryman's Uplifting Primer* (**2003**), dealing, respectively, with the Inquisition, Space Marine regalia, the origins of the Imperium, non-human intelligences, and the Imperial army.

Web Link
- *Warhammer 40,000: Dawn of War*: http://www.dawnofwargame.com/

X-COM

Series (from 1994). Mythos Games (MG). Designed by Julian Gollop.

UFO: Enemy Unknown (*1994* MG; also known as *X-COM: UFO Defense* in the United States) designed by Julian Gollop, the first X-COM game, puts a single player in the position of leading Earth's defense against marauding aliens. This background is clearly influenced by the UK TV series *UFO* (*1970–1971*) and probably also by 1970s episodes of *Doctor*

Who featuring UNIT, the United Nations Intelligence Taskforce. (X-COM is a similar abbreviation to UNIT, standing for Extraterrestrial Combat Unit.) Much of the game's flavor comes from its use of genuine UFO folklore, such as the appearance of small, big-headed "grays" (referred to as Sectoids within the game) and the significance attributed to the transuranic "Element 115." *UFO: Enemy Unknown* is played in two modes: the **real-time** Geoscape, in which players can manage their worldwide network of secret bases, perform research on captured aliens, and intercept UFOs, and the **isometric turn-based** Battlescape, where teams of X-COM operatives investigate downed alien spacecraft or fight off terror attacks on Earth's cities and ground assaults on X-COM bases. Much of the game's fascination originates in the fear and doubt that haunt the player in the Battlescape, as they move a small team of soldiers through an unexplored landscape occupied by aliens of unknown species and uncertain abilities. As the game progresses, players are able to learn more about the aliens by dissecting captured specimens and salvaging their technology, but they must still fear the future and the unpredictable new threats it conceals.

X-COM: Terror from the Deep (1995 MicroProse) designed by Paul Hibbard and Pete Morland is the immediate sequel to the first game, written by a different team while the original designers worked on a more innovative successor. Time constraints meant that *Terror from the Deep* was essentially a slightly improved version of the original work transferred to an underwater setting, with the defeated Sectoids replaced by the Aquatoids (relatives who had been living deep in Earth's oceans for millions of years), UFOs by unidentified submersible objects (USOs), and so on. Rather than the UFO legends used in the first game, *Terror from the Deep* invokes H P Lovecraft's **Cthulhu Mythos**. The resulting game plays well, though there are moments when the time pressures show; for example, X-COM soldiers cannot swim above the ocean floor without researching special technology, a restriction that matches the development and use of flying armor in *UFO: Enemy Unknown*. The next installment, *X-COM: Apocalypse* (1997 MG) designed by Julian Gollop, was intended to be a major development of the franchise. It is set in a domed city, under attack by aliens from another dimension (unrelated to the various species appearing in the first two games). This allowed for a greater variety of Battlescape mission types and for the introduction of multiple competing organizations that might cooperate with X-COM or oppose it depending on the player's actions. Arguably, not all of these features were implemented ideally in the final work, but it remains a novel and interesting piece of game design. In any case, it failed to sell as well as *Terror from the Deep*; the next few games in the series were spin-offs, some of which had little in common with the original game other than its name.

The franchise, long dormant after the commercial failure of the somewhat generic action game *X-COM: Enforcer* (*2001*), was revived with the release of *XCOM: Enemy Unknown* (*2012* FG) designed by Jacob Solomon and Ananda Gupta, a reimagining of the original *Enemy Unknown*. While Firaxis' game is also an isometric turn-based design, two decades of evolution in computer technology allowed it to offer a greatly improved visual representation of the series' core tropes. The aliens of *XCOM: Enemy Unknown* are essentially the same as those of *UFO: Enemy Unknown*, but the superiority of their graphic portrayal in the later game makes them seem far more threatening and more truly Other. These new technical affordances are also used to interleave brief cinematic sequences into the battles on the ground, fostering the appearance of **emergent** narrative as players increasingly come to identify with their chosen soldiers and tell their own stories of desperate victory and grueling defeat. The milieu of the new *Enemy Unknown* is a place of alien autopsies, **psionic** transcendence, black technologies, and secret wars, a vividly drawn world born from Gerry Anderson's *UFO* and the paranoia engendered by the USAF's Project Blue Book but one that is still uniquely itself.

Related works: *The Bureau: XCOM Declassified* (*2013* 2K Marin) designed by Morgan Gray and Zak McClendon is the latest spin-off from the main franchise, set in what appears to be an **alternate history** of its milieu, in which a similar group of aliens to those encountered in *UFO: Enemy Unknown* invade America in the 1960s. Where the original game drew upon British TV of the 1970s for its inspiration, this work seems more evocative of the US series *The X-Files* (*1993–2002*) and *Dark Skies* (*1996–1997*), as well as of the alien invasion movies of the 1950s. *The Bureau* was also the product of a prolonged development process that involved work done by three different studios on several versions of the concept over a 7-year period; arguably, the final game still shows signs of this troubled gestation. Its gameplay is reasonably effective, blending the design of a **third-person shooter** with that of a **CRPG**; players can choose between real-time and effectively turn-based approaches to combat, as in many modern **CRPGs**. However, while the 1960s setting is highly atmospheric, it never seems to quite make sense, being undermined both by a scattering of unfortunate anachronisms and the contrived interpolation of elements taken from earlier games in the series. Despite an interesting reversal in the game's **linear** plot and a variety of **multilinear** endings, *The Bureau*'s narrative ultimately seems less convincing than its gameplay.

X-COM: Interceptor (*1998* MicroProse) designed by Dave Ellis is an earlier spin-off set in the period between *Terror from the Deep* and *Apocalypse*, in interstellar space, where X-COM's task is to defend human mining ships from aggressive aliens. Gameplay is similar to that of the first two games, except that the Battlescape is replaced by a real-time space combat mode in which the player flies an X-COM interceptor against the aliens. *X-COM: em@il Games* (*1999* Hasbro Interactive; also known as *X-COM: First Alien Invasion*) is a two-person **play by e-mail** game based on a (perhaps overly simplified) version of the Battlescape combat seen in *UFO: Enemy Unknown*, while *X-COM: Enforcer* (*2001* MicroProse) is a third-person shooter that concentrates on providing intense (though often quite predictable) action sequences. More recently, the *Elite Soldier Pack* (*2012* FG) and *Slingshot* (*2012* FG) are expansions for *XCOM: Enemy Unknown* that add visual enhancements and several new missions, respectively. *XCOM: Enemy Within* (*2013* FG), however, is a major expansion that transforms the 2012 *Enemy Unknown* by adding the ability to enhance X-COM soldiers into partially alien organisms or **cyborg mecha**. To achieve victory in this variant of the game, the player's operatives must sacrifice their own humanity while fighting not only extraterrestrial invaders but also humans who have covertly allied themselves with the aliens. There is also a spin-off novel for the first game, *X-COM: UFO Defense* (**1995**) by Diane Duane; Duane is clearly writing for X-COM players rather than a general audience.

Web Links

- *XCOM: Enemy Unknown*: http://www.xcom.com/
- Dave Ellis on *X-COM: Interceptor*: http://www.thelastoutpost.co.uk/games/dave-ellis-early-days
- xcomufo (Tribute Site): http://www.xcomufo.com/

CHAPTER 14

4X Games

4X GAMES ARE A form of **videogame** of which the archetypal example is Steve Barcia's *Master of Orion* (*1993* Simtex). The phrase was coined by the journalist and designer Alan Emrich in a preview of that game, as an acronym of sorts for "eXplore, eXpand, eXploit, and eXterminate." This construction is in fact something of a misnomer; while 4X games typically involve players in exploring unknown regions, expanding into them, and exploiting their resources, there is no requirement that anything be exterminated. A more helpful definition might be that a 4X game models the evolution of a developing civilization over many years, simulating complex interactions between the economy, social system, scientific research and trade, diplomacy, and conflict with other (usually computer-controlled) cultures. Players will typically see events unfold on a **2D** map, with additional displays to represent more abstract developments. Such games are generally slow paced and intellectually demanding, with events proceeding turn by turn rather than continuously (in "**real time**"). Victory over other civilizations may be achieved by methods as diverse as military conquest; the achievement of economic, cultural, or political dominance; or (in *Sid Meier's Alpha Centauri* [*1999* Firaxis Games (FG)]) by unifying all the minds on the planet into a single transcendent consciousness.

While *Master of Orion* was the first game to be referred to as 4X, it was not the first of its kind. Precursors include the tabletop **wargames** *Stellar Conquest* (*1974* Metagaming Concepts) designed by Howard Thompson and *Outreach* (*1976* Simulations Publications Inc.) designed by Irad Hardy, as well as the Australian videogame *Reach for the Stars* (*1983* Strategic Studies Group [SSG]) designed by Roger Keating and Ian Trout. The earliest example of the form to become well known in the mass market, however, was *Civilization* (*1991* MicroProse) designed by Sid Meier, in which players can guide the evolution of their chosen civilization from the Bronze Age to the near future, competing with other cultures for territory and knowledge. *Civilization* itself appears to have been influenced by early **god games** as well as by such board games as the French *Risk* (*1957* Miro as *La Conquête du Monde*) designed by Albert Lamorisse and the UK *Civilization* (*1980* Hartland Trefoil) designed by Francis Tresham, which has a similar theme but quite different mechanics to its videogame namesake. A clear line of development can be drawn between *Stellar Conquest* and *Master of Orion*, however, suggesting that the 4X form may have grown from several similar seeds.

Other significant examples of the school include *VGA Planets* (*1992*) designed by Tim Wissemann, the pseudomedieval fantasy game *Master of Magic* (*1994* Simtex) designed by Steve Barcia, and *Galactic Civilizations* (*2003* Stardock) designed by Bradley Wardell. There have also been various sequels to and spin-offs from *Civilization*, including *Colonization* (*1994* MicroProse) designed by Brian Reynolds and Sid Meier—based on the early history of the Americas—*Sid Meier's Alpha Centauri* and the less commercially successful and less well-reviewed *Civilization: Call To Power* (*1999* Activision) designed by Cecilia Barajas, Mark Lamia, and William Westwater, a sequel made by other hands that extends from prehistory into the far future. Meanwhile, the Hungarian game *Imperium Galactica* (*1997* Digital Reality) designed by Gábor Fehér and István Kiss attempted (only partially successfully) to combine 4X gameplay with **real-time strategy** (**RTS**) elements and a **linear** story in which the player is an officer with a hidden past in the military of a future galactic empire.

Most 4X games are science fictional, with the exception of the *Civilization* series, which is science fiction (sf) only in the limited sense that it allows players to generate counterfactual **alternate histories** of Earth's development. Considered as sf, however, the **framing** narratives of otherwise excellently crafted members of the form can lack color and vitality, though this is by no means a universal failing; *Sid Meier's Alpha Centauri* and *Emperor of the Fading Suns* (*1996* Holistic Design [HD]) are both set in richly realized milieux. 4X games are essentially a niche form, but one that remains commercially viable. Recent releases include the **independent game** *Endless Space* (*2012* Amplitude Studios) designed by Romain de Waubert de Genlis and François Kmetty, *Sid Meier's Civilization V* (*2010* FG) designed by Jon Shafer—the fifth installment in the main *Civilization* series—and the Canadian game *Sins of a Solar Empire* (*2008* Ironclad Games), which follows *Imperium Galactica* by borrowing many gameplay elements from the **RTS** school. The form remains of considerable science-fictional interest for the way it enables players to act out the evolution of societies as an **interactive narrative**, a potential that is impressively explored in *Sid Meier's Alpha Centauri*.

Web Link

- The History of Civilization: http://www.gamasutra.com/view/ feature/1523/the_history_of_civilization.php

EMPEROR OF THE FADING SUNS

1996. Holistic Design (HD). Designed by Bill Bridges, Andrew Greenberg, Garner Halloran, Ken Lightner, and Ed Pike.

The *Fading Suns* setting is a Gothic interstellar empire, morally and intellectually decadent, which has reverted to medieval habits of thought. For unknown reasons, the stars are slowly going out. The society depicted is feudal and strongly religious, consciously evocative of Dark Ages Europe; the overall effect is reminiscent of both the tabletop **wargame** *Warhammer 40,000* (*1987* Games Workshop) and of such novels as Frank Herbert's *Dune* (**1965**). Unknown things lurk between the stars, while the Universal Church hunts the **psionically** gifted and creates its own occult miracles. Meanwhile, the noble houses, merchant guilds, and religious orders struggle for influence over the galaxy's Emperor.

In the **videogame**, players compete to become Emperor; success depends on both political maneuvering and strategic combat. The game is interesting for the degree to which the background is woven into the gameplay. It is possible, for example, for the player's noble house to research technologies banned by the Church, though this may attract unwelcome attention. Considered as a work of sf, *Emperor of the Fading Suns* is markedly superior to such predecessors as *Master of Orion* (*1993* Simtex) designed by Steve Barcia, but the balance struck between the abilities of various factions in *Emperor* is sufficiently askew to make it inferior as a game. Nevertheless, it remains one of the most vividly realized works of **medieval futurism** in the videogame form.

Related works: The milieu was developed by Bridges and Greenberg, who had previously worked on the innovative **World of Darkness** line of pen and paper **role-playing games (RPGs)**, and was also used as the basis for the tabletop **RPG** *Fading Suns* (*1996* HD; revised *1999*; revised *2001*) designed by Bill Bridges and Andrew Greenberg. *Passion Play* (*1999* HD) is a **live-action RPG** using the *Fading Suns* setting. *Noble Armada* (*1998* HD; revised *2002*; *2011* revised as *A Call to Arms: Noble Armada*) designed by Chris Wiese and Ken Lightner is a tabletop **wargame** that combines combat between miniature starships with boarding actions. *The Sinful Stars* (**1998**) is an anthology of spin-off fiction edited by Bill Bridges.

GALACTIC CIVILIZATIONS

2003. Stardock. Designed by Bradley Wardell.

Galactic Civilizations is a descendant of Steve Barcia's *Master of Orion* (*1993* Simtex), a **turn-based 4X game** played on a **2D** galactic map. More directly, its design is based on that of an earlier and less well-known version for the IBM PC OS/2 operating system, *Galactic Civilizations* (*1994* Stardock) designed by Bradley Wardell. As in *Master of Orion*, the player expands their civilization into a **space opera** galaxy, colonizing new planets, developing their scientific knowledge, and encountering alien races. In *Galactic Civilizations*, however, the player is always human. The gameplay is sophisticated, featuring a wide range of strategic options as well as a variety of nonhuman species with their own histories and "racial personalities." One interesting aspect is the economic model, which allows players to borrow money from human corporations. Victory is achievable in four ways: by military conquest, by cultural domination of other species, by achieving overwhelming political power, or by reaching a level of technology that allows humanity to transcend to a higher plane of existence.

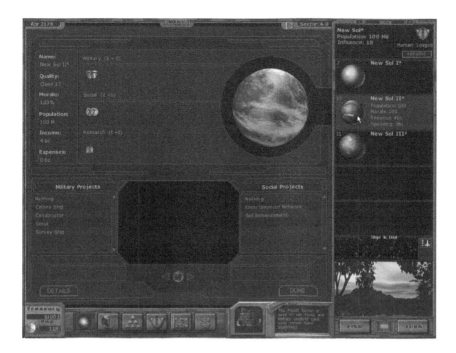

As is typical of **4X games**, most of the player's time in *Galactic Civilizations* is spent manipulating complex interfaces representing abstract concepts. Here, the player is beginning the colonization of a new world.

Galactic Civilizations II: The Dread Lords (*2006* Stardock) designed by Bradley Wardell is a reimagining of the first game, using detailed **3D** graphics displayed on a 2D plane. Additions to the gameplay include the ability to design unique spacecraft and a choice of playable races. The game also includes an optional **linear** story line involving the eponymous Lords, a **forerunner** species who attempted to enslave the galaxy before their mysterious disappearance. *Galactic Civilizations II: Dark Avatar* (*2007* Stardock) designed by Bradley Wardell is an expansion pack, adding new species and a story revolving around a civil war among factions of the imperialist Drengin race.

The well-developed personalities of the computer-controlled opponents in the *Galactic Civilizations* series give the games a strong sense of atmosphere, making playing them more than a purely strategic exercise. Players are often confronted with moral choices, such as the question of whether autochthonous inhabitants of a colonized world should be enslaved, sent to a reservation, or incorporated into the colony's political structure.

The game mechanics are neutral as to which option is superior; brutality may be helpful in the short term but will have diplomatic consequences later. The kind of galactic civilization that the player creates is, ultimately, up to them.

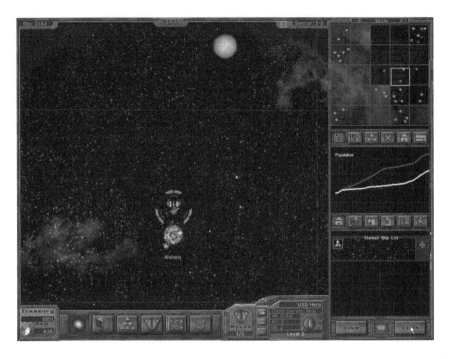

Exploration in *Galactic Civilizations* occurs on a **2D** map of the galaxy.

Related works: *Galactic Civilizations: Altarian Prophecy* (*2004* Stardock) designed by Bradley Wardell is an expansion pack for *Galactic Civilizations*, focusing on the Altarians, an alien species who seem strangely similar to humanity.

Web Links

- *Galactic Civilizations*: http://www.galciv.com/

- *Galactic Civilizations II* Postmortem: http://www.gamasutra.com/features/20060405/wardell_01.shtml

- Interview with Bradley Wardell: http://www.gamasutra.com/php-bin/news_index.php?story=14842

MASTER OF ORION

1993. Simtex. Designed by Steve Barcia.

Master of Orion is perhaps the best known of all **2D** space-based **4X games**, with gameplay that is a development of that seen in such earlier works as *Reach for the Stars* (*1983* SSG) designed by Roger Keating and Ian Trout. The central conceit is that a number of species are simultaneously beginning to expand into interstellar space, where they will colonize alien worlds, negotiate and trade with each other, develop advanced sciences, and fight for dominance. Participants begin the game by selecting a race to play; each species has its own unique strengths and, when not chosen by the player, its own strategy for success. Many races also have built-in attitudes toward other species, adding flavor to the game's diplomatic aspects. *Master of Orion* is a deep, cerebral game that offers players a wide range of options, from espionage to planetary assault to designing ever more advanced spacecraft with which to win the inevitable arms race. Typically, a final victory is gained when one race either defeats the others militarily or achieves political domination of the galaxy.

In the first game, Orion is the original solar system of a vanished **forerunner** race, possibly responsible for the **uplift** of the younger species; a common path to victory is to gain control of the titular star and make use of the ancient technologies found there. The next installment, *Master of Orion II: Battle at Antares* (*1996* Simtex) designed by Steve Barcia, presents a reimagining of this scenario. In this version, the Antarans, a species defeated and imprisoned by the Orions in the distant past, have begun to escape from their confinement. Players must compete with both the other new races and the Antarans; victory can be achieved either by conquest of all the younger civilizations or by defeating the elder race, thus awing the other species into submission. This game added a number of new features to the design of its predecessor, including the ability to add player-designed races and the option of competing against other humans online.

Master of Orion III (*2003* Quicksilver Software) is a direct sequel to *Master of Orion II*, based on the premise that the Antarans ultimately conquered the galaxy. The game is set a thousand years later, after most of the Antarans have mysteriously disappeared and the remainder have established themselves as the "New Orions," ruling the galaxy in the place of their former enemies; players select one of the subordinate races and attempt to take power from the Antarans. *Master of Orion III*'s gameplay is notable for involving far more detailed management of the player's empire than previous games in the series. The interface included a high degree of automation in a not entirely successful attempt to make this enjoyable; the game was released to generally mixed reviews.

Ultimately, the *Master of Orion* series sets the template for 4X games in space, but suffered from the relative weakness of its fiction compared to such later works as *Galactic Civilizations* (*2003* Stardock) designed by Bradley Wardell. Despite their historical significance, the games are little played today.

Related works: *Star Lords* (*1992* Simtex) designed by Steve Barcia is the original prototype for *Master of Orion*, made available for free download in 2001.

Web Links

• *Master of Orion III*: http://moo3.quicksilver.com/

• *Star Lords* download: http://moo3.quicksilver.com/game/starlords.html

REACH FOR THE STARS

1983. Strategic Studies Group (SSG). Designed by Roger Keating and Ian Trout.

Reach for the Stars is essentially a skillfully implemented conversion of Howard Thompson's board and counter game *Stellar Conquest* (*1974* Metagaming Concepts) to a form suitable for home computers. As such, it is the most important link between that seminal **wargame** and *Master of Orion* (*1993* Simtex) designed by Steve Barcia, the first work to be described as a **4X game**. Like *Stellar Conquest*, *Reach for the Stars* is a **turn-based** game that is entirely concerned with the strategy, as opposed to the tactics, of interstellar conquest. Unlike such earlier "space empire" **videogames** as *Galactic Empire* (*1979* Brøderbund Software) designed by Douglas Carlston and *Andromeda Conquest* (*1982* Avalon Hill) designed by David Peterson, this game allows players to develop the technology of their empire and effectively manage its economy as they expand out into space. While both the gameplay and the graphics are much simpler than those of such successors as *Master of Orion*, all the elements characteristic of 4X game design are present in *Reach for the Stars*.

Related works: *Reach for the Stars* (*2000* SSG) designed by Roger Keating and Ian Trout is an updated version of the original, which suffered from an unfortunate lack of sophistication compared to such contemporary examples of the form as *Master of Orion II: Battle at Antares* (*1996* Simtex) designed by Steve Barcia and *Sid Meier's Alpha Centauri* (*1999* FG) designed by Brian Reynolds and Sid Meier.

SID MEIER'S ALPHA CENTAURI

1999. Firaxis Games (FG). Designed by Brian Reynolds and Sid Meier.

Alpha Centauri is a **4X game** based on an attempt to colonize the eponymous solar system, with a design much influenced by that of the designers' *Civilization* series of historical games, particularly *Sid Meier's Civilization II* (*1996* MicroProse) designed by Brian Reynolds, Douglas Caspian-Kaufman, and Jeff Briggs (to which the 1999 game is an unofficial sequel). In *Civilization II*, the player guides their chosen culture through all of human history, achieving victory by various alternative means including destroying all other civilizations and dispatching a starship to our nearest neighbor in interstellar space, the Alpha Centauri star system. The game of *Alpha Centauri* begins with a **sublight** colonization expedition arriving in the titular solar system, after escaping from an Earth destroying itself through war and overpopulation. However, a mutiny occurs on board as the ship approaches its destination; seven different factions escape from the disintegrating vessel and succeed in landing on the planet's surface. The player adopts the role of the leader of one of these groups, with the aim of shaping humanity's future in accordance with the beliefs of their chosen faction.

Gameplay revolves around exploring and settling the planet, making use of its resources, researching improvements in science and technology, and trading, negotiating, and fighting with the other factions. Throughout the game, players also have to deal with attacks by **psionically** active native life; eventually, it emerges that the planet itself is a sentient **hive mind** that is resisting the human intrusion, an idea that may have been suggested by Harry Harrison's sf novel *Deathworld* (**1960**). A victory can be won by military conquest, by the achievement of economic dominance or diplomatic supremacy, or by triggering a worldwide transcendence. This last condition is satisfied by unifying human consciousness with the planetary mind, creating a global **posthuman** mentality. The need to balance many conflicting priorities and the wide selection of choices available to the player make *Alpha Centauri*'s gameplay a richly varied experience.

The true source of the game's fascination, however, may lie in the nature of its factions. Each expresses a different aspect of humanity, from military honor to enthusiastic capitalism to ecological pacifism. Thus, the player's choice of role represents a decision to adopt a particular persona within the game. That character is not fixed, however. As the game evolves, players often find that tactical necessities encourage them to take actions that change the nature of their chosen society, an evolution that is made personal by the game's use of miniature stories to illustrate the consequences of such decisions. So a player leading a peaceful ecological group being attacked by an aggressive capitalist faction might choose to use brutal mind control technologies to govern the population of a conquered enemy base and discover that the price of victory is becoming something they despise. *Alpha Centauri*'s fictional universe is informationally dense and cleverly constructed, with many subtle details and a rich science-fictional ambience somewhat reminiscent of Frank Herbert's world of **Dune**. The game itself is one of the most accomplished examples of **emergent** narrative in **videogames** to date.

Related works: *Sid Meier's Alien Crossfire* (*1999* FG) is an expansion pack that makes another seven factions available to the player, including two groups belonging to an alien race, which have taken different sides in a civil war. *GURPS Alpha Centauri* (*2003* Steve Jackson Games [SJG]) designed by Jon Zeigler is a sourcebook for the *GURPS* (*1986* SJG) tabletop **RPG**, which details the milieu. *Centauri Dawn* (**2000**), *Dragon Sun* (**2001**), and *Twilight of the Mind* (**2002**), all by the game's story developer, Michael Ely, are spin-off novels. Each focuses on one of the common conflicts that develop during gameplay, between such pairings as militarists and peacekeepers or religious believers and scientists. *Alpha Centauri: Power of the Mind Worms* (*2000*) is a graphic novel written by Steve Darnell, describing the first attempts to make psionic contact with the eponymous creatures. "Journey to Centauri" (1999) and "Centauri: Arrival" (1999), both by Michael Ely, are episodic short stories written to promote the game's initial release and published on the web.

Web Link
- *GURPS Alpha Centauri*: http://www.sjgames.com/gurps/books/alphacentauri/

VGA PLANETS

1992. Designed by Tim Wissemann.

VGA Planets is a game of galactic domination displayed on a **2D** map, broadly similar to its near contemporary *Master of Orion* (*1993* Simtex) designed by Steve Barcia. ("VGA" refers to a type of graphics hardware; its use in early versions made the game more visually appealing than some of its competitors.) After receiving mixed reviews on its initial release, *VGA Planets* became one of the earliest commercially successful **independent games**. The current version is **played by e-mail**; orders for a turn are created by every player in a game and sent to a central machine, which determines the results. As is conventional for this type of game, each player adopts the role of an entire civilization. One probable reason for the popularity of *VGA Planets* is its selection of playable races, many of which are based on well-known alien species and galactic empires from mass media sf, including *Battlestar Galactica*'s Cylons, *Star Trek*'s Romulans, and *Star Wars*' Empire. Each race has strengths and weaknesses appropriate to its model, allowing players to pit their favorite heroes and villains from different franchises against each other.

Web Link

- *VGA Planets*: http://www.planets4.com/

CHAPTER 15

God Games

G OD GAMES ARE A form of **videogame** in which the player has the powers of an actual or metaphorical god, as well as some of the limitations attributed to such entities by deist religions. The term itself appears to have been coined by Bob Wade of *ACE* magazine to describe Peter Molyneux's seminal *Populous* (*1989* Bullfrog Productions [BP]). A god game will typically contain a simulation of a world, a nation, or (more prosaically) a business, inhabited by mortals (or employees) conducting their own independent lives. The player is given specific powers—for example, the ability to cause divine earthquakes or to increase salaries—with which they can manipulate the scenario, and goals to achieve. In contrast to the similar **4X game** form, the player's abilities will generally not include the power to order their mortals to do whatever is necessary; instead, success must be achieved indirectly, by influencing the behavior of the simulated population. Another related form is that of the social simulation in which no goals are specified, making it more of a toy than a game; these works are considered in the section on **toy games**. Many members of the god game school can also be categorized as "construction and management simulations," a generic term used to denote games dealing with the simulation of business activities in the modern world. The god game proper, however, has historically been dominated by works created by developers associated with the UK designer Peter Molyneux, many of which are fantasy.

Several early videogames could be regarded as precursors of the god game form, including *The Sumer Game* (*1968*; *1973* revised as *Hamurabi*) designed by Doug Dyment, a text-based simulation of life in ancient Mesopotamia, and *Utopia* (*1981* Mattel Electronics) designed by Don Daglow, in which two players compete to build a better society on their own island than their opponent can on theirs. Science-fictional descendants of *The Sumer Game* include *Lost Colony* (*1981* Acorn Software) designed by David Feitelberg, in which the player must ensure the survival of a newly abandoned extraterrestrial colony. The first clear example of the god game form, however, is *Populous*, in which the player is a literal god, whose goal is to cause their worshippers to go forth and multiply faster than those of their computer-controlled opponent. As is conventional for games of this type, the player views events from a distant, elevated perspective. Other significant examples include *Theme Park* (*1994* BP) designed by Peter Molyneux and Demis Hassabis, in which participants must manage an amusement park; *Dungeon Keeper* (*1997* BP) designed by Peter Molyneux, where the player is the Dark Lord of a fantasy dungeon closely resembling those seen in early tabletop **role-playing games (RPGs)**; and *Black & White* (*2001* Lionhead) designed by Peter Molyneux. *Black & White* is one of the more impressive games in the form to date; the player, in the role of a god, must attempt to convert ordinary villagers into worshippers, but can choose to be good, evil, or somewhere in between. Arguably, however, the sequel—*Black & White 2* (*2005* Lionhead) designed by Peter Molyneux and Ronald Millar—offers a more playable approach to the same concept. Among the rare science fiction (sf) examples are the UK-created *Startopia* (*2001* Mucky Foot Productions) and *Evil Genius* (*2004* Elixir Studios) designed by Demis Hassabis and Sandro Sammarco, as well as the less-well-received US game *Outpost* (*1994* Sierra On-Line) designed by Bruce Balfour, in which the player must manage the colonization of a new world after the destruction of Earth. While god games are relatively uncommon, the form remains commercially and artistically significant, a point amply demonstrated by both Will Wright's recent *Spore* (*2008* Maxis) and Molyneux's own upcoming *Godus*.

```
TRY YOUR HAND AT GOVERNING ANCIENT SUMERIA
SUCCESSFULLY FOR A 10-YR TERM OF OFFICE.

HAMURABI:  I BEG TO REPORT TO YOU,

IN YEAR 1, 0 PEOPLE STARVED, 5 CAME TO THE CITY.
POPULATION IS NOW 100.
THE CITY NOW OWNS 1000 ACRES.
YOU HARVESTED 3 BUSHELS PER ACRE.
RATS ATE 200 BUSHELS.
YOU NOW HAVE 2800 BUSHELS IN STORE.

LAND IS TRADING AT 17 BUSHELS PER ACRE.
HOW MANY ACRES DO YOU WISH TO BUY 10
HOW MANY BUSHELS DO YOU WISH TO FEED YOUR PEOPLE 2000
HOW MANY ACRES DO YOU WISH TO PLANT WITH SEED 200


HAMURABI:  I BEG TO REPORT TO YOU,

IN YEAR 2, 0 PEOPLE STARVED, 10 CAME TO THE CITY.
POPULATION IS NOW 110.
THE CITY NOW OWNS 1010 ACRES.
YOU HARVESTED 5 BUSHELS PER ACRE.
RATS ATE 0 BUSHELS.
YOU NOW HAVE 3530 BUSHELS IN STORE.

LAND IS TRADING AT 22 BUSHELS PER ACRE.
HOW MANY ACRES DO YOU WISH TO BUY
```

Hamurabi, the version of *The Sumer Game* printed in David Ahl's 1973 book *101 BASIC Computer Games*, was the first social simulation game to become widely available.

EVIL GENIUS

2004. Elixir Studios. Designed by Demis Hassabis and Sandro Sammarco.

The setting of *Evil Genius* serves as a gentle, good-humored parody of such science-fictional "superspy" films and television programs as *Moonraker* (*1979*) and *The Avengers* (*1961–1969*). Within **videogames**, its clearest predecessor is perhaps *Dungeon Keeper* (*1997* BP) designed by Peter Molyneux, in which the player adopts the role of a Dark Lord in a generic fantasy milieu, charged with maintaining a vast underground complex designed to trap and destroy invading adventurers. In *Evil Genius*, the player's part is that of the classic supervillain, a criminal mastermind whose goal is to take over the world. This can be achieved by constructing one of three available superweapons, the activation of which will automatically result in global domination. Reaching this point, however, can be difficult.

The gameplay is divided into two parts. Much of the player's time is spent managing their secret lair, constructing training areas and elaborate traps in an **isometric** view while populating a private island with scientists, diplomats, technicians, and mercenaries. The other half of the game is played on an abstract map of the world, dispatching minions on missions including illicitly acquiring funds, stealing rare resources, and performing "acts of infamy," successful completion of which will increase the player's underworld notoriety and enable them to hire more powerful henchmen. Such activities, however, tend to attract the attention of intelligence agencies, causing them to send operatives to investigate the island. These inconvenient visitors can generally be disposed of by well-designed traps, though these devices do have an unfortunate tendency to eliminate the player's employees as well. In practice, *Evil Genius* is often quite slow to play, but the wide array of superscientific gadgets—from a device that literally washes brains to robots that give instruction in etiquette—make it consistently entertaining to watch.

Evil Genius' characters and situations are ingenious and densely referential. Among its many amusing small parodies are a mission whose goal is to rid the world of country and Western music and an apparently emotionless Russian superspy who can only be defeated by destroying her long-forgotten childhood toys, plunging her into existential despair. The visual style is also strong and highly evocative of the source material. *Evil Genius* can, however, be somewhat frustrating to play. The majority of the player's many minions can only be controlled indirectly—though executing one usually encourages the others—and they occasionally behave in unexpected and unfortunate ways. Nevertheless, the game remains a fine tribute to the megalomaniacal dreams of many a would-be world conqueror and a chance to reverse their unfortunate defeats.

Related works: *Evil Genius: WMD* (*2010* Rebellion) transposes the core concepts of the original game to the Facebook social network, with gameplay much influenced by that of the iconic *FarmVille* (*2009* Zynga).

FATE OF THE WORLD

2011. (Revised *2012* as *Fate of the World: Tipping Point.*) Red Redemption (RR). Designed by Gobion Rowlands and Ian Roberts.

Fate of the World is an **independent game**, created in the United Kingdom, which simulates the effects—physical, economic, and political—of climate change. Its design is essentially that of a **god game**; it resembles such "kingdom simulators" as the prototypal *Hamurabi* (also known as *The Sumer Game*), but with its scope expanded to cover every nation on Earth. Its ancestors include the developers' own far less ambitious precursor *Climate Challenge* (*2006* Red Redemption [RR]), as well as *SimEarth* (*1990* Maxis) designed by Will Wright and—perhaps most significantly—Chris Crawford's little played ecological simulation *Balance of the Planet* (1990). *Fate of the World* positions its player as the leader of a newly created world body, the Global Environmental Organization, which has been empowered to set worldwide policies to guide humanity through the twenty-first and twenty-second centuries. These powers, however, are not absolute; players can only operate in one of the various geopolitical regions into which the planet is divided if they have the broad consent of its population. Gameplay occurs in five-year turns, in each of which limited resources must be spent to play virtual cards enacting regional policies ranging from increased use of nuclear power to ecological awareness programs. Victory is declared when a set of conditions associated with the chosen scenario have been achieved; for example, players might be required to limit any rise in global temperature while maintaining human welfare over the course of a century. Available scenarios include ones that make simplifying assumptions—such as specifying that unlimited reserves of fossil fuels exist or that the global population is universally sympathetic to the player's aims—as well as full simulations. *Fate of the World*'s many options may seem complex, but this is surely necessary if the intricate interrelationships of humanity's global problems are to be convincingly represented.

Among the policies that can be implemented by players are a number of interesting covert options, including the destabilization of overly polluting regimes, the clandestine sterilization of uncooperative populations, and—*in extremis*—the deployment of tailored viruses designed to reduce the planet's population by means of carefully calculated genocide. Over the course of a full game, players are likely to foster a considerable amount of technological development; researchable options include **nanotechnology**, artificial intelligence, **geoengineering**, search for extraterrestrial intelligence (**SETI**), and cold fusion, which (appropriately) does nothing. As this last possibility suggests, a sly (if somewhat dark) sense of humor enlivens much of the game's fiction, most notably in the scenario that tasks the player with destroying as much of the Earth's ecology as possible while retaining the enthusiastic support of its population. It is probably also clear that the later turns of a long session of *Fate of the World* take place in a distinctly science-fictional environment; it is possible (though very difficult) to reach a utopian outcome in which a population whose energy is generated by clean nuclear fusion is made almost immortal by medical **nanomachines** or one in which the colonization of other worlds has begun.

It is, however, true that *Fate of the World* can be a frustrating game to play. Arguably, the desire to create balanced gameplay is here in conflict with the need to make the simulation as accurate as possible, an issue that has often manifested during the development of board and counter **wargames** that depict historical conflicts. More problematic, perhaps, is the opacity of that simulation. While much effort has clearly been spent on clarifying the complex underpinnings of the game's various approaches to modeling reality, comprehending the nature of the many links between cause and effect can still be difficult. As with both *SimEarth* and the sociological simulation *Republic: The Revolution* (*2003* Elixir Studios) designed by Demis Hassabis and Adrian Carless, grasping the totality of the system represented by the game is not an easy task. Notably, some events in *Fate of the World* seem to happen as a result of a prescripted narrative rather than evolving out of the underlying models; thus, continuing research into artificial intelligence will eventually produce a rogue entity that takes control of the global computer network, though this being can be a useful ally. Such occurrences cannot be predicted, making the game essentially impossible to master. It is also clear that, though the climate model included in *Fate of the World* is scientifically credible and physically realistic, its sociological predictions are subject to some debate, while its representations of technologies that might be invented in a hundred years' time are simply fictional. The best approach, perhaps, is not to treat *Fate of the World* as a true simulation of the future, or as an inherently winnable game, but as an experience to be explored. As a demonstration of many of Earth's possible near futures, and as a warning, it demands to be played.

Related works: Two expansions have been created for the game. *Migration* (*2011* RR) adds a new scenario that focuses on mass waves of refugees driven by climate change in the late twenty-first century, while *Denial* (*2011* RR) modifies the simulation to make the climate unchangeable, a variation in which players must still manage limited global resources as the world's population grows.

Web Link
- *Fate of the World*: http://fateoftheworld.net/

SPORE

2008. Maxis. Designed by Will Wright.

The panspermia theory formulated by the Nobel Prize–winning scientist Svante Arrhenius hypothesizes that the life is spread throughout the universe by drifting seeds or spores. The game of *Spore* begins with a single cell, deposited in the ocean of an unknown planet by a convenient meteor; the player's goal is to evolve this organism into an intelligent species capable of building a starfaring civilization. Gameplay is divided into five distinct phases, beginning with a **2D** subgame in which the player must survive in the primordial soup, eating and avoiding being eaten. Food can be either other creatures or vegetable matter, depending on whether the player has chosen to adopt an herbivorous or carnivorous nature. The process of evolution is mimicked by the acquisition of body parts that can be combined with the creature's existing form, using a remarkably sophisticated and powerful software tool. At the end of this phase, the player's creation emerges from the oceans and moves on to dry land. There, it participates in a similar **3D** subgame in which it can either prey on others or attempt to ally with them, with the eventual goal of evolving a brain. Once this stage is complete, the physical form of the species is fixed, and it moves through phases representing tribal and technological civilizations, both of which resemble simple 3D **real-time strategy** games. Again, it is possible to either cooperate with other cultures (the herbivore's approach) or conquer them (the carnivore's preference). These phases end with the (peaceful or otherwise) unification of the entire planet under the aegis of the player's civilization. The fifth, and final, stage of the game (for which the sf author Walter Jon Williams wrote the dialogue) is by far the most flexible and open ended, recalling *Spore*'s working title of "SimEverything." In this phase, the player can roam the galaxy in their own spacecraft, **terraforming** and colonizing other planets, engaging in conflict or diplomacy with alien civilizations, and involving themselves in the development of primitive species. The design draws on both the exploration form of **space sim** and **god games**, in a universe that has been modeled with considerable attention to detail.

Games of *Spore* begin in the primordial soup.

Powerful editing tools allow players of Spore to evolve their creations.

The overall effect of the gameplay is remarkably charming. The player-created species are consistently appealing, with a "phenotype" of elegant and amusing animations generated automatically from the "genotype" supplied by the player's decisions in the creation tool. While the central themes of the game are evolution and social development, they are approached in a manner reminiscent of a children's cartoon; the biology is poetically rather than scientifically accurate. New physical characteristics are either found or taken from other creatures and then passed on to offspring, a model that only vaguely resembles the Darwinian theory of evolution. *Spore* is also notable for its status as the first "massively single-player online game." Unlike **massively multiplayer online games**, only one player at a time participates directly in the game. However, each player's experience is informed by the others' actions. The various species created by *Spore*'s users, and the behavioral patterns demonstrated by them during play, are distributed across the internet and appear in the worlds inhabited and visited by each participant. Considerable effort has been devoted to supplying players with powerful tools that make constructing their own creatures, buildings, and vehicles as easy as possible, employing the collective creativity of huge numbers of individuals to populate the game's simulated universe.

Structurally, *Spore* is perhaps best described as a god game in which the player molds the physical and social evolution of an entire species. It is, however, not a flawless work. While the first stage is well crafted and the last is an excellently designed, highly involving experience, the intermediate phases can become repetitive. A potentially more fundamental problem is the limited degree to which the player's actions in earlier phases affect their creations in later ones. With the exception of the basic approach taken to other creatures—peaceful or aggressive—acquired characteristics are generally only important in the stage after which they were gained. The physical form of the species, for example, has little impact on the final phase. Regardless, the creatures are clearly the stars of the show. The true goal of *Spore* is not, perhaps, to progress through the phases, but simply to experience the joy of shared creation.

Related works: *Spore Creature Creator* (*2008* Maxis) designed by Will Wright is a stand-alone version of the tools used to build species in *Spore*, released before the main game. *Spore: Creepy & Cute Parts Pack* (*2008* Maxis) is an expansion pack for the original game that supplies new components from which species can be constructed. *Spore: Galactic*

Adventures (*2009* Maxis) is another expansion pack, one that adds additional complexity to the play of the game's fifth (and final) phase. Notably, players are able to create their own missions and share them with other participants on the Internet, similarly to the way in which new creatures are distributed in the original work.

Many associated works have also been created, some of which appear to have little in common with their original beyond a desire to take advantage of its marketing budget. *Spore Creatures* (*2008* Foundation 9) is a **console RPG** in which the player adopts the role of a creature kidnapped from their home planet and transported to a hostile world, an action that players of *Spore* can perform in the fifth stage of the game. *Spore Origins* (*2008* Barbaroga/Tricky Software) is an extended version of the first (2D) phase of *Spore*. *Spore Islands* (*2009* Max/Area Code Entertainment) is a much simplified version of the original game in which every participant controls a single island, but every island is inhabited by species created by multiple players, played on social networks. *Spore Hero* (*2009* Electronic Arts) is similar to *Spore Creatures* but distinguished by the presence of a computer-controlled opponent that must be defeated. *Spore Hero Arena* (*2009* Maxis) is a more combat-oriented variant of *Spore Hero*; its gameplay seems more suggestive of that of the *Pokémon* series of monster fighting games than that of the original *Spore*. *Darkspore* (*2011* Maxis) is an **action RPG** in which participants form teams of creatures with which to play through a **linear** story of galactic war against the eponymous **hive mind**; reviews were mixed.

Web Links

- *Spore*: http://www.spore.com/

- Soren Johnson on *Spore*: http://www.gamasutra.com/view/feature/3722/interview_soren_johnson__spores_.php

STARTOPIA

2001. Mucky Foot Productions.

The setting of *Startopia* is a series of derelict space stations that the player must rebuild after an interstellar war. Its developers had previously been part of Peter Molyneux's BP, and the design is much influenced by such non-sf Molyneux games as *Theme Park* (*1994* BP), in which players build and operate modern-day amusement parks. Similarly to *Theme Park*, players of *Startopia* must set up various facilities, hire aliens to run them, and ensure that their customers are kept satisfied. Rather than providing family entertainment, however, *Startopia*'s space stations supply rest, recreation, and medical facilities for a variety of exotic alien species, from the **psionically** psychoactive Karmaramans to the two-headed, scientifically inclined Turrakken. To succeed, a player must watch the inhabitants of their space stations closely and adjust their environment to maximize their happiness and minimize unnecessary conflicts. There is also an antagonistic aspect to the gameplay; other sections of the stations are controlled by different governors, against whom the player must compete for business.

Startopia is a light-hearted game, with a humorous tone that seems suggestive of both the fiction of Douglas Adams and the television series *Red Dwarf (1988–2012)*. Its game world is also strongly evocative of many previous works of sf set on space stations inhabited by a variety of alien species. Notably, there are moments that are reminiscent of episodes of both *Babylon 5 (1993–1998)* and *Star Trek: Deep Space Nine (1993–1999)*, as well as the written works that make up James White's **Sector General** series. Such echoes are, however, perhaps less the result of actual influence than of the game's emphasis on the need to balance the conflicting demands of many different species, combined with the inclusion of such random events as the arrival of aliens in need of medical attention or seeking spiritual fulfillment, all of which represent tropes that are common in earlier fictions with a similar theme.

CHAPTER 16

Toy Games

Toy GAME IS A term used in this book to describe a form of **videogame** in which, unlike most games, the player is given no explicit goals to achieve. Such games are typically simulations of a complex technological or sociological system that can be experimented within the manner of a toy; the US designer Will Wright has described his own contributions to the form as "software toys." The earliest toy games modeled vehicles such as aircraft, as in *Flight Simulator* (*1979* subLOGIC) designed by Bruce Artwick; such works were often marketed as home equivalents of the expensive simulators used to train pilots and other professionals. This variant remains moderately popular today and is represented in science fiction (sf) by spaceship simulations including *Space Travel* (*1969*) designed by Ken Thompson—a game credited with spurring the initial development of the UNIX computer operating system—the **2D** *The Halley Project* (*1985* Tom Snyder), *Microsoft Space Simulator* (*1994* Bruce Artwick Organization) designed by Charles Guy, the freely available *Orbiter* (*2000* Schweiger InterActive) designed by Martin Schweiger, and *Noctis* (*2001* Home Sweet Pixel) designed by Alessandro Ghignola. More recently, a Mexican development house has released preliminary versions of the impressive **independent game** *Kerbal Space Program* (*2011*–current Squad) designed by Felipe Falanghe, in which amusingly enthusiastic frog-like aliens can be instructed to build a wide variety of realistic spacecraft with which they will attempt to master interplanetary travel. Similarly, the upcoming independent game *Space Engineers* (*2013*–current Keen Software House), developed in the Czech Republic, is intended to model the construction of colonies in space, a frequent preoccupation of the written sf genre.

A small step for a Kerbal, but a giant leap for a player of *Kerbal Space Program*.

A separate line of development is primarily associated with Wright, who has created a number of games that model biological, economic, and sociological systems, allowing their players to manipulate the scenario as they wish while observing events from an overhead view. The first of these was *Sim City* (*1989* Maxis), a game partly inspired by Stanisław Lem's "The Seventh Sally or How Trurl's Own Perfection Led to No Good" (in *Cyberiada* **1965**), a short story in which the artificial citizens of an urban simulation rebel against their tyrannical owner. The game presents a model of a modern industrial city in which the player, in the role of mayor, can set taxes, construct buildings, react to natural disasters, and otherwise experiment with the inhabitants' lives. Precursors to *Sim City* are rare but include the "modern life simulator" *Alter Ego* (*1986* Activision) designed by Peter Favaro and *Little Computer People* (*1985* Activision) designed by David Crane, in which the player keeps human pets. Later games designed by Wright include the science-fictional *SimEarth* (*1990* Maxis) and the remarkably commercially successful *The Sims* (*2000* Maxis). This latter work is a kind of digital dollhouse or human zoo in which the player employs effectively supernatural powers to manage their own private soap opera (or satire on capitalist consumerism); it is remarkably effective at creating the appearance of real human interactions among the virtual people who inhabit it. *The Sims* and its various sequels have had few successful competitors, perhaps because the creation of such works has proved to be remarkably difficult; one science-fictional example is *Space Colony* (*2003* Firefly Studios) designed by Simon Bradbury. Arguably, such games are in any case less works of sf than they are embodiments of a common sf trope, that of the artificial world that becomes a toy for its creator, of which the canonical example is perhaps the "neoteric" civilization of Theodore Sturgeon's short story "Microcosmic God" (April 1941 *Astounding Science Fiction*).

MICROSOFT SPACE SIMULATOR

1994. Bruce Artwick Organization (BAO). Designed by Charles Guy.

Microsoft Space Simulator is a **toy game** that simulates historical and technologically extrapolated forms of space exploration, much influenced by the developers' line of flight simulators beginning with Bruce Artwick's *Flight Simulator* (*1979* subLOGIC) and continuing as the *Microsoft Flight Simulator* series. (It could also be considered a descendant of *Space Vikings* [*1982* subLOGIC] designed by Mitchell Robbins, an obscure early example of the combat-based form of **space sim** published by the creators of the first version of *Flight Simulator.*) The majority of players' time is typically spent in the "free-flight" mode, exploring the solar system and the planetary systems the developers created for such stars as Achernar and Polaris. It is also possible to use the software as an observatory and to play through some prepared scenarios, such as the Apollo 17 moon landing and docking the Space Shuttle with the projected Space Station Freedom.

The simulation is based on Newtonian physics; relativistic effects are broadly ignored, though acceleration decreases as a spacecraft approaches the speed of light and it is impossible to exceed it. A variety of options are included to make spaceflight easier and more enjoyable, from using an autopilot to a flight mode that ignores many of the more inconvenient physical realities. A wide range of spacecrafts is available, from actual vehicles such as Apollo's Lunar Module and Shuttle's Manned Maneuvering Unit (which allowed space-suited astronauts to navigate in Earth orbit) to an alien vessel with an **antigravity** engine and a somewhat optimistically engineered starship based on the physicist Robert Bussard's 1960 design for an interstellar ramjet. Many maneuvers used in actual spatial navigation are achievable within the simulator, including the Hohmann transfer orbits, aerobraking in a planetary atmosphere, gravitational slingshots around celestial bodies, and accelerating toward a target until a "turnover" point is reached, at which point the spacecraft is reversed and begins deceleration. In practice, however, most players adopt a more instinctive approach to spaceflight, chasing planets through the sky; this attitude is encouraged by the software's lack of a system for planning interplanetary navigation in advance.

While the developers' enthusiasm for the project is clearly visible, *Microsoft Space Simulator* is a far less accessible game than its flight-simulator-based cousins; little happens in space between occasional course corrections. In essence, this is a game for dedicated spaceflight enthusiasts only.

Web Link

- MS Space Simulator Central (Tribute Site): http://www.planetmic. com/orbit/spasim01.htm

SIMEARTH

1990. Maxis. Designed by Will Wright.

SimEarth is a simulation of the evolution of a terrestrial planet, with an underlying model much influenced by James Lovelock's **Gaia** hypothesis (a description of the Earth as a self-regulating system somewhat analogous to a living organism). Players have access to a wide variety of options, including the ability to control the rate of mutation for living species, the level of greenhouse effect in the atmosphere, and the planet's degree of volcanic activity. It is also possible to trigger mass extinctions, by such means as greatly increasing the frequency of meteoric impacts, and introduce artificial devices, including an intelligence-increasing Monolith modeled on the alien artifact that appears in Stanley Kubrick and Arthur C Clarke's film *2001: A Space Odyssey* (*1968*).

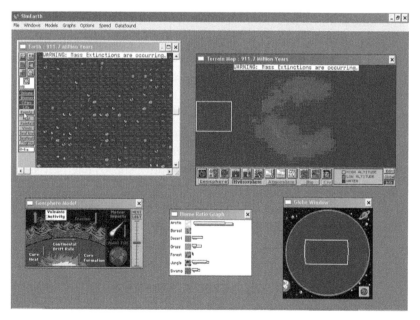

SimEarth's model of Earth in the Cambrian era.

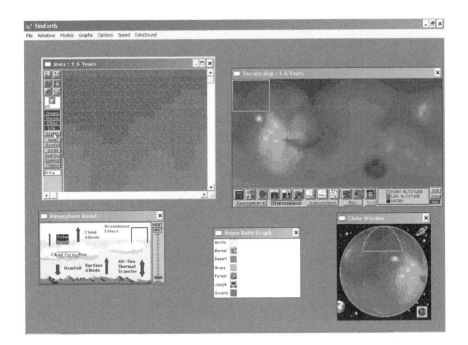

Terraforming Mars in *SimEarth*.

As is generally true in **toy games**, players must set their own goals; a commonly chosen one is to evolve intelligent life and create an advanced civilization. Amusingly, all taxa are created equal; it is entirely possible to generate a planet populated by sentient carnivorous plants or (as a successor civilization after the first has suffered a nuclear war) self-reproducing machines similar to those described in Poul Anderson's short story "Epilogue" (March 1962 *Analog Science Fact—Science Fiction*). Available starting worlds for the game include Earth in the Cambrian era, Mars and Venus (which the player can attempt to **terraform**), present-day Earth, and "Daisyworld," a simple simulation used by Lovelock and Andrew Watson to illustrate the Gaia hypothesis when it was first published in 1983.

Unfortunately, *SimEarth* lacks the intuitive responsiveness of such related games as the urban simulator *Sim City* (*1989* Maxis) designed by Will Wright; it is often difficult to understand the relationships between a player's actions and events in the simulation. The end result is a game that is hard to learn and harder to master; *SimEarth* is generally more admired than played.

Space Sims

A SPACE SIM IS A type of **videogame** in which the player is the commander or (typically) pilot and sole crew of their own spaceship. The behavior of the spacecraft generally resembles that of a World War II era fighter aircraft rather more closely than it does that of any likely actual space vehicle; as in the *Star Wars* films, accuracy in this area does not necessarily add to the enjoyment. Two main variants exist: the space combat game and the space exploration game. There are also a limited number of pure spaceflight simulators that model the control of actual or credibly fictional spacecraft, as in *Microsoft Space Simulator* (*1994* Bruce Artwick Organization) designed by Charles Guy; these works are considered in the section dealing with **toy games**.

To be effective, a space combat game of this kind must be played in **real time**, with a **3D** display representing the pilot's eye view. One significant precursor to the form is the appropriately named *Spasim* (*1974*) designed by Jim Bowery, a game played on the educational Programmed Logic for Automated Teaching Operations (PLATO) network in which up to 32 participants could attack each other in 3D interplanetary space. However, this game updated the positions of spacecraft once a second and hence cannot really be regarded as real time. Early games with similar themes on home machines and in videogame arcades concentrated entirely on the reflex and coordination-based gameplay of shooting enemy spacecraft and dodging incoming attacks, as in *Starship 1* (*1977* Atari; *1977* revised as *Star Ship*) designed by Steve Mayer, Dave Shepperd, and Dennis Koble. The first true example of the form thus appears to have been *Star Raiders* (*1979* Atari) designed by Doug Neubauer, which added strategic elements to the play of those earlier works by incorporating a larger universe within which the participant could travel and the need to conserve limited energy resources. All of the fundamental features seen in later space combat games are already present in *Star Raiders*; from this point on, the form developed by adding **linear** story lines while gradually improving the visuals and the sophistication of the gameplay. Important members of the school include *Wing Commander* (*1990* Origin Systems [OS]) designed by Chris Roberts, *Star Wars: X-Wing* (*1993* Totally Games [TG]) designed by Lawrence Holland and Edward Kilham, the United Kingdom's *Independence War: The Starship Simulator* (*1997* Particle Systems [PS]) designed by Glyn Williams, Michael Powell—notable for its use of realistic physics—and *Descent: Freespace—The Great War* (*1998* Volition). While most of these works were intended for play on personal computers, several games with similar designs were also released for home consoles, including *StarFox* (*1993* Nintendo/Argonaut; also known as *StarWing* in Europe) designed by Shigeru Miyamoto and Katsuya Eguchi—an excellently crafted work featuring anthropomorphic animals as space pilots that was intended primarily for children—and the rather more adult *Colony Wars* (*1997* Psygnosis) designed by Mike Ellis. Few new space combat games have been released since *Freespace*, however, and the form seems largely extinct. One possible reason for its apparent demise is that, as the gameplay was progressively refined in order to appeal to owners of previous titles, the games simply became too difficult for casual players to enjoy.

Space exploration games depend on the simulation of a universe that allows the player considerable freedom of action, a personal sandbox built on a galactic scale. While games such as the text-based *Star Trader* (*1974*)—designed by Dave Kaufman and later published by the People's Computer Company in the book *What to Do After You Hit Return* (**1975**)—the UK-developed *Trader Trilogy* (*1982* Pixel Productions) designed by Joe Gillespie, *Universe* (*1983* Omnitrend Software) designed by Thomas Carbone and William Leslie III, and *Sundog: Frozen Legacy* (*1984* FTL Games) designed by Bruce Webster can be seen as precursors of the form, its true prototype is the UK game *Elite* (*1984*) designed by David Braben and Ian Bell. That game's fusion of 3D real-time space travel and combat with exploration of a large universe within which many activities are possible, from trading and mining to piracy and bounty hunting, established a shape for the form that has remained essentially the same ever since. Refinements have been made, as improving technology allowed for better graphics and enhancements to the quality of the simulation, but the core concepts remain unchanged. Significant examples of the school include *Space Rogue* (*1989* OS) designed by Paul Neurath, *Wing Commander: Privateer* (*1993* OS) designed by Joel Manners and Chris Roberts, the less than successful *Battlecruiser 3000 AD* (*1996* 3000AD) designed by Derek Smart, *Freelancer* (*2003* Digital Anvil) designed by Chris Roberts, and the German *X Series* (from *1999* Egosoft). The popularity of the form in the 1990s also resulted in the transposition of its core mechanics to games that were not set in interstellar space, as in the train-based *Transarctica* (*1993* Silmarils) designed by André Rocques and *Pirates of Realmspace* (*1992* Cybertech) designed by Al Escudero, set in the pseudo-Aristotelian fantasy universe of **Spelljammer**, where planetary systems enclosed in crystal spheres float in an endless ocean of phlogiston.

A related line of development can be seen in *Starflight* (*1986* Binary Systems), *Star Control II* (*1992* Toys for Bob [TFB]) designed by Fred Ford and Paul Reiche III, and the Russian *Space Rangers* (*2002* Elemental Games [EG]). These latter games, while generally considered to be members of other forms, share many features with *Elite*. They are, however, distinguished by their largely **2D** graphics and their focus on story and character beyond the **environmental** narrative elements that predominate in many space exploration games. While the descendants of *Elite* have proved to be less popular with players in the twenty-first century than they were in the 1990s, they have also been one of the forms revived by the crowdfunding website Kickstarter, which has enabled the fans of many cult schools of videogame design to fund the development of new works of their favorite type despite major publishers' insistence that the audience was too small to justify the creation of new games in the form. Upcoming space sims, all of the exploration type, include *Elite: Dangerous*, a reinvention of the original *Elite* designed by one of its creators, David Braben; *Star Citizen*, a combination of **massively multiplayer** and single, player game designed by Chris Roberts, the inspiration behind the early *Wing Commander* games and *Freelancer*; and the **independent game** *No Man's Sky*. Meanwhile, the Icelandic game *EVE Online* (*2003* CCP [Crowd Control Productions] Games) designed by Reynir Harðarson has achieved considerable commercial success by transposing the form into a **massively multiplayer online game**. Arguably, this work represents a kind of apotheosis for the form, in which its historical weaknesses—notably a certain dryness of tone and lack of human interest—are resolved by the transformation of its simulated space into a shared galaxy. Significantly, both *Star Citizen* and *Elite: Dangerous* are expected to include mechanics allowing players to cooperate in the creation of their fictional universes.

FURTHER READING

- Francis Spufford. *Backroom Boys: The Secret Return of the British Boffin*. 2003. (Chapter 3 explores the origins of *Elite*.)

ARCHIMEDEAN DYNASTY

1996. (Also known as *Silent Running* in Germany.) Massive Development (MD). Designed by Alexander Jorias, Helmut Halfmann.

Archimedean Dynasty is an example of an unusual **videogame** form, the "subsim"—a **space sim** that has been transposed from an inter-planetary to an underwater milieu. Its ocean world is displayed **three-dimensionally** in **real time** when the player is piloting their character's submarine and as a series of static images when they are talking to the inhabitants of the game's various undersea cities. As in many space sims, the gameplay revolves around a variety of missions that the player can undertake, including transporting cargo, escorting other ships, and sal-vaging equipment, most of which involve frequent combat; any profits can be spent on upgrading the player's vessel.

Players of *Archimedean Dynasty* adopt the role of an amoral mer-cenary on a postholocaust Earth so ruined by war and environmental collapse that humanity can only survive under the sea. This is a world without a sky; not only has the land been flooded by the effects of global warming, frozen by nuclear winter, and poisoned by fallout, but the sur-face of every sea is covered in a thick layer of radioactive debris, which forever blocks out the sun. The oceans seem only marginally less hostile than the land. Humans subsist on artificially created food and "breath-ing gases," manufactured with energy supplied by giant fusion reactors. The details of the marine ecology are unclear, but it appears that in the absence of sunlight, most forms of sea life have become extinct. While the tone of the game's dialogue veers between undersea noir and ludi-crous melodrama, its visuals are consistently beautiful and atmospheric. A broadly **linear** plot gradually emerges as the player makes their way through the various missions, revealing the hidden threat posed by a **hive mind** composed of aggressive **cyborgs** to the competing power blocs of the game's politically complex future. Ultimately, *Archimedean Dynasty* offers a convincing simulation of future submarine combat fused with a moody, claustrophobic vision of life in the last surviving remnant of Earth's biosphere, a far darker picture than that presented in such con-temporary examples of "submarine science fiction (sf)" as the TV series *seaQuest DSV (1993–1996)*.

Related works: *AquaNox* (*2001* Massive Development [MD]) designed by Björn Braun, Philipp Schreiber, and Helmut Halfmann is a sequel in which the player again adopts the role of the first game's protagonist. Gameplay is similar to that of its predecessor, but far simpler; *AquaNox* focuses on action and visual appeal at the expense of tactical complexity and narrative depth. The physics of its submarine simulation is also far less believable than that of the earlier work, presumably because the designers were hoping to create a faster-paced, more immediately thrilling game. Any such hopes were not, however, fully realized. *AquaNox 2: Revelation* (*2003* MD) designed by Björn Braun, Philipp Schreiber, and Helmut Halfmann is a further sequel, though with a different protagonist. Its design and gameplay are generally similar to those of *AquaNox*, but the story line and dialogue are markedly worse.

BATTLECRUISER 3000 AD

1996. 3000AD. Designed by Derek Smart.

The *Battlecruiser* franchise is famous both for the length of time it has spent in development and for the combative personality of its designer. The first iteration, *Battlecruiser 3000 AD*, was intended to be a universal **space sim** using **3D** graphics, in which players could roam through a simulated galaxy without restrictions. It was released after 7 years of work to exceptionally poor reviews; the game was generally agreed to be both remarkably hard to understand and full of bugs. Considerable disagreement ensued between Derek Smart and the then publisher, Take Two Interactive. Smart continued development and *Battlecruiser 3000 AD v2.0* was released in 1998 by Interplay Entertainment. This version, while much superior to the first, received little attention from players. A third release, *Battlecruiser Millennium* (*2001* 3000AD; *2003* revised as *Battlecruiser Millennium Gold*), came much closer to embodying the original design vision for *Battlecruiser 3000 AD*; this iteration was self-published by Smart, making it an **independent game**.

In *Battlecruiser Millennium*, the player can choose a character from any of several species and pick a career ranging from starship commander to space marine. The best developed option is the one inherited from *Battlecruiser 3000 AD*, that of military starship captain. In this role, the player commands an interstellar battlecruiser and is responsible for personally managing a wide variety of power, weapon, and shield systems, as well as issuing orders to individual crew members and dispatching smaller fighter ships on independent missions. It is also possible to leave the ship by means of a shuttle and land on planets, dock at space stations, assault manned installations using boarding parties, and mine asteroids for resources. The galaxy in which the game is set contains several competing factions; battlecruiser commanders generally adopt a role resembling that of a privateer, an independent military commander who is personally responsible for arming and resupplying their own ship.

Unfortunately, the game suffers from a strikingly obscure interface. A wide variety of complex options are presented to the player in a distinctly idiosyncratic way, making the game difficult to learn. More fundamentally, the *Battlecruiser Millennium* games suffer from a failure of **environmental** narrative. The universe made available for exploration is impressively broad and detailed, though the details often lack atmosphere, but the general absence of characterization and plot elements means that the story fails to evolve. The games are perhaps best described as extremely detailed simulations of fictional spacecraft and their environment; they are compelling only to those who enjoy the simulation for its own sake and are happy to create their own goals within the game. Ultimately, *Battlecruiser Millennium* is less interesting for what it achieves than for what it sets out to do. The idea of simulating an entire universe in which players can adopt any role they choose is an old one in **videogame** development; it seems likely, however, that the future of this dream lies with **massively multiplayer online games** such as *EVE Online* (*2003* CCP Games) designed by Reynir Harðarson.

Related works: *Universal Combat* (*2004* 3000AD; *2005* revised as *Universal Combat Gold*) designed by Derek Smart is a development of the *Battlecruiser* series that focuses on combat-based gameplay in air, land, and space environments and includes an **online world**; it received mixed reviews. *Universal Combat: A World Apart* (*2005* 3000AD) designed by Derek Smart is an expansion that adds new missions and equipment to the original. *Galactic Command: Echo Squad* (*2007* 3000AD; *2008* revised as *Galactic Command: Echo Squad SE*) designed by Derek Smart began another sequence within the franchise that is generally similar to its predecessors but has a far more strongly defined—if not markedly original— plot. Derivatives of *Echo Squad* include *All Aspect Warfare* (*2009* 3000AD) and *Angle of Attack* (*2009* 3000AD), both of which are designed by Derek Smart and set on planetary surfaces.

Web Link
- 3000AD: http://www.3000ad.com/

CAPTAIN BLOOD

1988. (Also known as *The Ark of Captain Blood* in continental Europe.) ERE Informatique. Designed by Philippe Ulrich, Didier Bouchon.

The protagonist of *Captain Blood* is Bob Morlok, a computer game designer who somehow injects himself into the fictional universe of the game he is working on, apparently by virtue of his sheer creativity. There, he merges with his *alter ego* within the game, the eponymous Captain. Shortly after his arrival in the game world, Blood/Morlok is multiply duplicated during an aberrant **hyperspace** jump, an event that leaves the original critically short of "vital fluids." In an apparent reference to the evils of software piracy, the Captain realizes that he must hunt down and eradicate every last copy if he is to survive. Soon, his ship's computer begins the process of converting him into a **cyborg** to help him withstand the damaging side effects of the copies' creation; as more and more of his original parts are replaced, it becomes clear that in the end he could be entirely remade, leaving only a robot. Hundreds of years later, at the beginning of the game proper, Blood has managed to eliminate most of his duplicates, but is running out of time to find and destroy the remaining five.

The actual game places the player on the bridge of Blood's gigantic biomechanical starship, the Ark. From there, they can travel to many different (though often quite similar) planets searching for clues to the copies' location; once a duplicate has been discovered, its stolen fluids can be extracted and returned to the player. Unsurprisingly, this is a fatal experience for the copy. While the actions available to the player are different, the sense of freedom to travel within a simulated galaxy is reminiscent of the exploration form of **space sim** game.

For reasons that are never explained, every being in this artificial universe can be found at the end of a long, narrow trench cut into the surface of a planet (displayed as a set of **3D** outlines for technical reasons). On arriving at an inhabited world, the player must fly a living probe down into the appropriate channel, continuing until they find the resident alien (there is never more than one). They can then negotiate with this individual, offering information or interstellar transportation in return for news of the duplicates' whereabouts. This is the real heart of the game. An iconic communications system allows the player to communicate with any of the game's many alien species, despite the assumed lack of a shared language, by using a set of symbols representing emotional and conceptual states. The deliberately primitive nature of this interface cleverly disguises the limited nature of the intelligence, which could be bestowed upon the game's nonhumans by its programmers. Thus, the game's characters can obsess about obscure concepts or spout utter nonsense without breaking the illusion of real interaction, since their lapses in communication can be attributed to the difficulties of translating an alien language into a simple symbolic code. Many of the aliens (not to mention the Captain's duplicates) will cheat and lie during these discussions; it is common (though by no means necessary) for players to do the same. Interestingly, the approach taken to representing conversations in *Captain Blood* greatly resembles that of *Trust and Betrayal: The Legacy of Siboot* (*1987*) designed by Chris Crawford, another unusual **videogame** created in the 1980s.

Captain Blood is noteworthy in many ways, among them its offbeat sense of humor and the eclectic combination of disparate elements that make up its gameplay design. It features many quirky alien races of varying intelligence and disposition: two species are dedicated to the destruction of each other, a third express their feelings by the projection of human fantasies, while a fourth are the senile remnants of ancient **berserkers**. The title music is an early example of a licensed videogame soundtrack, having been adapted from Jean Michel Jarre's album *Zoolook* (*1984*). Ultimately, the game's appeal depends on the conversation system. Some players fail to find this interesting, but others are fascinated by the challenge of decoding a complex web of lies, truth, and gibberish woven by an assortment of bizarre aliens, using a language consisting of only 150 hieroglyphs. Very few, however, find this easy.

The sequel is *Commander Blood* (*1994* Cryo Interactive [CI]) designed by Philippe Ulrich and Didier Bouchon. As the title suggests, this time the player adopts the role of Commander rather than Captain. The titular character is a biological construct created by the original game's Bob Morlok (here "Morlock"), now the oldest (and possibly richest) being in the universe. Knowing that it will soon become impossible to further prolong his life, Morlock has decided that he should see the Big Bang before he dies. So the places himself in **suspended animation** and sends his body back in time, having built the player's character to pilot his new Ark through a series of **black holes**.

The mechanics of *Commander Blood* are quite different from those of its predecessor. As in the first game, the player's character remains on the bridge of their spacecraft throughout, but here, **full motion video** and **real-time** 3D graphics are used to display the visuals. All actions, including conversation, are performed by activating a control on the bridge or selecting an option from a simple menu; the exotic communications system of the original is not used. Instead, the gameplay revolves around puzzle solving, as in an **adventure** game. Similarly, in contrast to *Captain Blood*'s open universe, the extensive plot of *Commander Blood* is entirely **linear**. While the various times visited by the player are beautifully portrayed, and the assorted alien designs—including many not seen in the first game—are as eccentrically inventive as ever, *Commander Blood* is arguably a less interesting, if much easier, game than its original.

Related works: A third entry in the series, *Big Bug Bang: Le Retour de Commander Blood* ("Big Bang Bug: The Return of Commander Blood") (*1996* CI) designed by Philippe Ulrich and Didier Bouchon, was only released in French. This game begins after Morlock and Commander Blood have reached the Big Bang, only to discover that they have broken the universe with their meddling; the player must solve various puzzles to foster the evolution of life in the new reality that will replace Blood's original continuum.

Web Links

- ARGanoid's Captain Blood Worship Page (Tribute Site): http://argnet.fatal-design.com/bluddian.php

- Captain Blood Shrine (Tribute Site): http://www.oldskool.org/shrines/captainblood/

ELITE

1984. (Revised *1991* as *ArcElite*; revised *1991* as *Elite Plus*.) Designed by David Braben, Ian Bell.

Elite's gameplay is a perfect fusion of exploration, trading, mining, and combat that created its own subtype of **space sim**; later examples of the school include *Wing Commander: Privateer* (*1993* OS) designed by Joel Manners and Chris Roberts and the **massively multiplayer online game** *EVE Online* (*2003* CCP Games) designed by Reynir Harðarson. **Real-time 3D** graphics are used for the display, though technical limitations meant that only the outlines of shapes could be drawn before *Elite Plus*, which filled in the lines with solid colors. The player begins the game with their own starship, in a **space opera** universe much influenced by the tabletop **RPGs** *Traveller* (*1977* Game Designers' Workshop) designed by Marc Miller and *Space Opera* (*1980* Fantasy Games Unlimited) designed by Edward Simbalist, A Mark Ratner, and Phil McGregor. They are then free to wander through the galaxies, buying and selling goods, fighting pirates and (more rarely) aliens, and carrying out occasional special missions. *Elite* has a strong **hard sf** flavor, including such atmospheric details as the ability to scoop fuel from the outer fringes of a star and (in some versions) the occasional appearance of **generation starships**. Additional ambience is supplied by the detailed specifications provided for many different types of spacecrafts—a touch that is particularly reminiscent of *Traveller*—and the sociological and xenobiological classifications of planetary systems. Nevertheless, *Elite* is not a flawless game. Partly as a result of technical restrictions, its universe is broad but shallow, leading to an eventual realization that its many different solar systems are, in fact, quite similar. Missions are rare, and the gameplay can become repetitive, with little sense of an ongoing narrative. Descendants such as the *X Series* (from *1999* Egosoft) and *Freelancer* (*2003* Digital Anvil) designed by Chris Roberts have considerably improved on *Elite* in these areas while retaining the same basic gameplay. However, it can be argued that *Elite* is the best game of its kind that was achievable on the hardware platforms available, evoking a remarkable sense of openness and freedom in an unpredictable universe. It was highly popular in the United Kingdom, with considerable competition among players to reach the highest pilot rating, after which the game was named.

Frontier: Elite II (1993) designed by David Braben is a sequel with a broadly similar design, but much improved visuals and a fictional universe that is a smaller but deeper version of that seen in the first game. Unfortunately, this more detailed background lacks novelty; some players found it less intriguing than the personal visions that they could project onto the blanker canvas of the original. *Frontier* also made several major changes to the gameplay, adding the ability to land on planets and an accurate implementation of Newtonian physics. These alterations met with mixed reviews; most importantly, the use of accurate physics without a simulated flight computer meant that players had to fly their spacecraft manually in a Newtonian universe, which many found frustrating. *Frontier: First Encounters* (*1995* Frontier Developments) designed by David Braben is a further sequel, which adds many more narrative elements to the basic design of *Frontier*. Notably, *First Encounters* includes journals reporting news from the game universe and specially designed missions that combine to form a **linear** plot, in contrast to its predecessors' purely **environmental** approach to story.

Related works: *Elite* included a novella by the sf and fantasy writer Robert Holdstock, *The Dark Wheel* (**1984**), a well-crafted story of young adult adventure that was one of several such works sold with UK-developed **videogames** in the 1980s. *The Dark Wheel* was not made available with the revised *Elite Plus*, which instead incorporated a different work—"Imprint" (1991) by Andy Redman—in the game's manual. This literary association was continued in the sequels with the inclusion of the collections *Stories of Life on the Frontier* (**1993**) and *Further Stories of Life on the Frontier* (**1995**), both edited by David Braben, in *Frontier* and *First Encounters*. The contents of these works are mostly routine; *Further Stories of Life on the Frontier* includes a story previously published in the August 1992 issue of *Interzone* magazine, Julian Flood's "Children of a Greater God."

Web Links

- Ian Bell's *Elite* Page: http://www.iancgbell.clara.net/elite/

- FrontierAstro (Tribute Site): http://www.frontierastro.co.uk/

- Life on the Frontier (Tribute Site): http://www.lotf.co.uk/

FREELANCER

2003. Digital Anvil (DA). Designed by Chris Roberts.

Freelancer is a **real-time 3D** game that combines the open exploratory gameplay of such predecessors as *Elite* (*1984*) designed by David Braben and Ian Bell with an integrated **linear** plot. The player's character is Edison Trent, a down on his luck "freelancer" who needs a new ship. Soon, the player is involved with a secret alien invasion, searching for a mysterious artifact that can eventually be used to help save humanity. The setting is a **space opera** universe in which different solar systems have been settled by particular nation states from Earth, leading to a range of somewhat stereotypical future cultures. Many different factions inhabit this milieu, including pirates, corporations, and naval forces; the player can decide which to ally with or oppose. While not participating in plot developments, participants can choose to mine asteroids, salvage wrecked ships, trade, or go on bounty-hunting missions. After the story has concluded, they can continue with these activities, wandering freely through space.

Space itself is very crowded in *Freelancer*. In contrast to the realistic *X Series* (from *1999* Egosoft), distance and time scales are manipulated to ensure that the player's environment is always interesting and involving. Combat is also made as entertaining as possible; as in *Star Wars: X-Wing*

(*1993* TG) designed by Lawrence Holland and Edward Kilham, it has been modeled on aerial dogfighting, with an interface that emphasizes ease of use. While its story is not entirely credible and the free-roaming gameplay can become repetitive, *Freelancer* is an entirely competent example of its form. It has proved popular as a multiplayer game, where many players share a single persistent **online world**, trading, fighting, and cooperating with each other and with computer-controlled characters.

Related works: *Starlancer* (*2000* DA/Warthog) designed by Erin Roberts is a combat-based **space sim**, strongly influenced by the early games in the *Wing Commander* series (from *1990* OS). It is set in a future version of the solar system that has been extensively colonized, during a war that broadly recapitulates the East versus West standoff of the late twentieth century. In *Starlancer*, however, the war has turned hot, and the player, as a starfighter pilot for the (Western) Alliance, appears to be on the losing side; a linear narrative is effectively integrated into the player's complexly designed missions. This game also serves as a prequel to *Freelancer*, whose interstellar colonies are said to have been founded by refugees from the defeated Alliance.

FREESPACE

Series (from 1998). Volition.

Descent: Freespace—The Great War (*1998* Volition; also known as *Conflict: Freespace—The Great War* in Europe) is a combat-based **space sim** in which the player pilots a single-seat starfighter, a descendant of *Star Wars: X-Wing* (*1993* TG) designed by Lawrence Holland and Edward Kilham and *Wing Commander* (*1990* OS) designed by Chris Roberts. *Conflict: Freespace* was released almost 20 years after the first such game, *Star Raiders* (*1979* Atari) designed by Doug Neubauer, and the gameplay is an extremely refined version of the essential mix of **real-time** tactical choices and first-person dogfights in space. The game is notable for the air of desperation that pervades its essentially **linear** story. It begins with humanity involved in a pointless war with the alien Vasudans. Without warning, both sides are attacked by an unknown enemy, the technologically superior Shivans. The plot then follows the increasingly hopeless attempts of the now allied humans and Vasudans to survive against overwhelming force; in the end, the Shivans are defeated but Earth is lost. *Descent: Freespace—Silent Threat* (*1998* Volition; also known as *Conflict: Freespace—Silent Threat*) is an expansion pack, dealing with the attempt of a rogue human intelligence unit to destabilize the new alliance between humans and Vasudans.

Freespace 2 (*1999* Volition) is a sequel, set 30 years after the first game, when a human rebellion and the return of the Shivans confront the alliance with a war on two fronts. Again, the player is on the losing side; this time, the game ends with the Shivans abandoning the war on the brink of victory. Throughout the series, the enemy remains unknowable and their motives unexplained, though it is suggested that they have exterminated other species in the past. Aspects of the *Freespace* universe are reminiscent of the TV series *Babylon 5* (*1993–1998*), notably the impressive space battle scenes and the alien races; Vasudans have something in common with Minbari and Shivans with Shadows. The series ended with *Freespace 2* for business reasons, after which Volition released the *Freespace 2* software for noncommercial use. An improved version, *Freespace Open*, is available for public download.

Web Link
- *Freespace Open* download: http://www.fsoinstaller.com/

INDEPENDENCE WAR: THE STARSHIP SIMULATOR

1997. Particle Systems (PS). Designed by Glyn Williams, Michael Powell.

Independence War is a combat-oriented **space sim**, with views displayed in **real time** using **3D** graphics. It is remarkable both for its use of accurate Newtonian physics and for the fact that the player's ship is a corvette with a crew of four, rather than the more conventional single-pilot starfighter. The game's **multilinear** plot unfolds during a war between the Earth Commonwealth and rebellious colonists; the player is the captain of an Earth starship. A detailed story is effectively told through a combination of events within the player's assigned missions and precreated scenes outside them. Several different endings are available, including one in which a peace is negotiated after the player discovers that the war is perpetuated by shadowy forces within the Commonwealth. As in such **military sf** novels as Elizabeth Moon's *Once a Hero* (**1997**), *Independence War's* story takes an equivocal view of the glories of war.

Gameplay is focused on the solution of physically based puzzles and ship-to-ship combat. The simulation of real-world physics gives the game a very different feel to such predecessors as *Star Wars: X-Wing* (*1993* TG) designed by Lawrence Holland and Edward Kilham, which reproduce World War II's aerial dogfights in space. In *Independence War*, the player must move and accelerate in three dimensions while subject to the effects of inertia, a task that is made considerably easier by a simulated flight computer and sophisticated head-up displays. Any of the four crew stations can be occupied by the player, including navigation and weaponry; unoccupied stations will be handled automatically by the game. The combination of realistic physics and informationally dense graphical overlays allows *Independence War* to present a remarkably convincing simulation of the kind of near-future space warfare frequently described in such works of military sf as David Weber's *On Basilisk Station* (**1993**) or David Feintuch's *Midshipman's Hope* (**1994**), which emphasize the apparent realism of their iconic space battles.

Related works: Additional missions telling the same story from the rebel perspective were added to the basic game for *Independence War Special Edition* (*1999* PS; also known as *Independence War Deluxe Edition* in the United States). *Independence War 2: Edge of Chaos* (*2001* PS) is a sequel, set a hundred years after the original game, in a distant region of space known as the "Badlands Cluster." The player takes the role of a rebel against the oppressive corporations that dominate this region of space. Gameplay resembles that of the first game, with the addition of free-roaming piracy and simple trading options similar to those available in *Wing Commander: Privateer* (*1993* OS) designed by Joel Manners and Chris Roberts.

Web Link
- *Independence War* Tribute Site: http://www.i-war2.com/

SPACE RANGERS

2002. Elemental Games (EG).

Space Rangers is a game that includes features from an eclectic range of forms. Notably, menu-driven text **adventures** are used for many submissions, including ones set on planets, and the default **turn-based** space combat model is replaced by an **arcade game** resembling *Spacewar* (*1962*) designed by Stephen Russell, J M Graetz, and Wayne Wiitanen inside **black holes**. The core gameplay focuses on exploration, trade, mining, diplomacy, and combat within an impressively dynamic universe; the galaxy has a working economy, and many events occur independently of the player's actions. The main display is 2D, serving more as a symbolic interface than as a realistic depiction of space. While reminiscent of such exploratory space games as *Star Control II* (*1992* TFB) designed by Fred Ford and Paul Reiche III and *Starflight* (*1986* Binary Systems), *Space Rangers* does not have a predefined plot. Nevertheless, its use of structured missions with complex goals within an independently evolving universe is often successful at creating **emergent** narrative. Players are all members of the Space Rangers, recruited to fight an invasion of a **space opera** future galaxy by the technologically superior Klissans. However, budgetary limitations mean that Rangers must support themselves economically; most of the player's activities will be unrelated to the invasion. Throughout, the game exhibits a quirky sense of individuality and a cheerful enthusiasm about its subject matter evocative of such low-budget 1980s sf films as *Spacehunter: Adventures in the Forbidden Zone (1983)*.

Related works: *Space Rangers 2: Dominators* (*2005* EG; also known as *Space Rangers 2: Rise of the Dominators* in the United States) is a sequel, expanding *Space Rangers'* gameplay to include basic **real-time strategy** and **first-person shooter** modes. Set 200 years after the first game, it features another invasion, this time by out-of-control war robots; the ingenuity and immersive gameplay of the original are preserved. *Space Rangers 2: Reboot* (*2008* EG) is an expansion pack for *Dominators* that adds new missions and equipment.

STAR CONTROL

Series (from 1990). Toys For Bob (TFB).

The original *Star Control* (1990 TFB), designed by Fred Ford and Paul Reiche III, is a competently executed computer wargame set during an interstellar war between the Alliance of Free Stars and the Hierarchy of Battle Thralls. (The titular Star Control is the military arm of Earth's United Nations, a member of the Alliance.) A wide variety of ship designs are featured, with varied abilities that are nevertheless well balanced in gameplay terms. Combat between individual ships is handled using a 2D system modeled on that of Spacewar (1962) designed by Stephen Russell, J M Graetz, and Wayne Wiitanen. The sequel, *Star Control II* (1992 TFB) designed by Fred Ford and Paul Reiche III, is a rather more interesting game, much influenced by Starflight (1986 Binary Systems) and sharing its focus on exploration of a simulated galaxy, in the manner of a 2D space sim. In its future history, the Alliance of Free Stars has lost the war described in *Star Control*. However, an isolated human scientific expedition discovered the ruins of a powerful alien civilization in the last days of the war, and 20 years later, they have used its technology to construct a working, if incomplete, starship. The player takes the role of captain of this vessel, which has just succeeded in reaching Earth.

A strongly modular plot focuses on the player's attempts to recruit allies, rescue enslaved worlds, and finish assembling their ship, in preparation for freeing the galaxy from the Hierarchy. In practice, the game's most important characters are the various alien species with which the player can negotiate, each of which has a strongly developed "racial personality." (David Brin's Uplift War series and the Known Space stories of Larry Niven were both influential on the designs of these races, among other works.) While the story of *Star Control II* rarely rises above the level of generic space opera, the game is remarkably effective at generating a sense of an open, freely explorable universe in which any choice is available and all actions are meaningful.

Related works: *Star Control 3* (*1996* Legend Entertainment) designed by George MacDonald and Michael Lindner is a sequel created by a different developer that attempted unsuccessfully to reproduce the formula established in the second game. This iteration of the series adds the ability to found colonies, but changes the default combat view to an **isometric 3D** perspective that is notably difficult to use. More fundamentally, the story—which begins with an expedition to another region of space containing the source of a mysterious effect that has disabled normal forms of **faster-than-light** travel—often feels forced, with the player required to proceed down paths they might not otherwise follow. *The Ur-Quan Masters* (*2002*) is a somewhat modified release of *Star Control II*, based on a version of the software that was made freely available. *Star Control: Interbellum* (**1996**), by William Quick, is a spin-off novel.

Web Link
  • *The Ur-Quan Masters*: http://sc2.sourceforge.net/

STAR RAIDERS

1979. (Also known as *ST Star Raiders*.) Atari. Designed by Doug Neubauer.

Star Raiders was the first **real-time 3D** space combat game that combined arcade style action with strategic concerns. (These latter elements were derived from text-based **computer wargames** inspired by the *Star Trek* TV series, most notably *Super Star Trek* [*circa 1975*] designed by David Matuszek and Paul Reynolds.) The game's universe is a **2D** grid of "sectors," travel between which is achieved using a **hyperspace** jump. These spatial zones may contain enemy ships or friendly starbases, which must be protected. Within a sector, players fly their starfighters from a first-person view, expending their limited energy reserves to activate shields and weapons with which to fight the hostile "Zylons" (an apparent reference to the original version of *Battlestar Galactica* [*1978–1979*]). While of largely historical interest today, *Star Raiders* is notable for containing all the core gameplay concepts seen in later space combat simulations, from *Star Wars: X-Wing* (*1993* TG) designed by Lawrence Holland and Edward Kilham to the *Freespace* series (from *1998* Volition).

Related works: The sequel, *Star Raiders II* (*1986* Atari), was adapted from a game based on the film *The Last Starfighter* (*1984*) after Atari lost the license to create works derived from the movie; it was less well received than the original. A *Star Raiders* graphic novel was published by DC Comics in 1981, written by Elliot S Maggin and illustrated by Jose Luis Garcia Lopez.

Web Links

- Doug Neubauer on *Star Raiders*: http://www.dadgum.com/halcyon/ BOOK/NEUBAUER.HTM

- *Star Raiders* Tribute Page: http://www.sonic.net/%7Enbs/ star-raiders/

STAR WARS: X-WING

1993. Totally Games (TG). Designed by Lawrence Holland, Edward Kilham.

Star Wars: X-Wing is the first in a series of combat-focused **space sims** set in the *Star Wars* universe. Written by developers who had previously worked on World War II aerial conflict simulations, they present spatial conflict as primarily a form of dogfighting between single-pilot starfighters, as do the films they reference. *X-Wing* and its competitor *Wing Commander* (*1990* OS) designed by Chris Roberts popularized space combat as a game form, one that perhaps reached its apotheosis with the *Freespace* series (from *1998* Volition). All of the games in the series are well crafted, with diverse and challenging mission designs, entertaining gameplay, and **linear** plots that are well integrated into the timeline of the original trilogy of *Star Wars* films. Thus, *Star Wars: X-Wing* takes place during *Star Wars: Episode IV—A New Hope* (*1977*) and its sequel *Star Wars: TIE Fighter* during both *Star Wars: Episode V—The Empire Strikes Back* (*1980*) and *Star Wars: Episode VI—Return of the Jedi* (*1983*), ending before its final battle, while the last installment, *Star Wars: X-Wing Alliance*, is also set during episodes V and VI, but on the rebel side. The atmosphere and visual style of the films are conveyed with skill.

In *X-Wing*, the player adopts the role of a pilot for the films' Rebel Alliance. The game's missions are split into three tours; in the third, the player mysteriously takes Luke Skywalker's place during the final assault on the Empire's Death Star at the end of *A New Hope*. There are two expansion packs, *Star Wars: X-Wing—Imperial Pursuit* (*1993* TG) and *Star Wars: X-Wing—B-Wing* (*1993* TG), covering, respectively, the retreat from the rebel base on Yavin after the end of *A New Hope* and the arrival of the eponymous new Alliance fighter. The next entry in the series, *Star Wars: TIE Fighter* (*1994* TG) designed by Lawrence Holland and Edward Kilham, refined the gameplay while interestingly inverting the premise; the player becomes a pilot for the Alliance's opponents, the evil Empire. While there are some amusingly melodramatic moments between missions, the game is reluctant to place its players in truly malevolent roles; the majority of the story concentrates on the destruction of pirates and rogue Imperials rather than the Rebel Alliance. *TIE Fighter* has one expansion pack, *Star Wars: TIE Fighter—Defender of the Empire* (*1994* TG), which continues the base game's story of a war against a Grand Admiral who has rebelled in the hope of gaining personal power. This plot was concluded in *Enemies of the Empire*, a campaign included in the 1995 Collector's edition of *TIE Fighter*. Finally, *Star Wars: X-Wing Alliance* (*1999* TG) designed by Lawrence Holland offers a stronger story line than the previous two games, as well as the chance to fly larger ships. The player's character is the youngest son in a family of interstellar traders who sympathize with the Alliance; eventually, he joins the rebellion, taking part in a series of missions that end with *Return of the Jedi*'s climactic Battle of Endor.

Related works: *Star Wars: X-Wing vs. TIE Fighter* (*1997* TG) designed by Lawrence Holland is primarily intended for online competitive play, though it has a limited plot. *Star Wars: X-Wing vs. TIE Fighter—Balance of Power* (*1997* TG) is an expansion that adds some new ships and a single-player story line focusing on the struggle between Empire and Rebel pilots in a remote sector of space.

TRANSARCTICA

1993. (Also known as *Arctic Baron* in the United States.) Silmarils. Designed by André Rocques.

Transarctica is set in the world of **La Compagnie des Glaces** ("The Ice Company"), a sequence of novels by G J Arnaud. In Arnaud's fiction, a twenty-first-century attempt to mitigate global warming caused by the greenhouse effect goes badly wrong, surrounding the Earth with eternal dust clouds and blotting out the sky. Civilization is shattered by the abrupt arrival of a new Ice Age; centuries later, all that remains are a few shrunken towns and the giant armored steam trains that travel endlessly between them. The player adopts the role of the "Arctic Baron," an idealistic rebel and master of one such train—the titular *Transarctica*—who is dedicated to bringing back the sun.

The visuals are a mixture of **2D** displays and static images; the most commonly used screen is a map on which the course of the player's train can be guided in plan view. The gameplay, however, is essentially that of a **space sim** on rails. Players must spend much of their time mining coal and trading in mammoths, slaves, and other items if they are to acquire the resources needed to maintain their train and its crew. Meanwhile, they must fight or avoid the battle trains of the Viking Union, which dominates this winter world and does not want to see it change, while searching for clues that might reveal the long-lost nature of the catastrophe. As is traditional for the exploration form of space sim, the player's train can be upgraded in several ways, including the addition of missile launchers, goods wagons, and observation cars as well as the purchase of small railroad cars for reconnaissance. Various kinds of wanderers can be met in the ice fields, including nomadic merchants and the degenerate descendants of the workers who built the global railway network. Despite the erratic quality of the English translation and its occasionally frustrating gameplay, *Transarctica* is a unique work that makes good use of its exotic world.

UNIVERSE

1983. Omnitrend Software. Designed by Thomas Carbone, William Leslie III.

Universe, a largely text-based game with some outline graphics that is played in turns, is an interesting precursor to the exploratory form of **space sim**, normally played in **real time** with **3D** displays. As in a space exploration game, players each possess their own spacecraft but must mine, trade, transport cargo and passengers, and possibly engage in piracy to keep it running. *Universe* also shares some elements of its structure with **computer role-playing games** such as *Starflight* (1986 Binary Systems); the player's ship has a full crew, though their representations are unsophisticated. The design focuses on strategic gameplay in a complex model of a **space opera** universe, including such activities as boarding enemy ships and landing mining probes on newly discovered worlds. While the wealth of available options can make players feel deeply immersed in their role as starship commander, the level of detail that must be dealt with manually—including such esoterica as calculating optimal orbits around planets—may prove frustrating. Certainly, *Universe* is of largely historical interest today.

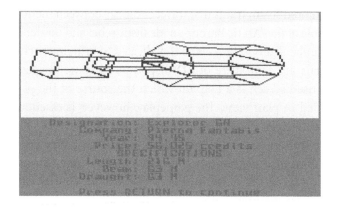

The universe of *Universe* is displayed using a mixture of text and **3D** outlines.

Universe's interface represents its simulated reality in mathematical terms, which would be unlikely to be used in a modern game.

The game is set in a remote area of space that humans have colonized using an alien technology, the **hyperspace** booster, which greatly extends the range of their spacecraft. This artifact has apparently stopped working, meaning that vital supplies are no longer arriving from Earth; the player's primary mission is to locate another such device. The milieu includes a remarkable amount of (somewhat generic) fictional detail, much influenced by the tabletop **role-playing game** *Traveller* (*1977* Game Designers' Workshop) designed by Marc Miller. This background was reused for the sequel, *Universe II* (*1985* Omnitrend Software) designed by William Leslie III. *Universe II* is similar to its predecessor, but more closely resembles a computer role-playing game set in space than it does a space sim; the player's character has a clear identity as an undercover operative for an interstellar government, and members of the ship's crew have individual names and professions. This game also includes sequences set in planetary starports that are played in the manner of a text **adventure**, though these received mixed reviews. A further sequel, *Universe 3* (*1989* Omnitrend Software) designed by William Leslie

III, is essentially a graphical adventure, with a **linear** plot and many puzzles to be solved, though the display takes the form of a **2D** plan view rather than the 3D landscapes commonly seen in such works.

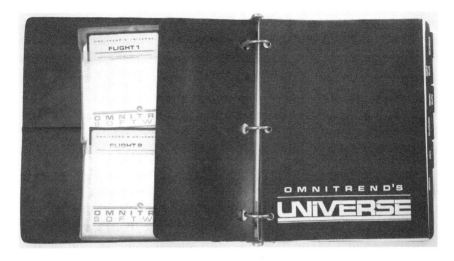

Early computer games were often sold in nonstandard packaging, such as *Universe's* ring binder (containing a thick bundle of manual pages and four floppy disks in plastic pouches).

Related works: *Breach* (*1987* Omnitrend Software) designed by Thomas Carbone and William Leslie III; *Breach 2* (*1990* Omnitrend Software) designed by Thomas Carbone; and *Breach 3* (*1995* Omnitrend Software) designed by Chris Bamford, Thomas Carbone, and Scott Woodrick are a series of squad-based tactical combat games using the same background as *Universe*. *Breach* and *Breach 2* reuse much of the design of *Universe II's* **turn-based** spaceship boarding system, while *Breach 3* is an early **real-time tactics** game. *Rules of Engagement* (*1991* Omnitrend Software) and its sequel *Rules of Engagement 2* (*1993* Omnitrend Software), both designed by Thomas Carbone and Maurice Molyneaux, are spaceship combat games, also set in the *Universe* milieu.

WING COMMANDER

1990. (Revised *1994* as *Super Wing Commander.*) Origin Systems (OS). Designed by Chris Roberts.

    Wing Commander is a combat-based **space sim**, a descendant of *Star Raiders* (*1979* Atari) designed by Doug Neubauer. The background is a **space opera** universe in which the Terran Confederation is fighting an interstellar war against the feline Kilrathi; the tone is much influenced by World War II aircraft carrier operations and the aerial action film *Top Gun* (*1986*). The dogfight-based gameplay is well crafted; notably, the player can issue instructions to their wingmen in combat, though those orders may not always be obeyed. *Wing Commander* is also interesting for its early use of noninteractive animated scenes to immerse the player in its fictional world and for its **multilinear** plot. Actual gameplay occurs during missions against the Kilrathi; if the player fails to complete their assigned tasks, the plot branches, changing the nature of future missions. The game received two expansion packs, which continued the story line on the assumption that the player had won the original game: *Wing Commander: The Secret Missions* (*1990* OS) designed by Aaron Allston and Steve Cantrell and *Wing Commander: The Secret Missions 2—Crusade* (*1991* OS) designed by Ellen Guon and John Watson. A revised version of the game, including *The Secret Missions* and additional material that replaced *The Secret Missions 2*, was released as *Super Wing Commander*.

Several sequels followed, with broadly similar gameplay and steadily improving graphics. The games established a consistent story line featuring the player as Christopher Blair, who begins as a raw recruit and is eventually acclaimed as the savior of the Confederation. From *Wing Commander III* onwards, the series made extensive use of **full motion video** starring well-known actors to tell the parts of the story that occurred between missions. Perhaps as a result of the expense of filming, the plots became increasingly **linear** as the quality of their delivery grew ever more impressive. Taken as a whole, the series is somewhat analogous to a 1930s serial film with a strong **military sf** flavor, reminiscent of the novels of such writers as David Weber and Elizabeth Moon. Each game begins from the most successful ending of the previous one, assembling a grand, if somewhat melodramatic, tale of betrayal, dishonor, revenge, and eventual victory. Entries in the main sequence include *Wing Commander II: Vengeance of the Kilrathi* (*1991* OS) designed by Chris Roberts, Stephen Beeman, and Ellen Guon, *Wing Commander III: Heart of the Tiger* (*1994* OS) designed by Chris Roberts and Frank Savage, *Wing Commander IV: The Price of Freedom* (*1995* OS) designed by Anthony Morone and Chris Roberts, and *Wing Commander: Prophecy* (*1997* OS) designed by Adam Foshko and Billy Joe Cain. The Kilrathi are finally defeated at the end of *Heart of the Tiger*; *The Price of Freedom* deals with a civil war in the Confederation. *Prophecy* has a new hero, the son of a character from the earlier games, who must fight an invasion by the alien Nephilim; Christopher Blair dies heroically at the end. Two of these games had expansions that further extended the plot: *Wing Commander II: Vengeance of the Kilrathi—Special Operations 1* (*1991* OS) designed by Kevin Potter, *Wing Commander II: Vengeance of the Kilrathi—Special Operations 2* (*1992* OS) designed by Kevin Potter, and *Wing Commander: Prophecy—Secret Ops* (*1998* OS) designed by Cinco Barnes, initially released as a free download and later included in *Wing Commander Prophecy Gold* (*1998* OS).

A different sequence set in the same universe began with *Wing Commander: Privateer* (*1993* OS) designed by Joel Manners and Chris Roberts, a game with a linear plot in which the player adopts the role of a freelance mercenary. *Privateer*'s gameplay is similar to that of *Elite* (*1984*) designed by David Braben and Ian Bell, with the player able to trade, prey on other vessels, or hunt pirates as they choose, both during the main story line and after its completion. *Wing Commander: Privateer—Righteous Fire* (*1994* OS) designed by Tom Kassebaum and Phil Wattenbarger is an expansion pack that continues the story and adds new spacecraft and weapons, while *Privateer 2: The Darkening* (*1996* Electronic Arts) is a sequel to *Privateer* with similar gameplay, set over a century later than the other *Wing Commander* games. Of the two major entries in the sequence, the first has inspired considerable loyalty in its players. Two separate amateur remakes are available for free download: *Wing Commander Privateer Remake* (*2005*), which attempts to improve on the original, and *Wing Commander Privateer Gemini Gold* (*2005*), which prefers to replicate it. For many players, especially those in the United States, the *Privateer* series as a whole came to epitomize the exploratory form of space sim, which had previously been little played outside the United Kingdom.

Related works: *Wing Commander Academy* (*1993* OS) puts the player in the position of a new recruit to the Confederation, practicing their starfighting skills in a simulator; players can design their own test missions. *Wing Commander Armada* (*1994* OS) designed by Jeff Everett and Whitney Ayres contains both a **turn-based computer wargame** of space warfare set in the *Wing Commander* milieu and a space dogfighting game, but no story line. The game can be played cooperatively or competitively by two players using various methods, including telephone modem connections. *Wing Commander Armada: Proving Grounds* (*1994* OS) is an expansion that was made freely available as a download. *Wing Commander Arena* (*2007* Gaia Industries) is a space combat game based on the franchise with single- and multiplayer options; uniquely among *Wing Commander* games, it is played in a **2D** overhead view. *Wing Commander* (*1995* Mag Force 7) designed by Jeff Grubb and Don Perrin is a **collectible card game** based on *Wing Commander III.*

Wing Commander (*1999*; also known as *Wing Commander: Space Will Never Be the Same*) is a remarkably bad film based on the series (and directed by Chris Roberts, its lead designer) that serves as a loose pre-quel to the events of the original *Wing Commander. Wing Commander Academy* (*1996*), meanwhile, is an associated animated television series. Both of these works are to some extent incompatible with the continuity established in the games. Several *Wing Commander*–related novels have been published, including *Freedom Flight* (**1992**) by Mercedes Lackey and Ellen Guon, *End Run* (**1993**) by William R Forstchen and Christopher Stasheff, *Fleet Action* (**1994**) and *Action Stations* (**1998**) both by Forstchen solo, and *False Colors* (**1998**) by Forstchen and Andrew Keith. *Heart of the Tiger* (**1995**), by Forstchen and Keith and *The Price of Freedom* (**1996**) by Forstchen and Ben Ohlander are novelizations of *Wing Commander III* and *Wing Commander IV,* respectively. *Wing Commander* (**1999**) by Peter Telep is a novelization of the *Wing Commander* film; *Pilgrim Stars* (**1999**) also by Telep is a sequel. A third Telep novel, *Pilgrim Truth,* was canceled by the publisher but eventually appeared online (see the following links).

Web Links

- Wing Commander Combat Information Center (Tribute Site): http://www.wcnews.com/

- *Wing Commander Privateer Gemini Gold* download: http://privateer.sourceforge.net/

- Peter Telep's *Pilgrim Truth*: http://www.wcnews.com/articles/truth/cover.shtml

X SERIES, THE

Series (from 1999). Egosoft.

The *X Series* is a line of exploratory **space sims**, directly descended from the prototypal *Elite* (*1984*) designed by David Braben and Ian Bell. Players have considerable freedom to explore, trade, mine asteroids, fight pirates (or become one), carry out missions (including bounty hunting and passenger transport), or create a commercial empire of space-based factories and fleets of starships. The game universe itself is impressively realistic and dynamic, with a working economy based on the principles of supply and demand; considerable attention is also paid to the scientific details of planetary orbits and the vast distances that separate them. However, the games' plots are generally weak and the characters emotionally uninvolving; the focus is on free exploration of simulated space. The series is set in the **space opera** "X Universe," a volume of space containing a large number of solar systems linked by **faster-than-light** gates and inhabited by a variety of species, including humans.

In the first game, *X: Beyond the Frontier* (*1999* Egosoft) designed by Bernd Lehahn, the player's character is Kyle Brennan, a pilot from Earth who accidentally travels to the X Universe through a **wormhole** while testing a new spacecraft. Unable to return, he must find a way to survive in this alien region of space. The game suffers from something of a slow start, but offers a wide variety of gameplay options once the player has spent some time improving their ship and learning the facts of their new life. It also has an optional story line revolving around the Argons, a group of humans who reached the X Universe hundreds of years earlier during a war with rogue **terraforming** machines. To protect Earth, the Argons sealed the wormhole they used behind them, preventing both themselves and the machines from returning. *X-Tension* (*2000* Egosoft) designed by Bernd Lehahn and Alexander Preuss is an expansion pack that adds new spacecraft and solar systems to the game, but no new plot; it is designed to allow players to roam more freely through the series' simulated galaxy.

Lovingly designed fictional spacecraft are a major feature of Egosoft's *X Series*.

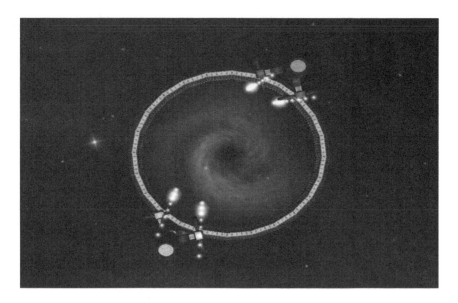

In *X2: The Threat,* **forerunner stargates**—known in the game as jump gates—connect different regions of space.

X2: The Threat (*2003* Egosoft) designed by Bernd Lehahn is a sequel that improves on the basic model provided by the first game, adding such options as the ability to blockade hostile space stations and use spy satellites. The player's character is Kyle's son, Julian; the plot centers on an invasion of the X Universe by the unknown Kha'ak race. While the plot is stronger than that of *X: Beyond the Frontier,* it is still episodic in nature, with story-related events occurring at prolonged intervals as the player continues to trade and explore. After finding Julian's father, the player can discover that the Kha'ak are attacking because natives of the X Universe have mined some of the asteroids in which they live, an act they interpret as a declaration of war. *X3: Reunion* (*2005* Egosoft) designed by Bernd Lehahn, Markus Pohl, and Christian Vogel is a further sequel, with a stronger story line than any of the previous games, though following its **linear** plot remains optional. *Reunion* depicts a hunt for an artifact capable of opening new **stargates**, created by a **forerunner** race; it ends with a new gate being opened to Earth through which a human fleet arrives to defeat the Kha'ak. *X3: Terran Conflict* (*2008* Egosoft) designed by Bernd Lehahn, Markus Pohl, and Christian Vogel is an expansion for *Reunion,* which can be played alone and which brings the series' ongoing story arc to a temporary close. In the end, the terraforming machines return and are revealed as genocidal **berserkers**; the player, in the guise of one of several available characters, must assist in their defeat.

The release of *X: Rebirth* (*2013* Egosoft) designed by Bernd Lehahn marked an apparent attempt to reach a larger audience by creating a game set further into the future of the X Universe, and thus largely disconnected from the existing continuity, with an interface resembling that of a modern console game and a more detailed and highly linear story line. Reviews to date have been mixed; notably, while the player can enter space stations in this iteration of the franchise, the activities available within them seem somewhat limited and repetitive. Considered as a whole, the *X Series* shares something with its contemporary, the TV series *Farscape* (*1999–2003, 2005*), including many extremely impressive visuals, but in place of the latter's vivid characterization, the games provide a deep and involving simulation of interstellar exploration and trading. Ultimately, the universe of the *X* games is beautiful, but somewhat cold.

Related works: *X3: Albion Prelude* (*2011* Egosoft) is an expansion for *X3: Terran Conflict*, which adds new missions, spacecraft, and regions of space to the base game. Several novels have been published in the setting, including Helge Kautz's *Farnham's Legend* (**2005**) and *Plutarch Rising* (**2013**), as well as *X-Universe Volume One* (**2006**), an omnibus containing Darren Astles' *Dominion* and Steve Miller's *Rogues Testament*.

Web Link
- *X: Beyond the Frontier*: http://www.egosoft.com/games/x/

CHAPTER **18**

Others

T HIS SECTION INCLUDES ENTRIES for science-fictional videogames that do not fit into any of the types previously described. While some—such as *Deus Ex Machina* (*1984* Automata UK) designed by Mel Croucher—are truly *sui generis*, most are simply members of recognized forms that have little relevance to science fiction (sf) and thus have not been given their own chapters. These forms include flight simulators (where the player must pilot some form of aircraft and sometimes also engage in combat with opponents), **platform games** (in which the game-play revolves around jumping and climbing over obstacles), **puzzle games** (which depend on the solution of—typically spatial—problems in **real time**), **racing games** (in which players must race against vehicles controlled by each other or the computer), "shoot em ups" (whose players must eliminate a large number of enemies, usually in a **2D** view), and **sports games** (which simulate the play of a—generally, but not always, real—sport). Many of them are also categorized either as **arcade games** (early works designed for use on coin-operated cabinets in public arcades) or a few as "casual games" (relatively simple efforts created for the twenty-first-century mass market and typically played on the web or on mobile phones).

ANGRY BIRDS SPACE

2012. Rovio Entertainment (RE). Designed by Jaakko Iisalo.

The original *Angry Birds* (*2009* RE) designed by Jaakko Iisalo was created by a small studio in Finland, though its subsequent popularity has enriched its developers to a degree where it no longer seems appropriate to view such sequels as *Angry Birds Space* as **independent games**. *Angry Birds* is a **2D puzzle game** in which the player fires flightless birds from slingshots at pigs who have stolen their eggs, solving simple physics problems to ensure that the birds hit their targets, demolishing themselves, their enemies, and any structures that the swine may be using for shelter. Progress in the game thus depends on successfully catapulting the various types of birds on carefully chosen ballistic trajectories through Earth's gravitational field. In the space-based sequel, however, the pigs are either placed on small planetoids—each of which has its own gravity well—or in empty space, where they float far from the pull of other celestial bodies. These innovations allow the developers to create a variety of novel scenarios, including ones in which the player's projectiles must be set on paths that enter one planetoid's sphere of influence before being slingshot out into another. *Angry Birds Space* is as highly playable as its original, easy to start but hard to finish, comical and cartoon-like; the eponymous missiles remain endearingly cheerful despite the inescapable knowledge that their every assignment is a suicide mission.

Such games as *Angry Birds* and its various spin-offs are perhaps best understood as modern equivalents of the vastly popular but not overly complex **arcade games** of the 1970s and 1980s. Certainly, *Angry Birds Space* contains explicit homages to both *Space Invaders* (*1978* Taito) designed by Toshihiro Nishikado and its block-smashing ancestor *Breakout* (*1976* Atari). *Angry Birds* and its many cousins are cheap and pervasive, running on such widespread computing platforms as the iPhone and iPad. Over a billion copies of games from the franchise have been downloaded to date, one for every seven people on Earth (though only some of those copies were paid for). As with *Space Invaders* and *Missile Command* (*1980* Atari) before them, these works have become pop culture icons; *Angry Birds Space* was launched with the assistance of a demonstration filmed on board the International Space Station. For long-time sf enthusiasts, the game may have a special significance. The effect, perhaps, is of an artifact recovered from some abandoned 1960s future of universal space travel, something the **Jetsons** might have used to teach their children the basics of orbital mechanics.

Web Link

- *Angry Birds*: http://www.angrybirds.com/

ANOTHER WORLD

1991. (Also known as *Out of This World* in the United States; also known as *Outer World* in Japan.) Delphine Software. Designed by Éric Chahi.

Another World is a **platform game** set on an alien planet, much influenced by cinematic conventions and visual storytelling techniques. Its design echoes that of such predecessors as the martial arts game *Karateka* (*1984* Brøderbund Software) designed by Jordan Mechner and prefigures the more sophisticated narratives of the dark fairy tales *Ico* (*2002* Sony) and *Shadow of the Colossus* (*2006* Sony), both designed by Fumito Ueda. All of these games excel at telling a purely **linear** story without words; emotion is conveyed by facial expressions and body language alone. As in *Ico*, there is no visible interface in *Another World*; all indications of the game's state have been removed to enhance the player's **immersion**. Unlike that later game, the visuals of this work are entirely **2D**, seen from the side.

The game begins with the player's character, a young physicist, running an experiment on a particle accelerator. Lightning strikes the laboratory at a critical moment, and the experimenter is transported to an unknown planet. There they are captured by humanoid aliens; with the assistance of an imprisoned alien, they can escape and attempt to survive in the hostile environment of this ultramundane world. In the end, the wounded protagonist and their speechless friend are allowed to fly off together into an endless blue sky. The gameplay combines the need to perform sequences of perfectly timed actions typical of a platform game with the solution of inventively diverse physical puzzles, in a manner reminiscent of such action **adventure** precursors as *Metroid* (*1986* Nintendo) designed by Gunpei Yokoi and Yoshio Sakamoto. Success can be difficult to achieve; the game demands that the player execute a series of extremely precise movements, many of which can only be discovered by experiment, if they are to progress through its simulated world.

Nevertheless, *Another World* is remarkable for its ability to convey a striking sense of otherworldly beauty while depicting the player's movements with an air of balletic grace. It could be said to epitomize the "French touch"—the flair for visual design displayed in many early Gallic **videogames**, including *Captain Blood* (*1988* ERE Informatique) designed by Philippe Ulrich and Didier Bouchon and *B.A.T.* (*1990* Computer's Dream) designed by Hervé Lange and Olivier Cordoléani.

Related works: *Heart of the Alien* (*1994* Interplay) designed by Jeremy Barnes, Michael Burton, and Doug Nonast is a sequel built by other hands. Here the central relationship of the first game is inverted; the player adopts the role of *Another World*'s alien friend, while the human physicist appears as a computer-controlled ally. Unfortunately, this seems to work less well than the original's design, perhaps because players find it harder to identify with the alien than with the familiar. The game begins with an introduction that shows the events of its predecessor from the alien's point of view, as well as parts of his backstory; play then proceeds directly from the end of *Another World*. Arguably, this forced resolution of the original's deliberately ambiguous ending is less than felicitous. The mechanics are similar to those of the first game, but overcoming the various challenges presented by *Heart of the Alien* is noticeably more difficult. In the end, the alien can free his people, imprisoned by the villains of *Another World*, but the human must die.

Web Link
- *Another World*: http://www.anotherworld.fr/anotherworld_uk/

ASTEROIDS

1979. Atari. Designed by Lyle Rains and Ed Logg.

Asteroids is a **2D arcade game**, set in space and seen in plan view. Its often frenetic gameplay forces the player to shoot rapidly moving pieces of space debris before their spaceship is destroyed by a collision; unfortunately, most of these bodies simply split into smaller fragments when hit. The design was derived from a variant of the mainframe game *Spacewar* (*1962*) designed by Stephen Russell, J M Graetz, and Wayne Wiitanen, which included similar obstacles by increasing the number of celestial bodies and removing all other features of the game (such as its central sun and second player). Unlike the earlier *Spacewar*-derived game *Computer Space* (*1971* Nutting Associates) designed by Nolan Bushnell and Ted Dabney, *Asteroids* proved to be commercially very successful, illustrating the rise in popularity of arcade games in the United States during the 1970s. Of all the various space-based arcade machines of the late 1970s and early 1980s, *Asteroids'* relatively constant pattern of threat and maneuver may make it the game most suited to the achievement of a Zen-like trance of endless play.

Related works: *Asteroids Deluxe* (*1980* Atari) designed by Dave Sheppard made minor changes to the graphics and gameplay of the first game, while *Space Duel* (*1982* Atari) is a two-player version (with options for competitive or cooperative play) using colorful geometric shapes in place of the original's black and white asteroids. *Blasteroids* (*1987* Atari) is a more complex version of *Asteroids*, featuring much improved graphics, different ship variants, and similar two-player options to *Space Duel*.

CRIMSON SKIES

2000. Zipper Interactive. Designed by Jordan Weisman, David McCoy, and John Howard.

The original *Crimson Skies* tabletop **wargame** (*1998* FASA) designed by Jordan Weisman, Dave McCoy, and Michael Stackpole uses miniature models to represent small-scale aerial battles, using a simple, streamlined rules system. It is set in an **alternate history** of the 1930s in which the United States has fragmented into a multitude of independent nations. In this history, Prohibition is not enacted and an epidemic of influenza is brought home by soldiers returning from the Great War, two changes that cause states to barricade their borders against each other and the federal authorities. By the mid-1930s, the previously United States of America have been replaced by the Nation of Hollywood, the aggressively separatist Republic of Texas, the Christian Socialist People's Collective, and the Confederation of Dixie, among others. Intermittent warfare has crippled the continental road and railway networks, causing commerce to take to the air in Zeppelins, where air pirates hunt fat cargoes and militias and private bounty seekers hunt them. Exotic aircraft and bizarre weapons abound, many of them based on unsuccessful historical prototypes, from autogyros and flying wings to aerial torpedoes and "drill rockets." The atmosphere is one of carefully crafted **retro-pulp**, reminiscent of such "air war" magazines as *G-8 and His Battle Aces* (*1933–1944*), and of their later reinvention in films like *The Rocketeer* (*1991*) and *Sky Captain and the World of Tomorrow* (*2004*).

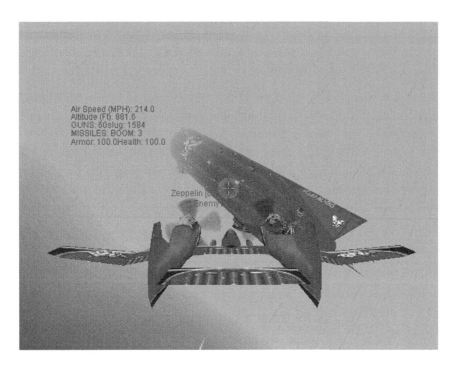

Air Speed (MPH): 214.0
Altitude (Ft): 881.6
GUNS: 60slug: 1584
MISSILES: BOOM: 3
Armor: 100.0Health: 100.0

Zeppelin [
Enemy

Many experimental designs for aircraft that in reality never left the drawing board can be flown in the alternate past of *Crimson Skies*.

The first **videogame** in the franchise, *Crimson Skies*, is essentially a flight simulator, with a strong **linear** plot set in the wargame's vividly realized milieu. The player adopts the role of a new recruit to the Fortune Hunters, a group of air bandits led by Nathan Zachary, ladykiller and gentleman pirate. Gameplay revolves around flying a series of combat missions in the player's choice of aircraft, with plentiful opportunities for performing daredevil stunts; the tone is flamboyant and knowing, a loving homage to the original **pulps**. In the end, Zachary and his pirates save Manhattan and become public heroes.

Related works: *Crimson Skies: High Road to Revenge* (*2003* FASA) designed by William Morrison is a less successful sequel to the original videogame in which the player character is Zachary himself, seeking revenge for the murder of his friend Dr Fassenbiender by a group of megalomaniac Nazis. While some of the original game's roguish charm is retained, the story and gameplay of *High Road to Revenge* are both much simplified in comparison.

Crimson Skies (*2003* WizKids) is a **collectible miniatures game** based on the franchise, featuring both ground-based brawls between pilots and aerial combat using model aircraft. A considerable amount of fiction was written to promote the wargame and published on the web, some of which was reprinted in the volumes *Spicy Air Tales Vol. 1* (**1999**) edited by Michael Stackpole, *Spicy Air Tales Vol. 2* (**1999**) edited by Robert E Vardeman and Loren L Coleman, and *Crimson Skies* (**2002**), edited by Eric Nylund, Mike Lee, Eric Trautmann, and Nancy Berman. Two novels have also been published: Stephen Kenson's *Wings of Fortune: Pirate's Gold* (**2000**), which features Nathan Zachary, and Loren L Coleman's *Wings of Justice: Rogue Flyer* (**2000**).

Web Link

- Crimson Skies: http://www.microsoft.com/games/crimsonskies/

DEFENDER

1980. Williams Electronics (WE). Designed by Eugene Jarvis and Larry DeMar.

Defender is a **2D arcade game** in which the player flies a small spaceship over a planet, protecting the humanoids who live on its surface from various types of invading aliens. The main display scrolls horizontally across the planetary surface to keep the player in the center of the screen, while an overview of the whole world is shown at the top of the display. Previous "shoot em up" games such as *Space Invaders* (*1978* Taito) designed by Toshihiro Nishikado had been limited to a single screen; *Defender*'s introduction of a larger playing field opened up many arcade players' concept of what a game world could be. The need to balance competing priorities (rescuing the humanoids, destroying the aliens, and checking the overview for dangerous situations developing elsewhere) makes *Defender* a surprisingly complex game to play, requiring participants to make frequent and rapid decisions as well as exercise their reflexes. Though generally seen as too complicated when it was first demonstrated, *Defender* eventually proved to be very successful commercially, prefiguring the kind of sophisticated high-speed gameplay later seen in **first-person shooters**.

Related works: There have been several sequels to *Defender*. *Stargate* (*1981* WE; also known as *Defender Stargate*; also known as *Defender II*) designed by Eugene Jarvis added new types of aliens and a **stargate** that could transport the player across the planet, while the less successful *Strike Force* (*1991* Midway) allowed two players to cooperate on multiple planets. Later remakes include *Defender 2000* (*1996* Atari) designed by Jeff Minter, with much improved visuals compared to those of the original, and *Defender* (*2002* Seven Studios), which converted the basic gameplay to a **3D** view.

DEUS EX MACHINA

1984. Automata UK. Designed by Mel Croucher.

Deus Ex Machina is a member of no recognizable school of **videogame** design, though its anarchic ethos can be seen in many other British works of the time. It is, rather, the computer game reconceived as concept album; it shares more with the work of such musicians as Frank Zappa or David Bowie than it does with that of any contemporary game designer. The game is set in a generically Orwellian near future, one that contains many references to late-twentieth-century computer technology and the "Seven Ages of Man" speech from the Shakespeare play *As You Like It* (**1623**). The structure of the work is based on an included rock album composed by Croucher; users play along with the music, which provides context and timing for the various miniature games that allow them to participate in the story. These games cannot be lost, since play must proceed through the album at a constant rate until it ends, but the player can score well or badly. Voice artists include Ian Dury (of Ian Dury and the Blockheads), Frankie Howerd, and the *Doctor Who* actor Jon Pertwee.

The early stages of the game follow a genetically altered human, created inside the rebellious central computer of its future dystopia, from conception through gestation to birth. After emerging from the machine, this godlet attempts to overthrow the system with his **psi powers**; eventually, he will conquer all, only to struggle against the temptations of power and finally be defeated by old age. *Deus Ex Machina* is a unique piece of experimental multimedia, but it is not a perfect work. Listening to the soundtrack and following the lyrics while simultaneously playing the synchronized miniature games are not easy, and the relevance of the games to the narrative is often obscure. It could be argued that *Deus Ex Machina*'s status as a game adds little and that it would be equally effective as a concept album with accompanying video.

Web Link

- Deus Ex Machina 2: http://www.deusexmachina2.com/

IT CAME FROM THE DESERT

1989. Cinemaware. Designed by David Riordan.

Much influenced by the "atomic ant" film *Them!* (*1954*), *It Came from the Desert* is also suggestive of such contemporary cinema as *Tremors*

(*1989*) in its loving homage to the monster movies of the 1950s. The game conspicuously references Hollywood traditions, especially the narrative conventions of the action movie. Unlike later "interactive movies" such as *Obsidian* (*1996* Rocket Science Games) designed by Howard Cushnir, Scott Kim, and Adam Wolff, *It Came from the Desert* is structured as a series of action sequences within a narrative framework. Most of the gameplay is provided by a collection of **real-time** action games—including **2D** plan view chases and **3D** first-person shooting galleries—linked by cinematic animations (using a succession of static images in the original and **full motion video** in the PCEngineCD version). The player adopts the role of a geologist in the small town of Lizard Breath in the early 1950s, somewhere in the American Midwest. A meteor lands near the town, a portent that is quickly followed by an outbreak of mysterious disappearances and other unexplained phenomena. It soon becomes clear both that the town is menaced by gigantic ants and that convincing the townsfolk of the reality of this threat will not be easy.

Although the player has considerable freedom to move around a map of Lizard Breath, investigating locations and talking to the locals as they choose, the game's story continues to unfold throughout, creating an essentially **linear** plot. The player cannot die until the end of the story, but if sufficient evidence has not been gathered to persuade the Mayor to call out the National Guard within two simulated weeks, the town will be completely destroyed, and the game will be lost. *It Came from the Desert* was not the first game to use a combination of action sequences and cinematic scenes to transpose this kind of narrative from the cinema to the computer; the basic approach was developed by Cinemaware in such predecessors as the **retro-pulp** *Rocket Ranger* (*1988* Cinemaware) designed by Kellyn Beck. (As *It Came from the Desert* echoed the B-movies of the 1950s, *Rocket Ranger*'s story of a US army scientist who must use a rocket pack sent back from the future to prevent the Nazis winning World War II prefigured Hollywood's own tribute to 1930s B-serials in *The Rocketeer* [*1991*].) Many of the miniature games included in *It Came from the Desert* revolve around real-time combat or chase scenes, which can become repetitive, but the strong sense of style and atmospheric evocation of the America of fifties teen movies make playing the game a memorable experience.

Related works: *Antheads: It Came from the Desert II* (*1990* Cinemaware) designed by David Riordan is an expansion for the original game, with a new story line set 5 years after the events of the original.

Web Link

- Cinemaware: http://www.cinemaware.com/

LUNAR LANDER

1969. Designed by Jim Storer.

The first version of *Lunar Lander*, distributed in 1969 as the *Lunar Landing Game* and designed by Jim Storer, was **turn based,** using a keyboard to accept commands and a teletype to print the results. In an homage to the Apollo missions, players had to land a lunar module on the surface of the Moon while conserving their limited supply of fuel. Storer was a student at a US high school when he wrote the original game; distinct versions, known as *Rocket* and *LEM*, were created in the early 1970s by other American students. Eventually, the code for all three programs was published in *101 BASIC Computer Games* (**1973**; **1978** revised as *BASIC Computer Games*) edited by David Ahl. An improved variant in which the player had to land the lunar module in **real time** on a **2D** visual representation of a mountainous moon was then commissioned by Digital Equipment Corporation (DEC) to demonstrate the capabilities of their GT40 graphics terminal. Developed by Jack Burness, this version—*Moonlander*—was freely distributed on DEC mainframes from 1973. In 1979, Atari Corporation converted the graphical design into an **arcade game**, adding more sophisticated controls and the ability to purchase extra fuel for more money. This version, the first major variant to be named *Lunar Lander*, proved to have enduring popularity, spawning an entire genealogy of copies, clones, and derivatives.

In contrast to such predecessors as the mainframe game of *Spacewar* (*1962*) designed by Stephen Russell, J M Graetz, and Wayne Wiitanen, the movement of the spacecraft in the *Lunar Landing Game* and its various descendants has always been modeled using realistic physics. In fact, nature's cold equations are the player's only enemy; there are no aliens to fight, or missiles to avoid. *Lunar Lander* remains one of the few **videogames** to be based on a real space program, as opposed to the many games inspired by fictional forms of space exploration.

MERCENARY

1985. Novagen Software (NS). Designed by Paul Woakes.

While it is of primarily historical interest today, *Mercenary* is notable as an early example of a **modular** plot structure in which the player has considerable freedom of action within clearly defined boundaries, an approach used in such later games as *Fallout* (*1997* Black Isle Studios) designed by Tim Cain, Leonard Boyarsky, and Christopher Taylor. The player adopts the role of an interstellar gun for hire who crashes in a city on the planet of Targ, which is at war with invading aliens. As in *Elite* (*1984*) designed by David Braben and Ian Bell, the visuals are **3D**, but only the outlines of objects are drawn due to technical limitations, an approach that is perhaps less successful when displaying an urban area than in empty space. Gameplay revolves around finding a way off Targ; there are a number of possibilities, including performing missions for either the invasion force or the defenders. The tone is perhaps best described as a somewhat sardonic blend of generic **space opera** and spaghetti Western.

The sequel, *Damocles* (*1990* NS; also known as *Mercenary II*) designed by Paul Woakes, uses solid colored graphics to depict the planet of Eris and its solar system, where the main character from *Mercenary* has again become trapped without a working spacecraft. The gameplay is similar to that of *Mercenary* but on a grander scale; the eponymous comet is due to the impact on Eris, and the player must find a way to divert it. *Mercenary III* (*1991* NS; also known as *Damocles II*) designed by Paul Woakes is set in the same solar system as *Damocles*, with similar graphics but a more interactive environment. The plot begins with the resignation of Eris' President and involves the player in preventing the election of a megalomaniac politician as her replacement. References to contemporary UK politics are frequent. The *Mercenary* series remains significant for the freedom afforded to players to explore their environment and follow different paths through the plot, an approach that has become central to the design of many **computer role-playing games**, as well as to that of the well-known *Grand Theft Auto* series of contemporary crime games.

Related works: Some versions of *Mercenary* included an anonymously penned novella, *Mercenary: Interlude on Targ* (**1985**). *Mercenary: The Second City* (*1986* NS) designed by Paul Woakes is an expansion pack for *Mercenary* that largely repeats the original game's plot in another city on the other side of Targ. *Damocles: Mission Disk 1* (*1990* NS) and *Damocles: Mission Disk 2* (*1990* NS), both designed by Paul Woakes, are expansions for *Damocles* containing additional missions. *MDDClone* (*2005*) is a freely available remake of all three *Mercenary* games.

Web Link
- *Mercenary* Tribute Site: http://mercenarysite.free.fr/merce.htm

METROID

1986. Nintendo. Designed by Gunpei Yokoi and Yoshio Sakamoto.

Similarly to its contemporary *Exile* (*1988* Superior Software) designed by Peter Irvin and Jeremy Smith, *Metroid* is a combination of **platform** and **puzzle game**, displayed from the side in two dimensions. As with many examples of the more recent action **adventure** form, the solution of simple physical problems is an important aspect of the gameplay. A great deal of wide-ranging exploration and potentially frustrating experimentation is required to complete the game, as the player acquires various powers—such as the ability to roll through tight spaces while curled up into a "morph ball"—and returns to previously encountered barriers to determine whether they can now be bypassed. The design of *Metroid* drew on three major influences: Shigeru Miyamoto's *Super Mario Bros* (*1985* Nintendo), from which it took the basic gameplay of jumping from pillar to platform in a side view; Miyamoto's *The Legend of Zelda* (*1986* Nintendo), which contributed the idea of exploring a single large world; and Ridley Scott's film *Alien* (*1979*), which inspired much of the game's background and its isolated, threatening ambience. While *Metroid* is not especially original as a work of sf, and its story is minimal, it deploys its mutated insectoid space pirates and eponymous hostile aliens with élan. The game's protagonist is the iconic Samus Aran, raised by a vanished **forerunner** race known as the Chozo, who gave her a unique suit of **powered armor** that she makes use of as a bounty hunter for the future "Galactic Federation." Perhaps the best remembered moments in *Metroid* are the various closing sequences in which, if the player achieves a sufficiently high score, the protagonist removes the helmet of their suit and—after wearing the gender-concealing armor throughout the preceding parts of the game and being referred to repeatedly as "he" in the English version of the game's manual—reveals herself to be a woman. This could not exactly be described as a feminist statement, however; the ending displayed for the best possible performance shows Aran in a skimpy bikini.

Metroid was later remade as *Metroid: Zero Mission* (*2004* Nintendo) designed by Yoshio Sakamoto. *Zero Mission*'s gameplay is similar to that of its original, but it adds additional locations and a great deal of guidance for the player, reducing the amount of trial and error required to progress through the game. *Metroid II: Return of Samus* (*1992* Nintendo) designed by Gunpei Yokoi, Hirojii Kiyotake, and Hiroyuki Kimura is a more combat-oriented sequel to *Metroid*, possibly inspired by the film *Aliens* (*1986*), in which Aran is given the task of exterminating the entire Metroid species.

Should the player complete the game, however, they will discover that their character eventually decides to spare one alien, a newly born specimen that imprints on Aran as its mother. In *Super Metroid* (*1994* Intelligent Systems/Nintendo) designed by Yoshio Sakamoto and Makoto Kanoh, this last survivor is then kidnapped by adversaries who intend to use it to breed a new generation of monsters. The design of *Super Metroid* returns to the gameplay model established in the original game but refines it to create an experience superior to that offered by its prototype. *Metroid Fusion* (*2002* Nintendo) designed by Yoshio Sakamoto replaces the now apparently extinct Metroids with a new enemy, the X-Parasites, which are capable of possessing human hosts. Eventually it is revealed that the Metroids were created by Samus Aran's forerunner benefactors to control the X-Parasites; now that their predators have been exterminated, the Parasites' population has exploded. While it is still a **2D** platform game displayed in side view, *Metroid Fusion* is less exploratory and more strongly plotted than its predecessors, with a broadly **linear** story line through which Aran is guided by a helpful artificial intelligence. Another sequel, *Metroid: Other M* (*2010* Team Ninja) designed by Yoshio Sakamoto, Yosuke Hayashi, and Takehiro Hosokawa, is a late interpolation in the series, taking place between *Super Metroid* and *Metroid Fusion*. This game begins with Aran responding to a distress call from a Galactic Federation research vessel, only to find it overrun by experimental bioweapons and artificially created Metroids controlled by a genocidal artificial intelligence. *Other M*'s gameplay is far more directed and less exploratory than that of most previous games in the franchise, concentrating on intense combat sequences, physical puzzles, and acrobatics resembling those found in many action adventures. **3D** graphics are used for the display, seen from a variety of angles including a side view and both third- and first-person cameras. In another departure for the series, the game presents a highly detailed linear narrative, though its story is dominated by melodramatic clichés.

A separate branch of the franchise began with *Metroid Prime* (*2002* Retro Studios [RS]) designed by Mark Pacini, a 3D game whose design draws upon both action adventures and **first-person shooters**. The earlier games' focus on exploration is retained, but the puzzles concentrate less on jumping from platform to platform and more on manipulating exotic machines in lushly visualized alien landscapes. An integrated targeting system can be used to automatically aim weapons, making the gameplay less dependent on physical skills than in most games influenced by first-person shooters. As with *Metroid*, there is little explicit narrative, but a considerable amount of backstory is **embedded** in the environment of the game. *Metroid Prime* is set between the original *Metroid* and *Metroid II*, including such canonical elements from the earlier games as space pirates and the ruins of the Chozo civilization as well as the newly invented Phazon, a mutagenic compound that creates dangerous new forms of Metroid. There are two sequels with broadly similar gameplay: *Metroid Prime 2: Echoes* (*2004* RS) designed by Mark Pacini—set on a planet at war with its own dark reflection—and *Metroid Prime 3: Corruption* (*2007* RS), also designed by Pacini.

Related works: *Metroid Prime: Hunters* (*2006* Nintendo) designed by Masamichi Abe is a spin-off from the *Metroid Prime* sequence that more closely resembles a typical first-person shooter and is generally better regarded as a competitive multiplayer game than as a single-player experience. Unusually for a member of the *Metroid* series, the eponymous aliens do not appear; the game is instead based on an extragalactic competition between various bounty hunters, including Aran. *Metroid Prime Pinball* (*2007* Fuse Games) designed by Adrian Barritt is a virtual pinball game that makes thematic use of various elements drawn from the *Metroid Prime* series.

Web Link
- *Metroid* Series: http://www.metroid.com/

MIRROR'S EDGE

2008. Digital Illusions CE. Designed by Thomas Andersson.

Mirror's Edge is a **platform game** that is displayed using **3D** graphics. Unusually for a **videogame** that depends on the "platform" mechanics of jumping and climbing, events are seen from the protagonist's perspective rather than from an external view. The setting is a totalitarian utopia, a nameless future city whose people have given up their freedom in exchange for security. This is not a grim dystopia; this is a happy city, depicted in bright primary colors, but it is still a place where dissent will not be tolerated. The player's character, Faith, is a runner, a courier who works for clients who do not want their messages to be monitored by the servants of the state. Faith and her terminally hip fellow runners are all skilled in an art resembling *parkour*, a French sport whose adepts treat urban structures as an obstacle course to be jumped over, scrambled across, and rolled under. This allows the runners to use the city's rooftops to make deliveries, evading the security forces. The game's story, scripted by Rhianna Pratchett—daughter of the comic fantasy writer Terry Pratchett—is a simple, human one with an entirely **linear** structure. When it ends, not much has changed, suggesting that a sequel may eventually appear.

The oppressively perfect city in which *Mirror's Edge* is set may be its most vividly depicted character.

Throughout the game, players must aim for a fluid state of constant motion; many experience an exhilarating sense of flow. While combat is sometimes unavoidable, the gameplay is more about flight than fight. Nevertheless, it seems ironic that a game so concerned with freedom should have such a restrictive structure, in which the player must follow the pattern of the plot through a preplanned sequence of environments, always choosing one of the few routes that can be successfully run in that particular place.

Players of *Mirror's Edge* can experience a remarkable sense of balletic grace as they sprint and tumble their way across the city's skyline.

Related works: *Mirror's Edge 2D* (*2009* Borne Games) designed by Brad Borne is a **2D** platform game, loosely based on the original work. Another variant, *Mirror's Edge* (*2010* IronMonkey Studios) designed by Jarrad Trudgen, is similar. *Mirror's Edge* (*2008–2009*) is a six-issue comic series that acts as a prequel to the original game, written by Rhianna Pratchett.

Web Links

- *Mirror's Edge*: http://www.ea.com/mirrors-edge

- *Mirror's Edge 2D*: http://www.ea.com/1/mirrors-edge-2d

MISSILE COMMAND

1980. Atari. Designed by Dave Theurer.

Missile Command is a **2D arcade game** in which the player must defend their home planet against endless waves of "interplanetary ballistic missiles," a task that is made much harder by the limited supply of antimissile missiles available. Unusually for a combat-based arcade machine, *Missile Command* is purely defensive; there is no way to strike back at the enemy. Another interesting aspect of the game is that, as was conventional for arcade machines at the time, it is impossible to win. As the player reaches higher levels of the game, the number of incoming missiles steadily increases until all their cities are inevitably destroyed. This evocation of the likely results of an actual nuclear war between the United States and the Soviet Union was sufficiently disturbing that the setting was changed during development from the American West Coast to a distant planet. Even so, the designer reportedly suffered from frequent nightmares while working on the game.

Related works: *Missile Command 3D* (*1995* Virtuality Entertainment) included a **3D** version of the basic game as well as a variant that could be used with Virtuality's unsuccessful **virtual reality** headset.

MULE

1983. Ozark Softscape. Designed by Danielle Bunten Berry.

MULE represents an important link between traditional board games, played by people who are spatially and socially close to one another, and **online worlds**, often inhabited by people who are spatially remote but socially close. Its gameplay resembles that of a board game, except that all of its players take turns at performing actions within its virtual world, rather than alternately moving pieces on a map. The concept was partially inspired by a sequence in Robert A Heinlein's sf novel *Time Enough for Love* (**1973**), in which genetically altered mules are used to homestead a remote frontier planet. In the game, players use robot MULEs (Multiple Use Labor Elements) to start a colony on an unexplored world, displayed in a **2D** overhead view. In each turn, resources must be gathered and new land settled, after which the players can sell items they have produced to each other through an auction system. Typically, participants find themselves alternately competing to obtain the best score and cooperating to ensure the survival of the colony as a whole.

MULE was influential on the development of later **4X games** such as *Sid Meier's Alpha Centauri* (*1999* Firaxis Games) designed by Brian Reynolds and Sid Meier. Considered on its own merits, it is an excellently designed and highly social game, combining practical applications of game theory and free market economics with a humorous, appealing presentation. The tragically early death of its designer—inducted into the Academy of Interactive Arts and Sciences Hall of Fame in 2007—remains a sad loss; one of the most respected **videogames** ever created, *The Sims* (*2000* Maxis), is dedicated to her memory.

Web Links

- Interview with Danielle Berry: http://www.dadgum.com/halcyon/BOOK/BERRY.HTM

- World of MULE (Tribute Site): http://www.worldofmule.net/

PSYCHONAUTS

2005. Double Fine Productions. Designed by Tim Schafer.

Psychonauts is a **3D platform game** with a strongly **linear** narrative and vividly drawn characters. There are many possible influences on its fictional world, though none can be positively identified. Thus, the game's story is informed by an absurdist sense of humor reminiscent of that seen in such animated series as *Invader Zim* (*2001–2006*), while its visual design is often suggestive of the work of the film director Tim Burton. The player's character, Razputin, has run away from a circus to join a summer camp for Psychonauts, specially trained children who use their **psi powers** to fight the War on Terror. The camp itself is built on deposits of psychoactive meteor rock that enhance psychic powers and have made the local bears **telekinetic**. Soon, however, the player discovers that their coach is stealing students' brains as part of his plan to take over the world.

Most of the player's time is spent inside other people's minds, each of which is constructed to reflect their subconscious desires and fears. In one such world, they can discover a cartoon version of the 1950s suburbia, complete with paranoid spies, while the militaristic coach has a mental landscape resembling a World War I battlefield, where even the bushes are made of ammunition belts. In the end, Razputin must engage in direct brain versus brain combat with the coach, after both of their brains have been extracted and stored in tanks. In essence, *Psychonauts* is a psychedelic trip through the minds of a procession of seriously disturbed individuals. Its gameplay successfully fuses the puzzles of an **adventure** with the running and jumping mechanics of a platform game; the story similarly mingles comedy with occasional tragedy.

Web Links

- *Psychonauts*: http://www.psychonauts.com/

- razputin.net (Tribute Site): http://v2.razputin.net/

ROBOTRON

2084 1982. Vid Kidz (VK). Designed by Eugene Jarvis and Larry DeMar.

Robotron is a **2D arcade game** in which the player must defend the last human family against unending waves of hostile robots. The game is notable for its frantic pace; enemies attack continuously from all sides, while the player must use two joysticks to fire and move simultaneously. Where the designers' earlier *Defender* (*1980* WE) emphasizes speed and freedom, *Robotron* concentrates on confinement and desperation. Its scenario prefigures that of the film *The Terminator* (*1984*); in the year 2084, the robots have rebelled and conquered the world. The player's nameless character is a genetically engineered superhuman, but as the game continues and more and more robots appear, it becomes clear that there is no hope of survival. *Robotron* is perhaps the most striking expression of technophobia in a **videogame** to date.

Related works: *Blaster* (*1983* VK) designed by Eugene Jarvis and Larry DeMar is a **3D** space game set in 2085, in which the player (presumed to be the last human) must shoot their way through waves of robots to reach a planet named "Paradise." *Robotron X* (*1996* Player1; also known as *Robotron 64*) is a remake of the original using 3D graphics.

Web Link

- Eugene Jarvis on *Robotron 2084* and *Defender*: http://www.dadgum.com/halcyon/BOOK/JARVIS.HTM

SENTINEL, THE

1986. (Also known as *The Sentry* in the United States.) Designed by Geoff Crammond.

In *The Sentinel*, topography is everything. The player adopts the role of a "synthoid," a robot in a **3D** chequerboard landscape overlooked by its eponymous guardian. The Sentinel's gaze slowly scans across the game's small world; if it catches sight of the player, it will begin to absorb the synthoid's energy until it is destroyed. In an almost nightmarish touch, the player cannot move. Instead, they can make new synthoid shells and transfer their consciousness to them. In order to defeat the Sentinel, they must create boulders on which to build higher synthoid bodies, until they can look down on the guardian and absorb its energy. Gaining height while avoiding the Sentinel's deadly gaze is an almost chess-like exercise in strategy, played out under strict time limits. As soon as one Sentinel is destroyed, the player moves to a new landscape, where the game begins again. Playing *The Sentinel* is a curiously compelling experience, absorbing and surreal in equal measure.

Related works: *Sentinel Returns* (*1998* Hookstone) designed by Geoff Crammond is a revised version with similar gameplay to the original; the visual design is eerie and disconcerting, blending metallic and organic elements in a darkly threatening world. There are three freely available remakes of *The Sentinel*: *Sentry* (*1998* Momor Productions) designed by Emmanuel Icart, *Zenith* (*2006* comp-sci) designed by John Valentine, and *Sentinel* (*2006*) designed by Georg Rottensteiner.

Web Links

- *Sentry* download: http://eicart.free.fr/sentry/

- *Zenith* download: http://johnvalentine.co.uk/d00014.html

SPACE INVADERS

1978. Taito. Designed by Toshihiro Nishikado.

Space Invaders was by no means the first **videogame**, but it was the first to achieve worldwide commercial success. The early versions only worked on expensive arcade machines, and its popularity helped foster the rapid growth of video arcades in the 1980s. The basic concept, in which wave after wave of hostile aliens move down the screen until the player inevitably runs out of lives and is destroyed, has achieved an iconic status in popular culture, as well as spawning its own videogame form—that of the "shoot em up." *Space Invaders* introduced several innovations to the arcades other than those represented by its core design, including the use of animating characters (an element made possible by its employment of the then novel microprocessor technology rather than the wholly dedicated circuitry built into earlier arcade machines) and the inclusion of a "high score" display, which would be preserved for other players to envy. In the end, the experience offered by the game was simply far more intense than that provided by such earlier works as *Pong* (*1972* Atari) designed by Allan Alcom.

Toshihiro Nishikado wrote the game after seeing publicity material for the film *Star Wars: Episode IV—A New Hope* (*1977*), which suggested the idea of a game set in space. The enemy designs, however, were inspired by the Martians in George Pal's 1953 film of H G Wells' *War of the Worlds*; the octopoid appearance of its interplanetary invaders led Nishikado to create a variety of aliens that resembled squid, crabs, and other sea creatures. Gameplay was heavily influenced by the early US videogame *Breakout* (*1976* Atari), in which the player uses a paddle to deflect a ball into a series of blocks, all of which must be broken to proceed to the next level. In *Space Invaders*, however, the targets could shoot back.

There have been a number of sequels to and remakes of *Space Invaders*. *Space Invaders Part II* (*1979* Taito; also known as *Space Invaders Deluxe*) is simply a full color version of the original game, while *Space Invaders DX* (*1994* Taito) is a collection of old Invaders games with some comedy options, but *Return of the Invaders* (*1985* Taito), *Majestic Twelve: The Space Invaders Part IV* (*1990* Taito; also known as *Super Space Invaders '91*), and *Space Invaders '95* (*1995* Taito) are all genuine sequels. Of these, *Majestic Twelve*, which changes the original gameplay by introducing a wide variety of "power-ups" (which give the player special weapons or other helpful gadgets), may be the most interesting. More recently, *Space Invaders: Revolution* (*2005* Taito) is a remake including new levels and visual effects, *Space Invaders: Evolution* (*2006* Marvelous Interactive) is a **3D** version, and *Space Invaders Extreme* (*2008* Taito) is an unusually fast-paced variant that includes options for competitive online play. The true legacy of *Space Invaders*, however, is the enormous influence it had on the development of videogame design, including the emphasis on sf and fantasy themes in early **arcade games**.

FURTHER READING

- Martin Amis. *Invasion of the Space Invaders*. 1982. (An enthusiast's guide to the arcades and arcade games of the early 1980s, including *Space Invaders*, *Defender*, *Missile Command*, and *Asteroids*, written in Amis' characteristically playful style.)

SPACEWAR

1962. Designed by Stephen Russell, J M Graetz, and Wayne Wiitanen.

While not the first game to be implemented using electronic hardware, *Spacewar* was the first such game with an original design and the first to be widely distributed. Inspired by E E Smith's **Lensman** and **Skylark** series, the developers decided to write a game for the new PDP-1 minicomputer at the Massachusetts Institute of Technology, based around the theme of interplanetary war. The programmers were among the first generation of computer hackers, working informally on one of the earliest digital computers that allowed a single user to interact directly with the system. Previous mainframe designs had been extremely large and expensive, operated by teams of professionals and surrounded by an almost religious air of reverence, an image that helped inspire the depiction of the computer as inhuman tyrant in much of the popular culture of the 1960s and 1970s. As the first **videogame** to become highly popular (though only among the computer academics and engineers who had access to the necessary hardware), *Spacewar* is an important step on the road that transformed the computer from inaccessible mainframe to ubiquitous microcomputer, from god to toy.

The game itself uses a simple **2D** display that shows two spaceships, a background of stars, and a central sun that exerts an intense gravitational attraction on the spacecraft. Two players can shoot at each other using "torpedoes" and maneuver round the screen; supplies of torpedoes and rocket fuel are limited. The actual gameplay is surprisingly sophisticated. The limitation on available fuel means that players must make strategic use of the central gravity field, adopting orbits that allow them to fire and evade without impacting the sun. Many different versions of *Spacewar* proliferated throughout the academic computing community during the 1960s, including minor changes and additions such as reversed gravity and **force fields** for the players' ships. Two of these variants became the first commercial videogames: the *Galaxy Game* (*1971*) designed by Bill Pitts and Hugh Tuck, a version running on a PDP-11-based machine installed at Stanford University that users had to pay to play, and *Computer Space* (*1971* Nutting Associates) designed by Nolan Bushnell and Ted Dabney, a dedicated hardware design implementing a simplified single-player version of the original game. *Computer Space* was sold as an amusement device to be installed in bars and college campuses; one cabinet appears as a futuristic prop in the film *Soylent Green* (*1973*). While *Computer Space* proved to be too complex to be successful in the mass market of 1971, it was the ancestor of all later **arcade games**, beginning with the far more popular table tennis–based *Pong* (*1972* Atari) designed by Allan Alcom. *Spacewar* remains of interest both for its influence on the development of action-based games and for its demonstration of a close connection between videogames and sf, a link that persists to this day.

Related works: *Space Wars* (*1977* Cinematronics) designed by Larry Rosenthal and *Space War* (*1978* Atari; also known as *Space Combat*) designed by Jeff Petkau, two commercial versions released in the late 1970s, both bear rather more resemblance to their original than does *Computer Space*.

FURTHER READING

- Steven Levy. *Hackers: Heroes of the Computer Revolution.* 1984. (An insightful analysis of the microcomputer revolution, including a detailed history of *Spacewar* as well as material on the early text **adventures** *Colossal Cave* [*1975*] and *Time Zone* [*1982* On-Line Systems].)

Web Link
- J M Graetz on *Spacewar*: http://www.wheels.org/spacewar/creative/SpacewarOrigin.html

SPEEDBALL

Series (from 1988). The Bitmap Brothers (TBB).

The *Speedball* series is a line of violent **sports games**, frequently evocative of the film *Rollerball* (*1975*). While there have been a number of well-received sports **videogames** with a fantasy theme, mostly derived from the American football–inspired tabletop **wargame** *Blood Bowl* (*1986* Games Workshop) designed by Jervis Johnson, the *Speedball* sequence is a rare case of a successful science-fictional example. The first game in the series was *Speedball* (*1988* TBB; also known as *KlashBall*), in which teams of twenty-first-century speedball players wear steel armor to kick a steel ball around a steel arena. Gameplay focuses on training players and bribing referees between events and putting the ball in the opposing team's goal during actual matches. During a match, human players automatically take control of whichever member of their team is closest to the ball, while the remainder are handled by the game. The visuals are **2D**, seen from above. This design proved to be too simple to hold the interest of most players, so TBB released a sequel that came to define the series: *Speedball 2: Brutal Deluxe* (*1990* TBB; revised *2007*) designed by Eric Matthews.

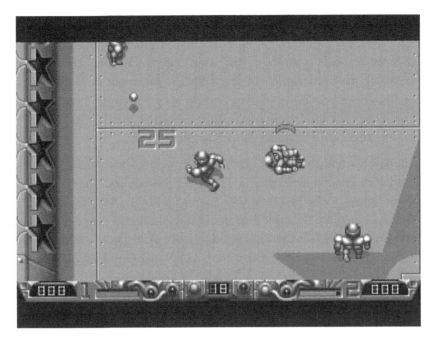

"The action is fast and furious in games of *Speedball 2: Brutal Deluxe*."

Brutal Deluxe is set in the twenty-second century, after radical changes have been made to the rules of its eponymous sport. Teams are larger than they are in the first game, and points can be scored in a variety of ways, including hitting targets spaced around the walls of the arena as well as scoring goals. Unrealistic elements are used to add to the intensity of the brief matches, with tokens scattered on the ground that allow a player to immobilize the opposing team or instantly win possession of the ball. The resulting bouts are frantic, unpredictable, and occasionally disorienting; this is very much a game that concentrates on providing constant action rather than on allowing players to execute carefully planned strategies. In essence, the version of speedball depicted in *Brutal Deluxe* resembles a cross between ice hockey and pinball, with the attitude of an exceptionally aggressive game of rollerball. The society in which the game is played is only cursorily drawn, though it bears a passing resemblance to those shown in many of the more routine comic strips included in contemporary issues of the UK anthology magazine *2000 AD*.

While written and filmed sf has typically viewed its ultraviolent future sports with horror and (occasionally rather prurient) contempt, *Brutal Deluxe* glories in its simulated carnage. Notably, players are awarded points for injuring members of the opposing team as well as for scoring goals (though the small size and stylized nature of the character depictions greatly reduce the emotional impact of this). Arguably, the key difference here is not so much a moral division as a disagreement about the nature of representation. The designers of *Brutal Deluxe* saw it not as an instructive story about the possibility of hyperviolent sports becoming real but as a virtual (and thus inherently nonviolent) game that used brutal competition as a provocative disguise for its basic design.

Related works: *Speedball 2100* (*2000* TBB) is a variant of *Brutal Deluxe* that uses **3D** graphics; reviews were mixed. *Speedball 2: Tournament* (*2007* Kylotonn) is a loose sequel to the first two games. Gameplay is generally similar to that of *Brutal Deluxe*, but there are differences; notably, there is more diversity in the types of players that can be selected to make up a team. In addition, it is possible to play *Tournament* against human opponents in a temporary **online world**. Reviews were again mixed. *Speedball 2: Evolution* (*2011* Vivid Games) is another remake of *Brutal Deluxe*, this time for handheld devices, which received better press than earlier attempts to reinvent the franchise.

Web Link
- TBB: http://www.bitmap-brothers.co.uk/

STAR SAGA

Series (from 1987). MasterPlay. Designed by Andrew Greenberg, Rick Dutton, Walter Freitag, and Michael Massimilla.

Star Saga is a series of "paragraph-system" board games, a type of game that combines the board-and-piece-based spatial gameplay typical of their form with the narrative flow and detailed fictional text of a **gamebook**. However, while such prior examples of the school as *Tales of the Arabian Nights* (*1985* West End Games; revised *2009*) designed by Eric Goldberg are built entirely from physical components, the *Star Saga* games are distinguished by the use of computer software to perform the necessary housekeeping tasks. Each turn begins with the players entering their actions into the game software; depending on the results generated by the system, they may then move across a flat map of the galaxy, read paragraphs of narrative from the included books, or talk to and trade with one another if they have arrived in the same region of space.

The first game in the series, *Star Saga: One—Beyond The Boundary* (*1987* MasterPlay), begins after humans have colonized the planets of several nearby stars using a **faster than light** drive. After suffering a devastating plague of extrasolar origin, Earth and its nearest colonies have isolated themselves from the rest of the galaxy. Each of the players selects a predesigned character with their own reasons for escaping this confinement (from recovering a sacred artifact for the Final Church of Man to performing a vital mission for the Space Patrol) and goes on to explore the universe and uncover its many secrets. The second game, *Star Saga: Two—The Clathran Menace* (*1989* MasterPlay), is a direct sequel in which the players continue to unravel the mysteries of the cosmos while struggling against an armada of genocidal aliens. A third game, which would have resolved the series' many tangled plots, was never released.

Both games succeed in capturing something of the spirit of such early **space operas** as Jack Williamson's **Legion of Space** (though uneasily combined with moments of undergraduate humor) and in enabling players to participate in an excellently constructed **multilinear** story. The approach taken to their design, however, is essentially an artifact of the available technology. Contemporary **computer role-playing games,** such as *Starflight* (*1986* Binary Systems), were already presenting interactive space opera narratives without depending on physical media when the *Star Saga* games were released, a path followed by all subsequent **videogames** with similar aims.

STRANGE ADVENTURES IN INFINITE SPACE

2002. Digital Eel (DE). Designed by Richard Carlson and Iikka Keränen.

Strange Adventures is an **independent game** of space exploration, much influenced by the board game *Voyage of the B.S.M. Pandora* (*1981* Simulations Publications Inc.) designed by John Butterfield and Edward Woods, but also suggestive of such early **space sims** as *Star Control II* (*1992* Toys For Bob) designed by Fred Ford and Paul Reiche III. Unsurprisingly for a game whose effect is that of a (somewhat whimsical) **space opera**, acknowledged sources include both *Star Trek* (*1966–1969*) and A E van Vogt's novel *The Voyage of the Space Beagle* (**1950**). The gameplay is generally simple. Players control a starship with which they explore a randomly created **2D** map, traveling to a different solar system each turn. When they reach a star, they are confronted with situations chosen by the game from a menu of predesigned possibilities. This can lead to players making **first contact** with alien races (who may want to trade, to fight, or simply to be left alone), discovering mysterious artifacts (with which it may be possible to enhance the player's ship), collecting exotic life-forms, falling into **black holes**, recruiting mercenary escorts, or even encountering the majestic whales of space. Combat can generally be avoided, but if players do choose to engage the enemy, the resulting space battles are uncomplicated, if visually appealing. Every play session terminates after a brief period of playing time when the starship's 10-year mission time is up, and it must return to its homeworld. In essence, *Strange Adventures* takes a highly **modular** approach to **interactive narrative**, making every encounter with the game a self-assembling episodic adventure.

Most of the alien species encountered during a mission are amusingly bizarre, whether they are evolved intelligences, **uplifted** beasts, incomprehensible artificial intelligences, or simply oddly formed plants and animals. Many of the star names refer to sf and fantasy authors and game designers, including Isaac Asimov, Arthur C Clarke, Gary Gygax, and Roger Zelazny. Similarly, the descriptions of discovered artifacts—which run heavily to the kind of technobabble associated with the TV series *Star Trek: The Next Generation* (*1987–1994*)—often quote from the corpus of the written genre, as when they reference the monolith from Clarke's short story "The Sentinel" (Spring 1951 *10 Story Fantasy*) or Larry Niven's use of **stasis fields**. As this may suggest, the game's science-fictional concepts are not especially original; the interest emerges from the diversity of the ways in which the various elements can be recombined. Notably, the player's ignorance of the current galactic map makes *Strange Adventures* a game that cannot reasonably be played to win. It is, rather, a magical mystery tour of the universe, full of peculiar juxtapositions and unexpected twists of fate.

Related works: Arguably, the missions players undertake in *Strange Adventures* can be too brief, and the number of unique elements from which their narratives are assembled too few. Both of these criticisms are addressed in the sequel, *Weird Worlds: Return to Infinite Space* (*2005* DE) designed by Richard Carlson and Iikka Keränen, which is essentially a much expanded and refined version of the original game. In *Weird Worlds*, the player chooses one of three different types of ship—piratical trader, scientific explorer, or military scout—each of which has a different set of goals for its mission and explores a more detailed galaxy, presented with greater attention to visual detail. In a different form, *Eat Electric Death!* (*2013* DE) is a board game focusing on tactical combat between starships, set in the *Infinite Space* milieu.

Web Link

- Strange Adventures in Infinite Space: http://www.digital-eel.com/sais/

TRUST AND BETRAYAL: THE LEGACY OF SIBOOT

1987. Designed by Chris Crawford.

Siboot is a rare example of an attempt to make use of **emergent** narrative techniques in a **videogame**. Players are competing for the "shepherdship" as one of a group of alien religious acolytes, each of whom has variable amounts of three different "auras"—tanaga, katsin, and shial. Every night the acolytes fight in their dreams, setting their auras against each other in a **telepathic** contest resembling the game of "scissors-paper-stone," where tanaga defeats katsin and katsin beats shial but shial trumps tanaga. Dreamers must choose which auras to use; the winner of any combat keeps the one selected by the loser. Since the shepherdship is awarded to the first acolyte to possess eight of each type of aura, it is helpful to know how many tanagas, katsins, and shials an opponent has and thus be able to predict which type of aura they might select in dream combat, based on what auras they most need. Discovering this information is the heart of the game.

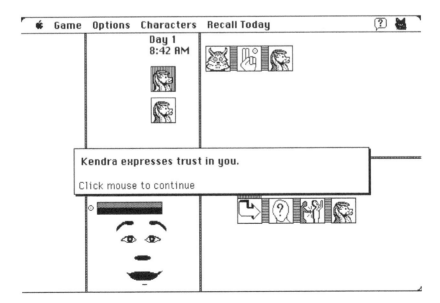

Players of *Trust and Betrayal: The Legacy of Siboot* communicate with computer-controlled characters using a symbolic language.

Every morning, each acolyte wakes up knowing the quantity of one type of aura (tanaga, katsin, or shial) possessed by each of the others. During the day, players can visit the other, computer-controlled, acolytes and talk to them in an iconic artificial language that accurately mirrors the limited reality of the game world, making it possible to offer to exchange information or betray others' confidences. These arrangements are not purely mechanical, however. Every alien has three basic feelings for each of the other acolytes: fear, trust, and affection. Players rapidly build up relationships with the simulated personalities of the other participants, becoming friends or enemies. Betrayals are taken seriously and can result in lasting enmity. Players can also find this affecting, feeling a sense of personal injury if a trusted ally reveals their aura count to their worst enemy. Another innovative aspect of *Siboot* is the use of micronarratives tailored to the player to add flavor to the world, an idea later revisited in *Sid Meier's Alpha Centauri* (*1999* Firaxis Games) designed by Brian Reynolds and Sid Meier. However, the text-based interface used for these miniature stories does not always combine pleasingly with the iconic language employed elsewhere, especially in the occasional metafictional moments when Crawford appears in person to lecture the player on the correct way to approach his work. *Siboot* is certainly an unusual game and was not commercially successful. While some of its innovations have been used in later videogames, many represent roads not taken in the history of game design. Most regrettable, perhaps, is the general absence of other games that use simulated personalities and a carefully designed world to generate narratives algorithmically.

WINGS OUT OF SHADOW

1983. Berserker Works (BW). Designed by Fred Saberhagen.

In 1983, the sf editor Jim Baen founded not only the sf and fantasy publishing house Baen Books but also the less well-known **videogame** publisher Baen Software (BS). At this time, the sf author Walter Jon Williams had been writing historical novels under the name of Jon Williams and designing associated games—including the eighteenth-century tabletop naval game *Tradition of Victory* (*1978* Erisian Games) and its revision *Privateers and Gentlemen* (*1983* Fantasy Games Unlimited)—variously as Walter Williams and Jon Williams. (*Tradition of Victory* includes both a **wargame**, *Promotions and Prizes*, and a pen and paper **role-playing game**, *Heart of Oak*, both of which were included in *Privateers and Gentlemen* with some additional material.) Baen hired Williams to work as a game designer for his new software company. Meanwhile, the sf author Fred Saberhagen and his wife Joan had become intrigued by the potential of the then new medium of the computer game (an interest that is clearly visible in the text of Saberhagen's novel *Octagon* [**1981**], inspired by the **play-by-mail** wargame *Starweb* [*1976* Flying Buffalo] designed by Rick Loomis) and had founded their own development studio in 1982 with assistance from Baen. This was Berserker Works, intended to create games that used stories by Saberhagen and other sf writers as the raw material for experiments in **interactive narrative**. A number of interesting works were produced by this complex of interrelated companies and individuals, including an early **computer wargame** dealing with galactic conquest—*Starclash II* (*1984* BS) designed by Stephen Walton—and the "Regency Romance" game *Pride and Prejudice* (*circa 1984* BW) designed by Walter Jon Williams, in which players compete to win the affections of a wealthy bachelor in a scenario inspired by the novels of Jane Austen. Saberhagen designed several products derived from his own **berserker** series, notably the computer wargame *Berserker Raids* (*1983* BW)—a game of space strategy created with Lloyd Johnson—and *Sign of the Wolf* (**1987**), an illustrated version of the short story "Sign of the Wolf" (May 1965 *If*) that was sold on a disk.

The most intriguing of the various games published by BS, however, is *Wings out of Shadow*, based on Saberhagen's short story of the same name (March/April 1974 *If*), in which simulated World War I fighter pilots battle **berserker** ships in interstellar space. The game adapts the story, giving the player a more active role than that of the protagonist of the original piece. Interestingly, this new version of the work includes some branches in its plot, making it an early example of **multilinear interactive narrative** in a videogame. The narrative is presented as text, with frequent detours into embedded games that represent the more action-oriented parts of the design. Thus, one of the included works is a simple **real-time** combat game that takes place in the player character's subconscious, while another is a **turn-based** tactical computer wargame set in deep space. Unfortunately, these disparate elements do not come together to form an especially harmonious whole. Regardless, it seems that *Wings out of Shadow* is almost completely unknown today not because of any inherent failings but as a result of the disastrous nature of the arrangements made to distribute it. This game—and all of the other products developed by BS and Berserker Works—was intended to be sold into bookshops by the sales force of Simon and Schuster, a book publisher. Regrettably, the sales team, the bookshop owners, and ultimately the potential customers all proved to be uninterested in this idea, and as a result, very few copies of the games were ever sold. (Competing US software publishers of the time reached their buyers through computer stores and mail order, avenues that BS did not explore.) The fact that most of these games were published during a downturn in the US market for personal computer software was presumably also unhelpful. In the late 1980s, Berserker Works was shut down and Baen abandoned the computer games industry to concentrate on book publishing, where he was far more successful. Nevertheless, it is interesting to speculate on an **alternate history** in which Baen adopted a different approach to distribution, and companies staffed by professional sf writers had a real chance to sell their works into the nascent computer gaming market. They might, perhaps, have come to look back on *Wings out of Shadow* as an early experiment that led on to greater things.

Web Link
- Illustrated version of *Sign of the Wolf*: http://www.berserker.com/story-wolfcover.htm

WIPEOUT

1995. Psygnosis. Designed by Nick Burcombe.

Wipeout is a **racing game** set in the mid-twenty-first century, in which players compete for first place using **antigravity** vehicles in tightly enclosed tracks. The gameplay is often frenetic, combining strikingly rapid movement through a variety of twisting, claustrophobic tunnels with the tactical options provided by a range of defensive and offensive weaponry that can be used to delay (though not destroy) competitors. It can, however, be frustrating to play, particularly when the exotic handling of the vehicles leads racers to brush against the track walls and come to a disconcertingly abrupt stop. The design was much influenced by *F-Zero* (*1990* Nintendo) designed by Shigeru Miyamoto and Kazunobu Shimizu, an earlier science-fictional racing game that was intended for younger players. As in that game, the sf elements are thin, though the visuals are often impressive.

The original game is significantly less due to its originality as a design than for its historical importance. *Wipeout* was marketed extensively to young club goers who had stopped playing **videogames** when they reached adulthood, with a soundtrack made up of cult UK dance tracks and a carefully crafted advertising campaign. Significantly, the game's title was often spelled *WipEout*, though a gameplay experience more distinct from the sensations induced by taking Ecstasy is hard to imagine. This marketing effort was highly successful, and the game became a symbol of the new generation of adult videogames for the mass audience who had grown up playing on home consoles and in arcades. Such games were initially often fundamentally similar to their predecessors—as is the case with *Wipeout* and *F-Zero*—but typically were displayed in three rather than two dimensions and exhibited a more conscious sense of visual style. Subsequently, these works have become increasingly diverse, replacing the old videogame market—split between console games for younger players and computer games for sf readers, computer enthusiasts, and other subcultures—with one dominated by (sometimes science-fictional) console and handheld games for adults.

Related works: *Wipeout 2097* (*1996* Psygnosis; also known as *Wipeout XL* in the United States) is a well-crafted sequel that improves on the original while greatly resembling it, resolving the frustrating aspects of the first game's design. Further sequels include *Wipeout 64* (*1998* Psygnosis) designed by Rob Francis, which adds a number of refinements to the gameplay and was generally better received than its predecessor. While *Wipeout 64* retained the core design elements of *Wipeout 2097*, *WipEout Pure* (*2006* Sony Computer Entertainment Europe [SCEE]) designed by Colin Berry deliberately rejected most of the alterations made after the second iteration of the series while adding some strikingly psychedelic visual effects. This approach to graphical design was retained in *WipEout Pulse* (*2007* SCEE) designed by Colin Berry, in which a number of gameplay innovations made in previous works reappeared. *WipEout HD* (*2008* SCEE) continued these trends, incorporating elements drawn from most of the previous games in the sequence; *WipEout HD: Fury* (*2009* SCEE) is an expansion pack. *WipEout 2048* (*2012* SCEE) is the most recent iteration of the series; its gameplay is similar to that of *WipEout HD*, but it is set in the near future rather than the more distant "medium future" of previous works in the franchise.

Glossary

2D: A term used to describe **videogame** graphics that are displayed with no apparent perspective, typically from a side or overhead view.

3D: A term used to describe **videogame** graphics that are drawn according to the laws of perspective, simulating three dimensions on a flat screen. Confusingly, it can also refer to true 3D graphics, for which special hardware is used to display the game as an animated hologram.

4X game: A form of **videogame** in which players "eXplore, eXpand, eXploit, and eXterminate," typically by manipulating the social, economic, scientific, diplomatic, and military evolution of a simulated civilization as it evolves over many years. The phrase was coined by the journalist and game designer Alan Emrich in a review of Steve Barcia's 1993 game *Master of Orion*, often regarded as the first member of the form.

Action RPG: A subtype of **computer role-playing game** in which the management of characters' simulated skills and the tactical complexity of conflicts are minimized, while highly **immersive real-time** combat is emphasized.

Adventure: A form of **videogame** in which the gameplay is largely based on the solution of puzzles, typically presented either as text (which may be illustrated with static images), as a largely **2D** graphical experience, or as a fast-moving **3D** action adventure that may also include sequences based around jumping, climbing, or fighting. The name refers to the first such work, the mainframe computer game *Adventure* (1975–1976; also known as *Colossal Cave*) designed by William Crowther and Don Woods.

Alternate cosmos: A critical term for a **parallel world** in which the laws of nature differ from those of our own universe; canonical examples in the written science fiction (sf) genre include Bob Shaw's

The Ragged Astronauts (**1986**), Stephen Baxter's *Raft* (**1991**), and Richard Garfinkle's *Celestial Matters* (**1996**), in which Ptolemy's concentric crystal spheres really do surround a central Earth.

Alternate history: A science-fictional term for a version of the history of Earth (or occasionally the universe) as it might have been if some crucial event or events had happened differently.

Alternate reality game: A form of **videogame** in which the gameplay revolves around the shared solution of puzzles by large numbers of players on the Internet and events related to the game are interpolated into the participants' everyday lives to make its story more significant, though these intrusions are deliberately made less than totally convincing. The phrase was first used by Sean Stacey to promote the amateur science-fictional game *Lockjaw* (*2002*).

Alternate world: A synonym for **parallel world**.

Amber: A universe of fantastic **parallel worlds** that forms the setting for a series of novels by Roger Zelazny, the first of which was *Nine Princes in Amber* (**1970**).

Android: A science-fictional term for an artificial human constructed from organic materials; its first use in sf appears to have been in Jack Williamson's *The Cometeers* (**1950**), originally published in the May–August 1936 issues of *Astounding Stories*.

Anime: A school of animated film and TV programs, historically associated with Japan and often featuring fantastic settings. The word is derived from a Japanese pronunciation of "animation."

Antigravity: A science-fictional term for a technology that somehow negates or neutralizes the effects of gravity.

Antimatter: A material that is identical to ordinary matter except that fundamental physical properties such as charge have the opposite sign. Famously, when matter and antimatter come into contact, they mutually annihilate with the release of a large amount of energy. The existence of antimatter was originally proposed by the physicist Paul Dirac in 1930, and the first such particle was discovered in 1932.

Arcade game: A form of **videogame** played in public arcades on coin-operated cabinets, often seen as descendants of pinball machines, and typically focused on immediate action and excitement. The term is also used to describe works for other systems—such as home computers or consoles—which are derived from cabinet games.

Arcology: A very large building, or "hyperstructure," that contains the population of a city. The term was coined by the architect Paolo Soleri in 1969.

ARG: An acronym for **alternate reality game**.

Asymmetric: A game design term for a balance between hostile forces in which the opponents are radically different in abilities, numbers, or both but are still evenly matched.

Berserker: A critical term for an independently acting machine dedicated to the extinction of intelligent life, named after the artificially intelligent spacecraft featured in a series of stories by Fred Saberhagen, many of which are collected in *Berserker* (**1967**) and *The Ultimate Enemy* (**1979**).

Big dumb object: A critical term coined by Roz Kaveney in "Science Fiction in the 1970s" (June 1981 *Foundation*) for a gigantic (and presumably unintelligent) artificial structure, generally on a planetary scale; the canonical example is probably the titular sun-girdling hoop of Larry Niven's *Ringworld* (**1970**).

Black hole: An astronomical body that contains a point of infinite density, from which nothing can escape. The term was coined by the physicist John Wheeler in 1969.

Bolo: A series of stories by Keith Laumer (many of which were collected in *Bolo: The Annals of the Dinochrome Brigade* [**1976**]) that focus on the eponymous artificially intelligent tanks.

Buck Rogers: The protagonist of a series of magazine stories from the 1920s by Philip Francis Nowlan, beginning with "Armageddon – 2419 A.D." (August 1928 *Amazing Stories*), who later appeared in a well-known comic strip as well as various films and TV series. Rogers was originally a contemporary American who spent several centuries in **suspended animation** before waking in America oppressed by Chinese conquerors but later became a more generic **space opera** hero.

Budayeen: A Middle Eastern city located in a **cyberpunk** near future, the setting for a series of stories by George Alec Effinger, of which the first was *When Gravity Fails* (**1987**).

Captain Future: The hero of the eponymous **pulp space opera** magazine (*1940–1944*), invented and largely written by Edmond Hamilton.

Changewar: A critical term for a war fought by time travelers, typically involving attempts to change the past in order to establish a preferred version of history. The word was derived from the title of a series of stories by Fritz Leiber, of which the most notable are the novel *The Big Time* (**1961**) and the shorter pieces assembled in the collection *The Change War* (**1978**; revised as *Changewar*).

Chronicles of the Black Company: A series of **sword and sorcery** novels by Glen Cook, beginning with *The Black Company* (**1984**), notable for their moral ambiguity and focus on military fantasy.

CoDominium: The setting for a series of stories by Jerry Pournelle, among them *A Spaceship for the King* (**1973**), *West of Honor* (**1976**), and *The Mercenary* (**1977**), in which the United States and the Soviet Union form an uneasy truce to explore the stars, which eventually disintegrates and is replaced by a succession of galactic empires ruled by hereditary aristocracies.

Collectible card game: A form of card game in which the cards are collectible (in the manner of trading cards) as well as being usable for a game.

Collectible miniatures game: A form of **wargame** that uses miniature figures collectible in the manner of a **collectible card game**.

Computer role-playing game: A form of **videogame** derived from tabletop **role-playing games**, in which a single player interacts with a detailed fictional world through the personas of one or more characters with simulated abilities quite different from those of the player.

Computer wargame: A form of **videogame** descended from the tabletop **wargame**, with a gameplay that focuses on largely intellectual contests of strategy and tactics.

Console role-playing game: A form of **videogame** that evolved from the **computer role-playing game** and typically features more **linear** stories and simpler mechanics than its ancestors, historically associated with Japan and played on games consoles rather than computers.

Corum: The protagonist of two series of fantasy novels by Michael Moorcock, one (beginning with *The Knight of the Swords* [**1971**]) concerned with the war between Law and Chaos that also appears in the **Elric** stories and the other (of which the first was *The Bull and the Spear* [**1973**]) inspired by Celtic legends.

CRPG: An acronym for computer (or console) role-playing game.

Cryogenics: The study of very low temperatures, sometimes used in sf to indicate the preservation of human bodies in **suspended animation** by freezing.

Cthulhu Mythos: A fictional setting, contributed to by many authors but originally derived from such writings of H P Lovecraft as "The Call of Cthulhu" (February 1928 *Weird Tales*), in which incomprehensibly alien beings of vast power constantly threaten humanity, symbolizing the "cosmic terror" of an uncaring universe.

Cyberpunk: A school of sf associated with near-future settings oppressed by corrupt corporations, biologically invasive technologies, and rebellious or criminal protagonists, inspired by such works as William Gibson's *Neuromancer* (**1984**). The term itself was probably coined by Bruce Bethke in "Cyberpunk" (November 1983 *Amazing Science Fiction Stories*).

Cyberspace: A science-fictional term originated by William Gibson in *Neuromancer* (**1984**), describing a networked **virtual reality** within which human minds and computer programs coexist.

Cyborg: A partially cybernetic organism, usually used to refer to a human who has been mechanically augmented.

Darkover: A planet on which lost human colonists have developed what is essentially a **sword and sorcery** society in which **psionics** take the place of magic, the setting for various novels by Marion Zimmer Bradley including *The Sword of Aldones* (**1962**), *The Heritage of Hastur* (**1975**), *The Shattered Chain* (**1976**), and *The Forbidden Tower* (**1977**).

Discworld: The setting for a series of humorous fantasy novels by Terry Pratchett, beginning with *The Colour of Magic* (**1983**).

Dominic Flandry: The flamboyant hero of various **space opera** stories by Poul Anderson, including *Ensign Flandry* (**1966**), *A Circus of Hells* (**1970**), and *A Knight of Ghosts and Shadows* (**1974**), set in a decaying galactic empire that is part of Anderson's **Technic History**.

Dorsai: A supremely dedicated and skilled military culture in a series of sf novels by Gordon R Dickson, of which the best known are perhaps *Tactics of Mistake* (**1971**) and *The Genetic General* (**1960**; also known as *Dorsai!*), in which he attempted to lay out a philosophical blueprint for the future evolution of humanity.

Dread Empire's Fall: A series of **space opera** novels by Walter Jon Williams beginning with *The Praxis* (**2002**), set in a future in which humanity was long ago conquered by an alien species that has shaped the society and technology of its galactic empire to resemble those seen in the more traditional works of the subgenre.

Dream hacking: A critical term for the process of directly entering an individual's mind in order to alter or examine its contents.

Dumarest: A long sequence of **space operas** by E C Tubb, beginning with *The Winds of Gath* (**1967**), whose titular protagonist searches for his lost homeworld of Earth in a colorfully fragmented future galaxy.

Dune: The primary setting for a series of novels by Frank Herbert of which the first was *Dune* (**1965**), a desert planet in a complexly religious galactic empire whose inhabitants use mystic "spices" to foretell the future.

Dyson Sphere: An artificial globe built from a solar system's planets and surrounding its sun, thus trapping all of the energy radiated by the star for use as a power source, named after a related concept proposed by the physicist Freeman Dyson in 1960 (who was himself apparently inspired by an idea suggested in Olaf Stapledon's early sf novel *Star Maker* [**1937**]).

Elric: The hero (or antihero) of various fantasy works by Michael Moorcock of which the best known is perhaps *Stormbringer* (**1965**), a doomed albino who both despises and depends upon his supernatural sword.

Embedded: A form of **interactive narrative** whose events occur before the game begins and which is split up into fragments that the player can reassemble into a coherent story as they are discovered.

Emergent: A form of **interactive narrative** in which there is little in the way of preplanned story, but a clear goal, considerable freedom of action, and detailed characterizations are used to encourage the appearance of a sense of narrative for a single player.

Environmental: A form of **interactive narrative** in which a "story-rich environment" containing characters, background details, and short missions for the players to perform is used to encourage the evolution of a sense of ongoing narrative among a group of participants.

ESP: An acronym for "extrasensory perception," the supposed ability to sense reality by nonphysical means (such as **telepathy**). The term was popularized in the book *Extra-Sensory Perception* (**1934**), by J B Rhine.

Esper: A science-fictional term for an individual gifted with **ESP** or with **psi powers** in general.

Eternal Champion: A sequence of stories by Michael Moorcock that comprises many largely separate series about heroes, such as **Elric,** who are all manifestations or incarnations of a single "champion."

Explorable: A form of **interactive narrative** in which there is only one sequence of events connecting a single beginning with a solitary end but in which those events can be traversed in more than one order.

Faster than light: Einstein's theories of relativity suggest that moving at velocities greater than that of light is impossible or at least is equivalent to time travel. Sf stories and games that depend on rapid travel from star to star thus have to invent some scientific principle to allow this, such as **hyperspace**. "Faster than light" is a common science-fictional term for any such concept.

Fighting game: A form of **videogame** in which two characters fight a duel, typically with their bare hands or using short-range weapons such as swords and spears.

First contact: A science-fictional term for the first meeting between humanity and an alien civilization; an early use occurs in Murray Leinster's story "First Contact" (May 1945 *Astounding Science-Fiction*).

First-person shooter: A form of **videogame** distinguished by a 3D character's eye view of the world and fast paced, often violent, gameplay; "first person" refers to the camera position and "shooter" to the player's most common action.

Flash Gordon: The hero of a lushly romantic **space opera** comic strip created in 1934 after the model of **Buck Rogers**, later the protagonist of various films and TV series.

Force field: A science-fictional term used to describe a shield or barrier constructed from energy rather than matter, apparently first used in this sense in the July–September 1931 *issues of Amazing Stories* in E E Smith's *Spacehounds of IPC* (republished in book form in 1947).

Forerunner: A critical term for an intelligent alien race that was once very widespread and powerful, but has long since mysteriously disappeared, after the eponymous species that makes frequent appearances in the sf novels of Andre Norton.

Forgotten Realms: A somewhat generic **heroic fantasy** setting for the **Dungeons and Dragons** tabletop **role-playing game** that has been its most popular milieu since the late 1980s.

FPS: An acronym for **first-person shooter**.

Frame: A form of **interactive narrative**, such as a short story or brief film, which provides context for a game but which is not important during actual play and is not itself interactive.

Free Traders: A sequence of sf novels by Andre Norton following the adventures of the crews of two interstellar tramp trading vessels, of which the most popular have been the books beginning with *Sargasso of Space* (1955) and featuring the "Solar Queen."

Full-motion video: A term used to refer to prerecorded film footage used in a **videogame**, generally as a way of establishing a **frame** narrative. More recent works often achieve a similar effect by interleaving prescripted episodes displayed using the game's normal rendering technology into the gameplay. Some attempts have been made to use filmed visuals to present entire games, as in the early *Dragon's Lair* (1983 Advanced Microcomputer Systems)—which used laserdiscs to store pregenerated animations—and the later B-movie horror game *The 7th Guest* (1993 Trilobyte) and the French time travel mystery *Lost in Time* (*1993* Coktel Vision). This type of design enjoyed a brief vogue in the mid-1990s but subsequently fell out of favor when it became clear that the superior visual presentation of such "interactive movies" did not compensate for the loss of interactivity necessitated by the requirement that all possible events be recorded in advance.

Fu-Manchu: An oriental genius and would-be master of the world who is featured as the villain in a series of novels by Sax Rohmer beginning with *The Mystery of Dr Fu-Manchu* (**1913**; also known as *The Insidious Dr Fu-Manchu*).

Future history: An overarching chronology of events in some imagined future, typically used as the backdrop for a sequence of novels and short stories. The phrase appears to have been coined by the magazine editor John W Campbell Jr in the February 1941 issue of *Astounding Science-Fiction*, referring to a timeline produced by Robert A Heinlein that placed many of his sf stories in a single continuity.

Gaia: A hypothesis proposed by the environmental scientist James Lovelock in the 1960s, which postulates that Earth's biosphere acts as a self-regulating system similar to a living organism.

Gamebook: A work of written fiction in which different paths can be followed through the (typically **multilinear**) story, leading to multiple endings, some of which represent victory and some of which stand for defeat. The term was originally coined by Steve Jackson and Ian Livingstone for their *Fighting Fantasy* books, of which the first was *The Warlock of Firetop Mountain* (1982) but is now used for all such works.

Gamemaster: The individual who, in a group participating in a **role-playing game**, serves as both arbitrator of the rules and personification of the setting. The term appears to have been first used in this sense in 1975 in the rules of the **sword and sorcery RPG** *Tunnels and Trolls*, after "Gamesmaster," a word used to designate the moderator of a **play-by-mail** game of the **wargame** *Diplomacy* originated by John Boardman in the October 1963 issue of his **fanzine** *Graustark*. Also, in **massively multiplayer** games, a gamemaster is an individual who operates within the simulated world to enforce the rules of the game and moderate disputes (a role referred to as "Wizard" or "Witch" in the earlier **multi-user dungeon** form).

Gas giant: A large planet composed primarily of light elements such as hydrogen and helium and an unusual case of a science-fictional term—invented by the writer James Blish in his story "Solar Plexus" as it appeared in the anthology *Beyond Human Ken* (1952)—which has been adopted by the astronomical community.

Generation starship: A science-fictional term for a starship that takes many years to travel to its destination, generally at **sublight** speeds, so that by the time it arrives, its original crew have died of old age and been replaced by their descendants.

Generative: A form of **interactive narrative** in which the story is created entirely as the game is being played, an approach which is typically only successful in a human-mediated work such as a session of a tabletop **role-playing game**.

Geoengineering: The application of engineering principles to humanity's interactions with the Earth, including the deliberate modification of the planet's climate.

Glorantha: A strikingly original and vividly mythopoeic fantasy world created by Greg Stafford and used as the setting for the **role-playing game** *RuneQuest* and the board and counter **wargame** *White Bear and Red Moon*, among other works.

God game: A form of **videogame** in which the player can manipulate the inhabitants of a simulated world, but only by indirect means, such as improving an area of land in the hope that farmers will then choose to settle it. The phrase was coined by the games journalist Bob Wade to describe Peter Molyneux's 1989 game *Populous*.

Godzilla: The "King of the Monsters," a 400 ft radioactive fire-breathing dinosaur, originally known as Gojira, who stars in a long series of Japanese films beginning with *Gojira* (*1954*; also known as *Godzilla*).

Gormenghast: The vast and labyrinthine castle that forms the world in which Mervyn Peake's grotesquely vivid novels *Titus Groan* (**1946**) and *Gormenghast* (**1950**) take place and is arguably their central character.

Hard sf: A form of sf in which explorations and extrapolations of scientific concepts are the primary concern; the phrase was coined by P Schuyler Miller in the November 1957 issue of *Astounding Science-Fiction*.

Heechee: A series of sf stories by Frederik Pohl, beginning with *Gateway* (**1977**), in which humans explore the galaxy using devices abandoned by the eponymous alien race.

Heroic fantasy: A story set in a fantastic world, typically involving magic and featuring suitably heroic protagonists.

Hive mind: A science-fictional term for a group mind in which many individual consciousnesses are aggregated, somewhat in the manner of ants in an anthill.

Hyperfiction: A form of written narrative constructed as **hypertext**, of which the first significant work was Michael Joyce's *Afternoon, a Story* (**1990**).

Hyperspace: A science-fictional term for a kind of alternate space through which vessels can move more rapidly than they can in "normal" space, making it possible to travel between stars in a reasonably brief period of time. The term appears to have been introduced by John W Campbell Jr in *Islands of Space* (**1957**), originally published in the Spring 1931 issue of *Amazing Stories Quarterly*.

Hypertext: A way of organizing textual information that allows users to move from one section, or node, to another along various routes, or links. The term was apparently first used (as "hypertext") by Ted Nelson in 1965, as mentioned in the Vassar College *Miscellany News* for February 3, 1965.

Illuminatus: A series of novels by Robert Anton Wilson and Robert Shea, beginning with *The Eye in the Pyramid* (**1975**), which detail an endlessly recomplicated but essentially light-hearted conspiracy theory embracing almost every aspect of contemporary culture and which can be read as embodying a kind of countercultural Zen koan.

Immersive: The ability of a simulated world to take on a compelling appearance of reality and thus to involve a participant in its fiction.

Independent game: A game created without the involvement of a major publisher, analogous to an independent film or indie music.

Interactive fiction: A text **adventure**, particularly one considered to have artistic merit. The term was originally coined by Robert Lafore to describe the menu-driven textual games he wrote for Adventure International, among them the Victorian murder mystery *Local Call For Death* (*1979*), but was popularized by the development house Infocom when it was used to promote such works as *A Mind Forever Voyaging* (*1985*).

Interactive narrative: A generic term for the story of a game, which can be **embedded, explorable, linear, multilinear, modular, emergent, environmental, generative,** or a **frame**, or some combination of those forms, and which can potentially offer more than one way to reach a multiplicity of endings.

Isometric: A form of perspective projection used to create **3D** displays in some **videogames** in which the lines of perspective are parallel, as in classical Chinese art, rather than linear, as in the tradition of the European Renaissance. Games that use isometric graphics are typically displayed in an overhead view.

Ivalice: A **science and sorcery** world, the setting for a number of *Final Fantasy* games, which combines influences from a variety of medieval cultures, notably those of the Iberian peninsula.

James Bond: The mythic hero created by Ian Fleming as the protagonist of a series of (occasionally sf-like) spy thrillers, of which the first was *Casino Royale* (1953).

Jetsons: An animated television series originally transmitted from 1962 to 1963 in the United States, in which the titular twenty-first-century family has satirical adventures in a world that juxtaposes the social conventions of the 1960s suburbia with the technologies of an imagined Space Age.

Jonbar point: A critical term used to describe a crucial point in history, whose manipulation by time travelers can fundamentally alter subsequent events. The phrase is derived from Jack Williamson's novel *The Legion of Time* (**1952**), originally published in the May–July 1938 issues of *Astounding Stories*.

Known Space: The setting for a sequence of stories by Larry Niven in which a variety of intelligent species compete and cooperate in a complicated milieu littered with artifacts created by various **fore-runner** races, most notably the sun-girdling artificial structure described in *Ringworld* (**1970**).

Kôr: A lost city built by a pre-Egyptian civilization, ruled by the titular character of H Rider Haggard's novel *She: A History of Adventure* (**1887**).

La Compagnie des Glaces: A long series of novels by the French sf writer G J Arnaud, of which the first was *La Compagnie des Glaces* (**1980**), set in a world locked in a new Ice Age and dominated by the railway companies that control the only means of transportation.

Legion of Space: A series of influential space operas by Jack Williamson, of which the first to be published was *The Legion of Space* in the April–September 1934 issues of *Astounding Stories*, remembered for their weirdly menacing aliens and superscientific doomsday weapon.

Lensman: An agent of the Galactic Patrol who has gained **psi powers** as a result of their possession of a superscientific "lens," in a series of **space operas** written for sf magazines in the 1930s and 1940s by E E Smith and later published in book form beginning with *Triplanetary* (1948).

Libertarian: A political philosophy that aims to minimize or eliminate the involvement of states in the personal and economic lives of their citizens, thus combining the influences of anarchism with those of capitalism.

Linear: A form of **interactive narrative** in which the plot proceeds in a broadly straightforward fashion from beginning to end, but the player (typically) has considerable freedom of action within the smaller sections that make up the overall narrative.

Literary god game: A critical term for a story whose events are controlled from behind the scenes by an entity of godlike power, first used by the writer John Fowles to describe the scheme of his novel *The Magus* (1965).

Live-action role playing: An activity similar to participating in a tabletop **role-playing game** but characterized by the acting out of players' parts in a physical space, with combat represented by the use of symbolic weapons or simple game systems.

Living Dead: A trilogy of films directed by George A Romero, beginning with *Night of the Living Dead* (1968), which exerted a strong influence on many subsequent horror movies and could be said to have kick-started the tradition of zombies as reanimated cannibals.

Long night: A critical term for the interregnum between the collapse of one galactic civilization and the rise of its successor, named after the use of the phrase in Poul Anderson's **Technic History**; several stories set during such periods in this **future history** are included in his collection *The Long Night* (**1983**).

Machinima: A term used to describe (usually amateur) films created by recording the output from a **videogame** as it is being played and then manipulating the results. The word was coined by Hugh Hancock by misspelling the earlier (and less widely known) machinema, itself a neologism created by Anthony Bailey from "machine" and "cinema."

Manga: A Japanese style of comic strip, often featuring fantastic settings or characters; the English word is derived from the Japanese term for any comic strip or comic book.

Massively multiplayer: A term used to describe a form of **videogame** in which large numbers of players interact with each other in a virtual world whose history continues from one visit to the next.

Massively multiplayer online game: A **massively multiplayer videogame**.

Massively multiplayer online role-playing game: A form of **videogame** resembling a **computer role-playing game** but being played online by large numbers of participants in a shared world.

Matter of Britain: A term used to denote Britain's national mythology, traditionally referring to the Arthurian legends.

Matter transmitter: A science-fictional term for a device that can transport physical objects from one location to another without passing through the intervening space.

Mecha: A human-piloted robot or humanoid machine, historically associated with Japanese **anime** and **manga**; the term is derived from a Japanese pronunciation of the English word "mechanism."

Medieval futurism: A critical term for works of sf that combine medieval societies with future technology, coined by John Carnell in the introduction to *New Writings in SF 12* (**1967**).

Merchanters: A series of sf novels by C J Cherryh of which the best known is perhaps *Downbelow Station* (**1981**), in which an Alliance of eponymous traders competes with the ruthlessly expansionist Union for influence over interstellar space.

Middle Earth: The enormously detailed fantasy setting established by J R R Tolkien as the basis for his private mythology and later used as the background for *The Hobbit* (**1937**) as well as *The Fellowship of the Ring* (**1954**) and its sequels.

Military sf: A subgenre of sf that concentrates on the realistic (and occasionally militaristic) depiction of future warfare.

MMOG: An acronym for **massively multiplayer online game**.

MMORPG: An acronym for **massively multiplayer online role-playing game**.

MOBA: An acronym for **multiplayer online battle arena**.

Modular: A form of **interactive narrative** constructed from a number of largely independent "modules," in a similar manner to the separate episodes of a picaresque novel.

MUD: An acronym for **multi-user dungeon**.

Multilinear: A form of **interactive narrative** in which the plot can follow various paths through a branching tree of possibilities, though practical considerations often result in branches that diverge only to recombine with a more **linear** story line.

Multiplayer online battle arena: A more action-oriented variant of the **real-time strategy** form in which teams of players fight each other online, of which the first examples were versions of Blizzard Entertainment's games *Starcraft and Warcraft III: Reign of Chaos* created by fans.

Multi-user dungeon: A form of **videogame** in which many players coexist in the same virtual world, historically often presented entirely in text but distinguished from **massively multiplayer** games primarily by the smaller number of users supported by a dungeon. The term was coined by Roy Trubshaw, who named the first example of the form after *DUNGEN* (or *Dungeon*), a variant of the single-player **adventure** game *Zork*.

Mystara: A largely routine medieval fantasy setting that became the default milieu for later editions of the original *Dungeons and Dragons* tabletop **role-playing game**, while other worlds (such as the **Forgotten Realms** or **Spelljammer**) were published for *Advanced Dungeons and Dragons*.

Nanomachine: A very small machine that operates on the basis of **nanotechnology**.

Nanotechnology: A term used to describe science-fictional devices built on a very small scale, which could in principle be used to construct and change organic bodies and material objects almost at will. The word appears to have been coined by the futurologist K Eric Drexler in 1976 and popularized in his book *Engines of Creation* (**1986**).

Omega Point: A metaphysical term coined by the Jesuit philosopher Pierre Teilhard de Chardin in *The Future of Man* (**1950**) to mean the state of maximum consciousness toward that he believed the universe to be evolving. Later, the phrase came to be used in various works of sf and "speculative physics" as a shorthand for a future in which a near-infinite amount of computational power would become available, allowing the recreation of all past and possible worlds in virtual form.

Online world: A virtual location accessed on the Internet by players of online **videogames** in which the participants compete or cooperate with each other. Such worlds can be long lasting, or persistent (as is typically true in **multi-user dungeons** and **massively multiplayer** games), or temporary (as is generally the case with the worlds created to contain the duels fought by players of **first-person shooters**).

Opar: A lost colony of Atlantis situated in the jungles of Africa and frequently visited by Edgar Rice Burroughs' iconic hero **Tarzan**, possibly inspired by H Rider Haggard's **Kôr**. Its first appearance is in *The Return of Tarzan* (**1913**).

Operator #5: The hero of a series of **pulp** novels published in magazine format between April 1934 and November/December 1939, in which the eponymous secret agent must defeat a series of increasingly apocalyptic (and science-fictional) invasions of the United States by a remarkable variety of hostile powers.

Oswald Bastable: The protagonist of a trilogy of proto **steampunk** novels by Michael Moorcock of which the first was *The Warlord of the Air* (**1971**), named after the narrator of Edith Nesbit's *The Story of the Treasure Seekers* (**1899**).

Oulipo: *L'Ouvroir de Littérature Potentielle* ("The Workshop of Possible Fictions"), a literary movement founded in 1960 by Raymond Queneau and François Le Lionnais devoted to the construction of literary machines and the writing of fiction within various self-imposed formal constraints.

Parallel world: A science-fictional term used to denote another universe that is similar to but different from our own.

Pellucidar: The milieu for a series of stories by Edgar Rice Burroughs, beginning with *At the Earth's Core* (**1922**), which are set in the hollow center of the Earth, where prehistoric survivals and anachronistic refugees from the surface world struggle to survive under an eternal sun.

Planescape: A notably original fantasy setting for the *Dungeons and Dragons* tabletop **role-playing game**, in which the inhabitants of many planes of existence struggle to enforce the tenets of their various philosophies across an arrangement of metaphysical dimensions and in the fantasticated Victorian city that endures at reality's center.

Planetary romance: A critical term for a form of sf set on a planet, the exploration of whose romantic mysteries dominates the story; the phrase appears to have been coined by Russell Letson in his introduction to a 1978 reprint of Philip José Farmer's *The Green Odyssey* (**1957**).

Platform game: A form of **videogame** in which the gameplay is based on jumping and climbing.

Play by e-mail: A form of game that is played similarly to **play-by-mail** works but with the moves dispatched by e-mail rather than the physical post.

Play by mail: A form of game that is played by physically separated participants who send their moves to each other, or to a central moderator, by post.

Pocket universe: A science-fictional term for an isolated (and usually artificial) universe; it may have been coined by Murray Leinster in "Pocket Universes" (October 1946 *Thrilling Wonder Stories*).

Polesotechnic League: An interstellar mercantile organization that dominates the early period of Poul Anderson's **Technic History**, featuring in various works including *War of the Wing Men* (**1958**; also known as *The Man Who Counts*) and the stories collected in *Trader to the Stars* (**1964**).

Posthuman: A science-fictional term for the (usually artificially created) successors to contemporary humanity.

Powered armor: A science-fictional term for body armor that mechanically supports and amplifies the wearer's movements, a concept originated by Robert A Heinlein in his novel *Starship Troopers* (**1959**).

Pressor beam: A science-fictional term for a directed beam of force that pushes objects away from the projector, coined by E E Smith in *Spacehounds of IPC* (July–September 1931 *Amazing Stories*), a novel that was republished in book form in 1947.

Psionics: A generic science-fictional term for such mental powers as **telepathy** or **psychokinesis**; it seems to have first been used in Jack Williamson's story "The Greatest Invention" (July 1951 *Astounding Science-Fiction*).

Psi powers: An alternative term for **psionic** powers.

Psychohistory: A science-fictional term for a social science that allows the prediction and manipulation of the behavior of large groups of intelligent beings, invented by Isaac Asimov for "Foundation" (May 1942 *Astounding Science-Fiction*) and its sequels.

Psychokinesis: The ability to move objects using only the mind.

Pulp: A cheaply produced type of fiction magazine that was extremely popular in the United States for a period lasting roughly from the start of the twentieth century to the end of World War II, characterized by colorful heroics, flamboyant plotting, and an often low level of literary quality.

Puppetmaster: An individual who mediates an **alternate reality game**, controlling game events that occur in the real world and modifying the predesigned plot as necessary in response to players' actions.

Puzzle game: A form of **videogame** whose players must solve (typically spatial) puzzles and problems, generally in **real time**.

Racing game: A form of **videogame** in which players race against each other or the computer using simulated vehicles.

Real time: A term used to describe a **videogame** in which both human- and computer-controlled entities act continuously and simultaneously.

Real-time strategy: A form of **real-time computer wargame** that represents conflicts in a highly stylized fashion. Typically, players must simultaneously research new technologies and gather resources while using those resources to build structures and produce military units that can be used in tactical combat. The term appears to have been coined by Brett Sperry to promote the 1992 release of the **videogame** *Dune II: The Building of a Dynasty*, generally considered to be the first example of the form.

Real-time tactics: A form of **real-time computer wargame** in which players fight small-scale military battles, typically adopting the role of a squad commander.

Retropulp: A term for works that postdate the **pulp** era but deliberately attempt to replicate its themes and style, though not the quality of its printing processes.

Riftwar Saga: A series of epic fantasy novels by Raymond Feist, beginning with *Magician* (**1982**), in which a medieval European culture is invaded by a militaristic oriental civilization from another world. Interestingly, the medieval world is derived from the setting of a tabletop **role-playing game** in which Feist participated, parts of which were later published by Midkemia Press, while the invaders' culture is much influenced by the background of M A R Barker's pen and paper **RPG** *Empire of the Petal Throne* (*1975* Tactical Studies Rules).

Role-playing game: A type of game played with maps, documents, and dice around a table rather than with a computer, in which players, typically guided by a **gamemaster**, explore a fictional world and create an **interactive narrative**, adopting the roles of simulated personalities whose actions are constrained by a system of rules. The term may have first been used in this sense in an article written for the Games Workshop **fanzine** *Owl and Weasel* by Steve Jackson in 1975.

RPG: An acronym for **role-playing game**.

RTS: An acronym for **real-time strategy**.

RTT: An acronym for **real-time tactics**.

Science and sorcery: A critical term for fictional works that combine science-fictional ideas with those of **sword and sorcery**, often (but by no means always) in two separate worlds.

Science fantasy: A form of sf that uses the themes of **sword and sorcery** but justifies them in sf terms.

Scientific romance: A term used to describe early works of sf published (primarily in the United Kingdom) before the end of World War II; typically such works offer a rather less triumphant and more contemplative tone than such contemporaries as the stories published in US **pulp** sf magazines.

Scientology: A religious cult founded by the sf writer L Ron Hubbard as an outgrowth of Dianetics, his pseudoscientific replacement for psychotherapy.

Secondary world: A critical term invented by J R R Tolkien to describe an internally consistent fictional reality such as his own **Middle-Earth** and an important theme in the lecture "On Fairy Tales" he delivered at the University of St Andrews in 1939.

Sector General: A series of stories by James White concentrating on the diagnosis and treatment of the medical problems suffered by a wide variety of exotic aliens, mostly set on a space station known as the "Sector 12 General Hospital" and published in such books as *Hospital Station* (**1962**).

Sense of wonder: A critical term used to describe the sense of shock and awe that some works of sf can inspire when experienced for the first time.

SETI: The search for extraterrestrial intelligence, a term used to describe programs that search for signals generated by civilizations outside our solar system, typically using data from radio telescopes.

Skylark: A series of novels by E E Smith beginning with *The Skylark of Space* (August–October 1928 *Amazing Stories*), whose extravagant superscience, cosmic conflicts, and unconvincing characters helped create the subgenre of **space opera**.

Slower than light: A science-fictional term for interstellar travel by means that are not **faster than light**.

Social Darwinism: A system of thought that attempts to interpret human society in terms of the biological theory of evolution, often with a presumption that evolutionary fitness is determined by the ability to compete more aggressively than other species. The term first appeared in the 1870s and was popularized by the American historian Richard Hofstadter in *Social Darwinism in American Thought* (**1944**).

Space elevator: A structure that links the surface of a planet to a point in orbit, so that payloads can be cheaply lifted into space in an elevator cab; the basic concept was first proposed in 1895 by Konstantin Tsiolkovsky.

Space opera: A form of sf set in space whose themes echo those of the medieval romance, historically dominated by colorful tales of interstellar adventure but subsequently encompassing more thoughtful work. The term was originated by Wilson Tucker in 1941, after the use of "soap opera" for contemporary radio serials that promoted soap powder through melodrama.

Space sim: A form of **videogame** in which the player is a commander or (typically) pilot and sole crew of their own spaceship. Two major forms exist, one concerned largely with combat and the other with exploration and trading.

Space Wolf: A series of novels by William King, of which the first was *Space Wolf* (**1999**), dealing with the eponymous chapter of superhuman Space Marines within the universe of the *Warhammer 40,000* tabletop **wargame**.

Spelljammer: A setting for the *Dungeons and Dragons* tabletop **role-playing game** in which magically empowered ships sail through a pseudo-Aristotelian universe of crystal spheres and visitable planets.

Sports game: A form of **videogame** that simulates the play of a (usually real, but occasionally fictional) sport.

Stargate: A science-fictional term for a device that rapidly translates objects that pass through it to a distant point in space, typically one in another solar system; an early use appears (as "Star Gate") in Arthur C Clarke's *2001: A Space Odyssey* (**1968**).

Stasis field: A science-fictional term for a type of **force field** within which time is stopped, meaning that it functions as a kind of **suspended animation**, introduced by Robert A Heinlein in *Beyond This Horizon* (**1948**).

Steampunk: A form of sf set in a fantasticated (but still scientific) version of the Victorian era; the term was coined by the writer K W Jeter in an April 1987 letter to *Locus* magazine, by analogy with **cyberpunk**.

Sublight: A science-fictional term for travel at velocities less than that of light, meaning that centuries may pass on interstellar journeys. The word appears to have been introduced by Poul Anderson in "A Sun Invisible" (April 1966 *Analog Science Fiction-Science Fact*).

Survival horror: A form of **videogame** characterized by vulnerable protagonists attempting to escape from menacing and disturbing situations, typically of a fantastic nature; the term was first used by the developers Capcom to promote their 1996 game *Resident Evil*.

Suspended animation: A science-fictional term used to describe the preservation of individuals in a state in which they are not animate, and do not age, but from which they can be revived.

Sword and sorcery: A form of fantasy fiction involving magic, swordplay, and entertaining adventures, similar to **heroic fantasy**; the term itself was coined by Fritz Leiber in 1960.

Symmetric: A game design term for a balance between hostile forces in which the opponents are similar in numbers and type, thus ensuring that they are evenly matched.

Tactical RPG: A form of **videogame** descended from the **console role-playing game**, but emphasizing detailed tactical combat in a manner suggestive of a **computer wargame**.

Takeshi Kovacs: The protagonist of a series of novels by Richard Morgan beginning with *Altered Carbon* (**2002**), set in a brutally capitalist future featuring interstellar colonies and personal immortality.

Tarzan: The protagonist of a long series of novels by Edgar Rice Burroughs beginning with *Tarzan of the Apes* (originally published in the October 1912 issue of *The All-Story*) and subsequently appearing in various comics, films, and television programs, a scion of the English aristocracy who is raised by apes and thus gains the physical abilities of a mythic hero while embodying the moral virtues of the eighteenth-century "noble savage" or "nature's gentleman."

Technic History: A series of **space operas** by Poul Anderson that follow the rise and fall of successive galactic civilizations, encompassing the **future histories** of both the **Polesotechnic League** and **Dominic Flandry**.

Tékumel: A remarkably original **secondary world** created by M A R Barker, who combined primarily Indian and Mesoamerican influences to construct a richly elaborated human culture, used as the setting for various **role-playing games, wargames**, and novels beginning with 1975s *Empire of the Petal Throne*.

Telekinesis: A synonym for **psychokinesis**.

Telepathy: A form of **ESP** that enables direct mental communication.

Teleportation: A **psi power** using which individuals can move directly from one place to another without traveling through the intervening space.

Terraforming: A science-fictional term used to describe the process of modifying a world to make it more Earthlike; the word was introduced by Jack Williamson in *Seetee Ship* (**1951**), originally published in *Astounding Science-Fiction* in 1942 and 1943.

The Fleet: A series of short-story anthologies edited by David A Drake and Bill Fawcett, set in a shared **military sf** background, of which the first to be published was *The Fleet* (**1988**).

The World of Tiers: A pocket universe, in which various peoples transplanted from Earth live on the mutually inaccessible levels of an artificial world shaped like a wedding cake. Also, it is used as the setting of *The Maker of Universes* (**1965**), the first book in a series by Philip José Farmer about such worlds and their godlike creators, many of whom are inspired by characters in the private mythology of the poet William Blake.

Third Imperium: The default setting for the *Traveller* **role-playing game**, a far-future galactic empire ruled by a cosmopolitan aristocracy and surrounded by various alien civilizations.

Third-person shooter: A form of **videogame** similar to a **first-person shooter**, but in which the player's character is seen in an external view.

Tie: A term for a work of fiction whose setting or characters are derived from an existing film, game, TV series, or other franchise, after "tie-in."

Time police: A critical term used to describe an organization dedicated to protecting humanity from the potential consequences of travel through time or into **parallel worlds**.

Toy game: A form of **videogame** in which the player is given no explicit goals to achieve. Typically, such games model some complex technological or sociological system, with which the player is encouraged to experiment, as if it were a toy. The term is derived from "software toy," the phrase used by Will Wright to describe his 1989 game Sim City.

Tractor beam: A science-fictional term for a directed beam of force that pulls objects toward the projector, coined by E E Smith in *Spacehounds of IPC* (July–September 1931 *Amazing Stories*), a novel that was republished in book form in 1947.

Transmedia: An approach to fiction that presents a single experience across multiple media, such as television, novels, and **videogames**. The term was coined by Marsha Kinder in *Playing with Power in Movies, Television, and Video Games: From Muppet Babies to Teenage Mutant Ninja Turtles* (**1991**).

Turn based: A term used to describe a **videogame** in which various human- or computer-controlled entities make alternate moves, with each waiting for the others to finish before taking their turn.

Unorthodox engineers: A series of **hard sf** stories by Colin Kapp, collected in *The Unorthodox Engineers* (**1979**).

Uplift: A science-fictional term for the raising of animal species to human or greater levels of intelligence by genetic modification or some similar process, popularized by David Brin in his **Uplift War** novels.

Uplift War: A series of **hard sf** novels by David Brin that focus on humanity's anomalous status as the only intelligent species in the galaxy that has apparently not been **uplifted** into sentience, beginning with *Sundiver* (**1980**).

Uploading: A science-fictional term for the copying of the personality and memories of an intelligent organic being into a computer, after its use in computer science to describe the transfer of data to a remote system across a network.

Videogame: A form of game played on a computer.

Virtual reality: A synthetic analogue of reality, typically generated by a computer; the term appears to have been coined circa 1981 by Jaron Lanier.

Wargame: A form of game that models a military conflict using physical components, typically either miniature figures on a table or cardboard counters on a flat mapboard.

World of Darkness: A Gothically dark and supernaturally inhabited version of contemporary Earth that is the setting for various **role-playing games** created by Mark Rein·Hagen and the White Wolf studio, beginning with 1991s *Vampire: The Masquerade*.

Worldwar: A series of novels by Harry Turtledove of which the first was *Worldwar: In the Balance* (**1994**), set in an **alternate history** in which aliens invade Earth during World War II, forcing humanity to unite against them.

Wormhole: A science-fictional term for a (typically natural) phenomenon that allows direct travel from one location to another without passing through the intervening space, borrowed from the hypothetical physical concept proposed by the physicist John Wheeler in 1957.

Bibliography

The following resources proved particularly helpful in the preparation of this work.

BOOKS

Aarseth, E.J. *Cybertext: Perspectives on Ergodic Literature*. Baltimore, MD: The Johns Hopkins University Press, 1997.

Adams, E. and A. Rollings. *Fundamentals of Game Design*. Upper Saddle River, NJ: Prentice-Hall, 2006.

Adams, R.R. III. *The Best Apple Software*. Skokie, IL: Publications International, 1984.

Ahl, D.H. ed. *BASIC Computer Games (Microcomputer Edition)*. Morris Plains, NJ: Creative Computing Press, 1978.

Albrecht, B. *What to Do After You Hit Return*. Rochelle Park, NJ: Hayden Book Company, 1980.

Aldiss, B. *Billion Year Spree: The History of Science Fiction*. London, U.K.: Weidenfeld & Nicolson, 1973.

Amis, M. *Invasion of the Space Invaders*. London, U.K.: Hutchinson, 1982.

Anderson, M. and R. Levene. *Grand Thieves & Tomb Raiders: How British Videogames Conquered the World*. London, U.K.: Aurum Press, 2012.

Appelcline, S. *Designers & Dragons: A History of the Roleplaying Game Industry*. Swindon, Wiltshire, U.K.: Mongoose Publishing, 2011.

Atkins, B. *More Than a Game: The Computer Game as Fictional Form*. Manchester, U.K.: Manchester University Press, 2003.

Barthes, R. *S/Z*. Paris, France: Éditions du Seuil, 1970.

Bartle, R. *Designing Virtual Worlds*. Berkeley, CA: New Riders Publishing, 2003.

Barton, M. *Dungeons & Desktops: The History of Computer Role-Playing Games*. Wellesley, MA: A K Peters, 2008.

Barton, M. *Honoring the Code: Conversations with Great Game Designers*. Boca Raton, FL: CRC Press, 2013.

Bateman, C. ed. *Game Writing: Narrative Skills for Videogames*. Boston, MA: Charles River Media, 2006.

Bills, R.N. *BattleTech: 25 Years of Art & Fiction*. Lake Stevens, WA: Catalyst Game Labs, 2009.

Bloom, S. *Video Invaders*. New York: Arco Publishing, 1982.

Brand, S. ed. *Whole Earth Software Catalog 2.0*. New York: Quantum Press/ Doubleday, 1985.

Briceno, H., W. Chao, A. Glenn, S. Hu, A. Krishnamurthy, and B. Tsuchida. *Down From the Top of Its Game: The Story of Infocom*. Springfield, NJ: Rolenta Press, 2010.

Bridge, T. and R. Carnell *Spectrum Adventures: A Guide to Playing and Writing Adventures*. London, U.K.: Sunshine Books, 1983.

Butterfield, J., D. Honigmann, and P. Parker. *What is Dungeons and Dragons?* Harmondsworth, Middlesex, U.K.: Penguin Books, 1982.

Carlston, D. *Software People: An Insider's Look at the Personal Computer Software Industry*. New York: Simon and Schuster, 1985.

Castronova, E. *Synthetic Worlds: The Business and Culture of Online Games*. Chicago, IL: University of Chicago Press, 2005.

Chaplin, H. and A. Ruby. *Smartbomb: The Quest for Art, Entertainment, and Big Bucks in the Videogame Revolution*. New York: Algonquin, 2005.

Clute, J. and J. Grant, ed. *The Encyclopedia of Fantasy*. London, U.K.: Orbit, 1997.

Clute, J. and P. Nicholls, ed. *The Encyclopedia of Science Fiction* (2nd edn.). London, U.K.: Orbit, 1993.

Collinson, T. *The Traveller Bibliography*. Sawbridgeworth, Hertfordshire, U.K.: British Isles Traveller Support, 1997.

Crawford, C. *The Art of Computer Game Design: Reflections of a Master Game Designer*. Berkeley, CA: Osborne/McGraw-Hill, 1984.

Crawford, C. *Chris Crawford on Game Design*. Indianapolis, IN: New Riders Publishing, 2003.

Crawford, C. *Chris Crawford on Interactive Storytelling*. Berkeley, CA: New Riders Publishing, 2004.

Dewey, P.R. *Adventure Games for Microcomputers: An Annotated Directory of Interactive Fiction*. Westport, CT: Meckler Publishing, 1991.

Dibbell, J. *My Tiny Life: Crime and Passion in a Virtual World*. New York: Henry Holt, 1999.

Ditlea, S., ed. *Digital Deli: The Comprehensive, User-Lovable Menu of Computer Lore, Culture, Lifestyles and Fancy*. New York: Workman Publishing, 1984.

Donovan, T. *Replay: The History of Video Games*. Lewes, East Sussex, U.K.: Yellow Ant, 2010.

Dunnigan, J.F. *Wargames Handbook*, 3rd edn: How to Play and Design Commercial and Professional Wargames. Lincoln, NE: Writers Club Press, 2000.

Dvorak, J. and P. Spear. *Dvorak's Guide to PC Games*. New York: Bantam Books, 1991.

Ellis, J. *The 8-Bit Book—1981 to 199x*. Loachapoka, AL: Hiive Books, 2009.

Emond, S. *Ultima: The Ultimate Collector's Guide*. Calgary, Alberta, Canada: Falcon Designs, 2012.

Fisher, A. *The Commodore 64 Book—1982 to 199x*. Auburn, AL: Hiive Books, 2008.

Freeman, J. *The Playboy Winner's Guide to Board Games*. Chicago, IL: Playboy Press, 1979.

Freeman, J. *The Complete Book of Wargames*. New York: Simon and Schuster, 1980.

Goldberg, H. *All Your Base Are Belong to Us: How Fifty Years of Videogames Conquered Pop Culture*. New York: Three Rivers Press, 2011.

Grossman, A. ed. *Postmortems from Game Developer*. San Francisco, CA: CMP Books, 2003.

Guest, T. *Second Lives: A Journey through Virtual Worlds*. London, U.K.: Hutchinson, 2007.

Gutman, D. and S. Addams. *The Greatest Games: The 93 Best Computer Games of All Time*. Greensboro, NC: COMPUTE! Publications, 1985.

Hallford, N. and J. Hallford. *Swords & Circuitry: A Designer's Guide to Computer Role-Playing Games*. Roseville, CA: Prima Publishing, 2001.

Hanson, M. *The End of Celluloid: Film Futures in the Digital Age*. Mies, Switzerland: RotoVision, 2004.

Harrigan, P. and N. Wardrip-Fruin, ed. *Second Person: Role-Playing and Story in Games and Playable Media*. Cambridge, MA: The MIT Press, 2007.

Harrigan, P. and N. Wardrip-Fruin, ed. *Third Person: Authoring and Exploring Vast Narratives*. Cambridge, MA: The MIT Press, 2009.

Herman, L. *Phoenix: The Fall & Rise of Home Videogames*. Union, NJ: Rolenta Press, 1994.

Herz, J.C. *Joystick Nation: How Videogames Ate Our Quarters, Won Our Hearts, and Rewired Our Minds*. New York: Little, Brown and Company, 1997.

Holmes, D. *A Mind Forever Voyaging: A History of Storytelling in Video Games*. No place given: CreateSpace, 2012.

Howard, D. *An Introduction to MUD: Multi-User Dungeon*. London, U.K.: Century Communications, 1985.

Huizinga, J. *Homo Ludens: A Study of the Play-Element in Culture*. London, U.K.: Routledge & Kegan Paul, 1949.

James, E. *Science Fiction in the Twentieth Century*. Oxford, U.K.: Oxford University Press, 1994.

James, E. and F. Mendlesohn, ed. *The Cambridge Companion to Science Fiction*. Cambridge, U.K.: Cambridge University Press, 2003.

Johnson, P. and D. Pettit. *Machinima: The Art and Practice of Virtual Filmmaking*. Jefferson, NC: McFarland, 2012.

Kalata, K. ed. *The Guide to Classic Graphic Adventures*. No place given: Hardcoregaming101.net, 2011.

Kent, S.L. *The Ultimate History of Video Games: From Pong to Pokemon*. New York: Three Rivers Press, 2001.

Killworth, P. *How to Write Adventure Games for the BBC Microcomputer Model B and Acorn Electron*. Harmondsworth, Middlesex, U.K.: Penguin Books, 1984.

King, B. and J. Borland. *Dungeons and Dreamers: The Rise of Computer Game Culture from Geek to Chic*. New York: McGraw-Hill/Osborne, 2003.

Kohler, C. *Power-Up: How Japanese Video Games Gave the World an Extra Life*. Indianapolis, IN: Brady Games, 2004.

Koster, R. *A Theory of Fun for Game Design*. Scottsdale, AZ: Paraglyph Press, 2004.

Kushner, D. *Masters of Doom: How Two Guys Created an Empire and Transformed Pop Culture*. New York: Random House, 2003.

Landow, G.P. *Hypertext: The Convergence of Contemporary Critical Theory and Technology.* Baltimore, MD: The Johns Hopkins University Press, 1992.

Landow, G.P. *Hypertext 3.0: Critical Theory and New Media in an Era of Globalization.* Baltimore, MD: The Johns Hopkins University Press, 2006.

Laurel, B. *Computers as Theatre.* Boston, MA: Addison-Wesley, 1991.

Le Diberder, A. and Frédéric. *L'Univers des Jeux Vidéo.* Paris, France: Éditions La Découverte, 1998.

Levering, R., M. Katz, and M. Moskowitz. *The Computer Entrepreneurs: Who's Making It Big and How in America's Upstart Industry.* New York: New American Library, 1984.

Levy, S. *Hackers: Heroes of the Computer Revolution.* New York: Anchor Press/ Doubleday, 1984.

Livingstone, I. *Dicing with Dragons: An Introduction to Role-Playing Games.* London, U.K.: Routledge & Kegan Paul, 1982.

Loguidice, B. and M. Barton. *Vintage Games: An Insider Look at the History of Grand Theft Auto, Super Mario and the Most Influential Games of All Time.* Waltham, MA: Focal Press, 2009.

McGath, G. *COMPUTE!'s Guide to Adventure Games.* Greensboro, NC: COMPUTE! Publications, 1984.

Montfort, N. *Twisty Little Passages: An Approach to Interactive Fiction.* Cambridge, MA: The MIT Press, 2003.

Murphy, B. *Sorcerers & Soldiers: Computer Wargames, Fantasies and Adventures.* Morris Plains, NJ: Creative Computing Press, 1984.

Murray, J.H. *Hamlet on the Holodeck: The Future of Narrative in Cyberspace.* New York: The Free Press, 1997.

Newman, J. and I. Simons. *100 Videogames.* London, U.K.: British Film Institute Publishing, 2007.

Nicholls, P. ed. *The Encyclopedia of Science Fiction.* London, U.K.: Granada Publishing, 1979.

Palmer, N. *The Best of Board Wargaming.* London, U.K.: Arthur Barker, 1980.

Palmer, N. *Beyond the Arcade: Adventures and Wargames on Your Computer.* London, U.K.: Mosaic Publishing, 1984.

Peterson, J. *Playing at the World: A History of Simulating Wars, People and Fantastic Adventures, from Chess to Role-Playing Games.* San Diego, CA: Unreason Press, 2012.

Platt, C. and D. Langford. *Micromania: The Whole Truth about Home Computers.* London, U.K.: Gollancz, 1984.

Poole, S. *Trigger Happy: The Inner Life of Videogames.* London, U.K.: Fourth Estate, 2000.

Prucher, J. ed. *Brave New Words: The Oxford Dictionary of Science Fiction.* New York: Oxford University Press, 2007.

Railton, J. *The A-Z of Cool Computer Games.* London, U.K.: Allison and Busby, 2005.

Redrup, B. *The Adventure Gamer's Manual.* Wilmslow, Cheshire, U.K.: Sigma Press, 1991.

Roberts, A. *Science Fiction.* London, U.K.: Routledge, 2000.

Rollings, A. *The ZX Spectrum Book—1982 to 199x.* Auburn, AL: Hiive Books, 2006.

Rose, M. *250 Indie Games You Must Play*. Boca Raton, FL: A K Peters/CRC Press, 2011.

Ryan, M.-L. *Avatars of Story*. Minneapolis, MN: University of Minnesota Press, 2006.

Sadlier, J. and J. Stanton, ed. *The Book of Apple Computer Software 1981*. Lawndale, CA: The Book Company, 1981.

Salen, K. and E. Zimmerman. *Rules of Play: Game Design Fundamentals*. Cambridge, MA: The MIT Press, 2003.

Saltzman, M. ed. *Game Design: Secrets of the Sages*. Indianapolis, IN: Brady Publishing, 1999.

Schick, L. *Heroic Worlds: A History and Guide to Role-Playing Games*. New York: Prometheus Books, 1991.

Schuette, K. *The Book of Adventure Games*. Los Angeles, CA: Arrays Inc, 1984.

Sheldon, L. *Character Development and Storytelling for Games*. Boston, MA: Thomson Course Technology, 2004.

Simons, I. *Inside Game Design*. London, U.K.: Laurence King Publishing, 2007.

Spencer, M., R. Bilboul, and J. Durrant, ed. *The Good Software Guide: BBC Micro and Acorn Electron*. London, U.K.: Fontana Paperbacks, 1984a.

Spencer, M., R. Bilboul, and J. Durrant, ed. *The Good Software Guide: Spectrum 16K, Spectrum 48K and ZX81*. London, U.K.: Fontana Paperbacks, 1984b.

Spufford, F. *Backroom Boys: The Secret Return of the British Boffin*. London, U.K.: Faber and Faber, 2003.

Stanton, J., R. Wells, and S. Rochowansky, ed. *The Book of Atari Software 1983*. Los Angeles, CA: The Book Company, 1983.

Suits, B. *The Grasshopper: Games, Life, and Utopia*. Toronto, Ontario, Canada: University of Toronto Press, 1978.

Szulborski, D. *This Is Not a Game: A Guide to Alternate Reality Gaming*. Macungie, PA: New-Fiction Publishing, 2005.

Townsend, C. *Conquering Adventure Games*. Beaverton, OR: Dilithium Press, 1984.

Walker, J. *The Which? Software Guide*. London, U.K.: Hodder & Stoughton/ Consumers' Association, 1985.

Wardrip-Fruin, N. and N. Montfort, ed. *The New Media Reader*. Cambridge, MA: The MIT Press, 2003.

Williamson, G. *Computer Adventures: The Secret Art*. Farnham, Surrey, Canada: Amazon Systems, 1990.

Wilson, A. *The Bomb and the Computer*. London, U.K.: Barrie and Rockliff, 1968.

Wimberley, D. and J. Samsel. *Interactive Writer's Handbook*. San Francisco, CA: The Carronade Group, 1996.

CD-ROMS

- Dr Dobb's *Programmers at Work* (Including *Halcyon Days: Interviews With Classic Computer and Video Game Programmers*), 1998, CD-ROM, Dr Dobb's Journal, San Mateo, CA.

- *Grolier Science Fiction: The Multimedia Encyclopedia of Science Fiction*, 1995, CD-ROM, Grolier Electronic Publishing, Danbury, CT.

FILMS

- *Get Lamp: A Documentary About Adventures In Text*, 2010, documentary, distributed via http://www.getlamp.com/, no place given.

MAGAZINES

- *Computer Gaming World*. Published by Golden Empire Publications of Anaheim, California from issues 1 to 111 inclusive (November/ December 1981–October 1993) and then by the Ziff-Davis Publishing Company of New York from issues 112 to 268 inclusive (November 1993–November 2006).

- *Game Developer*. Published by UBM Tech of London from volume 1 number 1 to volume 20 number 6 inclusive (April 1994–June/July 2013).

- *Micro Adventurer*. Published by Sunshine Books of London from issues 1 to 17 inclusive (November 1983–March 1985).

- *Retro Gamer*. Published by Live Publishing of Macclesfield, Cheshire from issues 1 to 18 inclusive (Spring 2004–July 2005) and then by Imagine Publishing of Bournemouth, Dorset from issue 19 (December 2005 to current).

- *The Space Gamer*. Published by Metagaming Concepts of Austin, Texas from issues 1 to 26 inclusive (Spring 1975 to January/February 1980) and then by Steve Jackson Games of Austin, Texas from issues 27 to 76 inclusive (March/April 1980–September/October 1985). (Issues from number 26 [January/February 1980] to number 76 [September/October 1985] inclusive regularly included articles and reviews covering the early US computer gaming industry, though far less frequently in 1983–1985 than in 1980–1982.)

WEB RESOURCES

- Adventureland: http://www.lysator.liu.se/adventure/

- Atarimania: http://www.atarimania.com/

- BoardGameGeek: http://www.boardgamegeek.com/

- Develop: http://www.develop-online.net/

- Gamasutra: http://www.gamasutra.com/

- GameRankings: http://www.gamerankings.com/

- GameSpot: http://www.gamespot.com/

- GOTCHA: the Gaming Obsession Throughout Computer History Association: http://planetromero.com/gotcha/

- Grand Comics Database: http://www.comics.org/

- Halcyon Days: http://www.dadgum.com/halcyon/

- Hardcore Gaming 101: http://www.hardcoregaming101.net/

- Hyperizons: http://www.duke.edu/~mshumate/hyperfic.html

- IGN: http://www.ign.com/

- Interactive Fiction Archive: http://www.ifarchive.org/

- Internet Movie Database: http://www.imdb.com/

- Internet Speculative Fiction Database: http://www.isfdb.org/

- Machinima: http://www.machinima.com/

- Metacritic: http://www.metacritic.com/

- MobyGames: http://www.mobygames.com/

- Museum of Computer Adventure Game History: http://mocagh.org/

- Rock Paper Shotgun: http://www.rockpapershotgun.com/

- RPGGeek: http://rpggeek.com/

- Stairway to Hell: http://www.stairwaytohell.com/

- The Escapist: http://www.escapistmagazine.com/

- Unfiction: http://www.unfiction.com/

- VideoGameGeek: http://videogamegeek.com/

- Web Archive: http://web.archive.org/

- Wikipedia: http://www.wikipedia.org/

- World of Spectrum: http://www.worldofspectrum.org/

- Ye Olde Infocom Shoppe Vault: http://yois.if-legends.org/vault.php

- Youtube: http://www.youtube.com/

Index